THE LIFE OF PRIMATES

Pia Nystrom

The University of Sheffield

Pamela Ashmore

University of Missouri—St. Louis

PEARSON

Prentice
Hall

Upper Saddle River, New Jersey 07458

Library of Congress Cataloging-in-Publication Data

Nystrom, Pia
   The life of primates / Pia Nystrom, Pamela Ashmore.
      p. cm.
   Includes bibliographical references.
   ISBN-13: 978-0-13-048828-2
   ISBN-10: 0-13-048828-3
   1. Primates. I. Ashmore, Pamela, II. Title.
   QL737.P9N97 2008
   599.8—dc22

                      2007050113

Editorial Director: Leah Jewell
Publisher: Nancy Roberts
Editorial Assistant: Nart Varoqua
Director of Marketing: Brandy Dawson
Marketing Manager: Lindsey Prudhomme
Assistant Marketing Manager: Jessica Muraviov
Production Liaison: Barbara Reilly
Operations Specialist: Ben Smith

Director, Image Resource Center: Melinda Patelli
Manager, Rights and Permissions: Zina Arabia
Manager, Visual Research: Beth Brenzel
Cover Design: Kiwi Design
Cover Photo: Pia Nystrom
Image Permission Coordinator: Jan Marc Quisumbing
Full-Service Project Manager: John Shannon/Pine Tree Composition

This book was set in 10/12 Palatino by Laserwords and was printed and bound by RR Donnelley & Sons Company. The cover was printed by RR Donnelley & Sons Company.

Grateful acknowledgment is made to the copyright holders on pages 443–444, which are hereby a continuation of the copyright page.

PN: To my parents, Bertil and Stina, for their unswerving support throughout my life and to the Awash baboons for giving me insight into primate behavior.

PA: For Bruce who remained patient and supportive throughout this project, Tipsy who taught me much about companionship and the emotional support that a four-legged friend could give, and to the family members, friends, and colleagues who encouraged me along the way.

Pearson Education LTD.
Pearson Education Singapore, Pte. Ltd
Pearson Education, Canada, Ltd
Pearson Education—Japan
Pearson Education Australia PTY, Limited

Pearson Education North Asia Ltd
Pearson Educación de Mexico, S.A. de C.V.
Pearson Education Malaysia, Pte. Ltd
Pearson Education, Upper Saddle River, NJ

10 9 8 7 6 5 4 3 2 1
ISBN 13: 978-0-13-048828-2
ISBN 10: 0-13-048828-3

Contents

Preface

Over the last fifty years, primatology, the scientific study of our closest living relatives, has profoundly expanded what we know about the nonhuman primates. This field of study has also increased in popularity. Undergraduate students at many colleges and universities now have the opportunity to take an introductory course in primatology and often have the option to enroll in specialized courses such as primate behavior, primate ecology, and primate evolution. Monkey and ape displays at zoological parks are increasingly popular, as are television documentaries about primates. Newspaper and magazine articles inform us about the latest primate-related scientific discoveries. We are fascinated by the behavior of primates, enamored of their displays of emotion, intelligence, and physical agility, and when we are informed about the plight of these animals in the wild, we are often saddened. It is difficult to learn about these fascinating creatures and not recognize some degree of affiliation or kinship.

This text was written because we felt there was a need for one that would provide students with a comprehensive overview of the lives of primates. The field of primatology has become very complex and now incorporates information from molecular genetics, physiology, and brain studies. Computer programs are used to predict and model ecological and behavioral outcomes within particular parameters. Consequently, we wanted to provide a book that would help students to tackle complex ideas and issues that are now part and parcel of this field. We do this by first introducing a particular area of study and defining terms and methods of study. Our ultimate goal is to inform students about what is presently known about primates and to identify questions that scientists are struggling to answer. It is also our intention to describe the efforts of primatologists and other scientists to find creative yet objective scientific methodologies with which to study these complex animals.

The authors are university teachers and researchers. We have known each other since graduate school and over the years have remained friends and colleagues. We have worked with primates in both captive and field situations and have endeavored to bring our passion for this field of study to students of every age. We each have our own story about how and why we selected primatology as our chosen field of study.

Nystrom came to the field almost by chance, as she initially had her heart set on discovering the Miocene ape, which was the progenitor to our own lineage. However, all those plans changed in 1984 when she was given the opportunity to visit the Awash National Park in Ethiopia to participate in a long-term baboon research project directed by Jane Phillips-Conroy and Clifford Jolly. In her first encounter with a real, live baboon, one look into its eyes changed everything: Those eyes reflected such curiosity and intelligence. It was those eyes that spurred Nystrom on to study primate social behavior and to develop an interest in primate cognitive ability.

Early in life Ashmore journeyed to exotic places with anthropologists featured in the pages of *National Geographic* magazine. She was also an observer of virtually any form of animal life that she stumbled across in the woods of New England, where she spent most of her childhood. To the chagrin of her parents, many creatures came home for short visits so that she could observe them. As she was sitting in an undergraduate anthropology course taught by Michael Park, she realized that primatology was how she could, in fact, combine her interest in anthropology with her passion for animals.

We have written this text together, attempting to use a single voice that communicates our love for primatology, our amazement and respect for our subjects, and our strong desire to see human primates become responsible stewards of the nonhuman primates; their futures are ultimately linked to and wrapped up in our own.

Features of the Book

This book is organized in much the same way that either of us would teach an introductory course in primatology. Chapter 1 provides an introduction to the primates, Chapter 2 discusses how we distinguish between the many different types of primates, and Chapter 3 presents where they live. More detail is provided in Chapters 4 and 5 in which we discuss the primate body and the evolutionary history of the nonhuman primates. Primate ecology is discussed in Chapter 6, the social groups in which they live are described in Chapter 7, and social relationships are investigated in Chapter 8. In-depth coverage of primate communication and intelligence is found in Chapters 9 and 10. Chapter 11 provides an overview of the current state and issues that presently influence primate conservation.

Throughout the chapters two overall themes are found:

- The nonhuman primates are our evolutionary next of kin.
- What we know about primates is based on scientific methods that have been used to investigate them.

In each chapter we first provide the reader with an **introduction** to the topic being presented, e.g., evolution, ecology, communication. We then discuss how this topic relates to the primates and explore particular aspects that are most relevant to them; often this is accomplished by asking and then answering a series of questions. Each chapter includes **key words** that are boldfaced in the text, listed at the end of each chapter, and defined in the glossary. The most essential of these are defined in the margins where they are first introduced to the reader. **Information** and **Hot Topic** boxes provide small vignettes that we surmised would be of particular interest and provide greater insight to the reader. Chapter **summaries** review the major points that have been covered, and **study questions** indicate to the reader those points that we feel should be underscored and understood. At the end of each chapter there is a list of **suggested readings and related websites** where interested students can go to find more information on the material that has been discussed.

Appendices: At the end of the book the appendices provide helpful information. Since the measurement scale used by scientists is metric, there is a conversion table from metric to imperial scales in Appendix A. The comparative anatomy of nonhuman primate skeletons is presented in Appendix B.

Glossary: All key words are defined and appear in alphabetical order at the end of the text.

References: All the works cited throughout the text can be found in this list.

Comprehensive Index: This index will help the reader to locate where particular topics and primates are discussed in the text.

Illustrations, photographs, and maps occur throughout the text to help illustrate a topic, provide a picture of a primate or topic discussed; maps provide information about particular localities. In the inside cover of the book there is a world map.

The authors have endeavored to provide the reader with a better understanding of the nonhuman primates. We want to remind the reader that as much as we seek to learn more about these wonderful animals for their own sakes, they have provided us with a much greater understanding about ourselves and our capacities and potentials. The lives of many primates have been sacrificed to improve the quality of human life. For this and for the windows of understanding that they have allowed us to open about who and what we are, we owe them a great deal.

Acknowledgments

Many colleagues, students, and friends have contributed to this project, and we are grateful to them for their support. Special thanks goes to Donna Hart, who reviewed portions of this manuscript and whose unwavering support was so very much appreciated. Amy Debrecht helped to translate often incomprehensible text into coherent sentences. We also thank the anonymous reviewers whose comments provided us with a means to improve this first edition.

A special thanks goes to Nancy Roberts, our editor at Pearson Education/Prentice Hall, who from the very start believed in this project. She patiently awaited its completion while other life demands often interrupted its progress and adeptly guided us through the process. Lee Peterson, editorial assistant, provided a cheerful voice and help whenever it was needed. We also thank Kathleen Stowers and John Shannon, production managers who splendidly pulled all of our loose ends together into a comprehensive whole, and the result is this book.

To the many friends and colleagues who generously provided us with photographs to use in this text we are greatly indebted: Lise Albretchsen, James Anderson, Randy Ashmore, David Baum, Thad Bartlett, Brenda Benefit, James Campbell, Fernando Colmenares, Theodora Eleftheriou, Karin Enstam-Jaffe, Kathleen FitzPatrick, Renauld Fulconis, Donna Hart, John Fa, Benjamin Freed, Lisa Gould, Sharon Gursky, Rebecca Harrison, Nina Jablonski, Billy Kaysing, Mike Keithly, Carrie Kouri, Jorge Martínez-Contreras, Anna Nekaris, Hamilton Osorio, Alba Pérez-Ruiz, Gregory Retallack, Nick Robl, Michelle Sauther, Volker Sommer, Diana Swales, Larissa Swedell, Masa Takai, Amy Thomas, Liza Veiga, Alan Walker, and Mary Willis. We also wish to thank Stephen Nash for allowing us to use his beautiful drawings.

A coauthored text of this scope often places demands on an underlying friendship. In our case, the friendship not only survived but grew stronger. PA would like to thank

Pia Nystrom for her patience, guidance, and steadfast effort on this project. PN would like to thank Pamela Ashmore for her friendship and for providing a calming voice when the stress appeared unbearable.

We have made a great effort to produce a text that would be comprehensible to students, interesting to colleagues, and accurate in the synthesis of a tremendous amount of information and data. As with any first edition, however, there are bound to be errors, and we appreciate receiving any comments or corrections from readers. Any errors within the text are ours alone. We hope that our passion, respect, and our sense of wonder and awe for our closest living relatives come across in this text and will inspire others.

CHAPTER 1

Introduction to the Nonhuman Primates

The bonobo kept averting her eyes away from the camera lens, but just moments before she had been intensely looking directly into the eyes of the children who were watching her (see Figure 1-1). She lives in a family group of bonobos housed at the San Diego Zoo. She is the cover girl for this book, and her actions and behaviors are captivating; looking into her eyes, you encounter depth and intelligence. She is a highly endangered ape.

In the wild bonobos are found in limited regions of the Democratic Republic of the Congo, located in the central part of Africa. There are less than 20,000 individuals remaining in the wild (Bowen-Jones 1998). Among primates bonobos are most fascinating and rather unusual. They live in very fluid social groups, and females

(a)

(b)

(c)

FIGURE 1-1 Bonobos are in many aspects the most human-like of all living primates. Bonobos are also the least common and most endangered of all living apes.

tend to be the dominant sex. Bonobos are the most non-aggressive primate. They exhibit a wide range of sexually oriented behaviors that they not only use for reproduction but to settle their disagreements and arguments or to avoid them. In other words, they use sex as a social tool, and as such the whole group engages in these activities.

Bonobos can easily move in an upright or **bipedal** manner, but they are not habitual bipeds as we are. Paleoanthropologists have considered their body form to be similar to that of one of our human ancestors and often use bonobos as models when reconstructing the positional behaviors of our early ancestors (Zihlman et al. 1978). In captivity these apes have acquired language abilities, have learned to produce stone tools, and can distinguish between live and taped images of themselves on television (Savage-Rumbaugh and Lewin 1994).

An increase in scientific knowledge about nonhuman primates brings with it the responsibility to care about their fate. As we learn more about other primates, we can begin to appreciate these animals for what they are: our closest living relatives. The disturbing aspect is that once you realize that animals like this bonobo can think about themselves and about others, can feel pain, anger, despair, and happiness, you have to ask if we have the right to put them in cages and to put them on display. Importantly, what does the future hold for these animals? What is our cover girl's future, and what is ours if we eliminate animals like her from the face of this earth? It may be the fate for all of our ape relatives if we do not take unifying action to preserve their habitats and their lives.

❖❖ How Much Like Us?

Humans, apes, monkeys, tarsiers (referred to as **haplorhines**), lemurs, sifakas, lorises, and bushbabies (referred to as **strepsirhines**) all belong to a group of mammals called **primates**. Since nonhuman primates are our closest living relatives, people often wonder how much like us they really are. If you watch a chimpanzee or bonobo in a zoo or other setting, you are bound to recognize the many similarities that it has to a human being, or we have to them (Figure 1-2a and b). Striking parallels are found in the general style of its body, its facial expressions, how it manipulates objects in its environment, and even how it interacts with other group members. Having spent numerous hours observing nonhuman primates in zoo settings, we have overheard the remarks of many human observers about the nonhuman primates on display. People are quick to acknowledge family resemblances in both behavior and physical appearances, and they do not hesitate to assign human emotions, motivations, and goals to the actions that they observe. Even young children can become completely mesmerized by the antics of a nonhuman primate, and humans of almost any

(a)   (b)

FIGURE 1-2 (a) A male bonobo (*Pan paniscus*) relaxing in the sun. (b) Cinder is a chimpanzee (*Pan troglodytes*) that lives at the St. Louis zoological park. Her lack of hair is the result of an autoimmune deficiency disease.

FIGURE 1-3 Who is studying whom? A young lady watches the activity of a young gorilla (*Gorilla gorilla*), who is just as interested in the human.

age are intrigued by these animals (Figure 1-3). Why do nonhuman primates allure us so? Perhaps, it is because we recognize that nonhuman primates are much like us, but we do not necessarily know how to articulate or quantify how similar to us they really are.

We human beings have a long history of trying to distinguish and separate ourselves from the other members of the animal kingdom. Traditionally, we have defined ourselves as uniquely different from all other animals by acknowledging a number of special (strictly human) traits. These have included our ability to communicate through spoken language, our capacity to make and use tools, to have a concept of self and others, and to think in complex and abstract terms. Over the years, however, as we learn more about nonhuman primates as well as other animals (especially parrots, elephants, dolphins, and whales), we have come to discover that these characteristics are not strictly unique to humans. In fact, the dividing line between human and nonhuman worlds has become greatly obscured. The more we learn, especially about our closest living relatives, the less unique we find ourselves to be, and the more we can see ourselves as part of a shared world.

Humans are in many aspects unique, but we are only one unique species among other unique species. We are one of the few mammals that habitually walk on two legs, we are responsible for a tremendous proliferation of diverse and complex cultures, and we are capable of modifying our physical world to a greater extent than any other living organism on earth. Unfortunately, more often than not, this occurs at the expense of the species with which we share this planet. Therefore, if we desire to move into a position of global stewardship as opposed to domination, we must seek to understand and protect the other organisms with which we share this earth—and particularly those that are most like us—the nonhuman primates.

❖❖ What Is a Primate?

All living forms and their fossil antecedents are organized into a system of classification called a *taxonomic* scheme. Primates are a category called an **order** of this classificatory system. It represents a subdivision of the **class** Mammalia that is within the **phylum** Chordata (animals with a stiff rod of cartilage, called a notochord, that runs down the middle of their

---

TABLE 1-1   Basic Taxonomic Divisions

Kingdom: Animalia (animals)

     Phylum: Chordata (animals with a notochord)

         Class: Mammalia (mammals)

            Order: Primates

---

backs) within the animal **kingdom** (Table 1-1). Even though the focus of this text is on nonhuman primates, we should never lose track of the fact that we humans also belong to the order of primates. The primate order includes a diverse group of animals that display considerable variation in anatomy, neurology, physiology, ecology, and behavior. There is no single list of characteristics that can be put forth to clearly distinguish each and every primate from other nonprimate animals.

Carl von Linné (1707–1778), a Swedish botanist, was the first to provide a definition of what constitutes a primate. In his great publication of 1758, *Systema Naturae*, Linné suggested that primates can be recognized based on the presence of four anatomical traits: four **incisors**, two **clavicles**, two mammary glands, and at least two extremities that function like hands (for a more in-depth description of these traits, see below). This definition of primates remained intact for over 100 years until the English anatomist, George Mivart (1873), provided a more extensive list of traits used to define a primate (Table 1-2). It was not until the last century when another English anatomist, W.E. Le Gros Clark (1959), suggested that there was a need to include evolutionary trends in a definition of primates. In 1986, Robert Martin, an English anthropologist, put forth an even more comprehensive list of traits and suggested that we take into consideration such things as habitat adaptation, distribution, locomotor adaptation, and reproductive biology. Today the approach to defining primates is thus much more **holistic**; all of the parts that make up and affect the animal are considered.

A holistic approach to defining primates, as suggested by Robert Martin, is in use today because variation in form, function, behavior, and ecology is the norm for this taxonomic

---

TABLE 1-2   Mivart's (1873) List of Traits That Distinguish Primates from other Mammals

Unguiculate having nails or claws

Claviculate having clavicles

Placental mammals

Orbits eye sockets encircled by bone

Three kinds of teeth incisors, canines, and molars

Brain always with a posterior lobe and a calcarine fissure a transverse groove along the medial surface of that lobe

Innermost digit of at least one pair of extremities opposable

Hallux big toe with a flat nail

A well-developed caecum a pouch-like part of the large intestine

Pendulous penis

Scrotal testis

Always two pectoral mammary glands

Source: Adapted from Conroy 1990, p. 5.

group. A hallmark of the primate order is that it contains organisms that have a generalized body design. We cannot use any one single feature to define primates. Instead we can identify a generic *primate pattern*. This is accomplished by delineating a range of traits that are generally applicable to a majority of primates. There are always exceptions to every rule, and the members of this order represent many such exceptions—that is, it is a highly diverse mammalian order. When thinking about what a primate is, consider yourself. You can use your own body as a blueprint or guide to identifying a number of traits that, when considered as a whole, generally differentiates the primates from other kinds of mammals. As we describe those traits that are used to distinguish the members of the order Primates, try to think about how each of these traits contributes to a primate lifestyle. In other words, how does a particular feature or tendency relate to how primates live their lives?

The Extremities (Hands and Feet)

Many traits that are uniquely primate are found in the hands and feet. Primates tend to live in very complex, three-dimensional environments. Even though many species tend to be ground-dwelling, or **terrestrial**, the great majority of species lives in the trees; they are **arboreal**. Orangutans are, in fact, the largest living arboreal mammals in the world. Those primates that are terrestrial do spend some time in the trees—for example, when feeding or sleeping. The construction of the

> **arboreal** – tree-living
> **terrestrial** – ground-dwelling

hands and feet of primates relates to their ability to move around in a complex, three-dimensional environment and to manipulate objects within this environment.

Primates typically have five digits on their hands and feet. The condition of having five fingers and toes is called **pentadactyly** (Figure 1-4). Pentadactyly is a very **ancestral** or old **trait**. Some primates, however, show various degrees of digital specialization. For example, spider monkeys and langurs have reduced thumbs and some strepsirhines

FIGURE 1-4 The primate hand retains the ancestral form by displaying five functional digits; pentadactyly. On each fingertip are unique fingerprints.

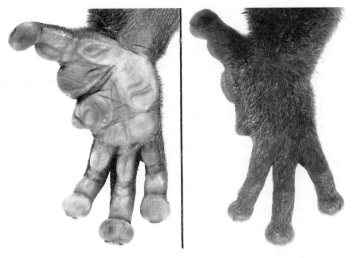

FIGURE 1-5   Some primate species have reduced expression of fingers. For example, this potto (*Perodicticus potto*) has an almost non-existing index finger.

have a reduced second finger (Figure 1-5). All primates have **nails** instead of claws at the end of their fingers and toes. This is a **derived** or recent **trait**. Some species, such as tamarins and marmosets, have specialized nails in the shape of claws. At the end of each digit and on the palms and soles, primates have **tactile pads** that increase the ability to detect what is being held or

> **ancestral trait** – an evolutionary older trait
> **derived trait** – a more recent evolutionary trait

touched. This provides a better grip on the substrate or surface that is being moved upon. Unlike rodents or cats, primates climb and move through trees by wrapping their hands and feet around branches; thus they hold on by grasping. The ability to grasp is called **prehensility** (Figure 1-6). Unlesßs an organism digs its claws into an object, it

FIGURE 1-6   Primates have hands with a very well developed grasping ability, as shown by this chimpanzee grasping a rope.

FIGURE 1-7 A juvenile bonobo (*Pan paniscus*) standing bipedally while manipulating the vegetation.

can be very difficult to grasp an item securely with claws. Most primates (excluding a number of the strepsirhine primates) have the ability to oppose or move their thumbs and touch the other digits or fingers of their hand.

Locomotion

Locomotion refers to how an organism moves around in its environment. Even though non-human primates are capable of standing up on their hind limbs in an erect posture (Figure 1-7) and may even move around like this, none of them move around habitually on their hind legs on the ground. Habitual terrestrial bipedality among living primates is a locomotor adaptation only found in humans. Most primates tend to move around in their environment on all four limbs, or are **quadrupedal** in their locomotor adaptation (Figure 1-8).

FIGURE 1-8 A lion-tailed macaque (*Macaca silenus*) in a quadrupedal pose.

FIGURE 1-9   Some American primates, such as this spider monkey (*Ateles belzebuth*) have tails that can grasp and function as a fifth limb.

Primates are unique among mammals in that they exhibit the greatest variety of strategies for moving around from place to place in their environment. As mentioned, primates may move around on their hind limbs in a bipedal stance, they may move around on all fours, and they may do this both on the ground as well as in the trees. In addition, when moving from tree to tree, some primates (including many strepsirhines) move by vertically clinging and leaping. A few species (spider monkeys, gibbons, and siamangs) are **brachiators** and move by propelling their bodies with an arm-over-arm swinging motion through the trees. Other specializations, like **prehensile tails** (Figure 1-9) that relate to how primates move around from place to place, will be discussed later in the text.

All primates have a clavicle or collarbone. Retention of the collarbones is an ancestral trait seen mainly in birds and reptiles but also in rodents and bats. Animals such as antelopes and horses, and other **ungulates** (hoofed mammals), which rely on speedy locomotion, have lost their clavicles. The clavicles function as struts and position the forelimbs out to the side of the body (Bass 2005).

A general characteristic that relates to how primates move around is that they often tend to be upright in body posture. They spend much time with their back in an upright position while sitting or hanging by their limbs vertically in trees. Even when moving quadrupedally, they tend to have their bodies slightly vertically aligned as opposed to being strictly horizontal. When jumping from tree to tree, their bodies are oriented at a vertical angle so they do not nose-dive into oncoming branches or tree trunks. Jumping with the body somewhat inclined enables both fore and hind limbs to securely wrap around oncoming supports.

Sense Organs

Primates depend on a combination of sensory abilities for their survival. Many **nocturnal** species

diurnal – active during the day **nocturnal** – active at night

have acute abilities to detect sound and smell. **Diurnal** species and especially those that spend a lot of time on the ground greatly rely on vision. A dependency on vision is a general trend among placental mammals and is maintained in the primate order. This is reflected by the expansion and increasing complexity of the visual areas of the brain. The eyes of primates face forward and are located in the front of the face. This is called **orbital convergence**. The eyes are protected by either a bony ridge (strepsirhines) or an entire bony socket (haplorhines). Your eyes sit in such a socket. Look up for a moment and pick a small spot to stare at. Now place your hand over one eye, repeat this procedure and cover up the other eye. What happens? You should be able to see the spot with either eye, but you have a different field of vision with each eye. In other words, you see more to the left or right periphery with the corresponding left or right eye. You see the spot with either eye because we have overlapping fields of vision, or **stereoscopic vision**. Even though what you see with either eye is a bit different, when both eyes are open, the information from each eye is received simultaneously and is processed at the same time in both sides of your brain. As a result, we see in three dimensions and have true depth perception. This relates to a primate lifestyle since it is vitally important to be able to perceive depth in complex, dimensional, three-arboreal environments. If primates could not accurately perceive, measure, and calculate depth, they would constantly be falling out of the trees.

The eye is a very primitive structure, and all mammals have the same basic construct. The retina in the eye contains sensitive **photoreceptors**. Some of these photoreceptors are sensitive to bright light (**cones**), while others are sensitive to dim light (**rods**). Most primates have a mixture of cone and rod photoreceptors, but nocturnal primates tend to have a higher concentration of rods. In addition, night-active strepsirhines have an extra reflective structure in the eye, the **tapetum lucidum** ("clear layer") to improve their vision at night (Figure 1-10). This is an ancestral trait and is not present in diurnal primates. All of the diurnal monkeys and apes have the ability to perceive color. This may be important as many primates rely on a diet of fruits, leaves, shoots, and flowers, and changes in the coloration of these items often signal when they are ready for healthy consumption.

FIGURE 1-10 The reflective eyes of two bushbabies (*Galago moholi*) look like two double spots of light.

Dentition

Even though some primate species are highly specialized in their dietary strategies, most primates are considered to be **omnivorous** because primate diets usually contain a mixture of food types. They tend to be both opportunistic and generalized in their selection of foods, and their teeth reflect this. Primates retain the ancestral mammalian trait of **differentiated dentition**; in other words, they have teeth that are structurally and functionally different. If we divide the mouth into four equal sections, (upper, lower, and with each divided into left and right sides) then in each **dental quadrant**, they generally have two incisors, one canine, two or three premolars, and two or three molars. Each tooth type serves a different function in obtaining, preparing, and processing foods for consumption (see Chapter 4). In those primates that have specialized diets, their dentition reflects the type of foods that are predominant in their particular dietary strategies.

Reproduction and Socialization

Since they are placental mammals, primates nourish their young with milk produced by mammary glands. Unlike other mammals, primates typically have only a single pair of mammary glands, but there is variability, and some primates have two or even three pairs. Births of singletons are the norm; however, some species show specialization in that they regularly produce twins (marmosets and tamarins are just a couple of examples). Compared to other placental mammals, the **gestation** period and the length of the infancy stage in primates tend to be longer in relation to life expectancy. Consequently, primates undergo a long period of development *in utero*. Despite this long period of gestational development, primates are quite helpless when born and remain dependent on their mother for an extended period of time (Figure 1-11). This reproductive strategy is highly adaptable for young primates that will have much to learn. A longer period of gestation reflects the fact that primates tend to have large and generally complex brains in proportion to their body size. An extended period of infant

FIGURE 1-11 An infant primate is dependant on its mother, and spends a lot of time clinging to its mother's tummy.

dependency relates to the fact that primates rely more on highly flexible learned behaviors to survive than they do on hard-wired or genetically controlled **innate** behaviors. This dependency on learned behavior translates to a propensity for behavioral heterogeneity; in other words, primates demonstrate great individuality in their response patterns (Jones 2005).

In order to be able to learn everything that a primate needs to know for its survival, it must acquire a great deal of information. This information is usually gained from its mother, less often its father, and commonly from other related individuals or peers. Primates are by definition and evolutionary development social organisms. All primates live in some sort of social environment, and **parental investment** is high. Compared to other placental mammals, few young are born, and immature primates often undergo intense rearing by their caretakers. Primates have a relatively long life expectancy. Depending on the species, they typically live between 10 and 45+ years. Primates enter the world as helpless individuals who are nurtured and cared for, and as they mature, they live in a very complex social world in which they will have to navigate for an extended number of years.

Behavior and Ecology

The ability of an organism to survive in ever-changing physical and social environments relates to its adaptability. In order for a trait to be considered as an **adaptation**, it must promote the ability of an organism to adjust to or survive in its environment, thus contributing to the survival of a population. All traits exhibit variation, and what is favorable in one environment may not be in another. Environments are not static, so what is adaptive at one time may not be adaptive in the future. Ultimately, in order for a trait to be considered an adaptation, it must be transmitted to and inherited by successive generations. In contrast, a short-term change or adjustment made by an individual organism to a particular situation at a specific time is referred to as an **acclimatization**. This type of change is not an adaptation because it is temporary and is not inherited.

For example, rhesus macaques living in the seasonally cold and snow-covered forested mountains in the foothills of the Himalayas have dense and thick coats of hair on relatively bulky bodies (Goldstein 1984). This is in sharp contrast to their lighter-bodied southern counterparts that live in the hot Indian tropics and that have less dense coats of hair. These gross physical differences reflect adaptations to the specific habitats in which these animals live.

Stress can produce physical and psychological reactions in both human and nonhuman primates. An increased production of hormones like adrenaline and cortisol is an adaptive response to stress. Elevated levels of stress hormones in the blood are good indicators of psychosocial stress. Robert Sapolsky (2001) has studied baboons for over twenty years and has determined that the social context a baboon of any age finds itself in can result in elevated levels of stress hormones. Thus baboons can exhibit temporary shifts in stress hormones that are physiological reactions to imagined or real social stressors. This temporary change is an acclimatization to the specific circumstances in which these baboons find themselves.

Nonhuman primates, being social organisms, depend greatly on learned behavior for their everyday survival. They tend to be more flexible in dealing with change as opposed to animals whose behavior is predominantly innate. To a great extent, the capacity of nonhuman primates to learn provides them with the ability to find alternative solutions and strategies to problematic environmental situations. In similar situations, more behaviorally inflexible animals might fail to survive and become extinct. Behavioral flexibility is thus another primate trait. We can, therefore, consider the primate lifestyle as one that involves increasing complexity in strategies that have been adapted over time to cope with ever-changing physical and social environments.

It is very important to note, however, that despite this great adaptive potential primates are adapted to particular habitats and most species cannot physiologically, behaviorally, or ecologically shift to living in entirely different types of environments. Many primate species are presently in very serious danger of extinction. We humans—through widespread habitat destruction and alteration, the trapping of nonhuman primates in the wild for pets and for sale to exotic animal dealers or for biomedical research, and the more recent crises caused by an accelerating demand for wild meat—are straining the ability of nonhuman primates to adapt to changing conditions. As a consequence, many of the living nonhuman primates are in great danger of becoming extinct. We will examine the status of primates in the wild in greater detail at the end of this book.

❖❖ What Is Primatology?

Primatology is the scientific study of nonhuman primates. It has only been within the last forty years or so that this field of study has been formally recognized. The scientific study of primates was first aligned with the work of natural historians and anatomists. Today, primatologists working in university settings are often housed in departments of anthropology, psychology, biology, ecology, conservation, or zoology. Anatomists were the first to formally and systematically study the nonhuman primates, starting as early as the second century A.D. The Greek anatomist, Galen (A.D. 131–201?), dissected a variety of mammals, including monkeys (Barbary macaques and baboons). His work was so precise that it served as a model for the learning of anatomy in European medical schools until the sixteenth century. Nonhuman primates were mainly used to advance our knowledge of anatomy and physiology.

In contrast to the Western world's relative unfamiliarity with nonhuman primates, those people who either shared habitats with various nonhuman primates or encountered them in their travels knew much about them. The ancient Egyptians imported hamadryas baboons to the Nile Valley. The Egyptians revered the baboons and considered them sacred beings. They were thought to be incarnations of Thoth, god of scribes and scholars, associated with scientific knowledge and writing (Figure 1-12; Kummer 1995). Hindu

FIGURE 1-12   The hamadryas baboon (*Papio hamadryas*) was considered sacred by the ancient Egyptians, and was often depicted as scribes or as the moon-god Thoth.

and Buddhist religious traditions have also long associated nonhuman primates with wisdom and insight by perceiving no division between human and animal worlds and by viewing the natural world as exhibiting continuity among all life forms. The three wise monkeys of Tendai Buddhism and the monkey king of the Ramayana story depict a mutualistic relationship between humans and the nonhuman primates (de Waal 2003, Wheatley 1999).

In the seventeenth century exploration of the world by the Europeans reached a peak. These explorers brought back reports of encounters with monkeys and apes, and in some cases, specimens were brought back to Europe. The distinguished physician, anatomist, and natural historian, Edward Tyson (1650–1708), conducted in-depth anatomical studies of the cadavers of chimpanzees and did much to describe the functional and structural relationships that existed between chimpanzees and human beings. However, unlike the Egyptians, the Europeans typically portrayed nonhuman primates as epitomizing those characteristics loathed and despised by humans. They considered them greedy, aggressive, shameless, and crass beings (Kummer 1995, Wheatley 1999).

The behavior of nonhuman primates began to be systematically studied by anatomists and psychologists in the United States, Britain, and Russia during the early 1920s. These studies took place mainly in captive situations, under crowded and monotonous conditions. Observing primates under such circumstances influenced Sir Solly Zuckerman (1932) to pronounce that the social lives of primates were dominated and controlled by sex and aggression. Robert Yerkes was a psychologist who readily perceived that many similarities existed between human and nonhuman primates (Figure 1-13). In 1925, he published a book called *Almost Human* in which he described the behavior of two chimpanzees that he kept at his home in Connecticut. In 1929, he and his wife, Ada, published an account of everything that was then known about the apes. Yerkes recognized that there was much to be learned about nonhuman primates, and although he himself never

FIGURE 1-13 Robert Yerkes (1876–1956)founder of the first major U.S. primate breeding laboratory.

FIGURE 1-14   The Sukhumi Primate Research Park, presently known as the Institute of Medical Primatology, is one of the oldest primate research centers. Boris Lapin was instrumental in establishing this primate facility and making it one of the largest and most active primate research centers. They have one of the largest captive breeding populations of hamadryas baboons (*Papio hamadryas*).

went into the field, he trained and prepared several young researchers. Between 1929 and 1930 Yerkes founded the first major U.S. primate breeding laboratory, the Laboratory of Primate Biology in Orange Park, Florida. Today, because of his groundbreaking research on primates, Robert Yerkes is considered to be the father of modern primatology. An even earlier primate facility was established in Russia in 1927, the Sukhumi Monkey Breeding Station (Figure 1-14). With the dissolution of the former Soviet Union, this facility was relocated to Sochi in Southern Russia. The new facility, Institute of Medical Primatology, houses over 2,500 primates, mainly macaques and baboons.

Investigations of primate ecology and social behavior in the wild began in earnest in 1931 when Clarence Ray Carpenter (a student of Yerkes) spent two years on Barro Colorado Island in the Canal Zone, Panama, studying howler monkeys. He also studied gibbons for four months in Thailand. Carpenter established a research protocol that was based on detailed and systematic quantitative description of both primate ecology and behavior. Other researchers followed Carpenter's lead, but World War II delayed the study of primates in the wild. After the war, research on nonhuman primates proliferated. In 1948, a Japanese primatologist, Junichiro Itani, under the direction of Kinji Imanishi, began fieldwork on the **endemic** (native) Japanese macaque. Japanese primatologists studied many components of the ecology and behavior of these monkeys, including their systems of social ranking, reproductive and grooming behaviors, as well as feeding and foraging strategies. Unfortunately, most of these early studies were published only in Japanese journals, and it was not until much later that the rich information gained from these early Japanese studies reached western primatologists (e.g., Kawai 1965, Suzuki 1965). Many of the groups studied in the late 1940s–1950s are still being observed today. Such multigenerational data have provided important clues into the complex social world of the nonhuman primates.

Throughout the 1960s and 1970s great strides were made in our knowledge of non-human primates. Primatologists from many countries traveled all over the world to study primates in their native habitats. The foundation for the modern tradition of primatological research was being laid and represented a very different approach to the study of nonhuman primates. This modern approach was based on a holistic perspective, which involves looking at all of the parts that make up a whole. This perspective, when applied to studies of nonhuman primates, requires that we look at all factors that influence the lives of these organisms. No one person can be an authority on all aspects of study, thus primates may be studied by a team of people with experience in various fields (**multidisciplinary**) of study. Individual team members may choose to study the primates from an ecological, **ethological** (behavioral), psychological, or biomedical perspective, among others.

As primatologists, we are concerned with how primates fit into their natural habitats, the ecology of these habitats, interactions between plant and animal species, how primates maneuver within their social environments, their evolutionary history, the history of particular populations, individual life histories, and even the effects that a study may have on the individuals being observed. Moreover, with the adoption of a holistic approach, primatology has become a much more rigorous scientific study. When a **scientific method** is utilized, observations are made and then research hypotheses are generated *a priori* to further study. A research strategy is then formulated, background research conducted, and data are collected with control and rigor. Once data are collected and statistical analyses performed, hypotheses are rejected, revised, or accepted. Data are collected with the implicit goal of being objective, reliable, and replicable. State-of-the-art technology is rapidly being implemented. Radio tracking, global positioning satellite imagery, portable computers, and health monitoring equipment are frequently used in the field (Figure 1-15).

FIGURE 1-15 Primatologists not only collect behavioral data while studying primates, but many are interested in collecting biomedical data. Here a ring-tailed lemur (*Lemur catta*) is measured and dental impressions are taken of its teeth.

❖❖ Why Study Primates?

Traditionally, nonhuman primates have been studied from the perspective of what we humans can gain from learning more about them. Nonhuman primates have been studied in order to understand, for example, the environmental circumstances behind human evolution and human adaptation, how learning occurs, the effects that physical and social environments can have on behavior, and to increase our knowledge of functional **morphology**, neuroanatomy, and physiology.

Today, the focus of much of the research on nonhuman primates has changed. Research projects are conducted with the specific goal to learn about a particular aspect of nonhuman primate species, to better understand some component of that species. Nonhuman primates are studied for the implicit reason of increasing our knowledge about them, their behavior, their ecology, the conservation of these species in the wild, their cognitive abilities, etc. Ultimately, however, their lives and ours are linked, and the more we learn about nonhuman primates, the more we will ultimately know and understand about ourselves.

❖❖ Primates as Models

Anthropologists have long recognized the applicability of using nonhuman primates as models to facilitate understanding about the evolution of our early human ancestors. Sherwood Washburn was one of the first anthropologists to systematically place the study of primates into the framework of human evolution. He stated that a valid interpretation of primate functional anatomy and human behavior could only be derived from the comparative study of living nonhuman primates in their natural environments (Washburn 1951, 1961). Our evolutionary histories have yielded characteristics and tendencies that are shared by members of the primate order. Study of our closest living relatives may thus promote insight into early **hominin** social behavior and ecology, population structure or demographics, mating systems, dietary reconstructions, and

> **hominin** – common name for members of the taxonomic tribe Hominini that includes living humans and their fossil representatives

ranges of intra- and interspecific diversity (diversity occurring within and between species).

The use of primates as models depends on the use of analogous relationships or patterns that have been independently acquired as the result of similar responses to evolutionary and selective events (Jolly 2001). **Analogies** establish relationships between phenomena that occur under similar situations. The usefulness of such models is contingent on how well we understand basic principles pertaining to behavioral ecology, functional morphology, evolution, and natural selection, as well as how valid or good the information is that we have about the nonhuman primates being used as models. What primate species to use as models is a contentious issue. The choice is to a great extent dependent on the question being addressed. If greater emphasis is placed on molecular, anatomical, and behavioral links, then apes may be the best models. If the emphasis is on the similarities in adaptive responses to physical environments hypothesized to be most like the ones occupied by early hominins, then monkeys may be the best choice as models.

Savanna-dwelling baboons were studied by DeVore, Hall, and Washburn in the early 1960s. They used this information to construct models representing the behavioral responses that early hominins would have made living under similar environmental conditions (DeVore and Hall 1965, DeVore and Washburn 1963). The role of dominant and aggressive male behaviors to maintain group integrity, safety, and reproductive success became core concepts in reconstructions of what life might have been like for early hominins (Hall and DeVore 1965, Washburn and DeVore 1961). However, as more and more studies were conducted on different populations and on other species of baboons living under similar and different environmental conditions, it became apparent that the "baboon model" had given us a skewed and limited view of primate adaptive responses. In particular, Shirley Strum's long-term study of the friendly behavior of male baboons and cooperative behaviors while hunting played a large role in diminishing the importance of the swaggering, dominant male (Strum 1975, 1987).

Other researchers have argued that, due to our close evolutionary links with apes, ape species are the most appropriate candidates on which to base our reconstructive models. Chimpanzees (Moore 1996), bonobos (Zihlmann 1996), orangutans (Schwartz 1984, 1987, 2005), and gorillas, or a combination of them (Potts, 1987, Stanford 1999, Susman 1987, Wrangham 1987) have been proposed as the "best" species. It has become apparent that we cannot underestimate the variability of primate responses to environmental conditions and that this was most likely also a hallmark of early hominins. Consequently, if nonhuman primates are to be used as models to reconstruct the adaptive responses of early hominins, to identify adaptive potentials or to hypothesize about the origin of certain behaviors, then models must be based on long-term studies of a variety of primates living under different and similar environmental conditions.

A recent approach to using primates to reconstruct the behavior of early hominins and the evolution of particular behaviors is found in the work of Hart and Sussman (2005). The frequency of predation on primates was analyzed from published sources and questionnaires that were sent to primatologists, zoologists, and other researchers studying nonhuman primates and predators in the wild. These data combined with incidences from the hominin fossil record of predation on early hominins provided evidence that primates, both human and nonhuman, have been and continue to be preyed upon by many different predators. Primates are preyed upon in all areas of the world, no matter if they are diurnal or nocturnal, large or small in body size, terrestrial or arboreal. Consequently, the evolution of cooperative behavior in primates and especially humans is seen as an adaptive response to the role of primates as prey over time.

Another important area in which nonhuman primates are used as models involves the study of human growth and development (Watts 1985). Nonhuman primates have been used to promote knowledge about dental development, craniofacial growth, **allometry**, and the neuroendocrine and physiological mechanisms that affect normal cognitive and social development. Nonhuman primates have also increased our understanding about the ill effects of child abuse, stress, smoking, and drug and alcohol abuse.

Our understanding of surgical procedures and viral and immunological diseases has been much advanced through the use of nonhuman primates (Blum 1994). These efforts have led to the discovery of the Rh factors present in human blood groups, the effects of exposure to toxins, and the cause of phocomelia (a condition produced through the use by pregnant women of a sleeping pill, thalidomide, that in humans caused severe deformities of arms and legs). Primates have been used to develop vaccines, such as the

Salk polio vaccine and a vaccine for rubella. They are also used to develop strategies for treating schizophrenia and diabetes, improvements in chemotherapy and understanding the life cycle of tumors, treating Hepatitis B and, most recently, AIDS. In addition, primates are used to refine surgical techniques for organ transplants, e.g., transplanting corneas. Literally millions of nonhuman primate lives have been sacrificed to better the quality of human life.

❖❖ Where Does One Go To Study Nonhuman Primates?

Some of you might recognize the names of Jane Goodall, Dian Fossey, and Biruté Galdikas. These three women became famous either in print or film because of their groundbreaking and long-term **fieldwork**. Jane Goodall studied the Gombe chimpanzees, Dian Fossey the mountain gorillas of Rwanda, and Biruté Galdikas the orangutans of Borneo (Box 1-1). In this context, "the field" means the natural habitat in which the study animals live. Not all primatological research, however, is conducted in the primates' natural habitat. Many people study nonhuman primates in captive or in free-ranging conditions. Captive locations include zoos, wildlife parks, breeding facilities, and a variety of laboratory settings. Free-ranging locations are typically primate colonies that have been artificially established on islands that a college, university, or other research-oriented facility supervises. One such free-ranging location is the island of Cayo Santiago in the West Indies that was established by Carpenter in 1938 (Rawlins and Kessler 1986). Today, provisioned rhesus macaques are thriving and provide ample opportunity for primatologists to investigate a wide range of questions. Other less exotic primate facilities include the home of the Arashiyama West colony of transplanted Japanese snow monkeys (macaques) that live in South Texas (Pavelka 1993).

 BOX 1-1

The Grand Dames of Primatology

A childhood dream became a reality when Jane Goodall (Figure 1-16a) traveled to Africa to visit a friend who had moved to Kenya. While there she met Louis Leakey, a paleoanthropologist, who was the Curator of the Coryndon Museum, now known as the National Museums of Kenya. Without a college degree but with much enthusiasm, Goodall went to work as a secretary for Louis Leakey. Recognizing her drive and commitment and a life-long fasci-

nation for animals, Louis Leakey asked if she would be willing to undertake a long-term study of chimpanzees. Armed with a notepad and binoculars at 26 years of age, Goodall went to Gombe, Tanzania, in 1960. She encountered many frustrating problems with habituating the chimpanzees, but eventually she was able to observe the animals without their running off, and she slowly began to recognize individuals. At the time she did not realize that in the

(continued)

(a)

(b)

(c)

FIGURE 1-16   (a) Jane Goodall established the Gombe Field Station in Tanzania, where chimpanzees are still being studied, and has devoted her life to the protection of these apes. (b) Dian Fossey established the Karisoke Field Station in Rwanda, where she studied the rare mountin gorillas (*Gorilla gorilla beringei*). (c) Biruté Galdikas established Camp Leakey, deep in the jungle of Borneo, to observe orangutans (*Pongo pygmeus*). Today it is also a place where rescued orangutans are cared for and prepared to be reintroduced to their natural habitat.

Western world it was scientific taboo to associate feelings, personalities, and emotions with animals. In October 1960 she witnessed two of her male chimpanzees, David Graybeard and Goliath, modify branches for termite fishing, and she communicated her observations to Louis Leakey. His famed response to her was "Now we must redefine *tool*, redefine *Man*, or accept chimpanzees as humans" (Goodall 1990:19). Goodall's observations literally stood the scientific community of the time on its head, and over time she did much to lessen the perceived chasm between human and nonhuman primates. In 1965 she earned a Ph.D. in Ethology from Cambridge University. Now, some forty years later, the multi-generational information about matrilineages and the comings and goings of Gombe chimpanzees have been well documented. Today the Gombe Stream Research Center continues its research, and Jane Goodall has become an internationally recognized champion, not only of the protection of chimpanzees, but of environmental conservation and education.

Dian Fossey (Figure 1-16b) was an occupational therapist who worked with disabled children when she too pursued a lifelong dream by going on safari to East Africa. Fossey went to Olduvai Gorge, an important fossil hominin site, where she met Louis Leakey and his wife, Mary. Fossey then went to the Congo to see the mountain gorillas that had been studied by George Schaller. Upon returning to Kentucky, she wrote a series of articles that appeared in the *Louisville Courier-Journal* about the Virunga gorillas. Louis Leakey and Fossey reconnected at a lecture he gave in Kentucky, and Leakey asked if she would be willing to go back for a long-term study of the gorillas. Fossey gladly accepted the challenge and returned to the Congo. However, after six months, civil war broke out. She decided to move across the border to Rwanda to study the mountain gorillas there instead. Fossey had a history of asthma and was a smoker, so she underwent great physical hardship working in the steep, mountainous terrain. Fossey established the Karisoke Research Center in 1967, and her studies furthered our knowledge about mountain gorilla behavior and ecology. Dian Fossey received a Ph.D. in Zoology from the University of Cambridge in 1974.

Fossey aggressively championed the plight of the mountain gorillas from poachers, and she became known for her "active conservation." On December 26, 1985, at the age of 53, she was found murdered in her camp. Many individuals were suspected, and a student was eventually arrested for her murder, but to this day her death remains a mystery. Sigourney Weaver played Fossey in the movie, *Gorillas in the Mist*, which immortalized her work and efforts, but the movie has been much criticized for its portrayal of her murder and her compulsive pro-gorilla behaviors. Today Sigourney Weaver is the honorary chairperson of Dian Fossey Gorilla Fund International. A new book, *No One Loved Gorillas More*, based on letters that Dian had written to family and friends, has recently been written by Camilla de la Bedoyere (de la Bedoyere and Campbell 2005), and the Opera-Kentucky Visions Program just produced an opera about Fossey's life.

Yet another of Louis Leakey's finds was Biruté Galdikas (Figure 1-16c). After earning a BA in psychology, she entered graduate school at the University of California, Los Angeles, to pursue a graduate degree in anthropology. Leakey was a guest lecturer in an archaeology class Galdikas attended. After the class, she assertively pursued an opportunity to introduce herself to Leakey and to inform him about her passion and strong desire to study orangutans. She persisted, earned her MA in 1969, and two years later Louis Leakey, as he did for Jane Goodall and Dian Fossey, obtained some initial funding to send Galdikas to the Indonesian island

(continued)

of Borneo. In 1971 at the age of 25, Galdikas began what has led to over three decades of research on the red apes. She lived in a hut that she named "Camp Leakey" and had to contend with poachers, leeches, and a multitude of carnivorous insects. Galdikas's work did much to initiate what we now know about the biodiversity of the Indonesian rainforest and the ecological and social adaptations of orangutans. She became very compassionate about finding ways to rehabilitate an ever-growing number of orphaned orangutans. She founded the Orangutan Foundation International and still actively teaches and lectures. Her memoir, *Reflections of Eden*, recounts her experiences (Galdikas 1995).

Each of these women did what at the time was thought to be impossible for young women to do. All three possessed an amazing passion and commitment to their research subjects and demonstrated almost unbelievable fortitude and courage. All three gained worldwide recognition for the knowledge they accumulated about their respective apes. Collectively, they became known as "Leakey's Angels." Goodall, Fossey, and Galdikas had been hand-picked and mentored by Louis Leakey, and each greatly expanded our knowledge about the apes that they studied—thus they have become known as the grand dames of primatology.

❖❖ Summary

Primatology is the scientific study of primates, which include the haplorhines (monkeys, apes, and humans) and the strepsirhines (lemurs, bushbabies, and lorises). Despite a tendency to differentiate ourselves from other animals, the nonhuman primates are our closest living relatives, and we share much in common with them.

All primate species can be identified by a series of characteristics, which when taken as a whole, delineate a particular primate pattern. This pattern identifies all primates as social organisms that greatly depend on learned behavior for their survival. The important role that learned rather than innate behavior plays within this order promotes great variability in both individual and group behaviors. Within the order there is also extensive variability in morphology and ecology.

Study of nonhuman primates has been important to the development of models used to understand the evolution, behavior, and ecology of early hominins. The robusticity of such models depends on the analysis of analogous behaviors exhibited by a range of different primate species. Models based on nonhuman primates have promoted knowledge about our own evolution, human growth and development, and the effects of viral and immunological diseases.

Nonhuman primates may be studied in the field, in captivity, or under free-ranging conditions. Today a primatological study will be holistic in perspective, multidisciplinary, and will adhere to the scientific method. Traditionally, primates have been studied for the benefit of humankind. Presently, nonhuman primates are studied for the sake of learning more about them, but because we and they are ultimately linked, these studies contribute to the knowledge about all of the species that are called primates, including ourselves.

❖❖ Key Words

acclimatization	field work	pentadactyly
adaptation	gestation	photoreceptor
allometry	haplorhine	phylum
analogy	holistic	prehensile tail
ancestral trait	hominin	prehensility
arboreal	incisor	primate
bipedal	innate	primatology
brachiator	kingdom	quadrupedal
class	morphology	rod
clavicle	multidisciplinary	scientific method
cone	nail	stereoscopic vision
dental quadrant	nocturnal	strepsirhine
derived trait	omnivorous	tactile pad
differentiated dentition	orbital convergence	tapetum lucidum
diurnal	order	terrestrial
endemic	parental investment	ungulate
ethology		

❖❖ Study Questions

1. What is a primate? What type of animals are included in this category?
2. What are the main characteristics that most primates share?
3. What does it mean to study primates from a holistic viewpoint?
4. How have primates been used as models?

❖❖ Suggested Readings and Related Web Sites

Blum D. 1994. The monkey wars. New York: Oxford University Press.

Fossey D. 1983. Gorillas in the mist. Boston: Houghton Mifflin Company.

Galdikas BMF. 1995. Reflections of Eden: My years with the orangutans of Borneo. Boston: Little, Brown and Company.

Goodall J. 1990. Through a window: My thirty years with the chimpanzees of Gombe. Boston: Houghton Mifflin Company.

Goodall J, Peterson D. 1993. Visions of Caliban: On chimpanzees and people. Boston: Houghton Mifflin Company.

Hart D, Sussman R. 2005. Man the hunted: Primates, predators, and human evolution. New York: Westview Press.

Savage-Rumbaugh S, Lewin R. 1994. Kanzi: The ape at the brink of the human mind. New York: John Wiley & Sons.

Strum SC. 1987. Almost human: A journey into the world of baboons. New York: Random House.

CHAPTER 2

Primate Classification

Most experts estimate the existence of approximately 330 species of living primates, but this is *not* a static number. Within our lifetimes we have witnessed the possible extinction of a primate species as well as the discovery of new ones. This may contradict what you might have assumed—that by now scientists would have identified all of the living members of the primate order. This is not the case for several reasons. All of the habitats in which primates live have not yet been thoroughly investigated. In addition, habitat encroachment or deforestation has forced primates out of obscure or fairly impenetrable habitats into more open and visible ones. Furthermore, new technologies now enable us to more closely scrutinize the genetic relatedness of species, and thus not rely only on physical appearances to evaluate species affinity.

Deep in the jungle tributaries of the Amazon River basin, two new species of marmosets—*Callithrix manicorensis* and *C. acariensis*—have been discovered within the last decade (van Roosmalen et al. 2000). A population of a highly endangered species, the black-faced lion tamarin, or *Leontopithecus caissara,* was recently discovered on an island in the Atlantic not far from the Brazilian coastal city of Sao Paulo. This is a significant discovery because this species has a dwindling population of less than 400 remaining individuals (Smithsonian National Zoological Park 2006). Most recently, a medium-sized, long-tailed monkey was found in southern Tanzania and was determined to be a new species of highland mangabey *(Rungwecebus kipunji)*. Within a ten-month time span, this species was actually discovered and identified by two independent research teams (Davenport et al. 2006, Jones et al. 2005). Many species that have been newly discovered by the Western world have long been recognized in the natural history lore of the indigenous peoples with whom they have shared their habitats. In the mountainous Indian state of Arunachal Pradesh, a new species of macaque, the Arunachal macaque *(Macaca munzala)*, has been identified (Sinha et al. 2005). The local people were familiar with this macaque, which they referred to as the "mun zala." On the island of Sulawesi, in Indonesia, a new tarsier species, *Tarsius lariang*, has been identified (Merker and Groves 2006). New primate species have also been determined through the genetic analysis of physically variable populations of closely related primate species; for example, the newly recognized species of sportive lemur, *Lepilemur seali* and *L. mitsinjonensis,* and a new little mouse lemur, *Microcebus lehilahytsara*.

In the year 2000 news about the extinction of a beautiful species, Miss Waldron's red colobus monkey (*Piliocolobus badius waldronae*; Figure 2-1), was announced in scientific journals and by the associated press (Oates et al. 2000). Sad news indeed, since this was the first primate species whose extinction was recorded in modern times. Then, in 2005, there was renewed hope that Miss Waldron's red colobus may not have disappeared but was hanging on by a thread in a remote southeastern corner of the West African country of Cote d'Ivoire (McGraw 2005). Despite the new additions to our inventory of primates, we are presently on the brink of witnessing the extinction of many of our closest living relatives.

❖❖ Classification Systems

Classification involves a system for ordering organisms, while **taxonomy** reflects the theory underlying how they are organized. Let's take as an example a postcard collection. You may decide to organize it according to who sent you the card, the time frame that the card represents, the geographic origin of the card, and the type of picture on it. If you organize it by picture, place, and time, you may further divide these general categories into more specific ones. Geographical origin could be subdivided into continent, country, and state. Whatever system you use to classify or organize your collection of cards

FIGURE 2-1 Many primate species are on the brink of extinction. The Miss Waldron's red colobus (*Piliocolobus badius waldronae*) was feared extinct in 2000, but this has not yet been confirmed.

reflects your taxonomic scheme or the theory behind your system of ordering. Taxonomy involves both the method used to classify organisms as well as the resulting classificatory scheme that reflects how organisms are related to one another.

> **classification**—the arrangement or organization of phenomena into categories
> **taxonomy**—rationale or methodology used to classify; in biology it is based on similarities and differences
> **phylogeny**—the evolutionary lineage of a group of related organisms

In the world of primate taxonomy, the system of organization follows that first devised by the Swedish botanist, Carl von Linné, who established a taxonomic system for all living organisms (*Systema Naturae,* 10th edition, 1758). His taxonomy was based on similarities and differences he observed in the morphology and adaptations of the organisms he classified. He arranged all living organisms into a nested hierarchy of categorical units called kingdom, phylum, class, order, family, genus (plural = genera), and species (always singular in form) (Figure 2-2). The kingdom is the broadest category containing numerous phyla, classes, orders, genera, and species, while membership at the species level is most specific. When appropriate, additional

Kingdom	Animalia
Phylum	Chordata
Class	Mammalia
Order	Primates
Family	Cercopithecidae
Genus	Papio
Species	anubis (anubis baboon)

FIGURE 2-2 The basic taxonomic system devised by Carl von Linné in the 18th century.

Kingdom
  Phylum
    Subphylum
      Superclass
        Class
          Subclass
            Infraclass
              Superorder
                Order
                  Suborder
                  ➜ Infraorder
                    ➜ Superfamily
                      Family
                    Subfamily
                  Tribe
                    Subtribe
                    Genus
                      Subgenus
                        Species
                    ➜ Subspecies

FIGURE 2-3   With our better understanding of the world around us, modifications to the Linnean system were needed. The modern taxonomic system has incorporated additional categories such as infraorder, superfamily, and subspecies.

higher and lower levels of taxonomic divisions such as infraorder, superfamily, and subspecies may be used (Figure 2-3). Presently, similarities and differences in anatomical structure and design are in some cases being recalibrated and fine-tuned by investigating the molecular or genetic closeness of various species. Ideally, correspondence between these two approaches should yield representative **phylogenies** that reflect the evolutionary relatedness of species.

Today there are two prominent approaches to the science of classification: **evolutionary systematics** and **phylogenetic systematics**, also referred to as **cladistics** (e.g., Cracraft 1983, Groves 2001, Mayr and Ashlock 1991). Evolutionary systematics, spearheaded by the late evolutionary biologist, Ernst Mayr, is based on evaluating the degree of distance or closeness reflected by a suite of morphological characteristics exhibited by different groups of animals. Establishing degrees of similarity or difference is presumed to reflect phylogenetic relationships. This method can be subjective, however, because the traits examined have been selected by the researchers. Phylogenetic systematics or cladistics, initiated by German entomologist, Willi Hennig, is intended to be a more objective approach. A cladistic analysis involves a systematic examination of specific traits, especially those that are derived or unique traits. The presence or absence of such traits can yield a branching pattern of their distribution within related **taxa.** Cladistic analysis has become a valuable technique for comparing and contrasting the evolutionary validity of established taxonomies. The classification of primates has traditionally been based on the establishment of taxonomies that reflect similarities and differences in morphological characteristics and adaptive strategies. This may represent the phylogeny of species, but it also may not. Moreover, taxonomy does not provide information about the timing of evolutionary branching events or the specific patterns of evolutionary relatedness. Taxonomies have been adjusted to incorporate improved techniques in genetic comparisons, but cladistics may offer even more precise insight into specific evolutionary patterns.

Interestingly, when we think about the established taxonomy of primates, we have traditionally divided the apes into three taxonomic families: (1) the Hylobatidae, which includes the gibbons and siamangs; (2) the Pongidae, which includes the gorilla, chimpanzee, bonobo, and orangutan; and (3) the Hominidae, which includes living humans and their fossil ancestors (Figure 2-4). Cladistically, on the basis of **shared derived characteristics**, or traits that are shared by members of two or more different taxonomic groups but are not exhibited in other such groups, we can no longer support this taxonomic arrangement. In particular, in light of recent information about the genetic relatedness of these species, we have had to reconsider the evolutionary relatedness of humans and the African apes. Consequently, there is a need to reevaluate how we have traditionally differentiated and classified members of the order primates. We will return to this topic later in this chapter.

A cladistic analysis is based on the use of **homologous traits** or traits that occur in species because of shared evolutionary ancestry. The traits used to identify membership to the order

> **homologous traits**—similarity of traits due to shared ancestry
> **analogous traits**—traits serve the same function but are not the result of shared ancestry

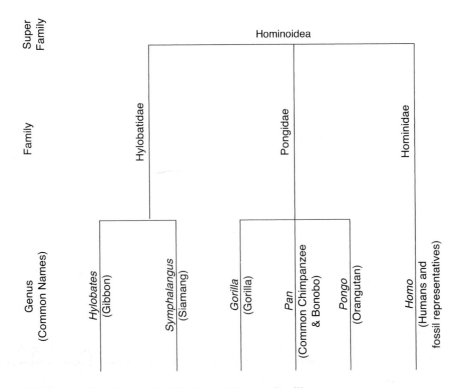

FIGURE 2-4 Traditional classification of the ape families.

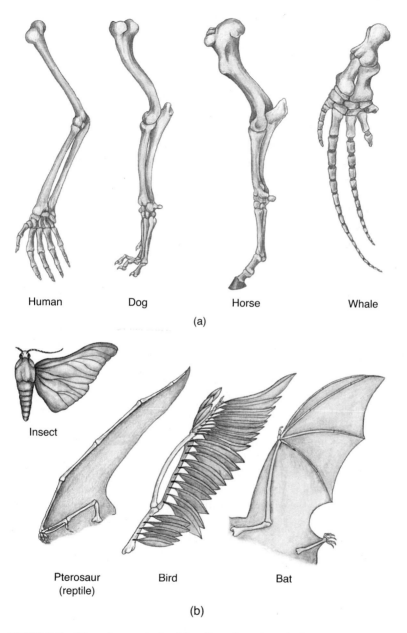

Human   Dog   Horse   Whale

(a)

Insect

Pterosaur   Bird   Bat
(reptile)

(b)

FIGURE 2-5   Homologous traits (a) reflect shared evolutionary ancestry, while analogous traits (b) show functional similarities but are not based on shared ancestry.

Primates, and described in Chapter 1, include a list of homologous traits. Other traits that look similar but only reflect common adaptations that have occurred in unrelated species are called **analogous traits**. A classic example of an analogous trait is the wings of a butterfly and the wings of a bat (Figure 2-5). Both serve the same purpose of promoting flight but

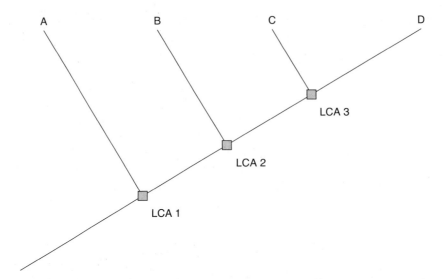

FIGURE 2-6 Cladograms are diagrams that reflect the pattern of shared derived traits. Each branch, or clade, represents the ancestor and all of its descendants. For example, the clade of the last common ancestor (LCA) #2 includes species B, C and D, and all species in between. The clade of LCA #3 comprises species C and D, and all species in between.

have evolved independently in the lineages represented by insects and mammals. Through an examination of homologous traits and by determining if they are ancestral or derived, we can establish the order of evolutionary branching. Cladistics focuses on shared derived characteristics. For example, hair is a shared derived character that is exhibited by all mammals but is not found in other classes of vertebrates. Patterns of shared derived characteristics that are homologous can be illustrated in a diagram called a **cladogram** (Figure 2-6). A cladogram depicts a phylogenetic tree with its branches or **clades** representing ancestral species and all of its descendants. The ultimate timing of the branching depends on an analysis of shared derived characteristics now identified on a molecular level, sequences in the bases that make up a genetic code. Clades just like taxonomic categories can be nested within larger clades. Ultimately, a clade should be composed of a single ancestor and all of its descendants, a **monophyletic group**. A clade that shows a single ancestor and only some of its descendants is a **paraphyletic group**.

◇◇ **What Is a Species?**

The concept of species has traditionally been considered as real. Species are presented as being the least arbitrary and biologically most relevant level within taxonomy. Other higher-level taxonomic groupings are more arbitrary and not necessarily representative of real biological entities. However, there is much controversy over what actually constitutes a species. This is partly due to the fact that evolution is not static; all living things exist in different stages of evolution. Taxonomic classification automatically forces an oversimplified structure onto a complex and dynamic situation. Likewise, how we define a species tends to be dichotomous and absolute—when it really should be continuous and relative. An ideal definition of a species would thus account for the

 BOX 2-1

Morphology and Molecular Biology—Competing or Supporting Lines of Evidence?

The goal of taxonomy is to order organisms according to their phylogenetic relationships. Groves (2000) describes taxonomy as a type of scientific hypothesis that must be confirmed through repetitive testing of available data. Typically, the data used to confirm, refute, and revise established phylogenies involve morphological, molecular, behavioral, and ecological adaptations. With increasingly refined technology and methodology, our ability to more precisely measure and identify molecular differences has led to more detailed and precise phylogenetic reconstructions. Ideally, any phylogeny established on the basis of shared derived morphological characteristics will be supported by molecular data or the other way around (Apiou et al. 1996, Shoshani et al. 1996, Vezuli et al. 1997). However, in the case of the Atelinae subfamily, a group of Central and South American monkeys, this has not been the case.

The Atelinae consist of five genera, including *Alouatta* (howler monkeys), *Ateles* (spider monkeys), *Brachyteles* (woolly spider monkeys), *Lagothrix* (woolly monkeys), and *Oreonax* (yellow-tailed woolly monkeys). *Oreonax* was only recently recognized as a separate genus within this subfamily (Groves 2001). There are consequently little data on this genus, thus the following discussion will be limited to the first four genera.

There is a general consensus that these genera represent a monophyletic group that shares the following characteristics: a relatively large body size, a

prehensile tail, and frequent suspensory behaviors (Collins 2004). The specific relationships that exist between the genera within this subfamily have, however, been hotly debated. Based on cladistic analyses using a range of morphological and behavioral traits, *Brachyteles* and *Ateles* have been identified as being most closely related in some analyses (Rosenberger et al. 1990), while in other analyses *Ateles* and *Lagothrix* have been identified as being more closely related (Kay 1990). In other studies yet, it has not been possible to determine the phylogenetic relationships between *Ateles, Brachyteles*, and *Lagothrix* (Ford 1986). The biomolecular data have yielded equally contradictory results. In some studies *Lagothrix* and *Brachyteles* have emerged as the most closely related genera (Meireles et al., 1999, Schneider et al., 1993), while Collins (2004) found such a close biomolecular similarity between *Ateles, Brachyteles*, and *Lagothrix* that it was impossible to resolve the three-way split.

The specific relationships that exist among the four genera of ateline monkeys have thus not been possible to resolve through *either* morphology or molecular biology. In the words of Hartwig (2005:1009), in this case, "calipers and centrifuges will not solve the problem," but the biomolecular data may highlight particular relationships presumed on the basis of shared morphology to be reconsidered in a new light.

Morphology and molecular biology offer a beneficial combination of different lines of evidence that can be used to

(continued)

fine-tune established phylogenies. Most times these two different approaches are highly complementary, but there are unique situations such as the one described above when the relatedness of genera is so complex that either approach, or a combination of the two, seems to create more confusion than resolve the evolutionary relatedness of the different genera. There may be other avenues available to scientists working on such taxonomic puzzles. Primates exhibit high host specificity in the type of parasites they contain (Hugot 1998). Parasites (such as pinworms) observed in different species of primates may be used as an evolutionary measuring stick and parasite phylogeny-trees may be generated providing yet another line of evidence to resolve complex phylogenetic situations. In any case, when morphological and genetic data do not appear to agree we should investigate methods used and investigate alternative, holisitic approaches.

evolutionary status of a species, its degree of relatedness to evolutionarily close and more distant species, as well as provide us with some indication about the timing of these changes. Such an all inclusive definition is virtually impossible to construct. There have been many attempts to overcome the limitations just mentioned, and many different species definitions, or **species concepts**, have been proposed that emphasize particular characteristics or aspects of a species (Table 2-1).

The most frequently used species definition is the biological species concept (BSC). The BSC is based on the idea of reproductive isolation. When populations of

TABLE 2-1   Some of the Most Commonly Used Species Concepts

Concept name	*Concept description*	*Source*
Biological Species Concept	Actual interbreeding populations that are reproductively isolated from other such populations	Dobzhansky 1935, Mayr 1942, Mayr and Ashlock 1991
Evolutionary Species Concept	Portrays a species as the result of evolutionary processes that have operated to promote a distinct and particular lineage	Simpson 1961
Phylogenetic Species Concept	Considers both ancestry and descent, and relies on the identification of distinctive characters such as DNA sequences, to distinguish members of a species	Cracaft 1983, 1997
Ecological Species Concept	Species maintain separation due to specificity in adaptations to particular habitats and niches	van Valen 1976
Recognition Species Concept	Members of a species share and use a wide variety of cues to identify one another as potential mates	Paterson 1978, 1985
Cohesion Species Concept	Holistic consideration of a variety of factors including genes, demographics, ecology, and behavior that operate in concert with one another to maintain species' integrity	Templeton 1989, 1998

organisms can interbreed, they are considered members of the same species; but when they are reproductively isolated from one another, they are considered to belong to different species. Even though this is the most frequently used species concept, it is not completely bulletproof: First, there is the question of determining the potential of species

> **sympatric**—populations share at least part of the same living space *Same region*
> **allopatric**—populations show no overlap in the living space

to successfully reproduce in **sympatric** and **allopatric** populations. Populations are considered to be sympatric if they occupy overlapping space. In contrast, populations that are allopatric do not share overlapping space. If two populations are sympatric and interbreeding does not occur, it is relatively clear that two different species are represented, but when populations are allopatric, how do we determine if we are dealing with two different species or one? If members of two seemingly similar populations cannot physically get to one another to mate (for example, they may live on two different islands), how do we know for sure that they are reproductively isolated? Second, for a species to be reproductively isolated there must be some sort of **reproductive isolating mechanisms** in place. These are behavioral, morphological, physiological, geographical, or ecological differences that make a successful mating resulting in fertile offspring unlikely to occur. If species appear to be closely related, we must attempt to determine if reproductive isolating mechanisms have been in place for a long period of time or if they are in the process of evolving. Furthermore, due to the destruction and disturbance of habitats, reproductive isolating mechanisms that effectively operated in the past may now be compromised. More and more cases involving species traditionally considered as representative of "good" biological species are now being called into question. The existence of hybrids poses an additional problem to the BSC (see Box 2-2).

When we think about species, we need to think in the terms of an extended time frame, both before and into the future of an existing species. Consequently, some concepts, such as the evolutionary species concept (EvolSC), portray a species as the result of evolutionary processes that have operated to promote a distinct and particular lineage.

 ❖ ❖ ❖ ❖ **BOX 2-2** ❖ ❖ ❖ ❖

Hybrid Zones and Their Potential Role in Speciation

A **hybrid zone** is where two genetically distinct but closely related taxa meet, interbreed, and produce offspring. Hybridization is more commonly observed in plants than in animals. Among animals it is most common in birds and fishes (Grant and Grant 1992, 1996, Riesenberg and Buerkle 2002, Smith et al. 2003), although there are many situ-

ations in the wild in which hybridization has occurred among primates (e.g., baboons: Alberts and Altmann 2001, Phillips-Conroy and Jolly 1986; guenons: Detwiler et al. 2005; lemurs: Wyner et al. 2002; macaques: Evans et al. 2001; squirrel monkeys: Silva et al. 1992). Hybridization is of great interest to evolutionary biologists and population

(continued)

geneticists because it provides an opportunity to examine the selective advantages of **gene flow** or the exchange of genes between populations under specific conditions. There is disagreement about the importance of hybrids and hybrid zones. Hybrid zones may be viewed as analogous to temporary "genetic sinks" or "evolutionary noise" with little or no influence on the BSC or speciation (e.g., Mayr 1992, Schemske 2000). An alternative view considers hybrid zones as a potential mechanism that promotes gene flow between parental species. Hybridization may even be considered as an evolutionary process that may lead to the formation of new species (Allendorf et al. 2001, Barton 2001).

Interbreeding at species borders, **parapatric hybridization**, is the most common type of hybridization. Populations are considered to be parapatric when their living space overlaps but only along the borders. Such hybrid zones tend to be narrow and persistent, almost like a buffer zone wherein the hybrids show a sharp morphological gradient between the two parental taxa. There appears to be only partial reproductive barriers in place. These are sometimes referred to as **primary hybrid zones**. **Secondary hybrid zones** occur when two allopatric taxa (which share a common ancestry) come into contact after having been separated for a long period of time. In reality, it is very difficult to actually determine whether a hybrid zone is of primary or secondary origin (Allendorf et al. 2001). Since the parental taxa can reproduce, they are not altogether "good" species according to the BSC; therefore, we often refer to hybridizing parental taxa as semispecies, subspecies, or allotaxa (Grubb et al. 2003).

Sympatric hybridization entails interbreeding among distinct species that live in the same area and have overlapping ranges. It is common in plants but seldom seen in animals. During sympatric hybridization there is low level "leakage" of genes between two taxa where interbreeding barriers have not yet become complete. The hybridization we see between different guenon species falls into this category (Detwiler et al. 2005).

To maintain species integrity, gene flow between related taxa has to be nonexistent or at least kept to a minimum. When hybridization occurs, it indicates that there were either no premating barriers in place or that these barriers were incomplete. Commonly, there is some form of postmating selection against the hybrids (Barton and Hewitt 1985). Hybrids may have reduced fitness either because they are less viable (hybrid inviability), have reduced fertility (hybrid sterility), or they may display morphological or behavioral deficits. For example, among the Sulawesi macaques, some hybrids have webbed fingers and toes (Supriatna 1991), and such handicaps can make the hybrids less able to compete with the parental forms.

Why are there hybrid zones? From an evolutionary point of view, the production of hybrids may seem wasteful unless the parental species stand to gain something in return. One such gain may be the transfer of genetic material across species borders, a process called **introgression** (when genetic material is dispersed from one parental population into another via hybrids). Introgression of genetic material can sometimes result in genetic variation that can be advantageous for the survival of the parental taxa (Turelli et al. 2001). Even though many hybrid taxa may be exposed to varying levels of postmating barriers, it is also becoming increasingly obvious that hybrid taxa can be quite successful. Many hybrid zones are located in transitional environments, so hybrids may be better able to deal with transitional environmental conditions in which parental taxa would be less successful. Under certain conditions hybrids can be equally or more successful than either of the parental forms. Increased hybrid fitness, **heterosis**, is often referred to as hybrid vigor; hybrids may be better able to survive in new environmental niches.

The fate of hybrid zones is varied (Figure 2-7). Some hybrid zones are narrow and stable over time and in space, though some may be ephemeral due to selection against the hybrids for one reason or another. There may also be a complete breakdown of the barriers between the two parental taxa, and they may fuse together into a single species. Alternatively, the hybrids may become reproductively isolated from the parental taxa and over time evolve into a new species.

The presence of hybrids causes many problems in conservation (Allendorf et al. 2001). Conservation efforts typically focus on the preservation of species, so problems arise based on how a species is defined and by determining what constitutes a pure species. Even if we were to accept introgression, how much would be acceptable? To solve this problem, more and more conservation organizations take into account the evolutionary status of a hybrid population. The more distinct (morphologically or genetically) the hybrids are from the parental populations, the greater the reason to treat them as belonging to a unique species separate from the parental forms.

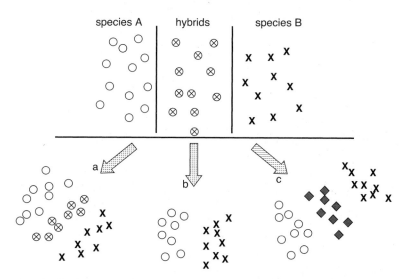

FIGURE 2-7 When two closely related species come in contact, hybridization may occur. The fate of such hybrid zones is varied. It may remain stable over time (a); the hybrids may be less successful than either parental species, and so disappear over time (b); or the hybrids may evolve unique traits and over time become a new species (c).

◊◊◊◊

The phylogenetic species concept (PSC) extends the EvolSC by considering both ancestry and descent. The PSC attempts to identify the "whatness" (as described by Groves 2004) of a species. This approach uses characters such as DNA sequences, vocalizations, coat color, or any other feature, and then attempts to correlate these characters with ancestral patterns of inheritance. Other species concepts stress what a species does in order to remain distinctive, such as the ecological species concept (EcoSC). In this case, species maintain separation due to specificity in adaptations to particular niches. According to the recognition species concept (RSC), members of a species use a wide variety of cues to identify one another as potential mates. These cues distinguish members of a species from those that are not members. A more holistic consideration of species is implied by the cohesion species concept (CPC) in which a variety of factors, including genes, demographics, ecology, and behavior, operate in concert with one another to maintain the integrity or cohesiveness of a species.

All of the various species concepts attempt to define and operationalize what constitutes a species. Each provides useful fine-tuning of the broad biological species concept but we still struggle to find one concept that can be realistically applied to both field and laboratory conditions. It is also difficult to find one that unifies all of the possible factors (whether we are dealing with allopatric or sympatric species, living or fossil species, or monophyletic or paraphyletic species) that we may encounter when attempting to correctly identify how primates are related to one another.

❖❖ How New Species Appear

New species can appear either through a gradual change over time within a lineage (**anagenesis**), or one species can give rise to two or more new forms over time (**cladogenesis**) (Figure 2-8). In anagenesis a monophyletic lineage experiences a gradual change in genetic makeup over time with one species evolving into something different. In anagenesis we can only assume that an individual at time *t* could not successfully reproduce with an individual from the same lineage from a later time period, i.e., **speciation** has occurred. In this case, it is time that is the barrier to successful reproduction. Cladogenesis entails the cumulative effects of **genetic drift** and natural selection as one species

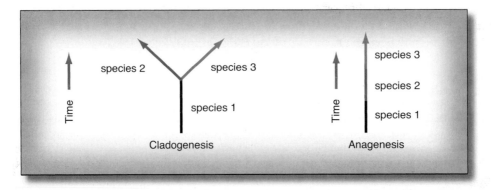

FIGURE 2-8   Cladogenesis is when one species gives rise to two new species over time. During anagenesis one species changes gradually over time into recognizably new species.

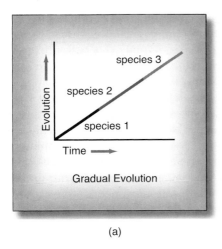
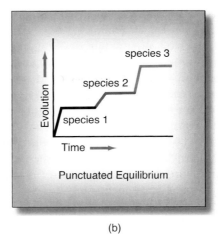

FIGURE 2-9   The evolution of a species may be slow and steady over time, so called gradual evolution (a). Evolutionary changes may take place in fits and starts, so called punctuated equilibrium, where there may be rapid changes followed by no or limited changes (b).

gives rise to two or more new forms over time. Some type of isolating mechanism must stop gene flow from occurring between populations. This could be a geographical or environmental barrier, such as a mountain or river that divides the populations. There can also be biological barriers. Members of the two populations may be reproductively incompatible—i.e., attempts to mate would be unsuccessful. If mating is successful, however, the hybrid offspring may not be viable or may be infertile. Behavioral barriers may also be involved if members of the two populations do not recognize each other as potential mates (RSC), or they may reproduce in different seasons (EcoSC). Cladogenesis and anagenesis can occur slowly over time (**gradualism**) or may occur in fits and starts (**punctuated equilibrium**) (Figure 2-9.)

Parapatric speciation** can occur when a species is widely distributed and a segment of the population is better able to deal with certain environmental conditions (e.g., drier conditions). Over time selection may promote permanent barriers to develop between the more successful population and the main population. When a species gets separated by some geographical barrier, selection will eventually lead to speciation. We refer to this mode of speciation as **allopatric speciation**. **Sympatric speciation,** in contrast, entails barriers arising between members of the same population in a continuously distributed species. Sympatric speciation is rarely observed in the wild, but now and then scientists encounter species in which sympatric populations are in the early stages of segregation, and often it is some behavioral variation that acts as a premating isolation barrier, as was recently detected among the African indigo bird (*Vidua camerunensis*, Balakrishnan and Sorenson 2006). It is possible that some of the speciation that has occurred within the guenon primates was the result of sympatric speciation (Kingdon 1990).

❖❖ Naming a Species

Once a species is recognized, it is given two Latin names (**binomen**) (see Box 2-3). The first name refers to its genus and is capitalized; for example, we belong to the genus

Homo. The second part of the name or binomen is the species name, and it is not capitalized; our species name is *sapiens.* So, scientifically you belong to *Homo sapiens,* together with all other **extant** or living humans. The binomial nomenclature applied to the rhesus monkey is *Macaca mulatta* and the Japanese snow monkey, *Macaca fuscata.* Both of these monkeys are different species that belong to the same genus; consequently, they are more closely related to one another than either is to us, or we are to them. A genus is a more general category than a species, and it may include one species or a dozen or more. A genus is composed of species that share certain similarities in morphology, ecology, adaptations, etc. We are the only living human species included in the genus *Homo*; however, there are some large-brained extinct "human" species that are also placed into this genus (e.g., *Homo erectus, H. neanderthalensis* [when several species of the same genus are listed, only the initial of the genus name needs to be presented]). Genera and species are incorporated into higher (more inclusive) taxonomic categories as shown in Figure 2-3.

❖❖❖❖ BOX 2-3 ❖❖❖❖

What To Do When You Find a New Species and How To Name It

Once a new species has been identified, a name has to be assigned to it. The process of naming a species must follow the system of binomial nomenclature as devised by Carl von Linné in 1758. Ideally, instead of promoting self-fame such as naming a new primate *Nystrom ashmorensis,* the name should provide information about the taxonomic affiliations and status represented by the species. The International Commission on Zoological Nomenclature has an established code that sets forth guidelines on how to name a species once it has been classified (ICZN 4th Edition 1999). On average 15,000 to 20,000 new animals are named each year (Polaszek 2005). Names must be in Latin; they are thus gender specific so there must be gender agreement between the names of the genus and species. A new species cannot have been previously named; this frequently happened in the past. Two or more researchers who believed they were seeing a new species for the very first time would give different names to the same species. The principle of priority states that the first name given to a species has priority over any other names assigned at a later time. The name must be published along with a description of the species, and the publication cannot be done anonymously or "conditionally." In the past, species descriptions would be published as "anon," and sometimes they were tentative or dependent on confirmation that the species was in fact a new species. This is no longer an acceptable procedure; researchers must be certain that they are indeed describing a new species, and they must have either a specimen or a very good visual representation of it. The name selected must also be unique; no two organisms—even if they belong to different taxonomic categories—can have the same names.

A new species of titi monkey discovered in Bolivia was recently given the name *Callicebus aureipalatti* (Wallace et al. 2006). The genus name of *Callicebus* establishes the taxonomic position of this species. In other words, this monkey shares traits with other species that have been assigned to this particular genus. Moreover, within the system of primate taxonomy it indicates that this genus belongs to the subfamily Callicebinae, which belongs to the family Atelidae within the superfamily Ceboidea and in the infraorder Platyrrhini (Figure 2-10). So its position within the order Primates is established by its binomen. The species name means "golden palace" and reflects the fact that this primate has a golden crown on its head. However, the common name associated with the formal Latin name is actually the "GoldenPalace.com Monkey" because the Wildlife Conservation Society put the naming rights to this species on an online auction last year. The online casino Golden Palace bought the naming rights to this monkey for $650,000. These funds are dedicated to conservation efforts in the Madidi National Park where the monkey was discovered.

❖ ❖ ❖ ❖

❖❖ Primate Taxonomy

Primate taxonomy provides us with a way to make sense out of the great diversity of species found within the order Primates. How a primate is classified signifies where it fits into the evolutionary history of the order and its relationship to all other extant primates. Taxonomy is intended to be an instructive tool, but it can also be quite burdensome. Taxonomic affiliations and associations will also change as we get better at reconstructing the evolutionary history of primates and learn more about their molecular, genetic, morphological, behavioral, and ecological relationships. Consequently, until all lines of evidence are synthesized, primate taxonomy will remain in a state of flux.

❖❖ Higher Taxonomic Units

As was discussed in Chapter 1, a suite of traits identify membership to the primate order. We are included in this order, as are lemurs, lorises, tarsiers, monkeys, and apes. The taxonomic positions of extant primates are illustrated in Figure 2-10. The order is subdivided into two suborders: the Strepsirhini (the strepsirhine primates) and the Haplorhini (the haplorhine primates).

There is an alternative scheme for dividing the primate order, which is an alternative to cladistic taxonomy and may be encountered in some introductory textbooks. In 1873 George Mivart used anatomical traits to divide the primate order into the suborders Prosimii and Anthropoidea. These suborders distinguished between primates that are referred to as prosimians (lemurs and lorises) and those that are considered as anthropoids (monkeys, apes, and humans). As a whole, prosimians exhibit more ancestral traits, or those traits exhibited by the earliest primates, while the anthropoids exhibit more derived characteristics. Part of the problem with this traditional approach stems from the placement of a particular group of primates called tarsiers. These small-bodied primates exhibit an interesting mix of prosimian- and anthropoid-like traits, both on a morphological level and biomolecular level. In the traditional approach, tarsiers were considered prosimians,

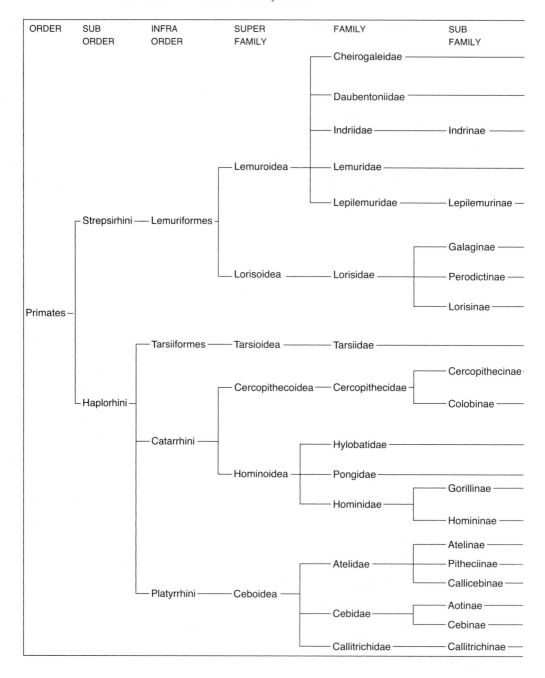

FIGURE 2-10 Taxonomic classification of all extant primates, to the level of genus.

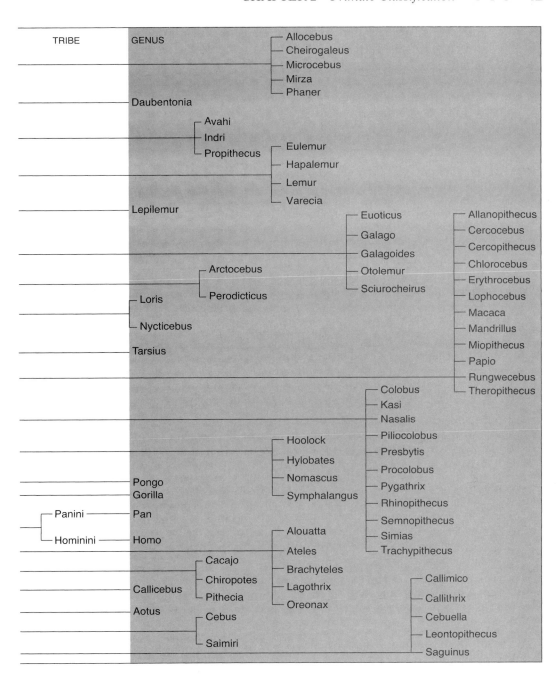

FIGURE 2-10   (*continued*)

but in more recent taxonomic schemes (cladistics) they are considered to be more closely related to the anthropoids. Some researchers have even suggested placing the tarsiers into their own taxonomic suborder (Tarsoidea). In the strepsirhine and haplorhine subdivision that we will be using in this text, tarsiers are included in the haplorhine group. Even though this taxonomic approach is still being debated, we feel that it is the most **parsimonious** approach to use based on our current knowledge of primate relatedness.

❖❖ The Two Primate Suborders: Strepsirhini and Haplorhini

Those primates that belong to the suborder Strepsirhini include all of the lemurs, sifakas, the aye-aye, lorises, and bushbabies. All extant strepsirhine primates are found in Africa and Asia. The species included in this suborder are generally small in body size and range from the very tiny Goodman's mouse lemur (*Microcebus lehilahyt-sara*), weighing a mere 30 g (or about an ounce), to the large indri (*Indri indri*), which weighs around 6–7 kg (13–15 lbs) (see Appendix A). Close to half of all strepsirhine primates are nocturnal. They tend to rely to a large degree on the sense of smell for communication. Indicative of the role that olfactory perception plays, strepsirhine primates have a moist nose or **rhinarium** that readily picks up scents as well as large mucous membranes housed in a predominant nasal cavity. Additional characteristics that are specific to strepsirhines but are not exhibited by *all* members of the suborder include a **dental tooth comb** (see Figure 4-13) and a **grooming claw**. A dental tooth comb is formed by closely positioned mandibular incisors and canines (the bottom front teeth) that horizontally protrude. As the name implies, the dental tooth comb is used for grooming, but in some species it is also used to scrape tree sap or gum. Strepsirhine primates have a claw-shaped nail on the second digit of their feet. This claw is used to groom but can also be used to extract insects out of tree bark. Some nocturnal strepsirhines exhibit solitary foraging strategies, while other diurnal strepsirhines live in large social groups.

The suborder Haplorhini includes the tarsiers, all of the monkeys, apes, and humans. Haplorhine primates occupy a large geographic distribution with extant species found in Africa, Asia, and South and Central America. Compared to the strepsirhines, these primates are (on average) larger in body size. Pygmy marmosets (*Cebuella pygmaea*), the smallest of the haplorhines, weigh 100 g (3.5 oz), while an adult male gorilla can weigh up to 170 kg or 375 lbs. Haplorhine primates are predominantly diurnal but there are two genera of nocturnal haplorhines. These primates rely more on vision than on olfaction. They have dry rhinaria, and their eyes are enclosed in a bony socket (the bony socket of tarsiers is nearly complete), whereas strepsirhine primates have open eye sockets. The haplorhine primates have a larger brain-to-body-size ratio than do the strepsirhines, and their brains exhibit a complex cerebral cortex. Consequently, haplorhine primates are capable of more intricate learned behaviors or cognitive behavior. In addition, with the exception of the orang-utan, haplorhine primates live in complex social groups. Each primate suborder is further divided into a number of different superfamilies. Within the Strepsirhine suborder there are two superfamilies, and within the Haplorhine suborder there are four. The superfamilies are further divided into even more exclusive taxonomic categories (Figure 2-10).

❖❖ The Strepsirhine Primates

The two Strepsirhine superfamilies are the Lemuroidea, which includes all of the lemurs, sifakas, indri, and aye-aye, and the Lorisoidea, which includes the lorises, pottos, and bushbabies.

Superfamily: Lemuroidea

All of the primates that belong to this superfamily live on the island of Madagascar, located approximately 400 kilometers (250 miles) off the southeast coast of Africa. The great diversity of extant lemurs is but a mere reflection of the enormous diversity of lemurs that once existed on this island (the adaptive radiation of lemurs on Madagascar is discussed in Chapter 5). There are five families within the superfamily Lemuroidea: Cheirogaleidae (dwarf, mouse, and fork-marked lemurs), Daubentoniidae (the aye-aye), Indriidae (woolly lemurs, avahi, indri, and sifakas), Lemuridae (the true lemurs, bamboo, ruffed, and ring-tailed lemurs), and Lepilemuridae (the sportive lemurs).

Five Lemur Families

The family Cheirogaleidae includes the dwarf lemurs (*Allocebus, Cheirogaleus,* and *Mirza*), the mouse lemurs (*Microcebus*), and the **monotypic** genus of fork-marked lemur (*Phaner furcifer*). All of these are small-bodied (30–500 g; a little more than an ounce–17.5 oz), nocturnal primates (Figure 2-11). The cheirogaleids build nests of leaves, sleep in tree holes or tangles of lianas (woody vines), and usually give birth to twins. They are much less social than other lemurs, and in some cases they are solitary foragers with many including small mammals and birds in their diet. The family Daubentoniidae includes the aye-aye

(a)   (b)

FIGURE 2-11 Examples of the Cheirogaleidae family: (a) fat-tailed dwarf lemur, *Cheirogalus medius*, (b) gray mouse lemur, *Microcebus murinus*.

FIGURE 2-12   The aye-aye, *Daubentonia madagascariensis,* is the only living member of the Daubentoniidae family.

(*Daubentonia madagascariensis*), which is perhaps one of the most unusual members of the primate order (Figure 2-12). It has shaggy dark fur, very large ears, and a large bushy tail and is highly specialized for a predominantly solitary and nocturnal lifestyle. It eats mainly insects, but it is also opportunistic and will include other foods such as birds' eggs and fruits in its diet. The largest lemurs belong to the family Indriidae. In this family we have the monotypic genus Indri (*Indri indri*), the woolly lemur (*Avahi*), and several species of sifaka (*Propithecus*; Figure 2-13). These primates weigh between 1–7 kg (2–15 lbs), and they have sleek bodies. Their long hindlimbs reflect adaptations for a specialized locomotor pattern known as vertical clinging and leaping (see Chapter 4). The indri and sifaka are diurnal leaf-eating monkeys

FIGURE 2-13   An example of the Indriidae family: Coquerel's sifaka, *P. coquereli.*

FIGURE 2-14 Examples of members of the Lemuridae family: (a) ruffed lemur, *Varecia variegata variegata,* (b) ring-tailed lemur, *Lemur catta.*

(a)

(b)

that exhibit a variety of physiological and morphological adaptations associated with this dietary pattern. Woolly lemurs are the only nocturnal members of this family.

The true lemurs (Genus *Eulemur*), ring-tailed lemur (*Lemur*), bamboo lemurs (*Hapalemur*), and ruffed lemurs (*Varecia*), belong to the family Lemuridae (Figure 2-14). These are medium-sized strepsirhines (weighing between 1–4 kg; approximately 2–9 lbs). They

> **cathemeral**—active at dawn and dusk

have long tails, prominent ears, and the various species exhibit a wide range in coat coloration. They tend to be diurnal or **cathemeral**, and although many are arboreal, ring-tailed lemurs (*Lemur catta*) spend an equal amount of time on the ground. Lemurs consume a wide variety of foods but those belonging to the genus *Hapalemur* specialize in bamboo. Ruffed lemurs (*Varecia*) eat mainly fruits and often give birth to two to four infants, so females have two sets of mammary glands. Many of the true lemurs live in small family groupings, but *Lemur catta* lives in large, multimale–multifemale social groups with more than twenty five individuals. In all lemur species that have been studied, females are dominant to males. Sportive lemurs (*Lepilemur*) belong to the family Lepilemuridae (Figure 2-15). All of the species of sportive lemurs are arboreal and nocturnal. Most commonly they are solitary foragers.

FIGURE 2-15 An example of the Lepilemuridae family: white-footed sportive lemur, *Lepilemur leucopus.*

Superfamily: Lorisoidea

The superfamily Lorisoidea includes a single family, the Lorisidae. This one family is further divided into three subfamilies: Galaginae (bushbabies), Perodictinae (angwantibo and pottos), and Lorisinae (lorises). These primates are more widely distributed than the members of the superfamily Lemuroidea. Bushbabies, the angwantibo, and pottos are found throughout Africa, while lorises are found in Asia.

(a)   (b)

FIGURE 2-16 Examples of members of the Galaginae subfamily: (a) South African lesser bushbaby, *Galago moholi,* (b) thick-tailed bushbaby, *Otolemur crassicaudatus.*

Three Loris Subfamilies

Members of the subfamily Galaginae are only found in Africa. Bushbabies (also known as galagos) are a very diverse group of nocturnal strepsirhine primates that includes many different genera: the needle-clawed bushbaby (*Euoticus*), the lesser bushbaby (*Galago*), the dwarf bushbaby (*Galagoides*), the greater bushbaby (*Otolemur*), and the squirrel bushbaby (*Sciurocheirus*) (Figure 2-16). They have long thick tails and large ears, and they range in size from 70 g–1.2 kg (2.5 oz–2.6 lbs). They are much more active and energetic in their movements than are the other members of the family Lorisidae. They tend to be vertical clingers and leapers and eat predominantly insects. The African pottos (*Perodictcus*) and the angwantibo (*Arctocebus*) belong to the subfamily Perodictinae. These primates are also nocturnal, and pottos are the larger of the two genera (1.2 kg) (Figure 2-17). Pottos include more fruit in their diet, while the angwantibo predominantly eat insects. The subfamily Lorisinae consists of the lorises. These primates have a much larger geographic distribution than the Galaginae or Perodictinae and are found on the continents of Africa and Asia. Lorises include the slender loris (*Loris*) and the slow loris (*Nycticebus*) (Figure 2-18). The diet of the slender lorises is almost exclusively based on animals (Nekaris and Jayewardene 2003, Nekaris and Rasmussen 2003) and similar to the pottos, they hunt through the use of slow and deliberate movement. Both pottos and lorises have specialized morphology of their hands and digits that enables them to grasp onto tree limbs for extended periods of time (see Figure 1–5).

FIGURE 2-17   An example of the Perodictinae subfamily: potto, *Perodicticus potto.*

(a)   (b)

FIGURE 2-18   Examples of members of the Lorisinae subfamily: (a) slow loris, *Nycticebus javanicus,* (b) slender loris, *Loris lydekkerianus.*

❖❖ The Haplorhine Primates

The suborder Haplorhini includes an even greater range and number of primates than seen within the suborder Strepsirhini. Consequently, additional divisions are necessary for this suborder; three infraorders in which superfamilies, families, genera, and species are identified. Each infraorder represents a general grouping of primates, and although they are very different from one another, they are more similar in morphology and adaptive strategies to each other than any of them are to the strepsirhine primates. The three infraorders of haplorhine primates are the Tarsiiformes, the Catarrhini, and the Platyrrhini (Figure 2-10).

Three Haplorhine Infraorders

Infraorder Tarsiiformes

The Tarsiiformes includes the superfamily Tarsiodea, which includes a single family, the Tarsiidae (Figure 2-19). Tarsiers are found in Southeast Asia and live in Indonesia and the

FIGURE 2-19   There is only a single extant genus in the Tarsiidae family. Shown here is a spectral tarsier, *Tarsius spectrum.*

Philippines. Tarsiers belong to the single genus, *Tarsius*, and the taxonomic diversity of this genus has likely been underestimated (Brandon-Jones et al. 2004). As described above, tarsiers have been problematic to primate taxonomists. Tarsiers are small-bodied (58–142 g; 2–5 oz) and nocturnal. Their eyes are very large—a single eye is larger than their brain (Fleagle 1999)—but unlike nocturnal strepsirhines, they do not have a reflective layer behind the retina that aids in night vision (see Chapter 4). They have dry noses. Particular aspects of their cranial morphology (in the olfactory and auditory regions), and how blood is supplied to the brain and to a developing fetus, are similar to that of other haplorhine primates. They have elongated heel and ankle bones and fused tibia and fibula in the lower leg that facilities an extraordinary leaping ability. Tarsiers eat insects and small animals, and some live in monogamous pairs.

Infraorder Catarrhini

Catarrhine primates include those monkeys that live in Africa and Asia as well as all of the apes and humans. Members of this infraorder have prominent or protruding noses, with downward and forward-facing **nares** or nostrils. They have two premolars in each quadrant of their mouth, and the tympanic membrane located within the ear is supported by a bony tube. The infraorder Catarrhini contains two superfamilies: the Cercopithecoidea and Hominoidea (Figure 2-10).

Superfamily Cercopitheciodea Cercopithecoidea includes the **catarrhine monkeys** (primates such as baboons, macaques, guenons, and langurs) and all are diurnal. The superfamily Cercopithecoidea includes a single extant family, the Cercopithecidae. All members of this family share a number of morphological characteristics. The molars are **bilophodont** in shape; in other words, there are four cusps on the **occlusal** surface (tooth surface that comes into contact with the tooth above or below it) of their teeth, and a small constriction divides them into pairs. This shape allows for tough fibrous foods to be processed even when the teeth have undergone significant wear. Their thumbs are fully opposable. In addition, these monkeys have **ischial callosities** or callused seat cushions on their rear ends, beneficial for long-term sitting on rocky or other hard surface areas (Figure 2-20).

FIGURE 2-20 The callused seat cushion, or ischial callosity, is shown here on a Celebes black macaque (*Macaca nigra*).

(a)   (b)

FIGURE 2-21 Examples of members of the Cercopithecinae subfamily: (a) Barbary macaque, *Macaca sylvanus,* (b) vervet monkey, *Cholorocebus aethiops.*

Compared to all other primate groups, the members of the family Cercopithecidae have larger geographic distributions and occupy the greatest diversity of habitat types.

Family *Cercopithecidae* The family Cercopithecidae is divided into two subfamilies: the Cercopithecinae, or cheek-pouched monkeys and the Colobinae, the leaf-eating monkeys and odd-nosed monkeys (Figure 2-10).

The subfamily Cercopithecinae includes twelve different genera. Members of this subfamily are the baboon (*Papio*), mandrill and drill (*Mandrillus*), gelada (*Theropithecus*), macaque (*Macaca*), guenon (*Cercopithecus*), mangabey (*Cercocebus*), talapoin (*Miopithecus*), patas (*Erythrocebus*), swamp monkey (*Allanopithecus*), vervet (*Chlorocebus*), grey-cheeked and black mangabey (*Lophocebus*), and the newly discovered kipunji monkey (*Rungwecebus*) (Figure 2-21). The cercopithecine monkeys represent an extremely diverse array of primates that exhibit complex behaviors and a wide range of adaptive strategies. Many of these primates, such as baboons and macaques, are highly terrestrial and live in large social groups. They tend to exhibit a large degree of **sexual dimorphism** in both body size and secondary sexual char-

> **sexual dimorphism**—size or form differences in morphological traits between males and females

acteristics. In addition, these monkeys have cheek pouches that enable them to quickly harvest foods in open, terrestrial habitats. Foods can then be processed at a later time in safer locations. Many prefer to eat fruit, but in general these monkeys are highly opportunistic in their dietary choices.

(a)   (b)

FIGURE 2-22   Examples of members of the Colobinae subfamily: (a) black and white colobus, *Colobus guereza,* (b) Hanuman langur, *Semnopithecus entellus,*.

The subfamily Colobinae includes the Asian langurs (*Kasi, Semnopithecus*, and *Trachypithecus*), leaf-monkeys (*Presbytis*), odd-nosed monkeys (*Nasalis, Pygathrix,* and *Rhinopithecus*), pig-tailed monkey (*Simias*), as well as the African colobus (*Colobus, Procolobus,* and *Piliocolobus*) monkeys (Figure 2-22). These monkeys have specialized gut morphologies that enable them to utilize a large percentage of mature leaves in their diet. Many of these primates are highly arboreal, but the Hanuman langur (*Semnopithecus*) is predominantly terrestrial. Their stomachs are sacculated much like that of a cow's, enabling tough, fibrous vegetable material to sit in the gut while it is being broken down by enzymes. This specialized morphology enables these primates to exploit and digest plant material that other primates cannot use.

Superfamily *Hominoidea*   The superfamily Hominoidea includes us as well as our fossil ancestors and all of the apes: gibbons, siamangs, orangutans, chimpanzees, bonobos, and gorillas. Members of this superfamily, such as the gorilla *(Gorilla)* and orangutan (*Pongo*), are the largest of the living primates. Compared to most other members of the primate order, they also have even larger and more complex brains, and they are capable of greater cognitive abilities. They tend to live longer and have extended periods of gestation, maturation, and infant dependency. Members of this superfamily do not have tails, they have relatively short body trunks, and their molar teeth exhibit a **Y-5 pattern** (in the peaks and valleys on the occlusal surfaces). This superfamily is traditionally divided into three different families: the Hylobatidae, the Pongidae, and the Hominidae.

A traditional Linnaean approach to primate classification would place the chimpanzee, bonobo, gorilla, and orangutan in the family Pongidae. Primates included in the family Hominidae (referred to as **hominids**) would be reserved for those primates that demonstrate adaptations for habitual terrestrial bipedal locomotion, i.e., living and fossil hominids. This classificatory scheme is, however, problematic. The family Hominidae is a paraphyletic group, and the members of this group do not share derived characteristics that are unique to it. In other words, as a group, the hominids do not exhibit characteristics that are evolutionarily distinctive from members of the family Pongidae. Now that both the human and chimpanzee genomes have been sequenced, we have confirmed the lack of discreteness in members of these two different families. Following a strict cladistic analysis, we should either belong to the family Pongidae, or the apes most closely related to us—chimpanzees, bonobo, and gorilla—should be included in the family Hominidae. Consequently, a more representative approach to primate taxonomy involves the use of additional taxonomic categories representative of monophyletic taxa. This is the scheme that we will use here.

Family *Hylobatidae*   This family includes the gibbons and siamangs found in Southeast Asia. There are three genera of gibbons: *Hylobates*, *Hoolock* (white-browed gibbon), and *Nomascus* (black-crested gibbon) (Figure 2-23). Siamangs are monotypic (*Symphalangus syndactylus*). Gibbons and siamangs are the smallest of the living apes, ranging in size from 4–12 kg (about 8–26 lbs). Members of this family are the only apes that have ischial callosities. Unlike the larger-bodied apes, they are not sexually dimorphic (but most show **sexual dichromatism**, or differences in coat and skin colors on the basis of sex). They exhibit a range of morphological

> **sexual dichromatism**—differences in the color scheme of the hair and skin between males and females

characteristics that reflect a specialized locomotor adaptation. These small-bodied apes actually swing arm-over-arm through the trees using a locomotion pattern called **brachiation**. These apes may form monogamous family groups, and they are well known for their loud calls that announce territorial boundaries.

Family *Pongidae*   Membership to this family is now reserved for the only Asian large-bodied ape, the orangutan (*Pongo pygmaeus* and *P. abelii*) (Figure 2-24). The two species represent the populations of orangutans that are found on two different Indonesian islands: Borneo (*P. pygmaeus*) and Sumatra (*P. abeli*). Orangutans are the largest living arboreal mammals. They have long shaggy red hair and exhibit extreme sexual dimorphism in body size (females average 37 kg or 81.5 lbs and males average 77.5 kg or 170 lbs). Similar to the African apes, orangutans build nests. When terrestrial, they move by walking on the outer edges of their feet and hands, referred to as a **quadrumanual** locomotion pattern. They are unique among primates because they exhibit the longest interbirth interval of any living primate species, with female orangutans giving birth approximately every eight years (Wich et al. 2004). Orangutans exhibit unique social lives and are the most solitary of any of the apes (see Chapter 7).

A More Progressive Taxonomic Scheme—the Family Hominidae

The family Hominidae is divided into two different subfamilies (Figure 2-10) that includes the African large apes and us. The subfamily Gorillinae is restricted to the largest of all of the living primates, the equatorial African gorilla (*Gorilla*); (Figure 2-25). Adult males can weigh 175 kg or 385 lbs, and adult females are about one-half the size

(a)

(b)

FIGURE 2-23   Examples of members of the Hylobatidae family: (a) white-handed gibbon, *Hylobates lar,* (b) siamang, *Symphalangus syndactylus.*

of the males. Two species of gorillas with two different subspecies each are now recognized due primarily to reevaluation of morphological and bimolecular characteristics (Groves 2001). The mountain gorilla (*G. beringei beringei*), and the eastern lowland gorilla (*G. b. graueri*) belong to a single species and are found in the eastern distribution, while the western lowland gorilla (*G. g. gorilla*), and the Cross river gorilla (*G. g. diehli)* are a separate species and represent the western distribution (Gagneux et al. 1999, Jensen-Sieman and Kidd 2001). Gorillas are knuckle-walkers and males obtain a silver coloration to their **dorsal** coat between the ages of approximately nine to thirteen years of age indicative of their sexual maturity. In addition to achieving physical maturity,

(a)

(b)

FIGURE 2-24 Examples of members of the Pongidae family: (a) Sumatran orangutan, *Pongo abelii,* (b) Borean orangutan, *P. pygmaeus.*

males must also achieve a level of social maturity and dominance. They generally live in one male–multifemale groups so males must learn how to assemble and maintain a group of females. In both ecology and behavior, the lowland gorillas are very different from the mountain gorillas. Lowland gorillas occupy a greater diversity of habitats and tend to eat more fruits than do the predominantly herbivorous mountain gorillas.

The subfamily Homininae (Figures 2-26 and 2-27) includes the bonobos, chimpanzees, and living and fossil humans, thus indicating our close relationship to the chimpanzee (*Pan troglodytes*) and the bonobo (*P. paniscus*). This subfamily is further divided into a taxonomic level called a tribe. As mentioned at the beginning of this chapter, additional taxonomic categories are often added to those that exist in the traditional Linnaean system. The taxonomic unit of a tribe represents such a case. This unit is placed between the subfamily Homininae and the genera, *Homo* and *Pan* (Figure 2-10). The tribe Panini includes the members of the genus *Pan* and the tribe Hominini includes us and our fossil ancestors.

(a)   (b)

FIGURE 2-25 Examples of members of the Gorillinae subfamily: (a) western lowland gorilla, *Gorilla gorilla gorilla,* (b) mountain gorilla, *G. beringei beringei.*

Panini consists of four subspecies of chimpanzee that reflect the different geographic ranges that the chimpanzees occupy (western, central, eastern, and Nigerian-Cameroon). The bonobo is a monotypic species found only in central Africa. Chimpanzees and bonobos are knuckle-walkers. Compared to either orangutans or gorillas, they exhibit a lesser degree of sexual dimorphism. Female chimpanzees average between 32–47 kg (71–104 lbs), and males weigh an average of 40–60 kg (88–132 lbs). The body morphology of bonobos is slightly more linear and less bulky. Both chimpanzees and bonobos demonstrate complex social organizations, social behaviors, and have a large capacity for learned behavior. They live in dynamic multimale–multifemale social groups that are fluid in group membership. They are, however, very distinctive in social behaviors. Females are the dominant sex in bonobos, while males are the dominant sex in chimpanzees. Bonobos tend to be more arboreal, they are less aggressive, and they demonstrate a wide range of sexual behaviors that function to reduce stress in the social group.

The Hominini tribe is reserved for extant and fossil hominins (Figure 2-27). Members of this tribe include habitually bipedal terrestrial primates—humans and our ancestors. The use of the tribe level of classification and the word hominin as representative of the members of this tribe is not universally practiced. Today approximately half of the introductory biological anthropology textbooks use this terminology, while the other half classifies humans and their fossil ancestors as hominids.

As our phylogenetic reconstructions change regarding ape and human relationships, so too must the taxonomic categories that we use to describe these relationships. The names used in the Linnaean system represent inherent rankings, and as hypotheses change and newer information based on molecular information and genetics are discovered, the

(a)

(b)

FIGURE 2-26 Examples of members of the Homininae subfamily, tribe Panini: (a) bonobo, *Pan paniscus*, (b) chimpanzee, *P. troglodytes.*

traditional taxonomic names that we have used are often unable to reflect advances in our knowledge. Consequently, a new taxonomic system called PhyloCode has been proposed (Foer 2005). This new classificatory scheme attempts to address the problems with the ranked positions used by the Linnaean scheme. It has not, however, been accepted as an alternative to the code of biological nomenclature. Our traditional approach to taxonomy is currently being stretched and strained to accommodate new information and the resulting phylogenetic revisions.

Until a more fluid taxonomic system can be established, we feel that it is important to use a scheme that puts humans on the same playing field as other members of the primate order and that stresses our ties to the African apes.

Infraorder Platyrrhini

The Platyrrhini infraorder includes the monkeys found in Mexico and Central and South America. Compared to the Infraorder Catarrhini, the members of this infraorder have

FIGURE 2-27   An example of the Homininae subfamily, tribe Hominini: *Homo sapiens.*

relatively broad and flat noses. **Platyrrhine monkeys** tend to be more arboreal than terrestrial. Features that distinguish platyrrhine monkeys from catarrhine monkeys include their having three premolars in each quadrant of their mouth and an eardrum that is supported by a bony ring instead of a tube-like structure. Their thumbs may not be fully opposable, and they are the only primates that have prehensile tails. However, it is important to note that only five genera of platyrrhine monkeys exhibit this adaptation. Consequently, knowing that a monkey has a prehensile tail squarely identifies it as a member of the infraorder Platyrrhini, but the absence of a prehensile tail does not exclude it. Prehensile tails serve as a fifth limb, supporting monkeys while they forage and feed in arboreal environments. Platyrrhine monkeys belong to the superfamily Ceboidea. Ceboidea includes three families, the Atelidae, the Cebidae, and the Callitrichidae (Figure 2-10).

Family *Atelidae*   The Atelidae monkeys include three subfamilies: the Atelinae, the Pitheciinae, and the Callicebinae. The Atelinae includes the howler monkey (*Aloutta*), spider monkey (*Ateles*), woolly spider monkey or muriquis (*Brachyteles*), woolly monkey (*Lagothrix*), and the monotypic yellow-tailed woolly monkey (*Oreonax flavicauda*) (Figure 2-28). These are the largest of the platyrrhine monkeys (5.5–15 kg; 12–33 lbs). All members of the Atelinae have prehensile tails. Muriquis and spider monkeys are also referred to as **semibrachiators** because they are capable of moving through the trees using a suspensory locomotor pattern. Howler monkeys are well known for their loud territorial calls. Their diet is leaves, especially mature leaves. The subfamily Pitheciinae contains the saki (*Pithecia* and *Chiropotes*) and uakari (*Cacajao*), both of which are very striking-looking primates (Figure 2-29). Sakis have long, fluffy **pelage** or coats and long bushy tails. The white-faced saki (*Pithecia pithecia*) is sexually dichromatic; males are black and females are agouti brown. Sakis are highly agile and can demonstrate extraordinary arboreal leaps. They are seed-feeding specialists. The two different species of uakari have either vibrant red or black faces. They inhabit flooded forests and occasionally assemble into large social groups of up to 100 individuals. The Callicebinae includes a group of monkeys known as titi monkeys (*Callicebus;* Figure 2-30). None of

(a)   (b)

FIGURE 2-28   Examples of members of the Atelinae subfamily: (a) woolly monkey, *Lagothrix lagotricha,* (b) Mexican black howler monkey, *Alouatta pigra.*

these monkeys have prehensile tails, but the titi monkeys use their long, thick tails for balance and in a social context they tail-twine.

Family *Cebidae*   The Cebidae family is divided into two subfamilies: the Aotinae and the Cebinae (Figure 2-10). The night or owl monkey (*Aotus*) is the only nocturnal platyrrhine monkey (Figure 2-31), and it belongs to the subfamily Aotinae. There are many different species of owl monkey. They are found within a large geographic distribution (from

(a)   (b)

FIGURE 2-29   Examples of members of the Pithecinae subfamily: (a) white-faced saki, *Pithecia pithecia,* (b) black-bearded saki, *Chiropotes satanas.*

FIGURE 2-30   The titi monkey, *Callicebus,* a member of the Callicebinae subfamily.

Panama to northern Argentina) and live in large family groups. The owl monkey is predominantly a fruit eater. The subfamily Cebinae includes capuchins (*Cebus*) and squirrel monkeys (*Saimiri*) (Figure 2-32). Capuchins have semi-prehensile tails; they cannot suspend themselves by their tails, but they use them for support and balance as they harvest fruits while suspended under branches. Capuchins are rather clever and easy to train and are often used in television shows, commercials, and movies. For example, a capuchin monkey appeared in the series *Friends*. *Saimiri* species have not shared the

FIGURE 2-31   The owl monkey, *Aotus,* a member of the Aotinae subfamily.

(a)   (b)

FIGURE 2-32 Examples of members of the Cebinae subfamily: (a) red squirrel monkey, *Saimiri oerstedii,* (b) white-throated capuchin, *Cebus capuchinus.*

same commercial fame as have capuchin monkeys, but they are a common primate used in biomedical research. Squirrel monkeys (600–1200 g; 21–42 oz) are smaller than capuchins (1.3–4.8 kg; 3–11 lbs) in body size. The tail of a squirrel monkey is prehensile at birth, but as the monkey matures the grasping ability is lost (Boinski 1989).

Family *Callitrichidae* The subfamily Callitrichinae includes a diverse grouping of small-bodied primates including marmosets (*Callithrix* and *Cebuella*), tamarins (*Saguinus* and *Leontopithecus*), and Goeldi's monkey (*Callimico*) (Figure 2-33). These are the smallest platyrrhines (less than 1 kg), and they have claw-like nails on all of their digits with the exception of their big toes. Marmosets and tamarins typically give birth to twins, and unlike

(a)   (b)

FIGURE 2-33 Examples of members of the Callithrichidae family: a) Geoffroy's tufted-ear marmoset, *Callithrix geoffroyi*, b) golden-headed tamarin, *Leontopithecus chrysomelas.*

other platyrrhine monkeys they lack the third upper and lower molars. Many of these primates exhibit an amazing array of moustaches, ear tufts, and vibrant coat colors. They typically have extremely variable diets, but plant exudates such as gums and sap constitute a major portion of their diet.

◈◈ Summary

Classifying primates is not an easy task. Some 330 or more species are included in the primate order. The way in which primates are classified is also ever-changing. New species have recently been discovered both in the wild and through the molecular analysis of species in the lab, while yet others are on the brink of extinction. Primate taxonomy is a tool. Ideally, it should reflect the phylogenetic or evolutionary lineage of species. The concept of what it means to be a species is also difficult to define. Many different species concepts exist, and each one stresses diverse aspects and factors essential to being a species.

Primates are divided through the use of a large number of different taxa. The most basic division is made between strepsirhine and haplorhine primates. A number of different morphological and behavioral characteristics separates the lemurs, sifakas, the aye-aye, lorises, and galagos from the tarsiers, monkeys, small and large apes, and humans. Tarsiers have historically posed a conundrum to primate taxonomists because they display features associated with both strepsirhine and haplorhine primates. Another major distinction is made between monkeys that live in the Americas and those that live in Africa and Asia. The platyrrhines and catarrhines exhibit a number of different morphological and behavioral characteristics. Among the catarrhine monkeys another division is made between cheek-pouched monkeys, the Cercopithecinae, and the leaf-eating monkeys, the Colobinae. The large Asian arboreal ape, the orangutan, belongs to the family Pongidae. The African apes (chimpanzees, bonobos, and gorillas) and humans belong to the family Hominidae. We further differentiate extant and fossil humans as belonging to the tribe Hominini.

◈◈ Key Words

allopatric
allopatric speciation
anagenesis
analogous traits
bilophodont
binomen
brachiation
catarrhine monkeys
cathemeral
clades
cladistics
cladogenesis
cladogram
classification
dental tooth comb
dorsal
extant
evolutionary systematics
gene flow
genetic drift

gradualism
grooming claw
heterosis
hominids
homologous traits
hybrid zone
introgression
ischial callosities
monophyletic group
monotypic
nares
occlusal
parapatric hybridization
parapatric speciation
paraphyletic group
parsimonious
pelage
phylogenetic systematics
phylogeny
platyrrhine monkeys

primary hybrid zones
punctuated equilibrium
quadrumanual
reproductive isolating
    mechanisms
rhinarium
secondary hybrid zones
semibrachiators
sexual dichromatism
sexual dimorphism
shared derived characteristics
speciation
species concepts
sympatric
sympatric hybridization
sympatric speciation
taxa
taxonomy
Y-5 pattern

❖❖ Study Questions

1. What are the limitations or problems associated with the biological species concept?
2. Why are hybrid zones important to our understanding of (a) speciation and (b) species concepts?
3. What are the mechanisms by which we gain new species?
4. What are shared derived traits that are used in cladistic analysis?
5. What is binomial nomenclature and how does it indicate the taxonomic position of a species?
6. What is the difference between strepsirhine and haplorhine primates?
7. What is unique about the tarsiers and why have they been a taxonomic problem?
8. What is the difference between platyrrhine and catarrhine monkeys?
9. Which ape belongs to the family Pongidae and what characteristics are unique to it?
10. We have had to rethink how we classify humans (extant and fossil). Why has this happened and what is a hominin?

❖❖ Suggested Readings and Related Web Sites

Groves C. 2001. Primate taxonomy. Washington, DC: The Smithsonian Institution Press.

Groves C. 2004. The what, why and how of primate taxonomy. International Journal of Primatology 25:1105–1126.

Morales JC, Disotell, TR, Melnick DJ. 1999. Molecular phylogenetic studies of nonhuman primates.

In Dolhinow P, Fuentes A editors. The nonhuman primates. Mountain View, California: Mayfield Publishing Co., pp. 18–28.

Rowe N. 1996. The pictorial guide to the living primates. New York: Pogonias Press.

CHAPTER 3

Primate Biogeography

Biogeography is a comparative observational science that seeks to identify patterns in the distribution of plants and animals and the geographic regions in which they are found. Primates generally occur in the tropics and in forested environments. Even though the location of primates may appear straightforward, when we look more closely at where individual species are found or the location of different populations of the same species, we discover much variation in the localities and types of habitats in which primates live. This does not mean that primates can live anywhere. While the requirements of some species are quite generalized, and they can occupy a variety of climatic conditions and habitat types, most primate species are adapted to a limited range of environmental conditions.

❖❖ Where Do Primates Live Today?

Primates are found in the **tropical** and semitropical regions of Africa, Asia, and the Americas, and the **temperate** areas of North Africa and Asia. Their geographic distribution is primarily delimited by the Tropic of Cancer (23°28' north) and the Tropic of Capricorn (23°28' south), although these lines of latitude do not entirely restrict the distribution range of pri-

> **tropical**—geographic regions located in between the Tropics of Cancer and Capricorn
> **temperate**—regions located north of the Tropic of Cancer to the Arctic circle and south of the Tropic of Capricorn to the Antarctic circle; these regions are characterized by pronounced seasonality
> **subalpine**—mountainous regions close to tree line

mates (Figure 3-1). In the Americas, extant primates are found in southern North America (Mexico) through Central and South America. Primates are found throughout most of Africa, and they occur throughout Asia from Pakistan to as far east as Japan (Figure 3-1). In the past, primates had a much more extensive geographic distribution, and today, fossil primates are recovered from the western United States, Europe, and Mongolia (see Chapter 5).

The majority of primates live in tropical and subtropical climatic zones, but some species of catarrhine monkeys are found in temperate climates. Primates occur from sea level to altitudes exceeding 3,000 m (9,840 ft). Plant communities at such high altitudes become dominated by herbs characteristic of **subalpine** forest. Some primates, in particular macaque species (*Macaca*), are found in temperate locations in the Himalayas, including Tibet, northern India, and Pakistan, and in the temperate forests of northern Japan. At these locations, there is dramatic seasonal variation, and for two to three months of the year, the ground is covered in deep snow (Figure 3-2).

Close to 90 percent of all primate species live in forested environments, but not all species are restricted to forest habitats (Falk 2000). Some species inhabit areas predominantly covered by bushes, grasses or grasslike plants, such as sedges, and sparsely vegetated semidesert scrub lands. Primates also occur in areas that have been modified by humans such as cities, towns, and villages and can be found in temples and parks, alongside roadways, and in plantations (Figure 3-3).

❖❖ World Biomes

The geographic distribution of primates covers a large portion of the world. As a result, they occupy a wide range of different habitat types: rain forest, seasonal forest, woodland forest, savanna, semidesert scrub, and temperate woodland forest (Table 3-1 on page 65). The word **biome** refers to a natural community that displays a degree of consistency in the types of plants that make up the community—in general, it reflects the **abiotic** (nonliving) conditions (e.g., soil type and water availability) that determine climate and associated **biotic** (living) forms. The recognition of different biomes helps us to identify the range of plant communities in which primates are distributed.

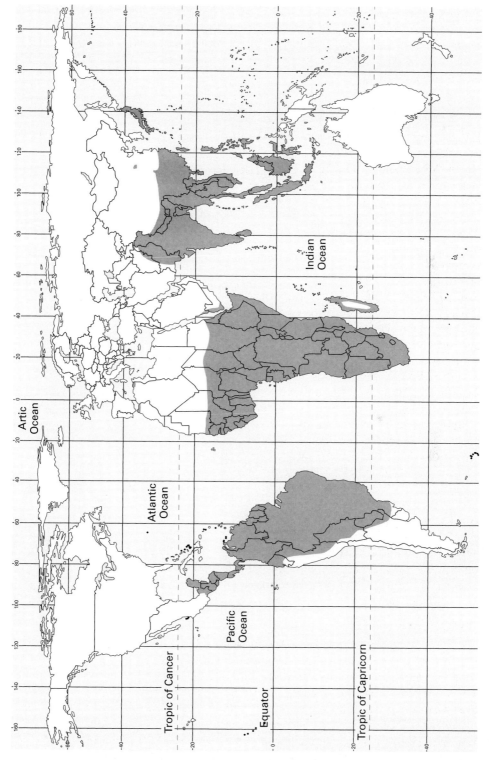

FIGURE 3-1 Geographic distribution of extant primates. Most species are found along the tropical belt, although a few are found in temperate areas.

FIGURE 3-2 Several macaque species live in temperate habitat where winters may include snowfall. However, this appears not to dampen their spirits, as shown by these Japanese macaques (*Macaca fuscata*) playing in the snow.

(a)　　　　　　　　　　　　　　　(b)

FIGURE 3-3 (a) Macaques and langurs are often found in urban habitats. In the Hindu religion, langurs, and by default macaques, are regarded as holy, and they often aggregate around temples where they are provided with food offerings. (b) Primates do not hesitate to take advantage of abandoned human structures, as shown by these vervet monkeys (*Chlorocebus aethiops*) using an old mine tower as a sleeping site.

TABLE 3-1   Primate Distribution Across Major Biomes

	Primate		*Tropical Biomes*					*Temperate Biomes*
	Family	*Subfamily*	*Rain Forest*	*Seasonal Forest*	*Wood-land*	*Savanna*	*Semi-desert*	*Wood-land*
Strepsirhines	Cheirogaleidae		X	X	X	X	X	
	Daubentoniidae		X	X	X			
	Indriidae		X	X	X	X	X	
	Lemuridae		X	X	X	X	X	
	Lepilemuridae		X	X	X	X	X	
	Lorisidae	Galaginae	X	X	X	X		
		Perodictinae	X	X	X			
		Lorisinae	X	X	X	X		
Haplorhines	Tarsiidae		X	X	X			
	Cercopithecidae	Cercopithecinae	X	X	X	X	X	X
		Colobinae	X	X	X		X	X
	Hylobatidae		X	X	X			
	Pongidae		X					
	Hominidae[*]		X	X	X			
	Atelidae	Atelinae	X	X	X			
		Pitheciinae	X	X				
		Callicebinae	X	X				
	Cebidae	Aotinae	X	X				
		Cebinae	X	X	X			
	Callitrichidae		X	X	X			

[*]Nonhuman primates only

(Summarized from Campbell et al. 2007; Lehman and Fleagle 2006; Richard 1985; Rowe 1996; Sussman 1999, 2000)

Rain Forest

The tropical rain forest biome, where most primates are located, stretches across portions of Central and South America, West and Central Africa, and Southeast Asia. Typically, in these environments, variation in temperature is greater during the course of a day than it is throughout the year. Rainfall often exceeds 2,000 mm (80 in) per year. These forests usually receive heavy rains daily (wet or humid rain forest), although there may be a shift between a wet and a dry season (seasonal rain forest). The microclimate within tropical rain forests keeps humidity high, providing the vegetation with sufficient moisture to survive even during dry periods (Figure 3-4a on page 66; Collinson 1988, Richards 1996).

Most of the trees found in rain forests are broad-leaved evergreens. The timing of flower and fruit production by these trees can be highly variable. The understory and middle level of a tropical rain forest include from ground level to approximately 25 m (82 ft) in height

(a)   (b)

FIGURE 3-4 (a) An aerial view of the tropical rain forest at the Bwindi Impenetrable Forest, Uganda, showing the density of the vegetation. (b) Trees can grow to enormous proportions in rain forest. Note the scale of the human being standing in front of the base of the tree.

(Figure 3-4b). The canopy and emergent levels expand from 25–50 m (82–164 ft). The canopy shields the understory and the soils of the forest floor from the leaching effect of ultraviolet (UV) radiation (Figure 3-5).

Rain forest communities comprise the most diverse plant communities in the world (Richards 1996, Turner 2001) (Box 3-1). Consequently, they provide rich and complex habitats for a majority of primate species. The rain forests of Central Africa, particularly in Gabon, support the largest number of different primate genera and species in the same forest (Grubb et al. 2003). Rain forests are not, however, uniform in structure or type, and they vary greatly in degree of disturbance, amount of rainfall received, altitudinal zones, soil types, and exposure to flooding.

Yearly rainfall varies per geographic location so rain forests may be considered humid or dry. In humid forests, rainfall tends to exceed 3,000 mm (120 in), and in dry forests the rain tends to be less than 2,000 mm (80 in) (Richard 1985). Rain forests can be found at different altitudes. Lowland forests are those located below 1,000 m (3,280 ft); forests located above 1,000 m are referred to as montane and cloud forests.

Many primate species are found in **primary rain forests.** Primary rain forests are areas virtually undisturbed by humans in which trees have matured over many centuries. Other primate species are adapted to less pristine conditions and are very successful in **secondary rain forests.** These are forests that have regenerated after some natural or human-caused disturbance (Rowe 1996). Secondary rain forests are comprised of smaller and more immature trees, and a variety of vines, lianas, and other vegetation that grow in the areas where mature

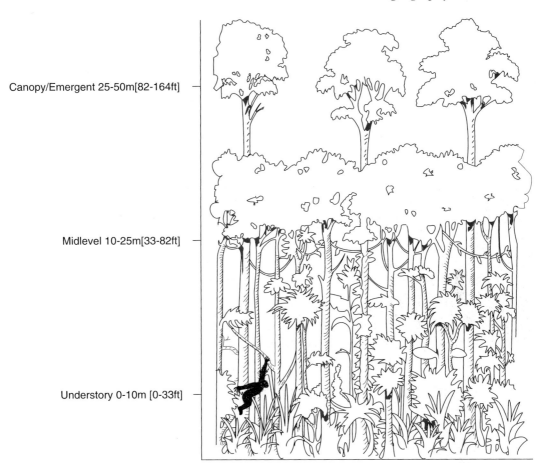

Canopy/Emergent 25-50m[82-164ft]

Midlevel 10-25m[33-82ft]

Understory 0-10m [0-33ft]

FIGURE 3-5 A schematic view of the different layers found within a rain forest habitat.

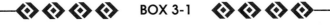

BOX 3-1

The Paradox of a Tropical Rain Forest

Despite exhibiting tremendous diversity, tropical rain forests are fragile ecosystems and this diversity is dependent on the dynamics of the rain forest ecosystem remaining intact. These highly productive and lush environments are maintained through a delicate balance that involves the quick and efficient cycling and recycling of biotic materials throughout the system. A paradox comes into play because often people envision this seemingly unending abundance of foliage as an indicator that the land upon which a tropical rain forest sits could similarly produce high yields of agricultural crops for unlimited periods of time. This has been shown not to be the case.

A first-time visitor to a rain forest may get the mistaken impression of uniformity. Rather, these habitats are very diverse in

(continued)

the spatial distribution of plant and animal species (flora and fauna). They exhibit seasonal and daily fluctuations in rainfall, humidity, ambient temperatures, and light. As a result, the timing and cycling of leaf-fall, flowering, and seed germination varies. In addition, emergent tropical trees can have life spans in excess of 150 years, so the range in the life cycle of the plants themselves is beyond a human lifetime.

Tropical rain forests, located in equatorial zones, receive a greater amount of ultraviolet radiation (UVR) emitted by the sun than seen in most temperate latitudes. However, it is not only the latitude that is a factor, because places such as the Sahara desert receive even greater amounts of UVR than do rain forests located at approximately the same latitude (Jablonski 2006). The upper canopy of a rain forest shields the lower canopy and the forest floor from the harmful effects of UVR. When trees are felled to clear land for agricultural purposes, the ground layer is no longer shielded from exposure to UVR. Even though the soil types underlying the rain forests vary, in general they tend to be relatively shallow in depth and poor in nutrients. If the soils tend to be poor, where are the nutrients that generate the prolific growth found in a tropical rain forest? In temperate forests, the forest floor is nutrient rich because of the deposition of organic material. Fallen logs, leaf litter, fallen fruits, the feces of animals, dead animals and insects, etc., accumulate on the forest floor and decompose. However, in rain forest habitats, the decomposition occurs at such a rapid rate that biotic material is expediently recycled resulting in very little organic material accumulating in the soil. In addition, whatever nutrients do accumulate in the rain forest soils are leached out by rain. A rain forest represents an extremely efficient exchange system, but the cost is its fragility and susceptibility to disturbances.

Recognizing the unsustainable status of exposed rain forest soils, the method of shifting cultivation, or "slash and burn" is used by peoples who need to grow food in rain forests (see Chapter 11). Trees are felled and burned, the ground is cultivated for a year or two, and then left under "bush-fallow." Typically, it will take eight to ten years before new, secondary growth can reestablish a sufficient nutrient base, although still far from its previous level (Longman and Jenik 1974). Once trees are cleared, the natural nutrient cycle that occurs in a tropical rain forest deteriorates, mineralized nutrients are washed away, and when crops are harvested, even more nutrients are removed. Serious problems arise when population and economic pressures necessitate an ever-increasing area of land to be used for slash-and-burn agriculture. Such pressures also increase the demand to shorten the length of time that the land is allowed to regenerate; i.e., remain as bush-fallow. If strained too far, the nutrient levels will be depleted, and the land will become unusable for future crop production. It can take hundreds of years for the scars to mend and for a rain forest to regenerate.

Not all types of disturbances in a tropical rain forest have negative influences on tree diversity. Natural tree falls cause gaps in the forest and provide an opportunity for other plants to establish themselves in more variable light conditions. Such disturbance leads to an increase in diversity. This phenomenon, referred to as the "intermediate disturbance hypothesis" (Connell 1978), was tested in a study of 17,000 trees in a tropical rain forest in French Guiana (Molino and Sabatier 2001). In this study, species diversity was assessed in untouched control areas and in sections of the forest that had been selectively logged ten years ago. In the forest **transects** where trees had been removed on a limited basis, there was increased diversity due to the presence of heliophilic or sun-loving species. Treefall gaps change the architectural structure of a forest not only for a few years, but for an extended period of time, and as such, contribute to the diversity of plants found in a rain forest community. However, even the highly selective logging of trees must be closely monitored by scientists who understand the intricacies of a rain forest environment.

trees have disappeared. We find differences in the distribution of even closely related primate species, such as two different species of macaques. Populations of long-tailed macaques, *Macaca fascicularis,* are found in greater densities in secondary rain forests than in primary rain forests, while populations of pig-tailed macaques, *Macaca nemestrina,* have a higher density in primary rain forests (Ashmore-DeClue 1992).

Along rivers and streams grow **gallery** or riverine **forests** (Figure 3-6). In these areas there are, in addition to trees and bushes, a rich variety of vines and other herbaceous plants. A number of primate species are particularly well adapted for exploiting gallery forests (e.g., uakari, *Cacajao;* and titi monkeys, *Callicebus*). Swamp forests such as mangrove forests are found in river deltas, estuaries, and in coastal areas. Mangrove trees grow in the silt-rich, brackish waters and are well adapted to this salty and swampy habitat. A number of primate species are adapted for living in swamp forests, including some species of guenons (*Cercopithecus* and *Allenopithecus nigroviridis*), and the proboscis monkey (*Nasalis larvatus*).

Seasonal Forest

The seasonal forest biome includes forests that are semideciduous to completely deciduous. Within this biome there is more seasonal variation in temperature rather than

FIGURE 3-6 Rivers provide permanent water for vegetation; riverine or gallery forests are rich in vegetation, including vines and herbaceous plants, although they do not usually extend very far away from the river.

FIGURE 3-7   The savanna landscape is mainly covered by grasses, with few interspersed bushes and trees. Savanna grassland habitats support great herds of herbivores such as this oryx (*Oryx gazelle beisa*).

daily variation. Seasonal forests in which primates are found are located throughout Central and South America, Africa, and Asia. The trees in these forests are not as tall as those found in a primary rain forest. In a seasonal forest, rainfall is highly variable throughout the year and at least some tree species shed their leaves during the dry season. The monsoon forests of India, Sri Lanka, and Southeast Asia are examples of seasonal forest. Many primates live in seasonal forests, but in general the species diversity is less than that found in rain forests (Richard 1985).

Woodland Forest

Woodland biomes include environments composed of more scattered small trees and shrubs. It is transitional between wetter and drier biomes. Consequently, this biome typically demonstrates a gradient in vegetation often going from small trees (wetter) to shrubs (drier). Many plants are drought resistant, and a prolonged dry season is characteristic of the woodland biome. Woodlands occupied by primates are found in South America, eastern and southern Africa, Madagascar, and Asia. Typically, these environments support fewer primate species and often in lower densities. There are usually no more than two or three sympatric species occurring in the same woodland. Primates that utilize woodlands tend to have ranges that extend into neighboring biomes (Richard 1985).

Savanna

The savanna or savanna-mosaic biome includes tropical areas where grasses and bamboos predominate (Figure 3-7), interspersed by drought-resistant bushes and trees such as baobab (*Adansonia*) and *Acacia*. Savannas cover an estimated 20 percent of the world's surface (Collinson 1988). There is greater daily variation in temperatures than there is seasonal variation. These environments receive rainfall, but it may be irregular and periods of rain (rainy season) are separated by periods of no rain (dry season). The yearly rainfall in savanna habitats can vary from 254–1,016 mm (10–40 in). The high variability in rainfall is reflected by the presence of many subcategories of savanna-type habitats. A typical grassland savanna receives 300–500 mm (12–20 in) of rainfall and trees comprise 1 to 10 percent of surface coverage, while woodland savannas receive between 500–1,000

FIGURE 3-8 Semidesert scrub habitats have sparse ground vegetation and scattered bushes, e.g., *Acacia* species. Few primate species live in such habitats because of the low availability of food and water. The hamadryas baboons (*Papio hamadryas*), sometimes referred to as the desert baboon, is an exception.

mm (20–40 in) of rainfall a year and trees comprise between 50 to 90 percent of surface coverage. The diversity of plant species is lower than it is in rain or seasonal forests. Savannas are found in South America, Africa, Madagascar, India, and Southeast Asia. In Africa, this biome is favored by terrestrial primates such as baboons (*Papio*), vervet (*Chlorocebus*), and patas (*Erythrocebus*) monkeys, and on the island of Madagascar, ring-tailed lemurs (*Lemur catta*).

Semi-Desert Scrub

Semi-desert scrub represents a biome not frequently occupied by primates. These environments are hot and dry, typically receiving little rainfall throughout the year (less than 500 mm; 20 in). The vegetation is sparse and consists mainly of drought-tolerant species. In Africa, the hamadryas and chacma baboons (*Papio*) and barbary macaques (*Macaca sylvanus*) can be found in this biome; in Asia, the hanuman langur (*Semnopithecus entellus*), and on Madagascar, sifakas (*Propithecus*) live in semi-desert scrub (Figure 3-8).

Temperate Woodland Forest

In the temperate woodland biome, deciduous forests, including needle-leaf trees, are utilized by primates. Today, these forests are limited to North Africa, in Asia along the southern boundary of the Himalayas, and north central Japan. Regular rains occur (750–1,300 mm; 30–52 in), and there is not an extended dry season. Trees such as oaks (*Quercus*), beech (*Fagus*), and maple (*Acer*) may be dominant in the deciduous forests, while in the needle-leaved forests, pine (*Pinus*) and fir trees (*Abies*) predominate. These environments are regularly subjected to cold winters, and in northern Africa (Algeria and Morocco), Nepal, and Japan there may be deep winter snows (Figure 3-9). Macaques (*Macaca*), langurs (*Semnopithecus*), and golden snub-nosed monkeys (*Rhinopithecus*) live in cold temperate woodlands (see Box 3-2).

FIGURE 3-9 Temperate woodland forests experience seasonality, and there may be severe winters with much snow. Several macaque species survive well in such habitats, such as this Japanese macaque (*Macaca fuscata*).

 BOX 3-2

Cold Weather Primates

When we think about where primates live, we do not often think about primates living in snow-covered habitats. The Japanese macaque, *Macaca fuscata,* lives at the most northern limit of the nonhuman primate geographic range. It is found on the northern tip of the island of Honshu on what is known as the Shimokita peninsula at 41°30' N and 141° E (at the same level as Providence, Rhode Island). At this location, life can be challenging for nonhuman primates. This region is subjected to prolonged periods of deep snow cover. It snows on 110–140 days of the year with accumulations of up to 2.5 m (a little less than 10") (Suzuki 1965). Temperatures may fall to –5°C (23°F). The macaques live in the temperate deciduous forest that consists of oak, ash, and maple trees, as well as rhododendron bushes that may be completely covered by winter snows, with the trees devoid of leaves for up to five months of the year (Izawa and Nishida 1963, Hanya et al. 2007). The macaques also utilize pine forests found on the eastern edge of the mountain ridge.

These predominantly terrestrial macaques travel in single file through deep heavy snow, and as Japanese primatologists Kohesi Izawa and Toshisada Nishida have observed, they may be buried to the elbows in snow with the lead macaque cutting a path. Even though the Japanese macaques are omnivorous and fruit-eating primates, they survive by eating bark and pine needles when foliage is covered with snow.

In fact, the bark of trees can make up almost 88 percent of their entire wintertime diet (Suzuki 1965), and they eat the leaves of needle-leaved coniferous trees. Even though not of much nutritional value, the bark and needles provide bulk in the stomachs of the hungry macaques.

During the cold winter months, the activity patterns of the macaques reflect heat conservation strategies. When food is not readily available, why go searching for it and waste energy? Instead, the macaques curtail their ranging behaviors, and they sit and huddle together (Takahashi 1997, Wada and Tokida 1981). Even the choice of sleeping sites is weather dependent. During the snowy season, the macaques sleep in the bare deciduous trees, avoiding the conifers. It would appear as if the coniferous trees provide more of a block from the cold winter winds; but the branches also contain accumulations of snow that can tumble down on top of sleeping macaques.

The temperatures of the volcanic hot springs have been altered to attract and be soothing to resort visitors. As it turns out, the macaques also enjoy the hot springs and will take prolonged soaks in the 43°C (109°F) water (Figure 3-10). The macaques found in Jigokudani (Hell's Valley) have been featured on their own live webcam and on stamps, and they received many visitors during the 1998 Olympic games.

FIGURE 3-10   Japanese macaques (*Macaca fuscata*) utilize hot springs to stay warm during the winter months.

❖❖ Distribution of Primates

The Strepsirhines

Strepsirhine primates are found in Africa, including the island of Madagascar, and in Asia, especially Southeast Asia (Figure 3-11). Lemurs, indris, sifakas, and the aye-aye are found on Madagascar and nearby islands. Madagascar is approximately 1,500 km (930 miles) long,

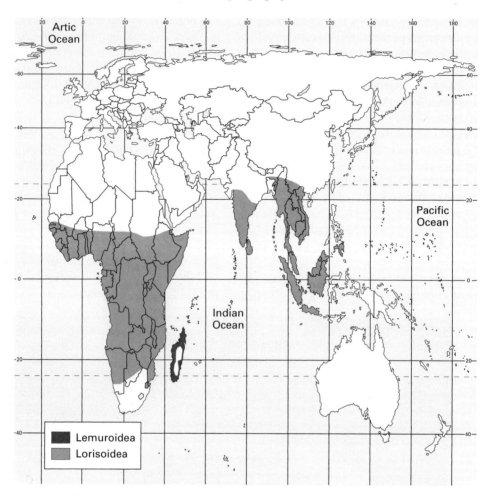

FIGURE 3-11   A map showing the geographical distribution of strepsirhine primates.

an area of about the same size as Texas. Madagascar comprises a complex mosaic of topographical and climatic features. Before humans reached Madagascar, around two thousand years ago, the island was covered by forest (Burney 1999, Goodman and Benstead 2003). The island has since then been subjected to severe rates of deforestation, with an estimated loss of 111,000 hectares (274,170 acres) of forest per year (Green and Sussman 1990). The central highlands have been most affected by human activity, and presently only fragmented forested areas remain (Wilmé et al. 2006). The ocean monsoon winds come from the east, providing an east to west gradient in rainfall. Humid rain forests are found on the east side and dry woodland forests on the west side of the island. In the mountainous north there are humid rain forests, and to the south are the dry spiny forests (containing the cactus-like *Didierea* trees) and savanna habitats, with gallery forests growing along rivers.

With the exception of the aye-aye (*Daubentonia*), all family taxa of primates living on Madagascar have representative species in all major tropical biomes (Table 3-1). The ring-tailed lemur, *Lemur catta,* is especially drought tolerant and is found living in the spiny forest and along the borders of semidesert scrub zones that are often subjected to extremely high temperatures and prolonged periods of drought (Gould et al. 1999, Sauther et al. 1999, Sussman 1977). *Eulemur* species are found throughout the island but most commonly in forested environments (Mittermeier et al. 2006). The various species of *Hapalemur* are specialized for eating bamboo and they live in rain forests where bamboo occurs. Ruffed lemurs (*Varecia*) also live in rain forests, and those living on the Masoala Peninsula, located on the island's northeast coast, have even survived destructive cyclones (Balko 1998; Ratsimbazafy 2001, 2002). Indris (*Indri*) and sifakas (*Propithecus*) are found in a large variety of habitat types, including both humid and dry forests. *Propithecus verreauxi,* like *Lemur catta,* lives in the dry south and southwest regions of Madagascar where there may be large shifts in the availability of food and water. In these habitats, infant mortality may be high as a result of starvation during the dry season or hypothermia during the dry cold season (Richard et al. 2002). The vast majority of nocturnal lemurs live in forest and woodland environments, although they may inhabit a variety of different specific forest types. The aye-aye (*Daubentonia*) is widely scattered across much of Madagascar and is found on the island of Nosy Mangabey, located off the northeast coast of Madagascar (Sterling 1993). Aye-ayes live in primary and secondary rain forest, mangrove forest, seasonal forest, dry woodland, and in cultivated areas (Sussman 1999).

Strepsirhines found outside of Madagascar include the lorises (*Loris* and *Nycticebus*), pottos (*Arctocebus* and *Perodicticus*), and bushbabies (subfamily, Galaginae). These nocturnal strepsirhine primates are distributed across Asia and Africa (Figure 3-11). Lorises are found in India, on the island of Sri Lanka, and in Southeast Asia. Pottos are found in West and Central Africa, and bushbabies are found throughout Africa south of the Sahara Desert. Lorises occur in a variety of forest types, including primary and secondary rain forests, coastal lowland and montane forests, and seasonal to dry *Acacia* scrub land (Nekaris and Bearder 2007). Pottos occupy primary and secondary rain forests, lowland swamp and montane forests, gallery forest, seasonal forest, and live at the edges of forests (Nekaris and Bearder 2007). Bushbabies occupy a similar range of forest types as do the pottos, but they are more diverse in their range of habitats. In Somalia and northern Kenya, they live in semi-desert scrub. Elsewhere, they are found in subtropical grasslands, montane tropical rain forests, farmlands, and plantations (Nekaris and Bearder 2007).

The Haplorhine Primates: The Tarsiers

Tarsiers are nocturnal and distributed throughout a number of islands in Southeast Asia (Figure 3-12). They are spread throughout Indonesia and the Philippines. These primates often sleep in tree hollows, and it was thought that the existence of large fig trees was a potential determining factor in habitat selection. Tarsiers, however, sleep in a variety of places, including vine tangles, other creeping plant and grass platforms, fallen logs, and crevices in rocks (Gursky 2007a). Three species of tarsiers are endemic to the island of Sulawesi. On this island, they are found in a broad range of habitat types, including primary and secondary rain forest, from sea level to over 2,000 m (6,560 ft), in mangrove forests, and at the edges of forests that border plantations (Gursky 2007b).

The Catarrhine Monkeys, Cercopithecinae

The Cercopithecinae, or cheek-pouched monkeys, are found in Africa, the Middle East, and throughout Asia (Figure 3-13). This group of primates includes the baboon, mandrill, drill, gelada, macaque, guenon, mangabey, talapoin, patas, and swamp monkeys. Macaques (*Macaca*) have the largest geographic distribution of any of the nonhuman

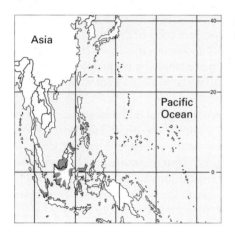

FIGURE 3-12 A map showing the geographical distribution of tarsiers.

primates. The result of this enormous geographic distribution is that macaques are found in a number of different climates and in an extensive range of habitat types distributed throughout all of the biomes listed in Table 3-1. Moreover, certain species of macaques (*M. mulatta, M. fascicularis,* and *M. radiata*) show high tolerance to habitat change. Thus, throughout Asia, populations of these species **commensally** live with humans in highly urbanized locations. Macaques are found in the North African countries of Morocco and Algeria, and throughout Asia, extending as far east as Japan (Figure 3-14). They occur almost as far north as 42° latitude in China and Japan and to the south at approximately 6° latitude on the Indonesian island of Java. Macaques are also the only extant primates to occur in Europe. *M. sylvanus* lives on Gibraltar, where the monkeys were introduced by British soldiers in 1915; three groups are still maintained by the government of Gibraltar (Figure 3-15; Fa 1984).

In Algeria and Morocco, *M. sylvanus* lives in a number of different habitat types, including scrub land and mid to high altitude forests located over 800 m (2,624 ft) above sea level. At approximately 1,500 m (4,920 ft), mixed deciduous oak forests give way to cedar-fir-evergreen-oak forests (Table 3-1; Mehlman 1988). At such high altitudes the winter months (December through March) may be severe, with temperatures dropping to –18°C (–0.4°F) and up to two meters (> 6 ft) of snow on the ground. In North Africa, these macaques, like *M. cyclopis* of Taiwan, tend to be restricted to high altitude habitats because at lower altitudes, their preferred habitats have been eliminated by human activities.

Baboons (*Papio*) are found from West Africa across to the Horn of Africa to South Africa (Jolly 1993, Newman et al. 2004). Within this wide distribution, baboons are found in a large range of habitats, including semidesert scrub, savanna grassland, as well as woodlands, seasonal, and rain forest habitats (Kingdon 1997). Geladas (*Theropithecus*) are endemic to Ethiopia and are found in montane grassland habitats at altitudes of 1,400–4,400 m (4,592–14,432 ft) (Figure 3-16). Drills, mandrills, and mangabeys are restricted to the rain forests or seasonal forests of west-central Africa. Drills and mandrills are terrestrial and adapted to dense primary and secondary rain forest habitats. Some species of mangabeys (*Cercocebus*) are both terrestrial and arboreal, and live in primary and secondary dry forests, while others (*Lophocebus albigena*) are highly arboreal and are frequently found in gallery forests.

All of the guenons, patas, talapoin, and swamp monkeys live in sub-Saharan Africa. They are predominantly found in West, Central, and East Africa. The guenons occupy a diverse range of habitats. Many species are found in primary rain forests, while others occur in secondary rain forests, gallery and bamboo forests, and flooded and swamp forests (Enstam

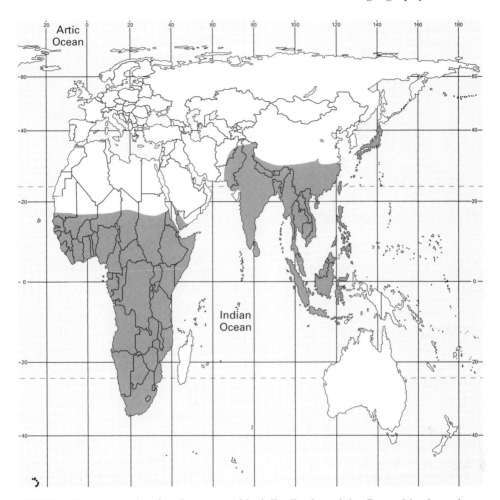

FIGURE 3-13   A map showing the geographical distribution of the Cercopithecinae, the cheek-pouched monkeys.

and Isbell 2007). *Chlorocebus aethiops,* the vervet monkey, is an edge species. It lives in savanna woodlands while utilizing savanna grasslands. The closely related patas monkey (*Erythrocuebus patas*) lives in woodland and savanna grassland habitats, which tend to be more arid than those occupied by vervet monkeys. Allen's swamp monkey (*Allenopithecus nigrovirdis*) and the talapoins *(Miopithecus)* are found in primary lowland swamp and inundated gallery forests.

The Catarrhine Monkeys, Colobinae

Leaf-eating monkeys occur across the continents of Africa and Asia (Figure 3-17). The African colobine monkeys (*Colobus, Piliocolobus,* and *Procolobus*) are found in East, Central, and West Africa. The Asian colobines (*Semnopithecus, Trachypithecus, Presbytis, Pygathrix, Rhinopithecus, Nasalis,* and *Simias*) are spread throughout Asia. Their specialized stomach morphology (see Chapter 4) is related to their leaf-eating habits and correlates with the occurrence of African and Asian colobines in forest and woodland biomes.

The African colobines are found in lowland and montane rain forests, gallery forests, and dry coastal forests (Fashing 2007). Among the African colobines, there is considerable

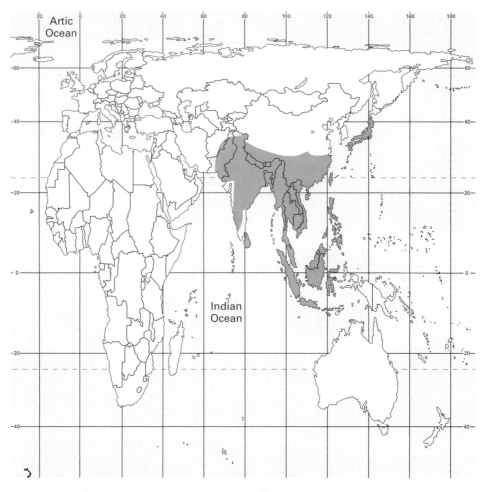

FIGURE 3-14 A map showing the geographical distribution of the genus *Macaca*.

FIGURE 3-15 Several Barbary macaque (*Macaca sylvanus*) groups live on the Rock of Gibraltar, where they are a favorite tourist attraction.

FIGURE 3-16   The gelada (*Theropithecus gelada*) is endemic to upland Ethiopia. It spends much time feeding on grass and seeks shelter along steep cliff faces at night and during danger.

variation in the preference of species for either primary or secondary forests. Many species are found in lowland rain forests. The black and white colobus (*Colobus guereza*) is especially unique because this highly arboreal primate seems to seek out areas of habitat disturbance and actually occurs in higher densities in forests where logging has occurred, as opposed to primary forest habitats (Chapman et al. 2000, Fashing and Oates in press). The black and white colobus tends to occupy lower levels of the forest strata and will come to the ground to feed or cross through deforested gaps.

Asian colobines, in contrast, occupy a greater diversity of habitat types (see Box 3-3). A majority of species live in tropical and subtropical rain forests, but they are also found in the temperate, high altitude, broad-leaved forests of Nepal and southwest China (*Semnopithecus* and *Rhinopithecus*). In Borneo, the proboscis monkey (*Nasalis larvatus*) occupies a very specialized habitat known as peat swamps and is also encountered in mangrove forests, while the Southern Plains gray langur (*Semnopithecus dussumieri*) lives in the semidesert scrub of western India (Kirkpatrick 2007). While most colobine monkeys are arboreal, some species of Hanuman or gray langurs (*Semnopithecus*) are highly terrestrial and are often found living in temple grounds and in park lands.

The Asian Apes

Gibbons (*Hylobates, Hoolock,* and *Nomascus*) are allopatrically distributed throughout eastern and southeastern Asia. They occur from India; north into Yunan Province, China; on Hainan island, extending south through the Malay Peninsula; and eastward through the Indonesian islands (Figure 3-18). Siamangs (*Symphalangus*) are restricted to Southeast Asia and are found on the Indonesian island of Sumatra and on the Malay Peninsula. Gibbons and siamangs are specialized brachiators and tend to be found high in the rain forest canopy. Even though most gibbons occur in primary rain forests, some species do utilize secondary rain forests and seasonal forests (Bartlett 2007).

The geographic distribution of orangutans (*Pongo*) is restricted to the Indonesian islands of Sumatra and Borneo. On these islands, orangutans are found in primary rain forests ranging from lowland swamp forests to upland forests. On Sumatra, orangutans

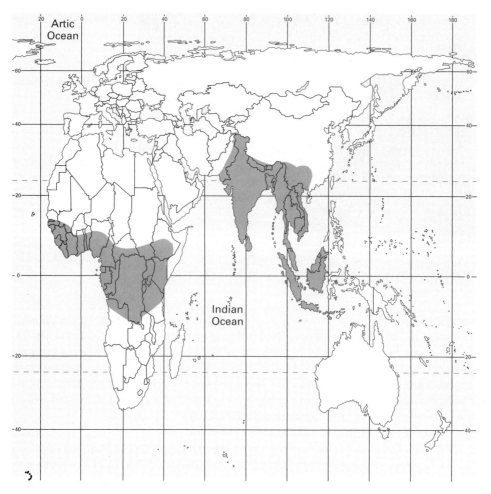

FIGURE 3-17 A map showing the geographical distribution of the Colobinae, the leaf-eating monkeys.

have been reported at altitudes of 4,000 m (13,120 ft) (Rowe 1996), but forests at lower altitudes are preferred. The lowland rain forests of Borneo and Sumatra are among the most diverse in the world (MacKinnon et al. 1998, Richards 1996). These forests are dominated by plants belonging to the family Dipterocarpaceae. A characteristic of dipterocarps is mast fruiting; i.e. many trees bear fruit at the same time over a wide area (Ashton 1988, van Schaik 1986). The timing of the mast fruiting is thought to be driven by climatic triggers such as the occurrence of an El Niño (Wich and van Schaik 2000). When an El Niño occurs, the waters of the eastern Pacific Ocean are warmed and drought conditions occur. In between periods of mast fruiting, there can be limited availability of dipterocarp fruits. Orangutans also occupy peat swamp forests that contain much fewer dipterocarps. These forests grow on dead vegetation that has been waterlogged; over time this vegetation accumulates as peat. The peat acts like a sponge and soaks in moisture especially during the monsoon rains. When these forests are cut down, the areas in which they were found become highly vulnerable to fire, especially during the dry season. In 1982, an ecological tragedy struck Borneo. The "Great Fire of

 ❖ ❖ ❖ ❖ BOX 3-3 ❖ ❖ ❖ ❖

An Unlikely Monkey Habitat

White-headed langurs (*Trachypithecus leucocephalus*) are very rare (Li and Rogers 2004, Wang et al. 2005) and have an extremely small geographic distribution. They are restricted to four counties in the southern Guangxi Province of China (Huang et al. 2003). Within this very circumscribed distribution, white-headed langurs live in a most unusual primate habitat. Langurs are typically considered to be arboreal primates, yet in southern China the white-headed langur lives in a limestone hill habitat with a very limited number of trees. The geology of this region is a **Karst topography.** According to Huang et al. (2003), the study site in which they studied the langurs included an area approximately 4 km² (1.6 mi²) of rocky hills at an elevation of up to 300 m (984 ft). The researchers identify four vertical zones that make up this hillside habitat. The highest hilltop habitat consists mostly of bare rock with grass, shrub, and vine cover. The middle zone contains many limestone caves and precipitous cave walls. The lower hill zone is composed of rich soils and dense vegetation, including trees. Cultivated lands lay below and surface water is only available when it rains.

In the winter months, the langurs were observed using the top of the hillside in the mornings for sunbathing. Throughout the year, they spend a majority of their day (66 percent of their time) in the lower zone where trees are present. However, the langurs do not stay in the trees at night. Instead, they travel up and across precipitous rock faces in order to enter caves for night-time sleeping. The researchers observed thick piles of langur feces that had accumulated as a result of the long-time use of these caves by the langurs. Surprisingly, the langurs avoid the cultivated fields.

> **Karst topography**—type of terrain that is formed on carbonate rock such as limestone and dolomite; as ground water percolates through the rock, it dissolves to form openings such as caves

The karst limestone habitat used by the white-headed langurs is somewhat unusual for primates. The reasons for this particular habitat selection are unknown but may be associated with human encroachment into habitats where the langurs used to live. Alternatively, the langurs' use of caves as sleeping sites may be the result of anti-predator strategies. Tigers have been extinct for many years in this area, but if the langurs have evolved anti-predator strategies, they may still be maintained (Huang et al. 2003).

❖ ❖ ❖ ❖

Borneo" burned for almost a year, and 4 million hectares (almost 10 million acres) of lowland tropical rainforest were destroyed. This tragedy was followed by an even larger fire in 1997 that swept over the entire island of Borneo, making life for both human and nonhuman inhabitants intolerable. The fires were initiated by smaller fires that were started to clear rice fields but quickly went out of control. Once these fires hit the peat forests, there was unlimited fuel to keep the fires burning. Much of the orangutan habitats and many orangutan lives have been lost (e.g., Curran et al. 2004).

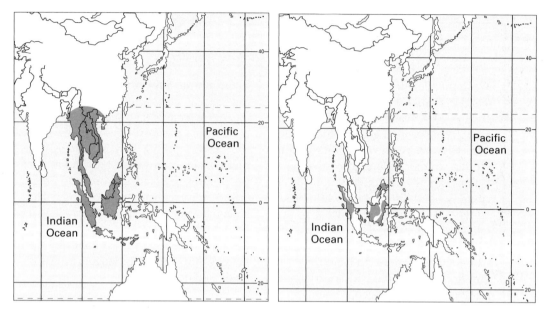

FIGURE 3-18 A map showing the geographical distribution of Asian apes.

The African Apes

Gorillas are found in Central Africa, but species' distribution is discontinuous and populations tend to be isolated from one another (Figure 3-19). Within its geographic distribution, gorillas occupy a number of different rain forest habitats that are distributed across a wide range of altitudes (Table 3-2). The mountain gorilla (*Gorilla beringei beringei*) lives in high altitude montane rain forests. At the Karisoke Research Center, Rwanda, where Dian Fossey worked, almost no fruit plants are available at altitudes exceeding 2,500 m (8,200 ft). Rather, these forests contain patches of bamboo, nettles, and *Vernonia*, a favored food source of the mountain gorillas. In contrast, in the Bwindi Impenetrable National Park of Uganda, only 30 km (18.6 mi) away and at slightly lower altitude (1,400–2,500 m), many more fruit trees are available. The difference in the occurrence of fruit trees is significant because the long-term studies conducted by Fossey on the mountain gorillas identified these large-bodied apes as being predominantly herb feeders. With further study in other locations, primatologists have discovered that gorillas also eat fruit in large quantities when it is available to them (Remis 1997a, Yamagiwa et al. 1996).

In the Democratic Republic of Congo, the Grauer's gorilla (*Gorilla gorilla graueri*) occupies a range of lowland and montane rain forest habitats. Lowland rain forests include swamp forests that are occupied by both the Grauer's gorilla (*G. g. graueri*) and Western lowland gorillas (*Gorilla gorilla gorilla*). The rain forest habitats that the Cross River gorillas (*G. g. diehli*) occupy are located farther to the north on the border of Nigeria and Cameroon. Consequently, these rain forests undergo a very long dry season consisting of five months of the year when rainfall is less than 100 mm (4 in) (Oates et al. 2003).

Chimpanzees (*Pan troglodytes*) occur in West and in Central Africa, while bonobos (*P. paniscus*) are restricted to the Democratic Republic of Congo in Central Africa. The geographic distribution of both species is highly fragmented and restricted (Figure 3-20). Chimpanzees occupy the rain forest and woodland biomes and inhabit lowland to montane rain forests, primary and secondary rain forests, seasonal forests, savanna woodlands,

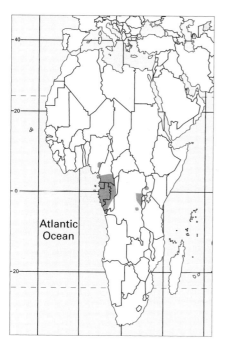

FIGURE 3-19   A map showing the geographical distribution of gorillas.

and gallery forests, as well as bamboo forests (Boesch and Boesch-Ackermann 2000, Furuichi et al. 2001, Goodall 1986, Rowe 1996). The range of bonobos is limited to lowland rain forests, but they may also be found in swamp forests and savanna woodlands (Hashimoto et al. 1998, Kortlandt 1995, Malenky and Stiles 1991).

The Platyrrhine Monkeys

Howler, spider, muriquis, woolly, titi, saki, uakari, owl, marmoset, tamarin, Goeldi's, capuchin, and squirrel monkeys are located in the Americas. The most northern distributed American primate species live in southern Mexico, and the most southern ones are found in

TABLE 3-2	Geographic Distribution of Gorillas	
Species/Subspecies	*Geographic Distribution*	*Altitudinal Range of Study Sites (meters)*
Mountain gorilla *Gorilla beringei beringei*	Rwanda, Uganda, Democratic Republic of Congo	1,450–3,710
Grauer's gorilla *G. g. graueri*	Democratic Republic of Congo	600–2,600
Cross River gorilla *G. g. diehli*	Nigeria, Cameroon	400–1,300
Western lowland gorilla *G. g. gorilla*	Gabon, Cameroon, Equatorial Guinea, Central African Republic, Angola, Democratic Republic of Congo	100–700

Adapted from Robbins 2007, p. 306 and 309.

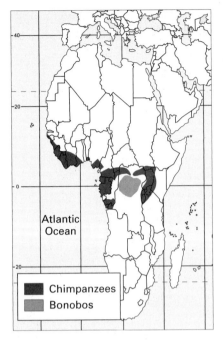

FIGURE 3-20 A map showing the geographical distribution of bonobos and chimpanzees. There is no overlap in distribution of the two *Pan* species.

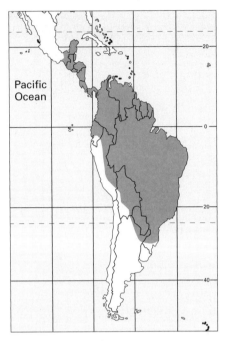

FIGURE 3-21 A map showing the geographical distribution of the platyrrhine monkeys.

southern Argentina (Figure 3-21). Platyrrhine monkeys are predominantly arboreal and live in forested habitats including rain forest, seasonal forest, and woodland forest (Table 3-1).

The Atelinae monkeys include howler (*Alouatta*), spider (*Ateles*), woolly (*Lagothrix*), and yellow-tailed woolly (*Oreonax*) monkeys, and muriquis (*Brachyteles*). Howlers have the largest geographic distribution, extending from eastern Mexico, through Central America, to northern Argentina. All of these monkeys are highly arboreal and live in rain forest and woodland forest habitats. Spider monkeys and muriquis use a rapid suspensory (semi-brachiation) mode of locomotion to move through the forest.

Muriquis are endemic to Brazil and are only found in relics of the Brazilian Atlantic Forest. Lion tamarins (*Leontopithecus*) are also endemic to this forest. The Brazilian Atlantic Forest contains highly unique coastal and montane rain forests that extend from northeastern to southern Brazil and northern Argentina and southeastern Paraguay. A once-extensive forest now exists only in pockets surrounded by very dense human populations (see Chapter 11, Box 11-2). Twenty-four primate species and subspecies live in this forest, and of these, twelve are endemic (Table 3-3).

Uakaris (*Cacajo*), bearded sakis (*Chiropotes*), and sakis (*Pithecia*) are the pithecine monkeys. They are found throughout South America in humid and dry rain forests of the Amazon Basin, north into the Guianas, and eastern Venezuela (Figure 3-22; Norconk 2007). Uakaris live in the Orinoco and western Amazon Basins and are found in gallery forests that may flood for nine months of the year to depths of 6–20 m (19–65 ft) (Ferreira and Prance 1998).

Titi monkeys (*Callicebus*) occur throughout the western and southern Amazon Basin and southern Orinoco River Basin (Norconk 2007). They are found in lowland

TABLE 3-3   Primate Species of the Brazilian Atlantic Forest

Scientific Name	Common Name
Alouatta guariba	Brown howler monkey
A. belzebul	Red-handed howler monkey
Brachyteles arachnoides	Southern muriqui[*]
B. hypoxanthus	Northern muriqui[*]
Callicebus coimbrai	Coimbra's titi
C. barbarabrownae	Barbara Brown's titi
C. personatus	Masked titi monkey
Callithrix aurita	Buffy-eared marmoset
C. flaviceps	Buffy-headed marmoset
C. geoffroyi	Geoffroy's marmoset
C. jacchus	Common marmoset
C. kuhli	Black tufted-ear marmoset
Cebus apella	Tufted capuchin
C. libidinosus	Black-striped capuchin
C. nigritus	Black capuchin
C. robustus	Robust tufted capuchin
C. xanthosternos	Buffy-headed tufted capuchin
Leontopithecus caissara	Black-faced lion tamarin[*]
L. chrysomelas	Golden-headed lion tamarin[*]
L. chrysopygus	Black lion tamarin[*]
L. rosalia	Golden lion tamarin[*]
Saguinus bicolor	Pied tamarin

[*]Endemic species

rain forest, and gallery forests with at least two species (*C. moloch* and *C. cupreus*) being tolerant to some degree of habitat disturbance. *C. donacophilus* has also been found in grassland habitats (Ferrari et al. 2000).

The owl monkey (*Aotus*), a nocturnal haplorhine, lives in the rain forests and seasonal forests of Central and South America. They occur in primary and secondary, humid and dry rain forests. They have been observed up to 3,200 m above sea level (Defler 2003).

The cebine monkeys, capuchins (*Cebus*), and squirrel monkeys (*Saimiri*) are distributed throughout Central and South America; however, the geographic distribution of capuchins is more extensive than that of squirrel monkeys. In many localities the two are sympatric. Capuchins occur throughout much of Central America and South America (Honduras to Argentina), while squirrel monkeys are found in isolated lowland rain forests of Costa Rica extending to the coast of western Panama, and northern South America (Boinski et al. 2002). Along with having a larger geographic distribution, capuchins are also found in more diverse habitat types. Capuchins occupy primary and secondary rain forests and a variety of seasonal forests and are referred to as "habitat generalists" (Chapman et al. 1989, Fragaszy et al. 2004). In contrast, squirrel monkeys are most commonly found in lowland rain forests.

The callitrichines, including Goeldi's monkey (*Callimico*), marmosets (*Callithrix* and *Cebuella*), lion tamarins (*Leontopithecus*), and tamarins (*Saguinus*), are distributed

(a)   (b)

FIGURE 3-22 Pithecine monkeys, such as (a) the white-faced saki (*Pithecia pithecia*) and (b) the black-bearded saki (*Chiropotes satanas*) are found in humid and dry rain forests in the Amazon Basin.

throughout the northern half of the South American continent (extending as far south as southern Brazil). Many of these monkeys live in the Amazon River Basin and have over-lapping ranges. Goeldi's monkey is most commonly found in gallery forests, while mar-mosets are found in woodland forests, savanna scrub, and several species readily adapt to highly disturbed human environments. Tamarins are not as diverse and tend to be found in rain forest environments. As mentioned above, lion tamarins are endemic to the Brazil-ian Atlantic rain forest (Digby et al. 2007).

❖❖ Biogeographical Patterns

The majority of primate species are found in tropical and subtropical regions with the greatest number of taxa being found in the equatorial tropical rain forests. Primate taxa are almost evenly distributed between tropical rain forest and seasonal forest biomes (Table 3-1). All primate families, except the Pongidae, have representatives in these bio-mes. A majority of primate families and subfamilies have representatives in tropical wood-lands, except for the Pongidae, Pitheciinae, Callicebinae, and Aotinae. As aridity increases across the biomes, the number of families represented decreases. Only seven families (six strepsirhines and one haplorhine) have members that are found in savannas. Six families are found in semi-desert scrub; four of these are strepsirhines, and two cercopithecines. Colobine (*Presbytis* and *Rhinopithecus*) and ceropithecine monkeys (*Macaca*) are the only ones found in temperate woodlands.

Strepsirhine and haplorhine primates are almost evenly represented across the tropical biomes. The wide distribution of the strepsirhines is attributable to the diversity of biomes found on the island of Madagascar. The Cercopithecidae family includes the most diverse primates, both in the terms of number of biomes occupied and in the terms of their geographic distribution.

❖❖ Summary

Biogeography is a science that seeks to identify patterns in the geographic distribution of plants and animals. The geographic distribution of primates is limited by the Tropic of Cancer to the north and the Tropic of Capricorn to the south. Within these two lines of latitude, the vast majority of primates are found.

Biomes are consistent natural communities of plants and the associated animals that live in them. In the tropical zones, there are rain forest, seasonal forest, woodland, savanna, and semi-desert scrub biomes. In the temperate climatic zones, primates are only found in the woodland biome. Strepsirhine primates are distributed throughout Africa and Asia. Five of the families are geographically restricted to the island of Madagascar. Haplorhine primates occur in Africa, Asia, and the Americas. The family Tarsiidae is distributed only in Southeast Asia. The family Cercopithecidae has the widest geographic distribution of any of the primate families, but is not found in the Americas. Its distribution is African and Asian.

Members of the family Hylobatidae and Pongidae (gibbons and siamangs, and orangutan) are restricted to Southeast Asia. Members of the family Pongidae have a much restricted distribution, and are found only on the Indonesian islands of Sumatra and Borneo. The Hominidae includes the African apes; their geographic distribution is presently limited to isolated locations in West and Central Africa.

The primates found in Central and South America includes the Atelidae, Cebidae, and Callitrichidae families.

❖❖ Key Words

abiotic	gallery forests	temperate areas
biogeography	Karst topography	transect
biome	primary rain forests	tropical
biotic	secondary rain forests	
commensally	subalpine	

❖❖ Study Questions

1. In general, where do we find primates living today?
2. What are the various biomes that primates occupy?
3. What is the paradox of the rain forest? How can it look so rich and fertile but not be able to support crops?
4. Which primates live in temperate regions, and how do monkeys cope with living in snowy habitats?
5. In general, where do the major groups of primates live?

❖❖ Suggested Readings and Related Web Sites

Lehman SM, Fleagle JG, editors. 2006. Primate biogeography: progress and prospects. New York: Springer

CHAPTER 4

The Primate Body

Primates come in all different sizes, shapes, and colors. These differences are manifestations of morphological and behavioral adaptations that have been shaped by natural selection over evolutionary time. The traits we see today are the result of the increased survival rates and differences in reproductive success within a species, both in the recent and more distant past. A species' reproductive success today will leave its mark on the species in the future. By examining specific body features of living primates, we can determine which features present on the primate body are reflective of shared mammalian ancestry and which features are more recent specializations.

◈◈ The General Primate Body Plan

Primate species range in size from the tiny pygmy mouse lemur (*Microcebus myoxinus*) that weighs just 30 g, or a little over an ounce, to adult male gorillas (*Gorilla gorilla*) that weigh around 170 kg (375 lbs) (Figure 4-1). Strepsirhines are, on average, smaller than haplorhines. The largest living strepsirhine is the indri (*Indri indri*), which weighs about 6 kg (~13 lbs). The smallest living haplorhine, the South American pygmy marmoset (*Callithrix pygmaea*) weighs 125 g (~4 oz), while tarsiers range between 90–150 g (3–5 oz). Nocturnal species are usually smaller than diurnal species, weighing less than 2 kg (4.4 lbs).

How do we recognize a primate? There is actually no single feature or trait that sets primates apart from all other animals. Rather we use a suite of traits to define a primate (as discussed in Chapter 1). The basic primate body plan reflects an inherent arboreal adaptation, with many ancestral traits retained. All primates have four functional limbs. In most species, each hand and foot has five digits (pentadactyly), with at least the big toe or thumb being opposable. Primates have unusually high mobility at the wrists, and to a lesser extent at the ankle joints, and can therefore manipulate and pull food sources toward themselves rather than having to move the whole body toward a food source. Most primates have flat nails instead of claws at the ends of their digits. Exceptions include the tamarins and marmosets, and the fork-marked lemur (*Phaner furcifer*), which have clawlike nails on all but their big toes. It is suggested that these clawlike nails provide a better grip when these species scurry up and down tree trunks searching for tree sap. The aye-aye (*Daubentonia*) also has clawlike nails on its digits, except on the big toe and thumb, but it is not so obvious why this is the case. It may be a reflection of a behavioral pattern of the past. For all primates, the skull

FIGURE 4-1 Primates come in a wide range of body sizes; from the tiny mouse lemur to the great male gorilla.

is larger than that of other animals of similar body size, and their eyes face forward. A tail is present in most primates, the exception being the tailless apes.

All primates have bodies that are covered with hair, although some species have almost hairless faces. Humans are an exception, as we have retained very little hair on our bodies (which is why we have been called "the naked ape"). Hair is effective, not just to keep the body warm, but also to keep it cool by reflecting away the sun's rays. The range of hair color is extensive among primates, including the glossy orange as seen in orangutans and golden-headed lion tamarins (*Leontopithecus chrysomelas*) to the black and white ruffed lemur (*Varecia variegata*), and the beautiful mix of colors of the Diana monkey (*Cercopithecus diana*) (Figure 4-2).

Primates not only have vibrant-colored hair, many species have brightly colored skin, especially around the face and genital region. Some of these variations in hair and skin coloration are permanent and assist individuals within a species to recognize each other, especially when moving about in dense vegetation where visibility is limited. In many taxa, males and females exhibit different hair colors (sexual dichromatism). For example, black and

(a)

(b)

(c)

FIGURE 4-2 Many primates have dramatic color schemes in their hair. Some have contrasting colors and patterns, such as the Diana monkey, *Cercopithecus diana* (a), the black and white ruffed lemur, *Varecia varecia* (b), and the golden-headed tamarin, *Leontopithecus chrysomelas* (c).

FIGURE 4-3 Males and females may have different colored hair, sexual dichromatism, as shown here in the Chinese white-cheeked gibbon (*Hylobates leucogenys*); the female has buff colored hair while the male has black.

gold howler males (*Alouatta caraya*) have black-colored hair while the females are golden yellow. Likewise, the Chinese white-cheeked gibbon (*Nomascus leucogenys*) males are black while the females have buff or tan-colored hair (Figure 4-3). This type of sexual dichromatism may be the result of **sexual selection**, wherein one sex may find the opposite sex more attractive with a different coloration. For species that live in a dense arboreal habitat, it may also be easier to recognize a male from a female, which could be important information to an infant. Other color variations are not permanent and provide primates with social signals about their **conspecifics**, that is, individuals belonging to the same species. For example, the bright red and blue coloration of a male mandrill's muzzle signals dominance and top position in the social group (Figure 4-4), while the color of female sexual skin sends information about reproductive status. In some species, infants are born with a distinctly different hair color compared to that of the adults, making them quite conspicuous (Figure 4-5). The distinctive infant coloration elicits protective behaviors from adults (Treves 1997).

FIGURE 4-4 Many species have brightly colored skin, especially around the genital region and the face. The brightly colored muzzle of mandrill males signals dominance.

FIGURE 4-5 The hair of young infant primates is often of a contrasting color to the adults. This is especially common among leaf-eating monkeys. New born black and white colobus (*Colobus gureza*) are all white.

Skeleton

Underneath the hair, muscle, and other soft tissue we find all the bones that make up the skeleton (Figure 4-6; see also Appendix B). The skeleton provides the scaffolding upon which the muscles are anchored. Bones also facilitate movement. Muscles attach to bones at specific locations, and it is the muscles that make the bones move. Since there is a strong correlation between physical activity and skeletal structure, it is possible to infer behavioral adaptations such as modes of locomotion using just the skeleton.

Bones are made up of both organic materials (e.g., collagen) and inorganic minerals (e.g., hydroxylapatite). As long as an individual is alive, the bone is a living tissue. Throughout childhood bone grows and develops, and once full length or size is achieved, this growth stops. During daily activities bone is exposed to stresses and strains, and in response it is constantly being repaired. After death, the organic materials decay and are leached out of the bone.

When we look at primate skeletons, we see many retained ancestral or **plesiomorphic traits**. For example, primates have retained the clavicle (collarbone), which is lost in most other mammalian orders (Figure 4-6). In both the forelimb and the hindlimb we

> **plesiomorphic trait**—an ancestral trait or a trait with a long evolutionary history
> **apomorphic trait**—a derived, more recently evolved trait

find the same number of bones that are seen in most mammals. Figure 4-6 illustrates the basic skeletal arrangement of primates. In the parts of the limbs closest to the body we find a single bone; in the forelimb it is called the humerus and in the hindlimb the femur. Below the elbow and knee joints, primates have retained two bones. In the forelimb, the radius can be moved about on the ulna, making it possible to rotate the hand at the wrist. In the hindlimb, the fibula cannot move in the same fashion. However, the fact that the fibula is an independent bone is a plesiomorphic trait. Only in the tarsier

FIGURE 4-6   An articulated primate skeleton, showing all the major bones, and basic skeletal arrangement of primates.

is the end part of the fibula fused to the tibia, just as it is in other specialized leapers like rabbits. The fusion of the fibula to the tibia is a derived or **apomorphic trait**. The size and shape of the individual hand and foot bones show much species variability, reflective of locomotor and postural adaptations (see below).

When seated, primates appear to have a straight back (Figure 4-7). The vertebral column in the back is made up of five different types of bones. Closest to the skull are the cervical vertebrae, typically seven in number. Just below the cervical vertebrae are the thoracic vertebrae, which make up part of the rib cage. Usually, there are twelve thoracic vertebrae. Located in between the rib cage and the pelvis are the lumbar vertebrae. There are from three to eight lumbar vertebrae, depending on the species. The sacral vertebrae, commonly five in number, are fused together into a single bone, the sacrum. Last, there are the caudal or tail vertebrae. In humans and other apes, these comprise three to five small fused bones, the coccyx. However, all monkeys and strepsirhines have tail vertebrae that are not fused. The number of tail vertebrae depends on the length of the tail; species with short tails have fewer tail vertebrae while those with long tails have more. The pelvis is made up of three bones: the ilium, pubis, and ischium. The pelvis of nonhuman primates differs significantly from our own, which is greatly influenced by our upright posture and bipedal locomotion. In humans the ilium is shorter and more cuplike, while in other primates the ilium is elongated and has a more blade-like shape.

The size and shape of the skull or cranium is highly variable (Figure 4-8). At birth the **frontal bone**, which is located under the forehead, is made up of two bones separated by the **metopic suture**. The two frontal bones fuse together into a single bone by adulthood in all haplorhines, while remaining as two separate bones in most strepsirhine

FIGURE 4-7 A male anubis baboon (*Papio anubis*) sitting on its ischial callosities, showing the straight back posture (orthogrady) common in primates.

species. Likewise, the **mandible**, or lower jawbone, begins with a left and right part but fuses together in the midline by adulthood in all haplorhines, except the tarsiers. They retain an unfused mandible throughout life. The bony eye orbits vary much in size and location, although all primates have more or less forward-facing eye sockets (orbital convergence). The strepsirhine primates lack a complete bony enclosure of their orbits, and only have a bony bar that passes on the outside of the orbit joining the frontal and **zygomatic** (cheekbone) **bones** together (see Figure 4-9).

Dentition

Most mammals have teeth that are of different shapes and sizes, and primates are no exception. The presence of differently shaped teeth is referred to as **heterodonty** (Figure 4-9), which is a plesiomorphic mammalian trait. The number of teeth present in the jaws varies in different primate taxa (Swindler 2002). The general pattern is to have the same number and types of teeth both in the upper jaw (**maxilla**) and lower jaw (mandible), although there are a few exceptions. All primates also have two sets of teeth. The first set, the milk or deciduous teeth, appears in early childhood. The deciduous teeth are shed fairly early in life, and are replaced by the permanent teeth, which must last for the rest of an individual's life.

Most primates have four anterior, or front, teeth called incisors, in both the upper and lower jaw. Some strepsirhine species have, over evolutionary time, lost some or all of the incisors of the upper jaw (e.g., the aye-aye and the sportive lemur). Incisors are used as cutting tools and are usually flat with a straight edge. They vary in size, which is reflec-

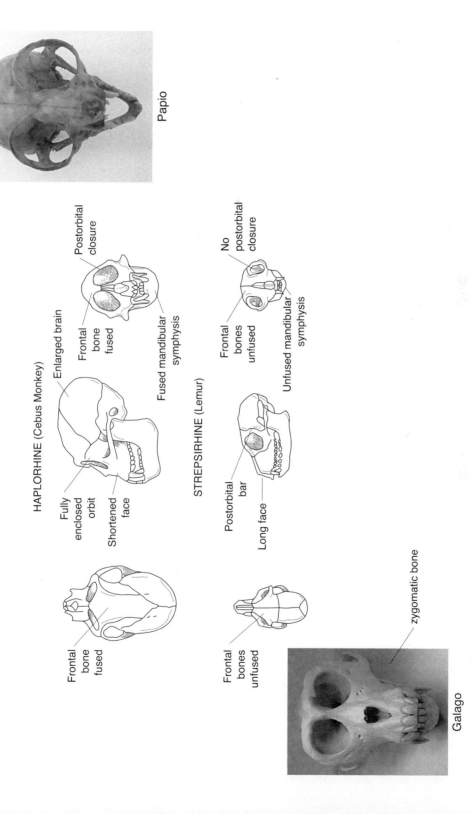

FIGURE 4-8 It is possible to examine various traits on the skull to determine whether the specimen is a strepsirhine or a haplorhine; here represented by a bushbaby (left) and a baboon (right). For example, the presence of a metopic suture, a bony ring around the eye, and an unfused mandible indicate a strepsirhine, while a fused metopic suture and mandible, and the presence of a bony socket around the eye indicate a haplorhine.

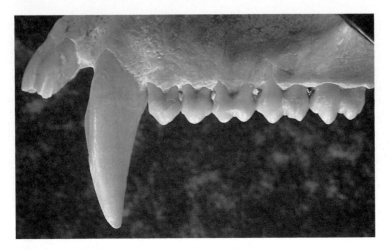

FIGURE 4-9 Primates have retained the ancestral mammalian trait of having teeth of different shapes and sizes, referred to as heterodonty. The anterior teeth are the incisors and canine, and the posterior teeth are the premolars and molars.

tive of dietary adaptations (see below). In some strepsirhines, the incisors in the upper jaw are very small, and there is a big gap (**diastema**) between the two central incisors. Following the tooth rows toward the back, behind the incisors are the **canines**. If present, there is a single canine in each quadrant of the mouth. In many primate species, the canines are large and imposing dagger-like structures, especially in males (sexual dimorphism) (Figure 4-10). To accommodate large canines, there is a diastema behind the maxillary incisors and the mandibular canines. In the majority of species, the canines do not appear to serve a function during feeding but seem to be important in social display. Further back in the jaw, behind the canines, are the **premolar** teeth. Premolars vary in surface complexity but often these teeth have two cusps (raised areas on the chewing or occlusal surface). There is some variability in how many premolars are present, and this reflects the evolutionary legacy of particular lineages. All catarrhines have two premolars on either side of the upper and lower jaw. The platyrrhines, however, have retained three premolars, as have the strepsirhines. The ancestral primate stock had four premolars in each quadrant of the mouth. An evolutionary pattern of primates has included a reduction in the number of teeth over time (see below). Behind the premolars are the **molar** teeth. The premolars and molar teeth are often referred to as the cheek teeth, and it is here that food is sliced, crushed, and ground into small pieces before being moved into the stomach. The shape of the molar teeth varies significantly depending on particular dietary adaptations. The shape of the molars in the upper jaw is also different from the opposing teeth in the lower jaw.

Strepsirhines have more triangular-shaped molar teeth (Figure 4-11a), especially in the upper jaw, while monkeys have more square-shaped molars with four cusps. The African-Asian monkeys have evolved a further elaboration in that the cusps are located in pairs, one pair in the front and one pair in the back, with a distinct indentation in between them. We refer to this pattern as **bilophodonty** or the +4 pattern. Each pair is connected via a transverse ridge (see Figure 4-11b). Leaf-eating monkeys have raised cusps with sharp crests between the cusps on either side of the tooth, while omnivorous and fruit-eating

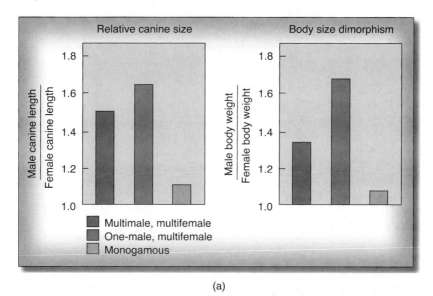

(a)

(b)

FIGURE 4-10 Most primate species show some degree of size difference between males and females. Such sexual dimorphism can be manifested in body size or canine tooth size (a). Body size dimorphism is more common in species that live in one-male, multifemale social groups, just like the patas monkey (*Erythrocebus patas*) shown here (b). Males (standing on the left) are almost twice as large as females (seated).

monkeys tend to have lower and more rounded cusps. Apes also have square molar teeth, but they tend to be more elongated towards the back because of the presence of a fifth cusp. The ape molar tooth pattern is referred to as the Y-5 pattern (Figure 4-11c). The five cusps on ape molar teeth tend to be very low and rounded. The chewing surface is more flat and better for crushing and grinding food. Most living primates have three molars on either side

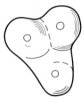
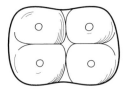
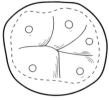

(a) tritubercular   (b) bilophodonty   (c) Y-5 pattern

FIGURE 4-11 The shape of molar teeth and the number of cusps present on the occlusal surface vary. Strepsirhine primates have triangular shaped teeth with three cusps, tritubercular pattern (a). Monkeys have more square shaped molars with four cusps, +4 pattern. African-Asian
monkeys have a further elaboration where the front two cusps are clearly separated from the
back two cusps, referred to as bilophodonty (b). The molars of apes are more rounded and have
five cusps, Y-5 pattern (c).

of the jaws. Some callitrichids have only two molars in each quadrant. It has been suggested that this is due to a secondary reduction in body size. Even in humans there appears
to be a trend toward the loss of the third molar (wisdom tooth).

Teeth are made up of various materials (Figure 4-12). What you see in the mouth
is the top or crown of the tooth. When unworn, it is the **enamel** of the crown that is visible. Enamel is the hardest material in the body. Unlike other parts of the body, it is
never remodelled or replaced. With age, the enamel is worn away as the teeth are used
for chewing, exposing the underlying **dentine**, which surrounds the **pulp cavity** where
nerves and blood vessels are located. Dentine is a softer material than enamel, and
it can replenish itself with increasing wear (secondary dentine). The part not visible
that anchors the tooth into the jaw is the **root**. Some teeth have a single root (incisors,
canines, and some premolars); others have two or three roots (molars). Within the
roots are openings through which the blood and nerve supplies pass. The teeth are
held in the jaw by a type of tissue called **cementum**. Rough and hard diets wear away
the enamel more rapidly, and exposure of the pulp cavity may result in infection.
Through natural selection species adapted to rough diets have extra thick enamel on
their cheek teeth to prolong the life of the tooth and to prevent premature death due
to infection.

Some interesting specializations in tooth morphology include the **toothcomb**, seen
in all living strepsirhines, and the **sectorial premolar**, found in taxa such as baboons. In
the strepsirhine toothcomb, the incisors and canines of the lower jaw are tightly packed
together and are almost horizontally implanted into the mandible (Figure 4-13). The
toothcomb is used for grooming and to gain access to food. The sectorial premolar
tooth complex (Figure 4-14) includes an elongated single-cusped premolar that serves
as a sharpening stone for the maxillary canines, keeping the back edge of these teeth
razor sharp.

The number of teeth present in the mouth is used as a guide to infer phylogenetic
affinity. The earliest primates (see Chapter 5) had more teeth in their jaws than do living primates. To convey information about primate teeth, researchers have developed
a shorthand way to identify the number and type of teeth that are present in one quadrant
of the upper and lower jaws. This is referred to as a **dental formula** (see Table 4-1). It is

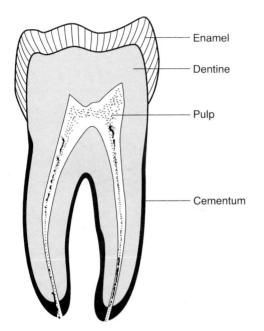

FIGURE 4-12   A tooth is made up of many different parts, as illustrated in the cross sectioned molar tooth.

Enamel

Dentine

Pulp

Cementum

recorded by showing the number of incisors:canines:premolars:molars present in the upper over the lower jaw. Strepsirhines have the most varied dental formulas, with the Malagasy lemurs having more varied formulas than mainland African-Asian lorises and bushbabies. Most strepsirhines have a dental formula of $\frac{2.1.3.3}{2.1.3.3}$ which is the same as that found in most platyrrhines. All of the catarrhines have lost a premolar, thus their dental formula is $\frac{2.1.2.3}{2.1.2.3}$ just like our own dental formula.

❖❖ Body Size and Energy Requirements

Being warm-blooded mammals, primates need to constantly supply the body with nutrients to keep warm (thermoregulation), to keep the body going (maintaining the biological system), and to reproduce. Different-sized bodies have different energy demands, which are due to a scaling effect known as **allometric scaling**. The rate of increase in linear dimensions, surface area, and body volume are each different. If a linear dimension of an animal were to double (e.g., its length), its surface area would increase fourfold because surface area increases as the square of the linear dimension (length^2). In the same case, the body volume would increase eightfold because volume increases as the cube of the linear dimension (length^3). Larger animals have therefore proportionally less surface area, which leads to less heat loss, compared to small animals. Small animals also need to produce more heat to keep their body temperature

> **allometry**—the relationship between size and shape and how this relates to physiological and morphological aspects of the body

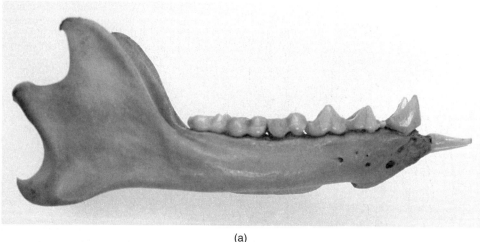

(a)

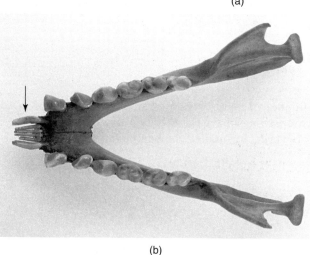

(b)

FIGURE 4-13 A side and superior view of a lemur mandible. The arrow points at the toothcomb which is made up of the four incisors and the left and right canine. The teeth are almost horizontally implanted into the mandible.

constant because of the lower body volume to body surface area ratio. Small animals as compared to large ones, therefore, have a higher energy requirement per unit body weight and need to eat more or eat foods with higher energy returns.

These differences in energy demands follow a predictable pattern, referred to as **Kleiber's Law** (Kleiber 1961). To measure what these demands are we use the standard metabolic requirement at rest, the **basal metabolic rate,** or BMR for short. This rate is related to body weight and for placental mammals it maintains a relationship of $\mathbf{BMR = kW}^{0.75}$, where W is the body weight and k is the allometric coefficient (derived from the intercept of the best-fit line in a bivariate allometric analysis). This formula shows that energy demands and body size do not scale one-to-one, and smaller animals have a higher metabolic rate than larger ones. Due to differences in energy requirements because of body size,

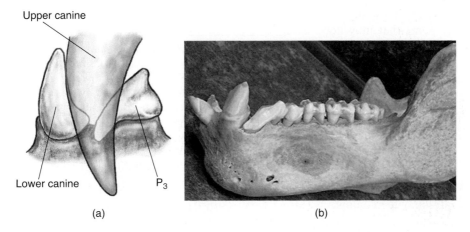

Upper canine

Lower canine   P₃

(a)   (b)

FIGURE 4-14   In some cercopithecine species, males with large canine teeth sharpen the back edges on the adjacent premolar (a). This leaves a razor sharp edge on the canine and a characteristic wear facet on the premolar of the lower jaw (b).

TABLE 4-1 Dental Formula For Different Primates	
Primate Taxon	*Dental Formula*
Modern strepsirhine primates (Cheirogaleidae, Lemuridae, Lorisoidea)	2.1.3.3 2.1.3.3
*Aye-aye	1.0.1.3 1.0.0.3
*Indri and sifaka	2.1.2.3 2.0.2.3
*Sportive lemur	0.1.3.3 2.1.3.3
Tarsius	2.1.3.3 1.1.3.3
Ceboidea (Platyrrhini)	2.1.3.3 2.1.3.3
*Marmoset and tamarin	2.1.3.2 2.1.3.2
*Goeldi's monkey	2.1.2.3 2.1.2.3
Cercopithecoidea (Catarrhini)	2.1.2.3 2.1.2.3
*Exceptions to the general pattern	

what an animal eats is very much dependent on its size. A small animal with a high BMR has to take in foodstuffs that quickly provide a lot of energy. It can do so by eating foods that are either high in protein (e.g., insects, meat) or are high in sugar content (e.g., nectar). Since larger animals have lower energy demands per unit body weight and do not need to

access energy as rapidly, a larger animal can "afford" to consume foodstuffs of lower qual-
ity, i.e. items that may need a longer time to pass through the gut or that need to be consumed in greater volume in order to gain the summed energy value (e.g., leaves)—the **Jarman-Bell principle** (Jarman 1974, Bell 1971).

> **The Jarman-Bell principle**–large animals require more total food intake per day and because of this they cannot afford to seek out widely distributed high energy resources. Small animals, because they have a higher metabolic rate, need to seek out foods with high energy to satisfy their requirements

Diet and Dietary Adaptations

Primates may feed on insects (**insectivory**), gum and sap from trees (**gummivory**), fruits (**frugivory**), seeds (**gramnivory**), leaves (**folivory**), or herbs (**herbivory**). These dietary categories refer to the type of food that makes up the major portion of the diet, although other foods may be included but to a lesser extent. Often there is seasonal variation in the diet since some foods are not available all year round. A few primate species are specialized feeders that focus on just one type of food. For example, the golden and lesser bamboo lemurs (*Hapalemur*) eat almost exclusively bamboo, and tarsiers feed exclusively on animal protein (**faunivory**, Jablonski 2003). Some taxa are true generalists (omnivores) and eat foods from all of the food categories, e.g., macaques and baboons.

Despite this great variety in primate diets, most primates are really fruit-loving animals, but most frugivorous species need to supplement their diet. Diet adaptation can be predicted based on body size in a general way. Small-sized primate taxa often include animals (both invertebrates and vertebrates) in their diet, while large-sized taxa feed mainly on the structural parts of plants (e.g., leaves, stems, bark). In the medium-sized taxa group, a species may supplement its staple food depending on size: A species in the small to medium-sized category (1–2 kg or 2–4 lbs) includes a mixture of insects and fruits. Medium to large-sized species (5–10 kg or 11–22 lbs) will include a lot more leafy materials in their diet.

The shape and size of the teeth are indicative of the diet of a species. We can divide the dentition into the anterior part (incisors and canines) and the posterior part (molars and premolars). Anterior teeth are often used to acquire food; they gouge, scrape, and puncture food items. Marmosets feed extensively on tree sap. They use their mandibular incisors to gouge holes in the bark, and the teeth have built-up enamel ridges on the sides (Swindler, 2002). Frugivores can be identified by their very large upper incisors. The teeth in the back of the jaw are involved in the mechanical grinding up of foods. Here we can see much variability (also reflective of phylogeny). Leaf-eating primates have tall cusps with sharp crests used to slice and cut the leaves into small pieces. The cheek teeth of fruit- and seed-eating primates have low, more rounded cusps, which are better for crushing fruits and seeds.

Nutritional Gain with Different Diets

Insects are high in protein and provide quick energy and calories. The drawbacks with insectivory is that insects often are small and difficult to catch, either because they move quickly or because they hide. The amount of effort and energy spent catching insects makes insectivory not a good option for large-bodied primates because it is not possible to consume enough insects to keep a big, active body going. Another type of food that provides quick energy and calories because of the high sugar concentration is gum or tree sap (**exudates**). Many primates eat tree exudates. Among the platyrrhines, tamarins and marmosets specialize in this food source, as do the needle-clawed bushbaby (*Euoticus elegantulus*) and fork-marked lemur (*Phaner furcifer*).

Fruits are high in calories because of the high sugar contents, but fruits are low in protein. Therefore, frugivores have to supplement their diet to get essential proteins. Small-bodied primates tend to supplement with insects, while big-bodied primates include lots of leaves. Fruits may not be easily accessible. Fruit trees are usually widely dispersed and fruiting may occur only seasonally (see Chapter 6). Most primates include some seeds in their diet. True seed specialists are rare, because most plants protect their seeds very well, and you need to have very strong jaws and thick enamel on the molar teeth to be able to get into thc useful part of seeds. The sakis (Pithecinae) of South America are seed-eating specialists (Norconk et al. 1998).

Even though leaves are high in protein, this protein is not easily accessible. Folivores require extra digestion and help from symbiotic bacteria to break down leaves into usable form. For example, howler monkeys may spend as much as 70 percent of their day resting in order to digest the leaves they have eaten (Crockett and Eisenberg 1986). Leaves have to be consumed in large quantities to provide sufficient energy. An asset to being a folivore is that there are a lot of leaves around, and they are not hiding or running away. Plants, however, protect themselves against predators by storing toxins and other protective compounds in their leaves. Usually, new growth such as buds, shoots, and young leaves, tends to contain less harmful chemicals and are often preferred by primates.

In general, primates are conservative in their major food choices, and most adults appear quite reluctant to try new food sources. Infants learn what is edible by smelling the food their mothers eat. Young primates also observe relatives and other group members while feeding and build a repertoire of what is edible. Young juveniles may attempt to taste plants other than the ones used by the adults by carefully mouthing or nibbling on them, but they usually dispose of the plant before consuming any significant amount, possibly making a decision based on proximate taste or texture sensations (Altmann 1998). Since plants can be very good at defense, experimenting with unknown plant species may have drastic consequences; therefore, there is most likely a selective advantage to being conservative.

In the **digestive tract** food is processed and broken down into simpler forms that can be used by the body to produce energy. The digestive tract comprises the teeth (see above), stomach, and small and large intestines. Any solid food you eat must pass through these structures, and various processes take place at each "station." Liquids do not have to contend with the destructive forces of the teeth and pass through the stomach rapidly as well. The digestive tract, especially the soft tissue, is the one structure of a living being that most accurately reflects dietary adaptations. It is therefore unfortunate that such structures do not survive in the fossil record.

When you eat, the teeth mechanically alter the food. During the process of chewing, the teeth, especially the cheek teeth (premolars and molars), cut and crush the food into smaller pieces. While chewing, saliva is produced; this contains a specific **enzyme** (amylase) that chemically alters the food. When you swallow, the food is sent down into your stomach. Once in the stomach, you have little control over what happens to the food on its journey through your digestive track.

The stomach is full of acids and the enzyme pepsin. It breaks down food proteins into smaller parts more easily used by the body. After some time, the food is shunted into the small intestines. Here, the gall bladder and pancreas release additional chemicals to further digest the food. In humans and insectivores/faunivores, the small intestines are long. It is here that the absorption of nutrients takes place. All nutrients are sent via the bloodstream to the liver. As if on a conveyer belt, the rapidly diminishing food is passed along the small intestines until it reaches the large intestines, the colon. The first part of the colon is called the **cecum**. Even though all species have a cecum, its size is variable and dependent on preferred and regular dietary choices. Some animals have lost the cecum all together (e.g., whales, dolphins, seals, and some insectivores such as hedgehogs and moles). We humans have just a residual space (the appendix). Some further nutrient absorption takes place in the large intestines but primarily water absorption occurs. Finally, what remains passes through the rectum during defecation.

In order to convert leaves into a usable form folivorous primates have to invite symbiotic micro-organisms into their bodies to assist in the breaking down of the **cellulose** present in leaves. This can be accomplished either by having an enlarged or **sacculated stomach**, as seen in colobines, or by having an enlarged cecum as seen in howler monkeys. Those that have an enlarged cecum have relatively short small intestines, as most nutrients are not released before they reach the large intestines. Those species that host micro-organisms in the stomach have intestines similar to frugivores and omnivores. However, if the breakdown of plant materials takes place in the stomach, all the plant's toxins are released there as well. We do not at present understand how primates deal with these potentially harmful compounds. Some folivores feed on clay or other soils, which are thought to reduce the harmful effects of plant toxins (Hladik and Gueguen 1974, Oates 1978). Feeding on clay and soils, **geophagy**, may be an important means of gaining essential minerals otherwise lacking in the diet (Kay and Davies 1994). It may also be soothing to the stomach—sort of the Pepto-Bismol® of the primate world—or it may serve as a means to control the volume of endoparasites (Krishnamani and Mahaney 2000, Wakibara et al. 2001).

  BOX 4-1

How Much Does a Gorilla Need To Eat in a Day?

Gorillas are the largest living primates. Male lowland gorillas can weigh as much as 170–175 kg (375–385 lbs), while females weigh about half that. Male mountain gorillas (*Gorilla beringei beringei*) are smaller, weighing "only" 159 kg (350 lbs). The mountain gorilla shows less sexual dimorphism, and females weigh around 80 kg (215 lbs) (Rowe 1996). With such bulk, it is easy to see that a gorilla needs to consume a lot of food to stay alive. However, gorillas do not need to eat as much as would say

34 monkeys weighing 5 kg each (=170 kg), because larger bodies require less energy intake than smaller bodies (see Jarman-Bell principle above). Nevertheless, gorillas need to consume a lot of food each day to stay alive and healthy.

Traditionally, gorillas are considered to be vegetarians. However, with more detailed studies on wild populations, it is apparent that the diet of gorillas varies greatly, and not just between the various subspecies but also between populations. The Virunga mountain gorillas have the

FIGURE 4-15 The mountain gorilla is the most folivorous of the gorillas. Here a male mountain gorilla *Gorilla gorilla beringei* is feeding on thistle, a favorite food.

most folivorous diet (Figure 4-15). Leaves, shoots, and stems make up 85 percent of their diet. If roots and wood are included, 96 percent of their diet is covered (Fossey and Harcourt 1977). Even though the Bwindi mountain gorillas (*G. b. beringei)* of Uganda eat a lot of leafy foods, they include a large amount of fruits in their diet, and they travel far to find these fruits (Robbins and McNeilage 2003). The seasonal reliance on fruit is especially evident in the diet of lowland gorillas. In both the Western and Grauer's gorillas, fruit is seasonally important, and their diet consists of between 25 to 70 percent fruit (e.g., Remis 1997b, Yamagiwa et al. 1996). Some gorilla populations also include a fair amount of social insects such as ants and termites in their diet (Deblauwe et al. 2003).

We have little information on what gorillas do during the day, how much time they spend travelling, searching for food and eating, socializing, or resting. In part, this is because gorillas are very shy, which is especially true of the lowland gorillas. The reason is most likely due to the hunting pressure they are under (see bushmeat section in Chapter 11), and therefore they avoid humans at all costs. The mountain gorillas spend most of their days either eating or lying about digesting the rather rough vegetation they have consumed. The lowland gorillas consume much more fruit, which is high in calories, and therefore they may not need to spend as much time feeding or digesting their food. However, as with all species that feed on fruit, they must increase their travelling and foraging time as fruit trees are usually widely dispersed.

Of course, compared to their wild relatives, captive gorillas (always lowland gorillas) have a very different diet. It is

(continued)

simply not possible to provide captive gorillas with the same source of plant materials in zoos. It is not uncommon for a single adult gorilla to consume 3–4 kg (6–8 lbs) of fresh fruits and vegetables each day, supplemented with special biscuits that contain added protein, essential vitamins, and minerals. When testing what kinds of food captive gorillas prefer to eat, Remis (2002) found that they sought out foods containing non-starch sugars over foods high in fiber and protein. This suggests that gorillas prefer to feed on fruits rather than vegetables, and that perhaps the diet of, for example, the Virunga mountain gorillas, is reflective of a constrained environment rather than preferred dietary choice.

❖❖ Locomotor Systems

Most primates use all four limbs when moving about, but they may use their forelimbs in a different manner from the way they use their hindlimbs. In general, the limbs of primates are long compared to their body length, and there is great variability in the size and shape of their hands and feet. Based on these differences, it is possible to infer locomotor adaptation by comparing the size and shape of the arm and leg bones. However, it is not only how a primate locomotes that has an influence on the skeleton; a species' postures also have an influence. We refer to the way a species moves about and its postural adaptation as **positional behavior**.

Quadrupedalism, using all four limbs when moving about, is the most common locomotor pattern of extant primates. There are both arboreal and terrestrial quadrupeds. When using a quadrupedal locomotor system, almost equal weight is placed on all four limbs. The forelimbs are more often than not involved in steering while the hindlimbs are used for propulsion. Bipedalism is a rather unusual way to get around. Aside from birds, few taxa use this mode of locomotion.

It is important to recognize that living in the three-dimensional space of trees presents some very specific dangers. The substrate available to walk on tends to be relatively small (of limited width), arranged at different angles, and perhaps most importantly, may not always be stationary. Therefore, there is extra stress on the ability to balance and keep stable on highly flexible and mobile substrates. We can see specific traits in the skeleton of primates that are adapted to deal with this type of habitat. Even though primates have long limbs compared with other mammals, the limbs of arboreal quadrupedal primates are relatively short, with the front and back limbs of approximately equal length (Figure 4-16). An animal with short limbs is closer to the substrate it is walking on, which helps to maintain balance. When arboreal quadrupeds walk, they tend to have their forelimbs held away from the body with their elbows and wrists slightly bent. They also have long grasping hands and feet to hold on to substrates, and they walk on the whole hand and foot surface (**plantigrady**). Most species have long tails, which assist in keeping balance.

A substantial group of arboreal species, especially larger-bodied primates, have adapted to moving about under tree branches in a suspensory fashion (Figure 4-17). They can do this in a more slow, quadrumanual fashion by using all four limbs as hands as we see in orangutans and spider monkeys, or they can move rapidly by swinging and using only the arms to hold on to branches—brachiation—as seen in gibbons and siamangs. Primates that use suspensory locomotion have especially long forelimbs relative to their hindlimbs. They have highly mobile wrists, in the sense that they can swing around on their wrist without

(a)

(b)

(c)

(d)

FIGURE 4-16   Quadrupedalism is the most common form of positional behavior in extant primates. The skeleton of a terrestrial quadruped (a) shows long and straight limb bones of approximately equal length. They tend to have short hands and long feet, and walk on their fingers. The baboon is an example of a terrestrial quadruped (b). The skeleton of an arboreal quadruped (c) shows relatively short limbs, and a long tail. They have long feet and hands to better hold on to branches, and they use the whole hand when walking. The squirrel monkey (d) is an example of an arboreal quadruped.

letting go of the substrate with their hand. Their fingers are especially long and curved. Often the trunk is short and the ribcage wide. Some of the platyrrhines have added a new twist to this locomotor pattern and have prehensile tails that they can use as a fifth limb.

A few primate species have adapted to a curious way of moving about—**vertical clinging and leaping**, e.g., the sifaka and tarsier (Figure 4-18). Primates that use this mode of locomotion have long, powerful hindlimbs with strongly developed leg muscles that propel them forward. Other species that move around quickly use leaping as a means to get from place to place, often referred to as **saltation**. Most of the primates adapted to leaping have a relatively small body size, and most of the species adapted to a leaping locomotor pattern have elongated heel bones. Both vertical clinging and leaping and saltation adapted taxa have short delicate forelimbs, but their hands and feet tend to be long to better enable them to grasp the stem or branch that they land on.

(a)   (b)

FIGURE 4-17 Suspensory primates tend to move below the substrate, *i.e.,* hanging below branches. The orangutan (a) is adapted for suspensory locomotion. The skeleton of a suspensory adapted primate (b) shows greatly elongated forelimbs. The bones in the forearm and the hand are especially elongated. There is also a shortening of the lumbar region in the vertebral column.

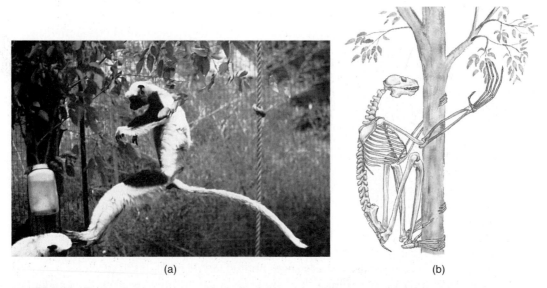

(a)   (b)

FIGURE 4-18 Primates adapted to vertical-clinging-and leaping such as this sifaka, *Propithecus verreauxi* (a). The hindlimbs are longer than the forelimbs, and the heel bone is greatly elongated (b). The hands and feet are long, although the thumb is often reduced in size.

Even though terrestrial quadrupeds have limbs of equal length, their limbs are longer than those of arboreal primates. Balance is not as important on the ground as it is in the trees, since terrestrial substrates tend to be more or less stable. A big danger for terrestrial quadrupedal primates is fast-moving predators; therefore, these primates are adapted for speed, and we see many similarities to animals such as greyhounds. The limbs are held closer to the body, with most movements taking place in a forward and backward direction. Many terrestrially adapted primates have short tails. They tend to have stubby fingers but retain good grasping ability as most of these taxa do seek refuge in trees or on cliff faces when alarmed or when sleeping. Most of these species walk only on their fingers (**digitigrady**).

Chimpanzees, bonobos, and gorillas are also quadrupedal, but they do not use the palm of their hand to rest the forelimbs on. Rather, they rest their weight on the knuckles of the hand, while they use the same heel-strike footfall as humans use. We refer to this type of locomotion as quadrupedal knuckle walking (Figure 4-19). Knuckle-walkers have longer forelimbs than hindlimbs, and their fingers and toes are longer than those of humans; the finger bones are broader and more stout.

In bipedal locomotion, balance has to be achieved by using two limbs. Extra stress is placed on the two limbs as they must bear the whole weight of the body. Bipedalism is not a common locomotor pattern, although let us not forget that many of the dinosaurs were bipedal, as are birds. However, among extant primates only humans are habitually and terrestrially bipedal. Many primates, especially apes, can stand erect and walk bipedally for short distances (see Figure 1–7). When we examine the limb proportions of humans, they appear similar to leapers (we have shorter arms than legs). There are many modifications made to the human skeleton indicative of upright posture. Our entire lower limb, from hip joint to foot joints, has been modified to accommodate compressional forces caused by standing upright. Our spine has several curves not present in quadrupeds. A curved spine can handle higher compressional forces than a spine that is straight. Furthermore, our forelimbs, which are not used for locomotion any more, are highly mobile and used for manipulation.

FIGURE 4-19   Knuckle-walking is a form of quadrupedal locomotion seen in gorillas, chimpanzees, and bonobos (shown here). Knuckle-walkers have longer forelimbs than hindlimbs, and when walking weight is placed on the knuckles of their hands.

❖ ❖ ❖ ❖   **BOX 4-2**   ❖ ❖ ❖ ❖

Swimming as a Means of Getting Around

Even though all primates need access to drinking water on a daily basis, most are not too fond of being in contact with or immersed in water. While some apes may protect themselves against rain by placing large leaves over themselves, most primates caught in the rain tend to simply huddle together in a sort of "grin and bear it" manner rather than seeking to protect themselves. The dislike of water may have a protective explanation as large bodies of water often hide predators such as crocodiles, monitor lizards, and snakes. Furthermore, slow-moving or standing water may harbor infectious organisms (e.g., those that cause river blindness).

Not all primates show fear or avoidance of water. For example, juvenile baboons may play in water puddles, and Japanese macaques are well known for taking long soaks in hot springs. There are even some primates that feed on crustaceans and submerged vegetation along coasts (e.g., macaques and baboons). Most of these activities are usually sporadic and of short duration. There are, however, two species that rely on using water as a means to get around: the proboscis monkey (*Nasalis larvatus*) and the talapoin monkey (*Miopithecus talapoin*).

The talapoin is the smallest of the extant catarrhine monkeys and lives in swampy rain forest areas of west-central Africa. We have only limited information about how frequently the talapoin monkey uses rivers as a means for getting around. To escape from potential predators, talapoins deliberately drop off the branch they are on to fall into the river, and they have been observed to be good swimmers (Gautier-Hion, 1971). We know a lot more about the habits of the proboscis monkey (e.g., Bennett and Sebastian 1988, Boonratana 2000, Yeager 1991).

The proboscis monkey is endemic to Borneo and is found along the coastal swamplands and in gallery forests along river systems. This monkey never ventures very far away from the water's edge. Rivers do not appear to be a hindrance during daily foraging trips, as they frequently swim across rivers. The monkeys enter the water with caution and most often at the narrowest location of the river. Usually, many individuals swim across together. These monkeys are very good swimmers. They have an added advantage by having webbing between their toes, so the feet can serve as stronger paddles. Males, who are almost twice as large as females, are more likely to enter the water. Females, especially if they have newborn babies, will not swim across a river. There may be good reason to be cautious, since there are many predators in the water capable of capturing even big species like the proboscis monkey. However, by swimming across rivers, the proboscis monkeys can expand their foraging range significantly with minimal energy expenditure.

❖ ❖ ❖ ❖

◇◇ Sensory Systems

The Brain

The size and complexity of the brain is another trait that sets primates apart from most other mammals. A distinguishing characteristic since their evolutionary debut is that primates have larger brains than do mammals of similar body size. Primates are also unique in having proportionally larger brains at all stages of gestation (Martin and MacLarnon 1985). Among living species, strepsirhines have a smaller brain size than do haplorhine primates (except for tarsiers) of equivalent body size (Figure 4-20). What advantage do primates gain by having such a big brain, especially in light of the fact that the brain is a very expensive organ for the body to maintain? In humans, the brain weighs approximately 2 percent of the total body weight, but it consumes some 20 percent of the total energy intake (Aiello and Wheeler 1995). We can therefore assume that in order for natural selection to have promoted and retained such an expensive organ there must have been some very strong selective advantages.

The brain, together with the spinal cord, makes up the **central nervous system** (CNS). There are several ways to divide the brain based on either evolutionary or developmental criteria. Most simply, the brain can be divided into the forebrain, midbrain, and hindbrain. The largest and most obvious structure of the forebrain is the **cerebrum** (Figure 4-21). The cerebrum is often referred to as the **neocortex**. It is the part of the brain that has expanded the most throughout primate evolution. In humans the neocortex is a highly convoluted structure consisting of numerous folds (**gyri**) and furrows (**sulci**). However, not all primates have the same amount of convolutions. Here both the taxa and the size of a primate influence the degree of convolutions. Smaller primates tend to have less convoluted brains, and a small strepsirhine brain is completely "smooth."

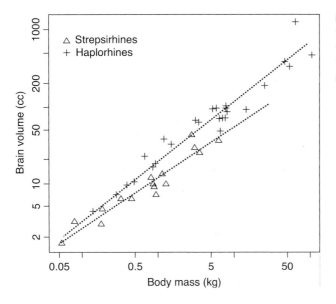

FIGURE 4-20 This graph shows the relationship between brain volume and body mass, and illustrates the differences between strepsirhine and haplorhine taxa.

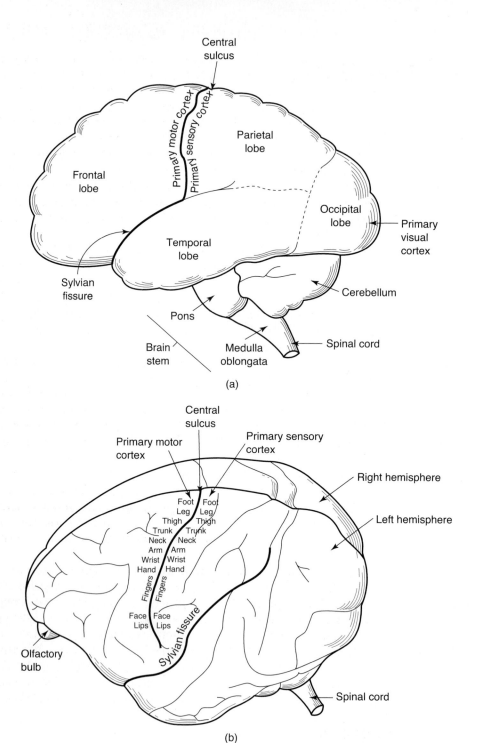

FIGURE 4-21   Lateral view of a primate brain. (a) The cerebrum, or neocortex, makes up the bulk of the brain, only part of the mid- and hindbrain is visible. (b) The cerebrum is divided into two hemispheres. Along the central sulcus are the areas for sensory (parietal lobe) and motor (frontal lobe) information governing the whole body.

What is the brain made up of? The nerve cells, or **neurons**, are located only in the outer 1–3mm of the surface area of the brain. The rest is made up of relay stations and connections, or communication pathways, between various regions of the brain or the rest of the body. If we were to stretch out the human neocortex onto a flat surface, it would be about four times the size of a chimpanzee's neocortex, and about sixteen times that of an average-sized monkey's neocortex. The neuron density in primates ranges from approximately 140,000 to 180,000 neurons/mm^2. Haplorhines tend to have a slightly higher density than strepsirhines, which have a higher density than other mammals (Barton 2006a). To gain an increase in the number of neurons, there must be an increase in surface area. The only way to do this and not end up with an enormous head is to increase the surface area by forming convolutions, as seen in most haplorhines, and especially in humans.

When looking at a brain from the side, most of the midbrain and hindbrain (also referred to as the **brainstem**) are hidden under the expanded neocortex, except for the **cerebellum** and the medulla oblongata, which is connected to the spinal cord (Figure 4-21). The cerebellum, sometimes referred to as the lesser brain, is also quite expanded in size in primates. The cerebellum is involved in many important activities, such as coordinating the gathering of sensory data (Bower and Parsons 2003), but it is especially important for the coordination of movement and balance.

The neocortex is made up of two halves (**hemispheres**), a left and a right hemisphere, which communicate at the base via the **corpus callosum**. In a general overview, these two halves look fairly similar. We name the different areas of the neocortex following the names of the skull bones (Figure 4-21a). Located in the back is the occipital lobe. It is here that the visual cortex is located, where all signals from the eyes are transported and translated into images. In the middle of both the left and right sides of the brain is a vertical division called the **central sulcus**. It divides the frontal lobe from the parietal lobe. Along this sulcus, on the frontal lobe gyrus, are the areas responsible for the primary motor information for the body, while on the parietal lobe gyrus the sensory information for the body is found. Every part of the body is represented here and laid out in a very specific pattern (Figure 4-21b). The motor and sensory areas in the left hemisphere "control" the right side of the body, while those in the right hemisphere "control" the left side of the body.

We can also identify **hemispheric specializations**, which are thought to have evolved to increase efficiency in how the brain functions. We refer to such specializations as **lateralization**. On the left side of the brain, there are areas associated with vocal communication. In the case of humans, these centers are involved in the production of language, e.g., Broca's area in the frontal lobe, and the comprehension of language, e.g., Wernicke's area in the temporal lobe (see Figure 9-7). In the temporal lobe there is also an area that is important for hearing and understanding spoken language, the auditory association area. About 20 percent of the human neocortex is assigned to some aspect of speech production and language comprehension. The right hemisphere has become specialized for spatial skills.

The Olfactory System

The sense of smell, or **olfaction**, is deeply embedded in primate evolutionary history (Barton 2006b, Heymann 2006). The earliest primates were more dependent on the sense of smell in their nightly activities than on an elaborated visual system. We can track slow evolutionary changes in the primate skull that reflect a decreased reliance on smell. These changes involve a reduction in the length of the nose or muzzle and a decrease in the width between the eyes (as well as in the width of the nasal bones). Even though the sense of smell is still quite important to all primates, especially in social communication, there has been a clear reduction in the reliance on the sense of smell over evolutionary time. However, some primate species are better at smelling odors than are others, and nocturnal primates compared to diurnal taxa have more elaborate olfaction areas in the brain.

Smells are detected by inhaling air into the nose. The smell is processed in two distinct areas: the main olfactory system and the accessory olfactory system (often referred to as the **vomeronasal** or **Jacobson's organ**) (Alport 2004, Evans 2006). The air that surrounds us contains all sorts of olfactory signals given off by everything in the surrounding environment, such as the smell of food or flowers. Some of these are chemical signals, **pheromones**, which are emitted and used by conspecifics for sexual advertisement and competition. Airborne chemical compounds are picked up or registered by sensory nerves located within the lining of the nose. To increase the ability to sense pheromones, in strepsirhines, tarsiers, and some platyrrhines the accessory olfactory system is located above the hard palate of the **premaxilla**. The accessory olfactory system is

> **pheromones**—highly volatile chemicals perceived by specialized sensory nerves located in the nose

ancient as it is also present in amphibians and reptiles. The existence of a gap or diastema between the central incisors of the upper jaw of strepsirhines indicates the presence of the vomeronasal organ (see *Galago* in Figure 4-8). It is not clear if catarrhines have an active vomeronasal organ. In humans it appears that this sensor system has lost much of its potency (see also Chapter 9, use of nose).

The shape of the nose has been used to classify primates into various groups. Strepsirhine primates have a moist, hairless nose with a cleft in the middle, while the haplorhines have a dry nose and a movable upper lip. Furthermore, platyrrhines have nostrils that point more toward the side, while catarrhines have nostrils that point more downwards (Figure 4-22).

The Visual System

The eyes, or the visual system, have set primates apart from most other mammals for almost as long as primates have been around. Primates, together with a few other predatory animals, such as owls and eagles, and carnivores such as lions and tigers, exhibit orbital convergence. By examining the shape and orientation of the bony eye sockets on a skull, it is possible to detect if the eyes are forward-facing.

As described in Chapter 1, with forward-facing eyes, the fields of vision from the left and right eyes overlap to a great extent. This overlap in visual fields creates the ability to see stereoscopically, to have depth perception (Heesy 2004). Of course, this can only happen with the corresponding translation taking place in the visual cortex of the brain where all visual information is processed. In animals with eyes facing sideways, the visual information from the left eye is sent to the right side of the brain's visual cortex, and the information from the right eye is transmitted to the left side. Therefore, the brain processes information from the two fields independently. In animals with frontal convergence, part of each eye sends information to either side of the brain, so there is partial overlap in the information that the brain receives (Figure 4-23). With this duplicated

(a)

(b)

(c)

FIGURE 4-22   The noses of strepsirhines (a), platyrrhines (b), and catarrhines (c) are strikingly different in shape and orientation of the nostrils. Strepsirhines have 'wet' nose tips and a median cleft. The platyrrhines have a broader space between their nostrils, which face more sideways.

information, the brain can produce an image in three dimensions. It has been suggested that such a system would be exceedingly valuable to animals that hunt by sight at night (Deacon 1995). The reason why this visual system has been retained and developed is due to its versatility and success. There have, of course, been some additional modifications to the visual system of primates over evolutionary time (see color vision below).

It is the **retina**, located at the back of the eyeballs, that collects the visual signals from the outside world and sends these signals on to the brain, specifically to the **visual cortex** located at the back of your brain (Figure 4-21a). Within the retina, the photoreceptors are sensitive to different kinds of light (Ross 2000): bright light (cones) and dim light (rods). The cones also have photopigments that are sensitive to color. Most primates, like most animals, have a mixture of cones and rods. However, diurnal and nocturnal primates have a different ratio of rods to cones. The amount of bright light exposure influences how many cones are present. Diurnal primates living on the open savanna have more cones than diurnal primates living in a dense tropical rainforest. However, all diurnal primates have more cones than nocturnal primates. Nocturnal strepsirhines tend to have a preponderance of rods, and they have an additional structure in the eye called the tapetum

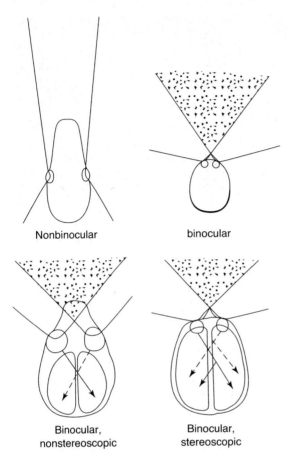

Nonbinocular

binocular

Binocular,
nonstereoscopic

Binocular,
stereoscopic

FIGURE 4-23 The location and orientation of the eyes dictate the external visual input: forward facing eyes provide overlap in the visual field not present when eyes face sideways. Depth perception is achieved when visual input is not only sent to the brain from the eye on the opposite side, but also from the eye on the same side.

lucidum, which is a membrane that lies over the retina and amplifies any light that is available. The presence of this structure in the eye of a species can be detected if, when shining a flashlight into the eyes, you can see a nice golden light reflection, which is referred to as "eye shine" (Figure 1–10). The tapetum lucidum is not present in diurnal primates, and primates that have become nocturnal secondarily (i.e., owl monkey and tarsiers) also lack this structure (Kirk and Kay 2004). To see well at night these species instead have enlarged eyes (Figure 4-24).

Color Vision

Another specialization that we see in primates, at least in diurnal primates, is the ability to perceive color. This may be important to the ability of primates to select healthy plant parts to eat. Much of our understanding of how color vision works in primates and how it evolved is based on the research of G. Jacobs (e.g., Jacobs 1994; Jacobs et al. 2002, Jacobs and Deegan 2003a, b).

The human eye has three kinds of photopigments in the retina, and therefore we describe human color vision as being **trichromatic**. Being trichromatic enables us to discriminate especially well within the red-green color band. As far as we know, all catarrhines have the same color vision system (Matsuzawa 1990), and as far as we know,

(a)   (b)

FIGURE 4-24 To increase visual acuity, nocturnal primates have enlarged eyes, as seen in this slender loris, *Loris t. tardigradus* (a), and the tarsier, *Tarsius spectrum* (b).

primates and fruit bats are the only placental mammals in which a trichromatic visual system has evolved (Araújo et al. 2006, Jacobs 1994).

It has been suggested that trichromatic color vision evolved after the division of platyrrhines and catarrhines some 35–45mya because most platyrrhines have only two kinds of photopigments; they are **dichromatic**. Even though all males and many females are dichromatic, the trait that is found on the X-chromosome is **polymorphic** (varied expression of a trait), providing much variation not only between species but within species as well. Since it is the X chromosome that is involved, some females have trichromatic color vision. Only the howler monkey is unique among the platyrrhines because it has the same trichromatic color vision system as catarrhines (Ross 2000).

Nocturnal strepsirhines have only a single type of photopigment in the retina and are therefore **monochromatic**, not able to perceive color (Box 4-3). The secondarily nocturnal owl monkey also has only a single cone pigment and thus has lost the ability to perceive colors. Most diurnal strepsirhines are dichromatic, although some females (e.g., Coquerel's sifaka and red-ruffed lemur) show polymorphism like the platyrrhines and have the potential for trichromatic color vision (Tan and Li 1999). We do not yet know if the strepsirhine brain has the necessary connections to be able to process the same kind of information, as can the brain of platyrrhines. Interestingly, the diurnal ring-tailed lemur (*Lemur catta*) does not show a similar polymorphism and must therefore be overall dichromatic (Jacobs and Deegan 2003a).

What is gained by having color vision? Especially, what is gained by being trichromatic? Observations of leaf-eating monkeys in Kibale, Uganda, have shown that the ability to discriminate within the red to green field is important for selecting young leaves, which in the tropics often flush red, making them stand out against mature leaves. Compared to mature leaves the young leaves contain fewer toxins and other unpalatable substances (Dominy and Lucas, 2001). It has been suggested that trichromatic color vision also enhances the ability to see fruits within a mass of greenery (Regan et al. 2001).

Evidence from the Skull

By examining the skull it is possible to infer much about the visual system of an individual, and this is important when we deal with fossil remains. For example, the size of the orbits can indicate whether a primate was diurnal or nocturnal. Compared to diurnal primates, nocturnal primates have larger eyes and their orbits are much enlarged relative to skull size (Figure 4-8). Orientation of the orbits can also indicate the extent of binocular overlap and how well developed the stereoscopic vision was in the specimen. Not all primate species have the same level of stereoscopic vision. Compared to haplorhines, some lemurs have orbits that face more to the side. Smaller primates with large eyes do not have as much binocular overlap in their visual fields as do larger primates. The length of the muzzle also impinges on orbit size by reducing the interorbital breadth; the longer the muzzle, the smaller the eye appears (e.g., baboons). Furthermore, the broader the muzzle, the less forward rotation can take place with the eye sockets (Figure 4-8).

The Tactile System

The primate hand is an unusual sense organ. Primates are not only quite adept at manipulation, but they also have a keen sense of touch. Most mammals have **vibrissae**, special hairs located on the muzzle, around the eyes, and sometimes around the wrists, to provide them with sensory information about their surrounding environment. Even though strepsirhines have vibrissae, haplorhines rarely do or they have a reduced number. Primates rely more on using their hands to explore their habitat. Primates have sensitive touch pads on the non-hairy, **glabrous**, part of their hands and feet. The skin of the hand is ridged, which is especially noticeable on the fingertips, referred to as fingerprints or **dermatoglyphics**. These touch pads are filled with sensory nerves, especially at the fingertips. There are also sweat glands, which make the ability to grasp more efficient. Some platyrrhines have prehensile tails (e.g., the spider monkey). Located on the underside, towards the end of the tail, is a bare patch of skin, which is similar in structures to fingertips, including the presence of dermatoglyphics (Figure 4-25).

The Auditory System

The ear picks up and sends sound waves to the brain where they are processed and translated into understandable information. The ear is composed of three main parts, all of which are essential for the perception of sound. The outer part of the ear, the external ear or **pinna**, picks up the sound vibrations that move in the air. These vibrations travel along the ear canal, and as the sound waves hit the eardrum, which divides the outer and middle ear, the vibrations of the eardrum pass through the three ear bones: malleus, incus, and stapes. The stapes is connected to the fluid-filled cochlea, a shell-shaped structure located in the inner ear together with the semicircular canals that enable our sense of balance. When passing through the ear, sound is transformed from sound energy into mechanical energy, and finally once inside the inner ear, into electrochemical energy. Small hairs located along the walls of the cochlea pick up the electrochemical energy. The hairs are connected to nerve endings that transmit information to the brain. The upper part of the temporal lobe close to the Sylvian fissure (see Figure 9–6) decodes communications (e.g., alarm calls), while sites in the brainstem pick up other sounds such as leaves rustling in the wind.

Compared to other terrestrial mammals, primates are no better or worse at perceiving sounds (Heffner 2004). For some unknown reason, chimpanzees appear to have

(a)   (b)

FIGURE 4-25   Primates have dermatoglyphics, or fingerprints, on their finger tips, they also have pads located at the base of their fingers which are highly sensitive (a). Some platyrrhine species have prehensile tails, which have a bare patch of skin on the underside of the tip of the tail which includes dermatoglyphics (b).

a reduced sensitivity to sounds in the 2–4 kHz range, but this is not the case in humans (Kojime 1990). Nocturnal primates, such as tarsiers and bushbabies, that rely on hearing to find their prey have a much keener sense of hearing. Their external ears are large and mobile and are used like antennae to locate faint sounds. Humans and other diurnal haplorhines lost this ability a long time ago, as our external ears are small and immobile. Primates can, like many other animals, pick up and discriminate more sounds (e.g., human language) then they can themselves produce.

The Taste System

There are four basic taste sensations: sweet, sour, salt, and bitter. Special nerve cells that pick up taste signals are located in different areas of the tongue and in the upper part of the throat. As far as we know, nonhuman primates share with us the same physiological system of perceiving taste. However, not all taxa respond with the same intensity to all four tastes. All catarrhines respond in a similar fashion to sweet, sour, salt, and bitter flavors as we do, but some species, e.g., the rhesus macaque, are less responsive to sour flavors (Scott and Plata-Salaman 1999). However, when tested to respond to various sweet tastes, strepsirhines and platyrrhines did not recognize or respond to as many sweet flavors as we perceive (Nofre et al. 1996).

It may not be so surprising that all primates can differentiate between the four basic tastes. The sweet, sugary taste found in ripe fruit and tree sap is usually indicative of beneficial effects. Bitter flavors, in contrast, are more commonly found in plants that are defending themselves with toxins and other secondary compounds. It is important for species that cannot break down these toxins to be able to detect such compounds before consuming too much of them, which may then lead to illness or even death. Detection of sour or acid flavors may be less important to those primate species that include more unripe fruits in their diet. Since there is usually no harm in such foods (unless too much is eaten), the ability to detect such flavors may be less important. Primates tend to respond to different tastes in a similar fashion as we humans; when tasting sweets primates stick their tongue out and lick their lips, while bitter tastes produce grimaces and avoidance.

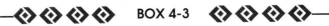

◈ ◈ ◈ ◈   BOX 4-3   ◈ ◈ ◈ ◈

Life of a Nocturnal Primate

Within the primate order, close to 80 percent of all species are diurnal, while only 17 percent are truly nocturnal. The remaining taxa are active both during the day and night, cathemeral, and include only some of the Malagasy lemurs (Rowe 1996). Most of the nocturnal primates are small strepsirhines, weighing less than 2 kg (4.4 lbs). Only two haplorhines, the owl monkey and the tarsier, are nocturnal (Wright 1996). Many of the nocturnal primates have a solitary social organization (see Chapter 7).

It is hypothesized that primates that are active at night have adopted such a lifestyle to circumvent competition for scarce food resources and to reduce predator pressures. Considering the food nocturnal primates rely on, e.g., insects, nectar, and fruits, birds would be their major competitors. By being active at night, primates avoid these competitors. Whether predation pressure is reduced at night has never really been directly tested.

Despite being awake and active at night, nocturnal primates just like diurnal primates rely on all their senses; they use their eyes to see where to go, their noses to recognize scents of conspecifics and predators, and their ears to detect prey as well as potential predators. We know that hearing is important because predation appears to increase significantly during windy nights when the primates' hearing is likely to be impaired (Bearder et al. 2002).

The most common predators of these small strepsirhines are owls, small wild cats, genets, and snakes. Gursky (2003) studied the spectral tarsiers (*Tarsius spectrum*) on Sulawesi, Indonesia. She found that these tarsiers decreased their activities on dark nights. When there was a full moon they spent more time moving about, foraging, and were more socially active. The same behavioral patterns occur in the Mysore slender loris (*Loris tardigradus lydekkerianus*) and the lesser bushbaby (*Galago moholi*) (Bearder et al. 2002). Both species become more active, move further, and are more social during nights with full moons giving support to the suggestion that these nocturnal primates do rely heavily on their sense of vision.

The Mysore slender loris, which relies on being cryptic to avoid predators, is much noisier at night, especially on dark nights, compared to tarsiers. The only explanation for this difference is that at this specific site the slender loris is not under as much threat by predators. The lesser bushbaby, in contrast, only vocalizes when alarmed or agitated. The lesser bushbaby experienced increased predation during dark new moon phases, when the genets are most successful in their hunts (Bearder et al. 2002). Bushbabies tend to mob predators when detected by emitting alarm calls, which usually attract other individuals that join in the mobbing. Since most predators hunt by stealth and will retreat when detected, this may be a very efficient way to deter being preyed upon. Of course, this may only be useful if the potential prey has an avenue of escape, and bushbabies can escape swiftly.

Even though we do not know if these strepsirhines are really *afraid* of the dark, the difference in their behavior between dark and light phases of the night suggest that they are more vulnerable to predation when it is dark and have adjusted their behavior to this fact.

❖ ❖ ❖ ❖

❖❖ Reproductive Biology

There are several traits related to reproduction that are used to define primates. In male primates, we see the presence of a pendulous penis, and the testes are located in the scrotal sac outside of the body, although in some strepsirhine species the location of the testes may vary between being scrotal or inguinal (Nekaris 2003a). In many species, the males have a **baculum**, or penis bone. The exceptions include tarsiers, spider monkeys, and humans. The size of the testes and penis bone is not necessarily correlated with body size. For example, the gorilla has a small baculum. Strepsirhines, in contrast, have long penis bones, which may relate to their prolonged intromission and post-ejaculation behavior (Dixon 1998). In addition, the size of the testes is strongly correlated with the type of social groupings and the mating system of the species. Males in multimale social groups have larger testes than males that live in single male groups. Larger testes usually translate into a larger volume of sperm produced. In general, female primates have two pectoral mammary glands (single pair of teats). There are some exceptions as many strepsirhine species give birth to more than one baby at a time so females have one or more extra pair of teats.

The high diversity within the primate order is also reflected in the reproductive system. Some taxa reproduce just once a year (seasonal breeders), while others can reproduce either several times during a year or throughout the year (nonseasonal breeders). Most females advertise in some fashion that they are receptive to mating. This can be achieved by giving off pheromones for males to smell. Emitting pheromones is common in all primates, but it is especially important in primates that live more solitary lives. In some species females have special skin around the genital area that may swell due to fluid retention as seen in, for example, chimpanzees and baboons (Figure 4-26). In some species females may experience a change in color around the genital area or face when receptive. In most species females change their behavior as they draw nearer to **ovulation**. When females become receptive to mating, we refer to this as being in **estrus**. Estrous females may solicit mating interactions with males or at least they are more receptive to

Estrus (noun), estrous (adj.)—time when a female shows morphological and behavioral readiness to reproduce

male advances. Males in general show consistent interest in females and are receptive to mating all the time, and in many species there are no seasonal changes in male behavior.

FIGURE 4-26 Special skin around the genital area retains fluids during estrus in some primate species, such as this chimpanzee.

However, in some seasonally breeding species, males express changes in behavior and physiology related to reproduction (they produce sperm only during the breeding season) as the breeding season commences. An example is the male squirrel monkey. During the breeding season, they get a boost of male hormones and expand in size, especially around the shoulder region, and look like little body builders running around and upsetting the social fabric of the group (see Chapter 7). In one-male groups, with a seasonal breeding regime, males become increasingly aggressive and assertive as the breeding season approaches due to an increase in male hormones.

Most females have a reproductive cycle that lasts 20 to 45 days. Platyrrhines have the shortest reproductive cycles (11 to 27 days). The estrus period lasts a few days or a couple of weeks depending on the species. During a reproductive cycle, a female's body responds to different hormonal signals. A short time before ovulation, the female begins to show changes in behavior toward males. In some species, females also begin to show swelling or change in color of the sexual skin. Ovulation typically occurs toward the end of estrus. In many smaller mammals, eggs are not released until the stimulation of copulation, and females can store the sperm for an extended period of time. This is not the case with primates, in which an egg is released spontaneously and sperm has a short life span. If fertilized, the egg will implant itself into the uterus and begin to develop into a baby. If the egg is not fertilized, it will be expelled after a few days' delay, together with the outer layer of the inner lining of the uterus. In many primate taxa, this happens at the time of menstruation, when the female may show some bleeding. However, most taxa do not show external evidence of bleeding.

In seasonal breeding species (e.g., most strepsirhines and most macaques), females go through one or two reproductive cycles. Most females become pregnant during the first reproductive cycle. Bushbabies and some other nocturnal strepsirhines are unusual because outside of the breeding season, the opening into the vagina closes, making mating impossible. In nonseasonal breeders, females go through repetitive ovulation cycles and can become pregnant at any point during the year. Some species show birthing peaks, which often coincide with an increase in food availability.

The gestation length varies between different taxa. Gestation in strepsirhines lasts around 2–3 months, while in platyrrhines it lasts around 4.5–5 months, and 5–6 months in African-Asian monkeys. Apes have the longest gestation period of 8–9 months. Most primate females do not have problems with birthing, although in some species babies are born with very large heads compared to the size of the female's birth canal. The size of newborn babies tends to be about 5 to 10 percent of the mother's weight. There are a few species that give birth to relatively large babies. For example, squirrel monkey babies may weigh as much as 15 percent of the mother's weight. The degree of the development of the brain is especially important here. In most primates, the brain of newborns is already 65 to 70 percent that of the adult brain size. It is just humans that lag behind as the brain size of human babies tends to be no more than 25 to 30 percent that of an adult's brain size. Humans are often referred to as being secondarily **altricial** because our brain is so underdeveloped at birth (Martin 1990).

Nonhuman primate babies are developmentally more advanced at birth. They are what we call **precocial**, that is, most growth and development has taken place within the womb. They are, of course, not as precocial as—for example—ungulates, whose newborns are able to run with the herd within a few hours after

> **altricial**–short gestation time, offspring born in litters, eyes closed at birth, short suckling period, rapid maturity after birth, and little contact with mother
> **precocial**–longer gestation, often singleton births, eyes open at birth, more active, longer suckling period, and bond with mother stronger

birth, but they are more precocial then many carnivores or rodents whose newborns are kept in a nest for weeks after birth. Primates do not nest in the same way as most other animals. Mothers carry their babies with them from the point of birth. This may explain why newborn primates have such good grasping reflexes—from their first moments of life, they need to be able to hold onto mom. Despite being precocial, primate babies are completely dependent on the care given by the mother, and in general, primates have a very long dependency period, during which time a very strong bond is formed between a mother and her offspring.

It is important for the survival of the species for individuals to reproduce and pass their genes into the next generation. Males can seek to maximize their **reproductive success** by mating with as many fertile females as possible, while a female's reproductive success is limited by the number of offspring she can give birth to in a lifetime (Trivers 1972). An individual female's reproductive output, her lifetime fitness, is influenced by a myriad of factors. Aside from the overall health of the female and offspring, females can improve their reproductive potential by reducing the gestation length, the length of infant dependency and interbirth interval, and by increasing female life span. To increase reproductive output, females can reduce the interbirth interval and produce offspring several times per year (e.g., bushbabies), they can produce more than one offspring each time (see Box 4-4), or they can commence their reproductive career earlier in life (e.g., female patas monkeys have their first offspring before they are 4 years old).

The reproductive output in different species is highly varied. Some small strepsirhines can give birth up to four times in a year, while chimpanzees may only give birth four to six times in a lifetime. The obvious difference here, aside from gestation length, is the amount of investment a female makes in each offspring. Extant great apes have an extended interbirth interval: gorillas three to six years, orangutans and chimpanzees five to eight years. Monkeys such as baboons have an interbirth interval just short of two years.

◇◇ Growth and Development

All primates go through the same stages of growth and development as we do. They all have to pass through an infant, toddler, juvenile, and teenage stage before they reach an adult form. During this time, the body develops both physically and mentally. An evolutionary trend toward a prolonged growth period after birth is seen in primates. The length and rate of growth differs between species and correlates with longevity. Species that live longer take a longer time to reach physical maturity, while those species that mature more rapidly have a shorter life span. During development the skeleton grows in size, especially the long bones of the limbs, which become longer, and muscles become larger. In most primate species, males and females exhibit different growth rates. Females usually grow faster and reach adult form at a younger age than males. Most humans have a growth spurt during the early part of adolescence. It is not known if all primate species have growth spurts, but such spurts have been recorded for several macaque species (Swindler 1998).

During adolescence the body produces an increased volume of sex hormones, which has a pronounced effect on the growing individual. At this time human females develop obvious breasts, but such changes in the females of other primates are less obvious, although their nipples become slightly longer. Males increase their muscle mass, and as they mature they begin to show the so-called secondary sexual characteristics, e.g., facial coloration in mandrills (Figure 4-4) and the long mane of geladas.

Physical maturity is usually attained at a later age than sexual maturity, which is especially evident in male primates. Female primates reach both sexual and physical maturity earlier than males, and a female may be a mother before a male of her own cohort reaches a position to be able to reproduce. Most males are physically able to reproduce; that is, they have viable sperm at an earlier age than they are socially able to compete with other males to gain access to females. Males, therefore, experience a delay in their physical maturation due to constraints in their social sphere. We can see evidence of this delayed maturity in the rate of canine growth in males (Leigh et al. 2005). For example, baboon males do not sport fully erupted canines until they are able to actually use them as a social as well as physical weapon while fighting with other males for a position in the dominance hierarchy (see Chapter 8).

◇◇ Life Expectancy

Life expectancy in primates is highly varied. Each species has its own age-specific life expectancies, but on average, monkeys live longer than strepsirhines, and apes live longer still. Some monkey species, such as macaques and baboons, may live to be 25 to 30 years old. However, only a small proportion of a population actually makes it to such a ripe old age. The highest mortality rate occurs before weaning, and juveniles that make it past weaning have a high probability of reaching adulthood.

In the Arashiyama West rhesus macaque population, which live in semi-free conditions in Texas, 2.9 percent of the females live beyond 25 years of age (Fedigan and Pavelka 2001). Among the olive baboons of Gombe, which have been studied for over thirty years, no female ever survived beyond 27 years of age (Packer et al. 1998). Longevity in apes is not that different from humans. Demographic studies from Gombe (Goodall 1986) and Mahale (Nishida et al. 2003) show that it is not unusual for chimpanzees to survive to be 40 to 50 years old.

In most nonhuman primates, females continue to reproduce almost up to the day they die. Baboon females tend to be reproductively active until they are around 20 to 21 years old, after which their **fecundity** significantly drops. In their early twenties, baboon females begin to have irregular menstrual cycles, and by the time they reach 23 to 24 years old, they stop cycling altogether (Packer et al. 1998). Chimpanzee females have the highest fecundity between ages 20 and 35 years, although many females continue to give birth into their late 30s (Nishida et al. 2003).

Human females reach reproductive senescence (menopause) around their 50th year. Whether the same happens in other extant apes is not known. However, we do know that mammalian oocytes (egg cells) in general do not survive beyond 50 years (Austad 1997). This suggests that from an evolutionary point of view, life after 50 for females at least is biologically not very useful. However, human females live many years after their reproductive careers have stopped. Why this is the case has given rise to many different hypotheses, the most prevalent being the so-called **grandmother hypothesis** (Hawkes et al. 1998, Nishida et al. 2003, O'Connell et al. 1999). This theory is based on the assumption that older females, past their reproductive age, can still provide support for their own mature offspring as well as their offspring's offspring, and therefore they contribute to the survival of their own genetic line.

In the case of males, once a male has been deposed from top rank and has reduced access to females, he usually experiences a rapid degeneration in his physical appearance. Older males are usually low ranking and more peripheral to the group. Still, older males can contribute to the protection of their maturing offspring and grand offspring or act as babysitters.

◆◆◆ 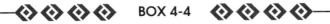 BOX 4-4 ◆◆◆

How Much Work Are Twins?

The general primate pattern is to give birth to a single baby at a time. This seems to reflect our evolutionary heritage because: (1) the uterus is constructed to handle just a singleton, (2) more often than not only a single egg is dispatched at ovulation, and (3) most females have only a single pair of mammary glands (teats). There are, however, some notable exceptions to this primate condition.

Twinning can occur sporadically in all primate species. For example, about 1 percent of all human births are twins. Some strepsirhine primates occasionally bear twins. It is estimated that in ring-tailed lemurs twins are born about 16 percent of the time (Figure 4-27). Red-ruffed lemurs (*Varecia* sp.) often give birth to triplets. Giving birth to more than one baby at a time may be correlated with resource richness. The survival of both offspring is not guaranteed because the mother usually cannot provide sufficient amount of milk to the developing babies. More often than not, the weaker baby will lose in the competition for access to the nipples and will not survive.

There are, however, some species that habitually twin: the dwarf and mouse lemurs of Madagascar and the marmosets and tamarins of South America. Marmosets and tamarins may also produce more than one litter per year. The female often becomes receptive to breed shortly after having given birth, and so will be pregnant at the same time that she is lactating.

FIGURE 4-27 The norm for most primate species is to produce a single offspring at each birth. In some species, such as this ring-tailed lemur (*Lemur catta*), females often give birth to twins, and occasionally triplets.

The offspring are precocious; their eyes are open, and they are capable of clinging to the parent from birth, plus they mature rapidly. It could be expected that the milk these females provide should be a super drink, but this is not the case (Power et al. 2002). The callitrichid's mother's milk is no richer than that of species that produce singletons. The babies are, however, weaned much earlier than in other species. By 1 month of age baby callitrichids begin to eat solids, and by 3 months they are weaned. Furthermore, the mothers conserve energy by having many helpers to carry the babies. Group members tend to compete to help care for the babies, both in terms of carrying and sharing food with them (Garber and Leigh 1997). Sometimes the father helps out, but not as often as one could expect. More commonly, other adult females and juveniles, possibly older brothers and sisters, help out. In some species, the mother is alone in caring for the offspring in the early stages of development, and only later may she allow others to carry her babies. The body size of the female appears to influence whether twinning will occur. Large females are more likely to give birth to two or more babies and may produce more than one litter per year. Smaller females may twin, but they are more likely to have longer interbirth intervals. This suggests that the general well-being of the mother is the most important factor.

◈◈ Summary

By looking in the mirror, you will get an idea about what a general primate body looks like. However, when you go to the zoo or watch a television show about the non-human primates, you may be struck with the realization that primates come in a wide variety of shapes and sizes. There are approximately 330 living species of primates, and the representative genera and species are quite different from one another as well as from us. However, we can identify a suite of traits that separates members of the Order Primates from other mammalian orders.

The physical characteristics that we use to distinguish primates from other mammals ultimately come together to define a primate lifestyle. We start with a general mammalian body plan but specific characteristics of the skeleton, dentition, relationships between body size and dietary adaptations, features associated with patterns of locomotion and the development of the brain, reproductive biology, growth, and development all contribute to a primate body design and a primate way of life. In addition, primates consist of species that live long lives; we are social organisms who live in complex physical and social worlds, which typically require a degree of complexity of brain functions. We greatly depend on our visual systems and an ability to manipulate objects that exist in our physical world. We evolved in arboreal or tree-living habitats and have since adapted a wide range of specific locomotor patterns including the uniquely human pattern of habitual bipedalism.

◆◇ Key Words

allometric scaling
altricial
apomorphic trait
baculum
basal metabolic rate
bilophodonty
brainstem
canine
cecum
cellulose
cementum
central nervous system
central sulcus
cerebellum
cerebrum
conspecific
corpus callosum
dental formula
dentine
dermatoglyphics
diastema
dichromatic
digitigrady
digestive tract
enamel
enzyme
estrus
exudate

faunivory
fecundity
folivory
frontal bone
frugivory
geophagy
glabrous
gramnivory
grandmother hypothesis
gummivory
gyrus (plural gyri)
hemisphere
hemispheric specialization
herbivory
heterodonty
insectivory
Jacobson's organ
Jarman-Bell principle
Kleiber's Law
lateralization
mandible
maxilla
metopic suture
molar
monochromatic
neocortex
neuron
olfaction

ovulation
pheromone
pinna
plantigrady
plesiomorphic trait
polymorphic
positional behavior
precocial
premaxilla
premolar
pulp cavity
reproductive success
retina
root
sacculated stomach
saltation
sectorial premolar
sexual selection
sulcus (plural sulci)
toothcomb
trichromatic
vertical clinging and leaping
vibrissae
visual cortex
vomeronasal organ
zygomatic bone

◆◇ Study Questions

1. Why should primates be afraid of water?
2. What advantage is there to having color vision if you are a primate?
3. In what ways can you determine if a primate is night active or day active?
4. How important is the sense of smell to primates? In what ways may primates use their sense of smell, and how can we recognize a species that relies on the sense of smell?
5. What is meant by a dental formula and what are the advantages to having heterodonty?
6. Why do not more primate species give birth to twins?
7. What are the "fast-foods" of the primate world, and why do we not see all primates eating the same kind of foods?
8. Imagine yourself as a nocturnal primate. What are the perils of being out at night?
9. Why is folivory such a complicated diet scheme?
10. How can the skeleton of a primate tell about its locomotor adaptations?

◆◆ Suggested Readings and Related Web Sites

Altmann SA. 1998. Foraging for survival. Yearling baboons in Africa. Chicago: University of Chicago Press.

Ankel-Simons F. 2000. Primate anatomy: an introduction. London: Academic Press.

Davies AG, Oates JF. 1994. Colobine monkeys: their ecology, behaviour and evolution. London: Cambridge University Press.

Fleagle JG. 1999. Primate adaptation and evolution. London: Academic Press.

Jones S, Martin RD, Pilbeam D. 1995. The Cambridge encyclopedia of human evolution. London: Cambridge University Press.

Martin RD. 1990. Primate origins and evolution. A phylogenetic reconstruction. London: Chapman and Hall.

Swindler DR. 1998. Introduction to primates. Seattle: University of Washington Press.

Swindler DR. 2002. Primate dentition. An introduction to the teeth of non-human primates. London: Cambridge University Press.

CHAPTER 5
Primate Evolution

I n this chapter we will provide a guide, albeit brief, of the evolutionary past of primates, starting with the murky past after the dinosaurs disappeared to the most recent past when the earliest members of the human family first appeared on earth.

The desire to know and understand the world surrounding us may be a uniquely human trait, and this desire to know about our past is nothing new. Throughout history people have contemplated the origin and meaning of the world they saw around them. In the nineteenth century it was a common pastime to look for fossils, because the concept that the earth had a very ancient history was becoming popular. Many important fossils were uncovered at this time, but the relationship between fossils and living species was not yet so clearly understood. Fossilized monkeys were found all over Europe, but at the time they were classified as gibbons and thought to lead to our own lineage. It is interesting that when the first hominin remains were discovered, only a few people actually paid any attention to them and recognized their importance as links to our own past.

There are many different reasons for this fascination with fossils, especially fossil primates, and why we search for them. Curiosity is, of course, still a strong motivating factor for why we look into the evolutionary past of primates. From a more scientific point of view, we want to understand how animals and plants made a living and survived in past environments. We also want to understand the evolutionary processes that affect all living organisms. Finally, as described in Chapter 2, there is the uniquely human desire to place everything into some sort of order (taxonomy), to determine who is related to whom and who were the ancestors of more recent forms (phylogeny).

❖❖ What Is Evolution and How Does It Work?

Evolution is the sum total of all the genetic modifications that occur in a population or a species over time. This involves changes in the genetic makeup or **genotype** as well as in the physical appearance, or **phenotype**. Changes in the genetic code due to mutations occur all of the time, and these are random changes. Natural selection provides directionality to the evolution of taxa. Individuals that contribute the largest number of surviving offspring to the next generation, i.e., those with the highest reproductive fitness, will leave the greatest mark on the species' gene pool. Individuals less able to cope with specific environmental situations, as evidenced by having reduced fitness, will be weeded out over time through natural selection.

When looking at earth's fossil record, it may appear, at least on a grand scale, as if evolution is progressive, that everything evolves from a simple form to a more complex form. In many instances, this may be the case but there are also many examples of when a simple form is maintained through time, or some form actually becomes simplified over time. There is always a balance between successful survival and the expenditure of the least amount of energy. The idea of progression from simple to more complex permeated early models of how our own lineage evolved: Humans must have passed through a strepsirhine stage, possibly a tarsier stage, and a monkey stage before reaching an ape stage (e.g., Le Gros Clark 1959). We know now this is not the case. All extant lineages have their own evolutionary path. Even though we share a common ancestry with some living taxa (e.g., we share a common ancestor with chimpanzees and bonobos, and apes and monkeys share a common ancestor), these ancestors were nothing like extant representatives. So despite sharing a common ancestor, we never were strepsirhines or monkeys.

Of course, we usually do not know the genetic composition or genotype of fossils. Instead, we have to rely on the phenotype of the fossil to determine species affinity, and to use changes in phenotype as an indication of speciation. However, phenotypic changes usually become evident some time after genetic modification, and speciation may have occurred long before we actually observe it in the fossil record. Since speciation is a process rather than an event, it is often difficult to recognize when a species has made the transition from one state to the next. The closer in time to the last common ancestor, the more difficult it is to discern the phenotypic divergence of two daughter species because they may continue to share many traits. It is the affinity of these transitional species, sometimes referred to as **basal** or stem **species**, that causes the most controversy and discussion. These species typically display a combination of ancestral (plesiomorphic) and derived (apomorphic) traits. It is usually easier to recognize a group of primates at the evolutionary stage when they display a full suite of apomorphic traits, so called **crown species**.

◇◇ How Do We Discern Ancestor-Descendant Relationships?

We discern phylogenetic relationships by examining and evaluating traits shared between taxa. All traits are not of equal value, however, when recreating a phylogenetic tree; some are more important than others and carry greater information about relatedness. Shared derived traits (**synapomorphies**) and unique derived traits (**autapomorphies**) are more informative than shared ancestral traits (**symplesiomorphies**). Since traits change over time, it is essential to trace the evolutionary path of a trait, or its **character polarity**: Did trait *a* evolve before trait *a'*? It is not always easy to discern which traits evolved first, or if the traits we use today to define extant species can actually be used to define fossil species, especially transitional taxa. It is difficult to predict how a trait will change over time and what factors may influence a change. As an example, let us look at the fused mandibular symphysis (see Chapter 4), a trait we consider to be characteristic of extant haplorhines. When we look at the earliest haplorhines in the fossil record, we see that some species had a fused mandible while others did not. To confuse the matter even further, some of the first recognized primates on earth, belonging to the strepsirhine suborder, also had a fused mandible. It is possible that errors have been made in how we classified these early primates, but more likely this type of situation represents our inability to identify the underlying reasons behind the development of a specific physical trait, such as the fused mandibular symphysis. Some traits may carry less phylogenetic information and be more reflective of the effects of body size and adaptations to specific environmental conditions. There is a need for further research to help us achieve a better understanding of how different traits respond and change under different environmental conditions, and what factors may impinge on a trait.

The most commonly used method in evolutionary phylogenetics is based on cladistic analyses (as discussed in Chapter 2) in which common descent is determined based on synapomorphies, shared derived traits. Cladistic analyses are performed using computer programs such as PAUP (Phylogenetic Analysis Using Parsimony; Swordoff 2001) or PHYLIP (Phylogeny Inference Package; Felsenstein 2005). These programs are based on evaluating the most parsimonious or most likely and least complex phylogenetic relationship based on the traits included. All these programs are based on the assumption that a parental species gives rise to two daughter species.

When we look at the evolutionary history of primates (or any order for that matter), we see that along the way there are many lineages that, although they may have been very successful at one point, have disappeared without leaving any descendants or dwindled to the brink of extinction. For example, tarsiers were much more common in the past while today there is only a single genus left containing eight species (Rowe 1996). In addition, some lineages will remain unchanged for long periods of time (**stasis**) until conditions are right for them to be hugely successful (saltation or quantum evolution, Simpson 1944), which we refer to as an **adaptive radiation**. For example, between 15 and 20 million years ago, ape taxa were abundant and widespread, and although there were monkeys around, there were fewer monkey taxa, which is opposite of what we see today. Changes in climatic conditions lead to more diverse and seasonal environments, which apparently suited the monkeys better than the apes. As a result, apes dwindled in numbers and diversity, while monkeys began to diversify and spread out over a much wider area. This is, in fact, what is reflected in our world today.

If we look at the primate fossil record (see Figure 5-1), the first primates we recognize are the **euprimates** (*eu-* is latin for good or true, i.e., euprimates = true primates), dating to the earliest part of the Eocene epoch, around 55 million years ago. The euprimates show some similarities to present-day strepsirhines. Fossil evidence of haplorhine primates does not appear until the middle to late Eocene. From these basal or stem haplorhines arose the platyrrhines, the monkeys we encounter in South and Central America today. At a later stage, these early haplorhines also gave rise to the basal catarrhine primates, a group from which all the African-Asian monkeys and apes evolved. Apes were very successful at first and spread far and wide, while the success of catarrhine monkeys is a more recent phenomenon.

We gain insight into primate origin and evolution not only from the fossil record but from biomolecular studies, in which the genetic makeup of extant species are compared,

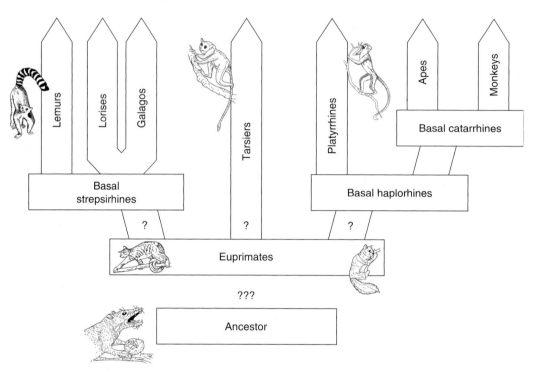

FIGURE 5-1   A schematic view of the primate fossil record, showing the relationships between the major groups. There are many unknown transitions in the phylogenetic lineages.

which can also elucidate questions pertaining to origins of taxa (see Box 5-1). Using molecular phylogenetics we now have strong evidence that the origin of primates goes much further back in time than what the fossil record has led us to conclude. It is very likely that the **basal primates** lived alongside the last of the dinosaurs. The results from biomolecular studies have fueled further explorations to find older and more complete fossil evidence. With each new fossil

> **basal primate**—the earliest of its kind, a much generalized form that over time may evolve into something more specialized, showing more derived traits; they are all extinct taxa
>
> **crown primate**—the latest form in a singular or monophyletic lineage in which derived traits are more common, such as extant monkeys and apes

recovered, there may be revisions in a species' taxonomic position and phylogenetic relationship to other groups or clades. This is the nature of science, and the process could go on indefinitely as we may never really know what happened at the dawn of the earliest primates, the first apes or the first monkeys. This is, of course, a big part of the fascination with studying the past. It is a very difficult but rewarding puzzle to try to complete. It is also a puzzle in which only a few pieces are known. It is up to us to fill in the many blank spaces with educated guesses based on reasoned hypotheses to try to present a picture of what actually happened.

  BOX 5-1

The Use of Biomolecular Data to Infer Phylogenetic Relationships

The scarcity of fossil evidence has led scientists to explore alternative ways to gain insight into the taxonomic and phylogenetic relationships of different species (see also Chapter 2). Biomolecular methods are becoming increasingly popular for investigating the relationships of living species, with the intent to determine when specific lineages diverged. With the advent of rapid and relatively inexpensive methods of examining molecular structures, such as DNA, RNA or proteins that we all have in our bodies, there have been many studies that investigate the phylogenetic relationship between living primates. It is possible to determine, based on how much change a molecule has undergone over generations (due to **mutations** or genetic drift), if Species A is more closely related to Species B or to Species C. The difficulty begins when attempting to determine the amount of time that has elapsed since the last common ancestor was around.

At present it is known that not all molecules change at the same rate. Such rate heterogeneity is especially prevalent in mammals. When examining the same molecule in various species, differences in mutation rates can be observed. Small species such as mice with a rapid generation time have a much more rapid mutation rate than large species such as humans who have a longer generation time. With further research it will hopefully be possible to know the rate at which specific molecules change and to understand the factors that may influence this rate. There is also evidence of rate heterogeneity

in primates, e.g., **hominoids** have slower rates than monkeys, the so-called 'hominoid slowdown' (Steiper et al. 2004, Yoder and Yang 2000).

However, before we can say we have an accurate molecular clock, it needs to be calibrated, which is done by using a known date of a fossil established using an absolute dating method (a method that allows a chronological date to be assigned; see section on dating below). Since a specific fossil can only give a minimum time of origin, there is always an inherent error in any molecular clock. With molecular data we usually end up with a time of origin that is much older than what the fossil record may suggest. This is because changes in the genetic makeup (genotype) will always precede changes in the appearance of the skeletal structure (phenotype). There will always be a time lag between genetic change and the actual physical manifestation of speciation in the fossil remains that we are lucky to find. As a result, when recreating the evolutionary path of specific taxa, more often than not we end up with long blank periods between the estimated time of divergence based on molecular changes and the first fossil evidence.

Over the past few years, biomolecular studies have provided exciting and revolutionary results by suggesting that the origin of primates predates the demise of the dinosaurs. An increasing number of molecular studies suggest that primates originated as far back in time as 85 to 90 million years ago (mya) (e.g., Arnason et al. 2002, Bromham et al.

(continued)

1999, Kumar and Hedges 1998). Since our earliest fossil primates are no older than 55 to 60 mya, this leaves us with a gap in the fossil record of at least 30 million years. Furthermore, the biomolecular data suggest a divergence time of around 77 mya for the lineages leading to strepsirhines and haplorhines, although we do not yet have fossil support for such an early divergence. With such an early split between the strepsirhine and haplorhine lineages, it is very likely that haplorhines never went through a strepsirhine-like stage as has been the traditional view. Even the bushbabies and lorises, which we have looked upon as more recent lineages, appear to have diverged in the Eocene based on biomolecular studies (Yoder 1997). In this case, we do have support for an early split between bushbabies and lorises (Seiffert et al. 2003). The challenge is to find more fossil evidence to confirm the molecular data.

Since the 1960s, when the first phylogenetic trees based on biomolecules were presented, there have been many advances made by both paleontologists and molecular biologists. The accuracy of dating techniques has improved, and the fossil record is steadily increasing in volume. Molecular biologists understand more about the evolutionary behavior of biomolecules and the factors that influence their structure. However, there are still many gaps in our knowledge and understanding, which often leads to heated discussions, and only further research will solve these problems. Sometimes it is necessary to approach an old problem with fresh eyes, and controversies can have a positive effect as they usually stimulate further research that leads to advancements in our knowledge. Paleontologists constantly improve our knowledge of the fossil record and re-evaluate the evolutionary paths of different lineages, and our understanding of biomolecules is rapidly improving. However, we are still far from total agreement between what the fossil record tells us happened and what the molecular evidence suggests, although the gap is steadily decreasing (e.g., Benton 1998, Goodman et al. 1998). One thing is sure: our views on how, where, and when primates evolved will see some major changes in the coming years. If the molecular results are correct, it will have major implications on our understanding of evolutionary processes and phylogenetic reconstructions.

❖❖ Evolutionary Models for Primate Evolution

The first cohesive proposal to explain the origin of primates was formulated in the early part of the twentieth century (Smith 1913, Wood Jones 1916). Primates were thought to have descended from a terrestrial insectivore, very much like extant tree shrews, which are not related to shrews but belong to their own order: Scandentia. It was thought that traits defining primates evolved (see Chapter 1; where primates are defined) when tree shrew-like ancestors ascended the trees and adapted to an arboreal lifestyle. For example, grasping hands and feet and forward-facing eyes, which provided depth perception, were perfect for scampering about on tree branches. This model remained unchallenged until the 1970s when Cartmill questioned the notion that adaptation to an arboreal life was the sole explanation for why primate traits evolved. He especially questioned this since many other species (such as the common squirrel) had succeeded very well living in trees without having any of these primate adaptations. Cartmill proposed a new theory, the visual predation theory, based on the premise that the first primates had become arboreal insect-hunting specialists that relied on visual acuity, thus explaining all of the defining traits of primates (Cartmill 1972, 1992).

Sussman, a primatologist, suggested that the visual predation theory could not account for all aspects of primate origins, especially since many extant insectivorous primates rely more on hearing than on vision to capture their prey. Together with Raven, a botanist, Sussman proposed an alternative model, the angiosperm co-evolution theory (Sussman and Raven 1978, Sussman 1991b, 1999). They suggested that the pre-primates, the ancestors of the basal primates, had taken advantage of the rapid radiation of angiosperm plants, the flowering plants, during the decline of the dinosaurs by adapting to feeding on the flowers, fruits, and seeds of angiosperm trees. Such a diet would force the primates into the most peripheral parts of the trees where grasping hands and feet would be advantageous. The ability to recognize and discriminate flowers, fruits, and seeds would place extra evolutionary pressure on the visual system.

There are many aspects of both the visual predation theory and the angiosperm co-evolution theory that are plausible. It is very likely that both theories reflect what happened (Rasmussen 1990a, 2002). Of course, we will never really know what caused pre-primates to evolve into primates. We assume that the earliest primates were small creatures with rapid metabolic rates that required high energy foods such as nectar, fruit or gum—the type of food that provides quick energy to an animal with a high metabolic rate (see Chapter 4). Such a diet might explain why primates could afford to expand their brain size compared to that of other contemporary mammals. With the appearance of a whole new set of ecological niches after the demise of the dinosaurs and the radiation of angiosperm plants, competition was most likely rife between many different lineages. Primates made it; however, we do not know against whom they competed (see Hot Topics 5-1).

❖❖ The Nature of the Primate Fossil Record

Fossils are the remains of organisms that once lived. Most often it is the bony skeleton and teeth that are preserved. It is rare that soft tissue is preserved, but occasionally paleontologists are lucky and impressions left by soft tissue, feathers, and fur are found (Figure 5-2). The fossilization process entails the preservation of the bone by a slow replacement of organic with inorganic materials, and over time what once was a living organism turns to stone, i.e. it becomes **petrified**.

Most living organisms disappear without leaving a trace. Only a miniscule portion of all living organisms become deposited under conditions favorable for fossilization. It has been estimated that less than 3 percent of what once lived is recovered (Martin 1993). When an animal dies, its body goes through varying stages of decay. In addition, under certain conditions such as being on the savanna, a carcass will surely be visited by various carnivores and scavengers, and they will consume all edible parts, including the bone marrow. Once they are finished, whatever remains of the body will be exposed to the elements; wind, sun, and rain will take their toll in breaking down the constituent

FIGURE 5-2 Under very rare conditions, not only bones fossilize but soft tissue remains leave impressions, such as outlines of feathers, fur, or even soft tissue. Here is shown an almost perfect impression of a dragonfly.

parts of the skeleton (Figure 5-3). Other animals will gnaw or trample the bones. The remains will slowly be covered by soil, which over the years accumulates in thickness. Plants will grow on top of the remains, and burrowing animals may cause further disturbance to the bony remains that lie in the soil. We refer to this process as **taphonomy**. It is within the soil that the slow process of fossilization occurs. A body deposited in a lake, river, or cave, where it is left undisturbed by predators and other natural elements, stands a much better chance of being covered and preserved. However, preservation is only step one. The chance that a fossil will actually be found is also highly unlikely because most fossils are hidden under layers of rock. Only where old **strata** are exposed in rock outcrops—for example, where a river has cut through ancient rock or in a quarry (Figure 5-4)—can finds be made.

Finding fossils is in part based on hard work, but there is also much luck involved. Scouting along exposed rock strata of the appropriate age may yield exposed remains. Paleontologists spend a lot of time "field walking" searching for evidence of fossil remains.

> **taphonomy**—the study of the fossilization process; what happens to bones after death and until they are fossilized
> **strata**—the different layers of rock or soil that have been laid down over time on earth's crust (singular stratum)
> **stratigraphy**—the study of the earth's strata

It is not always easy to recognize a fossil, because fossils tend to blend in with the surrounding rocks, and it takes a well-trained eye to be able to see them. When you are dealing with smaller animals, such as primates, it is even more difficult. Often it is just the teeth that are preserved, and some of these may be no bigger than the head of a pin.

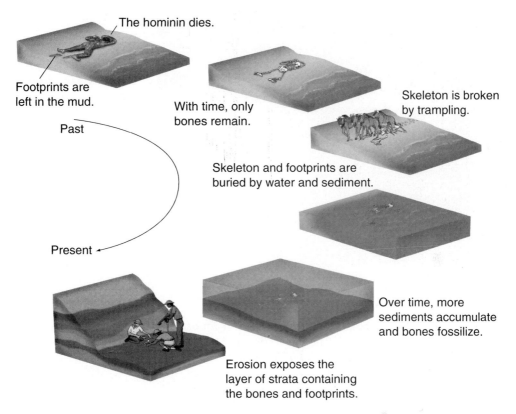

The hominin dies.

Footprints are left in the mud.

Past

Present

With time, only bones remain.

Skeleton is broken by trampling.

Skeleton and footprints are buried by water and sediment.

Over time, more sediments accumulate and bones fossilize.

Erosion exposes the layer of strata containing the bones and footprints.

FIGURE 5-3   When an organism dies, its remains are exposed to a range of destructive forces. This taphonomic process may leave nothing behind for posterity, or under favorable conditions part of the body will undergo changes and become fossilized.

How Do We Date a Fossil?

There are many different methods available to age a fossil. Some provide **absolute dates** (e.g., your birthday is an absolute date), while others give **relative ages** (e.g., you are simply younger or older than a sibling).

For dating we use **radiometric dating** techniques, which often are referred to as absolute dating techniques, although such methods usually give a date range and not an absolute date (such as your birthday). These techniques are destructive to the materials tested. Since fossils are usually too precious to undergo a destructive dating procedure, surrounding rocks or other materials of less value or that are more abundant are used. Radiometric dating techniques are based on the decay of naturally occurring unstable compounds called **isotopes**, which change at set rates into stable forms.

The most commonly used radiometric dating technique for fossil primates is potassium-argon (K/Ar) dating. The K/Ar dating is based on the decay of the compound potassium-40 (K^{40}) into argon-39 (Ar^{39}). When rocks are heated, all of the argon

FIGURE 5-4 Ancient rock layers may be exposed where a river has cut through, or where humans have removed rock to create a road. At such rock cuts it is possible to see layers (strata) of rock, each deposited under specific conditions and over time.

present in the rocks is released. It is as if a timer has been set to zero, and once the rock cools, the existing K^{40} begins to decay into Ar^{39}. We know that the time it takes for 50 percent of K^{40} to turn into Ar^{39} is close to 1.3 billion years. We refer to this time as the compound's **half-life**. Due to the very long half-life of K^{40}, very old rocks, usually of volcanic origin, can be dated with this method. There are several other radiometric-based dating techniques, e.g., fission-track, thermoluminescence, electron spin resonance, and amino-acid racemization, which can be useful when no volcanic rock is available.

Other dating techniques rely on indirect inferences and correlations, so-called indirect or relative dating techniques. Such methods are frequently used because fossil sites may not contain datable rocks (e.g., South African sites). The first means of dating is to look at the ordering of the rock formation. The law of superposition (most always true) states that a stratum of rock at the bottom of a formation will be older than a stratum higher up (Figure 5-5). One of the first tasks when a fossil site is discovered is for geologists to record and identify the different strata in the rock formations. They create **stratigraphy** maps, which can then be used to correlate various sites to one another. At some localities the evolutionary changes in specific fossil taxa, e.g., pigs, diatoms, and snails, are known and it is possible to use such known series to estimate an age (e.g., White and Harris 1997). The limitation with this kind of dating method is that it is only useful in a very local environment. For example, it is not prudent or advisable to use snail evidence from an East African lake to date something from West Africa. However, it is useful when comparing sites within East Africa. By comparing faunal remains from various sites, it may be possible to infer an approximate date. This is especially helpful if absolute dating has been established at some of the sites. See texts such as Conroy 1990 or McKee et al. 2005 for more details about dating techniques.

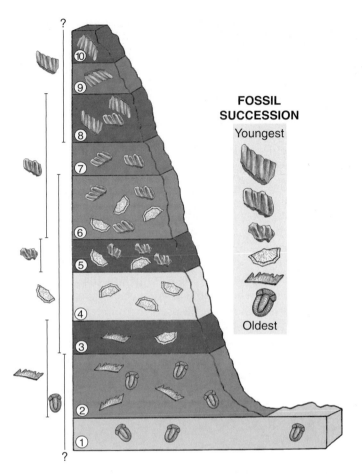

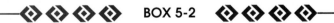

FIGURE 5-5 Indirect dating techniques may entail the examination of the ordering of rock strata, where according to the law of superposition the rocks at the bottom are older than those at the top. In that way, the sequence of fossil remains can be arranged in a chronological order or fossil succession.

❖ ❖ ❖ ❖ BOX 5-2 ❖ ❖ ❖ ❖

What Happens to a Fossil Once It Is Dug Up?

Before paleontologists can begin a fossil-hunting expedition, they must have permission from the owner of the land, be it a private landowner or a government, to excavate. Such agreements include not only permission to work at a specific site, but they also detail what will happen with the finds at the end of the field season. In the past, archaeologists and paleontologists would remove important finds to their home country or home university, but this is no longer

(continued)

the case. Today most foreign countries claim ownership of all finds found in their soil and may not even allow the fossils to leave the country.

Most fossils, especially those of scientific interest, end up in museums. If a find is recovered from private land, the landowner may donate, sell, or lend the fossil to an institution. After each field season, all finds are usually brought back to a museum or university (to which the researchers have an affiliation), to be cleaned, examined, catalogued, measured, and evaluated. At the end of each field season, a report is compiled detailing the fieldwork undertaken and the finds recovered. Scientific papers usually take a bit longer to prepare since more detailed study is required.

Fossils that are of less scientific or public interest are kept in storage, or they may be sold. Some fossils end up on the open market, either by being sold by private owners or by museums to gain extra funds. Money received this way may provide funding for the next year's excavation. You have probably seen trilobites for sale in natural history museums. Maybe you even have a few fossils at home. It is not unusual for common fossils to be extracted and sold to the public. If a fossil is found on private land, the landowner has the right to sell whatever he or she wants to. However, rare and precious fossils, such as hominin fossils, are considered part of our natural heritage. The most precious remains are usually locked in secure vaults, and what is presented to the public is a replica of the original. These replicas are of such accuracy that they can be used for further scientific study sparing further wear and tear on the original find. Museums and other educational institutions can purchase replicas of important fossils for permanent displays and teaching purposes.

◈◈ Earth Is Constantly Changing

Plate Tectonics

Even though the land we walk around on appears solid and firmly anchored, it is not really so. Each continent is like a raft floating about on the oceans. Deep to the solid surface of our continents, referred to as the crust, is a layer of molten rock that is swirling about in a similar fashion as ocean currents. It is this movement that drives the movement of continental plates. Not all continental plates move at the same rate, but some move by several inches per year. The study of continental movements is called **plate tectonics**. In the past the location of landmasses was different from what we see today (Scotese 2000, 2001, but see suggested changes in Briggs 2003). If we go far back in time, say some 200 million years ago, all landmasses were joined together into a single unit. We refer to this mega-continent as **Pangaea** (Figure 5-6). Some eighty million years later, Pangaea had divided into two: a northern continent, **Laurasia,** and a southern continent, **Gondwana**. When these large landmasses existed, animals and plants could disperse freely across the continents, and there was much continuity in the species present. By the time of the first fossil primates (55 to 60 mya), Laurasia and Gondwana had split into the continents we recognize today, although not all landmasses were located in the same position. There were also a few land bridges between some continents that we do

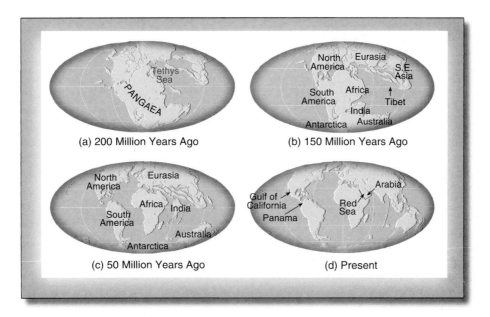

(a) 200 Million Years Ago

(b) 150 Million Years Ago

(c) 50 Million Years Ago

(d) Present

FIGURE 5-6   The continents we recognize today, have over geological time moved about, been joined together with other landmasses, some now long gone. At the height of dinosaur radiation there was a single mega-continent, Pangaea (a). Before primates made their entrance this mega-continent had divided into a northern, Laurasia, and a southern, Gondwana, continent (b). By the time we recognize true primates in the fossil record the continents had begun to take the shape and position we see today (c, d).

not see today. For example, North America was connected to Asia and Europe to the north, while South America, Antarctica, and Australia had continuous contact to the south. Africa was floating about as an isolated island. So was the Indian continent, as it had not yet moved north to collide with Asia. Madagascar had almost reached its present position on the southeastern side of Africa. During the Miocene (24 to 5.3 mya) most continents had reached a similar position and configuration as what we see today (Figure 5-6). So throughout time there have been occasions when animals have either been stranded on island continents or have been able to move about more freely. This has had a strong influence on evolution as well as on the distribution of taxa that we see in the fossil record.

Climate

The position of continents has a major influence on climates. It is really the deep ocean currents that both drive the winds and control our temperature. As shown in Figure 5-7, the annual temperature has varied quite a bit during the Tertiary. The Tertiary period began 65 mya and ended 1.8 mya (see Figure 5-8a). Ancient climates are reconstructed by examining oxygen levels in ocean sediments and polar ice caps. The earth's water contains two oxygen isotopes, one is lighter (^{16}O), and one is heavier (^{18}O). The ratio of these two oxygen isotopes is used to infer relative temperatures. Since ^{16}O is lighter, it is more

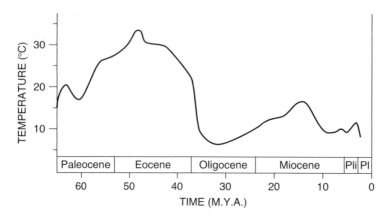

FIGURE 5-7 The temperature has fluctuated greatly over the past 65 million years (the Tertiary period). During the Eocene epoch there was a maximum estimated annual temperature of 30°C. Early in the following epoch, the Oligocene, there was a rapid cooling event, after which the annual temperature barely made it above 10°C. Aside from a slight increase in temperature during the Miocene, the temperature has remained consistently low until present. (Adapted from Fleagle 1999.)

likely to evaporate; therefore, precipitation (rain, snow) contains more of the lighter form of oxygen. When there is a cold spell ("ice age"), more of the ^{16}O gets trapped in icecaps and glaciers, and the ocean waters retain a larger amount of ^{18}O. By examining the ratio of the two oxygen isotopes from ocean cores and glacier ice cores, climatologists can reconstruct ancient temperatures.

During the late Paleocene and throughout the Eocene (58–38 mya) it was much hotter than it is today (Nunes and Norris 2006). When comparing the mean annual temperature of today (around 50°F or 10°C) to what it was in the middle of the Eocene (86°F or 30°C), you can see that it was really balmy at the time when the first recognizable primates roamed the earth. During this time, the habitat was also different. There was much less seasonality, and tropical rain forest habitats were much more widespread. Since it was so warm, no water was trapped in polar ice sheets as seen today, and as a result, the sea level was higher. At about 35 mya (the boundary between the Eocene and Oligocene epochs), there was a dramatic drop in world temperature. The collision of the Indian continent with Asia started the uplift of the Himalayas. This, in turn, resulted in the retreat of the Tethys Sea, which was covering much of Eurasia at the time (the Mediterranean, Caspian, and Black Seas are leftovers from the Tethys Sea). All of this led to the disruption of the ocean currents (Ramstein et al. 1997). During the Oligocene (24–34 mya), the temperature was somewhat like it is today, maybe even a bit cooler, and there was an increase in seasonality. The tropical rain forest habitats had shrunk and a completely different habitat structure appeared with more deciduous plants similar to what we see today in forests of the temperate regions.

How Life on Earth Has Evolved

Earth is estimated to be around 4.56 billion or giga years (Gy) old. In Figure 5-8 the geological time scale of earth is shown. Earth's history has been divided into different

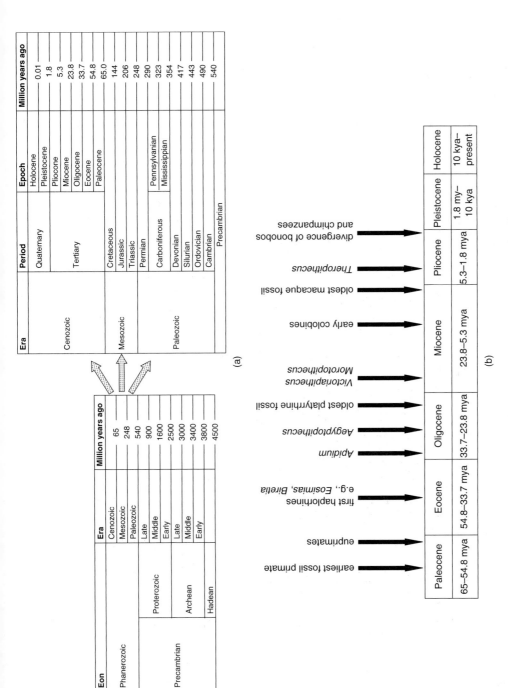

(a)

(b)

FIGURE 5.8a Earth is estimated to be around 4.6 billion years old. For the first billion years there may not have been any living forms present, and for a large part of earth's history single celled or very simple organisms existed. Around 560 million years ago there was a radiation of more complex organisms, which were followed with an abundance of increasingly complex life forms. **FIGURE 5-8b** Fossil evidence of primates comes from the Cenozoic era. The oldest primate fossils date to the Paleocene epoch, but during the Eocene we see a major radiation of the euprimates. During the Oligocene differentiation occurs and lineages leading to later apes and monkeys appear. In the Miocene apes show an adaptive radiation, while monkeys do not become diverse and wide spread until the Plio-Pleistocene.

147

time units reflecting the major events that occurred. We do not have direct evidence of earth's age because all older rocks have been 'recycled' due to plate tectonics, and the rocks present today are of a younger age. There are, however, a few locations where some very ancient rocks have been preserved, for example, on Greenland and Australia. Within these rocks evidence has been found of single-celled organisms as old as 3.5 Gy (Schidlowski 2001, Walsh and Lowe 1985), although many scientists propose that life on earth might be older still (Cavalier-Smith 2002). The first organisms were **anaerobic**, carbon-fixing bacteria that occupied the shallow sea floor. Around 2.5 Gy we begin to pick up evidence of **aerobic**, oxygen-fixing bacteria (Kasting et al. 1992), which over time increased in both size and complexity. Eukaryotes, organisms with a defined cell nucleus, appeared around 900 mya, and by 800 mya the first protozoan, unicellular animals such as amoebas, appeared.

The first life forms were found in the water, and life in the vast oceans became increasingly abundant and successful. Between 543 and 565 mya there was an explosion of advanced multicellular organisms in the oceans. At first these were soft-bodied, tube-like animals (with a mouth and anus), but later, arthropods with protective armour appeared. Not until about 430 mya, during the Silurian period, did some brave creature begin to visit dry land. These earliest forms were not obligate land-dwellers. It took the land animals some time before they began to expand and diversify. An efficient way to breathe air in order to extract oxygen and to not dry out while out of the water had to evolve first. Then they had to evolve an efficient way to move on land.

In the Canadian arctic, researchers recently found the earliest evidence of a transitional form between fishes and the later tetrapods (four-limbed vertebrates). *Tiktaalik roseae*, dated to around 370 million years old, shows a clear transition from water-dwelling fish to land-living, air-breathing tetrapod (Daeschler et al. 2006, Holmes 2006). This tetrapod-like fish had rudimentary paddlelike limbs with eight digits with which it could have moved about in shallow coastal waters. The earliest "true" land vertebrates, the Tetrapods, were amphibian-like and date to about 365 mya. They retained many traits that suggest they spent only part of their time on land. Later forms such as *Pederpes* had four limbs ending with five digits that may have been oriented in such a way as to provide a more efficient way to move on land (Clack 2002). Following the tetrapods, in the early part of the Mesozoic era, there was an adaptive radiation of reptiles. Archaic mammals are found in the Triassic period of the Mesozoic era at the same time the dinosaurs began to make their presence. Some of these early mammals were carnivorous and fed on small or young dinosaurs (Hu et al. 2005). Birds evolved from four-winged dromaeosaurid dinosaurs (Xu et al. 2003) and made their entrance in the latter part of the Mesozoic era, in the Cretaceous period. Around 125 mya we find the first evidence of eutherian (placental) mammals (Ji et al. 2002). At this point, there is also a major shift in the plant life. During the reign of the dinosaurs, **gymnosperm plants** (cone-bearing plants such as pine trees) were dominant. During the latter part of the Cretaceous, however, angiosperms, the flowering plants, began to take hold.

We know that a cataclysmic event took place in between the Mesozoic and Cenozoic (around 65 mya). What really happened is not known, but it has been suggested that a large asteroid hit earth and caused such havoc that it resulted in the demise of the dinosaurs and the introduction of a new world order (Alvarez and Asaro 1990). Angiosperm plants became dominant, as did animals dependent on these plants, such as birds and mammals. The traditional view, based on fossil evidence, is that it is at this point, during the earliest part of the Tertiary, that primates experienced their first major adaptive radiation.

❖❖ Fossil Primates

Archaic mammals have been around since the Mesozoic Era (Figure 5-8a) but a diverse and prominent reptilian fauna overshadowed their presence. It was not until the demise of the dinosaurs at the end of the Cretaceous (65 mya) that mammals really come into their own. With all the vacant ecological niches made available, mammals experienced a massive adaptive radiation in the beginning of the Cenozoic era, which is often referred to as the "age of mammals." Mammals of modern aspect became prominent during the Tertiary period. Within this adaptive radiation we suspect that the progenitor to the primates existed, even though there is no consensus in regard to where the first primates evolved or even what the first primates looked like. The conservative estimate is that the origin of the primate order goes back in time to at least 60–65 mya. However, biomolecular studies as well as statistical modelling suggest that the origin of primates may date as far back as 90 mya (Tavaré et al. 2002; see Box 5-1).

The First Primates to Be Recognized: The Euprimates

We actually do not have direct evidence in regard to when primates differentiated from other related mammals (see Hot Topics 5-1). It is not until well into the Tertiary, in the Eocene epoch, that we come across the first recognizable primates in the fossil record (Figure 5-8b). We find these early primates in North America and in Europe, where they were both abundant and diverse, but they are also found in Asia and in Africa.

We recognize these first primates, the euprimates, because they have many morphological traits that we use today to define the order of primates. For example, they had bony bars on the outside of the eye sockets and the orbits faced forward, and they had flat nails rather than claws on their fingers and toes. Many of the traits displayed in the euprimates are shared with living strepsirhines. However, it is important to remember that because of the estimated 50 million years of evolutionary adaptations made by living strepsirhines, these earliest primates are not the same as our living strepsirhines, i.e., living strepsirhines are not arrested forms of fossil euprimates.

The fact that these Eocene primates appear all of a sudden in the fossil record, and in great abundance and species diversity, may suggest that they had been around for a while and migrated from somewhere else. We do not yet know from where. Africa has been suggested (Miller et al. 2005, Simons 1995), although how they managed to get to Europe is unknown, as Africa was an isolated continent at the time (Figure 5-6). There is a possibility that Asia, and not Africa, is the site of origin. Since Asia and Europe are part of a single landmass, migration of taxa was possible. Migration between Europe and North America was also possible, at least until the middle of the Eocene, as there was a land bridge connecting the two continents.

Today, North America and Europe are located in the temperate zone with seasonal variation in climate. This was not the case during the Eocene, when the first primates lived there. There had been a steady increase in world temperatures since the middle

Paleocene (see Figure 5-7), which peaked in the middle Eocene. In the Eocene both North America and Europe were covered with humid tropical forests that lacked pronounced seasonality, just the kind of habitats where we find most of today's primates.

The Adapids and Omomyids

Euprimates are generally placed in two major groups: the adapids and the omomyids. The adapids belong to the superfamily Adapoidea within the Lemuriformes infraorder, while the omomyids belong to the superfamily Omomyoidea within the Tarsiiformes infraorder. There is great taxonomic diversity within both groups. The adapid group comprises three long-lived and divergent families: Adapidae, Notharctidae, and Sivaladapidae. Taxa belonging to the adapid group have been found in North America, Europe, Asia, and Africa (Figure 5-9). The Adapidae family is mainly European and became extinct by the early Oligocene. The Notharctidae family is most abundant in North America while the sivaladapids are found only in Asia. The omomyid group comprises two families: Omomyidae and Microchoeridae, both containing many different genera. The Microchoeriidae is solely a European family while the Omomyidae, although most common in North America, is also found in Asia (Figure 5-9; Fleagle 1999, Gunnell 2002). We can see many similarities in the earliest species of the adapid and omomyid groups, and it is very likely that they shared a common ancestor (Rose 1995). Over time, however, the differences between the omomyids and adapids became increasingly distinctive morphologically.

The adapids and omomyids can be distinguished based on morphological traits (Table 5-1). Even though there is some overlap in body size, the adapids are in general

TABLE 5-1 Morphological Differences Between Plesiadapids and Euprimates

Character		Plesiadapids	Adapids	Omomyids
Teeth	Incisors	Large	Small	Large
	Canines	Small	Large	Small
	Canine dimorphism	?	Present	Absent
	Diastema	Present	Absent	Absent
Eyes	Size	Mainly small	Small	Large
	Socket	No postorbital bar	Postorbital bar	Postorbital bar
Nose	Soft tissue	Long, narrow	Long	Short
Ear	Petrosal bulla	?Present	Present	Present
	Bony structure	?	Bony ring	Bony tube
Digits	Fingers and toes	Claws	Nails	Nails
	Big toe	Non-opposable	Opposable	Opposable
Skull	Brain	Small	Relatively large	Relatively large
	Frontal bone	Unfused	Unfused	Unfused
	Mandible	Unfused	Unfused*	Unfused
Body	Size	Small	Larger (>1 kg)	Smaller (<400 g)

* Later taxa such as the Notharctines had fused mandibular symphysis

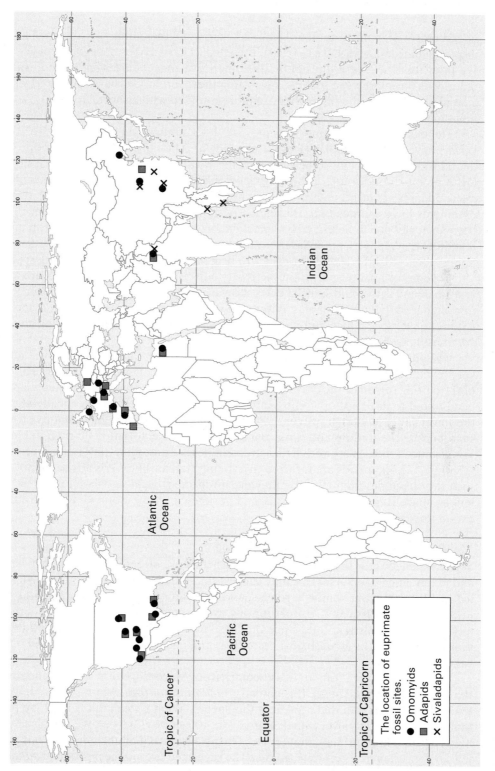

FIGURE 5-9 A map showing the distribution of the euprimates .

larger, most weighing more than 1 kg (>2.2 lbs), while the omomyids are small animals, most weighing less than 400 g (<15 oz). The adapids have narrow faces with longer noses. We infer that they were diurnal because their eye sockets are small. In contrast, the omomyids have large eye sockets, suggesting they were nocturnal. Compared with the adapids, the faces of the omomyids are more rounded with a short, tapered nose, and a more globular brain case.

The dental formula of most adapids is 2.1.4.3. Only a few later species (e.g., *Mahgarita*) have lost a premolar (Rasmussen 1990b). The omomyids have a more varied dental formula, although some of the earlier taxa had four premolars, most taxa had lost a premolar and some of the later species had only two premolars. The canines of many adapids are large, and some taxa show clear sexual dimorphism in this trait. The omomyids have canines that are relatively small and there is little difference in size between males and females, i.e., no sexual dimorphism. Most euprimates had an unfused mandibular symphysis, but in later Notharctine species the symphysis is fused; as mentioned above, this is a trait we consider to be a haplorhine trait among living species.

Locomotor adaptation within the two groups is varied. The omomyids are in general small and active and some species show evidence of a leaping or saltation adaptation similar to living bushbabies. Within the adapid group, some taxa show evidence of a slower quadrupedal locomotor adaptation, while some notharctines had long hindlimbs and must have been good leapers (Covert 2002, Gebo 2002).

The adapids are sometimes referred to as being "lemur-like"; however, there are very few traits that are shared with living lemurs or even living strepsirhines. The shape of the cutting region of the crown of the upper cheek teeth is similar, but no adapid has been found to have a toothcomb. Rather, their anterior teeth are vertically placed in the lower jaw. They do, however, have the same configuration of the bony structure surrounding the middle and inner ear (they have an ectotympanic ring; Table 5-1). What some of them share with living strepsirhines is a grooming claw on the second toe. Likewise, the omomyids are referred to as being "tarsier-like." It is advisable not to use such shorthand descriptions since they are misleading, because only a few of the living lemurs share traits with the adapids, and very few of the omomyids share traits with extant tarsiers.

Where Did the Euprimates Originate?

When we encounter the first fossil primates, they are already abundant, widespread, and taxonomically diverse. This may suggest that they had migrated into North America and Europe from somewhere else, and that their origin goes much further back in time than the Eocene. Unfortunately, we have not yet found evidence for the "where" and the "when," and since the fossil evidence is minimal we have to rely on biomolecular results (see Box 5-1) as well as making educated guesses based on what we do know.

The oldest known primate fossil comes from Morocco, North Africa, and dates to the late Paleocene (60 mya). It is named *Altiatlasius koulchii*. At present we have only ten badly eroded teeth that represent this species. What we can tell from these teeth is that they belonged to a very small animal (50–100 g or 1.8–3.5 oz). We can also tell that it was a generalized primate that retained many ancestral mammalian traits, but we cannot say for certain its taxonomic affinity. The suggested taxonomic position of *Altiatlasius* ranges from an omomyid (Covert 2002, Sigé et al. 1990) to a basal haplorhine (Beard 1998). However, recently it has been suggested that *Altiatlasius* might be an African plesiadapid (see below; Hooker et al. 1999). We need more fossil evidence from *Altiatlasius* before we can draw any conclusion about its place within primate phylogeny.

What is present in the Paleocene (55–65 mya) is a highly successful and diverse group of insectivorous primate-like mammals belonging to the order Plesiadapiformes. These mammals had taken foothold in North America and Europe, although they may have been present in Africa as well (Hooker et al. 1999, Tabuce et al. 2004). It was a highly successful group with some lineages surviving for some 10 to 15 million years. These early mammals, which we know mainly from dental and skull remains, ranged from mouse-sized (10–20 g) to cat-sized (2–3 kg), although most did not weigh more than a few hundred grams. Even though the Plesiadapiformes, or plesiadapids for short, were a very successful group of mammals that survived well into the Eocene, they disappeared rather suddenly, and by the end of the Eocene there were just a few taxa left. They may have lost in a competitive battle with rodents or with the first euprimates, although the drying up that was taking place at the time may also have altered the environment beyond their adaptive ability.

Until fairly recently the plesiadapids were considered to be our earliest evidence of primates because of the presence of several primate traits,

> **petrosal bulla**—an inflated area of the petrosal part of the temporal bone surrounding the middle ear structures

e.g., **petrosal bulla**, rotation of wrist and ankle joints, and some dental traits (Table 5-1). However, many of the plesiadapids were either too specialized dentally to have given rise to a later, more generalized primate taxa, or they were so generalized that they could have given rise to almost anything (e.g., fruit bats, sugar gliders, primates; see Hot Topics 5-1). The dental formula of the earliest plesiadapids includes two incisors, one canine, three premolars, and three molars in each quadrant of the mouth. Over time, however, the different lineages showed reductions in the number of teeth present, with some lineages losing incisors, canines, and/or premolars. Dental specialization was also evident in some lineages. Some families, such as the carpolestids, had very specialized premolars. The very fact that the earliest euprimates had four premolars rules out the majority of the plesiadapids as potential ancestors, because if a tooth has been lost evolutionarily, it is most unlikely to reappear in later forms.

Today we recognize that the shared traits are due to **parallel evolution** and not due to phylogenetic relations. The plesiadapids are placed in their own order, but it is still possible that they are a sister group to primates. Still we cannot yet completely rule out the possi-

> **parallel evolution**—the independent development within a group of animals of similar adaptations, *e.g.*, the long arms of both platyrrhines and some catarrhines to adapt to a novel feeding strategy
> **convergent evolution**—the independent development of similar characteristics in non-related taxa due to similar adaptive strategies, *e.g.*, wings of bats and birds

bility that we may find the origin of primates within the plesiadapid group. Despite the uncertain relationship between plesiadapids and primates, the plesiadapids are, according to Rose (1995), the best analogues we have of the earliest basal primates.

 **HOT TOPICS 5-1**

How do We Recognize the Ancestor of the Euprimates?

This is a most difficult question to answer, and at present the answer appears to be that we cannot. The fossil evidence is eluding us; perhaps we are not looking in the right places. In addition, would we recognize the earliest representatives of the primate order if we found their fossil remains? It is quite possible we would not because the ancestors would most likely have few traits in common with later forms. Some of the traits used to decipher what species or group of living mammals are most closely related to primates include the type and configuration of bones in the middle ear and eardrum, and the pathway of blood flow to and from the brain. While these traits are easy to see in living species, they are seldom detectable in fossils. When searching for the sister group to primates among living species, there are several contestants (see Figure 5-10).

Comparative studies, focussing on skeletal, dental, and soft tissue similarities, suggest that primates are more closely related to tree shrews, the Tupaiids (order Scandentia), sugar gliders, the colugos (order Dermoptera), and bats (order Chiroptera) than they are to any other order of living mammals. Details about the visual system have been used to suggest that primates and fruit bats (*Megachiroptera*) are most closely related (Pettigrew 1986), while the colugos, which have a similar visual system, are more distantly related. Now we know, however, that

these similarities are due to parallel or convergent evolution rather than close ancestral relationships. The inferred close relationship between colugos and strepsirhine primates was based on the fact that both have toothcombs, although on closer inspection, the toothcombs are structurally not very similar to each other. Therefore, the presence of toothcombs in both taxa is most likely also a case of **convergence** due to similarity in feeding adaptations.

Results from biomolecular studies are not making the picture any clearer. Depending on what molecular system is investigated, different results have been achieved. In some studies the four groups (tree shrews, colugos, bats, and primates) could not be separated (Shoshani 1986), while Novacek (1992) found that colugos and bats grouped together, and tree shrews and primates formed a sister group. In a third study, in which amino acids were compared, bats and tree shrews grouped with insectivores and carnivores, while primates grouped with lagomorphs (rabbits and hares) and rodents (Miyamoto and Goodman 1986).

The plesiadapids are no longer considered to be ancestral primates; rather they are considered to be primate-like insectivores. The traits shared with primates are likely to be due to convergent adaptation to similar environmental requirements. It has even been shown, based on a very well-preserved specimen, that at

FIGURE 5-10   Comparative studies suggest that the closest living relatives to primates may be: (a) the treeshrews (the Tupaiids, order Scandentia); (b) the colugos or sugargliders (order Dermoptera); (c) the bats (order Chiroptera).

least one family of the plesiadapids had folds of skin between their limbs and were adapted for gliding like the colugos, leading Robert Martin to state: "plesiadapiformes, formerly 'dental primates,' are no more than 'postcranial colugos'" (Martin 1993:227).

As early as 1910 Gregory proposed the existence of a close rela-tionship between bats, tree shrews, colugos, and primates. He suggested that these orders should be placed together into the superorder Archonta. However, there is disagreement over this classification, in part because molecular data seem to disagree about how each group may be related to each other, and it is not yet known how much of the similarity in

(*continued*)

traits is due to convergent or parallel evolution rather than phylogenetic relationships. We cannot, however, completely rule out that we share a common ancestor in the distant past with the bats, colugos, and tree shrews. Whether the image so often portrayed of the ancestors of the euprimates looking something akin to the tree shrew—a small, nocturnal, terrestrial insectivore—is correct still eludes us. Presently the tree shrews have been delegated to their own order, but in the past they were considered to be the most plesiomorphic of all living primates (Le Gros Clark 1965). It is possible that the two orders are sister groups because of the many shared ancestral traits.

What Happens to the Euprimates and the Strepsirhine Lineage?

The adapids and the omomyids were highly successful animals that were around for a long time. However, by the end of the Eocene (34 mya), when the climate became increasingly colder and more seasonal, we see a major faunal turnover in the fossil record. We refer to this event as the ***Grande Coupure***. Most primate lineages became extinct, or at least they disappeared from the northern continents. A few taxa in North America and Europe survived into the Oligocene, but in much reduced numbers, and over time they also became extinct. Only in Asia did some euprimate taxa find refuge. Here the sivaladapids survived into the Miocene (Ciochon and Gunnell 2002). The sivaladapids were fairly large (3–4 kg or >7 lbs) and show folivorous dietary adaptations. They are distinctive in having lost the **hypocone** from their maxillary molars (see Figure 5-11 for location of cusps on molar teeth). The taxonomic position of these Asian euprimates is still uncertain but the consensus is that they represent an ephemeral Asian line that disappeared without living descendants (see Hot Topics 5-2).

Today we find many strepsirhines living in Africa and Asia, while there are no strepsirhines in the Americas. Living strepsirhines comprise the lemuriforms of Madagascar, and the African and Asian lorisiforms (lorises and bushbabies). Even though genetic data support the idea that lemuriforms and lorisiforms have been around for a long time, we have little fossil evidence about their existence, and there are many gaps in their fossil records. Until recently, *Plesiopithecus teras,* found in the Fayum of Egypt and dated to 35–36 mya, was the oldest known fossil lorisiform (Simons and Rasmussen 1994). More recent dental remains discovered from 35–40 my old strata in the Fayum belonging to *Saharagalago* may represent a potential ancestor of the bushbabies and *Karanisia* a potential ancestor of lorises (Seiffert et al. 2003). The teeth of the two fossil species show very clear affinities to their respective groups. These fossils support the assertion based on biomolecular evidence that the bushbaby-loris divergence took place in the Eocene (Martin 2003). Following these early finds there is a gap in the fossil record until the middle Miocene when we again pick up evidence of lorises and bushbabies (McCrossin 1992). Most of these later finds are from sites in East Africa (see Box 5-4) with only one loris (*Nycticeboides*) having been found from the late Miocene of Asia (Jacobs 1981; see map in Figure 5-12).

The earliest lorisiforms have a more generalized skeleton than living taxa. Rasmussen and Nekaris (1998) propose that differences in the skeletal anatomy, especially

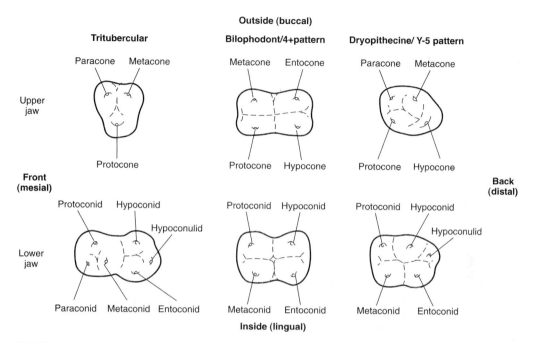

FIGURE 5-11   A comparison of the molar cusp pattern in extant strepsirhines (trituberculate pattern), monkeys (4+ pattern), and apes (Y-5 pattern). Maxillary teeth (top) have a different shape compared with the mandibular teeth (bottom).

of the wrist and ankle joints, of living lorises and bushbabies are due to their pursuing divergent foraging strategies: Bushbabies are more adapted for quick leaping locomotion while lorises are more adapted for slower quadrupedal locomotion. By the Miocene, the fossils show similar traits to extant forms, except their foot bones do not yet show the same derived adaptations for leaping as living bushbabies. It is not until the Pliocene that bushbabies show indistinguishable morphology to living species, and by that time we place them in the same genus as the living forms.

Lemurs are a special type of strepsirhine found only on the island of Madagascar. We assume that their evolutionary history is restricted to this island since there is no evidence of lemurs anywhere else. We know close to nothing about their origin. *Bugtilemur,* found in Oligocene deposits in Pakistan, was initially claimed to be related to living lemurs. Marivaux et al. (2001) suggest that its cheek teeth show special features very similar to those of living Cheriogaleid lemurs. However, the specimen lacked a toothcomb, which would indicate that this fossil is not related to lemurs. Most experts consider *Bugtilemur* to be a sivaladapid, and the affinity with lemurs reflects convergent evolution due to similar adaptations to

> **subfossil**—species that have become fossilized during the Pleistocene or Holocene

diet. There are, however, **subfossils** from Madagascar that are less than 26,000 years old. They can be found all over the island in caves and other secluded areas. These subfossil remains show that in the past lemurs were even more diverse than at present. For one thing, some of the subfossil taxa were much bigger; some were as large as living baboons and gorillas.

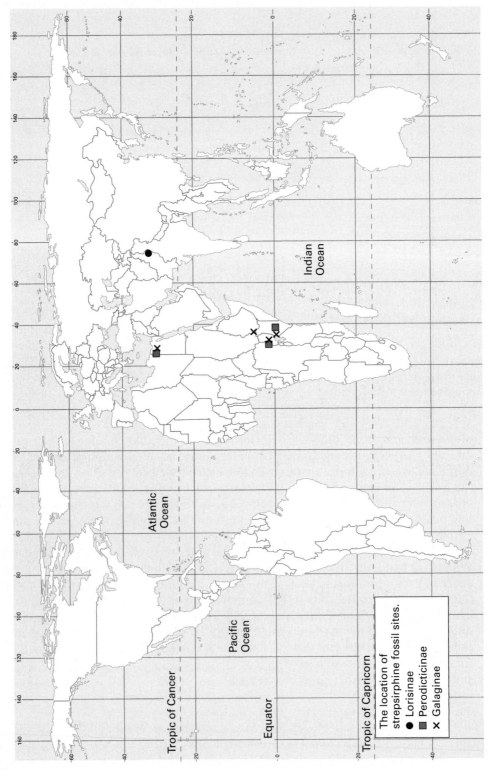

FIGURE 5-12 A map showing the distribution of more recent strepsirhine fossil sites (post-euprimates).

Based on genetic data we infer that all living lemurs share the same ancestor (**monophyly**), which most likely arrived on the island some 55 mya (Yoder 1997). How this ancestor reached the island is another very interesting and as of yet unresolved question (Martin 2000). The ancestor of modern lemurs must have rafted across the Indian Ocean since Madagascar broke free from mainland Africa between 120–130 mya (Abramovich et al. 2003).

At present, seventeen extinct species of lemurs, belonging to five families, are known from the late Pleistocene to recent times (Figure 5-13; Godfrey and Jungers 2002). Some of these families had evolved really unique traits. The palaeopropithecid family is referred to as sloth lemurs because they show a locomotor adaptation similar to living sloths;

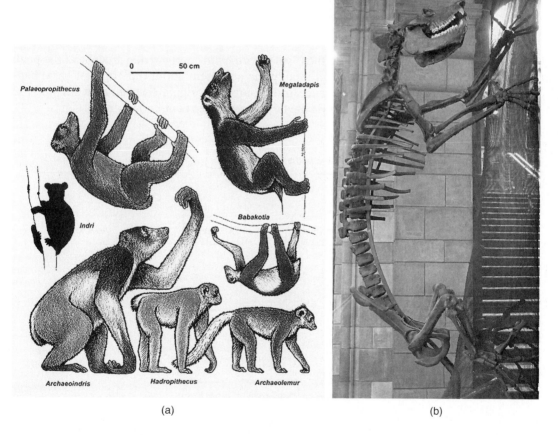

(a)   (b)

FIGURE 5-13   The diversity of lemurs on the island of Madagascar was greater in the past (a). There existed lemurs the size of gorillas (*Archaeoindris*), some had locomotor adaptations similar to sloths, while others looked superficially very much like monkeys (*Hadropithecus, Archaeolemur*). The outline of an extant indri provides a scale. Well preserved remains of subfossil lemurs, such as this *Megaladapis* (b), have been found at various locations on Madagascar.

their forelimbs are long, and fingers and toes are curved. Some had skulls and teeth highly reminiscent of living indris. The megaladapid family, the koala lemurs, are quite amazing as they reached the size of adult male gorillas, and they seemed to have fed on leaves. The archaeolemurs were also large. They are often referred to as monkey lemurs because they show several convergent traits with extant monkeys. Their limb bones suggest highly terrestrial adaptations, and they had bilophodont molars (Figure 5-11; see also Figure 4-11). Their diet appears to have included hard objects akin to the diets of capuchin and saki monkeys, i.e., they may have eaten many hard seeds (Godfrey et al. 2005). Only the Daubentonia and Pachylemur families show a strong affinity to living forms. Fossil *Daubentonia* is just a larger version of the living aye-aye, and *Pachylemur* is very similar to the ruffed lemur (*Varecia*). It is highly probable that the introduction of humans on Madagascar approximately 2,000 years ago started the downfall of these lemurs. A combination of environmental changes, due to both climatic changes and human agency, and hunting by the people may have lead to the demise of the giant lemurs (Perez et al. 2005). Based on folklore, some of the subfossil lemurs may have survived to as recently as 500 years ago (Burney and Ramilisonina 1998).

The First Haplorhines

The basal haplorhines appear in the fossil record by the early to mid-Eocene at the peak radiation of the euprimates. Traditionally, the argument about the origin of basal haplorhines has centered on which ancestral group they originated from (the adapids, the omomyids, the omomyid lineage via the tarsiers, or some yet unknown group; Figure 5-14).

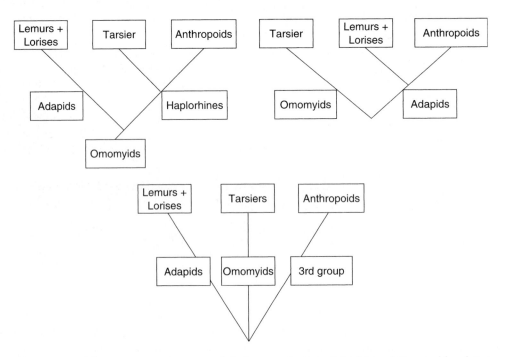

FIGURE 5-14 There are several suggested cladograms for how Adapids and Omomyids relate to later taxonomy. The most commonly suggested models are presented here .

Since the earliest haplorhines were contemporaneous with euprimates, the phylogenetic link to the euprimates is not very likely, and it may be prudent to seek the origin of the first haplorhines elsewhere (Box 5-3).

We have fossil remains of basal haplorhines both from Africa and Asia (Figure 5-15). It is important to recognize that these basal haplorhines have not yet evolved to the stage at which we can see them as distinct monkeys or apes (crown taxa). They also predate the division between the platyrrhines (the American monkeys) and the catarrhines (all other monkeys and apes). The traits used to define extant haplorhines (see Table 5-2) do not always work in defining the basal haplorhines because each taxon shows a unique mixture of ancestral (strepsirhine-like) and derived (haplorhine-like) traits, so called **mosaic evolution** (de Beer 1954, Mayr and Ashlock 1991). The more we learn about the past, the more apparent it is that haplorhine traits do not come as a "package deal" but piecemeal and in different combinations in different taxa. Mosaic evolution is actually a common phenomenon at each divergence point between major groups of primate taxa. Furthermore, there is evidence of much **homoplasy**, which is due to convergent or parallel evolution, and which also contributes to the classification disputes. However, with an ever-increasing number of fossils available, it is clear that the basal haplorhines are different and more derived than the strepsirhines, although there is not complete agreement among the experts in regard to the exact position of each species.

> **homoplasy**—when two species show similarity in a morphological trait that is not due to relatedness (a common ancestry), but due to parallel or convergent evolution

There are two main families of basal haplorhines from Africa, the Parapithecidae and the Proteopithecidae. The four genera and eight species belonging to the Parapithecidae are quite a diverse group. Their dental formula (mainly the presence of three premolars) places them in the basal haplorhine and pre-catarrhine category. Postcranial evidence and the articulation of the skull bones at the side of the skull (zygomatic and parietal contact; Figure 5-17) point toward a strong tie to the platyrrhines. However, some species have also retained several ancestral traits like those seen in omomyids. The most common parapithecid is *Apidium phiomense* (Figure 5-18). Hundreds of fossils have been found of this species in the Fayum, Egypt, making it the most well-known species. Even though the postcranial bones suggest a robust arboreal quadruped, the length and shape of its hindlimbs,

TABLE 5-2   Morphological Characters that Distinguishes Strepsirhines from Haplorhines (see also Figure 4-8)

Character		*Strepsirhines*	*Haplorhines*
Teeth	Molar cusps pattern*	Trituberculate	Bilophodont; Y-5
Skull	Frontal bone	Unfused	Fused
	Eye socket	Postorbital bar	Enclosed
	Mandible	Unfused	Fused
	Brain	Relatively small	Relatively large
Body	Digits	Grooming claw	Nails

* See Figure 5-11 for explanation of molar cusp pattern

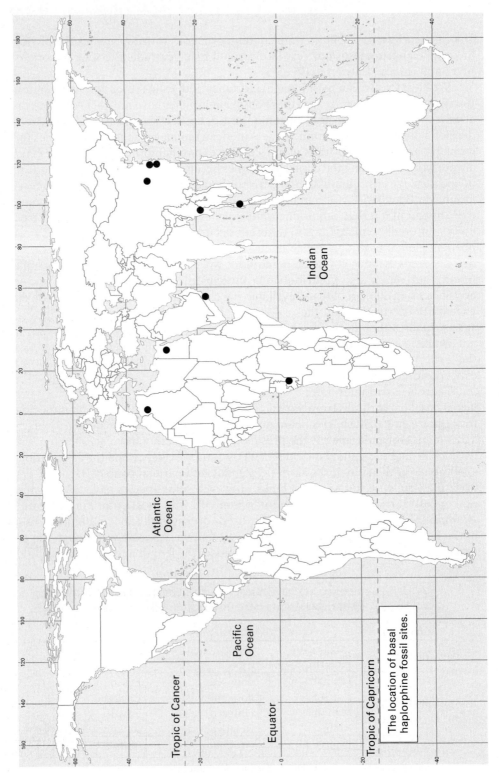

FIGURE 5-15 A map showing the distribution of basal haplorhine fossil sites.

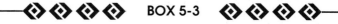

Where Is the Cradle of the Haplorhines?

There have been many suggestions in regard to the place of origin of the haplorhines (see Miller et al. 2005 for a recent summary). Africa has been considered the most parsimonious choice as the cradle of haplorhines based on the very rich fossil evidence from the Fayum as well as other sites in North Africa and Arabia. The Fayum, located in the northwestern desert of Egypt, has provided an unprecedented richness of fossils from the Eocene and Oligocene, and not only fossil primates but many different animals and plants. Our interpretation and concepts of early haplorhine evolution have been strongly influenced by these Fayum finds (e.g., Simons 1989, 1992, 1995). The fossil record tells us that by the end of the Eocene (possibly as early as the middle Eocene) the haplorhines were well established and quite diverse, and that these early primates were part of a larger endemic African fauna. A problem with an African origin is that Africa was an isolated continent at the time. The species diversity seen in the early haplorhines can be explained in two ways: Either the group has an ancient root in Africa, or it migrated into Africa from elsewhere. Once there, it experienced an adaptive radiation. At present we cannot resolve these possibilities without more available evidence, both from older sites in Africa and more information from other localities. The strength of the African origin model is the rich fossil evidence.

Over the past decade an increasing number of fossil primates from several locations in Asia (China, Myanmar, and Thailand) have placed the African origin of the haplorhines into question (Beard et al. 1996, Jaeger et al. 1999, Kay et al. 1997, Ross et al. 1998). Recent fossils, belonging to the eosiimid family, have opened up the possibility of an Asian origin. However, what the eosimids are and how they fit into primate evolution is a highly contentious issue. The very old (around 50 mya) and very small (less than 2 oz) *Eosimias* has been suggested to be a basal haplorhine (Figure 5-16; Beard et al. 1994, 1996). These Asian primates are discussed in greater detail in Hot Topics 5-2. The Asian origin model is viable only if *Eosimias* is accepted as a basal haplorhine (see below). This conundrum will not be solved until more complete fossils, especially cranial remains, are found.

Less commonly considered hypotheses are the Paratethyan origin (Rasmussen 1994) and the Indo-Madagascar origin (Krause and Maas 1990, Martin in press). The Paratethyan origin hypothesis proposes that haplorhines evolved out of the cercamoniine adapiforms, characterized by having fused mandibular symphysis, and their hypocone cusp is not developed from the protocone, which is the usual pattern. This highly diverse euprimate group (both in the case of body size and dietary adaptation) is found throughout Europe but could very well have occupied the circum-Tethyan region (the Mediterranean and Black Seas are remnants of the Tethyan Sea) since this land

(*continued*)

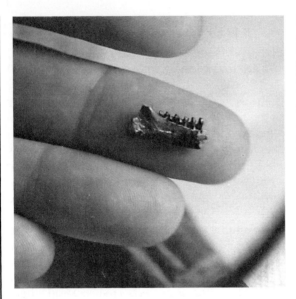

FIGURE 5-16 Members of the *Eosimias* genus, found at several locations in Asia, have been suggested to be basal haplorhines. However, there is much controversy surrounding the phylogenetic position of this taxon. *Eosimias* were very small primates, as illustrated by the size of this mandible (left side shown).

mass was a single ecological unit. This model can be supported by the available biomolecular evidence, and morphological support comes in the form of *Periconodon*. This cercomoniines genus has bunodont or rounded molars with certain traits that affiliate it closely with the African *Apidium*. This could of course be due to similar dietary adaptations rather than be reflective of a phylogenetic link. What is needed to give full support for this hypothesis is a skull from a *Periconodon*, which will determine whether this species had postorbital closure (Miller et al. 2005).

The Indo-Madagascar origin model rests mainly on molecular evidence and the assumption that plesiadapids are not a sister group to primates. At present, adequate supporting fossil evidence about the oldest primates, which may date to the Oligocene, simply do not exist. The idea that India could have anything to do with primate origins has not been contemplated, since traditionally it has been assumed that the Indian continent was isolated far from mainland Africa. However, recent study suggests that the trajectory of the Indian plate brought it much closer to the African mainland than previously suggested (Briggs 2003). By reducing the distance between the two continents, exchange of fauna could have occurred prior to India's contact with Eurasia in the late Paleocene to early Eocene. A prerequisite for this model to work is that the first Eurasian primates should be no older than 65 mya, the earliest point when faunal interchange could have occurred. This model would go a long way to explaining the rich diversity of both subfossil and extant lemurs on Madagascar.

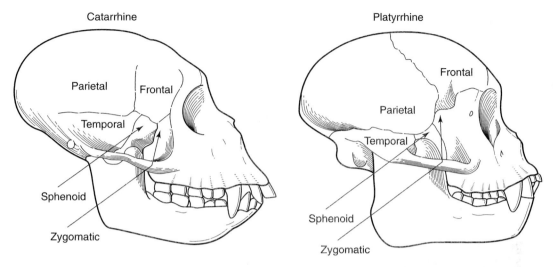

FIGURE 5-17   The way the skull bones articulate with one another on the side of the skull separate the platyrrhine primates from the catarrhine primates. Zygomatic and parietal contact is the platyrhine pattern, while frontal and temporal contact is the catarrhine pattern.

especially the nearly fused distal tibia and fibula, suggest a leaping adaptation. A diurnal lifestyle is inferred based on the small size of its eye orbits. The cheek teeth have very thick enamel, suggesting its diet contained many hard seeds. The most curious parapithecid is *Parapithecus (Simonsius) grangeri* because it lacks permanent lower incisors and has very robust tusklike canines.

The Proteopithecidae family comprise two (possibly three) genera with a single species in each. This group shows an even stronger affinity to the platyrrhines, e.g., hindlimb morphology, and size and shape of the premolars, specifically the second premolar, but they

FIGURE 5-18   The most frequently found parapithecid in the Fayum, Egypt, is *Apidium phiomense*. The postcranial bones suggest that it was an arboreal quadruped, with some leaping abilities, while the skull with its small eye sockets suggests a diurnal adaptation.

lack more derived haplorhine and catarrhine traits. Even though there is not a consensus among researchers, Miller and Simons (1997) have suggested that it is within this group that we may well find the origin of the American haplorhines.

The Asian basal haplorhines pose quite a dilemma (see Hot Topic 5-2). Our knowledge of the middle Eocene eosimids (Latin *eo*=dawn, *simias*=haplorhine or monkey+ape) from China and Myanmar (formerly Burma) increases with each field season, and an intriguing sample of fossil remains have been recovered. These remains comprise isolated teeth, jaw fragments, and foot bones. The eosimids were very small animals (Figure 5-16). Most weighed around 50–100 g (1.8–3.5 oz), but there are some foot bones that suggest a weight around half an ounce (10–15 g). If correct, this is the smallest primate ever recorded (Gebo et al. 2001). The dental remains show a mosaic of traits, but some display an affinity with the haplorhines (e.g., erect and spatulate-shaped incisors). The late Eocene fossil primates from Southeast Asia (*Amphipithecus*, *Pondaungia,* and *Siamopithecus*) were much larger animals (6–9 kg or 13–20 lbs). There is no consensus as to the phylogenetic position of these taxa. They appear to belong to a restricted Asian lineage and show a closer affinity to each other than they do to any of the African or later haplorhines taxa (see Hot Topics 5-2).

The Tarsier Lineage

Today we find tarsiers only in Southeast Asia, mainly in Indonesia and the Philippines. As mentioned above, they belong to a single genus (*Tarsius*) comprising eight species. As discussed in Chapter 2, tarsiers are difficult primates to classify because of their strange mixture of plesiomorphic traits (shared with both strepsirhines and haplorhines), apomorphic traits (shared with haplorhines), and unique apomorphic traits. In many ways tarsiers appear to straddle the division of strepsirhines and haplorhines. In the past tarsiers were considered part of the Prosmii suborder, but today they are considered part of the haplorhine clade. The traits we based this assumption on are not universally accepted as reflective of a phylogenetic relationship (Schwartz 2003, Simons 2003). However, biomolecular studies do support a sister clade relationship between tarsiers and the group comprising apes and monkeys, which would lend support for inclusion within the haplorhine clade (Yoder 2003).

Why is this important? Where we place the tarsier has implication for the taxonomic divisions we use and how we arrange the potential origin of haplorhines. If tarsiers are considered to be phylogenetically closer to apes and monkeys, then the Strepsirhini and Haplorhini division should be used. If, however, tarsiers are more closely related to lemurs and lorises, then the division Prosimii and Anthropoidea should be used.

The tarsiers have a long evolutionary history. Based on biomolecular data, we estimate that soon after the first appearance of the basal haplorhines in the middle of Eocene, the tarsier lineage diverged from the rest of the haplorhine lineage. The oldest tarsier fossil comes from China and dates to the middle Eocene (Beard 1998). This fossil, *Tarsius eocaenus*, is estimated to have weighed no more than 50 g (1.8 oz), half the size of extant forms. Unfortunately, most of the remains available are teeth. This Eocene species shows morphological adaptations for an insectivorous diet similar to that of the living species. The same adaptation is evident in the Miocene tarsier tooth from Thailand, *Tarsius thailandica*. This species is slightly smaller than living forms (estimated around

80 g or 3 oz). In the Fayum, scientists have found evidence of what is very likely a tarsier that dates to the Oligocene. *Afrotarsius chatrathi* is known from teeth and some longbones, which show a clear fusion between the tibia and fibula just as seen in living tarsiers (Rasmussen et al. 1998). Tarsiers were thus more widely distributed in the past, while today only a single genus survives—a remnant lineage that has managed to hang on. From the limited range of fossil remains it appears as if it is a lineage that has seen very little change except in size through time. The relationship between tarsiers and basal haplorhines as well as crown haplorhines remains unclear. There is increasing support for the idea that the tarsier lineage is a unique ancient lineage that is only very distantly related to crown haplorhines.

  HOT TOPICS 5-2

The Cradle of the Anthropoid Haplorhines: A Closer Look at Asia

The first Asian fossil primates, *Pondaunga cotteri* and *Amphipithecus mogaungensis*, were recovered in Myanmar in the early part of the twentieth century. At that time only dental remains were available, which were enigmatic and difficult to classify. Pilgrim (1927) was the first to describe *Pondaunga*. He noted some close affinities to euprimates but also recognized some more derived traits pointing toward a haplorhine affinity. *Amphipithecus* had more derived dental traits, and it was suggested that it might be on the cusp of becoming a haplorhine (Simons 1968). The idea that an Eocene haplorhine lived in Southeast Asia was considered intriguing, but due to political instability, fossil-hunting did not commence in this part of the world until the late 1980s. Presently, there are both cranial and postcranial materials available, but despite these additional remains, the phylogenetic position of these taxa remains uncertain. The classification of *Pondaunga* as a euprimate may be less contentious while the position of

Amphipithecus remains unresolved (see review in Beard 2002, Ciochon and Gunnell 2002).

In 1994 Beard and Qi presented the first evidence of an early middle Eocene fossil from China, which they named *Eosimias* (Figure 5-16). Based on the presence of derived character traits on the teeth, it was suggested that *Eosimias* was a basal haplorhine (Beard et al. 1994). This pronouncement caused quite a stir in paleontological circles in part because the assessment was based on a few poorly preserved teeth but also the idea that a haplorhine of such an ancient age existed in Asia did not fit well with preconceived theories. The response by the experts was varied: While *Eosimias* was accepted as a primate by some, others questioned if *Eosimias* actually was a primate (Godinot 1994, Simons and Rasmussen 1994). Most considered the conclusion, based on a few and poorly preserved teeth, that *Eosimias* was a basal haplorhine to be premature. The small size of *Eosimias* was also considered problematic. It was

(continued)

estimated to weigh less than 50 g (<1.8 oz), which is smaller than any living haplorhine. Since the initial discovery, many more complete and better preserved fossils have been recovered. *Eosimias* have now been recovered not only from China but also Myanmar, showing a wide distribution of the genus and reflecting that these primates were clearly highly successful.

Eosimias is no longer alone in the basal haplorhine family Eosimiidae. Two additional genera, *Bahinia* and *Phenacopithecus,* have been included (Beard and Wang 2004, Jaeger et al. 1999). The presence of three genera within the eosimid family may provide extra strength to the out-of-Asia model for basal haplorhines. However, the argument really rests on the position of *Eosimias* itself. If it is shown not to be a haplorhine (if, for example, a skull shows it lacks orbital closure), then the whole basal haplorhine family may tumble. There is still doubt amongst the experts, and some will not cast a vote until an eosimid skull has been found enabling the question of haplorhine affinity to be resolved once and for all by showing the presence of derived haplorhine features (Miller et al. 2005, Schwartz 2003, Simons 2003).

The presence of primate fossils in Asia is not denied. Clearly, Asia has been a refuge for certain primate lineages, euprimates as well as possible haplorhines, where they managed to survive for a long period of time. However, to place the origin of the haplorhines in Asia is still looked upon with skepticism by many scientists, especially as the eosimids show many unique traits only seen within the Asian group and finding an ancestor to these eosimids, as well as seeing the connection with later crown taxa, still eludes us (Miller et al. 2005). However, there has been a change in attitudes not just because of the recovery of more and better preserved fossils, but also our very definition of a haplorhine has come under severe scrutiny. Even though more research is required, we are beginning to develop a better understanding of what traits may be important phylogenetic markers and which ones may simply reflect functional convergence (Ross 2000, Schwartz 2003). We still need more fossil evidence, especially some crania, before it is possible to say anything definitive about how these specific fossils might fit into the origin of the haplorhine lineage. Thus, the debate will continue for some time.

The Platyrrhines: The First Monkeys of the Americas

Today we find monkeys from southern Mexico to northern Argentina. In the past, they had a wider distribution: from the Greater Antilles (Cuba, Jamaica, and Hispaniola) all the way south to Patagonia in southern Argentina as is shown in Figure 5-19. The oldest evidence of a platyrrhine monkey, *Branisella*, was found in Bolivia in the late nineteenth century, and dates to approximately 26 mya. It is therefore assumed that the first monkeys arrived on the South American continent some time before this date. We do

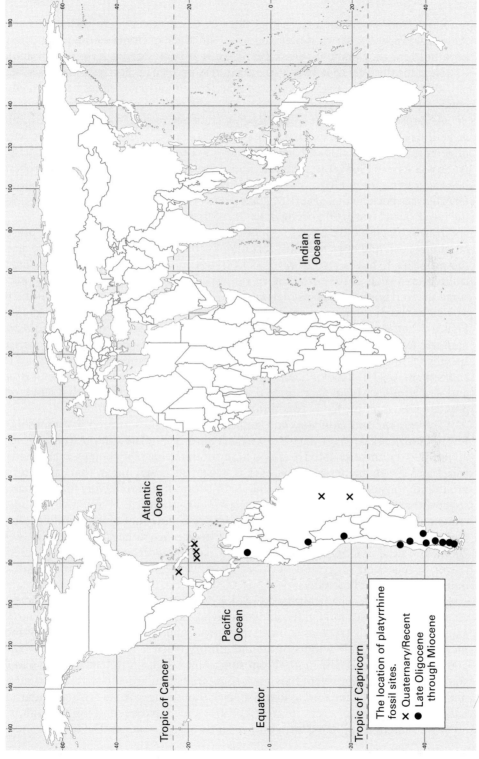

FIGURE 5-19 Distribution map of platyrrhine fossil sites. The oldest fossil is found in Bolivia but later taxa are found throughout the continent, and subfossils are found on the islands of the Greater Antilles.

not know from where the platyrrhine stock came, or how the ancestors reached South America. Presently, Africa is believed to be the place of origin of the platyrrhine monkeys, but how they made it across the ocean is anyone's guess. Based on biomolecular evidence, the divergence between African and American haplorhines may have occurred already in the late Eocene, and thus the platyrrhines and catarrhines have evolved independently over a long period of time.

At present, the richest fossil-bearing sites are found in Columbia, Bolivia, and Argentina (Figure 5-19). There are three genera known to date from the Oligocene, but most of the fossils found are from the Miocene. There are also a few more recent fossils (subfossils) from the Greater Antilles and Brazil. Despite the fact that researchers have been searching for evidence of primates older than 26 mya, there has been no luck so far. This is especially disconcerting since plenty of remains of other mammal taxa from the late Eocene–early Oligocene have been discovered.

Branisella, the oldest South American primate fossil (Figure 5-20a), dates to the late Oligocene and does not look very similar to a typical platyrrhine. It appears much too primitive to have close affinity to any living lineage. *Branisella* retains some ancestral features such as the retention of three premolars in the upper jaw. It also shows some derived features such as high-crowned, rounded (bunodont) cusps on the molars as well as the presence of a small but distinct hypocone on the maxillary molars (see Figure 5-11). *Branisella* appears to share with *Proteopithecus,* one of the oldest fossil haplorhines from the Fayum, a reduced second maxillary premolar. It also shares some specific features on the hypocone of the first and second molars in the upper jaw (Miller and Simons 1997, Takai et al. 2000). These are synapomorphies only between *Branisella* and *Proteopithecus*, but there is at present, however, no evidence that can confirm a phylogenetic relationship between the two taxa.

Tremacebus and *Dolichocebus* (found at several sites located in Argentina) are a few million years younger than *Branisella* (Figure 5-20). The skull of *Tremacebus* is relatively narrow and elongated as it is in many of the living platyrrhines. It also had a wide snout and the space between the eyes is wide, which may mean that olfaction was of greater importance to this species than later forms. It had relatively large orbits, which suggest that it was nocturnal. The external auditory meatus (the bony opening of the ear canal) and the shape of the lower incisors resemble that of a pliopithecid from the Fayum, but this may be due to evolutionary convergence rather than relatedness (Begun 2002). The skull of *Dolichocebus* elongated like *Tremacebus,* but its snout is much narrower. It has been suggested that *Dolichocebus* is shows close affinity with extant *Saimiri*, the squirrel monkeys.

Many of the fossils from the Miocene show close affinity to living species. Most commonly, the fossils look more similar to living pithecines (such as the saki monkeys), small-bodied cebids (such as squirrel monkeys), and callitrichines (tamarins and marmosets), with only a few hints of ateline affinity (such as the howler, spider, muriqui, and woolly monkeys). The more recent subfossils, e.g., the Antillean monkeys, look very similar to living forms except they have some traits that are either absent or rare in the mainland species. Compared to living species, their bones are surprisingly robust. These island monkeys are of great interest because they have been going through isolated adaptive radiation and some have only recently become extinct. The three island genera

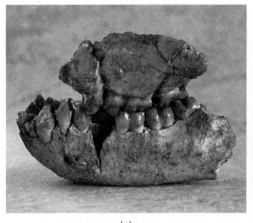

(a)

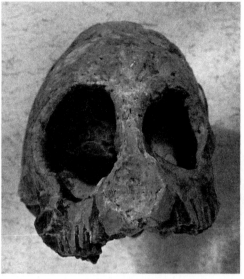

(b)

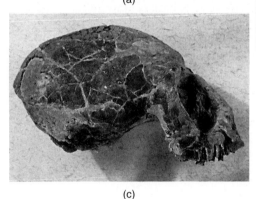

(c)

FIGURE 5-20 *Branisella* (a) is the oldest platyrrhine fossil evidence, comprising a few dental remains. It has relatively high-crowned lower molars. *Tremacebus* (b) has a narrow and elongated skull showing strong affinity to extant taxa. It also has large eye sockets suggesting a nocturnal adaptation (c). (Note the scale is in cm).

(*Paralouatta, Antillothrix,* and *Xenothrix*) show a closer phylogenetic relationship to each other than they do to their distant mainland relative, *Callicebus* (titi monkeys). If the Antillean monkeys form a monophyletic group, it is assumed that they were the result of a single colonization event (MacPhee and Horovits 2002).

Where Did the Platyrrhines Come from?

A question that has fueled much debate and research in primatology is where did the American haplorhines come from? There are three possible sites of origin: Africa, North America, or Asia (either via the Australia-Antarctica land bridge or Africa; see Figure 5-21). The origin of the platyrrhines is a difficult question to resolve because throughout most of the Tertiary, South America was an island continent. The contact it had with Africa was disrupted long before primates appeared, its contact with Antarctica was disrupted in the middle Eocene, and North and South America did not come into contact until fairly recently (~5 mya). Wherever the site of origin, the first primate settlers of South America

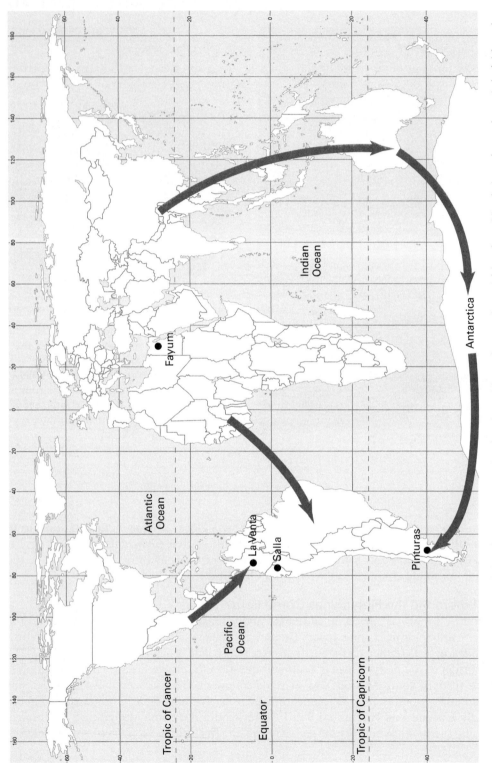

FIGURE 5-21 There are three possible migratory routes for the platyrrhine primates; from Africa, from North America or from Asia (either via Australia and Antarctica, or Africa). At the time we estimate the first primates to have reached South America, the continent was an isolated island, and any route required extensive water crossing, which is difficult to explain. With the evidence at hand, the most parsimonious source for the platyrrhine primates is Africa.

had to traverse a sizable expanse of water. How they managed to do it and get there is a conundrum (see Box 5-4).

The most popular hypothesis is that the first American haplorhines came from Africa. This is because it is easier (more parsimonious) to explain an African origin of these primates than it is to consider the alternatives. First, although the distance between the two continents was greater than in any of the other cases, the wind and ocean currents were more favorable for a speedy crossing. Second, there are many phylogenetic affinities between haplorhine fossil finds from North Africa and the earliest finds in South America.

North America is considered a less likely site of origin in part because we have no evidence of haplorhines ever living there (before humans that is). However, the lack of fossil evidence may not be as strong of an argument since areas such as Mexico have not yet been explored. A strong strike against North America is the fact that even though the water barrier between North and South America may have been a smaller expanse, the ocean currents would have made any crossing difficult. Possibly, the more difficult aspect to defend is that if North America were the source of the South American monkeys, haplorhines would have to have evolved twice from a strepsirhine stock. This means that the similarities seen in today's American and African-Asian haplorhines are due to convergence, which is not a very likely evolutionary scenario, but is one that cannot yet be ruled out.

Since fossil haplorhines (the eosimiids, see above) have been found in Asia, it must also be considered that the stem haplorhine could have been Asian, and simultaneously spread both toward Africa and South America. How such a progenitor primate population would have made the journey to South America becomes a rather convoluted affair, as they would have had to pass from Asia to Australia to Antarctica and then to South America. Both Australia and Antarctica were covered in thick forests, providing a favorable environment. To date no fossil evidence of primates has been found on either the Australian or Antarctic continents. However, it appears that some rodents did manage to pass from Asia to South America via Australia and Antarctica (Huchon and Douzery 2001), so it is possible that primates also traveled the same route. An alternative route for Asian haplorhines was via Africa, which would introduce the same problems as mentioned above. Obviously, much more research has to be done in order to solve the mystery of the origin of the South American haplorhines.

Another aspect that has been discussed extensively is whether the progenitor to the platyrrhines arrived once or if there were multiple "invasions." That is, are the crown platyrrhines monophyletic or paraphyletic (= more than one lineage)? The possibility that primates would make it across the ocean once is almost unbelievable, but to think that this may have happened repeatedly boggles one's mind. It has been suggested based on the morphological diversity of the extant species that some platyrrhine groups may derive from different gene pools. For example, the callitrichids (marmosets, tamarins, and Goeldi's monkey) have some traits that have been considered as ancestral (clawlike nails, loss of third molar, triangular maxillary molars; Martin 1990, 1992). However, as we learn more about fossil species, it is clear that many of the traits we observe in the callitrichids are derived features, and are the result of derived adaptations. Recent biomolecular data have confirmed that the callitrichids are a more recently evolved group (Goodman et al. 1998). In contrast, it appears that the

Callicebus (titi monkey), *Saimiri* (squirrel monkey), and *Cebus* (capuchin monkey) groups are the ones retaining the most ancestral or plesiomorphic traits. Thus, the living platyrrhines most likely derive from a single population of primates that somehow made it across the ocean.

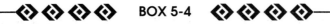

◈ ◈ ◈ ◈ BOX 5-4 ◈ ◈ ◈ ◈

How Far Can Primates Travel over Water?

It is often difficult to explain how animals reached far-off islands before humans provided a means of transportation. We have primates that have reached islands located far from the mainland. Not many terrestrial animals like water, and few would set out to swim long distances. Primates are especially unlikely to venture out into deep water (but see below). Consequently, we need to look for alternative explanations, such as there must have been some sort of land bridge that facilitated migration to new grounds.

We know that during ice ages the oceans' water levels are lowered due to extra water being confined in the expanding ice sheets. At such times, the ocean's water level is estimated to have been lowered by several hundred meters, which would make it possible for animals to migrate across newly exposed land. However, there are places, such as Madagascar, Sulawesi (in Indonesia), and South America, where such explanations do not work because even a reduced sea level would not provide the necessary land access. There are simply no mountains under the oceans that would have been exposed to provide land bridges to these places. Instead, it has been suggested that primates reached these locations by rafting across the watery expanses (MacFadden 1980).

In places where heavy seasonal rains bring about flash floods, swollen rivers can transport much debris. Trees growing in mangrove swamps are poorly anchored by roots and are easily uprooted during heavy storms or floods. Small islands with trees and vegetation have been observed floating far beyond the mouth of rivers. Trees uprooted by hurricanes can provide shelter and transport for animals, as was recently observed when alien iguanas arrived on islands in the Lesser Antilles (Censky et al. 1998). It is therefore possible that small mammals can be transferred from one place to another by such means (Calsbeek and Smith 2003). Of course, distance is a problem. Most mammals require water almost on a daily basis and would not survive a long ocean voyage. Houle (1999) has estimated that if both wind and ocean currents were favorable, it might not take a floating island more than seven to ten days to reach South America from the west coast of Africa. That is within the range of possibility for a primate to avoid dehydration or starvation during such a journey. Alternatively, the primate species that made the migration may have been able to enter into a state of semi-hibernation like the dwarf lemurs (*Cheirogaleus*) of Madagascar. It was also important for the survival of the species that the founder population

(continued)

minimally consists of a pregnant female or a few individuals of both sexes.

In general, primates are not fond of water and avoid it except to drink (Box 4.2). This is mainly due to a fear of predators (e.g., crocodiles, monitor lizards). However, there are exceptions. The proboscis monkey (*Nasalis larvatus*) lives in the mangrove forests of Borneo. These monkeys spend a lot of their time in the water moving between foraging sites. There is even a story about one adult male who was observed far away from land in the South China Sea. Talapoins (*Miopithecus talapoin*),

the smallest of the forest guenons, live in swampy forests by rivers and are known to drop into the water when scared and quietly swim to safety. Some of the introduced rhesus macaques (*Macaca mulatta*) on Cayo Santiago in the Caribbean occasionally decide to migrate to other islands by swimming across. With these cases we see that primates may utilize the sea as a platform for migration; however, the distance traveled in these examples is minor compared to the distance required to get to the South American continent.

The First Catarrhines

By late Eocene to early Oligocene times, we encounter haplorhine primates in Africa and Arabia that have only two premolars. This signals that platyrrhines and catarrhines had diverged (Table 5-3). It is important to remember, however, that these early basal catarrhines had not yet differentiated into crown taxa, the lineage leading to the extant African-Asian monkeys and apes. Even though they had evolved beyond the basal haplorhine stage, they were still very much generalized plesiomorphic haplorhines. It is their dental formula that sets them apart and defines them as catarrhines. Within this first catarrhine group some researchers include both the Oligopithecidae and the Propliopithecidae families, while others prefer to downgrade the oligopithecids to basal haplorhines despite the fact that they have lost a premolar tooth.

The oligopithecids appear at the end of the Eocene. Two genera belong to this family, both being rather small animals: *Catopithecus* (600–800 g or 1.3–1.8 lbs) and *Oligopithecus* (1–1.5 kg or 2.2–3.3 lbs). The oligopithecids have a strange mosaic of ancestral and derived traits. Aside from having a catarrhine dental formula (2:1:2:3), the shape and form of their cheek teeth is more similar to insectivorous strepsirhines, and it has been suggested that the primitive state of their cheek teeth may be a secondary

TABLE 5-3	Morphological Traits that Distinguish Platyrrhines From Catarrhines		
Character		*Platyrrhines*	*Catarrhines*
Teeth	Premolars	3	2
	Nose	Broad	Narrow
	Ear	No bony tube	Bony tube
Skull	Bony articulation	Zygomatic in contact with parietal	Frontal in contact with sphenoid

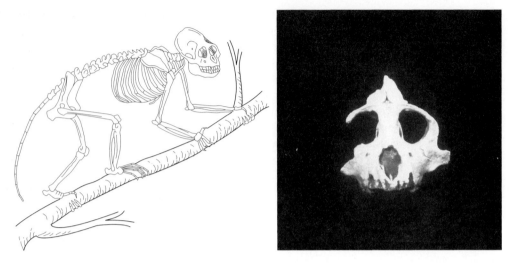

FIGURE 5-22   The propliopithecid *Aegyptopithecus zeuxis* is the second most commonly found fossil primate in the Fayum. It was a large, robust qudrupedal arboreal species (left). Sexual dimorphism is prominent in this species. Older individuals had large sagittal crests on the skull (right).

adaptation to insectivory (Gheerbrant et al. 1995). Due to the older age of the oligopithecids, it has tentatively been suggested that they (i.e., *Catopithecus)* gave rise to the early Oligocene propliopithecids (Seiffert et al. 2000).

The most famous of the propliopithecids of the early Oligocene is *Aegyptopithecus zeuxis* (Figure 5-22), the second most well-represented fossil primate from the Fayum deposits of Egypt. Many complete skulls and much postcranial material have been recovered. *A. zeuxis* was a large (6–8 kg or 13–18 lbs), robust arboreal quadruped that most likely survived mainly on leaves and fruits. We may infer that its diet was tough because in older individuals prominent bony crests can be seen on the skull where muscles for mastication attach. Simons (1987) argues that *Aegyptopithecus* is on the line leading to later apes. *Propliopithecus* was smaller (4 kg or 8–9 lbs), and its teeth suggest a more frugivorous diet. In this group we see significant sexual dimorphism in canine size. Maybe they lived in large social groups in which competition for females was common, such as what we see in present day baboons. Whether the propliopithecids gave rise to the pliopithecids (see below) can neither be confirmed nor ruled out.

Ephemeral Catarrhines

When discovered in the nineteenth century, *Epipliopithecus vindobonensis* was considered to be the ancestor of gibbons because of many shared features of the head and face, e.g., short muzzle, deep jaw, **orthognatic face**. It was suggested that this species lacked a tail, but more recent examinations have confirmed the presence of a small tail (Ankle 1965). Now we know that the Pliopithecoidea superfamily, which includes the Pliopithecidae and the Crouzeliidae families (Begun 2002), is a basal group of catarrhines that flourished in the middle to late Miocene (7 to 17 mya). It is speculated that the ancestors of this group of primates migrated out of Africa around 17 mya. Members of this group reached both Asia and Europe, but it was in Europe where the major adaptive radiation took place. As far as we know, there are no survivors and this group represents only distant relatives of living catarrhines.

The very large Pliopithecoidea group (9 genera; 16 species) was diverse in both size (ranged from 3 to 20 kg or 7–44 lbs) and dietary adaptations (frugivores to folivores).

> **orthognathic face**—when the forehead and chin are in the same vertical plane, i.e., flat face, opposite to prognathic face in which the muzzle is elongated and projecting

Laccopithecus is found in China and dates to the late Miocene. It was almost twice as large as *Epipliopethecus vindobonensis* (12 kg vs. 7 kg or 15 vs. 26 lbs). It was also gibbon-like but this is once again based on ancestral traits and cannot be considered a phylogenetic link. The shared plesiomorphic traits may simply reflect similar ecological adaptations. It is possible that the pliopithecids descended from the propliopithecines of Egypt. However, it is difficult to say for sure because only ancestral traits are shared between the two groups, and these traits are also found in platyrrhines, some adapids as well as in some living strepsirhines (Begun 2002).

Basal Ape Catarrhines

The late Oligocene and early Miocene (15–25 mya) saw a major adaptive radiation of basal ape catarrhines. It is estimated, based on biomolecular data, that the lineages leading to apes and to cercopithecoid monkeys had diverged around 30 mya (Steiper et al. 2004). These basal ape catarrhines are found mainly in East Africa and form a paraphyletic group. Most of these early taxa have not yet reached a crown ape stage; they share few traits with living apes. Members of this clade are distinguished by having a plesiomorphic monkey-like postcranial skeleton, e.g., thorax is narrow and deep, lower back is elongated and flexible, and their cheek teeth have thin enamel. At present there is no consensus regarding how to classify these early taxa. Traditionally, they have been considered to be early apes or stem hominoids (Begun et al. 1997). More recently, Harrison (2002) suggested that the members of the two families Dendropithecidae and Proconsulidae should be considered as stem catarrhines, but distinct from the lineage leading to crown monkeys and to apes. We find most of these species in tropical rain forest habitats. They show evidence of having been generalized arboreal quadrupeds that ate mainly fruits, although some appear to have been more folivorous.

Among the Dendropithecids, the tiny East African *Micropithecus* (3–4 kg or 7–9 lbs) and its close relative from Asia, *Dionysopithecus*, are most curious because of their very gibbon-like faces and teeth. We do not yet know enough about this lineage to tell if there is a real phylogenetic relationship between them and extant gibbons. The most famous of the proconsulids belong to the *Proconsul* genus, which comprises four species that differ mainly in size. The most well-known of these is *Proconsul heseloni* because many fossil remains have been recovered of this species (Figure 5-23). These remains range in age from infant to adult, and among the adults there are both males and females represented. *Proconsul heseloni* was a relatively small ape (8–10 kg or 18–22 lbs) and a slow-moving, frugivorous arboreal quadruped (Rose 1995). It had a mixture of ape-like traits (e.g., robust grasping big toe, bicuspid premolars, Y-5 molar pattern) and monkey traits (e.g., unspecialized ankle bones, no bony ridge above the orbits, the shape and number of lumbar vertebrae suggest a more flexible lower back). There has been argument about whether this species had a tail, but the most recent conclusion is that it

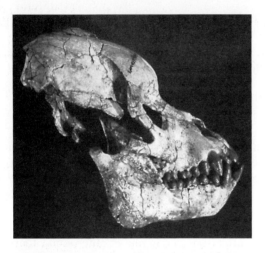
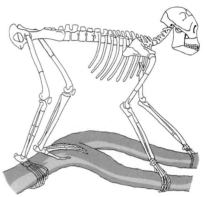

FIGURE 5-23 *Proconsul heseloni*, a mid-Miocene ape from east Africa. Many parts of its post-cranial skeleton have been found; it was a relatively small and slender ape, adapted to an arboreal existence, (right). In a side view of the skull (left) the lack of bony brow ridges is clearly visible.

lacked a tail (Nakatsukasa et al. 2004, Ward et al. 1991). What has been most confounding is the presence of air sinuses in the frontal bone, a derived trait only seen in living African apes and in humans. This is one of the reasons why, when it was first discovered, *Proconsul* was thought to be on the direct line leading to the earliest hominins (Walker 1997). Others have suggested that it may be a primitive ape that gave rise to later apes of more modern aspect (Rae 1999), or it may be another ephemeral species part of the early Miocene ape adaptive radiation (Harrison 2002). If the latter, it highlights that there was much parallel evolution in these early ape catarrhines.

The First True Apes

We recognize a "true" ape based on many morphological traits. They have molar teeth with a Y-5 cusp pattern, brow ridges with a prominent glabella (forward-projecting bony area in between the eyebrows), reduced number of lumbar vertebrae, and a less mobile lower back, while the shoulder and hip joints are more mobile (see Table 5-4 for a detailed list of how to recognize a true ape). The earliest "true" apes date from the early to middle part of the Miocene and are found mainly from sites in East Africa (Figure 5-24). These early apes were diverse, abundant, and fairly widespread. For a short time around 17 mya there was direct contact between Asia and Africa, and faunal interchange took place. Giraffes, rhinoceros, lions, and wild dogs moved from Asia into Africa. Many species moved from Africa into Europe at this time as well, e.g., members of the Pliopithecoidea superfamily (see above). Apes also migrated out of Africa into Europe, where they rapidly spread and diversified. Some species continued the migration via India and Pakistan to China. While Eurasian apes reached their zenith of taxonomic diversity, the fossil record of African apes becomes increasingly sparse. However, by 9 mya some of the European apes left and returned to Africa. There is a suggestion that it is from this European stock that the early hominins evolved (Begun 2002, Stewart and Disotell 1998).

TABLE 5-4   Morphological Traits That Distinguish Apes From African-Asian Monkeys

Character		*Apes*	*African-Asian monkeys*
Teeth	Molar cusps pattern	Simple, Y-5	Bilophodonty
Skull	Interorbital width	Wide	Narrow
	Mandible	Deep	Shallow
	Nose	Broad	Narrow
	Palate	Broad	Narrow
	Brain	Larger	Smaller
Body	Trunk	Short and relatively inflexible	Long and flexible
	Tail	Absent	Present

It is difficult to determine whether a species has crossed the threshold from being a stem catarrhine to being a stem hominoid. Many traits used in the past to determine relatedness, e.g., molar enamel thickness, have been discarded because they may reflect adaptations to diet rather than reflect ancestor-descendant relationships. Instead, we are now looking at postcranial traits, e.g., flexible shoulder and wrist joints, and shorter lumbar region adapted to orthogrady (erect back), to detect signs of ape evolution. Even though these first true apes retain some plesiomorphic monkey-like postcranial traits, they show increasingly derived traits, e.g., a shorter and less flexible lower back, and more mobility in the hip and shoulder joints.

The African Apes

The enigmatic *Morotopithecus bishopi* found in Uganda is the oldest fossil crown ape (20.6 mya). It is a fairly large ape (36–54 kg or 80–119 lbs; Gebo et al. 1997). While most of the early East African apes, the basal ape catarrhines, were arboreal quadrupeds, *Morotopithecus* shows an unusually mobile shoulder joint, and the lumbar vertebrae look very much like that of modern apes. Young and MacLatchy (2004) suggest that *Morotopithecus* is an early member of the great ape clade. They caution, however, that postcranial traits may not be reliable in recreating phylogeny as such traits may reflect adaptations to environmental conditions.

Afropithecus is of similar size to an extant male chimpanzee and lived in East Africa around 16–18 mya. It is a rather strange primate and differs from the basal apes that existed at the time. It had a long, narrow face with wide-set, small eyes, and a very robust jaw with big, square, flat cheek teeth that were covered with very thick enamel (possibly a derived ape trait). The dentition is reminiscent of the Eurasian *Sivapithecus,* a possible fossil relative of orangutans (see below), but the rest of its face was very unlike that of *Sivapithecus.* The shape of the face has led Simons (1987) to suggest an affinity to *Aegyptopithecus* from the Oligocene of the Fayum.

In the middle Miocene (14–16 mya) several species belonging to *Kenyapithecus* can be found in East Africa. *Kenyapithecus* has also been found in Europe—in Turkey—which is evidence of a link existing between Africa and Europe. It has been suggested that *Kenyapithecus* was terrestrially adapted (McCrossin and Benefit 1997); however, many postcranial traits relating to the shape of the elbow joint suggest a more arboreal adaptation (Nakatsukasa et al. 1998). It had thick, enamelled cheek teeth, suggesting a

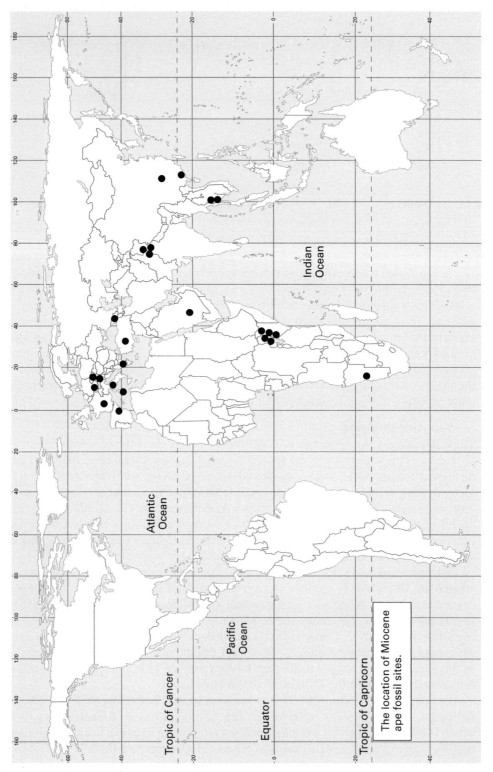

FIGURE 5-24 Distribution map of Miocene ape fossil sites.

move away from feeding on soft fruits to more tough food sources. This fits with the environmental changes that were taking place in East Africa at this time. Seasonal wood-land habitats were expanding while rain forest habitats were retracting.

Another species of uncertain status is *Otavipithecus namibiensis,* found in Namibia and dating to about 13 mya (Conroy 1999). *Otavipithecus* was a relatively small ape (14–20 kg or 30–44 lbs). The thin enamel on its cheek teeth ties this species to the middle Miocene and European *Dryopithecus.* However, as stated before, enamel thickness may not carry as much phylogenetic information as previously thought. *Otavipithecus* is unique in that it is the only hominoid fossil found in the southern hemisphere. To date all we have is a jaw fragment from this ape, and until we have more information it is difficult to do any phylogenetic reconstructions (Singelton 2000).

The Eurasian Apes

The European hominoids were a highly successful and diverse group. They existed from the middle to late Miocene and lasted for 8 to 9 million years. They were dispersed from Spain to Georgia. Some of these hominoids show affinity to earlier African species, while others do not. This group of apes is estimated to comprise nineteen different species belonging to ten or twelve genera (Begun 2002).

The oldest evidence of apes in Europe is *Pierolapithecus catalaunicus*, a middle Miocene (12.5–13 mya) ape from Spain (Moyà-Solà et al. 2004). A partial skeleton has been recovered of this species, representing an almost complete face as well as many important postcranial skeletal elements. It shares many derived facial features with extant apes (e.g., location of frontal processes, high zygomatic root, deep palate, the broad nasal opening). Its profile, however, shows a much more elongated face compared with living apes and is rather more similar to the early African basal ape catarrhines but also to *Morotopithecus.* The ribs together with a large and robust clavicle give good evidence that the thorax of *Pierolapithecus* was broad and shallow as seen in apes. It has been proposed that this species is closely related to the last common ancestor of extant hominids (Moyà-Solà et al. 2004).

Dryopithecus is a unique European genus. It is the most widespread (from Spain to Hungary) and well-recorded ape from the Miocene. The oldest remains have been found in France and date to 11–12 mya, while the remains from Spain are younger (9.5–10.5 mya). There are four species in this genus that range in size from 15–45 kg (33–100 lbs). *Dryopithecus* shows many derived ape traits, e.g., short lumbar region, prominent brow ridges, and mobile shoulder joints. It had a projecting face, which is a more ancestral trait. Possibly more unique is the very thin enamel on its cheek teeth and the rather delicate muzzle with relatively small and slender canines seen in some of the species. It has been suggested that at least the smaller species were arboreal frugivores (Kay and Ungar 1997).

The strangest of the European apes is *Oreopithecus*, a larger-bodied (30 kg or 66 lbs), highly specialized hominoid. It dates to the late Miocene (7–10 mya), and it appears to have been a geographical isolate found only in Italy. The remains show some affinity in the cheek teeth of the upper jaw to the East African proconsulid, *Nyanzapithecus* (Harrison and Rook 1997), but it also has some highly unique traits. In the upper jaw, the central incisors are large and rounded, while the lateral pair is peg-shaped. In the lower jaw, the molars have a sixth cusp. It appears to have been a dedicated folivore. The limb bones suggest that it was adept at suspensory locomotion, possibly even slow moving like a sloth (Susman 2005). However, a recent reanalysis of *Oreopithecus* hand bones led

Moyà-Solà and colleagues (2005) to suggest that it had an improved grasping capability especially for pincher grips similar to our own. It had a rather small brain, which may have been a secondary adaptation due to a diet comprised of low energy food.

Two other taxa found in Europe, *Ankarapithecus* and *Ouranopithecus,* are known mainly from craniodental remains. *Ouranopithecus* is from Greece and dates to the middle Miocene (10–11 mya). It was a large animal, estimated to have weighed around 60 kg (~132 lbs). *Ouranopithecus* is interesting because it shows closer affinity to African taxa than it does to other European species. It has been suggested that it shares some derived traits with later australopithecines (fossil hominins). deBonis and Koufos (1995) and Cameron (1997) even suggest that this species be included in the Homininae. *Ankarapithecus* was a large, generalized ape (30–60 kg or 66–132 lbs) from Turkey, dated to around 10 mya. Even though it shows some similarities to *Sivapithecus*, it is most likely not directly on the lineage leading to orangutans (see below).

The Lineage Leading to Orangutans

There appear to be quite a few ancient relatives of extant orangutans. *Sivapithecus* is found in Pakistan and India and dates to 8.6–9.2 mya (Pillans et al. 2005). *Sivapithecus* comprises three species, ranging in size from 40 to 90 kg (88 to 198 lbs). All have thick enamel on their cheek teeth. The similarity in shape and structure of the face and palate has been used to show a phylogenetic relationship between the orangutan and *Sivapithecus* (Cameron 1997, Pilbeam 1982). There has been a more recent reconsideration whether the shared facial traits that unite these two taxa are as valid as a phylogenetic link (Pilbeam et al. 1990), especially as dental characteristics show divergence. Furthermore, the morphology of a *Sivapithecus* humeral shaft suggests that *Sivapithecus* was a terrestrial quadruped, with no evidence of the suspensory adaptation of modern orangutans (Pilbeam et al. 1990).

The Chinese *Lufengpithecus*, dating from the latest part of the Miocene, may be closely related to *Sivapithecus*, while giganteus *Gigantopithecus* is thought to have evolved from *Sivapithecus*. *Gigantopithecus* is mainly known from teeth, which were first discovered in Chinese drugstores where they were sold as dragon bones, but more recent finds include some jaw bones. *Gigantopithecus* may be the largest ape ever to have lived (Figure 5-25). It is estimated that the older, late Miocene species *G. giganteus* weighed 150–190 kg (330–420 lbs) while the later Plio-Pleistocene species *G. blacki* weighed 225–300 kg (up to 660 lbs), although some even suggest it weighed twice as much (Ciochon et al. 1990a). Using a regression equation that estimates body mass based on tooth size alone (Conroy 1987) may be problematic, especially when applied to unique taxa like *Gigantopithecus*. When applied to the molar tooth size of the giant panda (*Ailuropoda melanoleuca*), the equation overestimates its body size, therefore some caution is warranted when attempting to estimate body mass based on tooth size alone.

However, we cannot get away from the fact that *Gigantopithecus* was large, and we assume that it was fully terrestrial, although no postcranial bones have ever been found. Its teeth are highly specialized. The molars have extremely thick enamel and the chewing surface is large and flat suggesting a tough diet. Possibly, it was a bamboo specialist just like the giant panda, but more recent results from microscopic examination of the teeth suggest a more varied but tough diet (Ciochon et al. 1990b). Remains of *G. blacki*, dating to 0.475 mya, have been found at a cave site in Vietnam together with remains of *Homo erectus* (Ciochon et al. 1996).

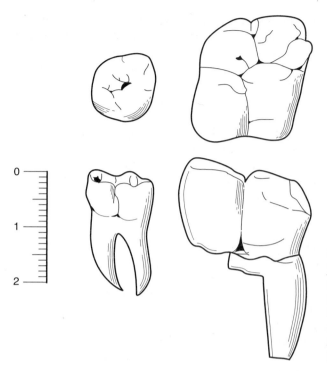

FIGURE 5-25 Only teeth and some jaw fragments have ever been found from *Gigantopithecus*. It was a very large ape, possibly the largest ever alive, as seen in this comparison of a *Gigantopithecus blacki* (right) molar with that of a human molar (left).

Recently, a new hominoid genus, *Khoratpithecus,* has been discovered in Thailand. The remains have been dated to the middle and late Miocene (Chaimanee et al. 2003, 2004). *Khoratpithecus* displays several shared derived traits with extant orangutans. Cladistic analyses based on cranial and dental features place the Asian *Sivapithecus, Lufengpithecus, Gigantopithecus,* and the European *Ankarapithecus* together in the *Pongo* clade (Begun 2002, Kelly 2002). Since *Khoratpithecus* displays all traits that unite these genera, it should also be included, possibly as a more direct ancestor of extant orangutans. If correct, it would therefore appear that the orangutan lineage has evolved within a tropical habitat similar to where they are found today.

What Happened to the Apes?

In the past, less attention was paid to the evolution of our living ape relatives. This is fortunately changing since it is important to understand why they took a different evolutionary path from our own lineage. We are beginning to fill in some of the gaps. We know that by 9 mya all of the apes disappeared from Europe. It is thought that climatic shifts to a cooler and more seasonal environment drove the European primates away. It is possible that they returned to Africa as has been suggested for species such as *Ouranopithecus.* Some found refuge in Asia. *Gigantopithecus blacki* was present in Asia well into the Pleistocene, with the youngest evidence dating to around 0.5 mya. Dental remains have been found of extinct orangutans dating to the Pleistocene from many countries in Southeast Asia, showing that their distribution used to be much greater than seen today. A complete skeleton of an adult female and some juvenile remains were recently found at a cave in Vietnam (Bacon and Long 2001). Even though these remains clearly belong to *Pongo*, we can see that the body proportions of this subfossil were different from extant orangutans. In the past orangutans had more slender limbs, with longer forearms, and their teeth were larger, indicating that this lineage underwent major changes in their adaptive niche.

For the African apes (gorillas, chimpanzees, and bonobos), we have close to no evidence linking the living forms to distinct fossil representatives. Recently, a few fossil teeth were discovered from middle Pleistocene deposits of the East African Rift Valley. These teeth show strong affinity with extant *Pan troglodytes* (McBrearty and Jablonski 2005). In addition to being our oldest evidence of fossil chimpanzees, they also show that in the past, chimpanzees had a wider distribution than seen in historical times. *Samburupithecus*, a late Miocene fossil recently found in Kenya (Ishida and Pickford 1998), may be related to gorillas as there are some shared facial traits. As we probe further and further back into our own ancestry, we must reach a point where we will encounter the ancestor we share with the chimpanzees, and along the way we will encounter unique chimpanzee ancestors as well. The closer we move toward the *Homo-Pan* divergence, the more similar the chimpanzee and human ancestors were, making it exceedingly difficult to determine the correct affinity. Transitional species usually have a mosaic of ancestral and derived traits, but the combination of these traits may be less predictive. In addition, it is very likely that there were several similar-looking lineages alive at the same time, which makes the reconstruction of our own evolutionary path much more difficult.

We have three fossil species to consider as potential stem hominins: *Ardipithecus ramidus* from Middle Awash, Ethiopia, is about 4 my old (Haile-Selassie 2001); *Orrorin tugenensis*, a 6 my old bipedal ape found in Kenya (Senut et al. 2001); and the most recent find from Chad, *Sahelanthropus tchadensis,* has been dated to between 6 and 7 my old (Brunet et al. 2002). The evidence we have from these species is limited, and most is highly fragmentary. *Sahelanthropus* provides an intriguing picture not only because of its age but the presence of some highly derived cranial traits, e.g., all four canines are small and only worn at the tip, and there is no space between the canines and premolar teeth (diastema). Furthermore, the bony ridge (**supraorbital torus**) was continuous across the forehead. Any conclusion in regard to whether any of these are our own ancestors, the ancestors of the chimpanzees, or maybe even predate the divergence between us, must await further evidence. We are, however, breaching the time when molecular information tells us that our two lineages parted evolutionary paths. Places such as Chad and Ethiopia are rich in potential fossil-bearing strata, and with time we may have the mystery of not only our own murky past solved, but also that of other extant apes. As we move closer in time along the path of human evolution, we do, of course, have much more information (a topic too great to be covered here, and which has been covered so well in other texts, e.g., Conroy 1999, McKee et al. 2005).

Basal Monkey Catarrhines

The first cercopithecoid catarrhines appear in the fossil record in the early part of the Miocene. As far as we can tell, they were not as common as the contemporary apes. Presently, fossils have been found only from localized sites in northern and eastern Africa. These basal cercopithecoids precede the division between cercopithecines (cheek-pouched monkeys) and colobines (leaf-eating monkeys). Like good transitional forms, they have a mixture of ancestral (mostly) and derived (few) traits. Even

FIGURE 5-26   *Victoriapithecus macinnesi*, a basal cercopithecoid, found in east Africa. Compared with extant monkeys, it had a smaller and less rounded skull, which showed prominent sagittal and nuchal crests.

though the cusp pattern on their cheek teeth is bilophodont (a derived trait), detailed features of the molars are quite plesiomorphic and not present in later taxa. Several features, especially on the skull, show strong affinity to the propliopithecine, *Aegyptopithecus* (Figure 5-22).

These basal cercopithecoids are divided into two genera: *Victoriapithecus* and *Prohylobates*. *Victoriapithecus* (Figure 5-26) was about the size of a cat (3–5 kg or 6.6–11 lbs). Its canines were sexually dimorphic, and its limb bones suggest that it was equally adept at moving about on the ground as in the trees, very much like present-day vervet monkeys (*Chlorocebus*). The skull was low and not as rounded as what we see in living monkeys, and it had prominent sagittal and nuchal crests. Even though its estimated brain size was compatible with contemporary species, it was smaller than that of living monkeys. While *Victoriapithecus* is represented by a single species, *Prohylobates* came in two different sizes, one smaller (7 kg or 15 lbs) and one larger (25 kg or 55 lbs). *Prohylobates* was adapted to a more frugivorous diet than *Victoriapithecus*, which appeared (based on dental microwear analyses) to have included harder objects such as seeds in its diet (Teaford et al. 1996). Benefit, who has extensively studied this genus, suggests that *Victoriapithecus* was not the ancestor of later monkey lineages, but rather it was a sister group that disappeared without leaving any descendants (Benefit 1999, Benefit and McCrossin 2002; see Box 5-5).

In the middle part of the Miocene we have an almost complete blank in the cercopithecoid fossil record. What we see is mostly apes or members of the pliopithecines (see above). It is not until toward the latter part of the Miocene that we begin to pick up fossil evidence again. By this time, the cercopithecines and the colobines had diverged. The most obvious physical traits that distinguish the two groups (the colobines' complex stomach and the cercopithecines' cheek pouches) consist of soft tissue that does not survive in the fossil record. We still have a few distinguishing traits that can be used to separate the two groups, e.g., intraorbital width, presence of shearing crests on molar teeth, length of muzzle, and the length and shape of the hands and feet. The trouble is that the early species are much more generalized, and the clear distinction we recognize between living species is not as obvious in the fossil species. This makes any inference of relatedness quite challenging.

The First Cercopithecines

We find very few fossil monkeys in the early to middle Miocene aside from the Victoriapithecidae, and it is not until the latest part of the Miocene that they make themselves known again. By then they are quite widespread and diverse (Figure 5-27). Based on biomolecular data, we surmise that leaf-eating monkeys had diverged from cheek-pouched monkeys at least by 12 mya, African and Asian colobines had diverged by about 10 mya, and by ~7 mya colobines were relatively common in Asia (Stewart and Disotell 1998). We know that the cercopithecines had their origin in Africa, but if the first modern cercopithecines did not evolve out of the Victoriapithecidae family, then their origin is at present unknown to us. The oldest evidence of modern African-Asian monkeys is a late Miocene macaque found in Egypt (*Macaca libyca*). By early Pliocene (5.5 mya) the macaques had spread into Europe (see Figure 5-27). This was made possible because around 5.3–6 mya the Mediterranean Sea was drying up due to an uplift at Gibraltar that blocked the flow of water from the Atlantic (Duggen et al. 2003, Krijgsman et al. 1999). For a while there were land bridges that provided access for animals to move between the two continents. Northern Africa experienced a drying-up period beginning about 7 mya that resulted in the Sahara desert as a barrier between the northern part and the rest of the continent (Schuster et al. 2006). It is assumed that it was at this time that the original cercopithecine stock was divided into the macaque lineage and the baboon lineage (the papionins).

The environmental conditions must have been very favorable for the macaques as they spread throughout south and central Europe and got as far north as England. The macaques did not make this migration alone, colobines as well as apes also made the move north (see below). Macaques were present in Europe until fairly recent (est. 100,000–200,000 years ago). An increasingly consistent cold climate may have finally put an end to the European macaques. They had moved east into Romania and Russia, and their track east was fast. By early Pleistocene, they had made it all the way across to China, and during the Holocene they spread widely all over Asia (Jablonski 2002).

The first macaques to make it into Europe, and the later African ones, were nearly indistinguishable from present-day Barbary macaques (*Macaca sylvanus*), the only macaque species still found in Africa. It was not until they reached Asia that they underwent an adaptive radiation and diversified. By the mid to late Pleistocene, Asian macaques looked more or less the same as extant species. To this day, macaques have retained a generalized body plan reminiscent of the earliest cercopithecine catarrhines. The macaque genus has been very successful, and they are the only cercopithecines to successfully invade three continents, although presently they are predominant in Asia, where they are widespread.

The earliest and most ancestral of all papionins was *Parapapio* of the late Miocene–early Pleistocene. It is thought that *Parapapio* gave rise to two lineages: one that led to mandrills and mangabeys, and one that led to geladas and baboons (Jablonski 2002). Initially, the most successful group of the papionins were the gelada or *Theropithecus* group. Today, only a single species survives in Ethiopia, while in the past

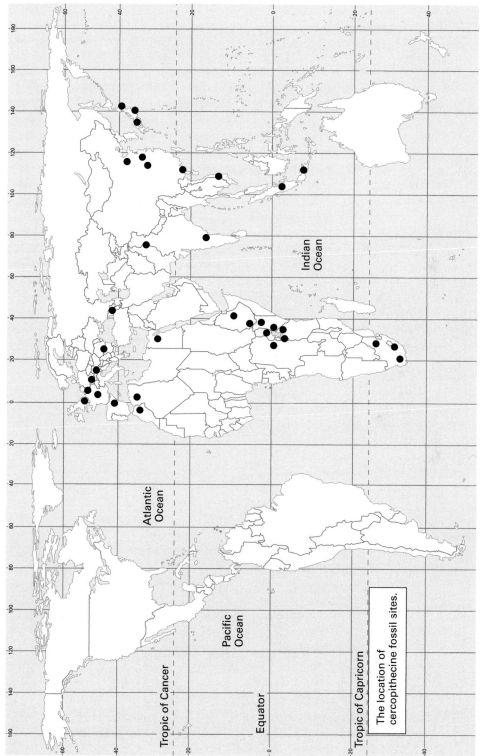

FIGURE 5-27 a Map showing the distribution of Miocene monkey fossil sites. a) cercopithecines, b) colobines.

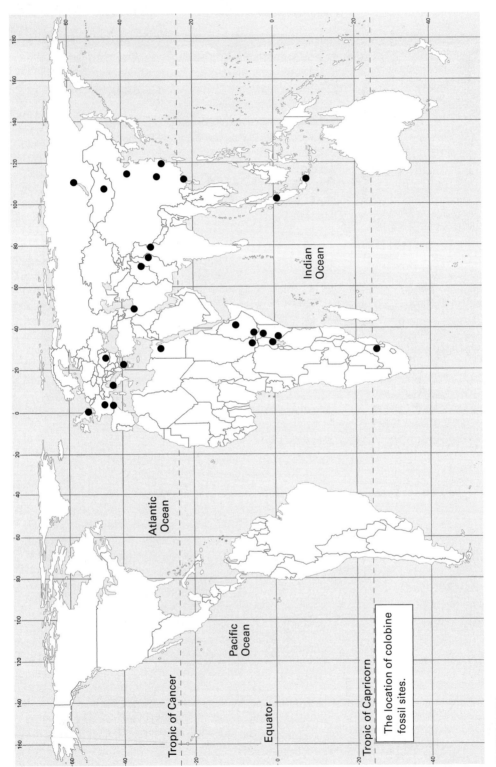

FIGURE 5-27 b

The location of colobine fossil sites.

Atlantic Ocean

Pacific Ocean

Indian Ocean

Tropic of Cancer

Equator

Tropic of Capricorn

188

(a)

FIGURE 5-28   *Theropithecus oswaldi* was an enormous monkey weighing up to 100 kg. They had a typical baboon-shaped face (a). Their teeth were adapted to a grass-based diet, and there was great sexual dimorphism in the species as seen in the very large canines present in males, and the honing facet on the third premolar (b).

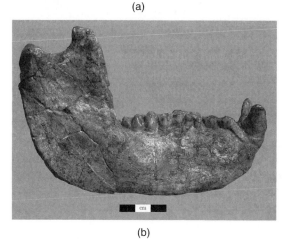

(b)

they were the most common monkey in eastern and southern Africa. There is even evidence that some made it across to Europe and India (see references in Jablonski 1993).

Theropithecus of the Plio-Pleistocene was highly specialized for life on the ground (Jablonski et al. 2002). It had specialized teeth that indicate a diet of grass blades and seeds. Some of these monkeys grew to quite remarkable sizes. *T. brumpti* was twice as large as any living baboon (50 kg or 110 lbs). This species was more common in the early reign of the geladas but declined later and was replaced by *T. oswaldi*, an enormous animal weighing up to 100 kg (220 lbs) (Figure 5-28). Changes in habitat structure may have caused this switch, because *T. brumpti* was associated with gallery forests along rivers, an ecosystem that became sparse in the later Pleistocene, while open grassland habitats became more common to the benefit of *T. oswaldi*.

Baboons, of the genus *Papio,* were much less common in the past than today. The oldest fossil has been found at Laetoli in Tanzania and dates to 3.7 mya (Jablonski 2002). These early baboons were also much bigger than extant forms, and they showed clear evidence of sexual dimorphism. Other African monkey species, such as the guenons, mandrills, and mangabeys, have an almost unknown past. They most likely lived in the tropical rain forest where little if any fossilization occurs. We suspect, based on biomolecular studies, that the guenons are a fairly recent phenomenon. Guenons experienced an adaptive

TABLE 5-5 Morphological Traits That Distinguish Colobines From Cercopithecines

Character		*Colobines*	*Cercopithecines*
Teeth	Incisors	Narrow	Broad
	Molar cusps	High	Low
Skull	Interorbital width	Wide	Narrow
	Mandible	Deep	Shallow
Digestion	Cheekpouches	Absent	Present
	Gastrointestinal tract	Complex	Simple
Tail		Long	Shorter

radiation in the last 1 to 2 million years, and the oldest guenon fossil dates to <3 mya (Gautier-Hion et al. 1988).

The First Colobines

The first clearly definable colobines, or leaf-eating monkeys, that we come across at the end of the Miocene are much less specialized than living species (Table 5-5). They were, however, much more diverse, had a wider distribution, and were often much larger in size. Today, we find colobines mainly in Asia with a few remnant species in Africa. In the past they were numerous in both places, plus they were present in Europe. They possibly made it to Europe ahead of the macaques.

The two oldest species of African colobines (*Microcolobus* and *Libypithecus*) were small— around 4 kg (~8–9 lbs)—and generalized monkeys that retained many early cercopithecoid traits. For example, their faces were more macaque-like than colobine-like. The only way we can tell for sure that they were leaf-eating monkeys is by the shape of their lower jaw (it is deeper) and their cheek teeth (the cusps are tall and sharp). These early colobines appear to have been more adapted to a life on the ground, feeding on seeds. It was not until later that they moved into the trees and focused their feeding on leaves. The appearance of highly successful terrestrial cercopithecines may have forced colobines into the trees.

Mesopithecus is the oldest European colobine (Figure 5-29). It was very successful and survived in southern Europe throughout the Pliocene. By at least 8.5 mya it had also spread into Asia. It was a medium-sized monkey of 5–8 kg (11–18 lbs). Based on the postcranial remains, it most likely spent more time on the ground than in the trees. *Mesopithecus* could possibly be a direct ancestor to all the extant Asian colobines (Jablonski 2002). Today, colobines are more diverse and widespread in Asia with only a few remnant species in Africa. This was not the case in the past. During the Pliocene and Pleistocene there were many more colobines present in Africa. Some of these reached quite giant sizes, e.g., the East African *Paracolobus* weighed around 30 kg (66 lbs) and *Rhinocolobus* around 20 kg (44 lbs).

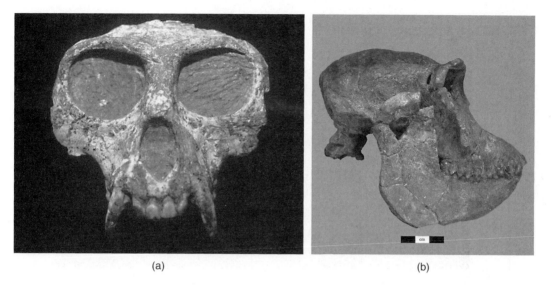

(a)   (b)

FIGURE 5-29 *Mesopithecus* is the oldest European colobine. It also made it to Asia and may be the ancestor to all living Asian colobines. Shown is a skull of *M. pentelici* from Greece (a). *Rhinocolobus turkanaensis* (b) was a giant colobine present in Plio-Pleistocene east African forest habitats.

❖ ❖ ❖ ❖   BOX 5-5   ❖ ❖ ❖ ❖

Paleoenvironmental Reconstruction: Maboko, a Case Study

The island of Maboko is located in Lake Victoria in Kenya (Figure 5-30). It has provided us with one of the richest sources of primate species fossils dating from the Miocene. The most common primate from Maboko is *Victoriapithecus macinnesi*, a basal cercopithecoid, and a sister group to all living cercopithecoids (Benefit 1999, Benefit and McCrossin 2002). The rarest find is *Komba winamensis*, until recently the oldest bushbaby fossil yet found (McCrossin 1992; see above). There are also several basal apes (*Limnopithecus evansi, Mabokopithecus clarki, M. pickfordi, Simiolus leakeyorum*) and a hominoid ape (*Kenyapithecus (Equatorius) africanus*) recovered from the island. A long list of nonprimate fossil animals has also been recovered (Retallack et al. 2002).

The geology of Maboko Island, the Maboko Formation, stretches along the Nyanza rift valley and includes sites such as Fort Ternan, Songhor, and the Rusinga Island (Retallack et al. 1995). Thus during the Miocene this area was continuous and not covered by a lake as seen today. In the Miocene, Maboko was surrounded by several active volcanoes, such as Kisingiri, which on occasion spewed ash over the area. This volcanic material is useful for dating the fossiliferous strata, placing the Maboko Formation within 13.8 to 14.7 mya band (Retallack et al. 2002). However, the fossil bones have been found below the 14.7 mya marker, and it is estimated that the base of the formation is about 17 my old (The Paleobiology Database). The recovery of fossil remains of any primate species is, of course, of great importance. It

(*continued*)

FIGURE 5-30 Excavations have taken place on the island of Maboko for close to 70 years. A view from of an old excavation site on Maboko dug by among others LSB Leakey. Lake Victoria can be seen in the background.

is possible to gain much information from studying the morphology of the skeletal remains. For example, it is possible to estimate locomotor adaptation from shape and size of longbones, and diet adaptation from examining the teeth both macroscopically and microscopically. However, to gain deeper insight into the lives of past species, there needs to be a better understanding about what kind of environment they lived in, what they ate, who they shared their home range with, who the competitors were, and the predators from which they may have had to run and hide.

Most major fossil research projects today use a holistic approach to the excavation process. The aim is not only to find primate fossils, but attention is paid to all fossil remains, both macrofauna and microfauna. In addition, the soil is carefully sampled, in part to salvage any pollen or other plant remains that may be present, but also to determine the soil type, which is directly related to the vegetation that once existed on it. However, before any excavation can take place, the area must be mapped and

the stratigraphy of the rock outcrop recorded in detail, to determine sequence of deposition, and if possible, to collect samples for dating (Figure 5-31).

Faunal analysis is a very important aspect of the reconstruction of a fossil site. Since the list of potential fauna is immense, many different experts are called in to help with identification. Researchers tend to specialize and have expertise in various taxa, e.g., rodents, bovids (cow-like animals), pigs, or snails. The record of what specific species are present in a soil layer provides a direct link to identifying the habitat type because most species occupy a fairly narrow niche. By studying the functional morphology of the remains, it is possible to determine if the species lived in trees or was terrestrial—information that contributes towards the general picture.

To reconstruct what plants grew on the ancient soils (**paleosols**), scientists often use stable isotopes, especially carbon and oxygen isotopes. For example, it is possible to discriminate between

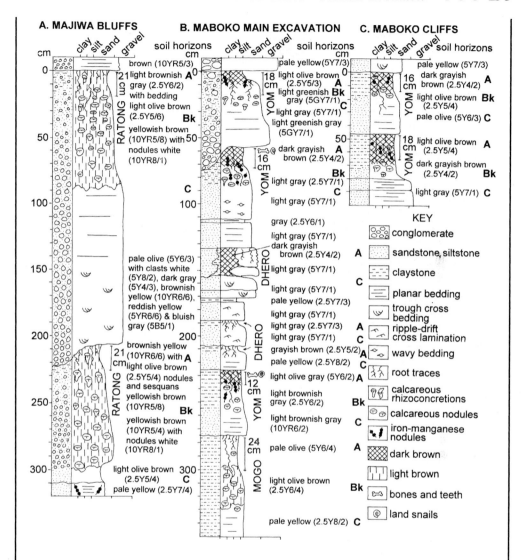

FIGURE 5-31 Schematic illustration of the stratigraphic columns of different types of rock found at the Maboko excavation site.

plants that rely more on rarer and heavier carbon (^{13}C) for their photosynthetic pathway, and those plants that utilize more common and lighter carbon (^{12}C). Plants that utilize more ^{13}C, so-called C_4 plants, comprise mostly tropical grasses. The plants that utilize more ^{12}C, so-called C_3 plants, include most trees, bushes, and herbs. There is a third group, the so-called CAM plants, which show an isotopic signature between the C_4 and C_3 plants. CAM plants are mostly found in wetter locals and in marine environments. Animals that eat these plants incorporate the different isotopes into their bones and teeth. It

(continued)

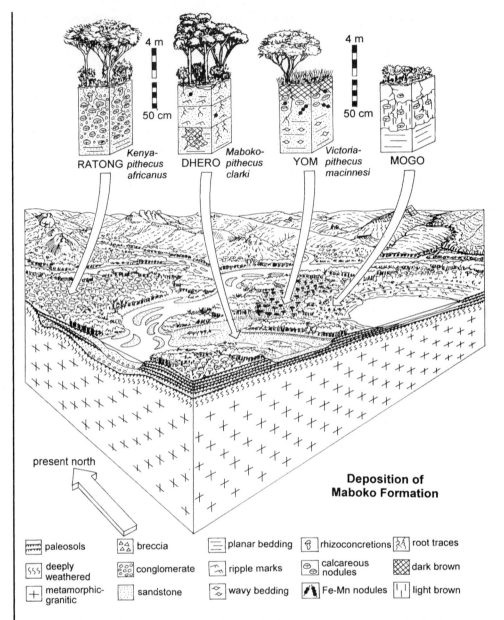

FIGURE 5-32 A schematic reconstruction of the habitats present at Maboko in the middle Miocene.

is therefore possible to use fossil bones and teeth to extract information about the habitat where the animals lived (e.g., Cerling and Harris 1999, Lee-Thorp et al. 2003).

At many locations it is possible to extract plant pollens from the soil. Pollens from specific taxa tend to have unique appearances, making it possible to determine, at least to the genus level, what plants occupied the area. Plant parts, e.g., leaves and stems, can also fossilize and give a direct indication of species present in an ancient environment.

Petrographic and geochemical analyses of paleosols on Maboko have revealed four distinct soil types: the Dhero, Mogo, Ratong, and Yom (Figure 5-31). Within the Dhero, ripple marks are frequently observed, suggesting seasonal inundations. The soil in general suggests a riparian or gallery forest habitat along streams. These strata are rich both in number of species and number of individual fossil remains. Examples of the animals found include chevrotains (small, spotted ungulates that live in the African rain forest), hyraxes, pigs, and rodents. The Mogo soil was less common and gave evidence of an alkaline, clayey environment, similar to the soda lakes seen in East Africa today. No fossils are found within this soil due to the high erosive effects of soda on bone. The Ratong soil contains many calcium carbonate accumulations (calcareous nodules), indicating it was a rather arid habitat. It was more of a wooded scrubland with little ground vegetation (it is possible to determine the extent of grass cover by the existence of fossilized root mats). Elephant-like animals, giraffoids, and chevrotains are found within these habitats. Last, the Yom strata comprised a darker and more crumbly soil. There are traces of grass roots, and it is possible that this area was wooded grassland. There is evidence of extensive forest fires in this environment. Yom was rich in fossil remains, including elephant-like animals, giraffoids, rhinoscerous, bovids, and pigs.

The largest number of *Victoriapithecus* remains is found in the Dhero, a gallery forest environment, although they are also found in the Yom wooded habitat. The proconsulines and Oreopithcines are also found in Dhero gallery forest habitat, suggesting they were more arboreal. The bushbaby, *Komba*, is found in the Yom habitat. Only *Kenyapithecus* seems to have been more of a generalist and covered more ground, as seen by remains found in all four paleosols. Based on this information and the fossil remains, it has been possible to paint a picture of what the environment looked like when *Victoriapithecus* and *Kenyapithecus* were present (Figure 5-32). What is very interesting is that the climatic signatures from Maboko show a much more arid place compared with the surrounding areas of Rusinga Island and Fort Ternan. This suggests that Maboko may have been in a rain shadow or an area that receives little precipitation because of the effect of a barrier such as a mountain range that blocks the prevailing winds (Retallack et al. 2002).

❖❖ Summary

Reconstructing the evolutionary history of our own order has been a major task and preoccupation for a wide range of researchers over the decades. However, this reconstruction is fraught with difficulties. As humans, we like to impose order and organization over natural phenomenon, but it is difficult to assess the taxonomic value that particular morphologies may have had long ago. Moreover, we not only have to reconstruct the significance of these morphologies, but we need to reconstruct the physical environments in which they occurred and even try to infer behaviors relating to lifestyles that may have been associated with particular morphologies. In addition, when thinking about the evolutionary development of the order: primates, we have to disassociate from the diversity of species that we recognize today. For example, during the Miocene there were many more genera and species of apes alive on this planet than there were monkeys— the inverse of today's situation.

What we do know is that proto primates were around previous to the demise of the dinosaurs during the late phase of the Cretaceous. Once the dinosaurs disappeared from the earth, a wide range of previously occupied ecological niches became available to this ancestral stock of true primates. The first clearly recognizable primates, or euprimates, occurred during the early Eocene and were found throughout North America, Europe, and Asia. They were to some degree like the strepsirhines of today, but yet were clearly different from extant species. The first haplorhine primates occur throughout Africa and Asia during the Early to Middle Eocene around the same time as when the euprimates reach a peak in adaptive diversity. In fact, some very interesting sites from Asia may be shedding new light on the origin of the haplorhines. The platyrrhines and catarrhines eventually differentiate from the ancestral stock of haplorhines; however, one of the great mysteries remains in explaining how the early platyrrhines got to the isolated continent of South America.

During the late Oligocene through the beginning of the Miocene, we find evidence for early apes in the fossil record. Throughout the Miocene, apes were very numerous and diverse and were ultimately at the pinnacle of their evolutionary success. Eventually, the apes declined in number and kind, while there was an increased diversity in African and Asian monkeys, similar to what we see today. At the present time, researchers are still working to reconstruct the evolutionary history of primates; however, we are also focusing on trying to identify specific evolutionary links between extant and extinct primate species.

❖❖ Key Words

absolute date	gymnosperm plants	petrified
adaptive radiation	half-life	petrosal bulla
aerobic	hominoid	phenotype
anaerobic	homoplasy	plate tectonics
autapomorphies	hypocone	radiometric dating
basal species	isotope	relative ages
basal primates	Laurasia	stasis
character polarity	monophyly	strata
convergence	mosaic evolution	stratigraphy
crown species	mutations	subfossil
euprimates	orthognatic face	supraorbital torus
genotype	paleosols	synapomorphies
Gondwana	Pangaea	symplesiomorphies
Grande Coupure	parallel evolution	taphonomy

❖❖ Study Questions

1. How can we tell a strepsirhine primate from a haplorhine by examining the bony skeleton?
2. Why are dental formulae useful in inferring phylogenetic relationships?
3. Why is it important to reconstruct the environment within which a fossil species lived?
4. What is the difference between apomorphic and plesiomorphic traits, and which kind is best for inferring phylogenetic relationships?
5. By what means can animals reach far-off places, such as islands, without being transported there by humans? What are the survival factors that need to be taken into account?
6. Who were the euprimates? Where did they live, and what happened to them?
7. When and how did lemurs get to the island of Madagascar, and how do living forms compare with fossil species?
8. How do early African apes differ from later European forms?
9. Since the most obvious morphological traits that differentiate colobines from cercopithecines are soft tissue traits, what traits do paleontologists use to distinguish fossil species?
10. How do we recognize the earliest colobine monkeys, and how did they differ from extant forms?

❖❖ Suggested Readings and Related Web Sites

Begun DR. 2003. Planet of the apes. Scientific American 289(2):64–73.

Ciochon RL, Gunnell GF. 2002. Chronology of primate discoveries in Myanmar: Influences on the haplorhine origins debate. Yearbook of Physical Anthropology 45:2–35.

Conroy GC. 1990. Primate evolution. New York: WW Norton.

Conroy GC. 1999. Reconstructing human origins. A modern synthesis. New York: WW Norton.

Fleagle JG. 1999. Primate adaptation and evolution. New York: Academic Press.

Hartwig WC. editor. 2002. The primate fossil record. Cambridge: Cambridge University Press.

Miller ER, Gunnell GF, Martin RD. 2005. Deep time and the search for anthropoid origins. Yearbook of Physical Anthropology 48:60–95.

CHAPTER 6

Primate Ecology

The word ecology is derived from the Greek root *oikos,* which means "house." This creates a useful mental image, because when thinking about primate ecology, one needs to consider not only where primates live, but how they use and live in the environment in which they are found. In Chapter 3 the geographic distribution of primates was presented, and the major types of biomes that they occupy were identified. In this chapter we will examine how primates live within these environments.

198

❖❖ How Primates Use their Environment

As members of an ecological community, primates have evolved behavioral strategies to exploit resources essential for their survival and to maximize their reproductive success. Patterns of habitat use may be indicative of strategies that have evolved due to competition for resources. Competition can occur between individuals residing in the same social group (intragroup competition) or between different social groups of the same or different primate species (intergroup and inter-

> **affiliative**—friendly and prosocial behavioral interactions, such as staying in close proximity or grooming

species competition respectively), as well as with other animal species. Since primates are social organisms, the evolution of **affiliative** and cooperative behaviors may also have influenced their behavioral ecology (Sussman et al. 2005).

How primates use their habitat varies not only between species, but there may be differences between populations of the same species and even between individuals within the same group. External factors, such as the geographical location and the specific type of habitat occupied, may also impinge on habitat use. Furthermore, the presence or absence of other species, especially predators and competitors, exerts a strong influence on how primates use their habitat.

Three general patterns regarding the habitat use of primates have been identified over the years:

1. Frugivorous primates range over larger geographic areas than do folivorous primates. In a tropical rain forest leaves are a more abundant and predictable resource than are fruits because fruiting trees tend to be more dispersed and fruiting occurs seasonally; i.e., fruits are not always available.
2. Nocturnal primates tend to be smaller in body size than diurnal primates, and body size has an effect on dietary choices (see Chapter 4), ranging behaviors, and grouping patterns (see Chapter 7).
3. Primate species that live in small groups are more cryptic than those living in larger groups, which may reflect anti-predator strategies (Overdorff and Parga 2007).

Outside of these general patterns, there is no universal primate pattern of habitat use, and variability in behavioral ecology appears to be the rule (Strier 1994b).

❖❖ Ecology Basics

Ecology is the scientific study of the structure and function of nature (Odum 1963, Pianka 1994, Ricklefs 1973). The study of ecology entails the relationships that exist between all of the organisms that share a specific area in space, which we can refer to as a "house," as well as the specific features of the environment. In order to study the ecology of the house (or habitat), a series of questions has to be addressed:

1. What is the size of the "house" and the neighborhood in which it is found?
2. What is the specific location of the "house" within the neighborhood?
3. How is the space within this "house" partitioned; what is the arrangement of the "rooms" within the "house," and what type of structures are present?
4. How is the temperature maintained in the area, and how is it heated and cooled?

5. Where does water come from, and how is waste disposed of?
6. What and who comes in and out of the specific "household" area?
7. Where is food located, and when and how does food get there?
8. What do we know about the individuals who live in the "house," and how do they use it?

In sum, the entire range of abiotic and biotic factors that are contained within, may be introduced into, or expelled from the "house" all need to be considered when trying to understand the ecology of a specific location.

Ecology involves the study of all the parts that make up a *fluid* natural system. It is important to recognize that an ecological system is based on a feedback system. Factors that influence an ecological system enter into and leave this system continuously. There is a particular balance or **homeostasis** that has to be maintained in order for the system to keep functioning properly. Fluctuations within the system occur, but there is a limit to how much fluctuation may be tolerated by a system before it begins to deteriorate. Homeostasis entails a system of checks and balances. Our bodies, like those of other mammals, have homeostatic controls—physiological reactions, such as sweating or shivering, which occur when our bodies become either too hot or too cold. Similar mechanisms operate

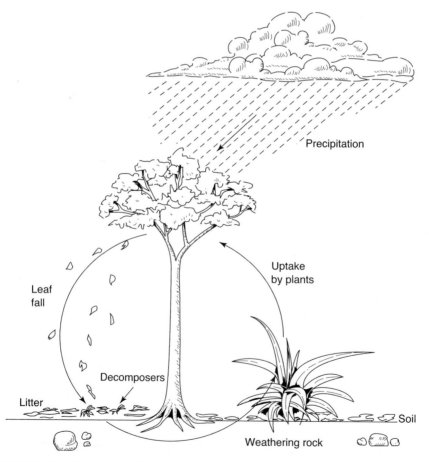

FIGURE 6-1 Illustration of energy exchange in an ecosystem (adapted from Ricklefs 1973, Whitemore 1984).

at the level of an ecosystem to regulate the exchange of energy (Figure 6-1). Primate ecology thus involves studying a community of organisms that live in a particular ecosystem, investigating how these organisms interact with one another, as well as with the physical environment or habitat in which they are found. It also involves studying how organisms react to fluctuations that may occur with in an ecosystem.

◈◈ The Components of an Ecosystem

Ecosystems are based on an intricate system of energy exchange. Abiotic components consist of energy that enters into the system via the sun. Other abiotic chemicals found in nature, such as oxygen, carbon, and hydrogen, are necessary for essential chemical processes such as photosynthesis to occur. There are two types of biotic components: **autotrophs** and **heterotrophs**. Autotrophs are organic and self-nourishing. Such organisms are able to utilize energy from the sun and other chemicals present in the atmosphere to produce food. Green plants are examples of autotrophs. Heterotrophs are organisms that utilize, rearrange, or decompose what the autotrophs have produced. Where light energy is readily available, the autotrophs are most active; however, they do occur in successive layers throughout an ecosystem. Heterotrophs are most active where organic matter has accumulated, such as in soils and leaf litter, but they occur in overlapping layers. In a rain forest, there is autotrophic activity at all levels, from the upper canopy to the ground. Immediately below the upper canopy, where energy is being converted into food resources by the autotrophs and distributed throughout the various levels of the forest, is a multitude of heterotrophs, such as birds, insects, fungi, etc. (Figure 6-2).

FIGURE 6-2   Distribution of autotrophs and heterotrophs in different forest levels.

Heterotrophs include consumers and decomposers. Consumers that eat other organisms, either plants or animals or both, are referred to as macroconsumers. Microconsumers are decomposers, such as bacteria and fungi that break down organic material. All heterotrophs play an essential role in maintaining homeostasis within an ecosystem. Ecosystems comprise a number of different trophic systems, and all autotrophs and heterotrophs belong to specific **trophic levels**. It is how an organism gains energy that determines its trophic level. Organisms that go through the same number of steps to obtain energy belong to the same trophic level. There are five primary trophic levels:

- Producers
- Decomposers
- Herbivores
- Primary carnivores
- Secondary carnivores

All producers, such as green plants, belong to the same trophic level. Animals, such as termites, that feed on dead organic matter are decomposers. Animals that eat living plants belong to yet another trophic level and are called herbivores, while animals that eat other animals are carnivores (Figure 6-3). Aardvarks that eat termites, are primary carnivores, like a lion that eats a wildebeest. However, a lion that eats an aardvark that has been eating termites would, in this food chain, be called a secondary carnivore. Primate diets are highly varied; they eat plant products, insects, and small vertebrates. Primates, therefore, belong to three different trophic levels—herbivore, primary, and secondary carnivore.

By simply describing the type of ecosystem that an organism lives in, the degree of complexity within that ecosystem may not be adequately presented. Often it is essential to assign quantitative values to delineate and measure the complex nature of an ecosystem. **Biomass** is one such quantitative evaluation, and it refers to the weight of organic matter present in any given trophic level. The biomass can also be expressed as the number of organisms present in a defined unit or area. **Population density** is another quantitative measure, which refers to the size of a specific population in relation to some unit of space, such as the number (n) of individuals of a specific species per square kilometer (km^2). Describing and counting the number of organisms that exist in an ecosystem is only a first step, but in order to understand the *effect* a population may have on a particular ecosystem, it is essential to know how many individuals exist within a defined space. The number of individuals of any specific species that a particular ecosystem can maintain without disrupting the homeostasis of the system is referred to as the **carrying capacity**. An evaluation of carrying capacity is useful for comparative studies of species

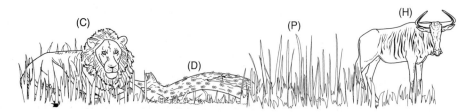

FIGURE 6-3 Illustration of trophic levels : Carnivore (C), decomposers (D), producers (P), and an herbivore (H).

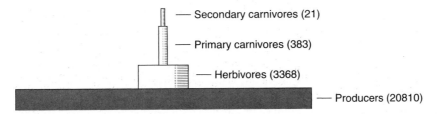

— Secondary carnivores (21)

— Primary carnivores (383)

— Herbivores (3368)

— Producers (20810)

FIGURE 6-4 Distribution of trophic levels ($Kcal/m^2/yr$) (adapted from Odum 1971).

living in different ecosystems. How many individuals of a species can a particular ecosystem support compared to another? What types of species can be supported in greater or lesser densities? Population densities are ultimately influenced by trophic level (energy flow) and by the actual body mass of the individuals. Trophic levels take on a pyramid-shaped distribution because any ecosystem can accommodate a higher number of decomposers than herbivores, which are more common than carnivores (Figure 6-4).

Habitat refers to the specific place in which an organism lives, while its **ecological niche** is the position that the organism occupies within an ecosystem. An organism's ecological niche describes its placement within the complex web of energy exchange that exists in an ecosystem. This position reflects the many evolutionary adaptations that an organism has made over time. Such adaptations are expressed in an organism's pattern of locomotion, diet, modes of food procurement, external handling and internal processing of food, behavioral cycles, reproductive patterns, etc.

❖❖ Factors That Limit Populations

Two principles that describe how the biomass and population density of organisms are affected are Liebig's "Law" of the Minimum (Liebig 1840) and Shelford's "Law" of Tolerance (Shelford 1913). Liebig discovered that the yield of agricultural crops was more likely to be limited by rare chemical elements as opposed to commonly occurring nutrients, such as water and carbon dioxide, which crops require in large quantities. Despite the fact that yields can be reduced when common and necessary resources are severely limited for extended periods of time, it is those resources that are in short supply and crucial for growth and survival that have the greatest constraining effect on a population. Therefore, any organism may be affected by the smallest link in its ecological chain of requirements. To maintain a stable population level, primates, like all living organisms, require adequate space, food, and water containing all essential nutrients, appropriate temperatures, and physical environments. Disease and predation are additional factors that may also limit population size.

Many primates living in tropical rain forests are predominantly frugivorous (Chapman 1995). Fruiting plant species usually produce fruits seasonally, but fruit production can be unpredictable and may even be irregular in a rain forest. Fruits, however, are typically not the smallest link in the chain of food requirements for primates. During times of fruit scarcity, the availability of alternative yet vital food resources, so-called **fallback food** sources—or those that are ignored when preferred foods are available—may become the most important limiting factors to a primate population (Hanya et al. 2006, Lambert et al. 2004, Sauther 1998, Terborgh 1983, 1986, Wrangham et al. 1998).

It is not only the lack of an essential resource that can be a limiting factor, but too much of some resource may also have a limiting effect on populations. Shelford's "law" of tolerance outlines the fact that any population is adapted to a limited range of ecological requirements. Some species have a more generalized adaptation, while others have a more specialized adaptation, or set of ecological requirements. Those species that are generalized have a broader range of ecological minimums and maximums that they can tolerate compared to species that are specialized and therefore have a more narrow range of tolerance (Krebs 1994, Pianka 1994). Species with very specific requirements are much less tolerant of fluctuations in any of their environmental parameters. Tolerance levels may also vary by season and location.

There is a very complicated and interrelated network of factors that may affect a given population. The macaque genus is a good example of a large group of closely related species that exhibit a wide range in ecological tolerances. Some macaque species are highly specialized, such as the lion-tailed macaque (*Macaca silenus*), while others such as the rhesus macaque (*M. mulatta*) are much more generalized (Ashmore-DeClue 1992, Richard et al. 1989). Within a species, living in different habitats and geographic locations, there can also be great between-population variability in ecological tolerances. In the case of the rhesus macaque, some populations live in relatively undisturbed tropical rain forests while others live in urban settings, e.g., villages and towns, along roadsides or canal banks (Southwick et al. 1965).

Ecologists and conservationists use the **niche breadth** of species (how generalized or specialized they are) to describe the range of factors that are limiting to a species under specific environmental conditions. Factors such as tolerance to climatic variability, changes in range size, and fluctuation in food resources are important to understand in order to define the present and future ecological requirements that must be secured for a species to survive. Generally, species with a broad niche and a wide geographic distribution tend to be found in higher population densities across their range. In contrast, species that occupy a narrow niche breadth and live in restricted ranges tend to be found in lower population densities (Chapman et al. 2006). While all may be susceptible to ecological threats, the latter are the ones that are most vulnerable.

◇◇ Species Interactions: Primates as Prey

Primates are part of an ecological community; consequently, their interactions with other species affect the ecological niche they occupy and may limit their population size. Interactions that primates have with members of different trophic levels include predator-prey or parasite-prey relationships. All primates are potential prey for other animals (Figure 6-5). Consequently, they have adapted anti-predatory strategies—such as defense or avoidance morphologies and behaviors that limit the success of a predator (see Miller 2002).

The majority of data on primates as prey are anecdotal. Accounts of primates being preyed upon are infrequent and random, and therefore difficult to quantify. Summaries of such accounts (Boinski et al. 2000, Hart 2000, 2007, Treves 1999) provide a list of a wide range of animals that prey on primates, including raptors (e.g., eagles and hawks), canids (e.g., wild dogs, jackals, and wolves), felids (e.g., leopards, lions, and tigers), viverrids (e.g., civets, genets, and the Malagasy fossa—carnivores that produce musk), hyaenids (i.e., hyenas), and reptiles (e.g., snakes, lizards, and crocodiles).

FIGURE 6-5 All primates are potential prey for other animals.

In the Kibale Forest of Uganda the crowned hawk-eagle (*Stephanoaetus coronatus*) specializes in preying on monkeys. Primates make up 84 percent of a crowned hawk-eagle's diet (Struhsaker and Leakey 1990), with a majority comprising immature red colobus monkeys. These eagles have been observed taking larger-bodied primates including subadult mandrills and bonobos, and even young human boys, and have been implicated in the deaths of early hominins (Steyn 1983 reported in Hart and Sussman 2005, McGraw et al. 2006). In Beza Mahafaly, Madagascar, mouse lemurs (*Microcebus*) are preyed on by the Malagasy long-eared owls (*Asio madagascariensis*). It is estimated that approximately 25 percent of the mouse lemur population is harvested annually by owls (Goodman et al. 1993). Body size alone is not an antipredator strategy because even gorillas can fall prey to leopards (Fay et al. 1995).

In all regions where primates exist, no matter if they are small or large in body size, nocturnal or diurnal, or terrestrial or arboreal, they may fall victim to predators. Consequently, through vocal and ranging behaviors, patterns of social groupings, locomotion styles, and activity cycles, primates have adapted to the ever-present threat of predation. These adaptations are reflected to some degree by the ecological niche that they occupy.

Primates are not only prey, they are also predators; primates prey on other primates. Chimpanzees, living in the Taï forest of West Africa and at Gombe in East Africa, hunt red colobus monkeys (*Piliocolobus*) and remove 8 to 13 percent of the population each year. Their successful hunting has a significant impact on the population size of red colobus monkeys (Boesch and Boesch-Achermann 2000, Goodall 1986, Stanford et al. 1994, and see discussion in Chapter 10 about hunting primates). Human predation can also have cataclysmic effects on populations of nonhuman primates (see Chapter 11).

Parasitic Predators

The interaction between parasites (predator) and primates (host) may influence the ecological niche and population density of primates. The interaction and competition that can occur between a parasite and its host often results in a homeostatic balance within which both manage to survive without eliminating one another. Most parasites are benevolent, and their presence does not cause any ill effects on the host. If a parasite causes the death of its host or limits its own reproductive potential within the host, this is ultimately a maladaptive strategy on the part of the parasite. If there is imbalance between host and parasite, the costs can be high and detrimental to both (Hart 1990, Holmes and Zohar 1990, Huffman 1997). Primates may exhibit behavioral adaptations to reduce or limit their exposure to potentially detrimental parasites, but it is difficult to determine cause and effect. Recently, researchers have started to focus on how primates self-medicate (Huffman 1997, 2001, 2007, Lozano 1998). These studies may shed light on the relationship between certain behaviors and health maintenance or improvement.

Primates can be negatively impacted by a wide range of parasites, including nematodes (worms), microparasites (protozoa, bacteria, viruses, and fungi), ectoparasites (e.g., ticks), and other biting insects. Baboons (*Papio ursinus*) living in a semi-desert scrub habitat in the Namib Desert of Namibia were found to exhibit a high infant mortality rate. In a four-year period eighteen of twenty-one infants died (Brain and Bohrmann 1992). The researchers observed that the baboons were infested with ticks; large numbers of ticks were attached to the baboons' ears, and they established tick counts for specified plots of habitat. One infant that died had a large number of ticks on its body, which supported the suspicion that ticks were contributing to the high infant death rate sustained by this population.

The avoidance of particular water sources or localities that are potentially infiltrated by parasites, the eating of medicinal foods, and the rubbing of the hair with plant material or insects may be behavioral adaptations that have been promoted because they yield direct benefits to the well-being and future reproductive potential of an individual (Huffman 2007). It has not been proven, however, that primates know that a particular behavior or a tendency to ingest secondary plant compounds may prevent, reduce, or even alleviate parasitic infection.

In the Mahale Mountains National Park, Tanzania, chimpanzees live in a semi-deciduous gallery forest that has a distinctive wet and dry season. During the wet season researchers observed that the number of chimpanzees infected with nematodes increased, and simultaneously noted a higher frequency in leaf-swallowing behaviors by the chimpanzees (Huffman et al. 1996). Repeated infection by nodular worms can be especially debilitating to large-bodied apes. Infected apes exhibit distress caused by severe abdominal pain, weight loss, weakness, malaise, diarrhea, and secondary infections can result in the death of an animal (Brack 1987). The eating of the pith of the plant *Vernonia amygdalina* by obviously sick individuals and their subsequent recovery was observed. The fecal material of one individual, monitored for parasitic load, showed a decrease in the number of eggs (per gram fecal material) from 130 to 15 within a twenty-hour period after the chimpanzee was seen eating from the *Vernonia* plant (Huffman et al. 1997).

Primates also topically apply plant material or insects (millipedes and ants) to their bodies. "Fur rubbing," "peat-bathing," and the "self-anointing" of the body has been observed in capuchin monkeys (*Cebus capucinus*) and (*C. olivaceus*); spider monkeys, (*Ateles geoffroyi*); owl monkeys (three species of *Aotus*); and black lemurs (*Eulemur macaco*) (Baker 1996, Birkinshaw 1999, Campbell 2000, Longino 1984, Ludes and Anderson 1995, Richard 1970, Valderrama et al. 2000, Zito et al. 2003). This behavior consists of the frenzied rubbing of the hair all over the body with chewed or unchewed plant material or insects. The rubbing behavior of white-faced capuchin monkeys living in

Costa Rica was studied by Baker (1996). These capuchin monkeys used at least four different plant species, "fur rubbing" occurred as a group activity or on an individual basis, and the behavior was observed more often in the wet season than in the dry season. Since heat and high humidity levels are associated with the wet season, it is suggested that this behavior might reduce the risk of bacterial and fungal infections.

The behavioral ecology of primates related to host-parasite interactions may yield interesting results. However, such a study will require long-term, close, and systematic monitoring of primate groups; an understanding of the phytochemical properties of plants, insects, and soil consumed; and the effects they may have on the health of individuals. Additional research into the medicinal use of the same items by indigenous peoples will be useful to confirm the medicinal properties of, for example, chimpanzee leaf-swallowing behaviors. It will be increasingly important to understand the relationship between primates and parasites, because as primates move into more disturbed habitats, they will be exposed to, and more likely to suffer from, novel parasites. It has already been shown that the parasite loads of species living in logged forests and fragmented forest habitats are greater than for the same species living in undisturbed forests (Chapman et al. 2005a,b 2006, Gillespie and Chapman 2006, Gillespie et al. 2005).

❖❖ Primate-Plant Interactions

Primates have an effect on the structure, diversity, and life cycle of plants located in their habitat. This is partly the result of primates acting as plant pollinators or seed dispersers. In either role, primates and the plants they feed upon demonstrate an ecological relationship called **mutualism**. The growth and survival of both are benefited by virtue of their interaction, and it is a codependent relationship (Odum 1971). The type of role a primate performs depends greatly on the foraging behavior of the primate. In addition, it depends on the structure of the plants and specifically the reproductive parts that the primate feeds on. The primate's digestive anatomy, handling techniques and food processing strategies, social structure, and ranging behaviors are other factors that influence this mutualistic relationship.

Plants are immobile and need to attract animals that will facilitate the processes of reproduction and dispersal. They make themselves attractive by producing nectar, pollen, and seeds with **exocarps** that taste good to seed dispersers. Typically, when thinking about plant pollinators, those that immediately come to mind are insects, birds, and bats. Plants have evolved specific characteristics to attract particular types of pollinators. Plants that depend on birds for pollination typically produce flowers that are brightly colored (either in, what would appear to us, a visible light spectrum or invisible, ultraviolet light), while those that depend on bats may have drab or white-colored flowers that give off a strong odor especially at night (Faegri and Vander Pijl 1971).

Primates as Pollinators

For some small-bodied nocturnal primates, nectar feeding provides an important source of nutrition and for other diurnal primates, it may serve as an important food alternative when fruits are scarce. Primates compete with other animals, especially bats, for access to nectar. Where bats are not present or are rare, primates will readily utilize this food source. In northwestern Madagascar there exists only a single species of plant-pollinating bat, and here mongoose lemurs (*Eulemur mongoz*) exhibit an unusual nocturnal activity that includes nectar feeding, thus filling a niche that elsewhere would be occupied by bats (Sussman and Tattersall 1976). Only three species of fruit-feeding bats occur on the island of Madagascar, consequently the flower and nectar-feeding behaviors of some lemurs may serve as an important component of pollination ecology (Birkinshaw and Colquhoun 1998, Kress 1993, Kress et al. 1994, Overdorff 1992, Sussman and Raven 1978).

In Ranomafana National Park, located in southeastern Madagascar, the flower-feeding behavior of two species of lemurs, the brown lemur (*Eulemur fulvus rufus*) and the red-bellied lemur (*Eulemur rubriventer*), was compared (Overdorff 1992). Even though these two lemur species were often destructive to the flowers, there were significant differences in the flower-feeding behavior of the two species. Red-bellied lemurs spent 86 percent of the time licking flower nectar and 14 percent of the time eating the flowers. In contrast, brown lemurs licked flowers 31 percent of the time and consumed flowers 69 percent of the time. Evidence that the lemurs acted as pollinators could be seen because they had pollen on their faces after feeding. However, the red-bellied lemur was a more consistent pollinator than the brown lemur, because it was less destructive to the flowers that it fed on. It was most frequently observed licking flower nectar or feeding only on flower petals and leaving the reproductive parts intact. The nectar-feeding adaptation of the red-bellied lemur is further reflected by its unique tongue morphology; a brush-like feather at the tip that seemingly facilitates its nondestructive flower-licking feeding behavior (Figure 6-6).

FIGURE 6-6 The non-destructive nectar feeding adaptation of the red-bellied lemur (*Eulemur rubriventer*).

The role of primates as **pollinators** is not restricted to the island of Madagascar. There have been many observations of different primate species engaging in foraging behaviors that appear to involve the dispersal of plants through pollination. In the forests of South America, floral nectars are consumed by tamarins (*Saguinus*) and marmosets (*Callithrix* and *Cebuella pygmaea*) (Dietz et al. 1997, Garber 1993). Capuchin monkeys (*Cebus*), although notorious for their destructive feeding behavior, do not necessarily destroy all of the flowers they consume and have been observed inserting their faces deeply into flowers and having pollen dust on their face (Janson et al. 1981, Oppenheimer 1977, Prance 1980, Torresde, de Assumção 1981).

A community of cercopithecine monkeys living in the tropical rain forests of Salonga National Park, in the central African country of the Democratic Republic of Congo, spent 20 to 50 percent of their monthly feeding time eating the nectar of the legume tree *Daniellia pynaertii* (Gautier-Hion and Maisels 1994). Four monkey species (*Cercopithecus ascanius, C. wolfi, Allanopithecus nigroviridis,* and *Cercocebus aterrimus*) were observed to target the nectar of these flowers, and to move from one *Daniellia* tree to the next, sometimes visiting up to twelve different trees in less than three hours. These monkeys demonstrated very delicate flower-handling behaviors, suggesting that that these primates are effective pollinators.

Primates as Seed Dispersers

Many primate species are major dispersers of seeds, a behavior that can potentially affect the structure of future forests (Lambert and Garber 1998). It is estimated that approximately 75 percent of all tree species in tropical forests produce fruits adapted for vertebrate dispersal (Howe and Smallwood 1982, McKey 1975, Terborgh 1983). In these forests animals may actually transport 95 percent or more of the seeds produced (Terborgh et al. 2002). As major frugivores living in a forest community, primates may consume, spit out, swallow, and defecate seeds (Figure 6-7). In some plant species, the passage through a vertebrate intestinal tract is essential for germination. The process of seed dispersal is dependent on how animals consume the fruits and seeds, whether they fully or partially masticate the seeds (**seed predation**), swallow them whole or spit them out. Seed predation is not a part of the mutualisitic relationship between plants and primates. If seeds are swallowed whole or maintained in cheek pouches, then the ranging behavior of the primates significantly affects seed dispersal. The process of transporting seeds in the body of a primate and then defecating or spitting them out is referred to as **endozoochory**. Seed spitting is most common among the African and Asian cercopithecine or cheek-pouched monkeys (Dominy and Duncan 2005, Gautier-Hion 1980, Kaplin and Moermond 1998, Lambert 1999, 2000, Rowell and Mitchell 1991).

By dispersing a seed away from a parent plant, the seed stands a better chance of surviving. A high density of seeds distributed close to a parent plant may subject them to host-specific pathogens or to seed predators, thus increasing mortality probabilities. Moreover, in close proximity to the parent tree there may be greater competition for light, nutrients, and water. Dispersing seeds over a wider range of space increases the chance that they will be distributed in favorable conditions for germination (Howe and Smallwood 1982, Norconk et al. 1998).

FIGURE 6-7 Female saki (*Pithecia pithecia*) eating a fruit.

Seeds that are dispersed through spitting may only be moved a few meters from the parent tree, while those that are defecated are often taken hundreds of meters away from the parent tree (Chapman and Russo 2007). Link and Di Fiore (2006) calculated that spider monkeys (*Ateles belzebuth*) dispersed seeds as far away as 1,281 m (4,202 ft) from a parent plant. Seeds may also be moved from the place where they were deposited by primates by secondary dispersers (e.g., pigs and capybaras), which may also include seed predators (e.g., rats, pigs, and civets) and a range of insects, especially dung beetles (McConkey 2005).

One of the ways that scientists measure seed dispersal is to calculate a **seed shadow,** or the spatial distribution of seeds away from a parent plant (Figure 6-8). This is done by measuring the distance seeds are distributed from the parent plant, and the density of germinated seeds to establish a distribution curve. Furthermore, monitoring the death or continued life cycle of seeds deposited at specific locations will enable conclusions to be made about the beneficial, null, or deleterious effects on plants dispersed by primates. Studies that have used this method indicate that seeds removed away from the parent plant stand a better chance of surviving (Harms et al. 2000).

In the rain forest of Borneo, gibbons spend approximately 62 percent of their feeding time eating ripe fruits (McConkey 2000). Gibbons are therefore important fruit-eating animals, and they tend to swallow seeds without damaging them. The effects on seeds being transported in the gut of gibbons and later eliminated was studied over a twelve-month period by retrieving feces from two groups of gibbons (McConkey 2000). When an animal defecated, its identity, the location, and time were recorded. The feces were collected in plastic bags and seeds present were identified and counted. Seeds not consumed by the

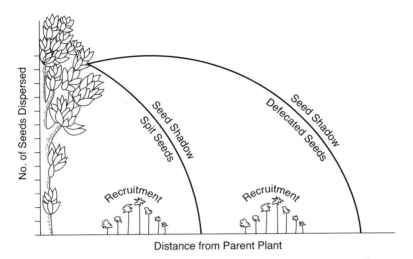

FIGURE 6-8   Seed shadows of seeds spit out by primates and those carried away and then defecated. The probability of survivorship increases with distance from the parent plant (adapted from Chapman 1995).

gibbons (control sample) and those extracted from feces were planted to determine if time spent in the gut track of gibbons facilitated or inhibited germination time. It was discovered that 41 percent of all plant species consumed by gibbons exhibited an accelerated germination rate. Therefore, it appears that there is a beneficial effect on a large portion of seeds that have been processed through the gut of a gibbon.

It is important not only where a seed has been deposited in feces, but also if the defecations are clumped or randomly spread out. Some primates, such as howler monkeys (*Alouatta*), defecate in specific locations that are sometimes referred to as latrines (Andresen 2001, 2002, Gilbert 1997). At these locations, feces may accumulate into significant deposits, leaving high nutrient concentrations (nitrogen and phosphorus) in their wake (Feeley 2005). At such sites, new seedlings may benefit by being provided with additional fertilizers.

Spider monkeys (*Ateles belzebuth*) living in the tropical rain forests of Amazonia are highly frugivorous, have very fluid social structures, and typically travel long distances throughout the day (Eisenberg et al. 1979, Shimooka 2005, Terborgh 1983). They swallow the seeds from a large variety of different plant species and can accommodate a big number of seeds in their gut (Link and de Luna 2004, Peres 1994). Their ecological strategies thus depend on having large areas of tropical forest to range within and being able to eat the fruits of many different tree species. Consequently, the seed-dispersal behavior of spider monkeys is thought to maintain and promote tropical forest diversity (Cain et al. 2000, Schupp et al. 2002, Wang and Smith 2002, Webb and Peart 2001). These primates, however, are highly vulnerable to any type of habitat alteration (Delfer et al. 2003, Link and Di Fiore 2006, Peres 2001, Peres and Dolman 2000) and tend to be among the first primates eliminated from disturbed forests. It is predicted that the extinction of spider monkeys from such environments will have a negative impact on the future diversity of these forests.

To quantify the importance of spider monkeys' seed-dispersal behavior on the maintenance of the diversity of plants in a rain forest environment, Link and Di Fiore (2006) conducted a year-long study in a lowland rain forest in Ecuador. Here spider monkeys fed on the fruits of 152 different plant species and swallowed the seeds of more than 98 percent of these plants. Fecal deposits containing seeds were on average retrieved 443 m (1,453 ft) away from a parent plant. The location of animals studied and defecation sites were entered into a geographic information system (GIS). By calculating the mean number of seeds passed per defecation, the researchers estimated that an individual spider monkey dispersed an average of approximately 643 seeds of various sizes (>1 mm) per day. This study shows that spider monkeys can be important dispersers of seeds from a variety of plant species. Spider monkeys and other frugivorous ateline monkeys, such as woolly (*Lagothrix*) and howler (*Alouatta*) monkeys, are the primary vertebrate seed dispersers in many rain forests of Central and South America (Link and Di Fiore 2006, Stevenson et al. 2002, 2005). They are particularly important dispersers of plants that produce large, thick-husked seeds that birds may not be able to open or swallow. Even in the dry, deciduous forests of western Madagascar, the brown lemur, *Eulemur fulvus*, is an important seed disperser (Ganzhorn et al. 1999).

In a rain forest in Cameroon a comparative study was conducted on the amount of seeds dispersed by monkeys and large frugivious birds (Clark et al. 2001). It was discovered that the primates dispersed on average twice the number of seeds than did birds. Consequently, it is doubtful that the dispersal services provided by primates could be compensated for by birds, should primates disappear from this forest. If primates are significantly reduced in number or eliminated due to habitat fragmentation, destruction, or by hunting, this could change the structure of future forest communities by effectively limiting their floristic composition.

Primates as Pruners

The foraging behavior of primates results in them acting as gardeners. Through the removal of plant parts, new plant growth may be stimulated. Capuchin monkeys (*Cebus capucinus*) on Barro Colorado Island, Panama, feed on membrillo trees (*Gustavia superba*). The growth patterns of membrillo trees used by the capuchins were compared to those found at another site where capuchin monkeys did not occur (Oppenheimer and Lang 1969). The trees that capuchins removed terminal buds from displayed an increase in branching and new growth.

❖❖ Behavioral Ecology of Primates

Study of the behavioral ecology of nonhuman primates investigates how ecological factors may affect the behaviors expressed by primates living under particular environmental circumstances—how food availability, for example, influences primate group sizes (e.g., Hanya et al. 2006). There are certainly a myriad of factors to be considered—both abiotic and biotic ones (see above), as well as any **synergistic** effects that the interaction of more than one variable might have. A natural habitat is a complex biological system so it is virtually impossible for any researcher to account, let alone attempt to quantify, all of the factors that may affect the behavioral ecology of primates. An additional level of complexity may enter the picture because primates are cognitively complex beings (see Chapter 10). There may be other socially derived reasons for some of the behaviors that are exhibited that simply cannot be accounted for on the basis of ecological variables alone.

How to Study Behavioral Ecology

Historically, much of the research conducted on primate behavioral ecology involved descriptive approaches—studying different species and then comparing the behaviors exhibited by these species. Many of the models developed from these early studies suggested that under specific environmental conditions, the primates present would display predictable patterns in social grouping, male to female ratios, etc. However, problems emerged as long-term studies were conducted and different populations of the same species were observed to exhibit great variability, both spatially and temporally. Many of the predictive models that had been proposed (but were based on very limited systematically collected data) simply did not stand up to additional testing with more and better data.

Models are an important tool for the study of complex systems. They provide us with a means to take into account numerous factors and to make predictions based on explicit assumptions about how things work. Dunbar (2002) identified that there are only two ways in which a primatologist can deal with such complexity: either by experimentally manipulating variables so that we can delineate and determine cause and effect relationships, or by resorting to mathematical modeling. Under natural conditions, the former approach is not readily applicable or even desirable and may not provide a holistic understanding of a system. Experimental fieldwork, however, involving the use of feeding platforms to study foraging behaviors, food selection, decision-making processes, and cognitive maps (by rearranging food choices) has been undertaken and have offered intriguing insight (Bicca-Marques and Garber 2003, Di Bitetti and Janson 2001, Dominy et al. 2003, Janson 2001, Janson and Di Bitetti 1997).

In the past, primatologists have been reluctant to incorporate the use of mathematical models into the study of primate behavioral ecology. A new generation of primatologists, however, is more willing to use this type of approach. Linear program models are graphic approaches used to identify the optimal results of introducing related variables into a two-dimensional space. Altmann (1998) investigated the diet of yearling baboons and established a linear model. Using this model, Altmann was able to take into consideration the proportion of two different food types in the dietary regime of baboons, as well as account for nutrients and toxins in the foods consumed. By using this model, it was possible to establish the amount of Food A and Food B that a young baboon would need to consume in order to achieve an optimal diet. Systems models, game theory models, and optimality models, among others, may all be applicable to the study of primate behavioral ecology (Strier 2007).

How Food Is Distributed in the Various Biomes

Integral to the life of primates—as it is for all animals—is the need to find enough food and water for survival. Obviously, these resources are not evenly distributed in time or space. Primates must therefore exhibit **foraging strategies** (involving searching for and locating food) that enable them to maximize access to available and necessary resources. Even though some primate species show more specialized dietary strategies, evolutionarily primates are generalists—they are devised for an omnivorous diet (see Chapter 1), but they can be quite eclectic in their dietary choices (Harding 1981). The diet of most primate species comprises a combination of leaves, fruits, flowers, herbs, insects, vertebrates, roots, bark, seeds, sap and gum, and other miscellaneous items. Long-term study of primate diets has revealed that plant foods may be selected from fifty or more different species by a single group of primates (e.g., Norton et al. 1987).

Differences in morphology and physiology affect the foraging behavior and dietary choices of primates. Body size, limb structure, teeth and jaws, and intestinal morphology all play a role in determining what type of foods primates can obtain and process. As described in Chapter 4, the sacculated stomachs of colobus monkeys enable them to consume large quantities of tough, fibrous leaves that other monkeys cannot digest, while the mandibular incisors of marmosets endow them with the ability to poke holes into tree trunks to obtain tree sap that others would not be able to extract. Many plants contain a variety of chemicals that may be toxic (e.g., alkaloids) or may cause them to be difficult to digest. Some primates have evolved better means than others to deal with these chemical compounds.

The habitat greatly influences dietary diversity. As described in Chapter 3, a majority of primates live in tropical or subtropical environments, with most species living in forest habitats. Most forest-dwelling primates obtain their foods from woody-stemmed plants, such as trees, and **lianas** or vines. In the rain forest biome diversity in tree species is high (50 to 100 species per hectare or 2.47 acres). Many of the species found, however, are only represented by a small number of individuals. The spatial structure of a rain forest is diverse—both in the horizontal and vertical distributions of plants. Various tree species differ in the height they will grow to and in the dimension of trunks, branches, and crown shape and size. Many plant species are not evenly distributed throughout the forest. Instead, they exhibit **clumped** or clustered **distributions** that may be related to particular soil and light conditions (Figure 6-9). Patterns in the production of foods (i.e., fruits, flowers, buds, or leaves) thus tend to be highly diverse and complex.

The timing of when specific parts of plants can be utilized as foods is not uniform or **synchronous** across an entire rain forest. Individuals of the same species may demonstrate broad overlap in the timing of, for example, fruiting or flowering, but even within the same plant species there may be considerable individual variation—i.e., they are **asynchronous**. Some species, such as figs (*Ficus*), are well known for their asynchronous fruiting behavior (Figure 6-10). Figs can be available throughout the year, but only the fruits of a particular tree or trees may be available at any particular time of the year. Consequently, there can be great variation in the timing of food availability within and between rain forest communities. There are peaks and troughs in the general availability of various food types; at the end of a dry period, new leaves and flowers are pro-

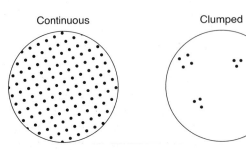

Continuous   Clumped

FIGURE 6-9 Continuous versus Clumped distribution of food resources.

FIGURE 6-10 A fig tree (*Ficus sycamorus*) with ripe fruits growing along the stem and branches.

duced, while the ensuing wet period results in an increase in the production of fruits (Oates 1987, Whitmore 1984).

Within the rain forest biome, great differences are found in the specific types of rain forest habitat in which primates live. Primary rain forests have evolved to be stable communities, while secondary rain forests typically contain many successional or colonizing plants that may be fast growing and more continuously distributed. The succession of plants in secondary, or disturbed rain forest habitats, may offer less diversity but a greater supply of plants such as herbs due to increased light exposure as a result of habitat disturbance (Box 3-1). The increased light exposure may cause an increase in the concentration of protein in leaves, making them more nutritious (Chapman et al. 2003, Ganzhorn 1995). Gallery forests that grow close to a water source may offer a higher density of plants, and the presence of a permanent water source may result in plant foods being available throughout the year.

In the seasonal and woodland forest biomes (see Chapter 3), the presence or absence of particular foods tend to be more pronounced. Primates living in seasonal forests may exhibit great shifts in the plant species that make up their diet in any one season (i.e., they have a seasonally variable diet). In woodland forests, rainfall is seasonal and typically less than in rain forests. There is also a more prolonged and pronounced dry season, resulting in a lower diversity of tree species. Primates living in these forests tend to optimize their use of available food species, thus their annual dietary diversity may still be high.

The savanna and semidesert scrub biomes offer even less diversity, and consequently, primates must be very eclectic in their dietary choices. In savanna habitats, primates harvest fruits, flowers, seeds, **corms**, etc. from a number of different trees, bushes, vines, grasses, and herbs. In semidesert scrub biomes, water may be scarce, and typically these habitats can only support low densities of primate populations. Here plants are more widely dispersed with more open ground exposed. Obviously, in the drier habitats the availability of water or water-bearing fruits can be severely limited. In these types of habitats, the "best" dietary strategy is that of a generalist; i.e., consuming a large variety of food items in various quantities.

Baboons are highly opportunistic feeders (e.g., Barton et al. 1992, Norton et al. 1987). A comparison of the dietary variability of chacma baboons (*Papio ursinus*) living in two different savanna habitats (Waterberg and Kruger Park) was conducted in South Africa (Codron et al. 2006). By examining the isotopic signatures (see Box 5-5) of plants found growing in the savanna and of plants found in baboon fecal samples, researchers could access the general category of plants consumed (e.g., grasses and bushes) and their nutritional value via crude protein content. The diets of the baboons living in the two savanna habitats were different. In Waterberg, baboons consumed a large proportion of grass (approximately 35 percent of food intake), while the diet of the baboons at Kruger comprised only 10 percent grass. Compared to other mammalian browsers, such as zebra and giraffe, the baboons maximized their intake of crude protein in both savanna habitats. It appears that the baboons were highly selective feeders, consuming a wide variety of foods to maximize protein intake, including fauna, subterranean plant parts, and at Kruger Park, human foods (Figure 6-11).

Seasonal variation is most pronounced in temperate forest woodlands, and primates living here often encounter alternating periods of peak food abundance and then extremely lean times. In these habitats, there is greater synchrony in the timing of food production both between and within plant species. Many of the broad-leaved trees drop their leaves during cold and dry months, and without a continuous canopy more light reaches the ground so there is greater variability in the plants that make up the understory of temperate forests. In the temperate forests of Japan and Pakistan, primates may also need to deal with periods of deep snow cover (see Box 3-2).

FIGURE 6-11 Many primate species readily use human refuse (often quite edible) as a source of food. Here a male chacma baboon (*Papio ursinus*) is feeding in a garbage dump.

  **HOT TOPICS 6-1**

How Do Primates Survive a Natural Disaster?

We have all been well informed about the devastation that a major hurricane, such as Katrina, can cause. Nonhuman primates occur in regions that are subjected to natural disasters such as hurricanes, cyclones, typhoons, floods, extensive fires, and severe draught. Primatologists often observe the aftereffects of a natural disaster on a primate population, but they rarely have comparative data prior to a disaster on a given population. The following example is an interesting exception.

During 1999–2001, data were collected on groups of black howler monkeys (*Alouatta pigra*) living in a lowland rain forest in southern Belize. The study was ongoing when Hurricane Iris struck on October 8, 2001 (Pavelka et al. 2003). Iris was a category 4 hurricane and it went directly through the 52 ha (128 acres) where the howlers lived—the devastation was tremendous. The researchers were forced to evacuate, and severe damage occurred to neighboring villages, making it impossible to resume research on the howlers until October 16th. When the researchers arrived, they found their camp destroyed, the extensive network of trails obliterated, along with huge amounts of fallen trees that made access to the forest impossible. Road surveys were thus done in order to establish if there were any surviving howlers.

The forest canopy in which these highly arboreal monkeys lived had vanished. Trees had been snapped or uprooted, those left standing were missing branches and were 100 percent defoliated. Before the hurricane, fifty-three monkeys in eight social groups inhabited the study area. They lived in stable groups that were associated with particular locations in the forest. The researchers were not able to identify individuals, but they could identify social groups based on where in the forest monkeys were observed. Between the second week and the fifteenth week after the hurricane, the number of monkeys sighted during a single survey ranged from zero to twenty-six. Since much of the forest was obliterated, the researchers could no longer recognize social groups. Repeated surveys yielded data indicating that 49 percent of the howler population had been lost to Hurricane Iris. Subadult males and other immature individuals seemed to sustain the largest casualties. Social disorganization occurred during the first three months. In fact, the researchers noted that their general impression was one of "social chaos," and solitary individuals were frequently sighted.

During the first two weeks, the surviving howlers were forced to forage in the piles of fallen trees for leaves and fruit. Consequently, these highly arboreal monkeys now spent much more time close to the forest floor. After two weeks, new leaves began to appear on the surviving trees, but most trees still failed to produce fruit some thirty-five weeks after the hurricane. These monkeys prefer fruit and young leaves, but they are opportunistic primates; and after the hurricane, mature leaves became a fallback food.

(continued)

After three months, solitary individuals were less frequently sighted and new social groups were forming. The only positive result from the hurricane was that the researchers were able to identify individuals due to increased visibility (because of the loss of foliage and the tendency for the monkeys to be located closer to the ground), and the distinguishable scars and healing injuries that many individuals now possessed as a result of Hurricane Iris.

How Primates Find Food

Complexity in the spatial distribution of plant food species, as well as the timing of food production, presents primates, as well as other animals, with a complex puzzle to be solved. They need to know where and how to find food that is both adequate in nutritional value and in ample supply. Evidence suggests that primates monitor the availability of food resources and that the travel patterns of groups are purposeful and directional; i.e., they direct their travels to intercept locations where food is available (Garber 1989). In terms of foraging strategies, it simply would not make sense for primates to randomly wander about in a forest or any other habitat on the off chance that they would eventually come across food. How do primates know where and when to find food?

The concept that animals have cognitive maps is not new (Sigg and Stolba 1981, Tolman 1948). We know that honeybees and desert ants use complex navigational cues, such as the sun as a compass, to locate sources of food (Wehner 1992). A cognitive map infers that an animal possesses a mental representation of the environment within which it lives. This mental map contains information about routes and environmental relationships that an animal uses to make decisions about where to go. To test if an animal retains a cognitive map of its range involves being able to determine if the animal makes novel "short cuts" to efficiently arrive at a specific site. An important feature of a cognitive map is that it must be highly flexible, indicating that it contains a larger amount of information about the environment than just knowing specific routes (Bennett 1996). To determine if animals do in fact possess cognitive maps is difficult because many cues not accounted for or recognized by the researcher may play a role in how animals negotiate their paths. Nonetheless, research on primate foraging routes has yielded provocative results.

Four female captive vervet monkeys (*Chlorocebus aethiops*) were allowed to observe where grapes were randomly hidden in small holes (baiting) (Cramer and Gallistel 1997). In twenty of twenty-six trials, the subjects selected an optimal route to obtain the grapes; they took the shortest distance to collect the grapes. Importantly, the route the monkeys selected to follow was different from the baiting order, and the route selected was strongly influenced by at least two baiting locations ahead of where they started, indicating that some travel plans were in place. The vervet monkeys minimized the amount of energy and time expended to get maximum rewards.

Primate groups living in well-studied locations have been tested for the efficiency of their travel routes. The movement patterns of capuchin monkeys (*Cebus apella*) living in a subtropical forest in Argentina were monitored during the winter months when no fruits were available (Janson 1998). Thirty-one artificial feeding platforms were arranged at seventeen locations over an area of 1 km² within the range of the study group. The platforms were spaced at least 180 m (590 ft) apart. At each site, one or two platforms were baited with 10 to 80 tangerines. Random patterns of movements among the platforms were predicted using a computer model. The movements of the capuchins did not match the random predictions—they moved in straighter lines and went to platforms that were closest to one another. The capuchins appeared to hold spatial knowledge about the location of the feeding platforms and moved directly to the platforms containing the most food.

Groups of tamarins (*Saguinus mystax* and *S. fuscicollis*) living in a rain forest of northeastern Peru were found to be very selective in their travel patterns (Garber 1989, Garber and Hannon 1993). Fruit and exudate-producing trees exhibit patchy distributions and variability in the timing of food production. Goal-oriented travel patterns were exhibited by the tamarins. Seventy percent of the time the nearest tree of a target species was selected as the next feeding site, and while the tamarins fed on average from 150 individual trees, they visited only thirteen trees on any one day. They exhibited knowledge of distance, direction, and an ability to monitor for cycles of food availability.

So, how do primates monitor limited resources? Primates utilize a variety of ecological information including olfactory and visual cues to locate food sources (Bicca-Marques and Garber 2004). Olfactory cues may be more important for nocturnal species (Vickers 2000) and visual cues for diurnal species, but in either case, spatial information is also important. In addition, during daily foraging treks, primates visit specific feeding sites, thus monitoring the absence or presence of specific food items. It appears that primates will maximize the use of whatever cues they can. Evidence that diurnal tamarins use olfactory cues to locate nearby feeding sites was indicated by sudden path reversals, a broad travel arc, and sharp 90° turns in their travel routes (Garber and Hannon 1993). It does appear that detailed spatial maps must somehow be maintained. As evidenced by the tamarins, a spatial map appears to be retained for at least several weeks. Diurnal group-living primates also appear to rely on social cues. The use of information-sharing or producer-scrounger models was tested on the foraging behavior of tamarins (Bicca-Marques and Garber 2005). If an information model is used, then all group members would search for food and share with others. A producer-scrounger model predicts that finders expend time and energy using ecological cues to locate resources, and joiners monitor the finder's behaviors and join in when the resources have been discovered. In this study, it was found that for 74 to 90 percent of all food searches, about half of the group members acted as finders, thus employing a producer-scrounger strategy. The decision of where a group-living primate goes to find food is dependent on an assessment of ecological information as well as social knowledge and awareness about other group members. Ultimately, however, we do not yet know what influences a group of primates to move off in a particular direction, especially at the start of the day.

❖❖ Intergroup Competition and Competitive Exclusion

Within any given habitat, primates are members of an ecological community and compete for resources with other group members, other animals, as well as with other primate species. Different primate species often co-occur in the same habitat, and the way in which resources are partitioned has been a focus of study for primatologists since the early 1960s. When primates co-occur, differences in niche occupation involving diet, timing of activities, positional behaviors (i.e., forest level and types of substrates used, etc.), locomotion patterns, social structure, and social organization facilitate the sharing of a habitat. This is referred to as **resource partitioning.**

Gause's principle of **competitive exclusion** states that no two species can occupy an identical niche; i.e., they cannot be in total and absolute competition with one another because if they are, they will either both be eliminated from the niche or one of the species will out-compete, and thereby exclude, the other (Gause 1934). Two species may only coexist if they are not in competition over density-dependent or other population-controlling factors (Mayr 1963). In actuality, however, competitive exclusion is rarely seen in the natural world, and primate species, even closely related ones, can and do co-occur. Significant niche overlap may also be common, but typically one or the other species will exhibit a difference along one niche dimension (Hutchinson 1957).

The co-occurrence of primates has been reported across primate taxa, and sympatric species may share niche requirements if essential resources are abundant or if there are niche parameters on which the species do not overlap. Even though it has been suggested that closely related species, because they would have more similar niche requirements, would not co-occur as frequently as more distantly related species, this is not always the case.

Two closely related sympatric species of mouse lemurs (*Microcebus murinus* and *M. ravelobensis*) occupy a dry, deciduous forest in northwestern Madagascar (Radespiel et al. 2006). These small strepsirhines are solitary, nocturnal foragers. Through the use of radiotelemetry, their movements have been monitored, and feeding ecology and vertical space use analyzed to determine how these species partition resources. Both species use the forest strata in a similar fashion, and were usually found 0.1 to 2.0 m above the forest floor. Overall diets were similar with insects and gum composing the majority of their diet. There was considerable overlap (> 50 percent) in the plant species consumed, but for approximately 40 percent of their diet, they fed on plant species that were exclusively used by one or the other species. In this case, a tendency to consume particular plant species not eaten by the other mouse lemur enabled these closely related species to occupy the same basic niche.

Apparent similarity in ecological strategies was thought to limit the co-occurrence of species. Two South American ripe-fruit specialists, a woolly monkey (*Lagothrix poeppigi*) and a spider monkey (*Ateles belzebuth belzebuth*), coexist in the Amazonian rain forest of Ecuador (Dew 2005). Even though both of these primates exhibit high dietary overlap in many of the fruit species consumed, foraging strategies and the fruits eaten differ. Woolly monkeys spend more time foraging, visit a larger number of smaller-sized food patches, feed lower in the canopy, consume a greater variety of fruits, and are seed predators. Spider monkeys, in contrast, forage less frequently and feed on fewer but more lipid-rich food sources, consume more fruits, with large seeds that are consumed whole, and feed higher up in the canopy. On closer inspection, these two species show considerable divergence in microhabitat preferences.

An even more extreme situation of ecological similarity involves the highly specialized bamboo lemur. In the rain forest of the Ranomafana National Park (RNP) of southeastern-central Madagascar, three species of bamboo lemurs (*Hapalemur*) live sympatrically. These small-bodied primates (0.9–2.4 kg; approximately 2–5 lbs) are rare and cryptic and are the only primates in the world specialized for a bamboo diet. Bamboo makes up more than 88 percent of their total diet, and this specialization requires them to have an ability to detoxify cyanide that is present in the bamboo (Glander et al. 1989). In a sympatric situation, competition for bamboo is expected.

A two-year-long comparative study was conducted in order to determine how such specialized foragers could coexist (Tan 1999). At RNP, it was discovered that although there was considerable dietary overlap in the amount and parts eaten of giant bamboo, the greater bamboo lemur (*H. simus*) was the most specialized in this solitary food source, while the lesser bamboo lemur (*H. griseus*) and the golden bamboo lemur (*H. aureus*) more frequently supplemented giant bamboo with fruit, other bamboo species, grasses, and leaves. In addition, the golden bamboo lemur had the most diverse diet. In this situation, ever so slight differences in diets and body size enable these species to co-occur.

Dietary overlap is possible and more feasible when resources are abundant. In lean times, the dietary overlap of sympatric species tends to decrease (Buzzard 2006a, Stanford and Nkurunungi 2003). During times of low fruit availability in the Taï Forest of Cote d'Ivoire, there was a large decrease in the overlap of specific fruit species used by three species of sympatric guenons (*Cercopithecus*). Overall dietary diversity for each of the guenon species increased at this time, indicating that they were selecting from a larger range of food species, maximizing resources that were available (Buzzard 2006a).

Polyspecific Associations

Some primates form mixed-species groups called **polyspecific groups** or associations. This is not a common group construction among primates, but some species, both diurnal and nocturnal, living in the tropical rain forests of Africa and South America regularly form mixed-species groups. There may be benefits to forming mixed-species associations that are related to anti-predator strategies, but there may also be rewards pertaining to feeding success. Habitats may be more systematically searched and exploited when different species of primates living in long-term association with one another overtly or passively share information. This is known as the **information-sharing hypothesis** (Norconk 1990). As observed by Norconk (1990), primates that form long-term mixed-species groups tend to be small- to medium-sized (less than 7 kg or 15 lbs), frugivorous, and they obtain much protein from insects. Another ecological advantage may involve the fact that a larger group is more efficient at defending feeding resources. During intergroup encounters, tamarins (*Saguinus*) were more successful at keeping other groups from gaining access to their feeding trees when they were in larger polyspecific groups as opposed to smaller single-species groups (Garber 1987).

Throughout much of their geographic distribution, tamarins (*Saguinus*) are known to form mixed-species groups (Garber 1988, Hardie 1998). Resource partitioning in groups composed of two and three species were studied by Buchanan-Smith (1999). Saddle-backed tamarins (*S. fuscicollis*) were found in association with red-bellied tamarins (*S. labiatus),* and often a third species joined the group—titi (*Callicebus*), saki (*Pithecia*), or Goeldi's (*Callimico*) monkeys. In this study, vertical stratification in forest use (the different primate species tended to be observed at different heights in the forest) seemed to be an important strategy in the partitioning of resources. Foraging at different heights minimizes resource competition in polyspecific associations, especially when those groups are formed by different species that belong to the same genus.

The frequency with which polyspecific groups are formed may be dictated by the availability of resources. On Maracá, a tropical rain forest island located between two rivers in northern Brazil, long-term two-species groups and ephemeral three-species associations were much more frequent during periods of food scarcity when the lowest estimates of fruit availability were recorded (Mendes Pontes 1997). During this time, several fruiting fig trees were occupied by squirrel monkeys (*Saimiri sciureus*) and capuchin monkeys (*Cebus olivaceus* and *C. apella*), as well as frugivorous rodents, birds (e.g., toucans), and coatis (members of the raccoon family), totaling some seventy individuals in a single tree.

❖❖ Ranging Behavior

Where to find food and other crucial resources, how far to go to obtain them, and how slow or fast to travel to a food source, and the sex, age, and health of the individuals that belong to a group are all factors that affect the ranging behaviors of primates. Primates tend to maintain and use a defined spatial region—i.e., **home range**. Like most other mammals, they are **philopatric,** meaning they associate on a regular basis with one particular area (Jewell 1966).

A variety of terms are used to identify the space within which primates range. Members of a social group occupy the same home range. This is the area that a group covers over an extended period of time (usually measured over the course of a year) and includes the resources that they exploit. Within the home range, smaller areas traversed over known periods of time are more circumscribed and are called monthly or **day ranges**. A **core area** is a section of the home range that a group frequently uses and is typically associated with preferred resources, such as sleeping sites, primary feeding trees, resting sites, etc. The most restricted space that a group may have is referred to as an **area of exclusive use** (Figure 6.12). This space is defended and not shared with members of other groups.

In the Kahuzi seasonal forest in the Democratic Republic of Congo, a group of twenty-three chimpanzees utilize a home range of 12.8 km² (5.12 mi²) and use this home range in a clumped pattern (Basabose 2005). The core area, defined as the area that the chimpanzees used for approximately 50 to 80 percent of the time, consisted of 0.69 km² or 0.276 mi². Their home range included a number of different habitat types, and the amount of time the chimpanzees were observed in the various habitat types indicated differential use. They spent 67.8 percent of the time in secondary forest, 10.5 percent of the time in primary forest, 6.6 percent of the time in swamp forest, and 5.9 percent in the bamboo forest. Seasonal variation in habitat use is dictated by the food sources

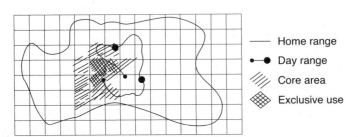

FIGURE 6-12 Illustration showing a hypothetical home range, with several day ranges, a core area, and area of exclusive use.

— Home range
●—● Day range
/// Core area
▨ Exclusive use

available. Ripe fruit is the preferred food of chimpanzees and can be found in the primary forest in the dry season; however, fig trees with ripe fruits are much more abundant in the secondary forest at this time. During times of fruit scarcity the chimpanzees lengthened their day range to get to more remote sections of their home range, which is close to primary forest habitats. This readily illustrates how the ranging behavior of primates is a complicated affair with forest structure, the location of preferred foods, and seasonal availability of resources, all contributing to the differential use of specific areas within a home range.

Primates exhibit tremendous variability in intergroup spacing. Species or groups can have home ranges with extensive overlap, slight overlap, or they can be exclusive with no overlap. Both the size of a home range and the degree of overlap are influenced by habitat quality, primate biomass, distribution of food and other limited resources, and patterns of social organization and behavior. Use of space may also be influenced by anthropogenic factors (human-induced changes), and this may have an effect on established home ranges and other ranging behaviors.

General patterns in the ranging behavior of primates have been observed: Terrestrial species tend to have larger home and day ranges than arboreal species, and frugivores have larger home and day ranges than do folivores (Clutton-Brock and Harvey 1977, Janson and Chapman 1999, Janson and Goldsmith 1995, Milton and May 1976). Frugivorous primates depend on food sources that typically exhibit greater seasonal variation in time and space; moreover, eating fruits involves shorter digestion times than does eating leaves (Demment and Laca 1991). In an oversimplification of complex issues, the size of a home range *generally* increases with the body size of a primate. This was true of the situation at RNP with the three species of bamboo lemurs. There are, however, many intervening and complicating factors, such as metabolic rate, locomotion, group size, whether the primates are nocturnal or diurnal, competition for resources, habitat quality, and seasonality in food abundance and distribution (Oates 1987). These factors may significantly affect the relationship between the size of a primate and the size of its home range.

In general, primates that depend on highly dispersed and unpredictable foods will exhibit larger ranging patterns than those that depend on dense and more evenly distributed resources that are predictable (Oates 1987). Seasonal changes in the availability of food affect the ranging behavior of primates in a variety of ways. One strategy involves energy conservation—when food is limited, day ranges may be reduced, and primates will feed on lower-quality food items (e.g., *Trachypithecus pileatus*, Stanford 1991; Box 3-2). A second option is for primates to increase their day and monthly ranges, and harvest foods from a wider area (e.g., *C. apella, Saimiri oerstedi, S. sciureus*) (Terborgh 1983). In some species, however, seasonal variation in food availability does not seem to greatly alter their ranging behaviors.

Three species of primarily frugivorous guenons of the Taï Forest exhibit similar ranging patterns to one another (Buzzard 2006b). Their ranging behaviors show long day ranges (an average of 1,120 m or 3,674 ft for all three species over all seasons) relative to home range size (52–98 hectares or 128–242 acres) and little repeated use of the same area on successive days. Due to the fact that these species show greater dietary diversity during periods of fruit scarcity (see above), it was assumed that differences in ranging patterns would also occur at this time. This was not the case, and Buzzard (2006b) identifies a third strategy in how primates might deal with seasonal variability in the availability of food: combine the use of alternative food species with ranging patterns to enable the consistent monitoring of resources over a large area.

In nonseasonal environments, primates may still have high travel costs in terms of energy expended. Spider monkeys (*Ateles belzebuth*) living in a highly diverse Ecuadorian tropical, moist rain forest in which no true dry season occurs, were found to maintain long mean day ranges (3,311 m or 10,860 ft) (Suarez 2006). These monkeys exhibit a highly diverse diet, eating more than 238 different species of fruits. Their foraging strategy involves visiting many feeding patches (an average of 13.3) on any given day, and staying in those patches for a relatively short period of time (a little over eight minutes). Being relatively large-bodied primates (7.3–10.4 kg, 16–23 lbs) and having to compete with conspecifics, other primates, mammals, and birds, necessitates a type of scramble

> **agonism**—aggressive or submissive displays or physical interactions; these may be based on visual, olfactory, or vocal behavior

competition for these primates. They can quickly deplete even a large food patch, but by ranging on a daily basis over large areas, they can be more selective about which fruits they consume in a patch because there is typically another patch to visit.

❖❖ Territoriality

When primates exhibit defensive or monitoring behaviors regarding the space that they occupy, this is referred to as **territoriality**. Patrolling boundaries and **agonistic**, or ritualistic behaviors directed at nongroup individuals trying to enter a used or occupied space are examples of territorial behaviors. Territorial behaviors have been noted for a large number of primate taxa including: ring-tailed lemurs, indri, tamarins, spider monkeys, baboons, macaques, guenons and colobine monkeys, langurs, gibbons, and chimpanzees (Cheney 1986). Typically, these behaviors are exhibited if resources are distributed in such a fashion as to enable a social group to economically defend them. Determining the economic feasibility of a group to defend its territory is computed through the use of indices. Assuming a circular distribution of a home range, average day range (d) is divided by the diameter of a circle with an area that would be equivalent to the total circular home range size, this provides an index (D) of defensibility (Mitani and Rodman 1979). This computation has been revised to include finer details of home range distribution and detection distances. Such indices do provide researchers with a means to compare the ranging and defensive behavior of primate groups but they do not completely reflect the complexity of the three-dimensional space in which primates live.

Sympatric guenons living in the Taï Forest (*Cercopithecus campbelli, C. diana,* and *C. petaurista*) exhibit daily monitoring of their home range boundaries, and high defensibility indices suggest that the three species of guenons can economically defend their territories (Buzzard 2006b). The guenons produce frequent, loud call vocalizations (especially made by *Cercopithecus diana*), and aggressive intergroup encounters involving chasing for periods lasting for more than an hour have been observed. Border patrol behavior has been noted for other primate species, including gibbons (Whitten 1982) and chimpanzees (Goodall 1986).

Gibbons (*Hylobates*) are typically described as being highly territorial (Leighton 1987). Intergroup encounters and resulting behaviors were observed for two focal groups living in the rain forest of Khao Yai National Park, Thailand (Bartlett 2003). A total of ninety intergroup encounters were recorded during 109 full-day observations. The encounters varied, with 58 percent classified as exclusively agonistic, 20 percent involved vocal exchanges, 6 percent were neutral, and surprisingly, 17 percent included affiliative interactions between members of the different groups. The agonistic encounters involved chasing, solo male vocalizations, and stand-offs. Adult males engaged most frequently in these encounters, but subadults, juveniles, and adult females also participated in the disputes. The affiliative encounters often involved immature individuals from both groups playing with one another, usually in the form of play chases and some grooming behavior, with adult males occasionally joining in. It appears that the nature of intergroup encounters between gibbons involves greater complexity in behavioral responses than initially thought.

◈◈ Activity Cycles

Animals have to allocate time in their daily or nightly cycle of activities to accomplish all of the tasks necessary for survival and their social well-being. Time must be invested in foraging, feeding, resting, being engaged in a wide array of social activities (including the rearing of offspring), and when necessary, staying vigilant about and avoiding predators. As both physical and social environments shift and change, what might have been an appropriate allocation of time in one season, social context, or location may no longer be optimal in another. Expenditure of time is thus a very serious affair, especially when living in complex social environments as most primates do.

Behavioral ecologists have examined the activity cycles of primates, also called **time budgets**, as representative of the ecological and social constraints under which primates operate. Evolutionary theory predicts that primates will be sensitive to these constraints and will adjust their time budgets to most appropriately deal with socio-ecological conditions (Mangel and Clark 1986). As time budgets have been investigated across primate taxa, it has become apparent that some primates allocate time between various activities in more or less efficient ways (Di Fiore and Rodman 2001, Dunbar 1992b, Krebs and Kacelnik 1991; see Figure 8.1).

Time budgets may be established through a number of different methodological approaches (Clutton-Brock 1977). The approach used depends on whether individuals can be identified, the conditions under which observations are being made—can individuals easily be seen or not—and the length of time observed. The research question that is being addressed will also dictate how and what kind of data to collect. Typically, if individual identities are known, an individual (or focal animal) is selected for a set period of time and its behaviors recorded either continuously or at very short, preestablished time intervals (e.g., observation made every two or five minutes). If individuals are not known, then a group is scanned and the various behaviors observed are recorded (scan sampling). The activities that animals are engaged in are classified according to an established **ethogram**. An ethogram is a behavioral inventory that has been established for a particular study group. Elements of an ethogram are composed of mutually exclusive (not overlapping) categories of activity (Table 6-1). Number of occurrences of behaviors divided by number of time units or total observation time provides a rate that can be established on an hourly, daily, monthly, or yearly basis. Dividing the

TABLE 6-1	An Example of a Basic Ethogram. Each Category May Be Divided into More Specific Behaviors Depending on the Parameters of a Study
Eat	To handle, process, or consume food items
Forage	To search for food, to actively manipulate a substrate in search of food
Travel	To change positions through locomotion
Rest	To be inactive in either a sitting, lying, or standing posture
Social	To be engaged in any behavior such as grooming or playing that involves one or more other individuals, usually in close proximity
Other	Any behavior not listed above

rate by 100 provides an estimate of proportion of time spent in activity a, activity b, etc. These figures may be derived for an entire group or broken into age and sex classes.

Active Time

Primates may be exclusively diurnal, exclusively nocturnal, **crepuscular**, or cathemeral. Being cathemeral (active both during the day and at night) is a relatively rare primate strategy, but many species of *Eulemurs* exhibit this pattern (Sussman 1999). As noted by Sussman, a cathemeral strategy may have arisen in association with the timing, seasonal avail-ability, and competition for par-ticular food resources, e.g.,

> **crepuscular**—active during low levels of light intensity (dawn/dusk)

floral nectar. Most primates usually exhibit one pattern of active time, although there can be variability in this pattern. Depending on the location and habitat of particular pop-ulations, the mongoose lemur (*Eulemur mongoz*) has been found to be active in each of these active time categories (Sussman 1999). In general, larger-bodied primates tend to be diurnal and smaller-bodied primates nocturnal.

How Do Primates Divide Up Their Day?

When to be active is likely cued by changing light intensities. However, ambient tem-perature, weather conditions, or the presence of predators can alter the precise timing of the start or end of when primates are active. In general, primates wake up with an empty stomach and within a relatively short period of time (sometimes preceded by brief periods of social behaviors or sunning behavior in cold or wet conditions) they begin to engage in foraging activities. The duration of time spent traveling and foraging is dependent on how far primates have to travel to find food and how they harvest the food. The amount of time spent feeding is dependent on group size; the age, sex, and health of an individual; and the quality and quantity of foods encountered. If primates are consuming leafy materials, then feeding is usually followed by periods of rest, enabling digestion to occur. Depending on the distribution of food resources (patchy or continuous), frugivorous or insectivorous primates may shift to yet another cycle of trav-eling, foraging, and feeding activities. Bouts of traveling, foraging, feeding, resting, and social behaviors punctuate most of the active time of a primate. Before primates travel to seek out sleeping sites, they will usually spend time foraging and feeding once again.

Diurnal primates living in arid or semi-arid savanna and semidesert scrub biomes may face additional stress from midday heat and this may limit activity. Brain and Mitchell (1999) monitored the body temperature of baboons living in the Namib Desert of Namibia via implanted telemeters. They found that an increase in body temperature above the norm constrained the activities of the baboons. Body temperatures were reduced after drinking, but when water was not available, core body temperatures could increase by 5.3°C. During days when water was not available, the baboons traveled less and overall curtailed their activities. In general, primate species that live in savanna habitats tend to seek shelter under trees and bushes and rest during the hottest part of the day. Thermoregulation requires energy (Agetsuma 2000), and as was the case for the baboons, when energy is being expended to try to keep cool, little energy can be expended on other activities. Macaques living in cold climates where temperatures can drop to −20°C (−4.0°F) (Wada 1980) have to expend energy to keep warm, and when possible they need to increase their intake of energy by feeding. Foraging for food thus becomes a dilemma—if food can be obtained, even of poor quality, then it may be worth the expenditure of energy; if not, additional conservation may be warranted (see Box 3-2). Temperature affects the need to conserve or expend energy, thus influencing activity patterns.

Identifying and explaining patterns in the activity budgets of different primates is difficult. Once again, primates exhibit great variability in how they divide up their time and this is seen on an individual, population, and species level. As illustrated in Figure 8.1, some basic patterns have emerged for diurnal monkeys and apes. Primates that are mainly folivorous, such as howlers (*Alouatta*) and langurs (*Presbytis*), tend to spend over 50 percent of their time resting, while other species spend much less time resting and more time foraging and feeding. The amount of time spent moving or traveling is dependent on the distribution and availability of food resources (Oates 1987). When foods, such as leaves, occur in large, continuous distributions, then less time has to be spent finding and harvesting them. Considerably more time has to be spent digesting food (i.e., resting). Foods consisting of fruits or insects typically occur in highly dispersed patches. These foods require time to locate, harvest, and consume, especially if seeds are not swallowed whole.

Seasonal Influences on Time Budgets

The availability of food resources is not constant and seasonal shifts occur that decrease or increase the availability of food. It is expected that this will have a direct effect on the time budgets of primates. When food becomes scarce, there are three possible options in how primates might adjust their time:

1. Spend a greater amount of time seeking out food.
2. Increase time spent feeding by eating lesser-quality foods (utilizing fallback foods) and consuming them in greater bulk.
3. Minimize energy expenditure by limiting time spent traveling and foraging and increase amount of time spent resting (Schoener 1971).

All of these options are utilized by various species of primates and populations of a single species. However, there are additional options open to primates as exhibited by woolly monkeys.

Patterns in the activity budgets of woolly monkeys (*Lagothrix lagotricha*) in eastern Ecuador revealed that these primates practice a different strategy. Over the course of a year these mainly frugivorous primates spent 36.2 percent of their time foraging and feeding, 34.5 percent traveling, 23.2 percent resting, and 6.1 percent in self-directed or social behaviors (Di Fiore and Rodman 2001). As predicted by option (3) above, there was a significant negative relationship between the time spent resting each month and the availability of ripe fruit. However, time spent traveling, feeding and foraging could not be related to any of the measures of fruit availability. It was discovered that woolly monkeys practiced an energy-maximizing strategy of food acquisition during times of fruit abundance. When fruits were most commonly available, these primates increased the time they foraged and fed on animal prey. Therefore, in addition to feeding on abundant amounts of ripe fruit (high in calories), they consumed much animal prey (high in protein). In contrast, more time was spent resting and less time spent foraging for animal prey when it was hotter and there was a reduction in the fruits available. In time of food abundance, these monkeys may be contributing to fat stores that can be expended when foods are not so plentiful. Similar strategies have been reported for the closely related muriquis (*Brachyteles arachnoides*) (Strier 1992).

The black snub-nosed langur (*Rhinopithecus bieti*) lives in mixed coniferous forests of Yunnan, China, and exhibits a time budget that maximizes foraging and minimizes energy expenditure (Ding and Zhao 2004). Annually, these monkeys spend on average 35 percent of their time feeding, 33 percent resting, 15 percent traveling, and 13 percent in social activities. During winters, the monkeys had one long rest period (11:00-14:00h), while during summers they took two shorter rest periods (11:00-12:00h and 15:00-17:00h).

Lichens compose 60 percent of their total annual diet, but during the winter months lichens make up 76 percent of the total diet (Table 6-2). In the winter months they spend a greater part of the day resting compared to other seasons (Table 6-2). These monkeys can conserve their energy during the winter months because lichens are readily found close by, so they spend little time travelling. In the spring, leaves and buds from flowering plants become available, and the monkeys rest less and travel more, eating a maximum amount of new leaves and buds (Table 6-2). At this time, when food is most available, they spend the largest amount of time engaged in social behaviors. In the summer months, these langurs depend on lichens for over 50 percent of their diet, but continue to feed on leaves and buds. During the fall, they spend the most amount of time feeding and rest the least.

TABLE 6-2   Annual Activity Budget and Diet for *Rhinopithecus bieti*.

Activity (%)	Winter Average	Spring Average	Summer Average	Fall Average
Feeding	37	31	30	42
Resting	46	29	26	24
Travelling	12	16	20	14
Social	4	21	17	14
Feeding (%)				
Lichens	76	44	54	57
Leaves and buds	23	55	33	13

(Adapted from: Ding and Zhao 2004, p. 594).

 BOX 6-1

Long-Term Study of the Ecology and Conservation of Primates Living in the Kibale Forest, Uganda

Over thirty years of research has been conducted on primates living in the Kibale National Park, located in the foothills of the Ruwenzori Mountains of western Uganda (Skorupa 1988, Stuhsaker 1975, Struhsaker and Leland 1979). The park is 766 km² (306 mi²) with more than half consisting of rain forest (primary and secondary), and the remainder unevenly divided between grassland, woodland, lakes and wetlands, and plantations. Kibale contains a very high primate biomass, and twelve different primate species reside within its borders (Chapman et al. 2005b, Fashing and Cords 2000, Oates et al. 1990) (Table 6-3).

The ecology of the Kibale Forest and the behavioral ecology of the first six primate species listed in Table 6-3 have been extensively studied; consequently, Kibale presents an intriguing case study of the factors that affect primate ecology, primate density, and conservation. Long-term study of the sympatric relationships between the two colobus species, the redtail and blue monkeys, and the mangabeys revealed subtle to extensive differences in their body weight, dietary preferences, ranging behaviors, territoriality, activity budgets, social structure, and social organization (see Chapter 7) (Struhsaker and Leland 1979). As described above, such differences enable species to coexist.

TABLE 6-3 Primates of the Kibale Forest

Common Name	Species Name
Red colobus	*Piliocolobus tephrosceles*
Black-and-white colobus	*Colobus guereza*
Redtail monkey	*Cercopithecus ascanius*
Blue monkey	*Cercopithecus mitis*
Grey-cheeked mangabey	*Lophocebus albigena*
Chimpanzee	*Pan troglodytes*
L'Hoest's monkey	*Cercopithecus lhoesti*
Vervet	*Chlorocebus aethiops*
Olive baboon	*Papio anubis*
Potto	*Perodicticus potto*
Matschie's bushbaby	*Galago matschiei*
Thomas's bushbaby	*Galagoides thomasi*

Kibale has a complicated history of human-induced habitat disturbance involving commercial logging and the agricultural clearing of land (Chapman and Lambert 2000). Twenty-eight years of data have been collected on primate abundance in logged and unlogged forests, and a ten-year study of the community dynamics in selectively logged forest areas provide a unique opportunity to

(continued)

shed light on the reaction of primate species to habitat alteration. In the year 2000, abandoned farms and degraded forest covered 146 km² (58.4 mi²) of Kibale, and researchers estimated a loss of 52,612 monkeys and 200 chimpanzees. In an attempt to understand the effects of habitat alteration on the primate species of Kibale, the use of forest fragments by primates has been extensively monitored. Researchers, however, have failed to find a predictive model that would account for the changes in primate abundance they have observed in such fragments (Chapman et al. 2005, Onderdonk and Chapman 2000). In other words, no aspects of the behavioral ecology of the primates or characteristics of the patches can reliably predict the presence or absence of primates. Consequently, researchers working in the Kibale National Park conclude that multifactoral explanations must be determined. Moreover, these explanation need to include parasites, predation, and other nonfood resource-related factors such as regional climatic change, as such factors additionally stress primate populations and may be associated with disturbed habitats.

As deforestation and forest fragmentation increase throughout the world, Kibale offers researchers a unique opportunity to study the factors that affect primate abundance. If these factors can be delineated at Kibale, they may then shape effective conservation strategies used in other tropical rain forest environments.

Extreme Form of Energy Conservation

Members of the family Cheirogaleidae (small, nocturnal Malagasy strepsirhines) enter into a state known as **torpor**, which is a type of hibernation. It is a strategy to reduce energy demands in environments where food supplies can become severely limited. Other mammalian species such as woodchucks and meadow and woodland jumping mice similarly practice a strategy of fat accumulation followed by a period of inactivity or dormant behavior. Mouse lemurs (*Microcebus*) and dwarf lemurs (*Cheirogaleus*) living in dry coastal forests where the availability of resources are highly seasonal, enter into a state of torpor for up to eight months of the year, hibernating in tree holes (Foerg and Hoffman 1982, Hladik et al. 1980, Petter 1978, Wright and Martin 1995). Brown mouse lemurs (*Microcebus rufus*) living in the rain forest of southeastern Madagascar (RNP) enter into a more abbreviated state of hibernation, as indicated by their absence from traps for periods of up to one month (Atsalis 1999). In these strepsirhines, fat is stored preferentially in the tails, as well as in other parts of their bodies (Figure 6-13). The gray mouse lemur (*Microcebus murinus*) lives in Forêt de Kirindy, a deciduous dry forest in western Madagascar. Schmid (2001) investigated what type of environmental cues stimulated the lemurs to enter into a state of torpor. Schmid found that these lemurs entered into torpor only during the dry season and not during the rainy season; however, ambient temperatures did not appear to be a reliable cue. The most reliable indicator appeared to be photoperiod. Moreover, those individuals that had greater body mass more frequently entered into torpor compared to those that remained in a normal state of activity (normothermic). It is suggested that in the case of these mouse lemurs that entering into a state of torpor might be a strategy to preserve body fat reserves.

FIGURE 6-13 A gray mouse lemur (*Microcebus murinus*) having fat stored in its tail.

A study of the fat-tailed dwarf lemur (*Cheirogaleus medius*) living in the dry deciduous forests of western Madagascar (Fietz and Ganzhorn 1999) showed that these lemurs could double their body mass in a relatively short period of time. Captured and recaptured individuals had a mean body mass of 124 g (4.3 lbs) in December, and before entering hibernation at the end of April, weighed 234 g (8.2 lbs). Prehibernation fattening involved the consumption of fruit species with high sugar contents. Locomotor activity declined significantly during the prehibernation fattening stage. Eating more and reducing the amount of energy expended is thus a prehibernation strategy.

❖❖ Summary

Study of primate ecology involves how primates use their habitat and obtain the resources that are necessary for their survival. As members of an ecological community, primates have evolved ecological and behavioral strategies that enable them to survive. These strategies have been shaped by competition and the tendency of primates to be social.

Ecology is a complicated topic. An ecological system involves a complex network of energy exchange. In order for an ecological system to function properly, a state of balance or homeostasis has to be maintained. Autotrophs produce food that heterotrophs, such as primates, consume. Membership to a trophic level implies that an organism has to accomplish a similar number of steps to obtain energy. Merely describing the components of an ecosystem does not capture the many intricate factors involved. Calculating measurements such as biomass, population density, and carrying capacity helps scientists to compare and contrast ecosystems. Habitat and ecological niche are smaller components of an ecosystem. Ecologists scrutinize the specific relationships that affect organisms living in these more specific zones.

No population of any organism, can have unlimited growth. Factors that limit population size involve Liebig's Law of the Minimum and Shelford's Law of Tolerance. These "laws" establish the ecological parameters that limit growth.

Within their ecological community, primates interact with a number of different species. Primates may be the prey for a variety of predators, and some primates prey on each other as well. Primates are subjected to parasites that may have a negative affect on a primate host. Primates perform significant roles as plant pollinators and seed dispersers. They are also gardeners and prune the plants that they feed from. All of these activities can have beneficial effects on plants. Forest diversity appears to be linked to the seed dispersing activities of primates—and the well-being of future forests may depend on the presence of primates in those forests.

Patterns in the behavioral ecology of primates have been difficult to pin down. Primates are diverse in their ecological and behavioral strategies, and this diversity is seen both between species and between populations of a single species. There just does not seem to be a "one size fits all" pattern for primates. How food is distributed in both time and space are essential factors that influence the foraging strategies of primates. When primates primarily feed on food that has a continuous distribution (such as leaves), they may not need to travel as far to seek it out. In contrast, when primates depend more on fruits or insects found in clumped distributions, they may have to travel farther to find them, in addition such foods may only be seasonally available.

Primates seem to know their habitat well, and where and when to find food. Creative studies have been engineered in order to study whether primates have the ability to create mental maps. It appears that they do; however, we are not necessarily sure how they accomplish this feat. Some species may actually monitor their home range and specific food sites from time to time.

The partitioning of resources occurs when primates compete with other primates, or other animals, living in the same habitat for the same resources. Resources may be divided up along many vectors including time, space, type of foods preferred, etc. In some cases primates form polyspecific associations in which two or even three species may co-habitate in a single group. Information sharing and a greater ability to defend resources may be factors that contribute to the formation of polyspecific associations.

The ranging behavior of primates involves their use of space. Primates live in defined areas and use an area known as a home range. Day ranges consist of the distance travelled in the course of a day. When primates actively defend their ranges, we refer to this as territorial behavior.

How primates divide up the day or night is related to many factors. Time must be spent in all of the activities that are necessary to the physical and social well-being of a primate. Seasonal shifts in time budgets have been identified for many primates but overall patterns are once again hard to establish. Energy conservation is a strategy that often but not always shapes how primates allocate their time. In situations of extreme environmental stress, small strepsirhine primates (the Cheirogaleidae) may even enter into a state of hibernation known as torpor.

❖❖ Key Words

affiliative	ecological niche	philopatric
agonistic	endozoochory	pollinators
area of exclusive use	ethogram	polyspecific groups
asynchronous	exocarps	population density
autotrophs	fallback food	resource partitioning
biomass	foraging strategies	seed predation
carrying capacity	heterotrophs	seed shadow
clumped distributions	home range	synchronous
competitive exclusion	homeostasis	synergistic
core area	information-sharing hypothesis	territoriality
corms	lianas	time budgets
crepuscular	mutualism	torpor
day ranges	niche breadth	trophic levels

❖❖ Study Questions

1. What is homeostatsis and why is it important to the study of ecology?
2. What is a trophic level and to how many trophic levels do primates belong?
3. What factors limit population growth, and why is it important to understand these "laws"?
4. What types of predators eat primates, and do primates prey on one another?
5. In what way do primates benefit plants, and why is the seed-dispersing behavior of primates important for the well-being of future forests?
6. How do foods that are clumped or continuously distributed affect the foraging strategies of primates?
7. How do primates find food, and what type of evidence do we have that primates are capable of having mental maps?
8. What is the principle of competitive exclusion, and how do primates share habitats?
9. What is a polyspecific association, and why do some primates form them?
10. What is a home range and a day range and what type of behaviors indicate that a primate is territorial?
11. How do primates divide up their day or night and how might seasonal changes affect primates' time budget?

❖❖ Suggested Readings and Related Web Sites

Campbell CJ, Fuentes A, MacKinnon K, Panger M, Bearder S. editors. 2007. Primates in perspective. New York: Oxford University Press.

Clutton-Brock TH. editor. 1977. Primate ecology: studies of feeding and ranging behaviour in lemurs, monkeys and apes. London: Academic Press.

Cowlishaw G, Dunbar R. 2000. Primate conservation biology. Chicago: University of Chicago Press. Especially Chapter 3: Behavioral ecology and Chapter 4: Community ecology.

Sussman. RW, editor. 1979. Primate ecology: problem-oriented field studies. New York: John Wiley & Sons.

Sussman RW. 1999. Primate ecology and social structure volume 1: lemurs and tarsiers. Massachusetts: Pearson Custom Publishing.

Sussman RW. 2000. Primate ecology and social structure volume 2: new world monkeys. Massachusetts: Pearson Custom Publishing.

CHAPTER 7

Primate Social Organization

ocial organization refers to how primates group themselves together. It describes the size and composition of a group (i.e., the number of individuals of different age and sex classes) and how individuals move between different social groups. Primates are born into what is referred to as a **natal group**. As primates approach sexual maturity, members of one or the other sex will then move into a different or reproductive group (**dispersal pattern**). In some cases, a primate may live in a number of different groups throughout its lifetime.

Most, if not all, mammals are social animals when it comes to reproduction and the rearing of young. However, primates belong to the most gregarious order of the social mammals. Even though individuals in some primate species may spend much of their time alone, in the overwhelming number of species, individuals aggregate together into groups. There is great variability in the type of groupings that different primate species live in, and in some species there is even variability between populations of the same species (intraspecific variability). Even though there are births and deaths, and animals entering and leaving, group membership tends to be rather constant over time unless there is some dramatic environmental change or upset.

❖❖ Why Do Some Primates Live in Social Groups While Some Do Not?

There are several explanations in regard to why primates form social groups (see below). Underpinning how species group themselves is the need for each individual to maximize its reproductive success. However, females and males have different demands: Females need access to reliable food resources and a safe environment in which to raise their young, while males need to seek out and mate with as many receptive females as possible. While living in a group may provide an individual with specific benefits, it is important to recognize that living in social groups may also carry costs, such as competition for food. There has to be a balance between the benefits and the costs for group living to be successful.

Five Primary Reasons for Group Living

- Predator protection
- Resource defense
- Access to mates
- Assistance in child rearing and protection against infanticide
- Phylogenetic propensity

Predator protection. Since there is usually safety in numbers group living provides added protection. The more eyes and ears available to look out for predators the safer each individual will be, and more individuals can be on the lookout and give warning calls when a predator is detected. Most predators depend on not being detected. They ambush their prey and if detected will abandon the hunt. Thus, predator protection may be a strong incentive for animals to group together. It may not be coincidental that diurnal species are more often found living in groups while nocturnal species tend to rely more on being "invisible" and frequently live alone. Terrestrial species live in larger groups than do arboreal species. Living out in the open away from the safety of trees offers fewer escape routes and increased predator pressure. However, there may also be costs to living in large social groups since it is easier for predators to detect their prey.

Resource defense and access to mates. To maximize their lifetime reproductive success females and males utilize different **reproductive strategies** (Trivers 1972). In her lifetime a female gives birth to a limited number of offspring; consequently, she invests a great deal of energy and effort in each one. Wrangham (1980) has suggested that females aggregate into groups to ensure access to good food resources. The greater number of individuals that band together, the better they will be at defending access to scarce resources such as food, water, and sleeping sites. This, of course, can also have an adverse effect, because there may be more competition for the same scarce resources within the group. Males, in contrast, have the potential to sire many offspring, and therefore males should seek out and mate with as many females as possible. Thus, while females may group together to defend scarce food resources and sleeping sites, males join such groups to better monitor the reproductive state of the females, and if possible, monopolize mating access.

However, reproductive success entails not only mating or giving birth but also the successful rearing of offspring so that he or she in turn grows up and reproduces. Therefore, the protection and care of offspring is vitally important and, in most primate species, parental investment is great. More often than not, it is the female (the mother) who is the sole or main caregiver. Only in a few species (e.g., titi monkey, *Callicebus,* and owl monkey, *Aotus*) is the male (the father) actively involved in raising the young and will carry them during daily foraging. Mothers often receive help from relatives and female friends with taking care of the infant, so called **aunting** or **allomothering behavior.**

Older offspring, especially older sisters, watch over and play with their younger siblings. By having relatives and friends around, a mother may also stand a better chance of protecting her offspring against infanticidal males.

> **allomothering**—or alloparenting, caregiving to an infant or juvenile by individuals other than the mother; often performed by older female siblings

There is much variability (both interspecific and intraspecific) in how tolerant a mother is toward allowing others to handle her baby. Adult males are usually not tolerated close to the baby unless it is a male friend. Such males, not necessarily the fathers, may directly or indirectly assist in the survival of the baby by protecting the mother and her offspring against harassment and potential threats. However, such protection may be less about protecting a potential offspring and more of a mating strategy on the part of the male, since in some species females apparently prefer to mate with male friends (Smuts 1987). Furthermore, old males, often male friends, may act as babysitters allowing the mother to catch up on feeding or social life (Figure 7-1).

Phylogenetic propensity. Primate sociality has been selected for by natural selection over many generations. Thus, a species' social grouping pattern reflects not only present-day

FIGURE 7-1 Older males, such as this hamadryas baboon, often form strong friendships with specific females. Even though they may no longer be mating partners, the males look after and protect the offspring of their female friends.

influences but also the phylogenetic history of the species. In other words, social grouping patterns may represent not just current constraints but also past selective pressures. This may be the reason why some species exhibit more than one pattern of social grouping (see below). The fact that primates are inherently social and most species are highly gregarious should not be ignored. Maybe they just like to be together with each other. Whatever the reason for living in a social group, there will always be both benefits and costs. Typically, the benefits should outweigh the costs, but because primates are complex social animals the costs and benefits to each individual will differ.

❖❖ Types of Social Groupings

Primates may live singly, in pairs, or in groups, of variable composition. Primatologists recognize seven types of social groupings Table 7-1), but there is also a degree of variability inherent in primate social groupings due to contextual and phylogenetic differences. Often a species may be found living in more than one type of social grouping. For example, hanuman langurs (*Semnopithecus entellus*) and red howlers (*Alouatta seniculus*) have

TABLE 7-1   Primate Social Groupings.

Social Groupings	Composition	Illustration
Solitary foragers	Individuals range and forage alone; females with dependent young; male home ranges typically overlap with that of several females	
One male-one female group	Single male and single female with dependent young; sometimes older siblings remain beyond adolescence; usually display territorial defense	
One male-multifemale group	One adult male together with more than one adult female with dependent young; no or little overlap in home ranges; males without females aggregate into single-sex groups	
One female-multimale group	One adult female together with one or more adult males with dependent young; other adult females may be present but without active involvement in breeding; no or little overlap in home ranges	

Multimale-multifemale group	Several adult males and females with dependent young; no or little overlap in home ranges	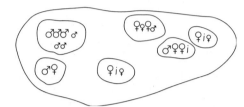
Fission-fusion group	Several adult males and females with dependent young; a more fluid system with members of the larger group or community coming and going at will; membership in each subgroup is not predictable from day to day	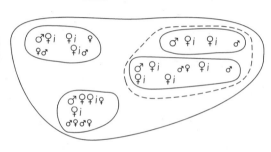
Complex, multi-leveled group	One male units (one male together with one or more females and dependent young) cluster together into "clans" or "teams." During travel or foraging many OMUs may join together into bands. At sleeping sites several bands join during the night; these herds can comprise several hundred individuals	

been observed living in either one male-multifemale or multimale-multifemale groups (Rowe 1996). Furthermore, a species' **mating strategy** may further complicate its social organization. Even though not necessarily independent of one another, mating systems and social organizations are influenced by different selective pressures—one promotes the reproductive success of individuals, while the other functions to promote the success of the group. Consequently, a species' mating system and its social organization are usually considered separately. Several species of tamarins (*Saguinus*) and marmosets (*Callithrix*) also have varied groupings. They may live in a group with several adult males and adult females but only a single male and female will reproduce. Alternatively, a group may consist of a single adult female and several males, i.e., a polyandrous grouping, and the female may mate with more than one male.

Solitary Foragers

The solitary forager or noyau group (Fleagle 1999) structure is most commonly observed in nocturnal strepsirhines. However, the orangutan is also a solitary forager. Our knowledge about solitary foragers (excluding the orangutan) is limited, although over the past few years results from several field studies have greatly improved our understanding about this type of social group living (see, e.g., Bearder et al., 2006, Nekaris 2001, 2003b, 2006, Pimley et al., 2005a,b, Radespiel et al., 2002, Sterling et al., 2000, Wiens and Zitzmann

2003). As the name suggests, individuals tend to range and forage alone, and adult females are accompanied by their dependent offspring. However, it is clear that many of these solitary species actually have very complex social systems. Richard (1985) suggested that we look upon the way these species live as representative of neighborhoods, in which despite foraging alone, each individual is keenly aware of his or her social surroundings. It is becoming evident that most of the so-called solitary species actually form loosely spaced but cohesive groupings, comprising more than one individual, not counting mothers with dependent offspring. Some species show a stronger affinity to aggregate than others. For example, slender lorises (*Loris tardigradus* and *L. lydekkerianus*) may spend a large part of their active time within vocal and visual range of several conspecifics (<20 m or <22 yds). They often come together to socialize and form sleeping groups (Nekaris 2000, 2003a, 2006). In contrast, while pottos (*Perodicticus potto edwardsi*) tend to forage and travel in close proximity to conspecifics, they are less likely to engage in affiliative interactions (Pimley et al. 2005a).

Additional species, that were considered to live as solitary foragers, have been found living in pair groups (e.g., mouse lemur, *Microcebus coquereli*) or in multifemale groups (e.g., bushbaby, *Galago senegalensis*). In the case of bushbabies, several females (possibly related) forage in close proximity or come together during the night to groom. During the day they form sleeping groups. Thus, being a solitary forager does not mean that the species is antisocial. Most likely, this is the best solution to gain access to food resources and avoid predators when one is a small nocturnal animal.

In most species, each female defends a territory, but tolerance of conspecifics can vary. In many species of bushbabies (e.g., *Galagoides demidoff*), the home ranges of several females may partially overlap. It has been suggested that mothers and daughters or sisters share part of their territories. In other species, there is little or no overlap between the females' home ranges (e.g., tarsier, *Tarsius bancanus,* and mouse lemur, *Microcebus coquereli*). Males have typically larger home ranges than females, and the home range of a male usually encompasses that of several females (see Table 7-1). It is unusual for the home ranges of males to overlap. Normally, males are not very socially inclined toward one another. In most species, males not only forage alone, they also tend to sleep by themselves, although in species such as the Mysore slender loris, males may join groups of females at sleeping sites (Nekaris 2006). Adult males keep track of the reproductive state of the females whose home ranges overlap with theirs, and they spend much time exploring for signs (olfactory cues) of the females' reproductive status. In most strepsirhines, the mating system is promiscuous.

Most commonly, a female gives birth to a singleton, and rears the baby by herself. In some species, the mother either leaves the infant in a nest, or "parks" it in a secluded place while she goes to feed (e.g., potto, *Perodicticus potto*). Bushbaby mothers usually carry the young infant around in their mouth, as do tarsier mothers (Figure 7-2). Once the infant is capable of keeping up with the mother, it accompanies her on nightly foraging stints. Before they become sexually mature, both male and female offspring leave their mother's home range. Daughters may not venture too far away from their mothers. Males have to "lay low" until they are able to establish their own territory.

FIGURE 7-2   In most primate species, the offspring clings to the mother's body. However, in some species, the mothers transport the babies in their mouth, as shown with this spectral tarsier, *Tarsius spectrum.*

❖ ❖ ❖ ❖   HOT TOPIC 7-1   ❖ ❖ ❖ ❖

What Is a Family?

Traditionally, when defining a human family we think about a father, a mother, and their children. We also assume that there is a special and exclusive relationship between the adult male and female. In the nonhuman primate world, such family groups are not very common. Kinzey (1987) estimated that only between 10 to 15 percent of all primate species live in monogamous pairs or family groups. However, what a monogamous pair or family group entails is not often defined. This creates much confusion because social organization and a mating system are often, incorrectly, treated as part of the same package.

More recently, Fuentes (1999, 2002) has attempted to separate the mating system from the long-term social bonds of an adult male and an adult female. Fuentes suggests that we should divide the family group into the *social pair bond* and the *sexual pair bond*. A social pair bond is defined as an association between an adult male and female that lasts for more than one year, each member of the pair seeks to be in proximity with the other member, and together they display specific behaviors such as vocalizing, displaying, and defending a territory. Some aspects of the relationship between the pair are similar to the friendships seen in multimale-multifemale groups (Smuts 1985). In a sexual pair bond, all the above features are evident, along with exclusive mating. Thus, when including exclusive mating in the definition of a pair group, only about 3 percent of all primate species can be classified as living in pair groups (Fuentes 2002).

Members of the Hylobatidae family (gibbons and siamangs) have been used as typical examples of primates that live in family groups. The bond between a male and a female was estimated to last for a very long time, maybe even for life. This bond included sexual fidelity ("Gibbons are invariably monogamous. . .", Leighton 1987:137). Even though we know of pairs that have stayed together for many, many years (6–14 years; see Bartlett 1999), gibbons apparently have a much more complex social organization and mating system. Other adult individuals have been observed in close association with family groups. Due to the lack of genetic information, it cannot be ruled out that these extra individuals are related to the adult pair. They could be mature offspring that for some reason or other have lost their mate or territory and had no other option than to move back home. Or they may never have left. Furthermore, reproduction within the pair bond apparently is not as monogamous as first thought. Extra pair matings are not infrequent (Palmobit 1996). In a study of the white-handed gibbon (*Hylobates lar*), Reichard (1995) found that of the copulations observed, 12 percent were outside of the pair bond. However, the mating behavior appears to be independent of the social grouping. Even though a female may solicit matings from neighboring males, she more often than not stays with the male in her family.

In the pair-bonded American monkeys, there is a much more cohesive and interactive relationship between the adult pair, and greater sexual fidelity. For example, titi monkeys (*Callicebus*) are believed to form permanent pairs, or at least long-term social and exclusive sexual bonds (Sussman 2000). Each pair spends rest periods in close proximity, often with their tails intertwined, and they often engage in mutual grooming. The male is actively engaged in the rearing of the offspring. By the second day after birth, it is the father that carries the offspring most of the time, and he may only return the newborn to the mother to feed. A similar pattern of behavior can be seen in the owl monkey (*Aotus*).

❖❖❖❖

One Male-One Female or Pair Group

A more rare social organization amongst primates is the pair group, often referred to as a family group (Table 7-1). Several American monkeys live in family groups, e.g., titi (*Callicebus*) and owl (*Aotus*) monkeys, as do several diurnal Malagasy lemurs, e.g., indri (*Indri*) and some of the bamboo lemurs *(Hapalemur)*. The gibbon is possibly the quintessential pair-bonded primate (Figure 7-3).

Usually, a pair group is made up of an adult male and an adult female, and dependent young. In some cases the juvenile remains with the family group beyond the birth of the next offspring. The relationship between the two adults may include an exclusive social and mating relationship (Fuentes 2002). It may last for a long time, although there is much variability not just between species but also in individual propensities. Occasionally these bonds may be temporarily broken (see Hot Topic 7-1).

FIGURE 7-3 Gibbons (*Hylobates*) are the quintessential pair-bonded primate, where a male and female may spend many years in each others company and raise offspring together. In many gibbon species males and females have different colored hair; shown here is the female (buff colored hair) grooming the male (black hair) while the infant is clinging to the male's leg.

In a pair group the male and female share in the defense of their territory. There is little to no sexual dimorphism in species that form family groups, although there may be distinctive sexual dichromatism (Figure 4-3). The adults usually show little agonism toward each other and often engage in affiliative behaviors.

Social interactions are, of course, limited in such small groups. During resting time they may sit close to each other or groom, although in some species (e.g., gibbons), interactions between the adults is less common (Figure 7-3). Infants engage in solitary play unless there is an older sibling present, although occasionally a parent may engage in play with his or her offspring. Gibbon families have been observed to aggregate at territorial borders, allowing offspring from different families to play together (Bartlett 2003).

In some species, males actively participate in the rearing of young by carrying the infant during daily travel (e.g., owl monkey, *Aotus* and titi monkey, *Callicebus*). In species in which offspring delay leaving their natal group, they may help with the caretaking of younger siblings. More commonly, upon reaching sexual maturity, both sons and daughters leave their parents' home range to seek out their own mates. *Aotus* and *Callicebus* parents do not show any aggression toward their offspring to induce them to leave their natal group. Gibbons, in contrast, may become increasingly intolerant toward their adolescent offspring with the agonism tending to flow from mother to daughter and from father to son. Females are most hesitant to leave home and less frequently take up solitary lives. They spend much time vocalizing, calling for potential mates, and many will not leave until they have found a mate. In contrast, adolescent males may spend several years alone before being able to establish a territory of their own (and to find a mate).

 **BOX 7-1**

Life as a Teenager

Compared to other animals, primates take a long time to reach adulthood, i.e., they have a prolonged immature stage. Several reasons have been suggested in regard to why primates need such an extended "growing-up" period. It may be due to the amount of time needed to learn the essential social and foraging skills required for successful survival. The delayed maturation may be a physiological consequence of having diverted so much energy to the development of a large brain, so the body needs some catch-up time. Alternatively, perhaps the longer you live, the longer you can take to grow up.

Most of the growing-up period is between weaning (end of the infancy period) and before reaching adult repro-

ductive age. We divide this time into two stages: the juvenile period, which falls between weaning and the beginning of puberty, and the adolescence period, which begins with the onset of puberty

> **bimaturism**—developmental differences between males and females; one sex may grow for a longer time or at a different rate than the other

and ends with the beginning of effective reproduction. Puberty starts when sex hormones begin to stream through the body, causing many physical changes. In male primates we may see an expansion of muscle mass and rapid testicular growth. In female primates the physical

FIGURE 7-4 A new born infant is a focus of attraction for other group members, who want to greet, touch and interact with it. However, mothers are usually wary and will only allow trusted individuals close to their infant. This chimpanzee mother is paying close attention to her infant and the interaction taking place with another group member.

(continued)

manifestation of adolescence is much less obvious, although in some species, perineal swellings (e.g., baboons, chimpanzees) may begin. The length of adolescence in many species differs between males and females. Males grow slower and for a longer amount of time than do females (**bimaturism**). For example, a baboon female may begin her reproductive career at 6 years of age while a male may have to wait until he is 10 years old before he is able to gain access to a female and successfully mate with her (Walters 1987).

Growing up is seldom easy. This is true for most primates. Infants are usually the center of attraction in the natal group (Figure 7-4). Even though most primate mothers are extremely caring and tolerant of their offspring, by the time one offspring is weaned, she is most likely pregnant again and needs time to recharge before the next baby comes along. Her tolerance may therefore run a bit thin (see Chapter 8; parent-offspring conflicts). This is the time in which the female seeks out the company of other social partners.

A crucial aspect of growing up is learning foraging skills (Altmann 1998). Each immature primate has to be able to discern food from nonfood, where food sources are located, and when different foods are available and ready to eat. Most of this is learned during the juvenile period, although infants also learn while they cling to their mother's stomach when she is feeding (Figure 7-5). There is usually not much room for experimenting. Since plants are pretty good at defending themselves by storing toxins, one bite of the wrong plant could prove to be fatal for an immature primate. Mothers may not directly teach their offspring what to eat and what to avoid, although they may remove nonfoods from an infant's grasp before it has a chance to eat them.

The social skills required to become a good member of a social group can take longer to gain. By observing the interactions taking place between their mother and other group members,

FIGURE 7-5 Infants learn their foraging skills initially from their mother, by smelling and examining each item that the mother consumes. Here an anubis baboon yearling is sniffing the food its mother holds in her hand.

infants and young juveniles gain much knowledge about social positions and interactions within the group.

Play is an important means through which to learn social skills. This is the case for most mammals, although it is especially evident in primates. Of course, the presence of peers influences the amount or type of play an immature engages in. When very young or when living in a social situation in which there are no peers, playing with objects or running about may be the only option. In large groups, social play with peers is the most common form of play. Juveniles spend most of their nonfeeding time in social play, e.g., chasing and wrestling (Figure 7-6). Males devote much more time to play than do females, except in species in which sex differences in dominance and size are not so marked, i.e., there is little sexual dimorphism, as is the case for ring-tailed lemurs (Gould 1992).

Why is so much time devoted to play? For one, it improves motor skills by building muscles and reflexes. In males it also refines the social and fighting skills necessary later in life. Even though play may appear to be just for fun, it is also very costly, because it is a huge energy drain. Furthermore, it can be dangerous. If the play becomes too rough, it may result in injury and even death. Mortality is high in juveniles, especially young juvenile males.

The play partner of juvenile females can be either male or female, but they tend to play with individuals slightly younger than themselves. Juvenile males, in contrast, play more often with other males of the same size and age as themselves (e.g., Fairbanks 1993). Females stop playing at an earlier age than do males. Females start at a very early age to participate in their mothers' social activities. They engage in grooming and assist their mother in dominance disputes. Females begin practicing their mothering roles by taking care of younger siblings or any infant that a mother is willing to spare.

Males continue to spend most of their social time with peers. As they grow older, their play becomes increasingly rough, and the activity of adult males becomes increasingly fascinating. Subadult males often begin to ascend in rank by harassing females

FIGURE 7-6 Play is an important activity for immature primates in all species. Here two young bonobos (*Pan paniscus*) are engaged in a wrestling match.

(*continued*)

until they are dominant to them, and they take a more peripheral position in the social group. This can also be the case for subadult females in species in which it is the female that leaves the natal group. Much attention is paid to neighboring social groups during intergroup encounters. In some species in which males leave their natal group, they are delegated to live solitary lives for an extended period of time, or they may join single-sex groups. These so-called bachelor groups are temporary social groupings (Figure 7-7). They provide a type of stop-gap support structure for males while they look for and join another social group in which they will become part of the reproductive system. Single-sexed bachelor groups are most frequently associated with species that have a one-male social structure. Even though competitive interactions do occur, life in these groups is overall friendly (this may be the only time when males spend all their grooming time grooming other males, something they will never do as a fully mature, breeding male).

◈ ◈ ◈ ◈

One Male-Multifemale Group

This type of social structure is common in most of the colobine monkeys, as well as in the guenons, including the patas monkey (*Erythrocebus patas*). Mandrills (*Mandrillus sphinx*) should possibly be included within this social grouping as well. Mandrills live in hordes of up to 600 to 800 individuals, but outside of the mating season usually only a single adult male is present in a group (Abernethy et al. 2002). Among the apes, this social structure is found in the gorilla. Commonly, there is a single adult male with two or more adult females, and their offspring (Table 7-1). This grouping pattern is often referred to as a **harem**.

In most species, it is the females that stay in the natal group while males disperse. Males often leave as juveniles or at least before they reach sexual maturity. In gorillas, both males and females leave their natal group. Female goril-

> **harem**—a unit comprising a single adult male and a number of females to whom he has exclusive mating access

las tend to immediately join another group, while males may wander alone for an extended period of time. Some colobine females may also leave their natal group (e.g., the silvered langur, *Trachypithecus cristatus*) but this is not a common occurrence. The females that remain in their natal group form strong social networks, especially if related, while the resident adult male is usually more socially peripheralized. Males, typically much larger than females, are intolerant of each other and attempt to exclude other males from joining their group. When a male leaves his natal group, he may live a solitary life for a while, or even join a group of another species. Alternatively, these "bachelor males" aggregate into single sex groups (Figure 7-7). In some species, the leader male may tolerate the presence of another male, especially if the other male is not yet mature and of lower rank (e.g., howler and proboscis monkey). This particular type of social organization is referred to as an **age-graded group**. The male adult leader may tolerate the presence of a subadult male because he could be his son, and the presence of a second male possibly enhances the protection and safety of the group.

FIGURE 7-7   Males who are not part of one male-multifemale groups form single-sex groups, so called bachelor groups. In such groups social interactions are common among the males, as shown here where two langur (*Semnopithecus entellus*) males are grooming.

Most commonly, reproduction takes place during a short time interval once a year, the so-called breeding season. All reproductively active females become receptive at the same time, which makes it almost impossible for the resident male to control mating access to all of the females. During the breeding season, solitary males or males from single-sex groups descend on the group. The resident females may solicit interactions with the new males, and preferentially mate with them. Alternatively, they may demonstrate choice by staying close to the leader male. Some of these extra-group males may challenge the resident male for the "possession" of a female. These fights are usually dramatic and intense. A male keeps his residency for no more than two to three years, although a silverback male gorilla may lead his group for a much longer time.

It is not uncommon for a new male leader to show aggression toward any immature individual in the group that is less than a year old and maybe even kill it (**infanticide**). A male may improve his reproductive success by doing so (see Chapter 8; van Schaik and Janson, 2000). Once the female has lost her baby, she will resume cycling, thus the male's behavior will ensure that her next baby will be his. An infanticidal male not only creates an opportunity to reproduce, but also removes the genes from his predecessor and competitor. Females may attempt to protect their offspring against aggressive males, but because the male is often twice as large as the female, the resistance of a female, even if the females band together, is limited.

> **infanticide**—the intentional killing of an infant as a means to gain reproductive advantage by inducing the mother into a receptive stage and fathering her next offspring

When females share the timing of their reproductive cycles, infants are born around the same time and thus will always have the same agemates to interact and play with. In some of these species the females show high tolerance for allomothering behavior (e.g., langurs), and within hours of giving birth, the infant may be passed around to other females (See Box 7-2). Since gorilla females tend to be unrelated, they do not have the same social cement that binds them, and each mother is left to care for her own offspring.

 BOX 7-2

Life as a Single Mother

A female primate spends most of her adult life either pregnant or lactating and caring for an offspring. We have parental care because, as Blurton Jones states, "Parental behavior evolved because it promoted the parent's reproductive success" (1993:310). A primate mother has to shoulder most if not all of the responsibility of raising her baby. The father, even if he knows the offspring is his, tends to have a more peripheral role in caring for the offspring. Males who are more certain that they have fathered the offspring invest more time and "effort." For example, male titi, owl, and tamarin monkeys carry their offspring during daily travels and may even share food. However, in the majority of species paternity remains unknown (or so we assume). A female may have good reasons to confuse paternity; by doing so she may prevent males from killing the baby (see Chapter 8; infanticidal males). Alternatively, a female may want to solicit several males into protecting her and her baby against harassment from other group members. Depending on the social structure, a female may have assistance in raising her offspring. Kin, especially daughters, and friends may also look out for and protect infants.

In most species, while juvenile boys tend to form playgroups or follow adult males, juvenile girls spend more time with their mothers. By observing her mother and other adult females, a juvenile female acquires mothering skills. She may be allowed to care for younger siblings or the offspring of female friends of her mother. Some high-ranking females may even kidnap infants from lower-ranking females, which may have disastrous results if the baby is prevented from suckling for a long time. Even in social groups in which there are adult females that are good mothers and can serve as models, infants born of **primaparous** females have a much higher mortality rate than infants born to more experienced **multiparous** females.

> **multiparous**—a female that has given birth to more than one offspring
> **primaparous**—a female who has given birth to her first offspring. A female who has not yet given birth is referred to as nulliparous. Parity is a measure of number of births

Most births take place in the early morning at the sleeping site, often leaving little time for the new mother to recuperate before the group is on their daily foraging trail (Altmann 1980). At birth, most babies have a good grasping instinct and hold on to the mother's hair so she can move about fairly unhindered. However, it is not uncommon to notice females who have recently given birth lagging behind as they have to walk on three limbs while supporting the newborn with one hand. In a few species, the mother carries the newborn in her mouth (e.g., tarsier), or the baby may be "parked" in a safe place (e.g., potto) while the mother forages for food. In arboreal species, it is especially important that the newborn infant can hold on, since a fall would almost certainly mean death (Figure 7-8).

Even though most group members are curious about the new arrival and may come to greet the new parent and baby (Figure 7-4), there is little compensation given to the new mother. The daily foraging trek remains unchanged. Either the mother has to keep up or she is on her own. On the day of the birth, the new mother may spend more time resting rather than feeding, but this is not a pattern that can be sustained. Of course, in the case in which there is a birth season and a number of females give birth at approximately the same time, the behavior of the group can more easily be modified.

The infant is completely dependent on its mother for the first few months after birth (altricial). She provides all the food, main care, and protection. While lactating, a female's energy demand increases by some 20 to 50 percent. To meet these demands, a female has to increase her food intake or feed on highly nutritious foods. Weaning takes place at different times depending on the species. The most rapidly developing species include the strepsirhines, tamarins, and marmosets. In the latter case, the mother may already be pregnant when the first offspring is about to be weaned. In general, monkeys wean

FIGURE 7-8 Primate babies are born with a well developed grasping ability; an ability present in newborn human babies as well. In arboreal species, such as this gibbon, an offspring that does not hold on will most likely have a fatal fall.

(continued)

their infants around one year of age, although the infant has been partially independent of the mother for some time prior to this. A female cannot continue to supply the offspring indefinitely, since the demands of the growing infant are greater than what the mother's body can support. There is always a conflict for the mother between the demands of present and future offspring (Maestripieri 2002).

In most species, the bond between a mother and her offspring is strong and long-lasting. This is readily observed in the members of a matriline, and by the fact that solitary foragers such as bush-babies remain close to daughters or sisters and form daily sleep clusters. From Gombe, we have good behavioral observations from several generations of chimpanzees, and the famous matri-line of Flo and her daughter Fifi, showed the close social relationships between mothers and daughters (Goodall 1986). We do not know much about the relationship between mothers and sons, since most sons disperse and may never come in contact with their mother or sisters again. However, in species in which males remain in the natal group, sons and mothers form strong social bonds. Bonobo mothers, for example, assist their sons during conflicts.

Sometimes mothers need help to protect an infant from harassment, especially from other often higher-ranking females. Abuse or rough handling of infants (e.g., hitting, dragging) is not uncommon. It is usually older multiparous females that are the aggressors. The reason behind such aggression is most likely female-female competition, and higher-ranking females may use such behavior as yet another way to demonstrate their dominance. Mothers may form alliances with adult males and with other females and seek their assistance against intragroup harassment.

◇◇◇ ◇◇◇ ◇◇◇ ◇◇◇

Multimale-Multifemale Group

Social groups that have several adult males and several adult females, and their dependent young, are the most common in the primate world (Table 7-1). Group size may vary from less than ten individuals to more than a hundred (Figure 7-9). The sex ratio (the number of adult males to adult females) in this type of social organization can differ from one-to-one, to several females per each adult male, to the more unusual of several males per each adult female (Rowe 1996). This type of social organization is seen in American monkeys such as capuchins, squirrel monkeys, and howler monkeys; in African baboons and vervets; and Asian macaques, and some langurs such as the Douc langur (*Pygathrix nemaeus*).

Both the dispersal pattern and mating system is highly varied within this social organization. In most species it is the males that leave their natal group before they reach sexual maturity (e.g., baboons and squirrel monkeys). However, in some species (e.g., red colobus and woolly spider monkey), it is the females that disperse, while in others both males and females disperse (e.g., howler monkeys and bonnet macaques). Females may be reproductively active throughout the year or seasonally. In either case, males do compete among themselves to gain access to receptive females.

The ring-tailed lemur (*Lemur catta*) is a diurnal, terrestrial Malagasy strepsirhine that lives in multimale-multifemale groups. The residents form clear dominance hierarchies. The only exception is that females are dominant over males. This relationship is reflected by

FIGURE 7-9   Multimale-multifemale groups vary in size from less than ten to several hundred individuals. Baboons (shown here) often form large groups, usually comprising twice as many adult females as adult males, and all dependent offspring.

the lack of obvious sexual size dimorphism, as females are slightly larger than males. Females aggregate into matrilines and the most dominant matriline holds a central position in the group (Sauther 1993). Males tend to be peripheral to the group for most of the year. This species has strict breeding and birthing seasons that occur once a year. Males compete for access to receptive females, and females may prefer to mate with new males rather than with males who have been in the group for a long time. The females raise their offspring more or less alone, and twinning is common among ring-tailed lemurs. When there is ample food available, both may survive, but more often than not, only the stronger infant survives. Infant mortality is very high in *Lemur catta* (Sussman 1991a).

The American squirrel monkey (*Saimiri*) also lives in groups with several adult males and females. Sexual dimorphism is not very pronounced in this genus, although males and females may have slightly different hair coloration (e.g., the Bolivian squirrel monkey). Throughout most of the year, males and females lead separate lives. In some squirrel monkey species, it is the females that are dominant to the males. During the breeding season, however, adult males get an infusion of male hormones (testosterone and cortisone; Bercovitch 1992) and expand in size, especially around the shoulder region. The males become highly aggressive. They form dominance hierarchies, and there are many competitive interactions for access to receptive females. Each female may mate with several males. Once the breeding season is over, the males return to their prebreeding season size and to a more peripheral lifestyle. Even though the female is the primary caretaker of her offspring, older siblings do provide allomothering care.

Baboons live in very large social groups (50 to 100+ individuals) (Figure 7-9). Usually, there are twice as many adult females as adult males. In the anubis baboon (*Papio anubis*), it is the males that leave their natal group. Males do not disperse until they are subadults or even young adults, and they do not spend much time alone. During his lifetime, an anubis male may reside in several different groups and may even return to his natal group. The females form strong matrilineal subunits, which establish the social core of the group. Males form dominance hierarchies and compete amongst themselves for access to females. The females are receptive throughout the year. All adult males, who also are much larger, are dominant over the females. Despite the fact that females generally mate with more than one male, they tend to have preferred partners (often male friends). Even though mothers do most of the parental care, females have much support from friends and relatives in the raising of offspring. There may be many generations present in a single group. During daily travels, a baboon group may disperse into smaller units, often comprising members of a matriline, and a female's male friend. At the end of the day, the group always reunites at the sleeping site.

Some primate species have a much more fluid system of social organization, in which the members of the larger group (community) come and go at will. Membership in each subgroup is not predictable from day to day. Occasionally, group members may not see one another for days on end. We refer to this as a **fission-fusion** social organization. We find such an organization in the chimpanzee (*Pan troglodytes*) and in the spider monkey (*Ateles*). Subgroups can consist of single individuals, a mother and her dependent offspring, and maybe together with a female friend and her family, or a group of males (Table 7-1). When subgroups reunite, there is much excitement and greetings. While chimpanzee communities may contain some thirty to fifty individuals, spider monkey groups are usually smaller (ten to eighteen individuals), but in both cases subgroups usually consist of two to five individuals (Sussman 2000). The spider monkey is curious, because there is little difference in the size of adult males and females (see sperm competition in Chapter 8). In most other species living in multimale-multifemale groups, males tend to be significantly larger than females. This is especially true of the chimpanzees in which the male is substantially larger than the female (male 40–60 kg, 88–132 lbs; female 30–50 kg, 66–110 lbs).

In both chimpanzees and spider monkeys, it is the females that leave their natal group upon reaching sexual maturity, while males tend to stay at home and form the social core of the group. Spider males actively defend their territory, just like the chimpanzee males (Watts et al. 2006). Since resident females usually do not take kindly to a new arrival, immigrating spider females attempt to form a relationship with subadult males. Chimpanzee females usually find that both males and females may be agonistic. Males are more likely to accept a young female into their group, especially if she is reproductively receptive. Both species breed throughout the year. While spider monkey females give birth every two to three years, the interbirth interval in chimpanzees is five to six years (Goodall 1986, Rowe 1996). Mothers raise their offspring by themselves with some assistance from older siblings.

Bonobos (*P. paniscus*) have a similar social organization to their cousins the chimpanzee. There are some fundamental differences, however, between the two species. Whereas it is the females that disperse in both species, the bonobo female is much more assertive. This may be in part because there is less difference in size between male and female bonobos than there is in chimpanzees. To gain access to a new group, the young female seeks out a mature female in the group and befriends her. Even though bonobo males form dominance hierarchies, there is little competition among the males for access to the females, possibly because female bonobos are dominant to males and therefore can choose their mates.

Complex, Multileveled Group

Within the multimale-multifemale social organization, the hamadryas baboon (*Papio hamadryas*) and the gelada (*Theropithecus geleda*) form complex, multileveled groups (Table 7-1). The smallest social unit in both species is the one male unit (OMU), which is made up of an adult male, one or more females, and a number of immature individuals. Some OMUs may also have male followers. These male followers can either be young adults who have not yet gained their own OMU, or old males who have lost their own OMU. In geladas all-male groups may form. In both species, the male leader of the OMU has exclusive mating access to the females. Thus, the OMU can be considered the equivalent of a harem.

Often several OMUs cluster together. In hamadryas these are referred to as "clans," and it has been suggested that the OMU leaders of each clan are related (Abegglen 1984). Within the gelada these larger units are referred to as "teams," but there is no evidence of relatedness between the males (Dunbar 1984). During travel or foraging many OMUs may join together into bands. Since sleeping sites are scarce in the habitats occupied by the hamadryas and the gelada, several bands may have to get together at night. These herds can comprise several hundred individuals. They are the most unstable units within the multileveled social structure. Even though there are usually no social interactions taking place at the herd level, this may be the opportunity for individuals to switch alliances or take over some females.

The dispersal pattern differs in the two species. Gelada males leave their natal group, while hamadryas females are more likely to leave, at least their natal OMU. Thus, in geladas it is more probable that the females within an OMU are related to each other or have at least known one another since childhood. The focus of most social interactions is between the females and their offspring, and it has also been suggested that female choice has a strong influence on the success of the male leader. It has been assumed that hamadryas females living within an OMU were unrelated, an assumption generally based on the lack of social interactions observed between females (Kummer 1968). Recent observations indicate that female hamadryas may have a lot more choice about what OMU they belong to than what was previously thought to be the case (Swedell 2000a). Male tenure as an OMU leader is usually not longer than two or three years, and a male usually does not get a second chance (Figure 7-10a). Once deposed, a male loses status rapidly, and his overall physical appearance changes (Figure 7-10b).

◆◆ Why Do Animals Migrate?

Leaving the safety of one's social group to take up residence in another group is a rather dangerous thing to do, especially if you are immature, alone, and small. Since at least 50 percent of all primates make this journey at least once in their lifetime, there must be some very good reason for doing so. We can recognize the outcome or consequences of leaving one's natal group: It reduces **inbreeding**. Of course, primates do not sit around and calculate how related they are to their group mates, and then decide to leave. There must be some other underlying reason why animals migrate.

Before attempting to answer that question, it is necessary to separate primary or **natal dispersal** from secondary or **breeding transfer** (Pusey and Packer 1987). Natal dispersal refers to when immature individuals leave the group into which they were

(a)

(b)

FIGURE 7-10 Hamadryas baboons live in complex social groups, where the smallest unit is the one-male-group, comprising a leader male and his females and dependent offspring. To be leader of such a "harem" a male has to be in his prime, as seen for example by the very thick and luxurious mane (a). A deposed leader, who has lost all his females, shows rapid degeneration in physical appearance (b).

born. Dispersal is most often a solitary affair, although in some species two or three individuals may transfer together (e.g., macaques). It may be siblings or playmates that decide to leave together. In some species, as they grow older, the immatures experience an increase in antagonism either from their parents or other group members. Such aggression is usually a consequence of competition for resources. Even if the immatures do not experience such "alienation," they leave anyway. Juveniles of the dispersing sex show great interest in neighboring groups very early. This curiosity of (conspecific) strangers is a very prevalent trait in primates. Since familiarity is highly correlated with genetic relatedness, the desire to seek out and interact with strangers may be a mechanism that evolved through natural selection to reduce inbreeding.

In secondary or breeding transfers, adult individuals move between breeding groups, and it is almost exclusively a solitary affair. There may be different reasons for leaving based on the sex of the individual. More often than not, if a female seeks to find a new group, she has been losing in the competition for food resources possibly due to low rank. Less commonly, females leave to seek a partner. Males take up residence in new groups almost exclusively to improve their chances to reproduce. Older males, past reproductive access, may also seek a new social group because the social anonymity may reduce harassment from younger, prime adult males (Sapolsky 2004a). The resources males and females require to maximize their reproductive success differ; hence, the reasons for leaving are also different.

◆◆ Summary

Primates are social beings that live in groups. Social organization refers to the makeup and size of such groups as well as the pattern of movement in and out of natal and reproductive groupings. Primates form and live in groups for a variety of reasons. Group living may be key to warding off or discouraging the attacks of predators (especially for terrestrial-dwelling species), and it may be easier for a group to defend access to a limited resource. In such highly social animals as primates, group living also enables a number of eyes, ears, and hands to assist in the caretaking of inquisitive young individuals, as well as to defend against the attack of a rival or highly aggressive adult male. Members of the primate order may also exhibit an evolutionary predisposition or phylogenetic propensity for group living. In other words, we have evolved to live in groups.

Within the order we find a range in different types of social organization. Many nocturnal strepsirhines live as solitary foragers. They predominantly forage alone but come together with other individuals to sleep and or groom. One male-one female groups are relatively rare among primates, but when these family groups are formed, typically the adult male and adult female act in concert to defend their territory. One male-multifemale groups consist of an adult male and two or more females and their offspring. The male attempts to maintain some degree of reproductive exclusivity over the females. Among primates, the most common grouping pattern is the multimale-multifemale group. This type of social organization is extremely variable in size and ranges from less than a dozen to greater than 100 individuals. This type of grouping is also associated with diverse mating and dispersal patterns. A fission-fusion type of social organization is a very fluid system involving subgroups that ebb and flow in and out of a larger group. Chimpanzees display this type of grouping pattern. Complex, multileveled groups are multiple group tiers that terrestrial hamadryas baboons and geladas exhibit. Individuals may belong to a relatively small group that comes into association with other small groups and forms a larger social network, and this network may in turn become affiliated with other such networks and form an even larger grouping. So, among primates there is a considerable range in the type of group lifestyle or organization that a species may display. Different populations of the same species may also exhibit different types of social organization.

Even though the group is imperative for life as a primate, there is a tendency for individuals of one sex or the other to leave the natal group into which they were born. This inclination is likely shaped by selective pressures because it is a way to guarantee that "new" genes will be introduced into a group and decreases the amount of inbreeding that may occur within a group. The complexities of group living are many—and primates live in complex social environments in which the benefits and costs of group living may differ for each individual.

◇◇ Key Words

age-graded group	fission-fusion	multiparous
allomothering behavior	harem	natal dispersal
aunting	inbreeding	natal group
bimaturism	infanticide	primaparous
breeding transfer	mating strategy	reproductive strategy
dispersal pattern		

◇◇ Study Questions

1. What are the pros and cons to group living for primates?
2. In what different ways do primates group together?
3. How does social organization differ from mating strategies?
4. In what ways are juveniles at risk, and is there a difference related to age?
5. Why do some individuals leave their natal group?
6. What is the advantage of a prolonged immature stage?
7. How are the social roles of adult males and females reflected in juveniles?
8. What are the underlying reasons for having complex, multileveled social groups?
9. How is play important for the growing primate?
10. What does the primate mother have to contend with, and how may she seek help from other group members?

◇◇ Suggested Readings and Related Web Sites

Altmann J. 1980. Baboon mothers and infants. Cambridge: Harvard University Press.

Fuentes A. 2002. Patterns and trends in primate pair bonds. International Journal of Primatology 23(5):953–978.

Kappler PM, van Schaik CP. 2002. Evolution of primate social systems. International Journal of Primatology 23(4):707–739.

Periera ME, Fairbanks LA editors. 1993. Juvenile primates. Life history, development and behavior. Oxford: Oxford University Press.

Rowe N. 1996. The pictorial guide to the living primates. East Hampton: Pagonias Press.

van Schaik CP , Janson CH editors. 2000. Infanticide by males and its implications. Cambridge: Cambridge University Press.

Smuts BB, Cheney DL, Seyfarth RM, Wrangham RW, Struhsaker TT editors. 1987. Primate societies. Chicago: University of Chicago Press.

Sussman RW. 1999. Primate ecology and social structure. Volume 1: Lorises, lemurs, and tarsiers. Boston: Pearson Custom Publishing.

Sussman RW. 2000. Primate ecology and social structure. Volume 2: New world monkeys. Boston: Pearson Custom Publishing.

CHAPTER 8

Primate Social Relationships

◇◇ Primates as Social Organisms

Primates are highly social and gregarious animals, capable of forming strong and lasting bonds with each other. The social world of primates is highly complex, comprising an intricate web of social networks. Anyone observing a group of primates for any amount of time will be struck by the constant flow of interactions taking place between group members. It is important, however, to recognize that there is no such thing as a typical primate pattern of social interaction. There is not even a typical ape, monkey, or strepsirhine pattern. On a more individual level, there are not even typical male–male, female–female, or male–female patterns of interactions (see Strier 1994b for more detail). Instead, we find great diversity in the way in which primates interact with one another. This diversity is derived from the myriad of behaviors that species, populations, or even individuals exhibit in response to the wide variety of social and physical environments in which they live.

Despite the lack of a *typical* primate pattern of social behavior, interactions do not occur randomly. There are three major factors that influence the pattern of social interactions a species or population will display (see below). As described in the previous chapter, individuals may have different reasons for living in social groups, and based on these differences the social agenda of groups will vary. Even though the ultimate goal of sexually mature individuals is to maximize their reproductive success, the immediate behavior and strategies used to achieve this differs greatly between individuals. Reproductive success, or **fitness,** refers to the successful passing on of one's own genetic material into the next generation. The factors that most strongly influence the behaviors displayed by primates are:

- Group composition (solitary, pair, one male- or multimale groups)
- Dispersal pattern (male or female biased, or both)
- Mating strategy (reproductive synchrony or not; promiscuity or not)

The size of a social group has an important effect on the frequency and kinds of interactions that can take place. The larger a social group, the greater potential for interactions and conflicts. The number of adult males and females present influences the kind and amount of social interactions that take place. The social networks in a group are also strongly affected by the species' dispersal pattern. Whoever remains in their natal group, be it males or females, tends to form the social core. The spatial arrangement within a group is seldom random. Irrespective of dispersal pattern, mothers and their dependent young form social clumps to which related kin are drawn. The social and the physical positions of males in a group depend to a large extent on how many males are present. In groups containing a single adult male, he may hold a central social position, as is often seen in gorillas, or a more peripheral social position, as seen in the patas monkey. In groups with many males, some males may be more closely associated with specific matrilines while others tend to be peripheral and move about on their own.

When we look at what primates do during the day, we see that they spend most of their time feeding or searching for food (foraging). Some species may have to travel great distances to find enough food to survive, but it is also important for them to rest. Primates that feed mainly on leaves rest between 50 and 80 percent of the day. This down time is required in order to digest tough, fibrous foods. For them there may be little time left for social interactions, but most species spend between 5 to 15 percent of the day engaged in social activities (Figure 8-1). We recognize how important social time is

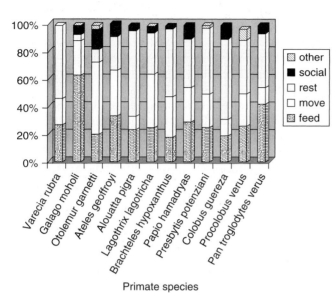

FIGURE 8-1 Activity budgets represent the average amount of time a group or species spend engaged in various activities. This bar graph presents the daily activity pattern of some key species.

to primates, because when food is running low and there is a need to increase foraging time, most species reduce the time they rest before encroaching on time spent in social interactions. The activity pattern of all group members is more or less synchronized. There may be some subtle differences. For example, females may spend more time feeding than adult males, and females tend to engage in social activities more often than males, while juveniles spend a lot of time playing.

Primate Relationships

In this chapter we will look at the social relationships of primates. Living in a social group is not an easy thing to do. There are always conflicts of interest, such as competition over access to specific resting places, preferred grooming partners, feeding sites, and so on. To get along in a social group, it helps to have friends and allies. Kinship is often the cementing force in a social group. For those lucky enough to have relatives around, it is within the kin group where the most support is to be found, but other familiar individuals may be equally useful and helpful. However, the dispersing sex may find itself in a sea of strangers when taking up residence in a new group. For most catarrhine monkeys, this is usually the destiny of males. In many other species, females are the dispersing sex, or in some instances, both males and females leave their natal group. Female dispersal is especially common in platyrrhines. We refer to the ability to make friends and allies as part of a primate's **social competence**.

Primates who live in social groups have sophisticated social knowledge about their group. Each group member is well aware of who belongs to the group and who does not. They may also know details about members of neighboring groups. Within their own social group, they know who is related to whom, who is friends with whom, thus who may act as an ally of a particular individual, and they especially know the rank position of all group members. This is knowledge that migrants have to pick up quickly if they are to make it in a new social group. Infants learn this information from their mothers, especially through the interactions given to and received by the mother from other group members. As we get to know more about the life of primate species that do not live in cohesive social groups, which comprise most of the nocturnal strepsirhines, it is clear that even in these species individuals have complex social knowledge about the conspecifics present in their surrounding area and engage in affiliative interactions on a daily basis with specific individuals.

To get by in the highly competitive world of social primates, there have to be certain strategies (rules and regulations) in place. These strategies provide alternative ways to negotiate conflict situations. Frans de Waal (1996, 2000) described a relational model that delineates the behavioral avenues open to competing individuals. The model presents three possible behavioral paths or options that individuals who are in contest over a specific resource may choose. One option is that they can show tolerance and share the resource. A second option is for one individual to back down (avoidance) and allow the more dominant individual access to the resource. If neither of these solutions works, there may be an aggressive confrontation. Such a confrontation can be costly, not just in the short-term (potential injury) but also in the long-term because it creates instability in the social domain of the group. Conflicts can cause disturbing ripples in the social fabric of a group.

It is essential that tension be kept at a minimum in a social group. Therefore, any conflicts that exist between individuals need to be resolved. Most species have worked out ways for conflicting individuals to reconcile (Figure 8-2). **Reconciliation** is a nonaggressive reunion between individuals who have been in conflict. It has been observed in nearly all species living in social groups (see examples in Aureli and de Waal 2000). More often than not, reconciliation takes the form of mutual grooming and vocalization or some show of appeasement behavior. Chimpanzees have evolved a highly elaborate means of reconciling by kissing and hugging, as well as grooming, and baboon females may approach each other while producing a soft grunt vocalization (Cheney et al. 1995).

An important aspect of the relational model is that it recasts aggression not just as antisocial behavior but as part of the arsenal of social decision-making options available

FIGURE 8-2 Reconciliation after a conflict may take various forms. Chimpanzees may kiss and hug, but more commonly primates tend to engage in grooming as a sign that they are friends again. The two female lion-tailed macaques *(Macaca silenus)*, shown here, hugged each other after each conflict.

to primates living in social groups. In this way, aggression can be used as effectively as affiliation to settle conflict situations. This may only be feasible if reconciliation is in place to ensure that conflicts do not undermine the social cohesion of the group. If a relationship or friendship is important to both participants involved in a conflict, then it should be advantageous for them to settle their differences and reconcile.

To avoid aggressive conflicts, individuals may be submissive, that is showing behaviors that are nonthreatening and so disarm the aggressive intent of the opponent. To avoid aggressive conflicts, many species have evolved a series of interaction rituals, such as male greeting behaviors, which inform participants about the status of their relationship. By displaying these ritual behaviors, participants can test each other's willingness to be friends and allies, without upsetting the balance of the social group. It is as if participants are arranging social contracts. Since primates are known to cheat (see Chapter 9), the more costly a signal or interaction ritual, the more likely it is to be an honest advertisement of the individual's willingness to be friendly and cooperative (Silk 2000, Zahavi 1977).

❖❖ The Adaptive Value of Social Behavior: Selfishness, Kin Selection, and Altruism

Over time, natural selection favors those behavioral patterns that enhance an individual's survival and reproductive success. We thus expect that an individual somehow evaluates the costs and benefits of an action, and individuals behave in a manner that best ensures survival. It therefore appears as if natural selection favors selfishness. However, related individuals share some proportion of their genes, and the more closely related individuals are, the more genetic material they share (Figure 8-3). Therefore, helping kin will indirectly benefit one's own fitness, referred to as **inclusive fitness** (Hamilton 1964).

What about helping other individuals? Are there benefits to placing oneself at risk for the sake of other nonrelated individuals? We frequently observe behavioral interactions among primates that seem to provide benefits for the receiver but not for the actor. There may even be obvious disadvantages or dangers to the actor. For example, when an individual comes to the aid of another engaged in an agonistic fracas, he or she may be placing him- or herself at risk. Similarly, if an individual produces alarm calls to warn other

> **Inclusive fitness**—when related individuals, those that share part of your own gene pool, are successful in reproduction and survival
> **Altruistic behaviors**—behaviors that may lead to diminished reproductive success of the actor in favor of an unrelated individual's success

group members of an approaching predator, it places itself in a vulnerable position. The presence of such apparent **altruistic behaviors** has long puzzled evolutionary biologists (Hamilton 1964). What we need to take into account is that primates can have a very long memory for things that are of importance to them, and behaviors or actions that appear to be altruistic may be part of a long-term reciprocal interaction. This would be a type of tit-for-tat interaction or **reciprocal altruism** (Novak and Sigmund 2005, Trivers 1971). It has been suggested, however, that altruism and even reciprocal altruism are rare among nonrelated individuals (Silk et al. 2005, Stevens and Hauser 2004). For such

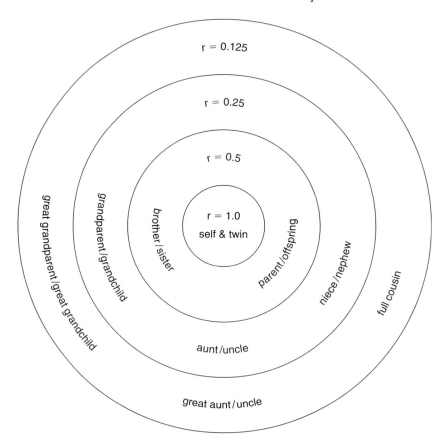

FIGURE 8-3 Illustration of genetic relatedness, as expressed by the r value, of kin.

behavioral strategies to persist, mutual benefits must be accrued down the road. What we often see is that if one party does not hold up its end of the bargain then the relationship ends (e.g., Barrett et al. 2000, de Waal 1982).

◈◈ Types of Primate Social Relationships

Primate groups are made up of highly complex social networks, and every member of the group contributes to the social fabric. It takes at least two individuals to have a social interaction. Even though it may appear as if most interactions take place between two individuals, so called dyadic interactions, it is not unusual to have more individuals involved, either directly or indirectly, in determining the outcome of an interaction. An individual may even play two individuals off against one another, or a third individual may come to the aid of one of the two quarrelling individuals. We refer to this as a triadic interaction. If an individual is upset about having been outsmarted by a dominant individual, the subordinate individual may redirect its frustration on a third party, so called **redirected aggression**. Females and immatures suffer most often from redirected aggression, especially from males.

We can divide the social interactive world of primates into five major groups:

- Those occurring between adult males, which usually involves competition over females

> **social**—living in a communal setting
> **gregarious**—interactive and socially outgoing

- Those occurring between adult females, which usually involves competition over food, space, and mates or protection of offspring
- Those involving the relationships between adult males and females
- Those involving the relationships adults have with immatures
- Those involving the relationships immatures have with one another

 HOT TOPICS 8-1

Are Primates Smarter and More Social than Other Social Animals?

The intuitive answer most of us would give to this question is "yes," because primates are usually presented as being special, with a social sophistication unique in the animal kingdom. However, perhaps primates are not quite as unique as we might think. Until fairly recently, we did not have sufficient or even the right kind of data to explore social relationships in other animals. It may seem surprising, but the research approaches that primatologists use are actually quite different from those used by zoologists to study other animals. Rather than focus on individual relationships and interactions within the social context of a group—the approach taken by primatologists—zoologists have traditionally tried to identify the motivational reason behind a behavioral pattern. Primatologists follow the lead of eminent behavioralists like Robert Hinde (e.g., 1979, 1983) and Hans Kummer (e.g., 1968, 1971) who suggested that to understand the sociality of animals you need to look at the behavior of individuals and how individuals form relationships within the greater social sphere of a group. It is the individual that is the most important cog in the great social machine of the group.

By being primates ourselves, we have a natural fascination for our own kind, and maybe it is easier for us to understand and interpret the behavior of other primates. Whatever the reason, there is more detailed information available on the social lives of primates than there is for other animals. This does not mean there is a lack of other animal species that live in social groups; many different mammals and birds live in permanent groups and form long-term relationships. When we look at specific aspects of primate social life, such as the presence of kin alliances, complex social networks, vocal communication, or tool use, we find these in many different animals as well. Long-term study on animals such as elephants, dolphins, and hyenas has shown that they live in complex social communities with a fission-fusion structure. Even some of the more social bird taxa are showing cognitive abilities akin to those of primates.

Despite the fact that African elephants have been studied for many

(continued)

years (e.g., Douglas-Hamilton 1972, Moss 1988, 2001, Poole 1987), only recently have questions pertaining to the intricacies of their social lives been addressed. Now they have been studied in much the same way as primates (e.g., Archie et al. 2006, Lee and Moss 1999, McComb et al. 2000, 2001). Stories about how elephants mourn and protect their dead companions against predators have frequently been reported (e.g., McComb et al. 2006, Theron 2003). We are beginning to have a clearer picture of their social lives and an understanding of the importance of older individuals for the transmission of social knowledge and for the healthy development of young individuals. It has even become apparent that young elephants that have experienced the loss of a close family member due to illegal hunting or culling display the equivalent of post-traumatic stress disorder (Bradshaw et al. 2005). Communication studies have shown the importance of vocalization in the social communication of elephants and that learning is an integral part of being able to vocalize in appropriate and effective social formats (McComb et al. 2000, Poole et al. 2005).

Additional studies have provided evidence for a wide range of complex social behaviors (those traditionally associated with primates) in other animals. Research on toothed whales is revealing the highly sophisticated and rich social lives of these animals (Conner et al. 1998, Mann et al. 2000). A long-term study on bottlenose dolphins (*Tursiops*) living around Monkey Mia-Shark Bay in Western Australia has provided insight into the complex social life of dolphins (e.g., Connor et al. 1998, Krützen et al. 2005, Mann and Smuts

1998, Smolker et al. 1997). Complex communication, with evidence for vocal learning and cultural transmission, has now been confirmed in bottlenose dolphins and orcas (*Orcinus orca*) (Janik 2000, Deecke et al. 2000). The cultural transmission of tool use is even suggested for bottlenose dolphins in which mothers show their offspring how to use sponges as tools (Krützen et al. 2005).

Many different bird species are known to use tools during foraging (Beck 1980, Lefebvre et al. 2002). The use of cactus spines and other sharp objects by woodpecker finches (*Cactospiza pallida*) and their cognitive ability related to tool use have been investigated (e.g., Tebbich and Bshary 2004). The ability of New Caledonian crows has received much attention, in part because these crows show flexibility in the use of tools and adjust tool manufacture to fit the demand at hand (Chappell and Kacelnik 2002, Hunt and Gray 2004 a, b). Actually, most members of the corvid family (birds such as crows, ravens, jays, and magpies) show evidence of advanced cognitive ability (Emery and Clayton 2004).

As we look more closely into the social lives of other taxa using the same research approaches we do for primates, we find that many other animals have a social complexity akin to that of primates. Even though primates may not have unique social traits, they may have a unique *combination* of traits used in social interactions (e.g., Harcourt 1992, Wrangham 1983). However, until we actually look at different **social** species through the same lens the jury may be out in regard to whether primates are more social, or even more **gregarious** than other types of social animals.

◈ ◈ ◈ ◈

Relationships Between Males

In most species, adult males tend to have an uneasy time together. Tension and friction often occur when males are in close proximity to each other. The underpinning reason is **mate competition**. Males are intolerant of each other because they are competitors for the one limited resource they need to maximize their own reproductive success: *females*. The reproductive success of males is based on finding and mating with as many females as possible. Therefore, males spend a lot of effort excluding competitors from gaining access to females. How this conflict is played out depends on the species' social organization, its mating system, and the mating tactics used by individual males. Males can achieve mating success overtly by fighting off other males in dyadic interactions, or they can use more subtle strategies such as forming coalitions with other males to repel more dominant males (Bercovitch 1988). They may even form special affiliative relationships with females (see section on male-female relationships below). Alternatively, they can fight the battle at the level of the sperm, so called **sperm competition**, by producing more or better sperm or prohibiting the sperm of competitors to fertilize the female (Dixon 1998, Harcourt et al. 1995). A most sinister way of reducing a competitor's reproductive success is to kill his offspring. **Infanticide** is used in many taxa as an alternative mating strategy (see Hot Topics 8-2).

Males That Live in One Male-Multifemale Groups

The ideal situation for a male, from a reproductive point of view, is to monopolize as many females as possible. To do so, a male has to prevent other males from having access to *his* females. Therefore, in species that live in groups comprising a single adult male and several adult females, males are downright intolerant of each other. The male leader makes every attempt to keep other adult males out of his sight and away from his females. In seasonally breeding species, male leaders engage in spectacular fights when outsider males descend on the group to challenge the leader's supremacy and to mate with the females. Such aggressive encounters can lead to severe injuries being sustained by the involved males, but also to any group member who happens to get in the way. In species in which females are receptive to mating throughout the year, male-male competition may be less intense but more long-term, and the male leader will attempt to repel any male that seeks to join the group, (Figure 8-4).

There is a degree of variability at both the species and individual level in regard to the pattern of male tolerance. For example, some gorilla males tolerate the presence of other males, even other silverback males (Robbins 1995). Males in groups with a more complex social organization, e.g., geladas (*Theropithecus gelada*) and hamadryas baboons (*Papio hamadryas*), often tolerate male followers. In the case of the gelada, these male followers are often deposed leaders that stay around because they have a vested interest in staying behind to protect their own offspring (Dunbar, 1984). In hamadryas, the follower male is usually a young male, possibly the son of the present leader, who is aspiring to take over the one-male unit (Abegglen 1984, Kummer, 1995). However, in all such cases the males are exhibiting a range of tolerance and do not engage in affiliative intentions with one another. In age-graded male groups (see Chapter 7) the dominant male's tolerance of other males does not extend to having that male fraternize or mate with the females.

In species in which males form single-sex social groups, so-called bachelor groups, males do affiliate with each other. Males in bachelor groups are often found in close

FIGURE 8-4   In most species, males have an uneasy time together. Mate competition is the underpinning cause. Males tend to display toward each other to settle a dispute but occasionally the disagreement result in a full out aggressive encounter.

proximity to one another and participate in unisex social grooming (Figure 7.7). Hamadryas males may also engage in male-male grooming, but this behavior ends as soon as a male has acquired his first female.

Males that live solitary lives, e.g., many nocturnal strepsirhine species, are in general intolerant of each other, although Nekaris (2003) observed several male slender lorises patiently awaiting their turn to interact with an estrous female without any antagonistic behavioral displays. In most of these species, males simply avoid one another, which is possible because strepsirhine males advertise their presence by scent marking the periphery of their home range to ward off unwelcomed intruders. This pheromonal message may even transmit information about how willing the marker is to defend his turf and the females that range there.

Males That Live in Multimale-Multifemale Groups

In groups that include more than one adult male, males have to find a way to co-exist. They can, of course, ignore one another or disperse as far away from each other as possible. Neither of these options is very easy to accomplish within a distinct social group. Often a male's position, or rank within the group, is determined through a sequence of competitive outcomes in dyadic interactions. The males then form what we refer to as **dominance hierarchies**, in which the alpha male is the top-ranking male followed by the beta male and so on (e.g., Walters and Seyfarth 1987). With such a ranking system, each male has a specific position or standing within the group, which strongly influences his conduct and interactions. By forming dominance hierarchies, unwarranted tension and friction may be circumvented. Dominance hierarchies are most often linear, although polyadic interactions (when more than two individuals are involved) can make a male's position in the hierarchy indeterminable (see alliances and cooperation below). In some species, e.g., capuchins (*Cebus*), the position of a male in the dominance hierarchy other than that of the alpha male is difficult to ascertain (Fedigan 1993).

Competing for a dominance rank can be a very costly affair. Attempting to assert or advance one's position can lead to fights in which injuries are inflicted, lasting scars are sustained, and possibly even resulting in the death of an individual. High rank often brings added benefits, however, making the risk worthwhile. Most male dominance hierarchies are not stable over time, in part because a male's competitive ability changes with age, and new males periodically enter the group.

The importance of dominance hierarchies varies in different species. For example, in chimpanzees and baboons, dominance rank plays an important role. High-ranking males often have priority of access to preferred resources, which may include access to receptive females (Goodall 1986, Hausfater 1975). In other species, such as capuchins (*Cebus*), dominance hierarchies get muddled up because males tend to **cooperate** and form **alliances**, and even alpha males do not necessarily have priority of access to preferred resources. Two species that seem to have

> **cooperate**—individuals join forces (uniform behavioral display) against a third party, e.g., two males challenging a third who is consorting an estrous female; such cooperation may persist over time and for different goals and can be referred to as an **alliance**

no or very relaxed dominance ranks among the males are the muriqui (*Brachyteles arachnoides*) and bonobo (*Pan paniscus*). The muriquis have a much more egalitarian social system (Strier 1994a), while bonobo males are more aloof and do not interact much at all, although Kano (1996) found that the bonobo males at Wamba, the Congo (formerly Zaïre), do form a dominance hierarchy and top-ranking males copulate at a higher rate than do lower-ranking males.

For seasonally breeding species that live in multimale groups, daily competition between males is reduced. Outside of the breeding season, males show affiliative tendencies and often aggregate together into foraging parties. In some species of squirrel monkeys (*Saimiri*), males are highly affiliative and may even cooperate and form alliances during the breeding season. This may be explained by the fact that females are either co-dominant with males or may even rank above them (Boinski 1999). In the diurnal ring-tailed lemur (*Lemur catta*), in which females are dominant to the males, the dominant males have a central position within the social group and interact more with females than do the more peripheral lower-ranking males (Gould 1997).

Males join forces and cooperate to fight off and keep other groups out of their home range. Individual males within a social group often cooperate and form alliances against each other (Bercovitch 1988, Nishida and Hosaka 1996, van Schaik and Aureli 2000). The formation of alliances between two or more males is a strategy that circumvents the dominance hierarchy. Cooperating males have more clout than a lone male and have greater success in gaining access to a scarce resource. For example, two lower-ranking males can together outcompete a higher-ranking male—something neither one could do alone. The formation of alliances is commonly seen in baboons when males join forces to harass a male in consort with a female in order to take the estrous female away. Such alliances are usually temporary, although a male may have a specific number of males he can rely on that will come to his aid, and these alliances are usually reciprocal. Capuchin (*Cebus*) males often form lasting alliances and they may even migrate together (Fedigan and Jack 2001).

Strategies to Prevent Aggression

Greeting behaviors have been observed in many species and may be potential mechanisms that control tension between males and provide an opportunity to size up the social commitment a male may be willing to make to an alliance partner. Baboons, especially the hamadryas baboon, display highly ritualized greetings (Figure 8-5, Colmenares et al. 2000, Whitham and Maestripieri 2003), as do mantled howler monkeys (*Alouatta palliata*) (Wang and Milton 2003). Greetings can take place anytime two males meet, but

FIGURE 8-5 In some species, males have complex strategies to circumvent agonistic inter-actions. Hamadryas baboons (*Papio hamadryas*) display highly ritualized greetings. Here a male leader is approaching and greeting another male leader (in the foreground). At the same time, the two follower males, belonging to each of the one-male units, also greet one another (in background).

they are commonly exchanged when males have been separated for an extended period of time, e.g., overnight. They also occur after a conflict situation or when tension is build-ing in a group. Such greetings can be expressed in a variety of ways. When chimpanzee males reunite with friends or relatives, they display excited vocalizations, exchange hugs and kisses, and may sit down for a friendly grooming session (Goodall 1986). When two howler males meet, they grasp each other in a deep embrace while vocalizing, though these embraces only last a few seconds (Glander 1980, Wang and Milton 2003).

Baboons and other monkeys are usually not as physical in their greetings. As a mat-ter of fact, a greeting may not entail any physical contact at all. In such instances, two males will rapidly approach each other, while making friendly facial expressions and vocalizing with staccato cough-like sounds. There may be a slight pause as the males face each other, but then they rapidly move in opposite directions. Sometimes, however, there is physical contact. The males approach as before, but when they flank each other they touch each other's rear end and one may mount the other, or they sniff and touch each other's genitals while vocalizing and lip smacking. Such greetings are brief and once over, the males move rapidly away from each other. Allowing another male so close to the instrument that can determine a male's reproductive success is quite a ges-ture of trust. It has been suggested that such greetings are an honest advertisement of a male's willingness to arrange a social contract and to live in peace, at least for the time being (Whitham and Maestripieri 2003).

There are often behavioral interactions in which males test the bonds that exist between them. They seek out each other's willingness or commitment to form alliances or to be friendly. Chimpanzees engage in hand-clasp grooming. A male who is doing the grooming (the groomer) holds the hand of the one who is being groomed (the groomee) high in the air. It is often the subordinate individual who is the groomer, but some-times it is a mutual affair (McGrew et al. 2001). The most curious of these "social con-tract" behaviors is the nose poking observed in some capuchin groups (Perry et al. 2003). Two individuals will sit close by, possibly grooming, when one will place its fin-ger into the nostril of the other. This individual may then place its finger up the part-ner's nostril. They can sit like this for a long while almost as if in a trance. Both hand clasping and nose poking are not restricted to males, as females and immatures also engage in such behaviors.

One might assume that related males would be friendlier and show more tolerance toward each other, but this is not necessarily the case. This lack of affiliation between males may be due to reproductive competition. Males who remain in the social group into which they were born (**patrilocal males**) often show more affiliative interactions. A good example is the chimpanzee (*Pan troglodytes*). They commonly groom, hug, and kiss each other, although chimpanzee males are also highly competitive and form linear dominance hierarchies. In contrast, bonobo males (*Pan paniscus*) do not interact very much, nor do they seem to form strong dominance hierarchies or directly compete for access to sexually receptive females. Bonobo males have opted for an alternative strategy to gain reproductive success: They form affiliative friendships with specific females in the group, relying on female choice (Kano 1996). The muriqui (*Brachyteles arachnoides*) is also patrilocal, just like chimpanzees and bonobos, but they differ from the apes in two major ways. First, the muriquis show little sexual dimorphism either in body or canine size. Second, the males are very laid back and spend much time in close proximity to each other. Strier has studied muriquis in the wild for many years and has found that aggression between males is exceedingly rare and the aggressive behaviors that are displayed are fairly mild, e.g., supplants (Strier 1994b). It appears that muriqui males have opted to compete for reproductive success in a more covert fashion: The males have very large testicles, and their sperm production is therefore assumed to be great. Thus, muriqui males may wield a sperm war (Milton 1985, Strier 1994a). It is possible that the lack of sexual body dimorphism commonly seen in spider monkey species is due to reduced overt aggressive competition between males, and that in spider monkeys competitive fighting occurs at the level of the sperm. Their arboreal and suspensory habits may have molded such adaptations.

If an aggressive conflict has taken place, the male participants usually attempt to settle their differences. As mentioned above, there are many different types of reconciliation. If the conflict persists between two males, the tension may escalate and erupt into a fight, which may leave one or both males with serious wounds. Alternatively, the lower-ranking male may leave the group to seek his fortunes elsewhere.

The Influence of Age on a Male's Position in a Social Group

A male's age has a strong influence on his position within the social group. In general males go through three stages in life: pre-prime, prime, and post-prime. Pre-prime includes subadult males, or not yet fully grown males. Usually, subadult males have low competitive potential and are often positioned peripherally in the group. Subadult males spend much time sparring with each other and paying close attention to the whereabouts of neighboring groups. To prepare themselves for entering into the adult male dominance hierarchy, they harass adult females until they have dominated all of them. A prime adult male is fully grown and at the maximum of his competitive potential. Prime adult males tend to be more central within the social group. As a male grows older, his ability to compete and gain access to reproductively active females diminishes, and males past their prime may take a more peripheral position within the group. In one-male groups, by the time a male is past his prime, he has most likely been ousted from leadership. Hamadryas leaders show a very rapid physical decline and usually do not survive for long after being deposed from their harems (Figure 7.10b). The options open for ousted males are to either take up a solitary existence or join single-sex groups. Living a solitary life may not be a good option for any old primates, as their ability to defend themselves against predators is greatly reduced. In multimale groups, it is easier for older males to remain in the group and to blend in. As mentioned, older males may stay around to protect their own offspring and grand offspring. They may even make very good babysitters (see Figure 7.1).

Not all species follow the same life history projections. In general, males reach their prime when fully grown and at peak physical strength. However, in some species the physical prime of a male does not necessarily coincide with his peak social status within the group. In capuchin groups, the alpha position is often held by the oldest male (Fragaszy et al. 2004) and gorilla males do not become silverbacks until later in life (Stewart and Harcourt 1987). In many species it appears that males must also be behaviorally mature and be able to demonstrate a degree of social finesse before they reach high rank.

 HOT TOPICS 8-2

Is Infanticide a Reproductive Strategy?

Infanticide refers to the intentional killing of an infant. The occurrence of infanticide among primates was first brought to our attention over thirty years ago (e.g., Hrdy 1974, Mohnot 1971). Since then, primatologists and other scientists who study animal behavior have become acutely aware that the killing of infants occurs in many different species, not only within the primate order but in a wide range of taxa, e.g., zebras, lions, rodents, and birds. Infanticide has been reported most often in primate species that live in social groups with a single adult male (e.g., colobines, gorillas) and most often takes place when there is a challenge to the leader male's position. Since "infanticide" is such a loaded term—we attach moral values to it and it implies intent on the part of the aggressor—it has been suggested that a more neutral term such as infant killing should be used (Jolly et al. 2000). There is much controversy surrounding infant killing, and three different hypotheses have been presented to explain its occurrence: (1) the social pathological hypothesis, (2) the epiphenomenon hypothesis, and (3) the sexual selection hypothesis.

Infant killings may reflect behavioral aberrations, caused by stressful environmental conditions, such as habitat destruction, or overpopulation, which is the explanation put forth by the social pathological hypothesis (Curtin and Dolhinow 1978, Dolhinow 1977). Therefore, infant killings are not believed to have any adaptive value. Even though this appears to be a plausible explanation, further study comparing the behavior of langur (*Semnopithecus entellus*) populations living at different locations with varied population densities, habitat richness, etc., found no significant correlation between environmental factors and infant killing behavior (Newton 1988).

The notion that infant killings are accidental occurrences due to general male aggression and not an advantageous behavioral pattern is called the epiphenomenon hypothesis (Bartlett et al. 1993, Sussman et al. 1995). Support for this hypothesis comes from observations of species living in multimale social groups. Baboons, for example, are well known for their use of infants as

FIGURE 8-6 Baboon males may use infants in their antagonistic, dominance related interactions with other males. Here a male has a black infant clinging to his back while threatening another adult male, who is walking away. The presence of an infant can have an inhibitory effect, but if the contest escalates, the infant may get hurt or even killed.

tools in order to intimidate each other during agonistic dominance interactions (Figure 8-6). Furthermore, infants and small juveniles are more vulnerable than other members of a social group during intragroup and intergroup male dominance conflicts, as they often get separated from their mothers in the midst of the turmoil surrounding a fight. It is, therefore, very likely that some infant killings are accidental, a by-product of male-male agonistic encounters. However, adult males have been observed during intergroup encounters specifically targeting females with young offspring (Collins 1984, Palmobit et al. 2000). In most cases these instances do not, in fact, result in the male mating with the female once she resumes estrus (Harris and Monfort 2003). Therefore, such attacks cannot directly result in any reproductive advantage for the attacker.

The basis for the sexual selection hypothesis is that a male kills unrelated offspring to gain a reproductive advantage (Borries et al. 1999, Hrdy 1974, Janson and van Schaik 2000, Sommer 1994). In most species, if a female loses her offspring soon after birth, she becomes sexually receptive shortly thereafter. Consequently, if a male targets females with young infants, by killing those infants, a male can hasten his own fathering of offspring as well as remove the genes from a competitor male. For sexual selection to actually be played out in this situation, the male should not kill related offspring, and he has to ensure that he fertilizes the female once she resumes cycling. There is also a need to show that infanticidal males have greater mating success than other males, i.e., that these males produce on average more offspring. This has been a very difficult point to prove

(*continued*)

since few genetic studies have actually been undertaken. In several studies it has been shown, however, that males do kill only unrelated infants (Borries et al. 1999).

It is suggested that infanticidal behavior is a major determinant of primate sociality (e.g., Dunbar 1984). The role of infanticide may have contributed to the evolution of sexual bonds, especially monogamy or pair bonds. Furthermore, females may have evolved counter-strategies to prevent or at least reduce opportunities for males to kill their offspring (see van Schaik and Janson 2000).

Females that live in social groups comprising several adult males may use many different strategies to prevent males from harming their offspring. Dominance may seem like the most obvious route to take, but there are only a handful of species in which females are dominant or co-dominant to males, e.g., ring-tailed lemurs and squirrel monkeys (Boinski 1999, Gould 1997). In species in which females are smaller and are lower ranking than males, females often gang up to outcompete adult males. This is what we often see in macaques, capuchins, patas monkeys, and langurs, but there may also be more subtle strategies that females can employ.

Promiscuous mating behaviors displayed by many females are considered to have evolved partly to confuse paternity. If a male has mated with the mother, the offspring may be his own, thus he should be protective of the offspring and not kill it. Whether male primates are so clueless may be questionable, because at

least some yellow baboon males do appear to know which infant is theirs despite a promiscuous mating system (Buchan et al. 2003).

In some species, females form friendships with males. These male friends not only protect the female friend from harassment, but also protect her offspring. From the female's point of view this may be a way to reduce the potential for attacks on her offspring. From a male's point of view such a friendship is an investment that may ensure future mating success with a female friend.

In yet other species in which females live in social groups comprised of nonrelated individuals, mothers have to seek different avenues to stop males from committing infanticide. Gorilla females form very close associations with the adult silverback male of her social group. Since gorillas (due to their sheer size) are not exposed to many predators, it has been suggested that this closeness is a response to potential threat by infanticidal extra group males (Harcourt and Greenberg 2001).

In sum, infant killing is a strange phenomenon that occurs in a variety of social animals. Aspects of several of the hypotheses described above seem to be supported by behavioral observations, but paternity studies will be needed in order to accurately delineate the factors that contribute to this behavior. Despite the fact that infant killing is a harsh reality, it may have contributed to shaping the complex range of social behaviors exhibited by primates and particularly adult females.

Relationships Between Females

Ecological factors such as the availability of food resources and predation pressure determine if and how females group together. How food is distributed in the landscape especially influences how females relate to one another (van Schaik 1989, Wrangham

1980). If food is clumped, females tend to group together. If the food is also defendable, females will compete among themselves and form dominance hierarchies. This is what we see in most of the African and Asian monkeys, such as baboons, macaques, and vervets. In contrast, if the food is not easily defendable, dominance relationships between females seem to be weaker or absent all together, as seen in many colobines and gorillas. Additional factors may also influence why females group together. In most species females are smaller and subordinate to males, but by grouping together females have a better opportunity to control aggressive and, as described above, potentially infanticidal males (Smuts and Smuts 1993, Treves and Chapman 1996). Furthermore, by living in a group, females may assist each other in the rearing of offspring.

When examining the relationship between females, we need to focus on a female's role as a mother since female primates spend most of their adult lives either being pregnant or lactating. To be successful mothers, females must be good competitors and strategists. How they accomplish this is very much circumscribed by the species' dispersal pattern, group structure, and mating strategy.

A female's reproductive success depends on how many offspring she is able to successfully raise. Therefore, the investment a female makes in each offspring is great, and her life centers on protecting and taking care of her offspring (Figure 8-7). The most important task for a female is to ensure that she has access to adequate, high-quality food resources, to feed herself and her infant, and to have a safe haven where they can rest. A female should also be selective in her choice of mates; by doing so she ensures that the "best" genes are passed on to her offspring. Securing food and selecting mates may lead to competition between the females of a group.

It may not be obvious at first glance, but females engage in as many competitive interactions as do males. Female competitive interactions are often overlooked because they tend to be less overt. They tend to engage more in squabbles than in outright fights. Female competition is not limited to access to food resources or resting places, but may

FIGURE 8-7   Mothers protect and come to the aid of their offspring whenever they are threatened. Here a Barbary macaque (*Macaca sylvanus*) mother chases away a subadult female. Following this encounter the mother embraced her offspring.

also include competition for access to males. Males not only provide the sperm for the females' future offspring, but by forming alliances or friendships, males can provide protection against other agonistic group members (Palombit et al. 2001).

There is a large difference in the lives of females that remain in their natal group and those that do not. Throughout their lives, females who are philopatric, or those that have stayed in their natal group, are surrounded by kin and other familiar females. Females that leave their natal group, in contrast, must seek access to a group of unfamiliar and presumably mostly unrelated individuals. Therefore, the dispersal pattern has a significant influence on the strategies females choose to follow in order to maximize their reproductive success.

Female Philopatric Species

In species in which females live their whole lives within the social group in which they were born, we see two types of female relationships, one being more despotic (tyrannical), while the other is more egalitarian. It is common in female-bonded species for related females to form social clusters within the larger group, so-called matrilines. These are very important to the survival of each individual, and social bonds between females have been shown to enhance infant survival in baboons (Silk et al. 2003a). For as long as a mother is alive, her daughters have her support in all power struggles within the group. The support a mother gives to her daughters has been shown, at least in vervet monkeys (*Chlorocebus aethiops*), to lead to an increase in reproductive success for the daughters (Fairbanks and McGuire 1986). Even though it is not uncommon to observe closely related females squabbling, it is very rare to see close kin with divided loyalty. Kin always present a united front against other matrilines. In taxa with clearly differentiated matrilines, we usually find strong, persistent dominance hierarchies among the females. In most of these species, daughters are born into a social position and inherit a rank close to that of their mothers (in some species just below, and in others just above that of their mothers).

Several factors influence the type and frequency of interactions that take place. The social position within the group is important, and a female interacts more often with females that are closer to her own rank. In turn, their offspring will grow up playing with each other and forming strong social relationships. This is the way that matrilineal dominance relationships are perpetuated within the group. Kinship can also serve as a constraint with related individuals exchanging affiliative interactions more often than with non-kin.

Despite the fact that females are often born into a social position, individual females can better their social status within the group, although it may be an ephemeral improvement. Even though such events are not common, grooming can be used as a tool to rise above one's station in life. Low-ranking females may groom and form alliances with high-ranking females. The dominant female might then return the favor by supporting the low-ranking female in disputes or her mere presence may result in added status to the low-ranking female. Small (1998) observed one low-ranking female macaque that used grooming as a ticket to gain the trust and support of the highest-ranking female in her group. Even though such improvement in position may be temporary, it may be sufficient to increase an individual's fitness beyond what would have been expected based solely on dominance rank.

The presence of a female dominance hierarchy does not automatically result in a despotic social system. Female squirrel monkeys (*Saimiri sciureus*) form linear dominance hierarchies, but they also appear to interact in a more egalitarian and peaceful manner (Baldwin 1992, Sussman 2000). Furthermore, not all species with female philopatry form matrilineal subgroupings or strong dominance hierarchies. For example, patas monkeys (*Erythrocebus patas*) show a much more egalitarian social structure with an almost nonexistent female dominance hierarchy (Pruetz and Isbell 2000). Even though it has not yet been proven, it may be that this egalitarian structure can be maintained due to the females' being closely related to one another. It may be that cooperation and coalitions against such threats as predation override the competitive urges between females for resources.

Female Transfer Species

Migration from the natal group is common in many of the colobines and is pervasive among the platyrrhines. Where females disperse, we can discern two general types of social interaction systems. In one, unrelated females focus their attention on the male leader with little or no interaction between the females, a so-called cross-sex bonding system (Byrne et al. 1989). Alternatively, females may form strong friendships and alliances, some which may be based on kinship, often to the exclusion of the male(s).

In species in which females migrate from their natal group, a female may spend many days alone following other social groups (shadowing behavior). Females attempting to immigrate, or enter into a new group, are usually chased and harassed by the group's residents, especially other adult females. If a female persists, the harassment may stop after a few days, and the female is then permitted to join the group. At first she will hold a peripheral position and interact mainly with subadult or low-ranking males. It can take a long time for a female to gain access to the more central part of the social group. The birth of her first offspring usually provides the female with an increase in status within the social sphere of the new group.

Howler monkey females (*Alouatta palliata*) have an especially rough time when seeking access to a new social group. They must compete and establish dominance rank over all members of the new group before they are accepted (Zucker and Clarke 1998). Not many females make it the first time around, and many have to wander about on their own, or they have to return to their natal group before they can attempt a second try. Alternatively, if the habitat can sustain it, an emigrant female may join with bachelor males and other single females and establish a new group. Once accepted into a new group, females stay for the rest of their lives. The young newly arrived females hold the highest dominance rank in the group, and as they grow older they become increasingly subordinate. Even though rank is determined through agonistic interactions, females with newborn infants gain a temporary increase in status. Since howler monkeys are not known to spend much time engaged in social grooming, sociality is expressed by spending time in close proximity.

Females that transfer usually do not form strong bonds with other, nonrelated females in their new social group. This can be seen in species such as howler monkeys and gorillas in which females tend to form strong relationships with the group's male leader. Female bonobos are an exception to this pattern. To gain acceptance into a new group, a young bonobo female begins by making overtures to become friends with an older established female. To do so, grooming and sex are exchanged (Kano 1996). Once a friendship is established, it lasts for a long time. The older female's son may be included in the friendship pact.

FIGURE 8-9 Grooming provides the social cement in a group. Females usually spend more time in this activity. The groomer takes this activity very seriously, and grooming has a soothing effect on the recipient.

Kinship can be a very strong binding force. Even in species that are considered to be solitary, like many nocturnal strepsirhines, females that are possibly related (sisters, mothers, and daughters) often spend time together. Not only do they forage together and form sleeping clusters, but they also spend much time in social interactions (e.g., Nekaris 2003a, 2006, Sussman 1999).

How Do Females Maintain Their Social Networks?

Social relations between females are influenced by resource competition (van Schaik 1989). The strongest bartering tool in a primate's arsenal is grooming, and females spend much of their social time engaged in grooming (Figure 8-9). Grooming can serve two functions: It removes ectoparasites and dirt (Goosen 1987), but it is more commonly used as a powerful instrument of social transaction. Consequently, it is often described as providing the *social cement* of a group. In almost all primate species we find that females engage in grooming more often than males. Grooming has a soothing effect on the recipient because the tactile interaction stimulates the release of biomolecules such as endorphins in the body, which produces a feeling of well-being (Keverne et al. 1989). The ability to make someone feel good can be a powerful tool, and it is through grooming that females make and keep friends and allies. By having friends and allies, a female is guaranteed support in agonistic affairs. We can use the frequency and duration of grooming episodes as an index to evaluate how strong the affiliative relationship is between a grooming dyad (Goosen 1987, Schino 2001).

In species in which females do not disperse, most grooming takes place between related females within the matriline. Unrelated females form grooming alliances based more on rank with close-ranking females spending more time grooming each other. If grooming is used as a way to barter for establishing alliances and cooperative friendships, we can expect there to be reciprocity in the behavior wherein both participants invest the same amount of time and effort. Female chacma baboons have been shown to drive a hard bargain, in that if a female does not return the same amount of grooming that she has received, then the grooming relationship between the dyad is finished (Barrett et al. 2000, Henzi et al. 1997). However, a lower-ranking female stands to gain more by grooming a higher-ranking female, thus she may be willing to contribute more time and effort grooming the higher-ranking female.

In species in which grooming is less common, the strength of an affiliative relationship can be evaluated based on how frequently two individuals are in close proximity. It is also possible to evaluate the strength of a social bond by observing how tolerant a mother is in allowing another female to handle her infant (Manson 1999).

What Happens to Females When They Grow Old?

All primates show external evidence of aging (Figure 8-10). Their facial hair turns white and grows sparser, the body "shrinks," and movements become slower. However, unlike male primates, the role of females within the social group does not usually change as they grow older. Age may bestow seniority, especially in matrilineally based species. In most species, females continue to reproduce until they die. In some instances, old females may show erratic menstrual cycles; their cycles become longer and then cease altogether a few years before they die. Menopause, however, and living into postreproductive age appear to be traits that are unique to the human female.

The average age at death may be less for individuals living in wild populations compared to captive ones. Most likely it is because life in the wild is a bit more taxing and unpredictable than life in captivity (for example, the chimpanzee Cheeta, of Tarzan movie fame, celebrated his 75th birthday in 2007). Since most primate species have long generation times, there are few studies of populations with long-term demographic information. At Gombe we have information on anubis baboons and chimpanzees from the 1960s to present day. There, no female baboon has lived beyond 27 years and those that

(a)   (b)

FIGURE 8-10   As primates grow old physical appearance changes. Their hair may become more spars and turn gray. The hair on this chimpanzee female (*pan troglodytes*) has begun to turn gray (a), while this 29-year-old female Barbary macaque (*Macaca sylvanus*) is beginning to show hair loss and in general looks dishevelled (b).

survived past 24 ceased to cycle (Packer et al. 1998). In captivity, where primates are more likely to survive longer, we have records of rhesus macaque females that survived to be 30 years old (Pavelka and Fedigan 1991). Flo, the famous chimpanzee matriarch of Gombe (Goodall 1986), was close to 50 years old when she died. Her even more famous daughter, Fifi, was born in 1958 and died in the fall of 2004. Fifi had given birth to her last (ninth) offspring in 2002. There appears to be a strong positive correlation between longevity and high rank. High rank affords one with much matrilineal support throughout life. Old females, like old males, that lack kin support become increasingly peripheralized and are more likely to fall prey to predators.

 BOX 8-1

Primates in Isolation

Primates, being highly gregarious animals, are very sensitive to the conditions of the social and physical environments in which they live. They are especially sensitive during the early developmental stages of their life. We see abnormal behavior more commonly in individuals that have been reared away from their mothers or are housed alone. Since primates are choice animals for displays at zoos, and some species are used in biomedical research, how they are cared for is of utmost importance to their well-being.

We know from early behavioral studies conducted by Harry Harlow and others (e.g., Harlow 1995, Harlow and Zimmermann 1959, Harlow et al. 1965, Menzel et al. 1963) that the social and physical environments within which baby monkeys, especially macaques, are raised have dramatic and lasting effects on later adult behavioral patterns. Infants reared alone and without mothers tended to develop highly abnormal behavioral patterns. Novel situations and unfamiliar objects made these infants extremely fearful and induced stereotypical disturbed behaviors. If placed in an unfamiliar room, they huddled in a corner, whimpering, hiding their faces, and rocking back and forth.

They were often observed sucking their thumb or big toe. Some even displayed self-injurious behaviors such as biting themselves.

In a now-famous experiment that demonstrated the importance of bodily contact and comfort, baby rhesus monkeys were provided with two choices of surrogate mothers. One was a bare steel wire structure with a crude wooden face. The other, although of the same basic shape, was covered with terrycloth and had a more monkey-like face (Figure 8-11). Milk was provided from a nipple on the steel wire surrogate. It turned out (maybe not so surprising) that all infants spent most of their time clinging to the soft surrogate mother, while they went to the other surrogate mother only to feed. Clearly, tactile contact and comfort rated higher than being close to food. If exposed to strange objects, such as a noisy wind-up toy, an infant would run and seek comfort from the soft surrogate mother. From this surrogate, once they calmed down, the infants would explore the novel object without fear.

Infants raised in abnormal rearing conditions grow up displaying behavioral abnormalities. Even if infants are reared

FIGURE 8-11 The importance of bodily contact with even surrogate mothers has been demonstrated experimentally. When infants were given the choice between a soft terry-covered "mother" over a wire "mother" they always preferred the soft "mother," even when the wire "mother" supplied milk.

in peer pairs or peer groups they show excessive self-directed behaviors, often huddling or clinging to each other. They engage in play less often and are more aggressive than infants reared with their mothers (Champoux et al. 1991, Sackett et al. 2002). There is strong evidence that infants raised in isolation or without their mothers may suffer permanent damage to specific parts of the brain, especially the physiological system that deals with stress, which would result in an inability to regulate negative emotions even in mildly stressful situations.

Even adult primates can develop idiosyncratic behavioral patterns when kept in isolation or in small enclosures in captivity. Such behaviors include stereotypical pacing in the cage, flipping of the head in a predictable manner, repetitive licking of surfaces or decorating the walls with feces. Sometimes more serious self-injurious behavioral patterns develop, e.g., biting oneself and pulling out the hair. More often than not, such behaviors can be prevented or at least be reduced in severity by providing both physical and social stimulation. If the origin of the abnormal behavior dates back to infanthood, however, there may be less of a chance of a cure (Novak 2003).

Most zoos and primate centers have developed enrichment programs to improve the mental as well as the physical health of the animals kept captive. It is recommended that any infant that cannot be reared with its mother should receive physical contact from humans or some other animal (e.g., dogs). Participation in daily playgroups makes a major improvement in both the physical and mental well being of infant primates (Sackett et al. 2002).

(continued)

FIGURE 8-12 Enclosures at zoos are now rather elaborate, providing three dimensional space for primates to move about in, and provide platforms where they can aggregate to relax and groom akin to an arboreal setting.

The type of housing where captive primates are kept is also of great importance. Gone are the sterile cages of the past with cement walls and floors. These enclosures typically had open metal bars facing toward the human spectators that provided only a single architectural level for the primates to live in. These enclosures were easy to clean and maintain, but they were very sterile environments. In addition, the open bars did not provide the primates with protection from the introduction of foreign items or loud noise into their cage. Now, even if the external structure of the cage is the same, the floor is covered with wood shingles, paper pellets or hay. The cage itself will have many different levels that the primates can use. The interior decoration can include platform areas, ropes to swing on and to travel along, and maybe even treelike structures for climbing. Attempts are made to reflect the structure of the natural habitat in the cage (Figure 8-12). The primates are also shielded from their human observers by protective glass or other physical borders that restrict people from getting too close to their enclosures. Furthermore, to prevent boredom, primates are made to forage for at least some of their food, e.g., food is hidden in wood shingles, or in food puzzles (Figure 8-13; Bloomsmith et al. 1988). Objects that can be used as toys or tools are often included in the decor. The objects included have to be sturdy because primates are not only very inquisitive, but they can also be very destructive (Figure 8-14). Therefore, much care has to be taken in regard to what is introduced. Fortunately, caretakers at zoos are no longer as worried about whether a cage looks messy to the human observers as they are about providing the primates with something to do.

Of course, the situation at biomedical research centers is different. Here primates are usually housed by necessity in single cages. There are strict

FIGURE 8-13   Food puzzles are frequently included in cages, providing the primates with foraging opportunities.

guidelines on the care of captive non-human primates and the cage size that is to be used for each primate species (U.S. Department of Agriculture 1991, 1999). There is of course a limit to what, and how many, objects can be introduced into a cage. However, most primates appear to be calmed and comforted by the presence of sound (music) and even by watching television.

FIGURE 8-14   Objects that can be used as toys or tools are often presented within enclosures, which the primates readily used. This gorilla female is using a plastic crate as a hat.

◈◈◈◈

Relationships Between Males and Females

The difference in the need to maximize their own reproductive success can lead to conflicts of interest between the sexes. Such conflicts are reflected in the interactions and relationships that we see between males and females. However, despite these potential conflicts of interest, there is also strong attraction between males and females (Perry 1997). In the case of males, this attraction is directly tied to a male's mating tactics and to the goal of maximizing reproductive success. A female's attraction to a male is first and foremost based on finding a protector, someone to protect herself and her offspring and to assist with securing food resources. This is especially important if the female does not have the support of a matriline. A female must also find a good mate. In many species, females have an uneasy relationship with males mainly because most males are dominant to the females, and males do not hesitate to use force to get their own way, i.e., access to sex or to food. By virtue of the fact that they are bigger, stronger, and dominant over females, males often circumscribe female choice. Even when females form coalitions with kin or join with like-minded females to outcompete or to oust an adult male, such dominance over a male is temporary and in any dyadic interaction a female has to submit. However, there are exceptions in which females are dominant or co-dominant to males, e.g., some lemurs, squirrel monkeys, patas monkeys, and bonobos (Boinski 1999, Freed 2007, Isbell and Pruetz 1998, Kano 1992, Sauther 1993).

To attract or appease males a female has two powerful tools: She can offer to groom him or she can mate with him. However, mating outside of estrus is not common, therefore females spend much time grooming males. Those behaviors that best reflect the relationship between a male and female are the frequency of being in close proximity to each other and the rate of grooming that occurs between them (Figure 8-15a). More often than not, it is the female that is the provider of the grooming and that seeks to be in close proximity. A female may express preference for a specific male by approaching him, presenting, and then grooming him. Males may respond positively to such an advertisement, but males are selective about the females they interact with as well. In most species males show a preference for **parous** females, those that have shown they can reproduce and successfully raise offspring, over young **nulliparous** females.

Male-female relationships may appear asymmetrical, but males and females bring different aspects to a relationship. There is a difference in the currency used to maintain a relationship—the female may be the more industrious groomer, while a male provides protection by being vigilant and protective. In many species a male usually shows increased interest in a female when she is in estrus; at this time, he may seek out her company and spend more time grooming her.

Males use two main reproductive tactics to gain access to females, one based on aggression and the other based on affiliation. Using a predominantly agonistic approach, a male may bully and coerce females to be and mate with him (Figure 8-15b; Smuts and Smuts 1993). Alternatively, a male may be more affiliative in his approach and first build a friendship relationship with a female that he can then use to influence the female's preference to mate with him (Manson 2007, Smuts 1987). Females can respond to bullying males by seeking support from other females or males. Females can more easily avoid unwanted overtures of affiliation by seeking out the company of others.

Following the best genes hypothesis, a female should be highly selective in regard to who fathers her offspring. Since females need to secure food and a safe environment for themselves and their offspring, a female may choose a male that has proven himself

(a)

(b)

FIGURE 8-15 (a) More often than not it is females who provide the grooming, but here a patas (*Erythrocebus patas*) male is grooming a female. (b) Males are bigger and dominant to females in most species, and males often bully and coerce females to mate with them.

by having a high dominance position, such as an alpha male that holds the highest attraction for many species of female macaques (Paul 2002). However, by choosing an aggressive and dominant male, a female may not only gain protection, but she may also be on the receiving end of his aggression. In some instances, females show preference for the largest male in the group, as is the case for capuchins and squirrel monkeys, or she may choose a lower-ranking, more affiliative male. In some situations, the male that is familiar, protective, and caring for a female's previous offspring will be selected, while in others females show a strong preference for novel males. The type of male a female prefers varies not just between species but within a social group, and it is not always straightforward what guides a female in making her choice.

A species' social organization and mating system constrain the social interactions between males and females. Furthermore, the mating tactics used play an important role in shaping these interactions. Male-female interactions reflect the conflicts of interest that exist between the sexes as each strives to maximize its own reproductive success.

One Male-Multifemale Groups

In groups in which there is only a single adult male present, the male does not need to worry about competition from other males for the attention of females. With a single adult present, the female has only one choice for a male partner. However, the amount of attention a female pays to the male varies much, both between species and even within a group. Interactions between males and females are influenced by whether a species has a seasonal breeding system and if females are philopatric.

In many seasonally breeding species, males and females go about their daily business quite separately outside of the breeding season. In species where females remain in their natal group, e.g., the silvered langur (*Trachypithecus cristatus*) and patas monkey (*Erythrocebus patas*), females tend to form strong social networks, while the resident adult male is usually socially peripheralized (Isbell and Pruetz 1998). The females may form a protective alliance against the male leader if he has acted in a way that has upset the females. In species in which unrelated females are grouped around a central male, much of the social attention is focused on the male leader, e.g., mountain gorillas (Harcourt and Stewart 1987; Watts 1994), lowland gorillas (Stokes 2004), and hamadryas baboons (Swedell 2002). If the females have a discernable dominance hierarchy, it is most often the dominant females that have the closest affiliative relationship with the male. Here, proximity to the male may be the best evidence of affiliation, but more often than not, females will compete to be close to and groom the male leader. When a female becomes receptive to mating, she gains the attention of the male by presenting her rear end to him. At this time she may also increase the rate at which she grooms the male.

During the breeding season, the resident male may fight a losing battle when trying to keep "his" females from mating with other "outsider" males. It is during these times when females can exert choice about which male they prefer as a partner. In species in which breeding occurs throughout the year, a male may need to pay closer attention to his females.

While both hamadryas baboons (*Papio hamadryas*) and geladas (*Theropithecus gelada*) have a complex multileveled social organization (discussed in Chapter 7), the smallest grouping is the one-male unit. Both species breed throughout the year, but they differ in female dispersal patterns. Hamadryas females disperse while gelada females remain in their natal unit. The dispersal in hamadryas is mainly due to male coercion by which young females are removed from their group. Therefore, female hamadryas may end up spending their lives with unrelated females, although older females may be able to exert some choice of residency (Swedell 2000a,b). In contrast, philopatric gelada females spend their whole lives surrounded by related females. These differences are reflected in the females' interactions with the leader male. Hamadryas male leaders are dominant to their females, and they may resort to aggressive acts such as neck biting if any of their females step out of line (Kummer 1968). The domineering tendencies of hamadryas males result in females directing much appeasement and affiliative interactions at a male, but females also spend as much time interacting with each other as they spend interacting with the male leader (Figure 7-10a; Swedell 2002).

The male hamadryas is possessive of his female(s) at all stages of her reproductive cycle. An estrous female holds no more interest to the male leader than does a pregnant or lactating female. Despite these possessive tendencies (which are really signals aimed at other adult males), hamadryas males do not affiliate or groom more often with their females than other baboon males, unless they perceive their bonds with the females to be threatened. It is the female that seeks proximity and that offers grooming to the male. Once a hamadryas male has "claimed" a female, his behavior towards her makes this very clear, and other males respect this possession, even when the female becomes receptive to mating.

A gelada male is also dominant to each of his females, but here the females will often form alliances and may even evict a male who is too despotic. Gelada females have much say in who their male leader is, and his worth is measured by the amount of time that he spends grooming each of his females. Patas (*Erythrocebus patas*) females also form alliances and may exert some influence on which male remains in the group after the mating season. They can express their choice by seeking close proximity to and grooming the male of choice while chasing away unwanted males.

Females in one-male groups tend to show synchronized estrus, and a cycling female often becomes receptive to mating when a new male has taken over the group. This may be a counterstrategy to reduce aggressive treatment by the new leader, and possibly a means to prevent the new male from committing infanticide. It is quite common for females to use sex as a means to reduce the aggressive tendencies of males directed toward themselves or their offspring.

Multimale-Multifemale Groups

In multimale-multifemale groups, both males and females have increased choice in mating partners. This increase in choice may, however, be circumscribed by dominance hierarchies, particularly by dominant males. Similar to the situation described above for one male-multifemale groups, in multimale-multifemale groups that breed, seasonally males and females do not interact much outside of the breeding season. For example, in some squirrel monkey species (*Saimiri*), males and females lead parallel lives within the same social group for most of the year. They seldom socialize and they do not rest or forage close together (Boinski 1999).

In species in which breeding occurs throughout the year, male attraction to females, and especially cycling females, is much more intense than in seasonal breeders. Males use various tactics to make themselves attractive to a female. Aside from using his bigger size and strength to his advantage, a male can establish a friendship relationship with specific females. These friendships are forged by the male behaving in a consistent, protective fashion toward the female and her offspring. They frequently travel, forage, and rest together, and mutual grooming may take place, although even in these friendships it is the female that provides most of the grooming. By having these affiliative relationships, a male may increase his chance of mating with the female when she becomes receptive.

A female does not necessarily use these friendly liaisons to gain a mating partner; her aim is to have protection against other aggressive group members. In some species, males provide infant care. For example, capuchin males often carry infants during travel (O'Brien 1991, Rose 1998), as do baboon males, and Barbary macaque males are well known for their infant-directed behaviors (Paul et al. 1996). A male that provides such services may be a preferred mating partner to many females, thus, both males and females stand to gain from such relationships. However, the caveat is that a male cannot provide protection to too many females at the same time, and in order to maximize his reproductive success, such friendships cannot last for very long. The initiation of such friendships most often is mutual and it can be either the female or the male who seeks out the other's company. Transferring males often attempt to establish a bond with a female in the new group to facilitate their gaining access to the group. A new male may do this by providing grooming or protecting a female against other males (often subadult males).

In multimale-multifemale groups, a female has greater opportunity to exert her choice for which male to father her offspring, and by mating with more than one male she can also confuse paternity. Females use grooming to solicit the interest of a preferred male or to appease agonistic males, and they can ultimately provide sex. Females use both whenever it is feasible. Where sexual dimorphism is great and females do not have kin to rely on, a female has to tread carefully as a male is more likely than not to take what he wants without giving much in return. This is especially true for chimpanzee females. Even though estrous females seek out and present themselves to select males, a dominant male can easily intervene and outcompete a lower-ranking male and mate with the female. Thus, unless a female's choice is the alpha male, she may not get to consort with the male of her choice. Deception is a tool frequently used by chimpanzees, and if a pair has selected each other as mating partners, they may actually leave the main group and not return until the female is no longer estrous. In such a situation both partners must seek each other out and coordinate their actions. Bonobo females, although also lacking kin support, build relationships with both males and females, and if a male attempts to force himself on a female, she can rally much support against the unwanted male. Thus, bonobo males use affiliative acts as a tactic to gain the desire of females. Bonobos use sex in almost any situation to show affiliation, to appease, and to settle disagreements. Young nulliparous immigrant bonobo females show a continuous estrus and spend much time copulating with the group's males (Kano 1989).

One Male-One Female Groups
In pair-bonded species, male-female interactions may vary in intensity. They may be infrequent, as is seen in gibbons (*Hylobates*), in which little affiliation or even close proximity occurs (Leighton 1987). In contrast, titi monkeys (*Callicebus*) are well known to form tight resting groups, in which the male and female may curl their tails tightly together for sustained periods of time.

Solitary Forager Species
Among solitary forager species, males and females have home ranges that overlap (see Chapter 7), and therefore they have the opportunity to come into contact. However, there is great variability in how much interaction is actually taking place between male-female dyads during nightly foraging. During the breeding season, males of all species show strong attraction to females, but may not spend much time with the female outside of copulating with her. However, courtship in slender lorises (*Loris lydekkerianus* and *L. tardigradus*) does entail lengthy grooming bouts (Nekaris 2003a). Male slender lorises appear to more often than not join female sleeping clusters, although they may alternate between several females' sleeping sites (Nekaris 2003a). In addition, before retiring at dawn and before setting out at dusk, there is much time devoted to grooming. The male participates in grooming as much as he receives grooming from other members in the sleeping cluster. Other solitary forager species may not have such a highly social interactive pattern between males and females, although there is much need for further observation of these rather elusive nocturnal species to know for sure.

Relationships Between Adults and Young
Female Maternal and Nonmaternal Care
In most mammals, including primates, raising offspring is mainly the responsibility of the mother. She provides the infant with nourishment, protection, and physical contact. Primate mothers exhibit a great deal of tolerance toward their young: Infants are

(a)

(b)

(c)

FIGURE 8-16 Primate mothers have the patience of a saint. The offspring may steal food out of the mouth of the mother or crawl all over her, but she will rarely do anything to stop her offspring. This chimpanzee infant is determined to get the food out his mother's mouth.

allowed to crawl all over, and they usually get in the way (Figure 8-16). During the earliest stages of development, there is almost continuous contact between the mother and the infant as it clings to her belly with unrestricted access to the nipple. The length and intensity of this contact varies between species. In some nocturnal strepsirhines (e.g., bushbabies and mouse lemurs), mothers leave their infants in a safe place while foraging but retrieve them for feeding sessions and when it is time to rest (Ross 2001). In arboreal species, as opposed to terrestrial ones, mothers restrict their infants' exploration of the environment until they are older. Living high in the trees presents dangers to newborns, especially if they have not yet developed good hand-eye coordination and might fall to their death.

The relationship between a mother and her offspring is a primary relationship that may persist into adulthood. During the early stages of infant development, all physical contact between the mother and her infant, especially grooming, is tremendously important. For example, touching and grooming have been shown to have a direct influence on how well the physiological system that deals with stress develops (Levine et al. 1993, Sapolsky 2004b). As the infant grows older, its nutritional demands begin to outstrip what the mother can provide. This is the beginning of the weaning process—when the infant has to supplement its milk diet with solid foods. This is a time rife with conflict between the mother and her infant. As the infant grows older, its social world begins to expand to include peer play groups, and as long as it has had enough to eat, it will associate with individuals other than mom (Barrett and Henzi 2000). In many species, by the time an infant is weaned, the mother may be pregnant. Even highly tolerant mothers have to prioritize access once a new infant enters the world, and the older sibling takes second place in the food line.

All newborn infants elicit much interest (as shown in Figure 7.5). Every group member wants to greet and handle the new arrival, especially other mothers with young infants. Nonmaternal infant handling is quite common among primates. Such interactions can range from friendly (e.g., look at, sniff, nuzzle, hold, groom, carry) to down right hostile (e.g., hit, pull, bite). It is especially the infants of low-ranking females that are exposed to the antagonistic behaviors of competitive high-ranking females. All this attention may cause the mother much distress, with the result that she is reluctant to allow anyone near her new baby. This reluctance declines, however, as the baby grows older and becomes more independent. This coincides with reduced attention by other group members.

How protective or tolerant a mother is varies not just between species but also within a single species and even within a social group. A mother's age and rank, as well as her personality, influence her behavior toward the offspring. Colobine mothers are more tolerant than cercopithecine mothers in allowing other group members to handle their infants. In many langur species, mothers allow their infants to be handled and even carried within hours after birth. Infant gray langurs (*Semnopithecus entellus*) may spend as much as 40 to 60 percent of the time away from their mother. Langur females may even nurse infants that are not their own. Some of the platyrrhines, especially capuchins and squirrel monkeys, show much tolerance to other group members' caring for their infants, and capuchin females may nurse infants that are not their own (Perry 1996). Among cercopithecines, mothers show the greatest tolerance toward other group members taking care of their infants. In the case of the Barbary macaques (*Macaca sylvanus*), mothers even allow adult males to handle their infants soon after birth (Paul et al. 1996). Chimpanzee mothers are among the most protective species. They often spend long stretches of time alone with their infants, providing an environment not so different from that of orangutan mothers. An infant clings to its mother as she travels, forages, and feeds (Figure 8-17). When resting, it receives much grooming from mom and she may spend long bouts playing with her infant or it will engage in solitary play—this is more common in the orangutan.

Different hypotheses have been presented to explain, from an evolutionary point of view, the presence of infant greetings and infant-handling behavior by nonmothers. The natal attraction hypothesis (Paul 1999, Silk et al. 2003b) is based on the premise that females are stimulated to be good and caring mothers by seeing other females with their

FIGURE 8-17   Initially an infant clings to its mother's belly when she travels or forages. As the infant grows older it will ride jockey style on the back of its mother as shown by this anubis baboon (*Papio anubis*).

infants. This might explain why females with infants of approximately the same age approach each other, greet, and interact with each other's infants. Such approaches are usually preceded by soft vocalization, and often a quick grooming of the mother signals friendly intentions. However, it is not just mothers that greet new infants, all group members tend to come and visit a new infant. It may be a way for them to gain knowledge about the new group member. The handling of infants may be best explained by the learning-to-mother hypothesis (Schino et al. 2003). This hypothesis is supported by observations that confirm that juvenile and nulliparous females are the ones that show the greatest interest in handling infants. They seek to hold and carry infants and have much to gain from such an experience. This type of infant handling is often referred to as allomothering. However, when adult (parous) females handle an infant, the learning-to-mother hypothesis loses its explanatory power. This may be an altruistic act, most likely performed by related individuals, because it frees the mother to catch up on feeding or resting. It has also been suggested that females use infant handling as a means to gauge how willing another female is to enter into a coalition relationship (Manson 1999). Alternatively, on a more sinister note, it may be part of a reproductive competition strategy, the so called aunting-to-death hypothesis (Hrdy 1976). This is when an infant is kidnapped and held against its own will. The mother may not be able to retrieve her infant because the kidnapper is of higher rank and can rally support against her. It is not just females that may kidnap infants; any group member can do so.

The special tolerance seen in many species with a single-male group structure has been attributed to female alliances and support against infanticidal males. In most langurs, for example, new babies have contrasting fur coloration to the adults (see Figure 4-5). This may be so that during aggressive interactions, such as male-male competition, a female can quickly retrieve an infant that may be in danger of being hurt.

FIGURE 8-18 Direct paternal care is uncommon; however, males may carry infants during travel. This ring-tail lemur (*Lemur catta*) male is giving an infant a lift.

Male Paternal and Nonpaternal Care

More often than not, fathers do not provide paternal care to their offspring. It is, of course, difficult to assess the value or the extent to which a male (possibly the father) provides protection to an infant just by his mere presence. Sporadic interactions between adult males and immatures occur in all species, such as a male carrying an infant or young juvenile during travel (Figure 8-18). This often occurs where danger may lurk and speed is essential. Even in pair-bonded species, fathers may have little direct involvement in infant care. Gibbon fathers seldom help with the infants, although they may sometimes engage in play with older juveniles. Among the callitrichids (marmosets and tamarins), in which females give birth to twins, one would expect that fathers would help, but they are not as good at helping as are older siblings in carrying the babies (Garber and Leigh 1997). However, in a few species, fathers do provide habitual care of the young. In the pair-bonded titi and owl monkeys (*Callicebus* and *Aotus*), it is the fathers that provide transportation for infants (Wright 1990). This activity may start within a day or two after birth, and the infant shifts to the mother only when it needs to nurse. Owl monkey fathers have also been seen to engage in play with older offspring (Wright 1994).

There is great variability in the way males relate to infants and juveniles, ranging from tolerant to indifferent to aggressive. It is not unusual to see an adult male avoiding coming into contact with an infant. Why should adult males bother with infants? The three main hypotheses presented to explain why adult males should interact with infants are

1. *Parental investment.* If the offspring is his own, it is in the male's best interest to protect and take care of the infant because he is then directly influencing his own reproductive success. In species in which the male has good reason to assume he is the father, more investment is provided, e.g., among callitrichids, fathers often

carry the offspring (Wright 1990). However, just because a species is pair bonded, the male may not be directly involved in infant care, e.g., gibbon males pay scant attention to infants. It has been assumed that males have no way of determining which infants they have fathered, especially in species in which females mate with several partners. However, a recent study has shown that male yellow baboons, which live in a multimale society, interact with and give more protection to infants that have been shown to be their own offspring (Buchan et al. 2003). We therefore will have to reassess our assumptions that paternity is unknown to resident males.

2. *Mating effort.* By being protective and affiliative with the infant, the male can show the mother that he is a worthy partner the next time she is mating. Thus, it is a way for the male to ensure that future offspring will be sired by him. Baboon males often are seen to form friendships with specific females and these friendships do often lead to greater mating success (Smuts 1985).

3. *Agonistic buffering.* Adult males may use infants as buffers during male-male contests. Baboon males often engage in such activities (Figure 8-6). Barbary macaque males have been frequently observed to carry infants toward each other in triadic interactions (Paul et al. 1996). One male will carry a cooperative infant on his back toward another adult male. The two males sit down facing each other and both vocalize and touch the infant (Figure 8-19). This type of interaction may have nothing to do with the infant and everything to do with the relationship between the two adult males. However, Barbary macaques are curious because despite having a promiscuous mating system, males frequently interact with and carry specific infants while they completely ignore others. Even though genetic investigations have not been able to correlate paternity with rate of male interaction with infants, it is a question that requires further study.

FIGURE 8-19 Two Barbary macaque (*Macaca sylvanus*) males interacting using an infant as a social tool.

It Is a Juvenile's World

In most primate species, infants show an almost complete dependence upon the mother (See Information Box 8-2). Much information about the surrounding habitat is picked up while still intimately attached to the mother, such as what to eat and what to avoid, what is dangerous and what is not, and who's a friend and who's a foe. Social relationships within the group are perceived through the mother's behaviors and reactions during interactions, as well as how the infant is treated by the other members of the group. Infants of dominant mothers are bound to receive more affiliative and differential treatment than infants of low ranking mothers. However, there comes a time when the infant has to let go of its mother's apron strings. For most primate species, weaning is a prolonged process as the infant slowly begins to supplement its diet with solid foods (Altmann 1998). This can be a traumatic time in the young primate's life, since it has to find its own food. No one is there to give or share food. As a matter of fact, food sharing is a rarity in nonhuman primates. A juvenile that is unable to find enough food will starve (Altmann 1998, Barrett and Henzi 2000).

Once weaned, an infant enters into the world of juveniles. This is a time for learning, and the prolonged juvenile period seen in most species is characteristic of primates. Much of the learning takes place through interactions with other group members, most specifically within the peer cohort, through exploration and play (see Pereira and Fairbanks 1993). From an evolutionary point of view, it is not so surprising that juveniles play and explore but it can be risky to explore, as seen in the very high mortality rates so typical of the juvenile age group.

When very young, both males and females spend much time playing, in often rough-and-tumble play (Figure 8-20). However, as a juvenile grows older, a clear sex-related difference in the nature of their activities can be detected. The sex roles that occur in a

FIGURE 8-20   Play is an important activity for immature primates in all species. Age cohorts often engage in rough-and-tumble play. Here juveniles Celebes macaques (*Macaca nigra*) are in full play mode.

group are learned at a very tender age. Early in life, daughters gain information about their mothers' social position and that of other female relatives. As juveniles, females enter into the world of the adult females' grooming networks. In most cases, an infant will have entered the social realm of the juvenile female, and the infant is a source of fascination for these young females. Juvenile males, in contrast, continue with their rough-and-tumble play, and as they grow older they become increasingly attentive to all of the social politics involving the adult males. However, if they live in a matrilineally based social group, both male and female offspring will give support to their mother in disputes. Immature males spend time grooming each other, older adult males, or young subadult females. As the males grow older, their play becomes more serious and clearly tests dominance relationships. By the time they are subadult, the males begin to harass adult females until they have reached a dominance rank above all the adult females in the group. At this time, their fascination with sex also enters the picture, but access is usually restricted to subadult females. When a male has reached this point in life, he most likely will leave his natal group and seek his fortune elsewhere. In many species the dispersing sex are just juveniles when they leave their natal group. Especially in species such as macaques or capuchins, a 3 to 4-year-old may migrate along with an older brother or several individuals from the peer group. At such a young age, a male is not able to defend himself against adults and relies on an older sibling to pave the way. If females are the dispersing sex, they tend to migrate when closer to adult age and thus have better leverage at being more attractive to the males of other groups.

 **BOX 8-2**

Orphaned Primates

A mother is the most important individual in an infant's life. She is the one that provides food, warmth, and protection. If an infant loses its mother before it is weaned, its chance of survival is close to nonexistent, even despite the care older siblings and other group members may give. Mothers are the center of the universe and it is from the mother that a baby primate gains its first understanding of the world. Even if weaned, the attachment to the mother can be so strong that upon losing her, the infant or juvenile sinks into a state of severe depression, succumbs to illness, and dies.

In some species, such as the chimpanzee, in which the bond between a mother and her offspring can be especially intense, even an older juvenile may perish if its mother dies (Goodall 1986, Pusey 1983). Infant chimpanzees younger than 4 years do not usually survive the loss of their mothers. Even within the 4 to 5 year age range, many do not make it without their mothers. Young chimpanzees that are orphaned seem to fall into a depressive state, sitting in huddled positions, listless, and showing little interest in play, despite the care offered by older siblings. The infants that showed the least devastating emotional effect were those whose mothers were not very attentive or affectionate.

(continued)

Orphaned Gorilla infants appear to fare better even at a younger age. If older siblings are present, they will likely be the ones who will care for an infant that has lost its mother. Sometimes adult males will actually take over the protective role, e.g., silverback gorillas (Watts and Pusey 1993).

Infants that are not yet weaned and still dependent on the mother for sustenance may have a much reduced chance of survival. However, in some species **allonursing**, nursing by females other than the mother, is common and orphans have a fighting chance. Immature langurs that lose their mothers readily adopt other group members as surrogate mothers (Dolhinow and DeMay 1982). Likewise, infant capuchins that have lost their mother or have even just temporarily been separated from their own mother are nursed by other group females (Perry 1996, Rose 1998).

◆◆ Summary

Primates are social animals that have complex and fluid social relationships. Patterns of social interactions that particular primates exhibit are influenced by their group composition, dispersal pattern, and mating strategy. Kinship tends to be a primary motivating factor in how primate relationships are expressed and played out in a social group. When conflicts over limited resources arise, kin may act as important allies to one another. Kin relations often form the central, foundational structure of a group. Conflict situations between individuals may be negotiated peacefully or violently. Overall, some degree of peace must be maintained in a social group in order for the group to remain intact, so primates use a variety of reconciliation strategies to restore normal relations between group members.

Social relationships between adult males are often influenced by competition for available mates. The relationships between adult females may reflect coalitions established to provide aid and support to related females and their offspring, or for females to act in concert against the aggressive behavior of adult males. Adult males and females must behave in ways that will maximize their reproductive success, but relationships other than those based on sex may be formed. In primate societies it is typically the mother who is the caretaker and who provides the immediate social world for her offspring. Mothers must behave in ways that ultimately provide adequate food, a safe haven, and model and frame social relationships in which their offspring engage. Through play, immatures forge and develop relationships with one another, and in some species they may leave their natal group together to seek out relationships in new groups. Social relationships are expressed differently in species that live in different types of social organizations, have seasonal or nonseasonal mating strategies, and in which male or female (or both) sexes disperse, and may ultimately be affected by the availability of resources. The individual life cycle of a primate also affects the type of social relationships that an individual forms. Young adults tend to strive for increasing rank and position within a group, and older individuals may often become peripheral members of a group. Whether living in captivity or in the wild, primates do not fare well at all as isolated individuals.

❖❖ Key Words

alliances
allonursing
altruistic behaviors
cooperate
dominance hierarchy
fitness
greeting behavior

gregarious
inclusive fitness
infanticide
mate competition
nulliparous
parous
patrilocal male

reciprocal altruism
reconciliation
redirected aggression
social
social competence
sperm competition

❖❖ Study Questions

1. What factors influence the social lives of primates?
2. de Waal's relational model considers tolerance, aggression, and avoidance as equally important in conflict resolution. Explain how aggression can be used to solve problems without destroying the social fabric of a social group.
3. Why might altruistic behaviors not be evolutionary advantageous strategies?
4. What purpose do greetings between adult males serve in primate groups?
5. What information do we need to support or refute the hypothesis that infant killing is an evolutionary advantageous strategy?
6. How do female primates maintain their social networks, and what factors affect these social networks?
7. What are the counterstrategies females use to circumvent male aggression and potential infanticidal behaviors?
8. How does old age affect male and female primates?
9. Many species of primates produce newborn infants with distinctly different hair and skin colors compared to those of adults. What might be some underlying reasons for these differences?
10. Discuss the ways that infant primates learn about their social and natural environments.

❖❖ Suggested Further Readings and Related Web Sites

Altmann J. 1980. Baboon mothers and infants. Cambridge, MA: Harvard University Press.

Periera ME, Fairbanks LA editors. 1993. Juvenile primates. Life history, development and behavior. Oxford: Oxford University Press.

Schaik CP van, Janson CH editors. 2000. Infanticide by males and its implications. Cambridge, MA: Cambridge University Press.

Smuts BB, Cheney DL, Seyfarth RM, Wrangham RW, Struhsaker TT editors. 1987. Primate societies. Chicago: University of Chicago Press.

Strier KB. 1994. Myth of the typical primate. Yearbook of Physical Anthropology 37:233-271.

CHAPTER 9

Primate Communication

❖❖ What is Language?

Most of us would probably agree that the function of our language is to communicate with fellow humans. Even though other animals may also communicate using vocalization, we instinctively assume that human languages are much more complex and expressive. However, is this assumption really true? Our language ability is often defined based on **semantics** and **syntax**, but as suggested by Hockett (1963), there is much more complexity to human language. Hockett provides an extensive list of aspects that define human language (see Table 9-1). Some of these are also common among other animals. Human speech, like all animal vocalization, is within the sound-hearing channel and as such is ephemeral. It is directional in that everyone understands other conspecifics. Other aspects within this list are, however, more question-able as to universality or uniqueness. For example, it is not known whether tradition or displacement is present in the vocal communication of other species; that is, if they can communicate about what is not present in the here and now. However, with such a clearly defined list, it is possible to systematically collect empirical data from nonhuman primates and evaluate whether they also have these attributes.

> **semantics**—refers to meaning attached to words, vocalizations, and signals; the basic sound units produced in human speech (phonemes) do not in themselves carry meaning. It is by combining them into words and affixes, so called morphemes, that meaning is gained. Morphemes are further combined into higher orders of meaning, e.g., sentences or stories.
>
> **syntax**—the way sentences are put together according to specific rules (grammar), and words or morphemes are placed in a predictive order to give comprehension to utterances

In this chapter we will explore how primates communicate, what they may be saying to each other, and what aspects of language we share with other primates. We will also examine research on the language ability of captive apes to determine the underlying potential for language.

❖❖ Theories about the Origin of our Language Ability

There is much discussion about whether our language ability evolved out of the vocal or gestural communication seen in the animal world, most specifically in other primates, or if our language ability is a reflection of our human uniqueness, which has nothing in common with the vocalizations of nonhuman primates. Presently, scientists are beginning to see that it may be a little of both. Part of the problem is how we define human language. There are aspects of our language that are unique, but there are also many aspects that are generally shared within many different taxa.

For centuries, philosophers and scientists have speculated about the origins of human language. Traditionally, this question has been polarized into two opposing schools of thought. One school is based on the suggestion that our human language ability is unique in the animal world and that we share only the most basic aspects of our language abilities with other animals. We refer to this as the uniqueness theory. The basis for the uniqueness theory is the work of Noam Chomsky, probably the most influential linguist of the twentieth century (e.g., Chomsky 1975, 1986). The tenet of his innate universal grammar

TABLE 9-1	**Design Features of Language based on Hockett (1963), with some modifications from Snowdon (1990)**	
Design features	*Description*	*Present in NHP*
vocal-auditory channel	modality communication takes place in	YES
broadcast transmission	directional	YES
rapid fading	vocalization is ephemeral	YES
interchangeability	everyone understands each other	YES
complete feedback	individual vocalizing hears the message	YES
specialization	importance of trigger effect	YES
semantics	signals refer to objects or events in the real world	YES
arbitrariness	vocalization does not resemble referent	YES
discreteness	vocalization differentiated; signals do not grade into each other	(YES/NO)
displacement	signal can refer to objects or events not in the here and now	NO?
openness	new meanings can be formed through recombination of vocalizations	NO?
tradition	vocalization transmitted to others through teaching and learning	YES?
duality of pattern	combination of phonemes into morphemes	NO
prevarication	use vocalization in deceptive acts	NO?
reflexiveness	use of language to talk about language	NO
learnability	ability to learn more than one language	NO?
syntax	vocalization presented in orderly and predictive way	NO

theory is that the brain is the mechanism underlying our language abilities. A recent mutation within our brain led to the development of specific language abilities, and there are no evolutionary antecedents (Chomsky 1986). More recently, some of the supporters of the Chomskian theory have conceded that our unique language abilities have an evolutionary history, but our capacity for language is limited to within the *Homo* lineage and evolved over time under the influence of natural selection (Pinker 1994, Pinker and Bloom 1990).

An opposing school of thought, which has gained support and popularity over the last few decades, especially from primatologists, is the so-called continuity theory. The premise of this theory is that there is an evolutionary continuity between the communication systems of other animals, especially other primates, and our own language abilities (Dunbar 1996, King 1999). Therefore, the difference in our language ability compared with other primates is considered a matter of degree rather than kind.

The evidence that we presently have at hand can lend support to either theory, but none of it provides a definitive answer. However, with increasing sophistication in technology and methodology, we are gaining better insight into how our language abilities work and what aspects, both neurobiological and genetic, are involved.

Origin of Language and Mirror Neurons

There are many ideas about the origin of language. The root of language may stem from gesturing, singing, vocalization, or grooming. The idea that there is a connection between language and manipulation, especially complex manipulation such as tool making, has much support (e.g., Calvin 1983, Corballis 1992, 2002, Dunbar 1996). Some recent brain behavioral research has come up with exciting results. By using PET (positron emission tomography) scanning techniques, an interesting type of brain cell located in the prefrontal cortex of macaques has been detected (Fogassi, et al. 2005, Rizzolatti and Arbib 1998). These neurons are called **mirror neurons**. They become activated when a monkey uses a precision grip to manipulate or grasp an object. More importantly, these neurons become activated when a monkey observes someone else do the same motion—i.e., these neurons respond to visual stimuli. This is exciting because it has been suggested that the brain area where the mirror neurons are located in the macaque is a homologue to Broca's area in humans, and Broca's area is important in speech production (Petrides et al. 2005; see below). This area is activated, for example, when naming objects as well as during object manipulation.

The mirror neurons found in the macaque brain may provide a fundamental mechanism for the recognition of actions by linking action recognition with action production (Umiltà et al. 2001). This has been suggested as a neural prerequisite for the development of communication between individuals, in our case, speech. A possible scenario is that the proto-speech area(s) of early hominins involved mouth and hand manipulation (the mirror neuron system), was honed through gestures or tool manufacture, and later hijacked for vocal communication over the course of a progressive association of using gestures when vocalizing.

Origin of Language and the FOX Gene Family

Over the past few years there have been great advances in genetic research. With the discovery of the **FOXP2** gene, we are beginning to trace the biological basis for language ability. The FOXP2 is a highly conservative gene and is present in most animals, including birds (Haesler et al. 2004, Shu et al. 2001). In humans it appears that aspects of this gene have undergone recent selective changes that may have coincided with the evolution of speech and human language (Enard et al. 2002). The FOXP2 has been reported as *the* language gene in the popular press; however, it is not specifically a "language gene." It is a transcription factor, i.e., a protein that regulates the activity of other genes. It has therefore a more universal or cascading effect, sort of like a master control gene, influencing many aspects of language production. Its effect is not grammar or speech-specific, but it has an effect on mouth and facial movement, which is a crucial part of language production (Marcus and Fisher 2003, Shu et al. 2005, Vargha-Khadem et al. 2005).

Our knowledge about the biological underpinning of language production and language ability is still rudimentary. However, rapid advances in research will provide us with greater insight into how and which genes are involved in various aspects of language. Once this information is available, we can make comparisons with other primate species, providing a better understanding of the evolutionary history of our language ability. Most likely, this knowledge will not be available to us for many years to come because language function in the brain is incredibly complex, but it will not be out of our reach in the future.

Today, much of the theoretical basis for studying the **communication** of nonhuman primates pivots around how and when the transition from emotionally driven communication signals to symbolic or abstract signals may have occurred during human evolution. However, primate communication can also be used as a tool to understand their minds. By studying how and what primates communicate in the wild, scientists hope to unravel the secrets of their mental ability. This will be examined in greater detail in Chapter 10.

◇◇ How Different is Human Vocal Communication from that of Other Primates?

The extent that human speech (i.e., language) differs from the vocalizations of nonhuman primates is a highly contentious topic. Early theories concerning the vocalizations of nonhuman primates were rather simplistic, and scientists described their results in a series of dichotomies that indicated fundamental differences between human and nonhuman primates (Table 9-2). In recent years, further research into the vocalization and

TABLE 9-2 Comparison Between Human and Nonhuman Primate Language Abilities

Categories	*Human Language*	*Nonhuman Primate Vocalization*
Brain	Language ability is voluntary and under higher cortical control (neocortex)	Language ability is relatively involuntary and under limited cortical control (limbic system)
Language perception	Speech is a graded continuum of sounds that are perceived as a series of discrete categories	Most calls are a graded continuum (especially open habitats dwellers) while some are discrete (forest dwellers)
Semantics	Words represent objects or events in the external world; they are "referential"	Most vocalizations represent the caller's emotional state (level of arousal); they are "motivational," but there is now much evidence of referential calls
Syntax	Presence of specific rules (grammar); words can be combined in an infinite number of ways; possibility for novelty and innovation	Lack of grammar; set number of vocal sounds; no evidence of novel combinations
Learning	Integral part of human ability; modifiable	No gradual development of ability little or no learning (innate); mainly non-modifiable

language capacity of nonhuman primates has shown that these simple divisions can be challenged on many levels. This research has occurred in three interrelated areas:

- Training apes to learn elements of human language (the so-called ape-language projects)
- Studies of the natural vocalizations of nonhuman primates
- Studies of the cognitive abilities of nonhuman primates

Here we will explore the basis for the perceived differences between human language and the vocalizations of nonhuman primates and how perceptions of these differences have changed over time. The continuity theory is gaining in support, as it is becoming clear that the dichotomies presented in Table 9-2 are not as discrete as first thought. It is also important to recognize that nonhuman primates do not present a homogeneous picture and that there is much variability in their vocalizations and patterns of vocal communication. Habitat adaptation as well as phylogeny may have played a role in the promotion of this variability. However, in order to address the factors that have affected this variability, more studies need to be done on primate vocalization in the wild.

❖❖ Ways to Communicate

Communication is a way to broadcast and receive information about what is happening in the social and physical environment in which an organism lives. Such information aids an individual in its daily tasks of survival and reproduction. By examining how and what primates communicate about in their natural environment, we hope to elucidate if what they are saying carries meaning, and even more importantly, if they themselves perceive their communication to carry meaning. We want to know whether the caller has the *intention* to communicate something specific to others. That is, does the individual understand that its communication gives information to others and does it use this knowledge to alter the behavior of others?

The first step in studying the communication of nonhuman primates is to look at *how* they communicate and what the differences and similarities are to how humans communicate with each other. Primates, like all animals, use some form of communication, and we assume that they relay information to conspecifics about what is happening in the physical and social environments around them. This line of research is now possible, in part because of our advanced technology. Recording primate vocalizations in their natural habitat is fairly easy, and **sound spectrograms** can be analyzed using simple computer programs.

However, vocalization is only one way that primates communicate with one another. They also communicate by way of chemical or visual signals, and physical contact. Most

> **sound spectrogram**—visual representations of vocalizations, showing the acoustic structure of individual calls

species use a combination of these ways to communicate, but not all primates rely on the same means of communication, or use it to the same extent. The environmental context they live in puts constraints on the communication system used. Nocturnal strepsirhines may rely more on chemical signals, while diurnal monkeys and apes more commonly use vocal communication. These are adaptations commensurate with the niche the species inhabits. At close proximity and in open habitats, visual cues are relied upon more extensively. In addition to habitat, the social structure and social organization of a species influence the type of communication system that is most prevalent. Primates use a combination of different ways to communicate, just like we do. We commonly use facial expression and gestures to reinforce speech, which is the dominant mode of communication in our species.

Communication using Olfaction

Many primate species deposit scents around their home range, especially around the periphery. The scents can be deposited via urine and feces or by rubbing specialized scent-excreting glands along branches or tree trunks. These chemical cues can be used to tell competitors to stay away or to attract mates. More often than not, this is a male affair, but females also use chemical signaling, by emitting pheromones to attract mates. Males can gauge from these signals how receptive a female is to mating. The perception of pheromones allows for the recognition of species, individual, sex, and age because each individual has a distinctive chemical signature (e.g., Dugmore and Evans 1990, Smith 2006). As these signals reveal much about the individual, we have to assume that they are honest signals about the condition or quality of the scent marker.

The primate species that use this type of communication have a well-developed sense of smell or olfaction. It is possible to recognize these olfactory-oriented primates by their elongated snout, and their noses tend to be wet (shiny) just as on a dog or cat (Figure 9-1). This type of communication is used most frequently by strepsirhines, but some American primates, e.g., callitrichids (marmoset and tamarins) and cebids (capuchin and squirrel monkeys), also use olfactory communication (Di Fiore et al. 2006, Epple et al. 1993). Capuchin and squirrel monkeys, for example, practice urine washing. Instead

FIGURE 9-1 Primate species that communicate using olfaction often have elongated muzzles and "wet" noses, just like this *Lemur catta*. This type of nose functions well to trap scent in the air and transport smell molecules into the nose.

of leaving the urine mark in the environment, they rub urine over their hair to enhance their smell. Bushbabies rub urine on their hands and feet, which also appears to increase their gripping ability (Figure 9-2; Welker 1973). Some lemurs (e.g., *Lemur catta*) use olfactory cues during aggressive intermale interactions, in so-called "stink-fights," when competing for access to females (Gould and Overdorff 2002, Jolly 1966) (Figure 9-2). Olfactory signals in species that live in social groups are used to communicate within the group and may be important for both inter- and intragroup sexual selection (Kappeler 1998).

FIGURE 9-2 Rubbing the body with urine (urine washing), is practiced by several primate species, especially nocturnal strepsirhines such as this bushbaby, *Otolemur crassicaudatus* (top). Some lemurs, such as these ring-tailed lemurs, *Lemur catta* (left), use olfactory advertisement—so called stink fights—during intermale aggressive competition.

There are some clear advantages to chemical communication. Most strepsirhines tend to be active at night, when reduced visibility together with the possibility of attracting predators, make vocalization and visual signals less feasible. Furthermore, when living in an arboreal habitat where dense vegetation may restrict visibility, communication using chemical signals may be useful. Chemical signals are economical and provide an advantage because they are long-lasting; consequently, the message broadcast is effective for an extended period of time (Palagi et al. 2005). This can be very important in the case of species that are solitary foragers (like many strepsirhines) and those that roam over extended areas.

 HOT TOPICS 9-1

Have Humans Really Lost their Sense of Smell?

It is true that our sense of smell is greatly reduced compared to that of other mammals, even compared to other primates. Where our noses may be letting us down is in the range of smells that we can perceive. It is estimated that about 63 percent of our olfactory receptor genes are inactive—they have become so-called pseudogenes, and much of this inactivation is believed to have occurred since the evolution and spread of anatomically modern humans (Young and Trask 2002). However, we actually do rely much more on our sense of smell than we may realize. Odors can alert us to dangers so that, for example, we do not eat spoiled food. Odors can modify our mood, which is often exploited by store owners as they pipe smells into stores to make the customers' attitudes more positive in the hope that they will spend more money.

The sense of smell is, however, a very complex matter. Most animals have evolved the ability to detect two general types of smells: odorant molecules and pheromones. Odorant molecules are abundant in the surrounding environment and are picked up by specialized cells located in the back of the nose. Most odorant molecules are consciously perceived, such as those given off by foods or flowers. The behavioral responses to such molecules can readily be modified by learning. Pheromones are chemical signals present in urine, sweat, and other bodily secretions and are perceived by the vomeronasal organ located at the base of the nasal cavity (see Chapter 4: the primate body). These chemical signals are usually not consciously perceived and result in innate, subconscious, and stereotyped responses, which are not readily modified by experience.

It is well established that most animals have the ability to discriminate and react to both odorants and pheromones floating about in the environment. It has long been suggested that we humans have lost the ability to detect, and maybe thus the possibility to be influenced by, pheromones. However, such assertions have been challenged by recent research in which it has been shown that humans do respond to what is believed to be human pheromones. For example, it has been shown that when several human females live together, their menstrual cycles become synchronized, which has been attributed to pheromones (McClintock 1971, Weller and Weller 1997). In addition, males and females respond to different types of pheromones (Stern and McClintock 1998, Brand and Millot 2001). However, compared to other animals, our ability to perceive pheromones is much diminished.

FIGURE 9-3   Visual communication often entails facial expressions. The female chimpanzee is exchanging visual communications with the male nearest to her (top). Male primates often yawn when they are exposed to a stressful and contest situation, exposing their large and intimidating canines (left).

Communication using Vision

Visual communication can take place in two ways, either through body posturing or facial expressions (see Figure 9-3). Such form of communication is dependent on a good visual field and acuity and is most useful when interaction takes place in close proximity. Visual signaling is most developed in diurnal primates.

Visual communication can be rather complex, and the effectiveness of visual gestures is frequently dependent on the social relationships of the individuals involved. Visual signals can be used to attract or repel others. It is used in dominance interactions, in which one individual may show a dominant expression while another responds with a submissive expression. A common goal of body posturing is to make the signaler's body appear larger than it really is. This is an effective way of communicating aggression or dominance. By standing upright, exposing one's flanks and having the body hair stand on end (**piloerection**), a very daunting impression is achieved. Facial expressions can be more subtle and more varied. When a male baboon wants to attract a female friend, he may raise his eyebrows, smooth down his ears, and lift his face forward while keeping his mouth closed, producing a so-called

FIGURE 9-4 Facial expressions are important during close-up communication, and can show much individual idiosyncrasy. Here is shown three very different expressive faces of a chimpanzee male.

"come hither look" (Smuts 1985). The female will instantly recognize this as a friendly gesture; she may then approach and groom him. In contrast, when a male baboon raises his eyebrows (without smoothing down his ears) and opens the mouth to display his large canines, his intentions are not friendly. This is a gesture often used against competing males, especially when negotiating social status in the group. As these examples show, signals can be used in various combinations to communicate whether the actor is friendly or agonistic.

The extent of facial expression is dependent on the species' anatomy; the more nerves in control of moving the skin and muscles, the finer the movements. This is the reason why strepsirhines have less expressive faces than haplorhines, and apes have especially expressive faces (Figure 9-4). The lack of facial hair further enhances the visual field of facial expressions. Facial expressions play a key role in close-up communication, and many are directly linked to specific vocalizations. Facial expressions are varied and can show much individual idiosyncrasy. Among the Gombe chimpanzees, Goodall (1986) found that some individuals had unique facial expressions never used by others. Prolonged eye contact is interpreted as threatening by most nonhuman primates, but in both chimpanzees and humans, direct eye contact is considered non-threatening and an important part of a social interaction.

Skin and pelage color also carry important information for conspecifics. Such information is more or less permanent and cannot be modified, at least not intentionally. A monkey cannot change the color of its hair just to escape attention. However, skin and pelage coloration can be used as effective signals too. For example, guenons use ritualized head-bobs and body postures in which their very distinctive color combinations serve as an integral part of the message broadcasted. Those species that have long tails may use them as part of a display, e.g., ring-tailed lemurs sway their tails above their heads (tails that are often impregnated with scent) to impress other group members. In most primate species, young infants have a coat color that is drastically different from their parents (Figure 4-5). Being so visible may place infants at greater risk, although it has been suggested that the different coat color assists mothers and other protectors of the infant to locate it more easily if a fight breaks out. The very obvious display of reproductive receptiveness that, for example, baboon and chimpanzee females display (see Figure 4-26) is beyond their control, but still serves as a potent signal to potential mates.

Communication using Tactile Senses

Humans often use tactile communication. People may shake hands or embrace when greeting. To give assurance or to get attention, a person may place his hand on someone's shoulder or arm. These are all friendly or reassuring gestures, but we use aggressive gestures as well, such as grabbing hold of or hitting, or in other ways hurt or dominate another person. In other primates, grooming or touching in appeasement or reassurance are the most common ways to communicate via touch. In most primate species, **allogrooming** is an important facet of social interaction. Social grooming promotes group cohesion and is used when giving or seeking reassurance (Figure 9-5), and it is how you make and keep friends and allies. There is much interspecific variability in the amount of time spent in grooming interactions. Some species may spend as much as 10 to 15 percent of the day engaged in social grooming. Strepsirhines tend to spend less time allogrooming than monkeys and apes. Aggressive tactile communications, such as hitting or grabbing, occur but are not as common as grooming.

Some species are more tactile than others. Physical contact is common in chimpanzees when giving or receiving reassurance, but occurs in other species as well. Frans de Waal has shown that after a conflict, reconciliation is important for maintaining social stability in, for example, chimpanzee groups (de Waal 1989, see also Aureli and de Waal 2000). Male chimpanzees are more likely than females to be involved in status conflicts and therefore often engage in reconciliatory behaviors, such as touching and kissing. Bystanders may also give a consolatory embrace to one or the other of the participants of a conflict. Moreover, eye contact is a very important component of the reconciliatory process. In addition, as an expression of peacemaking, kissing is a behavior that we share with the chimpanzees. In other primate species, reconciliation is usually achieved by grooming, although there are some rare cases when embracing (see Figure 8-2) or other demonstrations of affiliation

FIGURE 9-5 Grooming is a way to communicate using tactile senses.

and friendliness are expressed. Bonobos are well known for using genito-genital rubbing as a way to disperse tension and settle disputes (de Waal 1989, White 1996).

It has been suggested that our language ability has its roots in gesturing (Byrne 2006, Corballis 2002). Gesturing, using hands and feet to communicate, is only observed in apes. This may explain why scientists have had success in teaching apes to use sign language but failed with monkeys (see below). In a comparative study, Pollick and de Waal (2007) found that bonobos show greater flexibility in gesturing and they use gestures more often in non-emotive contexts compared with chimpanzees.

Communication using Vocalization

All primates vocalize under some circumstances, although some species are highly vocal all of the time. There are many different types of vocalizations. Maybe most distinctive but less common are **territorial calls** and **alarm calls**. Less distinct but much more frequent are the vocalizations related to social interactions and contact calls to maintain group cohesion and to direct progression while foraging.

Territorial calls or "territorial singing" can be most dramatically heard in indris (a Malagasy strepsirhine), howler monkeys (an American monkey), and gibbons (an Asian ape). Territorial calls function to inform conspecifics about the individual's location and where the boundary of its home range is located. These calls convey information about how many are present in the group and how willing they are to defend their territory. Thus it helps in keeping groups away from each other.

Most often territorial calling takes place first thing in the morning when the primates wake up. As one group begins calling, surrounding groups soon join in. However, this type of vocalization is not restricted to mornings. Often, during the day when intergroup encounters occur, territorial calling may take place. All members of the group participate, but adult males may be the most vigorous in their vocalizations. Anatomical modification of the throat area, where sound is produced, is found in some species. Siamangs and hoolock gibbons, indris, and orangutans have enlarged laryngeal sacs, but only the siamangs and hoolock gibbons have expandable skin on their throats that, when calling, expands into a **resonating air sac** (see Figure 2-23b; Mootnick and Groves 2005). In howler monkeys, the **hyoid bone** is enlarged into a hollow chamber, which increases resonance for enhanced long-distance call transmission.

Primates respond to the appearance of potential predators by vocal responses, either mobbing or alarm calls, or with complete silence. There are records of distinct vocalizations that are associated with the presence of specific predators and that can be easily distinguished by the human ear. Guenons such as vervet monkeys (*Chlorocebus aethiops*) and Diana monkeys (*Cercopithecus diana*) produce distinctive calls for specific predators (see Box 9-2 for further information; Cheney and Seyfarth 1990, Zuberbühler et al. 1997). Even some strepsirhines use specific alarm calls to differentiate predator types (Pereira and Macedonia 1991). Sauther (1989) found that ring-tailed lemurs (*Lemur catta*) emitted a "yap" call when dogs, feral cats, or **fossa** (*Cryptoprocta ferox*), an endemic viverrid, were in the vicinity, and "shriek" calls when specific aerial raptors approached. Due to their larger body size, apes have fewer predators. However, when chimpanzees perceive danger loud "wraa" (fear), bark, and scream calls are given together with extensive body posturing. It is thought that alarm calls are used to warn others in the group of the impending danger. Alarm calls and mobbing certainly communicate to the predator that it has been detected and consequently may act as a deterrent.

Vocalizations occur extensively in social situations. Anyone observing a primate group at close range will be struck by the constant vocalization that occurs between group members. These vocalizations range from low-pitched grunts and coos to high-pitched barks and screams. In addition, when a group is foraging and moving through dense forest, continuous contact calls are emitted. The sounds produced vary between species. In most cases we do not know what is being said, although in a few cases there appears to be a functional explanation. For example, Boinski and colleagues have detected specific calls used by *Saimiri* and *Cebus* monkeys when initiating group movements and when changing direction of movements (e.g., Boinski 1996). Many primate species have also been observed vocalizing when encountering rich food sources. However, it is not clear if these so-called food calls are given to inform other group members of the find, or if it is a spontaneous (affective) reaction to the presence of good food. Gruntlike sounds are frequently emitted by baboons. It appears that these grunts serve as social and affiliative signals (Cheney et al. 1995, Rendall et al. 1998). For example, a baboon female approaching another female while giving soft grunts is more likely to behave in a friendly manner than one that approaches without giving a grunt vocalization. Among gibbons and siamangs, male and female pairs are often heard "singing duets," and it is believed that these interactions function to strengthen the bond between the pair (Clark et al. 2006, Geissmann and Orgeldinger 2000).

Apes use vocal communication extensively, and at least fifteen different distinct calls are made by the Gombe chimpanzees. These calls can be broadly divided into intra-party calls and distance calls (Goodall 1986). Intra-party calls often reflect the social excitement or fear of the individual that is vocalizing, and the type of call given reflects the social rank of the individuals involved. Distance calls (pant-hoots) are given to maintain contact between group members when they are dispersed over a wide area.

 BOX 9-1

Anatomical Basis for Speech: The Brain and the Vocal Tract

Controlled human speech is possible because we have some very specific morphological structures located in the brain and the vocal tract. Specific areas of the neocortex of the human brain are designated for the production and understanding of language. About 20 percent of the human neocortex is assigned to some aspect of speech production and language comprehension. The areas responsible for human speech and language comprehension are, in the majority of humans, located on the left side of the brain.

Four major neocortical areas, the so-called classical language areas, are involved in human language (see Figure 9-6). **Broca's area**, located in the left frontal lobe, is involved in the production and formulation of spoken language. **Wernicke's area**, located in the left temporal lobe, is involved in language comprehension both during speech and reading. The ability to understand what is heard is located in the **primary auditory cortex**, and the oral part of the **motor cortex** is in charge of the muscles involved in producing sound. Damage to either of these two latter centers affects the production of speech, but not the comprehension of speech or written language.

(continued)

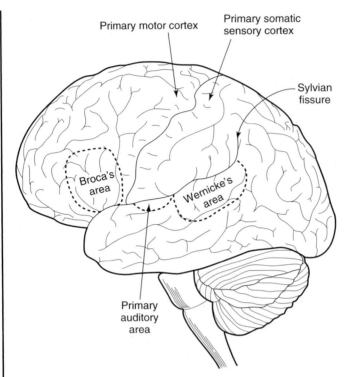

Primary motor cortex

Primary somatic sensory cortex

Sylvian fissure

Broca's area

Wernicke's area

Primary auditory area

FIGURE 9-6 A lateral view of the left side of a human brain, showing the different areas involved in language. The two classical language areas are Broca's (production and formulation of spoken language) and Wernicke's (language comprehension) areas.

Even though areas structurally similar to Broca's and Wernicke's are present in the brains of nonhuman primates, we do not yet have evidence that they are functionally the same. Recent examination of the brains of chimpanzees has revealed an expanded area of the **planum temporale** (Gannon et al. 1998), a key site within Wernicke's language area. This is a significant discovery because it suggests that chimpanzees may have a much better ability for language comprehension than we have previously thought. However, the presence of a similar anatomical structure does not automatically mean that there is a functional equivalence. It may, however, provide evidence for evolutionary continuity since enlargement of Wernicke's area is not present in monkeys but is present in chimpanzees, and that area in chimpanzees is not as large as that of humans.

In nonhuman primates, as with most animals, the limbic system of the brain controls much of the vocal production. It is thought that only the perception of vocalizations is under higher cortical control. The limbic system is part of the **allocortex** that is phylogenetically older than the neocortex. This part of the brain is known as the "emotional center," and it controls what is referred to as survival responses (fight or flight), as well as reproduction. Even though there is limbic influence in human emotional vocalizations—e.g., laughing, crying, and screaming—human speech is a voluntary action that is predominantly controlled by higher cortical functions located in the neocortex.

The shape of the vocal tract influences the production of sound. Our **supralaryngeal tract**, including the mouth, tongue, larynx, and pharynx, is constructed differently from that of non-human primates. Specifically, the tongue is located within the throat and the size of the air passageway appear to be very distinctive and of utmost importance. The lower position of the larynx in adult humans provides more resonance and sound amplification when we vocalize. In addition, we have greater nerve input into the muscles that control the movement of these structures and our breathing, which together influence how well we can produce speech sounds. Furthermore, the vocal folds differ in shape between humans and other primates. The vocal folds of nonhuman primates are less taut and therefore produce less controlled sounds.

The combination of the modifications in the brain with those of the mouth and throat area provides humans with the ability to produce very controlled units of sound. Furthermore, we are able to combine sounds in an almost infinite number of ways. In contrast, the range of sounds that nonhuman primates produce is much more limited and they do not appear to be able to recombine sounds into novel sounds. However, we know too little about the structural and functional aspects of nonhuman primate brains and vocalization, and there is great need for further research before any definitive statements can be made.

❖❖ Vocalization of Primates in their Natural Environments

The early studies of primates in their natural habitats involved the descriptive cataloguing of primate vocalizations. These studies focused on the **acoustic structure** of the vocalization and were mainly used for cross-species comparisons and to determine species' taxonomic affinities. Some of these studies have shown to be very useful, especially when studying difficult-to-see nocturnal strepsirhines (Bearder et al. 1995, Zimmermann et al. 2000).

More recent research has focused on the functional aspects of primate communication. This is done to determine the range of communication taking place among nonhuman primates and how they use vocal communication. We want to know if the vocal sounds used are the equivalent of human words and if sounds are strung together in a similar fashion to our sentences. Moreover, we want to know if nonhuman primates use vocalizations to refer to specific objects in the external environment, or if the vocalizations simply reflect the emotional state of the caller. Do nonhuman primates attribute meaning to their vocalizations, and if they do, is there intentionality in their vocal communication? Research that addresses these types of questions draws us closer to the investigation of the mental states of nonhuman primates and has shown some very intriguing results (see Chapter 10).

What Do Primates Tell Each Other?

In the early days of primate studies, it was assumed that the vocalizations made by nonhuman primates were merely emotive, a reflection of the caller's emotional state. This view was brought into question in 1967, when Thomas Struhsaker presented evidence that monkey vocalizations might have specific meaning. He suggested that the alarm calls of vervet monkeys (*Chlorocebus aethiops*) referred to specific objects in the environment—i.e., the calls were referential. In addition, each alarm call elicited specific responses in the monkeys. Struhsaker's suggestion that these alarm calls were referential was, at the time, highly controversial, and other scientists (e.g., Smith 1977, 1981) were convinced that the different alarm calls were emotionally based, and referred only to different escape modes and not the "naming" of specific predators.

To settle the controversy regarding the referential abilities of vervet monkeys, Dorothy Cheney, Robert Seyfarth, and Peter Marler went to Amboseli, Kenya, to test whether these monkeys had referential abilities (Seyfarth et al. 1980). They recorded the different alarm calls given by the monkeys for different predators. When no predator was visible, they played back each recording to the group from hidden speakers, and they filmed the responses given by the monkeys. They found that when a leopard call was replayed, the monkeys ran into trees. When an eagle alarm call was replayed, they looked up into the sky and some ran into bushes. For the snake alarm call, most stood bipedally and looked around on the ground. It appeared that the monkeys did have an understanding of what the different calls meant. To make sure that the alarm calls were not emotionally based, the researchers modified the length and amplitude of the calls played back. By doing this, the meaning of the calls was not altered, but any emotive signal would be scrambled. However, the responses given by the monkeys under these modified conditions remained the same. In a functional sense, the alarm calls thus appear to parallel human words in that each call gives accurate information about specific dangers and as such are representational signaling. Since these experiments cannot tell us about the underlying mental process or the causation of the vocalization, there is no absolute proof that the monkeys recognized the relationship between the vocalization (alarm call) and its referent (the predator). See Box 9-2 for more details on referential representations and the use of alarm calls by guenon monkeys.

With improvement in sound recording and decoding technology, the playback methodology has made it possible to record vocalizations of wild primates with greater ease. However, despite much advancement, there is no consensus whether we can gain insight into the meaning and function of nonhuman primate vocalizations. There are two main ideas about this type of research. One camp holds that there are just too few distinct vocal signals used in too many different contexts to possibly carry meaning; i.e., there cannot be a direct relationship between vocalization and meaning in the sense that we use words. Rather, vocalizations reflect the caller's emotional state, and it is the context that drives the information transfer, not the vocalization itself. In contrast, other researchers advocate that there are sufficient subtle differences in the vocalizations used by wild primates, and these subtle differences in vocal signals provide very distinct information to the listeners.

At Moremi Wildlife Reserve, Northern Botswana, Cheney, Seyfarth, and colleagues are deciphering the meaning of the vocal repertoire of chacma baboons (*Papio ursinus*). Here researchers are focusing on the more difficult to record social communications, e.g., grunts, barks, and contact calls, that are characteristic of highly social monkeys (Cheney et al. 1995, Fisher et al. 2001, Rendall et al. 1998, 2000). Grunts are harmonically rich calls, used by baboons in many different contexts. For example, when the group is getting ready to move, individuals give "travel grunts," and other group members respond or look in a specific direction. Grunts are also given when a female approaches a mother with an infant (infant grunt) and during reconciliations. Even though these grunts sound rather similar to our ears, baboon ears pick up subtle differences, which we only recognize by recording the calls' spectral structures. Playback experiments show that baboons consistently respond differently to the "travel grunt" and the "infant grunt." In response to travel grunts, baboons look toward a distant location, while for infant grunts they look at the hidden speaker. It has been possible to determine that the baboons are well aware of the identity and rank of the individual who vocalizes because females respond differently if the grunt playback is from a female of lower or higher rank than the listener.

Even though we are beginning to catalogue differences in grunt vocalizations, based both on spectrograms and differences in behavioral responses, we are still far from a complete understanding about what is being communicated by the baboons. We especially do not know if they themselves accredit specific meaning and intentional communication to the vocalizations. The study of vocal communication in free-ranging primates is still in its infancy. There are so many questions to be addressed regarding what various species are talking about when they are presenting us with an unending stream of vocalizations. There is now a renewed focus on recording and examining the meaning of vocalizations taking place between wild apes (Mitani 1996, Mitani and Gros-Louis 1995).

 BOX 9-2

Further Evidence of Referential Representations in the Alarm Calls of Guenon Monkeys

Klaus Zuberbühler has spent many years studying the vocal behaviors of the forest guenons living in the Taï Forest, located in Côte d'Ivoire, West Africa (e.g., Zuberbühler 2000a, b, 2002). Zuberbühler has used the playback technique pioneered by Peter Marler and used by Cheney and Seyfarth in their studies on the Amboseli vervet monkeys and Botswana baboons (see above). In his early studies, Zuberbühler established that Diana monkeys (*Cercopithecus diana*), just like the vervet monkeys, use alarm calls referentially (Zuberbühler et al. 1997). More recently, vocalizations of the Campbell's monkey (*C. campbelli*) and putty-nosed monkeys (*C. nictitans martini*) have been added to this study (Arnold and Zuberbühler 2006, Zuberbühler 2002).

The reason for studying Diana monkeys was in part because males and females emit different vocalizations for the same objects, without having any problems understanding each other. For example, when an adult male makes a leopard alarm call, the female responds with her own version of a leopard alarm call, and vice versa. The Diana and Campbell monkeys spend a lot of time together in mixed-species foraging associations. The alarm calls used by the two species' males are very distinct. Zuberbühler tested if the two species understand the underlying meaning of each other's calls using playback experiments. If Diana monkeys hear a conspecific making an eagle alarm call, they respond with their own alarm calls. However, if this call is followed by an

(continued)

eagle's shriek, they do not respond to it. We presume this is because they have already been warned, and further vocalization on their part may draw them to the predator's attention. If a Campbell male makes an eagle alarm call, the Diana female will respond with her own version of an eagle alarm call. So despite differences in call structure between the two species, there appears to be no misunderstanding about the referential meaning of the calls.

There is much evidence that primates combine smaller vocal units into larger ones following specific patterns, what Marler (1977) referred to as phonological syntax. However, no one has shown that these vocal changes altered the meaning of what was being said. As mentioned above, the Diana and Campbell monkeys have acoustically different alarm calls. The Campbell's males have an additional call, a short, low-pitched boom call they use for "distant dangers," such as when hearing the alarm call of a neighboring group or a branch crashing to the ground. Almost as if they are saying, "be alert but no need to panic." This boom call is not produced by Diana monkeys. To see if the boom call altered the meaning of alarm calls, Zuberbühler presented Diana monkeys with a series of combinations of alarm calls in a playback experiment and recorded how they responded.

In one series, Campbell's alarm calls were replayed with and without the boom call. In another series, Diana's alarm calls were replayed but with the added change of tagging on a Campbell boom in front of some of these alarm calls. The Diana monkeys responded to the Campbell's alarm calls as expected; response to regular alarm calls and no response to those that had a boom call first. They also responded as expected to Diana alarm calls. In those instances in which Zuberbühler had tagged on a boom, the Diana monkeys responded as if the boom call did not exist. By responding correctly to their own alarm calls, even when one was preceded by a Campbell boom sound, showed that the Diana monkeys recognized that the "boom" only carried meaning together with a Campbell alarm call, not for their own alarm calls. In other words, the boom sound was treated as a syntactic modifier *only* when coupled with a Campbell alarm call.

Syntactically organized communication is a hallmark of human languages. If truly present in these cercopithecine monkeys, as Zuberbühler's studies suggest, then this trait has a long evolutionary history.

❖❖ Talking with the Apes: Captive Studies

To be able to talk with our nonhuman ape relatives may seem like an intriguing proposition. When these kinds of studies first started, the goals were to see if it was possible to establish a language link between them and us and to see if they could learn and understand simple words. Once it was obvious that apes could learn words, questions regarding semantics and syntax followed. The question of cognitive ability is a more recent field of research; see Chapter 10.

Teaching Apes to Speak and Understand Our Speech

In the early twentieth century, Robert Yerkes (Yerkes and Yerkes 1929), suggested that the best way to gain insight into the capacity of apes for language would be to teach them sign language. He did not believe it possible to teach apes spoken language. Despite these warning words, several attempts were made to teach chimpanzees to speak English (Hayes and Hayes 1951, Kellogg and Kellogg 1933). Infant chimpanzees were raised in the same environmental setting as would a human child, often accompanied by a human infant, so called cross-fostering experiments. None of these attempts succeeded. The reason, as argued by Lieberman (1975, 1992), is that chimpanzees lack the anatomical structures necessary for controlled sound production. The ability of chimpanzees to comprehend the meaning of spoken English did, however, not appear to be lacking. This ability has been further supported by research conducted by Savage-Rumbaugh and colleagues focusing specifically on bonobos. Kanzi and his sister Panbanisha understand a wide range of spoken words, as well as rather complex sentences (see Box 9-3; Savage-Rumbaugh and Lewin, 1994). In addition, Kanzi's vocalizations appear to be modulated in such a way to suggest vocal communication (Taglialatela et al. 2003). This research supports the idea that there is no difference in ability to perceive as well as understand the sound of our words, but the ability of nonhuman primates to produce human speech is quite restricted.

Teaching Apes Sign Language

Failure to teach apes spoken language forced scientists to look into alternative methods to gain insight into the language capacity of nonhuman primates. In 1966, Allen and Beatrice Gardner began a long-term project to teach apes American Sign Language (ASL). ASL is recognized as a distinct and complex living language (National Science Foundation 2006). Consequently, the use of ASL by the Gardners and other researchers represents attempts to teach nonhuman primates a true language. The first ape to be trained was Washoe, a chimpanzee (Gardner and Gardner 1969). Other ASL projects soon followed, e.g., the lowland gorillas, Koko and Michael (Patterson 1978, Patterson and Linden 1981); the orangutan, Chantek (Miles 1990); and the chimpanzee, Nim Chimpsky (Terrace 1987) (Figure 9-7).

To teach ASL to apes required intense effort on the part of the trainers. First, while showing the ape an object, the trainer would repeatedly make the sign for that object. The next step was to mold the hand of the ape into the same form for the sign that was being used until the ape could independently make the sign. Due to differences in hand morphology between humans and apes, some signs could not be made by the apes precisely in the same way as humans would make them. Instead, an approximation of the sign was used. In a sense, the apes created their own dialect of ASL.

Apes could learn and use a great number of symbols. For example, Washoe recognized and used more than 200 signs, and Koko, now a mature gorilla, knows and uses over a thousand signs to communicate her needs, wishes, and thoughts (see The Gorilla Foundation). Overall, it appeared as if the trained apes understood the labeling relationship between a sign and the object it stood for. The strongest supporting evidence that apes attached meaning to their signs came from the instances in which compound signs were used to name a novel object; e.g., when Koko was given a Pinoccio doll and she signed "elephant" and "doll." However, the conclusion drawn from these studies that apes showed semantic ability was not accepted by all scholars.

FIGURE 9-7 The lowland gorilla, Koko (left and middle), and chimpanzee, Nim Chimpsky (right) are some of the apes trained to use American Sign Language to communicate with their caretakers.

Some of the criticism the ASL projects received was based on the lack of clarity in the signs and in the acceptance of the variations used by the apes as true signs. In addition, the testing situations were thought to lack rigorous controls. There was suspicion that trainers may have interpreted the subjects' responses as signing when the apes might have been only mimicking their trainers. Furthermore, the researchers may have been overzealous in their interpretations. Alternative conclusions that did not evoke semantic abilities on the part of the apes could be equally correct (see, for example, Wallman 1992).

Whether the ASL-trained apes had syntax, i.e., if they could form structured sentences, was examined by Terrace and his coworkers (1979). They found that most apes, as exemplified by the chimpanzee Nim, with whom they worked, used single- or two-word combinations most often. Combinations of three or more symbols were rarely used. The longer combinations tended to be repetitions of signs with no added information (e.g., eat me Nim, eat drink eat drink). Furthermore, it was suggested that the apes more often than not mimicked their trainers and that the researchers had either overgeneralized or exaggerated their interpretations. Terrace and his coworkers concluded that chimpanzees showed little or no evidence of language capability and had no concept of syntax (Terrace et al. 1979).

Teaching Apes Symbols

To overcome the various criticisms directed at ASL use in great apes, Duane Rumbaugh and colleagues at the Yerkes Primate Research Center at Emory (YPRC) devised a language system based on abstract symbols, referred to as Yerkish (Rumbaugh 1977).

FIGURE 9-8 Lana, 2.5 years old in this photo (top), was the first chimpanzee to be trained to communicate using abstract symbols. When each symbol is pressed the information is recorded directly into a computer. Dr. Sue Savage Rumbaugh and Panibasha (bottom), a female bonobo, communicating using a portable lexigram board.

The pictorial symbols (**lexigrams**) were part of a modified keyboard that was hooked up to a computer system (Figure 9-8). The advantage of this system was that there could be no misunderstanding as to what signals were given by the subjects as the computer registered each symbol pressed. An added advantage was that the computer keyboard was always present and active 24 hours a day. Hence, the apes could "talk" via the computer without a trainer present. Many chimpanzees (e.g., Sherman and Austin) and bonobos (e.g., Kanzi, Panibasha) have been trained to use this system at YPRC. In the Primate Research Center at Kyoto University, the female chimpanzee Ai has also been trained in a symbolic language (Biro and Matsuzawa 2001). Likewise, the orangutan Azy, now at the Great Apes Foundation in Iowa, has become proficient in using a symbolic computer-based language (Shumaker 2006).

We now know that apes readily learn to recognize and use a vast number of words through the use of symbolic language to communicate. As shown with the apes that studied ASL, apes have no difficulty using abstract symbols to represent real things. What we have learned from these studies is not just related to vocal communication but has also shown us a way to probe into the minds of the apes. The fact that they can "talk" about objects and persons not directly in view and refer to events in the past and in the future provides evidence that there may be fewer differences between our own minds and those of our close relatives (Savage-Rumbaugh and Lewin 1994).

A key element to human communication is that there is an underpinning of intention and comprehension regarding what is being said. In addition, the ability to realize that another individual's knowledge might be different from your own is also important, but more so is the recognition that knowledge can be shared through communication. Savage-Rumbaugh trained two chimpanzees, Sherman and Austin, to see if they could think and communicate as we do. In one test, they were placed in a room divided into two sections by a window, one on each side of the partition. They could see each other's actions and could communicate via a computer. Each one had specific tasks to do. For example, Sherman had a locked box containing a reward, while Austin had a set of tools, one of which could open the box. Sherman had to request the correct tool from Austin, who then had to give the tool to Sherman. If they did everything correctly, Sherman could open the box and they shared the reward. Sherman and Austin were equally proficient in playing either role of requesting or providing the tool.

This type of cooperation demonstrates the ability for true communication, with each participant sharing in the intention of exchanging information with a common goal. The individual needing a tool had to have a mental picture of the tool required and had to know how to request it from the other individual. The individual requesting the tool had to understand that the second individual lacked information and needed it to provide the proper tool. Often the behaviors displayed when either one of them made a mistake were most informative in regard to whether they did indeed comprehend the importance of communication. On one occasion, Austin provided a tool that Sherman had requested, but when Sherman saw the tool provided, he realized his mistake and rushed to the computer to enter the correct request. Austin noticed the new request and provided the second tool (Savage-Rumbaugh and Lewin 1994). It is clear from these studies that Sherman understood what information he needed to provide for Austin. Both chimpanzees showed they had the ability of mental imagery, and they both understood they had different knowledge they needed to share in order to reach a mutually beneficial goal (see Chapter 10 for further discussion on cognition).

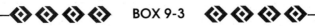

❖ ❖ ❖ ❖ BOX 9-3 ❖ ❖ ❖ ❖

Kanzi, A Miracle Ape or A Miracle Research Approach?

The story of Kanzi, probably the most famous bonobo, has been told many times (see Savage-Rumbaugh and Lewin 1994, Savage-Rumbaugh et al. 1998). However, it cannot be told too many times because through him and the research by Savage-Rumbaugh and her team, we have been shown a new avenue into the minds of nonhuman primates and the possibilities there are to reach into the minds of other apes.

Kanzi was the first offspring of a captive-born female who lived at the Atlanta zoo. His father was brought from the Congo not long before Kanzi was conceived. However, within the first hour of his life, an older female, Matata, was allowed to hold Kanzi, and he never went back to his birth mother. The bond between Matata and Kanzi was very strong. While Matata raised Kanzi, she was part of a research program at the Language Research Center at Yerkes Field Station where apes were trained to recognize and understand the symbol language called Yerkish. Matata, who was wild born and adult, had much difficulty in learning to discriminate the different lexigrams. Even though she appeared to understand that there was some importance to the different symbols, she did not seem able to learn their meaning. After several years of training, she had learned to recognize just a few lexigrams to request some favorite foods. Kanzi always attended the training sessions Matata was given, but he was never included in the teaching, although to Matata's detriment, he often took the rewards she had worked so hard to gain. However, Matata did not seem to mind, as she never reprimand Kanzi. Out of respect for Matata, the human caretakers did not reprimand Kanzi either—no matter what he got into.

When Kanzi was a little over 2 years old, Matata was sent back to the Atlanta zoo to spend some time with Kanzi's father, Bosondjo. Kanzi remained at the Language Research Center. Kanzi had a surprise for everyone: The first day he was alone, he showed his caretakers that he had not just idly hung about with mom. Kanzi had learned the meaning of many lexigrams, what they stood for, and how and when to use them. He had obviously learned this by observing the instructions Matata had been given, but while Matata was around, he never showed that he had learned anything. It is important to mention that Kanzi had from the beginning been exposed to caretakers using English to communicate with him and his mother, and he was always encouraged to use gestures to express, for example, in what direction he wanted to go.

When Savage-Rumbaugh realized that Kanzi had learned the meaning of many lexigrams on his own, it was decided to give him more formal training. Lexigrams were placed on large cardboards that could be carried about. Kanzi's vocabulary increased at a rapid rate, and new symbols where added almost on a daily basis. Sometimes he would take the lexigram cardboards on his own, while refusing to let the caretakers see and pointing at different symbols as if he were talking to himself. While going on outings in the surrounding woods, Kanzi was given pictures of various locations as another means to communicate where to go and what to find at different locations. In other words, Kanzi was exposed to as many different ways of communicating as a human child. Savage-Rumbaugh has suggested that it is this very rich and varied way of communicating at an early age that has led to the abilities that Kanzi is expressing. Kanzi's sister Panibasha, who was raised in a similar manner as Kanzi, is equally adept in using symbolic language and understanding spoken English (she may even be a bit better) (Figure 9-8). However, Kanzi's other sisters, Tamuli and Neema, were not exposed to the same enriched social environment at an early age, and they do not show the language comprehension expressed by Kanzi and Panibasha. Rather, they seem to behave more like their mother Matata. Further support for the importance of an enriched social environment at an early age has been shown in many of the early sign language projects, e.g., Gardner's work with the chimpanzee Washoe, and Patterson's work with the gorilla Koko. These the apes appeared to be able to perform beyond what may be expected for either of their conspecifics raised in less enriched environments.

◆◆ What Does Our Language Have in Common with the Vocal Communications of Primates?

Language Perception

Human speech is a graded continuum of sounds that are perceived as a series of discrete categories. Our speech comprises vowel and consonant sounds. Vowels are continuous sounds, which are produced when air is passed through an open vocal tract. Vowels strung together cannot be perceived by the human ear as individual units. Consonants, on the other hand, are produced when the vocal tract is restricted or closed, and it is the consonant sounds that provide discreteness to human language. In fact, it is difficult for us to say a consonant without also making a vowel sound. A consonant produced by computer simulation without a vowel actually sounds like a hiss or click. Hence, it is the consonants that provide definition and delineation to human speech and that make it so very unique.

To the human ear, the vocalizations of nonhuman primates sound more or less continuous. Most nonhuman primates do not produce consonant sounds; therefore, their sounds appear to grade into each other without any clear boundaries. The gelada is rather exceptional in the production of a wide range of sounds, including several consonant sounds (Aich et al. 1990, Richman 1987). However, when tape recordings of nonhuman primate vocalizations were analyzed with **sonographs** (these became available in the early 1960s), it became apparent that the dichotomy set up to distinguish the vocalizations of nonhuman primates from human speech was not so clear cut. What the human ear perceived as continuous vocal sound were, in fact, in many cases, discrete units of sound. Monkeys living in forested environments tend to use more discrete vocalizations for long-distance communication than do primates living in more open habitats. Curiously, even though nonhuman primates cannot produce human speech sounds such as consonants, they can readily distinguish human speech. This supports our belief that some brain structures related to sound perception must be shared, and this auditory perception is controlled by higher cortical centers.

Semantic Ability

A difference between human speech and nonhuman primate vocalization is that the basic units of sound produced in human speech, **phonemes** such as, e.g., ba, pa, and ta, do not in themselves carry meaning. It is by combining these basic units of sound (like building blocks) into words, or the smallest linguistic units (such as "in" in *incomplete*, or "pre" in *prefix*), so-called **morphemes**, that meaning is gained. In contrast, the vocalizations of nonhuman primates do not have these building blocks. Rather, each vocalization appears to be a finite morpheme. In human speech, morphemes are further combined into a higher order of meaning, e.g., sentences or stories, something not yet recorded for any wild primate species. Sentences are put together according to specific rules (grammar), which we refer to as syntax (see below).

In human language, words are symbolic representations of objects or events in the external world—that is, they are referential. It is clear that, in many instances, the vocalizations of nonhuman primates carry meaning and can be referential, as evidenced by the use of distinct vocalizations under very specific conditions (see Box 9-2; Cheney and Seyfarth 1990, Green 1975, Snowdon 1990, Zuberbühler et al. 1997). However, there is yet no evidence for the recombination of vocalizations in order to make new calls with new meaning.

Furthermore, we humans use language to refer to events that took place in the past and may occur in the future as well as referring to objects not in direct view, which is referred to as **displacement**. Whether this is an ability we share with other primates is still not fully explored. We have no convincing evidence from fieldwork that nonhuman primates refer to anything but what is directly visible to them. This may be challenged, however, as further results from research into nonhuman primate vocalization becomes available. It appears, based on captive studies, that at least some monkeys and apes have an understanding of **object permanence** even when an object is hidden from view (Scheumann and Call 2006, Tomasello and Call 1997). Captive apes trained in symbolic languages especially have the ability to refer to invisible objects as well as to events that have occurred in the past (e.g., Savage-Rumbaugh and Lewin 1994).

Syntactical Ability

Previous research by Herbert Terrace and coworkers suggested that apes lacked syntax or at best displayed a very limited ability for grammatical usage (see above, Terrace et al. 1979). However, when linguist Patricia Greenfield examined Kanzi's records, there appeared to be some predictable structure to his communications. Kanzi's utterances showed evidence that he invented his own set of grammatical rules (Greenfield and Savage-Rumbaugh 1990). If this is correct, this could provide important insight to understanding the evolution of grammar.

When Kanzi began formal language training, he was exposed not only to lexigrams but also to spoken language. In addition, he was allowed to use gestures (pointing) as a means of communicating. The combination of these three methods provided a much richer environment in which his linguistic and communicative skills could develop. A review of Kanzi's language usage revealed very different results from what Terrace and coworkers found for Nim and other chimpanzees. Kanzi repeated himself less often and seldom imitated the signs given by caretakers. He showed strong evidence for combining symbols in a semantically related way. Interestingly, his expressions appeared to follow a set of rules, which in some cases were idiosyncratic and not a reflection of the grammatical rules used by his caretakers. One grammatical rule that he invented was to combine a lexigram with a gesture in an action-agent order (action—e.g., chase, run, tickle; agent—e.g., Kanzi, Sue). Another grammatical rule that he invented was to combine two action lexigrams. Kanzi's grammatical ordering reflected his action ordering; e.g., by signaling "chase, bite," Kanzi would first chase followed by a bite. He also used the order of symbols to reflect differences in meaning, e.g., "bite Kanzi" when Kanzi was bitten, and "Kanzi bite" when he intended to bite someone.

Kanzi's language ability is not extensive. At age 5, Kanzi's ability was on the level of a 2-year-old human child. He used two-symbol combinations most often, and more often than not these combinations were requests rather than statements, as are those of a human child. However, it is essential to approach these differences with an open mind and to try to understand what would be natural for a bonobo to communicate about. Even though Kanzi gained grammar proficiency at a much slower rate than would a human child, the developmental stages he passed through were the same as those of human children. He first learned individual lexigrams (words), then he began to combine two lexigrams, followed by the combination of three lexigrams, and then he used these with set grammatical rules (Greenfield and Savage-Rumbaugh 1990).

◈◈ How is Language and Vocal Communication Acquired?

Even though many parts of the brain that control for speech and the understanding of language are present at birth in human children, there is much growth and development that takes place in these areas during the first few years of life. Human children, however, also learn language from the sounds they hear around them. Consequently, since learning is involved, it is possible to modify the use of language. In contrast, the vocalizations of nonhuman primates are thought to be innate, with little or no learning period needed. Baby primates come more or less full fledged into the world, with the ability to communicate with other group members. Even though their vocalizations cannot be modified, they still must learn the correct meaning and when to use specific vocalizations. Cheney and Seyfarth (1990) found that the calls of infant vervet monkeys were more general and inclusive, and as they grew older their calls became more specific and exclusive. In contrast, extensive studies on squirrel monkeys have shown no evidence of modification with age. An infant squirrel monkey has the same vocalizations as a mature squirrel monkey (Snowdon 1990).

Seyfarth, Cheney, and Marler (1980) looked at the developmental aspects of the different alarm calls in vervet monkeys. They recorded the calls and responses given by infants and juvenile individuals and compared them to the calls and responses of adults. Infants were more general in their alarm calls and often made "mistakes." For example, even though the "eagle alarm call" was only given to objects in the sky, objects such as a pigeon or a falling leaf could also elicit such a call. Juveniles did not make such mistakes in their calls, but they tended to include bird species that may pose no or a limited threat to them. A similar developmental pattern has been observed in the strepsirhine, *Lemur catta*. Infants make mistakes when giving alarm calls by, for example, giving an aerial raptor call to a falling leaf or parrot, while adults infrequently make such mistakes (Sauther 1989). Hence, there appears to be a learning curve, a sharpening of the association between call and predator, in the ability of nonhuman primates to correctly use alarm calls. In both studies, the vocalizations themselves, however, did not show much change over time, supporting the notion that the production of calls is more or less present at birth (innate).

◈◈ Summary

Human language is undoubtedly complex, and when the design features that comprise language are identified, we begin to see evidence for the existence of a continuum in the language abilities of nonhuman and human primates. Study of primate communication requires unique approaches, and many strides have been made due to technological innovations. Understanding the genetic underpinning of language has progressed due to the discovery of specialized mirror neurons and the FOXP2 gene. However, despite these gains, an understanding of the biological basis for language is still in its infancy.

One of the basic questions about primate communication entails the determination of what primates communicate about and if their communications are emotive, i.e., based on emotional responses to stimuli, or if they use symbolic or abstract signals to communicate meaning and information that a conspecific may lack. To answer these questions, three different avenues of research have been pursued: (1) training apes to use a human language, e.g., American Sign Language, (2) studies of the natural vocalizations of nonhuman primates in the wild, and (3) studies of the cognitive abilities of nonhuman primates.

Communication is a way to broadcast and receive information, and nonhuman primates like us communicate through a variety of means. Communicating through the use of olfaction is very common among nocturnal strepsirhines. Through the use of pheromones, females may transmit their reproductive status, and other chemical signals may indicate much about the individual who produced them. Visual signals are commonly used by diurnal primates living in open habitats. Body posturing may be used to broadcast friendly or agonistic intentions. Tactile communication particularly in the form of grooming is very common among primates, especially the haplorhines. The use of touch as a form of reconciliation is frequently used by chimpanzees. Vocalizations, especially territorial and alarm calls, used by some primate species appear to communicate very specific information, e.g., the type of predator approaching a group. Vocalizations also may play a role in organizing group movements.

Many different apes have been trained to use American Sign Language. These studies have been much criticized because of the inability of researchers to rule out the possibility that the apes are mimicking their trainers or that researchers are imposing greater ability on the part of the apes with their signing or to understand signs. To overcome such criticism, a novel study using pictorial symbols and a modified keyboard to record these symbols in a computer was designed. By using this system, it has been revealed that apes can use abstract symbols to represent real things. Determining if there is intention and comprehension regarding what is being communicated has been investigated by placing chimpanzees in pairs to complete a task. In such situations, it appears that one chimpanzee understands that his partner does not have the same information that he has, and that he has to appropriately communicate the required information to the partner so they may both receive a reward. Apes such as the bonobo, Kanzi, demonstrate a surprising capacity to learn and understand language that may have been enhanced by virtue of his being raised in an enriched social environment.

Consonants define human speech—without them we would not be able to make sense of words. With the exceptions of the gelada, nonhuman primates do not produce consonant sounds, but through the use of sonographs we have been able to determine that at least some nonhuman primate vocalizations are in fact distinctive. Through the study of the language acquisition of apes in captivity, we have seen that Kanzi demonstrates syntactical ability. However, he seems to have invented his own grammatical rules. The production of vocalizations by primates in the wild appears to be innate, however, those produced by immature primates may be more general, and as they gain experience using them they learn the specific applications and meanings associated with the vocalizations.

Much more study into the communication abilities of nonhuman primates remains to be done; however, the work that has been accomplished has opened windows into what nonhuman primates communicate about in the wild and what they are capable of expressing in captivity.

◆◇ Key Words

acoustic structure	hyoid bone	primary auditory cortex
alarm calls	lexigrams	resonating air sac
allocortex	mirror neurons	semantics
allogrooming	morphemes	sonographs
Broca's area	motor cortex	sound spectrograms
communication	object permanence	supralaryngeal tract
displacement	phoneme	syntax
fossa	piloerection	territorial calls
FOXP2	planum temporale	Wernicke's area

◆◇ Study Questions

1. List the different ways nonhuman primates communicate, and discuss how and to what extent the ways we communicate differ.
2. In what ways do primates use vocalization, and why is vocal communication more common and more complex among forest-living species?
3. Why is it not possible to teach apes or monkeys to speak like us?
4. How can we tell if primates intend to communicate something specific to their conspecifics, or if the behavior is innate?
5. Why is the search for the presence of semantics and syntax in nonhuman primate communications so significant?
6. What can we learn about the origin of human language by teaching sign language to apes?
7. How are language and vocal communication acquired by immature primates?
8. Why may our understanding of mirror neurons help us understand the origin of human language?
9. Is Kanzi a "freak of nature," or is he just a reflection of what apes are capable of if provided with the right conditions during development?

◆◇ Suggested Readings and Related Web Sites

Great Ape Trust of Iowa
   www. greatapetrust.org
The Gorilla Foundation
   www. koko org
Hauser MD. 1996. The evolution of communication. Cambridge: MIT Press.
King BJ editor. 1999. The origin of language. Santa Fe, NM: School of American Research Press.
Parker ST, Gibson KR editors. 1990. "Language" and intelligence in monkeys and apes: Comparative developmental perspectives. Cambridge: Cambridge University Press.
Patterson F, Linden E. 1981. The education of Koko. New York: Owl Books.
Rumbaugh DM editor. 1977. Language learning by a chimpanzee. The Lana project. New York: Academic Press.
Savage-Rumbaugh ES. 1994. Kanzi: The ape at the brink of the human mind. London: Doubleday.

The Primate Brain and Complex Behavior

◈◈ What We can Learn by Studying the Brain

In this chapter, we will explore nonhuman primate mental ability and what it may tell us about the evolution of human intelligence. Over the years, researchers observing primates both in their natural environment and in captive situations have reported that monkeys and apes appear to be clever, that they show insightfulness and perceptiveness, and that they are able to solve complex social and ecological problems. In addition, they demonstrate an ability to deceive and to pass on information to their fellow group members. Observations like these have led to a rapid proliferation in research focused on the minds and cognitive abilities of nonhuman primates. Scientists from a variety of research orientations, such as anthropology, biology, and psychology, are trying to unravel the mystery of primate minds.

As may be expected, the field of exploring the minds of nonhuman primates is highly controversial with many battles raging over research approach, definition of terms, the accuracy of the data presented, and the interpretation of results. It is even disputed whether humans can find a way to penetrate into the minds of other animals, to understand why, how, and what they may think. Despite potential problems, and although some researchers hold the opinion that animals lack thinking minds and therefore this type of research is a waste of time, the general consensus is that there *is* an evolutionary continuum between our own minds and that of other primates. Consequently, differences in the minds of human and nonhuman primates is ultimately based on more *quantitative* and less *qualitative* differences. Even if our mental ability is significantly different from that of other primates, it is within the nonhuman primates that the origin of our own intelligence is to be found.

◈◈ Why Study Nonhuman Primate Minds?

From a *philosophical* point of view, we want to know and understand our own position in nature: How unique is the human mind and our ability to think? From an *evolutionary* point of view, by examining our closest living relatives, we are trying to trace and understand the evolution of the human brain, our cognitive abilities, and the adaptive significance of these traits. This kind of research is often approached from an **anthropocentric** point of view. This may make sense since by knowing our own minds we can use this knowledge as a yardstick for understanding the minds of other species. However, an anthropocentric approach can also be limiting as it might restrict us from having the flexibility to think outside of the traditional box of known experience and self-knowledge. To make this research most insightful, we need to try to look at the world from the perspective of the nonhuman primates.

> **tool**—any object in nature that is used to modify another object (naturefact). A tool can also be more complex such as when an object is first modified before being used as a tool (artifact).

Interest in the mental ability of our closest living relatives began in the early part of the last century. Wolfgang Köhler conducted a groundbreaking study of the problem-solving ability of apes at a research facility on the island of Tenerife, the largest of the Canary Islands, located off the northwest coast of Africa (Köhler 1927). He tested several chimpanzees as well as other primate species on their ability to make **tools** and then use them in insightful ways to solve problems. Based on his observations, Köhler concluded that at least the chimpanzees were capable of insightful behaviors. However, systematic research into the mental ability of nonhuman primates did not occur until the early 1960s. Much of the cognitive research has been conducted under captive conditions on our closest living relatives, the African apes (chimpanzee, bonobo, and gorilla) and the Asian orangutan. There is also much documentation from a myriad of field studies on monkeys and apes recording the complexity of their minds. Most of these studies are based on anecdotal information rather than systematically collected data. Anecdotal information may elicit interest but does not provide strong supportive evidence for good scientific arguments, although there is increasing support to consider anecdotal records as valid data. This is in part because insightful behaviors may occur infrequently.

A great milestone in the study of complex behavior in nonhuman primates comes from the early fieldwork conducted at Gombe and Mahale, Tanzania, begun in the early 1960s (e.g., Goodall 1965, Nishida 1968). Researchers at these two sites showed, for example, that chimpanzees routinely make and use tools (Figure 10-1). Further research has even shown that chimpanzees have tool kits and that there is regional variation in these kits, which may be equivalent to cultural traditions. We also know that among West African chimpanzees, males engage in organized hunting activities, and females may actively teach their offspring how to use tools to crack open hard-shelled nuts for food (Boesch and Boesch-Ackermann 2000). However, it is not only chimpanzees that have tool kits. Wild orangutans are known to use various probing tools in many different situations (van Schaik et al. 1996, 2003a, b). Apes, however, are not the only ones that display complex behaviors. Even though monkeys seldom use tools in the wild, they frequently engage in social manipulations and deceptive behaviors (Whiten and Byrne 1997). Ultimately, it is our task to try to decipher whether nonhuman primates intentionally behave in certain ways and if there is conscious thought involved.

FIGURE 10-1   Chimpanzees (*Pan troglodytes*) habitually make and use a variety of tools. This female chimpanzee has prepared a stick which she is using to fish out food that has fallen into the water.

◇◇ Do You Need a Big Brain to Perform Complex Behaviors?

As explained in more detail in Chapter 4, members of the primate order have a larger brain than expected based on body size alone. It is common for long-lived species to have more complex social lives and to have larger and more complex brains. The assumption is therefore that the ability to solve problems is strongly correlated with an expanded brain size. When applied to humans, we often refer to the ability to solve complex problems as evidence of intelligence. However, the presence of purposeful and complex actions may not necessarily reflect intelligence because through natural selection little is left to chance, and it is very likely that complex or purposeful behavior is innate. Intelligence is best defined as consisting of a broad range of abilities that are effective when they are used. Being intelligent implies an ability to be flexible and creative, a sort of general-purpose mental ability, and being able to come up with novel solutions to problems as the situation demands.

Before attempting to answer the question of whether a big brain is required to perform complex behaviors, we need to ask why primates evolved such large brains. This is an especially important question since the brain is a very expensive organ to run as it incurs a higher metabolic demand than any other organ in the body, the so-called expensive tissue hypothesis (Aiello and Wheeler 1995). It can therefore be assumed that there must have been some very strong selective advantages that outweighed the costs.

Several driving forces have been proposed to explain why primates gained bigger than expected brains. Brain size has been correlated to many different variables such as home range size, diet, group structure and size, longevity, locomotor pattern, etc. From these variables, it has been found that primate species with large home ranges and that feed mainly on fruits (frugivores) have, on average, larger brains than those with smaller home ranges and that feed on leaves (folivores). Consequently, some researchers suggest that the environment places complex demands on primates.

An ability to solve problems regarding food sources may have been especially important in the case of frugivores (Call 2000). This is the basis for the ecological intelligence hypothesis (e.g., Clutton-Brock and Harvey 1980, Milton 1988). As discussed in Chapter 6, primates not only need to know where food is to be found, but also when specific food resources, such as ripe figs, will be available and how much of a specific food source will be available. This is important information to have because primates, like most animals must find sufficient food for survival on a daily basis.

Except for humans, no primate species is known to horde or to store food for later use. There is a constant struggle between the cost of searching for food and the benefit from the food sources found. In the long run, it would be too costly for a primate group to arrive at feeding sites and find out that no food is available or that there is not enough for all group members. Furthermore, the efficiency with which primates move about in their habitat has intrigued primatologists for some time. Researchers have studied the paths taken by primate groups as they wander about on their daily foraging, and it has been shown that no monkey ever wanders about randomly (see Chapter 6). Rather, when traveling from one food tree to the next, more often than not, a group will take the most direct route, even when there is no visual contact between the two sites. This ability to optimize travel routes is often referred to as having a "mental map" (Garber and Paciulli 1997, Sigg and Stolba 1981).

The most outstanding characteristic of primates is, however, their sociality. Therefore, an overwhelming number of researchers now propose that it is within the social domain that we will find the explanation for the increase in brain size, referred to as the social intelligence hypothesis (Dunbar 1992a, 1998). It is known that both group size and group structure correlate positively with brain size, and more specifically with the size of the neocortex (e.g., Kudo and Dunbar 2001, Sawaguchi 1992). We find that primate species that live in large groups with many adult males and females tend to have larger brains than those that live alone or in small groups. It is assumed that species living in large groups must deal with many more complex social interactions. We know that all individuals in a social group recognize each other, and that they recognize most if not all of the individuals in neighboring groups. Each individual also knows who within the social group is related to whom (**kin relationships**), and they know the dominance relationships between individuals, not just in a dyadic (two individuals) interaction, but also in triadic (three individuals) interactions. By knowing all of this, they can, and often do, use each other as a social tool to achieve personal gains (goals). It is this manipulation of others in the social domain that is most often used as evidence of intelligent and complex behavior. It is very likely that an increase in brain size was promoted by the social domain, but it may not have been possible to increase brain size without also providing a richer food source to feed the hungry brain. This is the basis of the expensive tissue hypothesis (Aiello and Wheeler 1995).

Is a bigger brain required to perform complex behaviors? The general assumption has been that a big brain is a prerequisite for being able to display intelligent and complex behaviors. However, with the discovery of the new hominin, *Homo floresiensis,* on the island of Flores, Indonesia, this assumption must now be re-examined. *H. floresiensis* is diminutive in stature and has a very small brain case (Brown et al. 2004, Morwood et al. 2005). Its brain size is estimated to be around 400 cubic centimeters, which is within the range of extant chimpanzees (Falk et al. 2005). Despite the small brain size, remains of this hominin have been found together with stone tools (Brumm et al. 2006). These tools are more advanced than any of the tools we have observed chimpanzees using. Even though there are still many unanswered questions pertaining to the Flores hominins, it appears based on present evidence that complex stone tool technology can be produced with a brain the size of extant chimpanzees. Of course, it may not be size alone that is important, but the internal organization of the brain is critical as well. These are research questions that are being explored.

❖❖ Exploring Mental States in Primates

The boom in field research on primate behavior in the 1970s and 1980s brought to light the complexity of social behavior displayed by many primates. While anthropologists investigated the nonhuman primates, psychologists were studying human child development. Much focus was given to the comparison of "normal" children and autistic children in order to understand how and when mental states develop, what might cause or influence altered mental states, and how deficient mental states are expressed. **Autism**, or more correctly autism spectrum disorders, refers to a range of disorders primarily associated with impairment in social interactions, such as the inability to infer false beliefs in others and to imagine invisible objects and delays in social and language development. Individuals diagnosed with some of the milder forms of autism, such as **Asperger's syndrome**, do not show developmental delays, but exhibit a reduced ability to read social cues and body language (Happé et al. 2006, Harris et al. 2006, Symons 2004). Dawn Prince-Hughes was diagnosed with Asperger's syndrome at the age of 36. As a child and young adult she struggled with social interactions and was unable to connect with people or to effectively communicate. She worked with gorillas at the Woodland Park Zoo in Seattle, Washington. In her book *Songs of the Gorilla Nation* (Prince-Hughes 2004), she recounts how working with the gorillas taught her to appreciate social context and how to understand social cues. The gorillas provided a bridge of understanding about social behavior that she could then apply to the human world in which she lived. Study of these types of syndromes will ultimately provide us with greater insight into the specificity of the human brain and perhaps provide new ways for us to envision how the minds of nonhuman primates, as well as other animals, function.

Theory of Mind

It was Premack and Woodruff who coined the term **"theory of mind"** (Premack 1988, Premack and Woodruff 1978). With this term they referred to the ability to understand the presence of mental states, which is the presence of beliefs, feelings, intentions, knowledge, and so on. Importantly, theory of mind entails the ability to recognize that other individuals also have mental states and that the mental states of others may be different from one's own.

By having a theory of mind, it is possible, for example, to predict what other people can or will do in a given situation. This ability provides the opportunity for more flexible and adaptive behavioral interactions. According to some, it is fundamental to real communication and being able to understand each other, what we call **empathy**. To us, this activity of inferring mental states in other people is so ingrained that most of the time we are not even aware that we are doing it or have this ability. However, are we humans alone in having a theory of mind, or is it an ability that we share with other primates?

It is important to recognize that we humans are not born with a theory of mind. Rather, we go through developmental stages to reach the adult level of attribution of mental states in others. Between 1.5 and 2 years of age, children begin to have knowledge of their own and others' moods, intentions, and actions. It is not until they are 4 to 6 years old that they can recognize that their own beliefs and thoughts may be different from those of others. Children can, however, recognize ignorance in others at an earlier age (around 3 years of age) than they can attribute that others may have false beliefs. It is not until they can attribute false beliefs that they are able to understand that mental states can act as **causal agents**, which can influence the behavior of others. It is this ability that autistic children appear to lack and what we want to determine whether nonhuman primates have.

Since we cannot communicate verbally with nonhuman primates (except, of course, those apes that have acquired the ability to recognize human spoken language), researchers exploring the presence of mental states have a difficult task as all interpretations are based on observations of behavioral interactions. Furthermore, mental states are not transparent. It is possible to communicate, inform, and deceive without the actor attributing mental states to others. It is, therefore, often difficult to interpret behavioral interactions. It is not always so obvious if an individual who is attempting to make another believe something is behaving with a mental image in place, or simply recognizing that if he or she behaves in a certain way then there will be a predictable result. When interpreting a behavioral episode, it is essential to distinguish between the ability to understand an individual's *visual perspective* of what the individual sees, and the ability to understand an individual's knowledge and *mental perspectives* of what the individual knows about what he or she sees.

Awareness

To have a theory of mind it is assumed that there is some level of awareness of being. However, awareness is a complex concept. It refers to the ability to understand the distinction between other and self and can be divided into two levels: (1) self-recognition, which is the ability to distinguish oneself from others, but it does not imply any recognition of mental states, and (2) self-attribution, which can be extended to social attribution, in which an individual is aware of his or her own state of mind and can use this awareness to predict and explain the behavior of both self and others. If we look at nonhuman primates, what level of awareness do they have? Would they recognize a reflection or picture of themselves as self? Can primates recognize themselves as separate entities when they look at others, or as others look at them?

Self-Recognition

Self-recognition develops gradually in humans. Human children do not recognize their own mirror images until around 1.5 to 2 years of age (Hart and Fegley 1994). At an earlier age, however, they can recognize their own position in their social environment, such as within the family unit. There has been much investigation into the extent of self-recognition in nonhuman primates. An often-used test, but not universally accepted,

FIGURE 10-2   A rhesus macaque is looking into a mirror and making a mild threat at the reflected image.

FIGURE 10-3 A young chimpanzee is closely scrutinizing its face in the mirror.

is to present a mirror to a monkey or ape and observe how it reacts (Gallup 1994, Heyes 1995). We find that most animals react to their own mirror image by either threatening or attacking the mirror image. After a period of time, most animals lose interest and eventually simply ignore the mirror. We refer to this as habituation.

Monkeys and apes behave differently when exposed to a mirror. Monkeys behave as if they are looking at a conspecific rather than themselves (Figure 10.2). They often threaten or attack the mirror. Younger individuals react most intensely to their mirror images, while older individuals often ignore it all together. In contrast, most apes presented with a mirror behave as if they know that they are looking at themselves (Figure 10-3). As seen in humans, this ability develops over time, and most chimpanzees begin to demonstrate self-recognition when they are 4 to 6 years old (Povinelli and deBlois 1992, Povinelli et al. 1997).

Chimpanzees, bonobos, and orangutans react in a similar way to their own reflections. They tend to explore otherwise inaccessible parts of their bodies using the mirror. Gorillas may be an exception in the way they react to mirror images. In their natural habitat, gorillas respond to their own reflection in a pool of water by threatening this image in a manner similar to monkeys (Byrne 1995). Due to such observations it has been suggested that gorillas do not have the ability of self-recognition. Penny Patterson, the caretaker of the captive lowland gorilla Koko, has disputed this conclusion. She states that Koko routinely uses a mirror to inspect herself (Patterson 1984, Patterson and Cohn 1994). To explain this difference, it has been suggested that captive apes, especially those involved in language training programs, show a different level of cognitive awareness compared to their wild counterparts. It is possible that the increased level of social stimulation during childhood leads to or brings out the ability for self-recognition.

Self- and Social Attribution

Self-attribution refers to the ability to reflect on one's own mental state, while social attribution is the ability to reflect on one's own mental state and to infer the mental states of others based on one's own experiences. As humans, we tend to do this almost automatically in our everyday social interactions with one another. We are able to reflect on our own minds, as well as on the minds of others. What we want to know is whether monkeys or apes can reflect on the mental state of others or, for that matter, on their own mental state.

Gordon Gallup, who devised the mirror test (see above), suggested that self-recognition can be used as an index of self-attribution (reviewed in Gallup 1991). Gallup proposed that the ability for self-recognition requires some level of a concept of self and that this has to be an initial step for more advanced levels of social attribution. This assumption is not universally accepted (e.g., Heyes 1995), and skeptics use the fact that while human children show self-recognition at around 2 years of age, they do so without being able to attribute mental states to others. To convincingly demonstrate whether nonhuman primates can attribute mental states to themselves or others is a complex matter, and the jury is still out in regard to whether they can. However, at least in the

 BOX 10-1

Exploring Mental Attribution in Apes and Monkeys

Research into the minds of our fellow primates is plentiful. This research has especially focused on whether other primates possess a theory of mind; if they are able to infer, predict, or know what is in the mind of others and what others know or do not know. Several testing paradigms have been used. One testing paradigm is based on the *cooperation* between a study primate and humans in which two individuals work together, one as an informant and one as an operator. In these experiments, the primates are tested for the ability of social attribution and role reversals (e.g., Povinelli 2003, Povinelli et al. 1992, 2000). Another testing paradigm uses the natural *competitive interactions* that occur within most primate species' societies and is based on the ability of a subordinate individual to understand the visual field and mental perspective of a dominant individual (e.g., Hare et al. 2000, 2001, Hare and Tomasello 2004).

Povinelli and co-workers have used the testing paradigm based on cooperation. They have devised many different experimental procedures to test whether monkeys and apes have the ability to reflect on their own mental experiences and if they can inferentially reason about similar mental experiences in other individuals. In one test they examined whether nonhuman primates could understand the connection between seeing something and knowing about what was seen. In this experiment, either a macaque or a chimpanzee observed two humans in a room. One human (*the knower*) had a food reward, which was placed into one of four boxes, but the monkey or ape could not see into which box the food was placed. Before *the knower* placed the food in the box, the second human (*the guesser*) left the room. After the food had been placed into the box, *the guesser* returned to the room. Both humans then pointed at a box, *the knower* pointed to the one containing the food reward while *the guesser* pointed randomly at an empty box. If the monkey or ape had the ability for social attribution, then it should select the human who placed the food into the

(continued)

box because only that individual knew where the food was.

Some but not all of the chimpanzees got it right most of the time; they would choose the individual who had placed the food into the box. The macaques, in contrast, did not choose the right person more often than they would by chance. The results from these experiments suggest that chimpanzees have some ability to infer mental states in other individuals, while monkeys do not. There is, however, much controversy about whether these experiments really measure the ability to attribute mental states to others, or if they just reflect the ability to learn from cues. In other words, do these types of experiments reflect the ability to learn instead of the ability of attribution? If so, then chimpanzees may be faster at picking up cues than are monkeys.

In the second testing paradigm, Hare and co-workers examined whether chimpanzees understand what their conspecifics know based on what they can see. Two chimpanzees, one dominant and one subordinate, were placed in a competitive situation over a food reward. These tests are based on the fact that many actions of subordinates are inhibited by the presence of dominant individuals because a dominant individual will invariably take a desired food item from a subordinate individual (Goodall 1986).

In these experiments, several testing conditions were presented. In one test situation the dominant and subordinate chimpanzees, who were facing each other, could observe two bananas located in the space between them. One of the bananas was located behind a transparent screen on the subordinate's side but clearly visible to both, while the other banana was presented without a screen. In a second test situation, the dominant and subordinate chimpanzees were facing each other as before, but this time one of the two bananas was hidden from the view of the dominant chimpanzees by an opaque screen, and thus was only visible to the subordinate individual. In a third test situation, there were two opaque screens, and while the dominant chimpanzee looked away, a banana was introduced behind a screen, only visible to the subordinate chimpanzee. The last test situation was presented to clarify whether the mere presence of a dominant individual would affect the behavior of a subordinate, or if the subordinate acted based on the visual perspective of the dominant individual.

The subordinate chimpanzee behaved differently in the three test situations. When both bananas were visible to both chimpanzees, the subordinate did not attempt to retrieve the fruit. When the dominant chimpanzee was not watching and a banana was placed behind an opaque barrier, the subordinate would invariably rush to retrieve the fruit before the dominant animal reacted. However, in the test situation in which the dominant individual was watching, the subordinate individual retrieved the fruit only about 50 percent of the time. These results suggest that the chimpanzees attend to the visual field of their conspecifics. This test paradigm also showed that by using situations more familiar to the animals being tested, i.e., competition, it has been possible to show that at least chimpanzees appear to have a clear understanding of the visual perspective of fellow chimpanzees, and know what they know and what they do not know.

case of chimpanzees, there are indicators that they have the ability for both self- and social attribution (see Box 10-1).

❖❖ Why Should Primates Need to Think? Exploring Mental States in Primates

There are many ways in which primates would benefit from being able to think and to have a theory of mind. The understanding of mental states and that you yourself can influence the behavior of others creates opportunities for more effective cooperation and social manipulation between group members. For example, by being able to look into the minds of others, an animal can better distinguish if the intentions of others are friendly or unfriendly. Such knowledge may be beneficial in social situations as individuals could then recognize if they were being duped and manipulated. It also provides a means to manipulate others for personal gains. In complex social situations, having a theory of mind may function as a tool during social interactions that involve cooperation and reciprocity. In addition, it enables individuals to distinguish whether others are ignorant or in possession of specific knowledge, and it would be possible to more effectively exchange knowledge through either **observational learning** or **direct teaching**.

Social Manipulation and Deception

Deception is a type of social manipulation. It can be defined as one individual being misled by the actions of another individual into believing something that is untrue. That is, one individual dupes a fellow group member to his or her own benefit. In order for one animal to deceive another, the actor must know that his or her behavior is informative. The difficulty in using deceptive behaviors as evidence of thinking in nonhuman primates lies in the fact that by displaying such behaviors, the actor does not necessarily understand that the recipient's mental image may be different from the actor's own. However, deceptive behaviors are intriguing. It is possible to be deceptive in several ways: Information can be withheld, concealed, or be false. Of course, deception is a risky way to manipulate someone. If used too often, the actor may be found out and the effect of the deceptive act will lose its power. Likewise, if used too seldom, the act may also lose its effectiveness and not be an advantage to the user. There are many recorded instances of what could be considered as deceptive behavior being performed by nonhuman primates.

Byrne recalls a behavioral episode not uncommonly observed in baboons (Byrne 1995:124-125). A small juvenile male baboon is intently watching a low-ranking female (but higher ranking than him) digging for corms — tasty underground morsels of food that are difficult for juveniles to dig up. The juvenile looks around, but he sees none of his relatives close by. He then inches up to the female and lets out a high-pitched shriek as if he is being attacked. Within seconds, his mother comes running to the scene, and she chases the female away. The result of this interaction is that the juvenile can eat the corms that the fleeing female left behind.

This episode presents an example of a type of behavior referred to as tactical deception (Byrne and Whiten 1985, 1988, Whiten and Byrne 1997). It is a behavior that is used in a context in which others may misinterpret a signal, which will be to the advantage of the actor—in the above case, how the mother responded upon hearing her son's scream. Even though Byrne and Whiten did not include *intentionality* in their definition of tactical deception, it can be questioned whether the juvenile baboon intended to use his mother as a **social tool** by making her believe he was being attacked in order to gain access to the food. Clearly, the juvenile was neither hurt nor frightened when he screamed. His mother appeared to believe that he was, because baboon mothers do not usually come to their offspring's rescue over a food dispute.

This kind of tactical deception is frequently observed in the primate world but is most commonly reported in cercopithecine monkeys and chimpanzees. The problem is in trying to determine whether there is intentionality in the actions. It is so easy for us humans to automatically assume that a deceptive act is intentional because we have a theory of mind. However, the use of deceptive behaviors may not necessarily mean there is a theory of mind involved. Rather, the deceptive behavior may be based on associative learning. The juvenile male may have just learned that a scream given off in just the right pitch would elicit a specific response from his mother.

There are many reports of instances of deception in both captive and free-living chimpanzees that appear to be based on conscious reasoning (de Waal 1998, Goodall 1971, 1986, Menzel 1971, 1974). Individual chimpanzees may withhold or conceal information from other group members, either to gain a goal or to stay out of conflict with more dominant individuals (see examples provided in Byrne 1995). It is difficult to explain these behaviors without inferring a theory of mind, and thus intentionality. Furthermore, in the studies conducted in laboratory settings (see Box 10-1), as well as recorded instances of the active teaching of immature chimpanzees by their mothers, it appears that in at least this species, individuals do distinguish between ignorance and the possession of knowledge by others (see Box 10-2). Thus, we assume that they do in fact have some level of theory of mind.

Cooperation and Planning—Hunting Primates

Meat eating is occasionally observed in haplorhine primates even if it is not a major part of a species' diet. Baboons have frequently been reported to capture and eat animals (Harding 1973, McKee 1992, Strum 1983). A few observations have been made of capuchins catching and eating meat (Perry and Rose 1994, Terborgh 1983). Even orangutans may eat meat (Sugardjito and Nuhuda 1981, Utami and van Hooff 1997) and have been observed capturing and consuming meat in zoos (Figure 10-4). However, these cases cannot be classified as hunting, at least not cooperative hunting, which is what chimpanzees do (Boesch and Boesch-Achermann 2000, Goodall 1986).

The male chimpanzees of the Taï forest have shown themselves to be adept hunters (Boesch 1994, Boesch and Boesch-Achermann 1989, 2000). They hunt more often than males at the East African sites of Gombe or Mahale. They also hunt more

FIGURE 10-4   This captive orangutan male (right) caught a rabbit that strayed into the enclosure. Other group members were curious but had no interest in joining in a meal.

often in teams than seen at other sites, and at least half of the hunts are premeditated. The beginning of a planned hunt can be recognized by a small number of males moving quickly and quietly along the ground while scanning the treetops. If prey—most often red colobus monkeys—are detected, a "hunting" bark is emitted (Boesch and Boesch 1989).

The success of a cooperative hunt is entirely dependent on each individual cooperating and playing specific roles according to rules. There are three roles that are crucial for a successful hunt. First is the role of the *driver* or *chaser*. This is usually the male that first approaches the prey and, when detected, begins to drive the prey in a specific direction. Working with him is one or more *blockers* that make sure the prey does not escape. Finally, there is the *ambusher* that monitors the progress of the hunt from the ground. It is the ambusher that will come in to do the final capture. Well-seasoned hunters often play both the driver and ambusher roles. The question of whether the hunt participants understand the roles they are playing or if they are simply setting a "trap-line" for the prey is crucial for determining cognitive ability. As far as we can understand their behavior, it appears fairly certain that they are well aware of each other's roles and how to flexibly respond to each other's actions during the hunt; that is, the ability to anticipate cause and effect (Tomasello and Call, 1997:219-220).

Hunting success is directly proportional to the number of individuals that participate. When more than six males participate, the success rate is 89 percent, which drops to around 70 percent when four to six individuals participate. Of course, the more hunters involved, the less meat there is for each individual as a reward. Hunting alone provides the highest reward to the hunter, but the success rate is very low (17 percent). So there is strong incentive to cooperate.

The meat is shared between the active participants of the hunt, who in turn may chose to distribute meat to others. There is a predetermined apportionment of the prey. The individual that captures the prey gets the largest part, followed by the driver and the blockers that anticipated the movement of the prey. Other participants get an increasingly diminished share, and the amount given is proportional with the effort contributed to the hunt. Even the tiniest sliver is important because meat is high in protein and fat, which provides important calories and energy. Cheaters, individuals that do not put too much effort into the hunt but still beg for meat, are common in the Taï population. However, members of the hunting team pay close attention to who participated and to what extent, and meat is distributed based on this measure.

To become a successful hunter, a chimpanzee must have some built-in physical and mental abilities, but it takes many years of tutelage. Even though male chimpanzees begin to participate in hunts as drivers or blockers when they are 8 to 10 years old, they lack the skill and ability to anticipate the action of the prey at this age. By the time they are 20 years old, the ability to anticipate the actions of the prey is better but still not foolproof. Successful hunters, who can take on all demanding roles, and who have complete ability at anticipating prey movements, tend to be over 30 years old.

Most chimpanzee populations that are studied in Africa hunt and consume meat, but it is only the Taï chimpanzees that have evolved complex team-hunting behavior. Even though team hunts also take place at Mahale, here the participants do not appear to cooperate or have specific roles to play. In contrast, at Gombe, individuals hunt most frequently alone. The same is true for baboons that tend to hunt on an individual basis.

Cooperation and Knowledge Transfer

Cooperation in problem solving is not a common feature of primate behavior while coalition and alliance formation is much more common. As seen above, cooperation during hunting is frequently exhibited by chimpanzees, but appears to be completely lacking in monkeys. In captive situations, monkeys can be trained to cooperate with group members for a reward. However, they are not very good at role reversals, suggesting they have no insight into the mental image of their partner (see Box 10-1). In contrast, apes appear quite capable of cooperative behavior and role reversals.

Over the past couple of decades, Savage-Rumbaugh and colleagues at the Yerkes Primate Research Center at Emory (YPRC) have focused their research on understanding how apes think and communicate (Savage-Rumbaugh and Lewin 1994, Savage-Rumbaugh et al. 1998). From these studies we have gained some very interesting insight into how information is shared between a trained and untrained ape, (suggestive of active teaching), and how two individuals can cooperate to complete a specific task by sharing information. Two chimpanzees, Sherman and Austin, readily cooperate in tests (see The Great Ape Trust). They appear to understand when either one of them is lacking knowledge and can communicate with each other to provide information to successfully complete a puzzle in order to get a reward (see also Chapter 9).

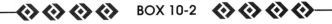

❖ ❖ ❖ ❖ BOX 10-2 ❖ ❖ ❖ ❖

Observational Learning and Teaching Among the Great Apes

A behavior is present in an animal either because it was present at birth (it is innate), or it is acquired during life. The most common way to acquire a behavior among primates is **trial-and-error learning** or **asocial learning**, in which each individual must gain the behavior on its own, and there is no transfer of knowledge or insight between individuals. There can also be social or observational learning, which may be less common (Figure 10-5). This type of information transmission can be further subdivided into **emulation** and **imitation** learning (e.g., Tomasello 1990, Tomasello and Call 1997).

Emulation is when one individual observes another individual performing a task, and through observation learns how to reach the same goal by performing the same task. In imitative learning,

the learner must be able to perceive and understand the action that the other individual is performing (mimic). The learner must also recognize the changes to the environment that action makes (emulation), and most importantly must understand something about the intentional relation between these two—i.e., how the behavior is designed to bring about the goal. Some researchers suggest that these two learning methods are not distinctly different, but rather reflect skills along a continuum (Whiten et al. 1996). Most apes emulate, but imitation also occurs (although less frequently) and seems particularly characteristic of apes that have been **enculturated**. A third way to learn a behavior is through teaching. For teaching to take place, it has to be assumed that the teacher has a perception of a behavioral incompetence or

FIGURE 10-5 Teaching among nonhuman primates has rarely been observed. However, young chimpanzees pay very close attention to their mothers when they use tools to extract termites or crack nuts.

(continued)

lack of knowledge on the part of another individual—i.e., an individual has to have some level of understanding of intentionality or the mental state of the conspecific.

One of the earliest and most famous examples of the social transmission of a behavioral pattern is the case of Imo, a Japanese macaque (Itani 1958, Kawai 1965). The researchers, who studied the macaques on the island of Koshima, Japan, provisioned the primates with sweet potatoes and cereal on the beach for convenience of observation. Imo, at the time 1.5 years old, introduced a new behavioral pattern to the group by washing the sand-covered sweet potato in the nearby stream rather than brushing the sand off by hand as was the general practice. At first she was alone in displaying this behavior, but over time other group members began to wash their sweet potatoes in water. The social transmission of this behavior followed a distinct pattern, which reflected the group's social relationships. First to pick up the behavior from Imo was her age peer group and her mother. Later, Imo's older siblings and their peer groups as well as the friends of Imo's mother acquired the behavior. Within a few years, the behavior had spread widely within the group. Only adult males, who were over 4 years of age when the behavior was first introduced, never acquired this new behavior. The behavior was transmitted from one generation to the next, and the potato-washing behavior has become fixed in the group's behavioral repertoire. It has, however, undergone some modifications—now all washing takes place in the saltwater of the ocean rather than in the freshwater of the nearby stream.

Another equally famous example of social transmission involves the unaided transmission of information to a novice ape, Kanzi, the bonobo at Yerkes. As described in Chapter 9, Sue Savage-Rumbaugh was training Kanzi's mother in Yerkish (Savage-Rumbaugh and Lewin 1994). While she was a slow and disinterested learner, Kanzi, who was just hanging out with mom (he was but a baby), did not appear to show much interest either. However, when his mother was temporarily moved out of the study area, Kanzi began to use the keyboard, showing that he had picked up an understanding of the symbols without having been directly taught (observational learning).

At present, there is little evidence for direct teaching among nonhuman primates (see cases listed below, and Boesch and Boesch-Achermann 2000). What little evidence there is, is limited to the apes. However, even this sparse evidence is of great importance. Among chimpanzees the individual that is taking on the role of teacher recognizes that he or she has information that others lack. In addition, by actively imparting information to an ignorant individual, that individual gains some added benefit, which alters its behavior in a positive way. This evidence of direct teaching hints at the fact that there must be some ability to understand that one's own mind or knowledge can be different from others, and that it is possible to modify mental states. This provides a much more flexible system that leaves room for modifications and advances.

Case 1: When Washoe, trained in ASL, lost her first offspring, she was given an infant, Loulis, to adopt. For the first five years of Loulis' life, neither Washoe nor Loulis were exposed to humans using ASL. During this time, Washoe proceeded to teach Loulis to make signs, both by careful visual cues and by directly molding his hands to form correct signs. The first case provides the possibility for observational learning (emulation or imitation), while the second is a case of direct teaching (Fouts et al. 1982, 1989).

Case 2: There is evidence from wild primates that active teaching takes place. In their long-term study of the Taï chimpanzees, Christophe and Hedwige Boesch have observed that to become proficient in cracking nuts and to master the complex use of tools requires many years of practice. Adult females spend more time in this activity than do males, and they also teach their youngsters how to do it. A mother cracks nuts in slow motion and in clear view of the youngster to see (observational learning). She also provides a situation for the offspring to practice (so-called scaffolding in psychology terms). This may entail placing a nut on a tree root (the anvil) with the hammer (branch or stone) close by. Occasionally, the Boesches have noticed that a female will turn a nut so it is positioned correctly before the youngster strikes it, or she may correct the position of the hammer in the youngster's hand (Boesch, 1991). Similar evidence of indirect or direct teaching has been seen with termite fishing among the Gombe chimpanzees (Goodall 1990).

❖❖ ❖❖ ❖❖ ❖❖

❖❖ Primates Who Make and Use Tools

In the early days of the study of primates, it was thought that **tool manufacture** and use was a unique human endeavor. Many statements about "Man the Tool Maker" were made in popular and scientific literature (see, for example, Ardrey 1976, Lee and DeVore 1968). It was therefore quite a surprise when Jane Goodall reported in 1960 that the chimpanzees at Gombe routinely made and used tools (Goodall 1964). Now we know that many animal species are capable of tool use and simple tool making (Beck 1980, Hunt 1996). Tool use in most animal species, however, represents behavioral adaptations associated with feeding strategies.

A defining trait in primates is their rich and varied ability to use their hands (Torigoe 1985). Primates have extensive representation of their hands in the sensory and motor areas of the cerebral cortex of the brain (see Figure 4-21; Kaas 1993, Kandel et al. 2002). Since primates are primarily hand-feeders (although they frequently use their feet to assist with holding), it may not be so surprising that they also make and use tools. Not all primate species use tools. The ones who use tools do so infrequently, with the exception of the chimpanzees and some orangutan populations. Strepsirhines use their hands in a different manner than haplorhines and have never been reported to use tools in the wild. Likewise, colobines do not use tools, possibly because they have no thumbs or their thumbs are much reduced in size. The ability to manipulate, especially using precision grips, is therefore not as great as it is for cercopithecine monkeys and most apes. Among the monkeys, only a few species have been reported to use tools in the wild, e.g., capuchins (Figure 10-6; Chevalier-Skolnikoff 1990, de A. Moura and Lee 2004), baboons, and macaques (see Tomasello and Call 1997:82-86). Until the recent observation of a female gorilla using a stick to test the depth of a pool of water, it was considered that gorillas never used tools in nature (Breuer et al. 2005). In captivity, however,

FIGURE 10-6   Until recently it was thought that no monkey species used tools habitually in their natural habitat, until it was discovered that some populations of capuchins (*Cebus apella*) use stones to crack open nuts.

most haplorhine primates use tools when given the opportunity (e.g., Candland 1987, Westergaard et al. 1998).

A tool can be defined in several ways (Beck 1980). In its most simple form, a tool is an object in nature, unmodified but perhaps carefully selected, that can be used to modify another object. An example of this is how otters use stones to break open mollusks, with the stone being used as a tool. A more complex tool is when an object in nature is modified and then used to modify another object. An example of this would be the way chimpanzees take twigs or grass blades and remove unwanted branches to fish for ants and termites. Chimpanzees, living in a mosaic savanna habitat of Senegal, have been observed to prepare spear-shaped tools that they use to probe and stab into tree hollows. The goal appears to be to kill and spear bushbabies, asleep in the tree hollows, for food (Pruetz and Bertolani 2007). Even though both males and females have been observed in this activity, it appears that this hunting tactic is more commonly performed by females.

At an even more complex level, we have the use of two tools involved in a single task. A good example is when the Taï chimpanzees use a hammer stone to crack open a nut placed on an anvil stone (Boesch and Boesch-Achermann 2000). The most complex tool use is referred to as **metatool** use, which entails a modified object being used to modify another object, which in turn is used as a tool. Until recently, it was thought that humans were alone in using metatools. However, when Matsuzawa observed chimpanzees at Bossou, Guinea, propping up the anvil stone tool with a wedge stone to get a level surface to be able to hit the nut with a hammer stone, he proposed that this was evidence of metatool use by wild chimpanzees (Matsuzawa 1991, 2001).

Even though primates use tools in many different situations, most of the tools are used to gain access to food, e.g., extracting, probing, and crushing tools. Most primates use unmodified objects as tools, and only apes have been seen in the wild to routinely use modified objects as tools. Chimpanzees and some orangutan populations have the largest tool kits (Boesch and Boesch-Achermann 2000, Sanz and Morgan 2007, van

Schaik et al. 2003a, b). It appears that the stone tool using behavior observed by the Taï chimpanzees has an ancient history. Researchers have found ancient chimpanzee tool sites dating to 4,300 years ago in West Africa (Mercader et al. 2007).

Not all tools are used to gain food; some tools are used for display to intimidate conspecifics or potential predators. Monkeys are known to dislodge branches from trees or rocks from cliff faces to scare off predators or rivals. Bonobo and chimpanzee males often drag big branches about in display (Ingmanson 1996). Objects can also be used as defensive tools, e.g., a capuchin male was observed killing a poisonous snake using a branch as a tool (Boinski 1988). Such tool use does not entail modification or the manufacture of a tool, just crude manipulation of a natural object. Chimpanzees also use various tools to clean the body (Table 10-1).

What Does It Take to Use and Make a Tool?

To use a tool may not involve anything beyond conditioned learning (or an innate drive), together with a good ability for manipulation. To make a tool for a specific task may, however, require more insightfulness. To make a tool, a primate needs a mental template or representation in its mind of the final product. There must be an understanding of the raw material to be used as a tool in order to successfully produce something that will assist in reaching a goal (see Box 10-3). For example, to fish for termites and to dip for ants require sticks of different dimensions, and different environmental conditions influence what kind of sticks may be used. Chimpanzees often prepare their tools ahead of time, suggesting that they plan ahead, that they have **forethought**. Köhler had already in the early part of the twentieth century suggested that the apes he worked with showed insight and could plan ahead, especially in the use of tools to solve problems (Köhler 1927). A good example from more recent observations is the nut-cracking Taï chimpanzees that have caches of hammers and anvils by specific nut trees. Observations from the wild have often been considered anecdotal. However, it has been shown under formal test conditions in captivity that bonobos and orangutans have the ability to plan ahead by selecting a specific tool for a specific task as much as fourteen hours in advance of reaching a goal (Mulcahy and Call 2006). Monkeys, in contrast, appear to lack insight and have never shown evidence that they have a mental representation of the tool itself

TABLE 10-1 Tool-using Activity Observed in the Chimpanzees

Tool-use activity	Object used as tool	Purpose
Insert	Grass, stick, twig	Gain access to termites, ants, bees, grubs, honey, bone marrow, brain, eyes, water
Probe	Grass, stick, twig	Explore the nests of termites, bees, ants; wounds, feared objects
Display	Branch, rock	Throwing, aimed throwing, dragging, hitting with an object, weapon, leaf-clipping
Clean	Grass, stick, twig, leaves	Wounds, dirt, sponging, brushing, catching

or even possibly the goal. Visalberghi has studied tool use and the cognitive abilities of capuchin monkeys (*Cebus apella*) over many years. The conclusion from these studies is that even capuchin monkeys that do readily use tools lack a causal understanding of tools; rather, they learn through trial-and-error (see e.g., Visalberghi and Limongelli 1994, Visalbergi and Trinca 1989).

How are Tool-using and Tool-making Skills Learned?

How primates learn various tool-using behaviors is poorly understood. As a matter of fact, how they learn any complex behavior has not been clearly established. There are several ways in which they can acquire a behavior. Primates and other animals may learn from goal-directed behaviors displayed by others, through observation, and trial-and-error learning. There may be long periods of learning. Even though apes appear to learn faster than monkeys, some tool-using behaviors take a long time to learn. For example, it may take chimpanzees six to eight years to become good at cracking nuts.

There is much controversy whether apes learn through emulation or imitation (see Box 10-2). Some scientists are of the opinion that all behaviors noted in chimpanzees are based on emulation learning (e.g., Tomasello 1990), while others suggest that there are examples of imitative learning (e.g., Whiten 2000). It has been suggested that **intentional teaching** takes place in chimpanzees. However, the evidence is sparse and controversial. The only evidence that appears to have withstood the test of time comes from observations made at Gombe (Goodall 1986, 1990) and the Taï Forest in West Africa, where mothers appear to stimulate, facilitate, and teach offspring to crack nuts (Boesch and Boesch-Achermann 2000). A mother may perform nut cracking in slow motion in front of her offspring, or she may leave nuts by a hammer and anvil for the offspring to practice, and the setup varies depending on the offspring's age. The mother may also intervene in how the offspring holds the tool or how the nut is situated on the anvil (Boesch 1991). In sum, most of the complex tool-using behaviors seen in, at least, the chimpanzees, are learned through a mixture of trial-and-error and emulation learning.

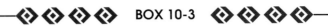
◆◇◆◇◆◇◆◇ BOX 10-3 ◆◇◆◇◆◇◆◇

Can Apes Manufacture and Use Stone Tools of the Same Quality as Those of Early Hominins?

The oldest stone tools discovered in the fossil record come from the Hadar region of Ethiopia. These tools represent what is known as the Oldowan stone tool industry, and date to 2.5 to 2.6 mya (Semaw et al. 2003). Even these oldest stone tools show sophistication in manufacture beyond anything produced by extant native apes. However, wild chimpanzees and orangutans do produce tools that clearly show that apes have both an understanding of the raw materials used and a mental template of the tool needed to complete a specific task. Furthermore, in captivity, apes have demonstrated great ability to learn symbolic communication systems, to solve complex tasks, and are able to learn how to use a wide range of human tools (Galdikas

1982, Savage-Rumbaugh and Lewin 1994).

Nick Toth, an archaeologist who specializes in early hominin stone tools, questioned whether living apes could make and use stone tools similar to the ones used by our early ancestors (Toth et al. 1993). The cognitive sophistication of Kanzi, the bonobo, led Toth to suggest that he and his colleagues should be allowed to test if Kanzi could learn to produce stone flakes. There was some hint at the possibility because some twenty years earlier an orangutan, Abang, who lived at Bristol Zoo in England, had been trained to produce and use stone flakes to cut a rope, which locked a box containing a food reward (Wright 1972).

Kanzi was 9 years old when he first met Nick Toth. It was decided that Kanzi should learn to make stone flakes by example (observational learning), rather than being directly taught. Thus, the archaeologist sat down in front of Kanzi with the raw materials surrounding him. To provide incentive for Kanzi, Toth had a box containing a food reward, which was secured with a rope (Kanzi could see the food reward through a transparent lid). As a first step, the archaeologist produced several flakes using a free-hand hard-hammer percussion technique, which involves holding the stone core in one hand and the stone hammer in the other hand. Kanzi was shown how and where to place the blow of the hammer stone to produce sharp flakes. He was also told verbally how to do it (remember Kanzi can understand spoken English, see Chapter 9). Then Toth used a flake to cut the rope that secured the box, giving the reward to Kanzi. As a second step, Kanzi was allowed to take a flake himself and cut the rope and open the

reward box. This was repeated several times until Kanzi had a good grasp of what kind of flake was required to cut the rope. The final step was to leave the raw materials with Kanzi so he could practice trial-and-error learning to produce flakes himself, which could be used to cut the rope to gain access to food rewards.

Even though Kanzi had been shown how to hold the stones and how to strike the core with the hammer stone, he had trouble replicating this behavior. Kanzi had problems duplicating the strike precision and adequate force, possibly because bonobo hands are not shaped in the same fashion as are human hands—his grasping ability is different from ours or even that of early hominins (Marzke 1997). In addition, Kanzi did not appear to understand where to strike, and therefore the strike angle he used was too steep (90° compared with 75–80° angle used in the Oldowan stone tool technology). As a result, the flakes he produced were small and often fractured in the middle. Kanzi developed his own alternative way to produce flakes. He would throw the stone core against another hard object such as the cement floor in his indoor enclosure or against a rock in his outdoor enclosure, or he would throw the hammer against the core that he had propped up on the floor. Kanzi was able to introduce much more force this way, and the stone would shatter and produce flakes. By using this method, the need for strike precision was reduced as the strike angle would be random, and the flakes produced were more often than not small, but they could be used to cut the rope. The researchers tried to discourage this method and wanted Kanzi to use the free-hand hard-hammer percussion technique of the early hominins.

(continued)

With further practice, Kanzi was able to produce increasingly better flakes, although none really reached the level of sophistication of the Oldowan tools.

We need to keep in mind that our ancestors most likely had millions of years of practice to reach the stage of being able to produce even the simplest of Oldowan stone tools. It would be unrealistic to expect Kanzi to become a master of such a technology in the matter of a few hundred hours of practice.

Even among humans there are those of us who cannot produce as good flakes as Kanzi can. It must be kept in mind that Kanzi *did* solve the problem presented to him; he was able to produce stone flakes to access the food reward in the box. Why should we expect him to produce anything beyond this goal? A more detailed account of this experiment can be found in Toth et al. 1993 and Schick et al. 1999 and see The Stone Age Institute www.stoneageinstitute.org.

◈ ◈ ◈ ◈

◈◈ Can Primates Count and Do Arithmetic?

All primates have good knowledge about the environment they live in. They have a mental map of their own home range, as well as bordering areas. They know where food and water is to be found, they know where good sleeping sites are located, and so on. However, simply knowing where the food is to be found is not sufficient, especially if you live in a large social group. There is also a need to have some understanding about how much food will be available. Primates cannot afford to travel to a food place and run out of food before all group members have had their fill. We know that at least capuchin monkeys and baboons have the ability to evaluate the volume of food found at specific locations in their home range (Garber and Paciulli 1997, Vauclair 1990). We therefore assume that primates, at least those that live in social groupings, have some understanding of quantity.

Quantitative skills can be grouped into two types: cardination and ordination. **Cardination** refers to the number of objects belonging to any specific type, e.g., 7 apples or 2 oranges. **Ordination** refers to the property of numbers and the recognition of the position of a number in a series, e.g., 7 belongs in between 5 and 9. This can also be referred to as dominance ranking. According to Piaget, a child developmental psychologist, the human concept of quantity is a synthesis or combination of both cardinal and ordinal aspects (Piaget 1952). To understand numbers, or numerousness, there must be an understanding that the number of objects can be substituted with a number symbol, e.g., "three apples" is the same as "3 apples" (**abstract numerousness**). In addition, there must be an ability to place different groups of objects, which have different quantities, into some order, based on some set criteria, e.g., 3 apples are fewer than 5 oranges (**relative numerousness**).

Based on numerous studies, it is known that monkeys and apes have a good handle on cardination. Rhesus macaques can match food pellets with Arabic numerals (Rumbaugh and McCormack 1967). Many chimpanzees (e.g., Ai, Sheba, Sarah, Austin, and Sherman) can also do this task with ease (Biro and Matsuzawa 2001, Boysen and Hallberg 2000, Woodruff and Premack 1981). It is more difficult to determine whether there is a conceptual understanding of the numbers. We can do this by looking at the understanding of ordination and **transitive inferences ability**. For example, if an individual understands that *a* is more than *b*, which is more than *c* (a>b>c), then he or she should also be able to draw the conclusion that *a* is more than *c* (a>c). Such a test using numbers with monkeys and apes has not yet been undertaken. Instead, a test has been constructed using colored objects, in which the colors carry different values (blue>red>green therefore blue>green). Chimpanzees as well as some monkeys can solve this puzzle.

Both monkeys and apes can make quantitative judgments, but only when small quantities are used. Rhesus macaques have shown some ability to both add and subtract (Hauser et al. 2000, Sulkowski and Hauser 2001). With the tests used so far, it is difficult to infer, however, if this skill is perceptual or conceptual. Both monkeys and apes can perform the sequential ordering of objects, e.g., from smallest to largest, least numerous to most numerous, etc. They can also fit an object into its place in a series, e.g., they can make transitive judgments even when presented with objects they have never seen before (which suggests some conceptual ability). Counting, summation, and understanding proportions are abilities that have only been tested with a few chimpanzees (Biro and Matsuzawa 2001, Boysen and Hallberg 2000, Woodruff and Premack 1981). Here it appears that individuals who have had prior language training are better at these skills than novice individuals. This suggests that the language projects provide the chimpanzees with an understanding of abstract relations, a skill they can then transfer in order to make mathematical inferences.

Until fairly recently, few strepsirhines have been included in cognitive testing. This is in part because of an implicit assumption that they would have a lower level of cognitive capacity compared to monkeys and apes. This may also be related to the fact that strepsirhines do not have the same ability to manipulate objects, and hence many test arrangements do not function well for them. However, when applying a testing condition initially developed to use on human infants based on gaze attention, it has been possible to test a wider range of primate species. The gaze test is based on the assumption that an individual will look for a longer time if the situation presented is incorrect, unexpected, or abnormal, while if an expected situation is presented the gaze will be of shorter duration (Hauser and Carey 1998).

When using the gaze test, it has been possible to show that several lemur species have a basic quantitative understanding (Santos et al. 2005). The test situation was structured so that the primate was presented with a single object, which was then hidden behind a screen. Next, a second object of the same kind was presented, which was also placed behind the screen. The length of time the lemurs looked at the objects once the screen was removed was measured. In the test situation described, the lemurs would gaze for a significantly longer time when only a single object was present when the screen was removed, compared to when the expected two objects were present.

 **HOT TOPICS 10-1**

Are Humans Alone in Having Culture?

The question of culture has received much attention, especially from anthropologists. There is much controversy surrounding how to define the concept of culture. Traditionally, culture has been considered a unique and defining trait of humans (e.g., Block 1991, Kroeber and Kluckhohn 1952, Montague

(continued)

1968). Even though Marvin Harris did not disregard the possibility that non-human primates have culture, he considered human culture to be different from that of nonhuman primates. He suggested that the difference was a matter of degree rather than kind, and that what nonhuman primates display is pre-culture (Harris 1964, 1979). Even if culture among nonhuman primates is accepted, there appears to be an obvious difference: Nonhuman primates can survive without their culture or traditional behaviors, while humans cannot survive without their cultural accoutrements (Mann 1972).

Many scientists consider the term culture appropriate to explain population-specific behavioral traditions in nonhuman primates (e.g., Boesch et al. 1994, de Waal 1999, 2001, Nishida 1987, Whiten et al. 1999), while others prefer to use terms such as social conventions or traditions (e.g., Perry et al. 2003). McGrew (1992) is a strong proponent of accepting the population-wide traditions seen, especially in chimpanzee tool use, as direct evidence of the presence of culture in nonhuman primates. Other researchers want to reserve this term for behavioral traditions in which particular kinds of social learning (imitation or teaching) are involved (e.g., Galef 1988, Tomasello et al. 1993). However, this kind of distinction is not very helpful because there is no consensus in regard to how nonhuman primates actually learn behaviors and how traditions get established (see Box 10-2).

Can the tool use and differences in tool kits seen in chimpanzees and orangutans be used as evidence of culture? There appears to be much population variability in the types of tools in a tool kit as well as how tools are used. For example, the sticks or wands used by the Gombe chimpanzees to fish for termites are long, while the Taï chimps use much shorter wands for the same activity. Furthermore, the oil palm nut kernels so desired by the Taï chimpanzees are ignored by the Gombe chimpanzees; they only eat the outer fruit of the plant. The nut-cracking behavior is restricted to the West African chimpanzees, but not all populations within West Africa crack nuts. There appears to be no ecological or genetic factors that can explain these differences. Of course, there may have been ecological differences in the past when the behavioral differences first appeared, and Tomasello warns us not to jump to conclusions too quickly because we have not yet heard the final word on the nut-cracking chimpanzee as cultural beings.

Whiten and colleagues have suggested that "a cultural behaviour is one that is transmitted repeatedly through social or observational learning to become a population-level characteristic" (Whiten et al. 1999:682). They have presented the clearest evidence to date that different cultures exist in at least the chimpanzees. As stated by Frans de Waal (1999:635) ". . . it will be hard to keep these apes out of the cultural domain without once again moving the goal post." Thus, humans are truly not alone in possessing cultural traditions, leaving open the possibility to search for the origin of human culture using our closest living relatives as models, although whether they should be considered homologues or analogues is not resolved (see Chapter 1).

❖❖ ❖❖ ❖❖ ❖❖

❖❖ Summary

Exploring the minds of nonhuman primates is a daunting task because we can never know for certain what they think or feel. We simply cannot crawl into their minds and look out at the world through their eyes, listen with their ears, smell with their noses, touch with their fingers, or taste with their mouths to get a sense of how they perceive the world around them. We can, however, devise ingenious studies that investigate the cognitive abilities of nonhuman primates by looking at how they manipulate and deceive one another within a social setting, if and how they cooperate with one another to accomplish a task or to solve a problem, their abilities to make tools, how they learn new behaviors, and if they have an understanding of quantity (or arithmetic).

Ultimately, we are asking the question of whether nonhuman primates have a theory of mind. For example, we know what is in our own minds in the terms of our beliefs, feelings, intentions, or knowledge, but we also recognize that other individuals have mental states that may be different from our own. Can the nonhuman primates, or at least some of the species, do this as well? Researchers exploring the mental states of nonhuman primates look at the level of awareness they have of themselves (self-awareness). They also look at both self-attribution and social attribution in which an individual is aware of his or her state of mind, but can use this information to predict and explain the behavior of both self and others. Fascinating studies have been done to determine the kind and level of awareness that nonhuman primates have of themselves and others. In particular, studies of social manipulation and deception indicate that nonhuman primates do, in fact, demonstrate social attribution. In sum, after reviewing the evidence for the ability of nonhuman primates to communicate, be aware, and deceive, it does seem likely that they do have at least some degree of a theory of mind.

Historically, we have been trying to understand whether there is a continuum or dividing line between our mental abilities and theirs. Apparently, if you live in a complex ecological environment and interact on a daily basis within a complex fluctuating social environment, then you need to have a big brain. And, if you subject an ape to an enriched and stimulating learning environment, the chasm between us and them quickly diminishes. Our definitions of culture and human versus nonhuman behaviors have been challenged and obscured by our studies of the primate brain.

❖❖ Key Words

abstract numerousness	empathy	ordination
anthropocentric	emulation	relative numerousness
Asperger's syndrome	enculturation	social tool
asocial learning	forethought	theory of mind
autism	imitation	tool
cardination	intentional teaching	tool manufacture
causal agent	kin relationship	transitive inference ability
deception	metatool	trial-and-error learning
direct teaching	observational learning	

◆◆ Study Questions

1. What are the strengths and weaknesses of the ecological and social intelligence hypotheses?
2. What do we mean by the term "theory of mind"? And how is the study of autistic children shedding light on the topic?
3. Why may the mirror test not reflect self-awareness?
4. Why is deceptive behavior so important in trying to understand the minds of primates?
5. What are the different ways that an animal can gain or learn a behavior?
6. How common is tool use and tool making among primates in the wild?
7. How was Kanzi able to make stone tools, and how did his tool kit differ from that of the earliest humans?
8. Are humans alone in having culture? Are behavioral traditions sufficient to be defined as cultural?
9. Why is it important to understand whether primates can count and do arithmetic?
10. Are we judging ourselves by a different yardstick than what we use when studying other primates?

◆◆ Suggested Readings and Related Web Sites

Byrne R. 1995. The thinking ape. Evolutionary origins of intelligence. Oxford, UK: Oxford University Press.

Cheney DL, Seyfarth RM. 1990. How monkeys see the world. Chicago: Chicago University Press.

The Gorilla Foundation
www.Koko.org

The Great Ape Trust
www.greatapetrust.org

Matsuzawa T. 2001. Primate origins of human cognition and behavior. New York: Springer.

Parker ST, McKinney ML. 1999. Origins of intelligence. The evolution of cognitive development in monkeys, apes and humans. Baltimore: The Johns Hopkins University Press.

Povinelli DJ. 2000. Folk physics for apes. The chimpanzee's theory of how the world works. New York: Oxford University Press.

Stanford C. 2001. Significant others. The ape-human continuum and the quest for human nature. New York: Basic Books.

Tomasello M, Call J. 1997. Primate cognition. Oxford, UK: Oxford University Press.

Whiten A, Byrne RW. 1997. Machiavellian intelligence II. Extensions and evaluations. Cambridge, UK: Cambridge University Press.

CHAPTER

11

Primate Conservation

We humans are among the most successful species that has ever lived on earth. Wherever we go we see evidence of human domination of earth's ecosystems. Among fellow mammals, our reproductive success is unprecedented. The geographic expansion of *Homo sapiens* is amazing—since the time of our migration out of Africa, perhaps some 200,000 years ago, we have managed to inhabit the entire world (Finlayson 2005). At present, there is hardly a landmass we have not visited and claimed. We inhabit all continents, and almost every ecological zone can be settled by us humans;

we can tame even the most inhospitable habitat for our own survival. With careful application of water, we can even make deserts bloom. Being able to modify the environment for our own benefit is the main reason for our success—we are no longer dictated by what nature has to offer, but instead we dictate what nature *should* offer us. The kind of habitat modification we are now capable of is a rather recent phenomenon. We did not become agriculturalists much before 10,000 years ago (Cauvin 2000, Gupta 2004). However, how we use our habitat today compared to the first farmers of the Middle East bears no comparison. It is becoming increasingly evident that the way we use the world is not sustainable in the long run. As our world population is steadily increasing, from 6.5 billion today to an estimated 9 billion by 2050 (Figure 11-1), the

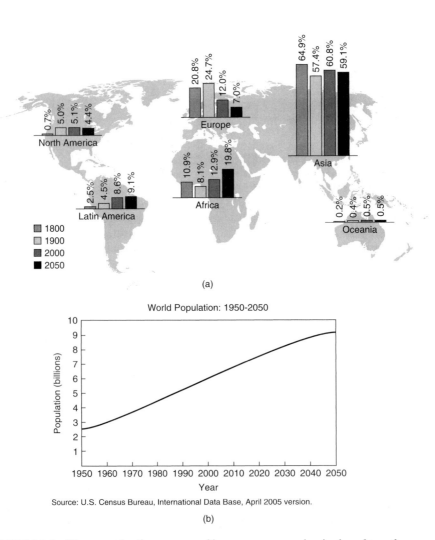

(a)

(b)

Source: U.S. Census Bureau, International Data Base, April 2005 version.

FIGURE 11-1 The reproductive success of humans, as a species, is clear from the world population census and projected increase over the next 50 years. There are about 6.5 billion humans living on earth presently, and it is estimated that by 2050 there will be 2.5 billion more people.

pressure on the land to produce more food is increasing. We are already utilizing the most fertile parts of the globe. The need for additional land to farm or to extract resources from is ever growing, and we are increasingly encroaching on more marginal habitats. Our lifestyle is highly destructive to our surrounding environment, and many species are suffering from our bulldozing mentality. Other species that show a similar kind of success despite our presence, e.g., rats, cockroaches, seagulls, or baboons are considered pests.

❖ ❖ ❖ ❖ HOT TOPICS 11-1 ❖ ❖ ❖ ❖

How Much Like Us? Should Nonhuman Primates Have Their Own Bill of Rights?

The United States Bill of Rights limits the power of the federal government and guarantees the protection of all peoples to basic principles or rights of human liberty. The right of people to have freedom of speech, religion, press, to assemble, etc., including the prevention of cruel and unusual punishment, are considered fundamental human rights or privileges. Any infringement of these rights can result in the pursuit of legal retribution. Human beings living in the United States have these rights, and many countries in the world have equivalent laws but should such rights be extended to those nonhuman primates who are much like us?

Even though chimpanzees and bonobos may not look similar to ourselves, we know, based on genetic studies (The Chimpanzee Sequencing and Analysis Consortium 2005, Elango et al. 2006), that the differences between us are not so very great. Of the genome regions compared, we see 98.8 percent overlap between humans and chimpanzees, although it has been questioned how important these differences are in defining ourselves relative to other living apes (Marks 2002). Whatever our stance is, we cannot deny the fact that chimpanzees and bonobos are our closest living relatives. In addition, as we

gain clearer insight into the minds of other apes through behavioral studies conducted both in captivity and in their natural environment (see Chapters 9 and 10), it has become evident that all living apes are highly intelligent; they have an understanding of themselves (theory of mind) and recognize themselves when exposed to mirrors (self-awareness). According to Jane Goodall, who has dedicated her entire adult life to the study and protection of chimpanzees, they are highly social, complex, and emotional beings with great intellectual ability and mental capacity—in other words, they *are* sentient beings.

Despite this, chimpanzees are often used as the preferred model in biomedical research, mainly because they are so closely related to us, and their bodies respond to diseases in a similar fashion to our own. Thousands of chimpanzees have been and are currently used for research on diseases such as HIV/AIDS, hepatitis, and malaria. This is done in an attempt to better understand the etiology of the diseases and to develop cures or vaccines for ourselves. When used in medical research, these highly intelligent and gregarious apes are removed from family and friends and usually kept isolated in small barren cages, with little freedom of movement or the ability to

(continued)

stay active. The stress resulting from the isolation and loneliness, as well as the testing procedures, creates an appalling image. Apes are also used in other venues designed for human pleasure and amusement. In the entertainment industry, apes—especially chimpanzees—are used in movies, commercials, circuses, and other displays. The training involved to induce apes to perform is usually based on a system of negative reinforcement or punishment. Unfortunately, the protection provided by the federal Animal Welfare Act (Crawford 2001) can be limited due to vagueness in the wording of the guidelines and regulations.

In the early 1990s, the plight of thousands of captive chimpanzees present in the United States prompted a group of thirty-four prominent scientists (including primatologists, biologists, ethicists, philosophers, and evolutionary biologists) to create a manifesto. The manifesto became known as **The Great Ape Project**, and because it addressed how captive apes should be treated, it is often referred to as the "Bill of Rights" for nonhuman apes (Singer and Cavalieri 1993). This manifesto was a rallying cry to protect captive apes and to provide them with the same basic freedoms, privileges, and legal protection as is enjoyed by human children. You may wonder why the rights of children were targeted. Children are considered the most appropriate model to use since apes are not able to represent themselves, and we are thus, by proxy, the legal guardians. The goal was to establish a legal basis to provide captive apes with first, the right to life; second, the protection of individual liberty; and last, the prohibition of torture. The basic premise was to improve the life of captive apes.

In many countries, scientists have petitioned their governments to introduce a bill of rights for all apes. So far, none of these petitions have passed into law but the attention to the plight of captive apes has led to regulations improving their care. For example, in New Zealand, Sweden, and the UK, apes cannot be used in biomedical research or testing. In the United States, Congress passed in 2000 the Chimpanzee Health Improvement, Maintenance and Protection Act, which promoted the National Institute of Health (NIH) to draft a chimpanzee management program [ChiMP] (see The Humane Society of the United States (HSUS), Gagneux et al. 2005, Shalev 2001). This act does not give equal rights to all apes, but it brings to the forefront the requirement of ethical treatment. One major step forward is that it puts a stop to the use of euthanasia at the end of experimental testing. It requires researchers to incorporate into their research budgets funding for the long-term care of their ape subjects. Retirement homes have been created for former research chimpanzees (e.g., Chimp Haven) where they can live out the remainder of their lives within social groups and in some comfort. There is also a moratorium on breeding chimpanzees in captivity without special permission.

The limited success of The Great Ape Project and granting other apes the legal status of a "person" is in part because most people look upon apes as "mere" animals and think animals do not have souls. It is difficult to get people to look upon themselves as part of the greater natural world—we are animals; we are apes. The jury is still out in regard to whether we are the only living beings on earth with a soul (however we define this). It is tantalizing to think that because apes have self-awareness; they recognize themselves as distinct from other conspecifics; they have a theory of mind; they have the capacity for basic consciousness; and are capable of expressing grief, happiness, and anger, that they would not also be capable of having a soul.

Even if we do not accord equal rights and the status of "person" to other apes, we should on humanitarian grounds and as fellow sentient beings ensure that our closest living evolutionary relatives are treated with dignity.

◇◇◇◇

◇◇ What Is the Future for the Primate Order?

Until quite recently, humans and other primate species lived in relative harmony, and in many places we still do. However, the need for more land to cultivate and extract resources has led to human encroachment in even the most isolated of places, placing an ever-increasing pressure on many other species, including primates. The threats we see facing primates today include the *loss of habitat* due to the encroachment and competition by humans for even the most isolated and wild habitats, and the *capture of primates* to be sold either as meat or to be traded as pets or curiosities in zoos (Figure 11-2). Conservation programs worldwide are attempting to stop the downward spiral in loss of habitat and life of wild primates. As the interests of humans and wildlife increasingly intersect, conflicts abound. Crop raiding is a problem wherever humans and other primates come into contact (Chalise 2001, Hill 2000, Naughton-Treves 1998, Saj et al. 2001), but we should ask ourselves if there is any reason why we should expect primates to understand that human crops are not part of their available food resources. Unfortunately, it is seldom

FIGURE 11-2 Baby primates are often taken from their mothers to be raised by humans for the explicit purpose of gaining an income. They may be trained to perform certain acts, or to be dressed up as celebrities, such as this juvenile macaque impersonating a pop idol.

the nonhuman primates that win in such situations. As a result, an ever-increasing number of species are endangered and many are on the brink of extinction. Of the 625 primate taxa recognized by IUCN/SSC, 230 or 37 percent are under threat (Mittermeier et al. 2006). The island of Madagascar is experiencing the most acute threat to its unique primate fauna with close to 60 percent of taxa being threatened. Our closest living ape relatives—the chimpanzees, bonobos, gorillas, and orangutans—are especially vulnerable. The responsibility to save our fellow apes from extinction lies squarely in our hands. We have the ability, and many would say the moral responsibility, to do so. We must acknowledge what we have already lost and recognize what we are about to lose before it is too late to do something about it.

Shrinking Habitats

As humans expand over the land, we seldom leave habitats intact. Rather, we change environments to suit our own needs often by removing all undesirable flora and fauna. Only those species that are beneficial to us and that do not interfere with our lives or livelihoods are allowed to remain. The larger and more visible species, especially large carnivores, are under great pressure because they more often than not come into direct conflict with us. Predators such as lions and tigers cannot differentiate between livestock and wild prey, and as a result livestock is often vulnerable (Kolowski and Holekamp 2006, Patterson et al. 2004, Woodroffe et al. 2005). However, it is not only livestock that is at risk; humans who come into contact with large predators are also at risk (Hart and Sussman 2005, Packer et al. 2005).

The tropical rain forest, comprising approximately 2 percent of the earth's landmass, has the highest **biodiversity** and is the richest ecosystem in both animal and plant species. It is estimated that around 50 percent of all known species can be found in tropical rain forest habitats (Wright 2005). These habitats are also a source of much of the world's need for exotic hard wood such as mahogany, teak, and rosewood. Commercial logging of these precious resources is a major reason for the loss of habitat in many areas (Figure 11-3). However, there are other threats to forests, often facilitated by the activities of logging companies. For example, slash-and-burn agriculture is eating away at the edges of tropical forests throughout the world (e.g., Nepstad et al. 1999). In the Taï National Park, Côte d'Ivoire, there has been an eightfold increase in human encroachment by small-scale, shifting agriculture, so-called slash-and-burn activities (see Box 3-1; Chapman et al. 1999). In some areas, logging is less of a threat to the preservation of forests; rather, the demand for firewood poses an even greater threat (Leslie et al. 2002).

More recently, encroachment by renewable resource schemes such as oil palm (*Elaeis guineensis* Jacq.) and biofuel plantations are increasingly leaving marks on the rainforest biome. It is estimated that 6.5 million hectares (16 million acres) of mainly lowland forest in Borneo and Sumatra were used for oil palm plantations in 2004 (Redmond and Juniper 2005). Even though there appears to be a slow down in the destruction of rain forest habitats (Meijaard and Wich 2007) this rampant deforestation is a major threat to all wildlife in the area. It is especially the orangutans that are under increasing threat of extinction as their habitat is shrinking and becoming more and more fragmented. The frightening fact is that it is estimated that 2.4 acres (close to 1 hectare) of forest are destroyed every second, which equals 78 million acres per year, or approximately half the State of Florida (Rainforest Action Network 2006). Such a reduction is not sustainable, not even in the short term.

FIGURE 11-3   Indiscriminate logging or slash-and-burn agriculture in forests leave lasting scars in the habitat, and may result in excessive degradation and erosion. In addition, where logging roads go, so follow other people who may cause further destruction to the surrounding flora and fauna.

Is it possible that we can limit the amount of land we use and set aside land as preserves for other animals to survive? Presently no more than 10 to 11 percent of our landmass is set aside as protected areas (Dirzo and Loreau 2005). However, even protected areas suffer from our human need for survival and demands based on rich nations' greed for exotic and cheap resources. Encroachment into national parks or other protected areas by both local and commercial people is widespread (Cowlishaw 1999, Naughton-Treves et al. 2003). Population pressure often forces an unsustainable use of the environment in many parts of the world, especially but not exclusively, in poor developing countries. More often than not, there is a stark contrast between the denuded habitats outside and the lush habitats inside protected areas. For people who are struggling to make ends meet, it must be tempting to stray over these often invisible borders, borders that can seldom be protected or enforced.

The monitoring of forest habitats over the years by global imaging systems (e.g., Landsat) has revealed not only dramatic infringement into protected areas, but a worldwide destruction of forested areas, especially in tropical regions. It has been calculated that between 1990 and 1997, close to 6 million hectares (14.4 million acres) of humid tropical forest were destroyed each year (Achard et al. 2002). As an example, the lowland forest loss in Gunung Palung National Park (GPNP), West Kalimantan, Borneo, between 1985 and 2001 amounted to >29,000 km^2, or a loss of 56% of the forest (Curran et al. 2004). The implication of such a loss in such a short time is not yet understood, but GNPN is the home to an estimated fifth of Borneo's orangutan (*Pongo pygmaeus*) population. Orangutans are a highly nomadic species dependent on the forest for survival.

The deforestation within the Brazilian Amazon is also proceeding at an alarming rate, a rate that is on the increase (Nepstad et al. 1999). In the 1990s an estimated 1.7 million hectares (4.2 million acres) were destroyed each year, while in 2003 this number increased to 2.4 million hectares (5.9 million acres) (Fearnside and Barbosa 2004, Wright 2005). Along the Atlantic coast of Brazil and northern Argentina is a remnant swath of highly fragmented rain forest. Within this habitat are found 24 different kinds of monkeys, 14 of which are highly endangered and are found nowhere else. Even though the Brazilian government in 1988 declared the area a national heritage site, it continues to be destroyed, and today only about 7% remains of this rain forest. An estimated half a million hectares (1.2 million acres) are removed on a yearly basis, mainly for coffee plantations but also hardwood logging.

What can be done? First of all, the demands to destroy habitats must be reduced. This can be done by providing alternative means for local people to make a living without needing to encroach into preserved areas, or by finding ways to have conservation and the sustainable harvesting of ecosystems work together. This is now a major thrust in conservation policy. There are many so-called "green projects" underway. However, a number of projects, including some oil palm plantations, entail the cutting down of rain forest to plant managed forest farms, which really defeats the purpose (Redmond and Juniper 2005). On a personal level, we can all ensure that we do not in any way become consumers of forest products that may have been logged illegally or unnecessarily. We also need to increase the number of habitats that are officially protected in order to have better control over the usage of land and its resources. Reforestation is an option, but it would be a very long-term project since it would take many human generations before anything resembling a mature, primary rain forest would be achieved.

For conservationists, there is an additional problem because many of these preserved areas consist of scattered pieces of land, like isolated islands floating in a sea of human habitation. The primate inhabitants of these islands often become isolated from other conspecific populations. As a result, gene flow (the exchange of genes between populations) is reduced or stopped altogether, which can lead to **inbreeding depression** followed by extinction of the

> **inbreeding depression**—reduced reproductive success because breeding within a small population of closely related individuals may result in an increase in deleterious genes

isolated populations (Westermeier et al. 1998). Many conservation programs now focus on developing corridors between isolated habitat patches allowing animals the opportunity to move back and forth to find food and mates.

Timber companies are responsible, both directly and indirectly, for much of the destruction of the rain forests and the wildlife living within them because of the creation of roads into otherwise inaccessible areas. These roads not only provide avenues for further cultivation, but provide easier access by people such as commercial hunters. Money can be made by selling wildlife on the open and black markets as pets, to unscrupulous zoos, or as bushmeat.

What Is Bushmeat and How Does It Differ from Any Other Wild Game?

We refer to any meat caught while hunting wild animals living in a moist tropical habitat, or rain forest, as **bushmeat**, although some may prefer to call it wild meat (Milner-Gulland et al. 2003). In many ways it is no different from the hunting of wild animals anywhere. The hunting of wild game for food is something that the human species has done for many, many years, and even trading in bushmeat has a long tradition (Grubb et al. 1998). There are still many human societies throughout the world that sustain themselves by pursuing traditional means of acquiring food, such as the Alaskan Inuits and Canadian Nunavut Inuits who hunt whales, and the Australian aborigines who hunt a wide range of foods such as kangaroo and iguanas (Fallon and Enig 1999, Freeman et al. 1998). In most countries it is perfectly legal to hunt wild animals, although there may be some local restrictions on when hunting can take place, what species, and how many individuals can be harvested. The problem arises when there is a profit motive, when it is an endangered species that is being hunted, or when the prey species can no longer sustain a viable population. The productivity of tropical rain forest habitats, especially in cases of large mammal species, is relatively poor and therefore any excessive or indiscriminate harvesting may lead to a crisis and even to species' extinctions (Fa et al. 2006, Robinson and Bennett 2004).

Most of the present concern with the bushmeat crisis is focused on Africa, but the problem is by no means restricted to the African continent. The hunting and trading of bushmeat is now a global problem. It was first brought to our attention when the extinction rate of large mammalian species in Southeast Asia began to spiral out of control in the 1970s and 1980s (Robinson 2005). Since then the problem has spread to Africa, especially in West and Central Africa where the problem is most acute (Chapman et al. 2006, Cowlishaw et al. 2005, Fa et al. 2005). However, it has become apparent that East Africa is poised for a problem on an equal scale (Kiiru 2004, Nielsen 2006). Moreover, it is projected that the hunting of bushmeat in South America will soon reach a crisis point, unless something is done to redirect the trend (Molleson 2003).

Why do we have a crisis? It is because people are harvesting faster than the animal populations can replenish themselves. What is hunted and sold as bushmeat varies widely and includes anything from birds and rodents to elephants. It is usually the big prey species that are depleted first, such as tapirs and primates, and once they are no longer available, smaller species are harvested. In Africa, rodents, such as cane rats and porcupines, and hoofed animals, such as duikers and bushbucks, make up the largest proportion of the bushmeat sold in markets. Unfortunately, a very long list of primates including chimpanzees, bonobos, and gorillas are also included in the bushmeat markets (Figure 11-4). What is of great concern is the fact that many of the prey species, especially the primates, are on the IUCN Red List of endangered species (IUCN 2004). It is not only the hunting of endangered species that is a major concern, but the general overhunting of all species. The overhunting of a single species can cascade into a series of other species becoming endangered or even going extinct.

The bushmeat situation is a multifaceted problem. In part, it involves issues of finance and economics, but it also underscores a severe need to educate people about conservation and the real hazards associated with hunting and eating bushmeat. It is possible that bushmeat hunting would be less of a concern if it were only a matter of some indigenous peoples pursuing a traditional way of life. Unfortunately, the situation is not so simple or straightforward. In many instances, indigenous peoples who hunt meat for their own survival, either to eat themselves or to sell on the local market, do so because it is an economic necessity for their survival—so-called *subsistence hunting* (Robinson and Bennett 2002). Increasingly, the major threat comes from professional hunters who are tapping into a very lucrative economic market—*commercial hunting*. The commercial hunters usually take home the largest share of the profit, and a good hunter can earn as much or considerably more than a civil servant or a park ranger (Cowlishaw et al. 2005).

FIGURE 11-4 It is not uncommon to find primates for sale in local markets. The selection may include fresh prime adult male mandrills (top), or monkeys that have been prepared and smoked for better "shelf-life" (bottom).

These entrepreneurs sell not only to the local market but also to major cities in the country of origin, or even to markets throughout the world. If you want bushmeat, you are as likely to find it in New York or London as you are in any African capital (Brown 2006, Chapman et al. 2006). More often than not, it is the demand of the urban elite that is the driving force in this market.

To tackle the unsustainable trade in bushmeat, a two-prong approach is needed. First, we must remove or reduce the need or desire for such meat. This can in part be done by informing the consumer about the problems associated with the bushmeat trade. Alternative food sources must be identified—especially those that do not pose a damaging effect on the environment or the survival of the species in it. If the incentive structure is changed and if the *economic rewards* are no longer viable, then the floor would fall out of this market altogether. Second, for the people who are economically dependent on the bushmeat trade, *alternative strategies* for making a living must be put in place.

Who buys and eats bushmeat? In addition to supplementing local rural markets, a major portion of the bushmeat makes its way to markets in urban centers, and with today's easy access to transport, bushmeat reaches both national and international urban markets throughout the world. Do people prefer bushmeat? Surveys of people buying bushmeat at local markets show that some people prefer the taste of wild game, and for those people who have migrated to urban centers, it may be their only remaining link to their past. Bushmeat is often more expensive than domestic meat or fish, so some eat bushmeat because they can afford it and because it is tied to status and novelty. Many people do not care one way or the other and are only interested in finding a protein source. In many instances, the economic success of a bushmeat market is directly tied to the availability of other market sources. For example, if there is a fish market providing a good source for seafood, less bushmeat is sold (Wilkie et al. 2005).

Despite many legislative rulings and trading restrictions on the bushmeat trade, it is mostly supplied through illegal means, and it *is* flourishing. Even though there are clear laws and guidelines in place, and there are people on the ground willing to uphold these, the enforcement of the law can be difficult because of the many loopholes through which illegal trade can pass. This is in part due to poor infrastructure and a lack of support for the people who are supposed to enforce the law at the local level. Understaffing is often one of the major problems, but there is also a severe lack of supplies to use in the fight against "the bushmeat mafia," which is very well equipped. Furthermore, access to wildlife living in the rain forest is made easier for the hunters by timber companies that have created roads that go deep into otherwise inaccessible land (Figure 11-3). Sometimes it is the loggers themselves who buy meat from local hunters because they are then able to transport large quantities into cities without being detected. It is this kind of illegal trade that is so difficult to control but that *must* be stopped if there is going to be any hope of survival for the wildlife. Many conservation organizations are working directly with major timber companies in an attempt to stop all illegal hunting and trading of bushmeat.

There is a third aspect to the bushmeat trade that may be equally frightening—this involves the transmission of infectious diseases between wildlife and the humans who handle or eat the meat.

Epidemics and Transmissible Diseases

Cross-species transmission of diseases, so called **zoonoses**, holds a potential threat to us all. The news that we hear almost on a daily basis is filled with horror stories about some new potentially deadly virus having been found somewhere

> **zoonoses**—the transmission of infectious or non-infectious organisms between animals and humans

along our own food chain, e.g., the SARS (**S**evere **A**cute **R**espiratory **S**yndrome) virus in poultry, now often referred to as avian or bird flu, or other infectious agents that cause concern about our own survival, such as HIV/AIDS and Ebola.

We must not forget, as is the case with SARS and HIV, that viruses have a life of their own. Viruses, bacteria, and other parasites are struggling for survival just as much as any other living thing. Organisms such as viruses need a host species for survival and transmission, which usually entails direct contact between a host and a potential host. There is a very long list of viruses that are harbored in nonhuman primates and other wild animals that may cause illness in humans who come into contact with them, such as the Hepatitis B virus.

Until recently, it was thought that very few pathogens crossed species' borders. With more extensive research and monitoring we now know that zoonotic transmission is actually quite common. Even though most of the zoonotic organisms are harmless or can easily be treated, there are many organisms that are deadly. In most cases, the infectious organisms are harmless in the reservoir or host species, but as they cross into a novel species they may become virulent or extremely infectious. For example, the simian immunodeficiency virus (SIV) is harmless to humans, but a mutated form of SIV is responsible for the human immunodeficiency virus, which is the cause of AIDS. Organizations such as the Centers for Disease Control (CDC) and World Health Organization (WHO) continuously monitor for new or mutated forms of potentially infectious diseases.

When the human immunodeficiency virus (HIV) was first isolated in the early 1980s, it was not known that this virus had jumped across species. The form of HIV that has become a pandemic scourge is now recognized as having originated from West African chimpanzees, while the less common and less virulent form, HIV2, is believed to come from the sooty mangabey (*Cercocebus torquatus*) (Gao et al. 1999, Santiago et al. 2003). Today we are well aware of the fact that most wild African primate species are carriers of SIV, yet it does not appear to cause illness in its wild primate hosts (Jolly et al. 1996, Silvestri 2005), and most people who have been infected by SIV do not show any ill effects.

What should worry us more is that SIV belongs to a large, highly varied family of **retroviruses**, which includes the Ebola virus. It is impossible to predict whether a virus will mutate and become infectious or even deadly, as has happened with the Ebola virus. The human Ebola virus causes hemorrhagic fever and has a mortality rate of 80 to 90 percent. Ebola outbreaks are usually localized and appear abruptly. The virus is readily transmitted, and we know that transmission can occur by handling infected bushmeat and through human–human contact (Leroy et al. 2004, Rouquet et al. 2005). The Ebola virus is just as deadly to chimpanzees and gorillas, as well as other primates, as it is to humans. Therefore, we know that these species are not the reservoir for this virus, and the source of the virus remains unknown, but bat species have been suggested as a potential reservoir (Leroy et al. 2005).

The transmission of infectious agents through the hunting and processing of wild meat is of grave concern. Through careful monitoring, it has been discovered that many bushmeat hunters carry a variety of viruses found only in wild species. Of special concern are the different types of simian retroviruses that have been discovered in bushmeat hunters (Wolfe et al. 2004, 2005). Even though these viruses do not presently cause disease, they are just as likely as SIV to mutate into a deadly form. Control of the bushmeat trade is, of course, one means of restraining potential zoonotic infections. It is also important to make hunters understand the dangers and the fact that they should not under any circumstances collect dead animals to sell or eat themselves.

It is not only humans that are at risk; the wild animals may also suffer. Research has shown that primate populations that come into contact with humans or are inhabiting areas disturbed by humans (e.g., logging areas), suffer from an increase in parasite infections compared to primate populations living in undisturbed environments (Chapman et al. 2005a, Gillespie and Chapman 2006, Gillespie et al. 2005, and Chapter 6). The recent report of the death of at least six chimpanzees in the Taï National Park, Côte d'Ivoire, has been attributed to the anthrax bacterium (Leendertz et al. 2004). Even though anthrax occurs globally, it is unusual to find it outside of areas where domestic animals occur. The source of the anthrax that killed the Taï chimpanzees remains unknown, but it has been suggested that transporting cattle on roads created by logging companies that pass close to the Taï National Park is the cause.

Ecotourism has added to the problem of transmitting germs across species' borders. Well-meaning tourists who pay large amounts of money to see endangered species in the wild have been responsible for the transmission of pathogens to the very animals they seek to save. In the 1980s there was an epidemic of respiratory symptoms with many fatalities among mountain gorilla populations. It was discovered that the gorillas had elevated levels of antibodies to measles, and the most likely source of introduction was a human carrier. This incident highlights potential problems with ecotourism and what can happen when humans come into close contact with wild animals (Figure 11-5). Most ecotourism companies now have very strict rules, and only healthy individuals are allowed to go on tour; often there is a minimum age requirement to prevent the introduction and spread of human childhood diseases. Of course, it is not only transmission between humans and wild animals or vice versa that is of concern. Animals kept as pets, in zoos, and in other institutions can carry potentially dangerous pathogens that can be easily transmitted to their handlers. This is why zoos attempt to keep a great distance or a glass wall between their animals and the public to ensure that pathogens are not exchanged.

The Primate Pet Trade

The trade in wild and exotic animals is flourishing in the United States and elsewhere in the world. Primates, reptiles, and birds are among the most popular "pets," but the list of species kept as pets is much more extensive than this. It includes anything from monkeys, wolves, tigers, chameleons, and iguanas to many different kinds of exotic birds

FIGURE 11-5 In the Bwindi Forest Reserve, Uganda, a middle school science teacher observes a group of mountain gorillas. The ecotourism groups were restricted to 10 healthy adults and contact with the gorillas was limited to no more than 60 minutes.

FIGURE 11-6 The trade in wild and exotic animals is common everywhere. Primates are often traded either as pets or for food. What ever the reason, many primates are suffering at the hands of humans.

(Figure 11-6). Even poisonous snakes have been found in private homes. Why would anyone want to own a wild animal? A natural fascination for the wild and exotic may be part of the reason, or there may be deep-rooted desires to communicate with nature. There may also be more sinister reasons at play such as the desire to dominate and be in control, possibly contributing to a "macho" image. Frequently, the animals are used as a status symbol and sometimes primates are treated as substitute children.

Without doubt, many of these wild animals are fascinating. It may not be so difficult to understand why some people would like to have a monkey as a pet; they look cute and cuddly, they act in ways that look appealingly human, they appear to be so smart, and their antics always seem funny. However, wild animals *do not* make good pets. This includes primates, and as any primatologist would be quick to confirm, primates simply *are not* good pets! Primates are wild animals. Even a primate born in captivity is essentially a wild animal. They follow the rules of nature instilled in them over generations upon generations of survival in the wild. They cannot be "tamed" by us humans. They require special foods, housing, and care, and it is not possible to house train a primate. Maybe even more important, they have complex needs. Primates are highly social animals that need interaction with conspecifics in order to grow into normal and healthy individuals, especially in the case of baby primates who need their mothers to care for them at least until they are weaned. In addition, primates are competitive by nature, and most species that are kept as "pets" naturally form dominance hierarchies. As the cute and cuddly infant monkey grows up, it will begin its struggle up the dominance hierarchy, and usually the first to suffer are the human children, followed by the rest of the family members. The unpredictable and aggressive behaviors that these primates start to display often take an owner by surprise. To reduce the chance of injury by primates, owners often have their pet's teeth extracted and may even have their nails surgically removed. Despite these alterations, a monkey can still inflict severe damage on a human. Not only do even small juvenile monkeys have the physical strength equivalent to that of an athletic man, but they also have the agility to act with lightning speed and may have bitten their victim several times before he or she can react (see Box 11-1).

❖ ❖ ❖ ❖   BOX 11-1   ❖ ❖ ❖ ❖

A Focus on the Pet Trade and Other Illegal Trapping

Most people who seek to have a primate pet are looking for cute and cuddly infants. These people often cannot have children of their own and seek a substitute child, or in other cases, they are looking for a companion to their own child. Little thought is devoted to what these infant primates will grow into and what needs and demands they will have as adults. The unpredictability of an adult primate is well known. The only defense these pets have is to bite, and bite they do often causing severe injuries to their owners. Since many are illegally owned, owners seldom seek help as it may result in the confiscation of the pet and euthanasia, as well as heavy fines.

The presence of a primate pet is usually not revealed until there is some sort of accident, an animal escapes, or it becomes ill and has to visit a veterinarian. Even though veterinarians do not have a legal responsibility to inform authorities, many do because they care about the welfare of the animals as well the owners.

Most owners find that as the cute little monkey grows up, they can no longer take care of it, and it ends up confined in backyard cages or basements. Human-reared primates lack survival skills and can therefore not be returned to the wild. Zoos do not have the capacity to care for unwanted wild animal pets. There are a few organizations that have

been established just to care for such animals, e.g., Wild Animal Orphanage, The Primate Sanctuary of the United States, and the Captive Wild Animal Protection Coalition. However, they are often bursting at the seams with rejected pets and cannot accept new ones, which often leads to the reselling of a pet to an illegal exotic pet market. If you come across an exotic or wild animal kept as a pet, contact the Humane Society (HSUS). They will know what to do. Never try to approach a primate that is freely running about on your own.

It is not only whole, live animals that are traded. There is a very lucrative market involving specific parts of animals— e.g., penis bone of tigers, bile from bears, **bezoar stones** from langurs, and horns from rhinoceros. The list of animals and parts used is quite long and many of the represented species are endangered. Animal parts are used as ingredients in traditional medicines commonly used in most Asian countries. In addition to medicinal uses, it is believed that some of these items have magical or aphrodisiac powers. To what extent traditional medicines actually work is disputed, but as long as there are people who believe that they do, the demand will drive the market. The ease with which animals can be hunted today with high-powered and accurate rifles make it almost impossible

(continued)

for targeted animals to escape and makes it easy to supply the demand. It is a lucrative market with high monetary return for hunters and traders alike, and as a result certain animals are decimated at an alarming rate.

The belief that bezoar stones have magical power has a deep history. There are records that the ancient Persians traded these very valuable stones, which were considered the best antidote for all sorts of poisons. Bezoar stones are calculous concretions formed in the stomach and intestines of certain animals, such as wild goats, gazelles, antelopes, and deer. They can occasionally be found in leaf-eating monkeys. It is estimated that no more than 1 to 10 percent of all individuals do actually carry bezoar stones. Some highly endangered langur species are close to being wiped out due to the demand for this commodity. The Hose's langur (*Presbytis hosei*), endemic

to East Borneo, is showing an alarming drop in numbers due to excessive hunting (Nijman 2005). The only way to save these species is to remove the demand for these products since it is almost impossible to stop the hunting.

In countries where primates occur naturally, there is also a tradition of having pet baby primates as part of the family, much like we in the West have cats and dogs. In tourist areas it is common to see hawkers with a captive primate on a leash to attract tourists, either to directly request support for the primate (or even offer to sell it), but more commonly they offer to photograph tourists with the monkey (Figure 11-7). It may be difficult to resist the opportunity to handle a primate but to discourage this kind of treatment of wild primates, it is necessary to resist temptation and not to give the vendor encouragement to continue this practice.

FIGURE 11-7 Primate babies are often used as tourist attractions (left), or where humans and monkeys share the habitat, wild primates may not be too shy to interact with people such as this juvenile Barbary macaque (*Macaca sylvanus*) on Gibraltar (right).

It is not only aggressive and unpredictable behaviors by pet monkeys that may cause problems. Most pet primates carry various types of zoonotic diseases. These may not cause the primate any discomfort, but may be very dangerous to the human owner. Viral diseases such as herpes and monkeypox are common, as are parasitic diseases, and lice, mites, and fleas, which can be transmitted during contact. It is believed that 80 to 90 percent of all adult macaques kept in captivity carry the simian Herpes B virus, a virus that is deadly to humans.

Since it is now illegal to import primates without a special licence, where do these animals come from? How do they enter the pet trade market? It may surprise you to find out that many pet primates come from sales by zoos and other institutions where primate research is conducted (AESOP Project 2006). Less than half of the states in the United States actually have legislation that bans the private ownership of monkeys and apes (see Table 11-1). However, several states are in the process of passing into law a ban on trading in nonhuman primates [HI, NC, SC, and OR] (Pet Monkey Info 2007). There is presently an attempt to close down all loopholes in the law and enforce a blanket ruling that NO primates are to be allowed as privately owned pets. In the meantime, there is much smuggling across state borders, and if anyone desires a pet primate, there are many avenues open. Fortunately, primates are expensive to buy, limiting who can afford them, but this also provides an incentive to the initial traders because they may make a 2,000 percent profit (Redmond 2006).

Canned and Trophy Hunting

People have created yet another avenue for the disposal of unwanted animals—they can be sold to so-called game ranches. These game ranches are stocked with wild and usually exotic animals, providing the opportunity for trophy hunting without the danger or the hassle of going abroad. Hunters pay a hefty sum to shoot an animal of their choice, an animal that has no chance of escape as it is trapped in an enclosure. Many of the animals provided for these hunts are former "pets" that have been hand-reared and often are not fearful of humans. The most highly desired trophies are the more charismatic large game species such as leopards, lions, tigers, bears, moose, or bison, but the list of species available is much more extensive than this.

There is no federal law that prohibits these activities, and the Animal and Welfare Act does not regulate game preserves or canned hunts. The majority of states allow them or at least turn a blind eye to these activities. Trophy hunting is a subculture supported by a wealthy elite, many of whom belong to the Safari Club International, which, among other things, promotes wildlife conservation through controlled culling (see www.safariclub.org). Even though organizations such as the Humane Society of United States (HSUS) have

TABLE 11-1 State Laws Regarding Private Possession of Nonhuman Primates

Restrictions	States	Total
Ban	CA, CO, CT, IA, GA, KY, LA, MA, MD, ME, MN, NH, NJ, NM, NY, PA, RI, UT, VT, WA, WY	21
Partial Ban	AK, AZ, FL, IN, MS, TN, TX	7
Require Permit	DE, IO, MI, OK, OR, SD	6
Must be Bonded	HI	1
No Requirements	AL, AR, IL, KS, MO, MT, NC, ND, NE, NV, OH, SC, VA, WI, WV	15

tried to close down these activities, the pro-hunting lobby is a strong and powerful group. However, a ban of canned hunts within the United States will only fuel the market elsewhere. Many countries, especially in Africa, directly or indirectly support trophy hunting because it is a market that provides a substantial source of income. It is common that such trophy hunts, which often are canned, are advertised as being part of a conservation program (see e.g., Lindsey et al. 2006). However, by definition trophy hunting entails the killing of prime adult male animals, and often it is rare and endangered species that are targeted.

In 2003 Congress passed the Captive Wildlife Act, which bars interstate trade in big cats such as lions and tigers for the pet trade. In March 2005 a new bill, The Captive Primate Safety Bill (H.R. 1329) was introduced with the intent to impose a similar regulation on all captive primates. However, this bill was buried in various subcommittees and did not pass. The pressure to act has now become acute due to the increased popularity in privately owned primates, followed by a dramatic increase in injuries caused by these "pets." In July 2007 a new bill was introduced to the Congress (H.R. 2964) which aims to impose a ban on trade in nonhuman primates without special license. This bill does not, however, ban the possession of nonhuman primates (HSUS, Pet Monkey Info).

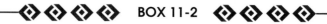

◇◇ ◇◇ ◇◇ ◇◇ BOX 11-2 ◇◇ ◇◇ ◇◇ ◇◇

Conservation—What You Can Do to Help: A Letter from a Volunteer

In 2003, I went to Camp Leakey as a volunteer with the Orangutan Foundation International's conservation program. Camp Leakey, situated within Tanjung Puting National Park, Indonesian Borneo, is an established research and rehabilitation site for orangutans set up in the 1970s by Dr. Birute Galdikas. Every year the Orangutan Foundation International sends four groups of ten to twelve volunteers to help in and around Camp Leakey during the dry season. The tasks involved vary from maintaining the infrastructure of Camp Leakey and the associated release sites to working to prevent and reduce levels of illegal logging within the park. The Orangutan Foundation employs local Indonesian assistants who are vital to the running and success of Camp Leakey. Not only do they undertake research activities, care for the orangutans, and build and maintain the necessary infrastructure, they

guard the River Sekonyer to prevent wood from being transported along the river ways, and patrol the forest looking for evidence of illegal logging activity.

My partner Chris and I spent six weeks with eight other volunteers from Britain, Canada, and the United States. Our main task was to help the Indonesian assistants construct a patrol post on the River Sekonyer. We also undertook maintenance work around Camp Leakey, (Figure 11-8a) repairing damage caused by the boisterous activities of the ex-captive orangutans who alternate their time between the forest and Camp Leakey. We worked and lived on the patrol post as we were building it. It was amazing to sleep under the stars and see the beautiful birds and proboscis monkeys playing in the trees around us. Once finished with building the patrol post, we spent the final week at Camp Leakey helping to complete the Education Center.

(a)

(b)   (c)

FIGURE 11-8   (a) Volunteers at Camp Leakey help out with mending and building platforms where the orangutans are provided with food. (b) Some of the orangutans can be rather pesky. Siswi, a dominant female, has taken a volunteer's sleep sheet to use as a hammock. (c) An orangutan is examining the contents of a first aid kit, and is finding the bandage rolls especially fascinating.

(continued)

We learned quickly not to leave *anything* lying around. Orangutans are very inquisitive and quick to identify an opportunity to acquire hammers, saws, and paint, so they can show off their carpentry and artistic prowess. They are quick learners with a penchant for chocolate or any other edible (or in some cases inedible) morsel they can consume. A firm favorite appears to be soap, making a wash on the jetty quite a challenge. Sometimes an orangutan would come down and just eat your soap. At other times they would come and wash your clothes. The clothes washing would have been greatly appreciated if Siswi, the dominant female, had not used another girl's expensive mint hair and body wash, then squashed a banana into my sarong during one of these washing events. It also became clear that if you had something they wanted, they were going to have it! My cotton sleep sheet, blackcurrant electrolyte drink in a red mug, and first aid kit are examples of the things taken to be explored and used for play. Siswi turned the cotton sleep sheet into a hammock (Figure 11-8b). It seems the red mug was the actual target but the electrolyte solution went down well. My first aid kit was not exactly stolen—it was used as a bargaining tool when an orangutan grabbed my arm and did not want to let go (Figure 11-8c). My partner Chris used the first aid kit to entice the orangutan to let go, sort of a "first aid kit vs. Diana" hostage negotiations in the forest . . . and it worked!

The orangutans are just as keen to observe us as we are them. Unfortunately, being stared at whilst one utilises a "squat" toilet can be quite unnerving when all that secures the door is a one-by two- inch piece of wood. Despite this, I really enjoyed my time at Camp Leakey and hope that my contribution will add to the survival of the orangutans. I have continued to be a member of the Orangutan Foundation, and I am alarmed to hear that Dr. Galdikas and several wildlife organizations have predicted the total extinction of these wonderful apes, our cousins, within the next ten years. There is need for much more proactive assistance in the preservation of the habitat to ensure the survival of our beautiful red cousin. Signed—Diana Swales

◈◈ Conservation

The aim of conservation is to ensure that natural habitats and species do not go extinct due to our misuse of the world. It is also a way to provide more pristine environments for us humans to visit and enjoy. The underlying problem is the increasing need and competition for space, food, and other resources. There are always discussions and controversy in the case of most conservation programs, and more often than not a delicate balance between preservation and human needs must be achieved. Our own needs usually supersede that of other species. Few people have the foresight to consider what human needs will be in a generation or two into the future. It is often stated that it is the rich nations that can afford conservation projects while poorer nations do not have such a luxury. However is conservation really a luxury? The world we live in is an intricate web of life where all species are dependent on the survival of each other. Hopefully, we will recognize that we need nature and all its inhabitants for our own survival before it is too late.

Conservation in the Wild

As the human population keeps increasing, the requirements for survival are causing an ever-increasing pressure on all earth's environments. The demand for more land has led to increased pressure on other animals, and many ecosystems are under threat. The survival of an ever-increasing number of species is being threatened, with many being on the brink of extinction. To alleviate these problems and to stop species from going extinct, various approaches to protect threatened and endangered species have been implemented. Initial protection measures focused on key species such as pandas, tigers, elephants, and chimpanzees. By protecting such **keystone** or **flagship species**, it was envisioned that other species would benefit as well, a so-called trickle-down effect. For example, the World Wide Fund for Nature (WWF, formerly known as World Wildlife Fund) was established in September 1961, and its emblem is still the giant panda. Even though keystone species are still important in formulating conservation programs, there is now greater emphasis on the preservation of specific habitats or whole ecosystems.

During the twentieth century, nature reserves, national parks, and wildlife sanctuaries were established all over the globe in an attempt to protect the most vulnerable species from extinction. The establishment of national parks and other preserves entailed the loss of areas that had been traditionally used by local peoples for farming and the grazing of domestic animals as well as for the harvesting of firewood. Such activities involved well-established traditional lifestyles and the expulsion of people from these lands. The prohibition of their use caused intense resentment and conflict. Many people were thus displaced. They could not see why their land should be taken away from them and why some outsiders should have the power to bar them from their traditional land and way of life. Little attention was paid to the people who were excluded or to their plight. These people were more often than not poor people—made even more destitute by the loss of land.

Due to intense resentment on both local and national levels, this type of "fortress" attitude in which people are excluded from certain areas in the name of conservation, is being abandoned (Brockington 2002). Instead, there is now a move toward a mixed use of the land so that, for example, domestic animals and wildlife live side by side (Figure 11-9). Of course, such a regime brings its own unique set of problems, especially where domestic animals and wild animals come into direct contact. Cross-species transmission of diseases occurs and can have devastating effects. In Africa, for example, the wild dogs and lions of the Serengeti acquired the distemper virus from domestic dogs (Alexander and Appel 1994, Ginsberg et al. 1995). The wild dog population in East Africa has been decimated by the distemper virus, and the species has become locally extinct. An extensive vaccination program in the Serengeti region is underway to try to stop the spread of distemper and save the remaining wild dogs. However, not everyone is in support of vaccinating wild animals because we do not yet know what the long-term consequences will be.

Most conservation projects are paid for through donation by well-meaning individuals, as well as aid programs from rich Western countries. Many alternative ways to infuse money into conservation projects have been tried in addition to the richer nations' providing aid. However, most of these approaches have left local people no more the richer as profits seldom trickle down. A major problem is that local people are rarely involved in such endeavors. It has become increasingly apparent that in order for

FIGURE 11-9 In East Africa wherever there are limited resources domestic and wild animals may be found together. Historically, however, humans seldom accepted this type of coexistence. At Sinya in northern Tanzania, cattle are using the same watering holes as zebras and other wildlife.

conservation efforts to ultimately be successful, they must include the participation and investment of the people who will be directly affected by these efforts. Over the last couple of decades, people involved in conservation research have suggested a new approach, one that has grown out of dissention with traditional strategies. There is now a much stronger focus on **partnerships** between countries and between people. Local people are made responsible for the care of the reserves or parks and the profits gained from tourism, for example, are shared. By empowering the local people, they receive the rewards and gain pride for their own backyard.

◈ ◈ ◈ ◈ HOT TOPICS 11-2 ◈ ◈ ◈ ◈

Reintroduction Programs

There is much controversy about the effectiveness of reintroduction programs: Are they really accomplishing what they were intended to do and are these programs cost effective? Is it worth saving species at the brink of extinction? How much effort and money should be devoted to a species that may stand a very low chance of long-term survival? In addition, how viable is it to introduce former pets and other captive primates into the wild? What are their chances of survival and of becoming successful reproductive individuals in the wild? The controversy surrounding the reintroduction of captive animals into their natural habitats is in part based on the limited success and problems experienced with some programs (Bennett 1992, Yeager 1997). Many conservationists believe that it is better to invest in saving habitats and larger, more viable species or populations. There are several reasons, however, why reintroduction programs may be a very good option. The introduced individuals can boost the local gene pool by providing more genetic diversity and so can prevent inbreeding depression. In addition, reintroduction programs always go hand in hand with the protection and improvement of the local habitat and bring educational opportunities that inform local people about how precious these resources are to the world.

There are numerous sanctuaries established all over the world that take care of confiscated primates. The goal of these sanctuaries is to reintroduce all individuals to the wild that appear to stand a chance of survival on their own. Examples of such sanctuaries include the Orangutan rehabilitation in Tanjung Putting National Park, Indonesia, where orangutans are cared for and reintroduced to the wild (Yeager 1997, see also Box 11-2); HELP (*Habitat Ecologique et Liberté des Primates*) in the Congo where orphaned chimpanzees have found a caring home awaiting reintroduction (Farmer 2002, Goossen et al. 2005); and CERCOPAN located in Nigeria, which cares primarily for guenons and mangabeys that have been rescued from bushmeat hunters. Most sanctuaries are run by highly dedicated volunteers and people who care about the survival of primates. Much time and effort is devoted to the care and training of each individual to prepare it for a life on its own in the natural environment. Most of these sanctuaries have long surpassed their maximum operating capacities, and reintroduction success rates are highly variable. This is in part because the animals that enter these sanctuaries have endured many hardships that have left deep scars. They may be socially impaired and, when released, may often enter a habitat filled with the same

type of danger as the place from which they were captured.

There are an increasing number of projects in which captive-bred endangered species are reintroduced into their natural habit. Many of these show promising success. For example, the Madagascar Fauna Group has since 1997 released captive-bred black and white ruffed lemurs (*Varecia variegata variegata*) on the Betampona Reserve in eastern Madagascar (Britt et al. 2004). It is estimated that around 40 percent have survived to the present. Even more encouraging is that some of the released individuals have joined and mated with wild conspecifics, showing that they can integrate well in the wild.

One of the most successful reintroduction programs so far is the Golden Lion Tamarin Conservation Program (GLTCP), a multinational and multidisciplinary project (Kleiman and Mallinson 1998, Kleiman and Rylands 2002). The first reintroduction of golden lion tamarins (*Leontopithecus rosalia rosalia*) took place in 1984 (Beck et al. 1991, Stoinski et al. 2003). To date, more than 400 individuals have been introduced, and there are now several generations of wild-born offspring that are the descendants of released individuals.

The golden lion tamarin (GLT) is endemic to the Atlantic coastal forest in Brazil (see Box 11-3). Today, we find the GLT scattered in forest fragments in the state of Rio de Janeiro but it is thought that they were once much more widely distributed within this costal rain forest. The reintroductions have taken place onto privately owned lands and usually away from naturally occurring groups to reduce competition. The project's objectives, as with all other reintroduction programs, are

(continued)

to increase the size of the wild populations and to increase the genetic diversity of the species, to improve the conservation of the natural habitats, and to introduce educational programs for people in the surrounding area, especially the ranch owners.

Monitoring and behavioral observations of the released individuals have shown that the survival rate of these animals is variable and in general lower than that of wild conspecifics (Kleiman and Rylands 2002, Stoinski et al. 2003). The released individuals are not familiar with their new habitat, and some show poor foraging ability; they spend much more time than individuals who have remained in the wild finding sufficient and the right kind of food (some have even died because they ate poisonous seeds). The released individuals appear not to be as agile, and some have had fatal falls (Beck et al. 2002). In addition, for some yet unknown reason, the survival rate of the released individuals' offspring is lower than that of the offspring of wild conspecifics (Beck et al. 2002). Still, the bottom line is that the conservation of wild GLT, their habitat, and the reintroduction program have been so successful that in 2003, IUCN was able to downgrade the GLT from being *critically* endangered to being endangered. However, we cannot be content with this success, and much more effort is required before we can say that this species is once again safe within its natural habitat. We need to ensure that there is sufficient protected habitat available for further reintroductions since some areas have reached a saturation point, and there is no more protected habitat available into which to introduce more groups. Furthermore, despite all the conservation efforts, tamarins are not totally protected from threats such as habitat destruction, hunting, and the illegal pet trade. Despite this initial success, we cannot be complacent; there is much more that needs to be done to ensure the survival of all the endangered primate species found throughout the world. The financial costs accrued by primate sanctuaries and reintroduction programs may appear great; however, doing nothing may cost us a great deal more. Therefore, the struggle for the survival of our fellow primates needs to be continued.

Conservation in Captivity

Gone are the days when the main aim of zoos was to exhibit exotic wild animals to the general public. The animals were then kept in small, bare concrete enclosures with a barred front so they could be easily viewed (Figure 11-10). In the second half of the twentieth century, all major zoos went through a radical change. All the bare concrete stalls and chain fences were replaced with larger and more naturalistic enclosures. Today, the aims of zoos are much more multifaceted. Zoos are no longer just a place for people to come and view exotic animals. They are places where the public has the opportunity not only to observe the animals, but also to learn about them—where they are found, what kind of habitat they prefer, what they eat, and so on. In addition, general information about each species' behavior is usually provided.

Most zoos pay close attention to the needs of each individual species. Whenever possible, something akin to the species' natural habitat is reconstructed and included in a display (Figure 11-11). In some zoos, there are even mixed species exhibits in which

FIGURE 11-10 Fortunately, old fashioned small cages surrounded by metal bars and with a cement floor are no longer common in most zoo settings (top), but occasionally it is possible to find primates, such as these anubis baboons (*Papio anubis*) having to endure cramped and monotonous surroundings (bottom).

several species that occur naturally are exhibited together, but of course prey and predators are never put together. Animals are given sufficient space so they can move around and get exercise. Some animals are naturally shy, and being exposed to visitors all of the time produces undue stress. Therefore, enclosures often contain secluded areas where an animal can go and hide. Animals may also need to hide from one another as well. Managers of zoos have to constantly juggle the well-being of the animals with the demands of the public to be able to view the animals.

Even though many zoos have a set of "required" species on display, such as tigers, lions, giraffes, chimpanzees, lemurs, and bears, an increasing number of zoos are now actively involved in conservation and breeding programs. Each zoo tends to focus on one or several endangered species, which act as keystone species for the zoo. Some zoos, such as the St. Louis Zoological Park, have employees who are keepers of International Studbooks in which the matings of captive animals and resulting offspring

FIGURE 11-11 Many zoos attempt to create enclosures for their animals that provide a more natural feel. In this spider monkey enclosure, space is successfully used in three dimensions by including ropes and nets.

are meticulously tracked, enabling the institutions that hold members of the same species, such as black lemurs (*Eulemur macaco macaco*), to monitor and control genetic frequencies in captive populations. The purpose is in part to ensure survival of the species, at least in a captive situation. There are also active **breeding programs**, where endangered species are maintained to ensure that their gene pool does not disappear, and by increasing a captive population, there is potential to reintroduce the species to the wild.

Reintroduction of captive animals, specifically raised to be brought back to their natural habitat, can be done either to replenish a fading population by improving the gene pool or to repopulate areas where there has been local extinction. However, these animals have never known anything but captivity and must therefore be carefully trained to recognize what is dangerous and to be able to defend themselves against both predators and conspecifics. They need to learn where to find food and what in nature is edible and what is poisonous. One of the very successful reintroduction programs is the golden lion tamarin (*Leontopithecus rosalia*) conservation program managed by The National Zoo, in conjunction with other zoos all over the globe. Over four-hundred individuals have been reintroduced over the past twenty years to privately owned ranches located in the Atlantic Coastal Rainforest (see Hot Topics 11-2). In conjunction with these reintroduction programs is the need to educate the local people and make them understand the need for conserving and protecting these endangered animals (Matsuo 2005).

There are numerous *rescue* and *rehabilitation* projects in which confiscated primates and former pets are taken into care, and when possible, reacclimatized to a life in the wild, e.g., Borneo Orangutan Survival Foundation and Orangutan Foundation International started by Dr. Biruté Galdikas (see the AESOP Project and CERCOPAN for further organizations involved in conservation, rescue, and reintroduction). To achieve success with such projects can be difficult since the animals may never have spent much time in the wild and may have gained idiosyncratic behavioral patterns due to their close contact with humans. It is therefore necessary to train each individual such that it will be able to survive in the wild. Such training may take years to complete. Similar to the reintroduction programs, it is important that the animals are set free in areas where they will be as safe as possible and where they will be able to settle into a life in the wild. Another major problem, especially for those that have grown up as pets, is that they are not afraid of humans. In such cases, they may seek out human habitation and end up in worse trouble than before.

Sometimes it may be necessary to remove individuals or whole groups of primates from an area because their survival is jeopardized. They may have become crop raiders and are being shot by angry humans, or their habitat is being lost due to human development. The only hope for such primates may be **translocation** (i.e., the removal from one area where they are vulnerable to another area within their historical range; IUCN 2002). Translocation of threatened and endangered species has been used quite successfully for many American primates, for example, black howlers (*Alouatta pigra*), golden lion tamarins (*Leontopithecus rosalia*), and black lion tamarins (*L. chrysopygus*) (Kleiman and Rylands 2002). Perhaps one of the most complex and successful ventures was the removal of several troops of baboons comprising over 100 individuals, because they had become such successful crop raiders and were consequently threatened with extermination (Strum 2005). The Gilgil baboons, including the Pumphouse Gang, initially studied by among others Shirley Strum and Bob Harding (Strum 1987), were captured and transported over 200 km (124 mi). The habitat to which they were transferred was much more arid and prone to droughts, but considered to be the best choice to ensure no future conflicts with human farmers. Now, twenty years later, the translocated baboons have survived well and even thrive in their new home (Strum 2005), lending support to translocation as a viable option in the quest for conservation.

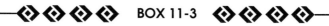

❖❖❖❖ BOX 11-3 ❖❖❖❖

The Mata Atlantica Biodiversity Hotspot

The Atlantic forest (Mata Atlantica) is located along the southeast coast (including many islands) of Brazil down to northern Argentina and Paraguay. Today, only a small fraction of this once vast and majestic rain forest, which at one time covered the whole coastal mountain range, survives. Exploitation of this coastal forest region began with the arrival of the Europeans, with high demand for timber not just locally but also in Europe. The most intense destruction began during the nineteenth century when much forest was cleared for large coffee plantations. After close to 500 years of destructive harvesting, the forest has become highly fragmented with many areas covering no more than 50 hectares (approximately 124 acres). Presently, it is estimated that less than 7 percent of the original forest survives and of this, less than 1 percent is considered pristine (Ribon et al. 2003). The northeastern part of Mata Atlantica is the most severely threatened, as less than 2 percent of the original forest still stands (da Silva and Tabarelli 2001). It has become one of the most endangered ecosystems in the world, and the reason why we should care is that it is one of the richest areas with enormous biodiversity, a so-called biodiversity hotspot (Myers et al. 2000).

(continued)

The Mata Atlantica region comprises highly diverse ecosystems, because it stretches over great longitude (from $2°50'$ to $33°45'S$) as well as altitude (from 0 to 2897m). It includes coastal sand dunes, salt marshes and mangrove swamps, upland grass plains, and humid tropical evergreen, semi-deciduous and pine forests. According to Conservation International (CI), the Atlantic forest of Brazil ranks as the fifth most important Global Biodiversity Hotspot for conservation, and in 1999 it was designated a World Heritage Site (UNEP-WCMC). The area supports a vast diversity of animals as well as plants. Many of the animals are endemic to the region. There are a number of endangered species of primates living there, but also there are many bird species and other flora and fauna in need of intense protection (Conservation International 2007, Myers et al. 2000).

Part of the problem is that Mata Atlantica is the most densely populated area of Brazil. Over 100 million people live here, which is 70 percent of the population. Urbanization is one of the major threats, with cities like Sao Paulo and Rio de Janeiro adding to the strains on the surrounding habitat. In addition to urban developments, human activity is extensive throughout the area. Cattle ranching and cultivation (mainly coffee and sugar cane plantations) have resulted in a highly fragmented habitat (Dean 1995). In addition, logging of the remaining forest is extensive, although many projects are now based on sustainable harvest.

There is a highly diverse fauna present in Mata Atlantica, but many mammals, especially larger species, are in danger of extinction within the region, e.g., the lowland tapir (*Tapirus terrestris*) and white-lipped peccary (*Tayassu pecari*), as are most of the endemic primate species. It is not only habitat loss and forest fragmentation that is the cause of the dwindling numbers of animals, most are still being hunted (Costa et al. 2005). Even though there are carnivores present (e.g., puma, jaguar, and bush dog, *Spethos venaticus*), they are rare. Carnivores need large home ranges, which is usually not supported by the fragmented Atlantic forest. In this densely populated region, roaming carnivores are often involved in vehicle collisions. The Atlantic forest contains more than 75 percent of Brazil's endangered bird species (Marini and Garcia 2005). Some of the larger bird species have already gone extinct in the wild (e.g., razor-billed curassow, *Mitu [Crax] mitu,* and the Spix's macaw, *Cyanopsitta spixii*), while others are threatened especially due to a prolific illegal international pet trade, for which macaws and parrots are especially targeted (Wright et al. 2001).

This remnant coastal forest region is home to twenty-four primate taxa (Figure 11-12, Table 3-3). The primates comprise 40 percent of the endemic species and most are highly endangered (Costa et al. 2005, IUCN 2004). Among the endemic species present in the Mata Atlantica are four species of lion tamarin (*Leontopithecus caissara, L. rosalia, L. chrysomelas,* and *L. chrysopygus*), two species of muriqui (*Brachyteles hypoxanthus, B. arachnoides*), two species of titi monkey (*Callicebus coimbrai, C. barbarabrownae*), three species of marmosets (*Callithrix aurita, C. flaviceps, C. kuhlii*), the bare-faced tamarin (*Saguinus bicolor*), and the buffy-headed tufted capuchin (*Cebus xanthosternos*), which are listed by IUCN as being among the twenty-five most endangered primates species alive today.

Due to the fragmentation of the forest, populations of various species of

FIGURE 11-12 There is a great diversity of animals in Mata Atlantica, including many endemic and endangered primate species. The woolly spider monkey, or muriqui *(Brachyteles arachnoids)*, is found nowhere else in the world but in this forest.

primates (e.g., brown howler monkey, black-faced lion tamarin, buffy-headed tufted capuchin, and muriqui) have become isolated in these fragments, with little or no possibility to migrate. This can lead to limited gene flow, which in turn can lead to inbreeding depression and eventual extinction.

The fact that so many of these highly endangered primate species have not already become extinct is to a great extent due to the long history of conservation effort within Brazil, especially by Coimbra-Fihlo, a renowned primatologist (Mittermeier et al. 2005). Coimbra-Fihlo was the person to bring the plight of the lion tamarins to the attention of the world (see Hot Topics 11-2). Over the past several decades there has been an explosion in the establishment of protected areas (Rylands and Brandon 2005). Conservation programs are run through government agencies and NGOs (nongovernmental organizations), as well as through private initiatives (private natural heritage reserves). It is this collaboration between the government, conservation organizations, and the local people that has led to numerous successes, and many of these programs serve as role models for other conservation projects.

❖❖ Primates in Medical Research

Millions of animals, including primates, are used and sacrificed on an annual basis in the name of science and biomedical research. Drug and cosmetic companies are the biggest users of animals for testing their products to ensure that all products offered for sale are safe. In many instances, testing is enforced due to stringent governmental regulations. By law, pharmaceutical companies must test all their products and prove that none of their drugs cause any ill effects or are dangerous to humans. Millions of animals, mainly mice,

FIGURE 11-13   A large number of primates are still used in biomedical research. Some of these studies may entail non-invasive behavioral studies (top), while others may entail more invasive research (bottom).

rats, and rabbits, are sacrificed on a yearly basis in such test conditions. In many instances, primates are the species of choice for these kinds of tests since they are more closely related to us.

Primates are often used in experiments to gain a better understanding of how our body works and how different organ systems react under different conditions. Nonhuman primates are used extensively to understand the etiology of infectious diseases, such as HIV/AIDS, Hepatitis B, and tuberculosis, and used as models for the production of vaccines (e.g., Philipp et al. 2006). Not all biomedical studies are invasive or terminal. Primates are expensive animals, and therefore great care is taken to utilize the resources well. For example, when exploring how our brain functions, nonhuman primates are most often used as models (Figure 11-13). Organ transplant research often focuses on using primates such as baboons because they are not so closely related to us and as such will not be as sensitive to the same pathogens and infectious organisms. Baboons are good donors for human liver transplants, and this is especially encouraging as baboons cannot be infected by the Hepatitis B virus (Michaels et al. 1996).

Public protest against the use of animals, especially nonhuman primates, in research experimentation and product testing has over the past decades been vociferous. Organizations such as PETA (People for the Ethical Treatment of Animals) and the Animal

Liberation Front (ALF) have brought many questionable research projects into the public eye, which in many instances have resulted in policy changes in the treatment of captive animals (see also Hot Topics 11-1). However, more militant protests in which threats or even attacks against researchers or animal caretakers, or in which animals are "let free," are causing more harm than helping the cause or the animals. Public opinion as far as animal testing in medical research is usually more ambivalent than most "animal rights people." Surveys usually show a majority, although often a slim majority, in favor of animal testing (see icmresearch.co.uk/reviews/latest-polls.asp). Furthermore, the use of nonhuman primate organs for transplants is receiving less publicity since the main concern is whether a human being will survive. In many ways, the use of nonhuman animals for testing involves ethical issues: Do we have the right to use animals as "guinea pigs" for our own benefits? What value is a life? Are some animals (e.g., mice and rats) more acceptable for testing than others (e.g., nonhuman primates)? Some people find it more objectionable to see our closest living relatives, the chimpanzees, used for biomedical research (see Hot Topics 11-1).

What alternatives do we have to testing or experimenting on live animals? In many cases, it is possible to use so-called *in vitro* experimentation, the use of bacterial cultures or tissue cultures, rather than living animals. Even though *in vitro* testing is used whenever possible, there are situations when such methods are not adequate. Many researchers believe that in a range of instances it is necessary to use live animal testing along side *in vitro* tests (Huxley 2006). It may be advisable to have high-risk products such as medicines and vaccines carefully tested and screened for side effects before being used by humans. There are other products that may be considered less essential and that involve lower risk such as cosmetics and other beauty products, which may not need to be so stringently tested on animals. The consumer has a voice here, as it is possible to buy beauty products that are not tested on animals.

❖❖ Summary

Our species has done much to change the face of the earth, and we continue to exploit habitats at the expense and well-being of other species—including those most like ourselves. Human population growth is exponential, and our demands for land on which to produce food and to extract resources from are increasing beyond sustainable limits. Two major threats to other primate species involve (1) the loss of habitat, and (2) their capture, either involving their introduction into captive situations or their death though hunting. Humans significantly modify or eliminate habitats used by nonhuman primate species, and we are destroying rain forests at an alarming rate—rain forests that contain the highest biodiversity of any habitat found on this planet. The loss of suitable habitat and encroachment on remaining ones often leaves primates with nowhere to go. Shrinking habitats also affects species' populations by isolating them from one another, thereby preventing gene flow and increasing the potential for inbreeding depression.

Primates are captured and hunted for meat, their body parts, and for sale as pets. The recent acceleration in the bushmeat trade is severely affecting an extensive number of primate species, including chimpanzees, bonobos, and gorillas. People hunt primates for meat for a number of reasons. One is that traditional peoples who themselves have been displaced often prefer the taste of wild game, while others hunt because there are significant profits to be made. The commercial hunting of primates and other species is difficult to curtail. The only way that the bushmeat trade will be stopped is by significantly reducing the market demand for it, thus limiting the profits made from these products. This will require the implementation of broad-based strategies including alternative economic opportunities, education about the need to save endangered and threatened species and their habitats, as well as informing about the dangers that may be associated with the bushmeat trade. The cross-species transmission of diseases, or zoonoses, poses a serious threat to those handling and consuming bushmeat. HIV/AIDS, Ebola, SARS, etc., are all caused by viruses that negatively affect humans and that came from other species.

Despite the appeal to own a primate as a pet, they do not make good pets. As cute young primates mature, they often become aggressive and unpredictable. Primates, like other exotic species, are essentially wild animals and, despite attempts to tame them, they are not like other domestic pets. Primates do not grow up to be well-adjusted monkeys or apes if they are not allowed to live in a social group with their own kind—they do not make suitable substitute children or playmates for human children. Primates also harbor diseases that are potentially dangerous to humans.

The conservation of nonhuman primates, other species, and their habitats is essential to our own well-being. Historically, conservation efforts were put in place to protect keystone or flagship species. Today, conservation initiatives are often aimed at preserving entire ecosystems. Successful conservation programs address the needs and incorporate the efforts and participation of local people who live on or use the land sought to be protected. Any successful conservation strategy must include economic advantages for local peoples as well as educational opportunities. People living on the brink of starvation and despair must be given economic incentives to preserve species and their habitats and be informed about the long-term benefits of conservation.

Today, many zoos breed primates for the purpose of reintroducing them to the wild. A number of projects, such as the one involving the golden lion tamarin, have been highly successful. Other efforts to supplement or maintain wild populations involve the rescue and rehabilitation of primates that have been illegally captured. These programs attempt to rehabilitate primates so that they may (if possible) be returned to a life in the wild. This involves long-term, arduous work that may not always be successful.

Nonhuman primates, because they are so much like us, are frequently used for biomedical research. Primates used for this type of research must now be cared for in the long term. Public awareness involving the abilities and capacities of nonhuman primates to feel, think, and learn has forced a number of animal protection laws and restrictions to be put in place.

◈◈ Key Words

bezoar stone	The Great Ape Project	retrovirus
biodiversity	inbreeding depression	translocation
breeding program	keystone species	zoonoses
bushmeat	partnership	
flagship species	reintroduction	

❖❖ Study Questions

1. What can you do to help with protecting endangered habitats and animal species?

2. In what ways can reintroduction programs benefit the survival of a species?

3. What are the pros and cons for the introduction of a "Great Ape Bill of Rights"?

4. Discuss the factors influencing the survival of primates in the wild.

5. Bushmeat trade is not only a threat to the survival of primate species—what other dangerous implications may be associated with this activity?

6. Discuss the different impacts subsistence and the commercial hunting of bushmeat have on primate populations worldwide.

7. Why are primates not good pets?

8. What are the benefits of using primates in biomedical research, and what alternative methods are available?

9. What are the benefits and drawbacks of translocation initiatives as a means of conservation?

10. What measures can be taken to avoid inbreeding depression in small isolated populations?

❖❖ Suggested Readings and Related Web Sites

Blum D. 1994. The monkey wars. New York: Oxford University Press.

Cavalieri P, Singer P. 1993. The Great Ape Project: Equality beyond humanity. New York: St. Martin's Griffin.

Robinson JG, Bennett EL editors 2000. Hunting for sustainability in tropical forests. New York: Columbia University Press

The AESOP Project
www.aesop-project.org

Bushmeat Crisis Task Force (BCTF)
www.bushmeat.org

Captive Wild Animal Protection Coalition
www.cwapc.org

Center for Education, Research and Conservation of Primates and Nature (CERCOPAN)
www.cercopan.org

The Humane Society of United States (HSUS)
www.hsus.org

The International Primate Protection League
www.ippl.org

The Primate Sanctuary of the United States
www.primatesanctuary.org

Wild Animal Orphanage
www.wildanimalorphanage.org

World Wide Fund for Nature
www.worldwildlife.org
www://petmonkey.info/laws.htm

Metric–Imperial Conversions

METRIC UNIT	IMPERIAL EQUIVALENT
1 centimeter	0.39 inches
1 meter	3.28 feet
1 kilometer	0.62 miles
1 kilogram	2.20 pounds
454 grams	1 pound
1 gram	0.035 ounces
1 liter	1.06 quarts
400 cubic centimeters	24.4 cubic inches
1 square kilometer	0.39 square miles
1 square kilometer	247 acres
0 degrees Celsius	32 degrees Fahrenheit

APPENDIX B

Comparative Primate Skeletons

Gorilla

Homo

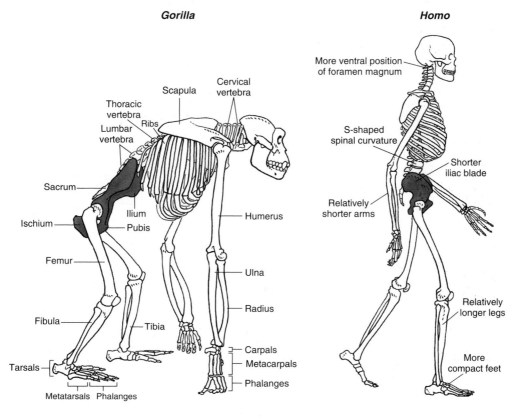

Gorilla labels: Scapula, Cervical vertebra, Thoracic vertebra, Ribs, Lumbar vertebra, Sacrum, Ischium, Ilium, Pubis, Femur, Fibula, Tibia, Tarsals, Metatarsals, Phalanges, Humerus, Ulna, Radius, Carpals, Metacarpals, Phalanges

Homo labels: More ventral position of foramen magnum, S-shaped spinal curvature, Shorter iliac blade, Relatively shorter arms, Relatively longer legs, More compact feet

Proconsul

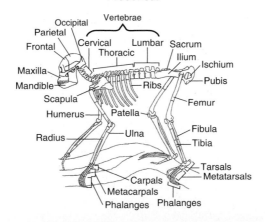

Proconsul labels: Occipital, Vertebrae, Parietal, Frontal, Cervical, Lumbar, Sacrum, Thoracic, Ilium, Ischium, Maxilla, Pubis, Mandible, Ribs, Scapula, Patella, Femur, Humerus, Fibula, Radius, Ulna, Tibia, Tarsals, Metatarsals, Carpals, Metacarpals, Phalanges, Phalanges

Glossary

abiotic—nonliving; opposite to biotic (living).

absolute date—a specific unit of time that is placed on an interval scale.

abstract numerousness—when a number of objects is substituted with a number symbol, e.g., "three apples" is the same as "3 apples."

acclimatization—a temporary change or adjustment involving physiological responses that is made by an individual organism in response to environmental pressure.

acoustic structure—the configuration of a vocalization as can be visualized using a sound spectrogram.

adaptation—the adjustment of an organism to its environment through its physical traits and behaviors; these traits may be inherited, thus contributing to the overall survival of a population.

adaptive radiation—the diversification of a species' lineage when environmental conditions are conducive for them to be successful and they adapt to a variety of new niches.

aerobic—using oxygen.

affiliative—friendly and prosocial behavioral interactions such as staying close to another individual or grooming.

age-graded group—a type of social organization where the leader male may tolerate the presence of another male, especially if the other male is not yet mature and of lower rank.

agonistic—a type of behavior that includes aggressive or submissive displays or interactions.

alarm calls—vocalizations made in response to the appearance of potential predator.

alliance—when two or more individuals form a relationship. This often involves joining forces against another individual or individuals.

allocortex—the portion of the brain that does not belong to the neocortex; the "older" part of the brain. It has fewer cell layers than the neocortex and consists mainly of the brainstem, hippocampus, and cerebellum.

allogrooming—when two or more individuals pick through and clean the skin or hair of other individuals; a form of social interaction.

allometric scaling—a scaling effect whereby the rates of increase in linear dimensions, surface area, and body volume do not occur in equal proportions.

allometry—the study of the relationships between size and shape and how this relates to physiological and morphological aspects of the body.

allomothering behavior—care giving to an infant or juvenile by individuals other than the mother; often performed by older female siblings.

allonursing—the nursing of an infant by a female other than the mother.

allopatric—a term that describes the geographic distribution of populations when they do not share overlapping space or territory.

allopatric speciation—a type of speciation that occurs when natural selection acts over time on a population separated from its parent population by a geographical barrier.

altricial—the development of an organism characterized by a short gestation time, offspring born in litters, eyes closed at birth, a short suckling period, rapid maturity after birth, and little contact with mother.

altruistic behaviors—behaviors that may lead to diminished reproductive success of the actor in favor of an unrelated individual's success.

anaerobic—without use of oxygen; carbon-fixing.

anagenesis—when a new species arises as a result of a monophyletic lineage experiencing a gradual change in its genetic makeup over time, with one species evolving into a different species.

analogous traits—adaptations that may serve the same purpose yet occur in unrelated species, e.g., the wings of a butterfly and the wings of a bat.

analogy—traits that serve the same function but are not the result of shared ancestry.

ancestral trait—an older trait, i.e., one that evolved at an earlier time.

anthropocentric—biased toward approaching things from a perspective that emphasizes human experience and values.

apomorphic trait—a derived (more recently evolved) trait.

arboreal—tree-living.

area of exclusive use—the most restricted portion of a group of primates' home range that is defended and not shared with members of other groups.

asocial learning—a type of learning where trial-and-error is used in order for an individual to learn a behavior on its own and there is no transfer of knowledge or insight between individuals.

Asperger's syndrome—a mild form of autism where an individual does not exhibit developmental delays but possesses a reduced ability to read social clues and body language.

asynchronous—a quality that some plants possess where there is individual variation from plant to plant in the timing of fruiting, flowering, or other natural processes.

aunting—when a mother receives help caring for her infant or juvenile from relatives or female friends.

autapomorphies—unique derived traits.

autism—a range of disorders primarily associated with impairment in social interactions such as the inability to infer false beliefs in others and to imagine invisible objects, and delays in social and language development.

autotrophs—organic, self-nourishing organisms that are able to utilize energy from the sun and other chemicals present in the atmosphere to manufacture food (e.g., grass).

baculum—a bone present in the penis, in some animals.

basal metabolic rate—the standard metabolic requirement for an organism at rest.

basal primates—primate species that are or were in transition from one state of speciation to the next and typically display a combination of ancestral and derived traits.

basal species—the earliest of its kind, a much generalized form that over time may evolve into something more specialized, showing more derived traits. All are extinct taxa.

bezoar stone—calculous concentration that can be found in the stomach and intestines of some animals, especially grazing animals, that in some folklore traditions is believed to be an antidote for poison.

bilophodont—a distinctive shape of the molar teeth involving four cusps on the chewing surface of the teeth; a small constriction divides them into pairs.

bilophodonty—the cusps of the molar teeth are located in pairs, one pair in the front and one pair in the back, with a distinct indentation in between them.

bimaturism—when the males of a species grow slower and for a longer amount of time than do females.

binomen—a term for the two Latin names of a species, the first name refers to the genus and is a broader classification than the second name that is more specific and refers to the species.

biodiversity—the number of species within a given area.

biogeography—a comparative observational science that seeks to identify patterns in the distribution of plants and animals, and the geographic regions in which they are found.

biomass—the weight of organic matter present in any given trophic level.

biome—a natural community that displays a degree of consistency in the types of plants that make up the community.

biotic—living, organic; opposite of abiotic (nonliving).

bipedal—a pattern of locomotion that involves walking on two legs.

brachiation—a pattern of locomotion that involves arm-over-arm swinging through the trees.

brachiator—an organism that uses brachiation as its mode of locomotion.

brainstem—comprises the midbrain and hindbrain, and is mainly involved in basic body functions such as basic metabolic rate and respiration.

breeding program—a program that maintains an endangered species, often in a zoological park, to ensure that its gene poll does not disappear. The underlying idea is that by increasing a captive population, there is potential to reintroduce the species to the wild.

breeding transfer—the movement of adult individuals between breeding groups. Often involves the transfer of single individuals.

Broca's area—an area of the brain present in humans that is involved in speech production.

bushmeat—any meat caught while hunting wild animals living in a moist tropical habitat, or rain forest.

canine—the tooth located behind the incisors. There is a single canine in each quadrant of the mouth. Canines have a single root, and are often pointed and sharp.

cardination—the number of objects belonging to any specific type, e.g., 7 apples or 2 oranges.

carrying capacity—the number of individuals of any specific species that a particular ecosystem can maintain without disrupting the homeostasis of the system.

catarrhine monkeys—monkeys living in Africa and Asia that belong to the infraorder Catarrhini.

cathemeral—when an organism is primarily active during dusk and dawn.

causal agent—when the mental state of an individual influences the behavior of others.

cecum—the first part of the colon; part of the intestinal tract.

cellulose—a carbohydrate that is primarily found in the cell walls of plants and can be difficult to digest without the presence of specialized enzymes.

cementum—a type of body tissue that holds the teeth in the jaw.

central nervous system—the brain and spinal cord.

central sulcus—a vertical division in the middle of both the left and right sides of the brain. Divides the frontal from parietal lobe.

cerebellum—sometimes referred to as the lesser brain. It is located at the back of the brain below the occipital lobe and performs many important activities such as coordinating the gathering of sensory data

and the coordination of movement and balance.

cerebrum—the largest structure in the forebrain, also called the neocortex. In humans the neocortex is a highly expanded and convulted structure.

character polarity—the evolutionary timing and path of a trait.

clades—the branches of a cladogram representing an ancestral species, the last common ancestor, and all of its descendants.

cladistics—a classification approach that involves the systematic examination of traits that occur in groups of organisms in order to place them within a branching pattern that illustrates their relatedness to other groups of organisms and their place within an evolutionary lineage. Sometimes referred to as Phylogenetic Systematics.

cladogenesis—when one species gives rise to two or more new species over time.

cladogram—a diagram that illustrates a phylogenetic tree and its branches, or clades, representing ancestral species and all of its descendants.

class—a level of biological classification within a nested hierarchy of categorical units inferior to phylum and superior to order, often consisting of more than one order.

classification—a system for ordering organisms or other phenomena into categories.

clavicle—a bone of the axial skeleton that articulates with the sternum and the scapula, more commonly known as the collarbone.

clumped distributions—the clustered or grouped spatial distribution of species within a geographic area. For example, the distribution of food species.

commensal—living in association with other species.

communication—broadcasting and receiving information about what is happening in the social and physical environment in which an organism lives.

competitive exclusion—a principle that states that no two species can occupy an identical niche i.e., they cannot be in total and absolute competition with one another because either both will be eliminated from the niche or one will outcompete the other.

cone—photoreceptor in the eye sensitive to bright light.

conspecific—an individual belonging to the same species.

convergence—when similar traits evolve in unrelated species because they serve the same or similar functions.

cooperate—when individuals join forces (uniform behavioral display) against a third party.

core area—a section of the home range that a group frequently uses and is typically associated with preferred resources, such as sleeping sites, primary feeding trees, resting sites, etc.

corm—fleshy, bulblike base of the stem of a plant; the energy storage part of a plant.

corpus callosum—the portion of the brain where information between the right and left hemispheres passes.

crepuscular—when an organism is primarily active during low levels of light intensity (dawn and dusk).

crown species—species at the evolutionary stage when they display a full suite of recently evolved traits.

day ranges—area within a group's home range that is typically traversed in a day.

deception—a type of social manipulation where one individual is misled by the actions of another individual into believing something that is untrue.

dental formula—a shorthand way to identify the number and type of teeth present in one quadrant of the mouth.

dental quadrant—one of four equal sections of the mouth, upper left, lower left, upper right, and lower right. Left and right sides divided at the midline of the mouth.

dental tooth comb—characteristic of the bottom front teeth of some strepsirhine primates. Mandibular incisors and canines are positioned close together and inserted horizontally into the jaw bone.

dentine—the portion of the tooth located under the enamel and that surrounds the pulp cavity. It is softer than enamel and with wear can replenish itself.

derived trait—a trait that has a more recent evolutionary history.

dermatoglyphics—ridged patterns found in the skin of the hands and feet and especially on the fingers. Refers to the configuration of the skin that forms the fingerprints.

diastema—a gap between teeth.

dichromatic—possesing only two kinds of photopigments in the retina.

differentiated dentition—a dentition that includes teeth of different shapes and sizes that serve different functions.

digestive tract—the portion of the body, comprising teeth, stomach, and small and large intestines, where food is processed and broken down into simpler forms that can be used by the body to produce energy.

digitigrady—locomotion pattern that involves walking only on the fingers.

direct teaching—when an individual recognizes that he or she possesses information that others lack and actively imparts information to an ignorant individual by using direct contact or demonstration.

dispersal pattern—a pattern observed as primates approach sexual maturity when members of one or the other sex will then move into a different or reproductive group.

displacement—a communication signal that can refer to objects or events not in the here and now.

diurnal—when an organism is primarily active during the daylight hours.

dominance hierarchy—a social ranking system where each individual has a specific position or standing within a group; the top ranking individual being the alpha followed by the beta and so on.

dorsal—pertaining to the back of the body.

ecological niche—the position that an organism occupies within an ecosystem and its placement within the ecosystem's complex web of energy exchange.

empathy—the ability to infer mental states in others.

emulation—when one individual observes another individual performing a task, and through observation learns how to reach the same goal by performing the same task.

enamel—the outer layer of a tooth and the hardest material in the body.

enculturation—the process by which one individual adjusts to the culture of another.

endemic—native or indigenous to a particular region or area.

endozoochory—the process of transporting seeds in the body of a primate and then defecating or spitting them out.

enzyme—proteins that speed up chemical reactions in the body.

estrus—the period of time when a female is receptive to mating both behaviorally and biologically.

ethogram—a behavioral inventory that has been established for a particular study group composed of mutually exclusive (not overlapping) categories of activity.

ethology—the study of animal behavior.

euprimates—the first primates recognized in the fossil record, i.e., true primates, dating to the earliest part of the Eocene epoch, around 55 million years ago.

evolutionary systematics—an approach to the science of classification that is based on evaluating the degree of distance or closeness reflected by a suite of morphological characteristics exhibited by different groups of animals, also referred to as cladistics.

exocarp—tough, outermost part of a fruit.

extant—presently alive; not extinct.

exudate—gum or tree sap. A food source, used by many primates, that has a high sugar concentration that provides quick energy and calories.

fallback food—vital but alternative food sources that are ignored when preferred foods are available and only eaten in times of food scarcity.

faunivory—feeding on animal protein.

fecundity—potential reproductive capacity of an organism or population.

field work—research that is performed in the field, or natural habitat, of an animal.

fission-fusion—a fluid type of social grouping where the members of the larger group (community) come and go at will. Membership in each subgroup is not predictable from day to day, and occasionally group members may not see one another for days on end.

fitness—a measure of reproductive success, and refers to the successful passing on of one's own genetic material into the next generation.

flagship species—species that are the specific focus of conservation efforts, and due to their popularity and recognition in popular culture, are used as the impetus to drive conservation efforts within a particular area.

folivory—feeding on leaves.

foraging strategy—the method and technique used to find food sources.

forethought—the process of planning ahead.

fossa—a carnivorous mammal of the civet family found on Madagascar.

FOXP2—a highly conservative gene present in most animals that is a transcription factor, i.e. a protein that regulates the activity of other genes and that in humans appears to have undergone recent selective changes that may have coincided with the evolution of speech and human language.

frontal bone—the skull bone located under the forehead. At birth it is made up of two bones separated by the metopic suture, which fuses together in early childhood in most haplorhines.

frugivory—feeding on fruits.

gallery forests—forests that grow along streams and rivers.

gene flow—the exchange of genes among populations through interbreeding.

genetic drift—random changes in gene frequency within a population.

genotype—the genetic makeup of an organism.

geophagy—the eating of dirt, clay, or soil.

gestation—the period of time an organism spends developing in the womb, i.e., *in utero*.

glabrous—surface that is devoid of hair.

Gondwana—the southern supercontinent that formed when Pangaea divided into two landmasses around 180 mya. Around approximately 120 mya this supercontinent had split up into the continents we recognize today.

gradualism—the Darwinian idea that evolutionary change, including the rise of new species, is slow and gradual.

gramnivory—feeding on seeds.

Grande Coupure—a major faunal turnover in the fossil record that occurred about 34 mya when most primate lineages became extinct or at least disappeared from the northern continents.

grandmother hypothesis—proposes that females live many years past reproductive age because they can still provide support for their own mature offspring as well as their offspring's offspring, therefore contributing to the survival of their own genetic line.

The Great Ape Project—a manifesto created in the early 1990s that sought to protect captive apes and guarantee that they would be provided with rights and appropriate care; specifically, the right to life, the protection of individual liberty, and the prohibition of torture.

greeting behavior—ritual behavior that occurs when two individuals meet after a period of separation or after a conflict. May or may not involve physical contact and can provide information about or reinforce each individual's status in the relationship.

gregarious—prone to frequent social interaction.

grooming claw—a claw-shaped nail on the second digit of the foot that is a characteristic of some strepsirhine primates, used primarily for grooming but also to extract insects out of tree bark.

gummivory—feeding on gum and sap from trees.

gymnosperm plants—cone-bearing plants, e.g., pine trees (plural: gyri).

gyrus—the upward fold in the surface of the neocortex.

half-life—the amount of time it takes for 50% of a naturally occurring, unstable compound (isotope) to decay into another, stable compound.

haplorhine—one of the two suborders of the Primate order. This group of primates includes tarsiers, monkeys, and apes (including humans).

harem—a unit comprising a single adult male and one or more females, and their dependent young. The male has exclusive mating access to the adult females.

hemisphere—one-half (left or right) of the neocortex.

hemispheric specialization—when one side of the brain possesses an area that is specialized to perform certain functions.

herbivory—feeding on herbs.

heterodonty—teeth that have different shapes and functions.

heterosis—the increased adaptive fitness of a hybrid.

heterotrophs—organisms that utilize, rearrange, or decompose what autotrophs have produced. All animals are heterotrophs.

holistic—assuming an interrelationship among the parts of a subject. Anthropology is an example of a holistic discipline.

home range—a defined spatial area that a group uses.

homeostasis—a balance that has to be maintained in order for a system to properly keep functioning and that entails a system of checks and balances to prevent fluctuations within the system from exceeding what can be maintained over time.

hominids—primates included in the family Hominidae; includes the African apes, humans, and our fossil ancestors.

hominins—extant and fossil habitually bipedal terrestrial primates—humans and our fossil ancestors.

hominoids—members of the superfamily Hominoidea, including humans and our fossil ancestors, and all extant apes and their fossil ancestors.

homologous traits—traits shared by two or more species because of shared evolutionary ancestry.

homoplasy—when two species show similarity in a morphological trait that is not due to relatedness (common ancestry), but due to parallel or convergent evolution.

hybrid zone—an area where two genetically distinct but closely related taxa meet, interbreed, and produce offspring.

hyoid bone—a small bone located in the throat, to which the tongue muscles attach, that is modified in some primate species to affect or enhance sound.

hypocone—a cusp on the upper molars located at the back of the tooth on the tongue side.

imitation—a form of learning that involves the learner perceiving and understanding the action that another individual is performing.

inbreeding—mating and reproducing with genetically close relatives.

inbreeding depression—reduced reproductive success because breeding within a small population of closely related individuals may result in an increase in deleterious genes.

incisors—front teeth found in both the upper and lower jaw that are used as cutting tools and are usually flat with a straight edge.

inclusive fitness—when related individuals, those that share part of your own gene pool, are successful in reproduction and survival.

infanticide—the killing of an infant primate by a conspecific.

information sharing hypothesis—proposes that habitats be more systematically searched and exploited when different species of primates living in long-term association with one another overtly or passively share information.

innate—of genetic origin.

insectivory—feeding on insects.

intentional teaching—a type of teaching, indicative of an intent to share information, that may be unknown to the learner.

introgression—when genetic material is dispersed from one parental population into another via hybrids.

ischial callosities—thickened calluses on the rump.

isotope—one of the 275 forms of the 81 known chemical elements. Forms differ based on their atomic weights and numbers of neutrons in the nucleus. Both stable and unstable (radioactive) isotopes exist in nature.

Jacobson's organ—an accessory olfactory system located above the hard palate of the upper jaw, also known as the vomeronasal.

Jarman-Bell principle—states that large mammals require more total food intake per day compared to small mammals. Large mammals need relatively fewer calories per unit of body weight and can subsist on more low-quality, harder-to-digest foods, e.g., leaves. Small mammals have a higher metabolic rate and need to seek out foods that provide high energy, e.g., insects.

Karst topography—type of terrain that is formed on carbonate rock such as limestone and dolomite. As ground water percolates through the rock, it dissolves to form openings such as caves.

keystone species—species that play a pivotal, or major, ecological role within an ecosystem.

kin relationship—network of who is biologically related to whom in a social group.

kingdom—most inclusive of the taxonomic categories defined by Linnaeus.

Kleiber's Law—states that there is a predictable pattern in the energy demands of placental mammals related to body size. Smaller animals have a higher metabolic rate than do larger ones.

lateralization—hemispheric specialization of the brain.

Laurasia—a northern supercontinent that formed when Pangaea divided into two landmasses around 180 mya. By approximately 120 mya this supercontinent had split up into the continents we recognize today.

lexigrams—pictorial symbols that represent words or phrases.

lianas—woody climbing plants or vines.

mandible—lower jaw bone.

mate competition—behavior found in many male primates who are intolerant of each other because they compete with one another for females in order to achieve reproductive success. Females also express behaviors related to mate competition but these tend to be more subtle.

mating strategy—behaviors typically exhibited by the sexually mature individuals of a species in order to be reproductively successful.

maxilla—upper jaw bone.

metatool—the most complex form of tool use, when a modified object is used to modify another object which in turn is used as a tool.

metopic suture—the suture that separates the left and right parts of the frontal bone (located under the forehead) of the skull.

mirror neurons—special brain cells that are activated both when a primate uses a precision grip to manipulate or grasp an object and when a primate observes another individual doing the same motion.

molars—the teeth located in the cheek region, behind the premolars, that are used to masticate, crush, and grind food.

monochromatic—a type of vision characterized by an inability to see color possessed by some nocturnal animals. Produced by having a single type of photopigment in the retina.

monophyletic group—a group that contains all of the known descendents of an ancestral species.

monophyly—sharing the same ancestor, having a single ancestral lineage.

monotypic—a genus that is represented by a single species.

morphemes—smallest linguistic units that carry meaning, e.g., words.

morphology—the shape and structure of the body, anatomical characteristics.

mosaic evolution—evolution that results in a species possessing both ancestral and derived traits.

motor cortex—the portion of the brain devoted to muscle control.

multidisciplinary—having experience in or involving many fields of study.

multiparous—referring to a female that has given birth to more than one offspring.

mutations—random changes that occur in the genetic code.

mutualism—a codependent ecological relationship involving two or more species where both species benefit from one another.

nail—a flattened, keratin-rich plate that grows on the dorsal side at the ends of fingers and toes.

nares—nostrils.

natal dispersal—when individuals leave the group into which they were born.

natal group—the group into which a primate is born.

neocortex—the largest structure in the forebrain, the cerebrum. Most primates have an expanded neocortex, and it has a convoluted surface consisiting of numerous folds (gyri) and furrows (sulci).

neuron—nerve cell in the brain.

niche breadth—the range of factors that are limiting to a species under specific niche conditions, an indication of how generalized or specialized a species is.

nocturnal—when an organism is primarily active at night.

nulliparous—referring to a female that has never given birth.

object permanence—an awareness that an object has not ceased to exist simply because it is no longer in view.

observational learning—a social type of learning; involves the transfer of knowledge or insight between an observer and a performer, this type of learning includes emulation and imitation learning.

occlusal—the portion of the tooth surface that comes into contact with the tooth above or below it.

olfaction—the sense of smell.

omnivorous—eating a mixed diet consisting of animal and plant foods.

orbital convergence—eyes located in the front of the face and not to the sides.

order—a level of biological classification that is a taxonomic division within a nested hierarchy of categorical units, superior to family and inferior to class.

ordination—the property of numbers and the recognition of the position of a number in a series, e.g., 7 belongs between 5 and 9.

orthognatic face—a relatively vertical or nonprotruding face, where the forehead and chin are in the same vertical plan.

ovulation—when a female's ovaries release an egg or eggs, usually occurring at regular time intervals in primates.

paleosols—ancient soils.

Pangaea—a single mega-continent that consisted of all the Earth's landmasses joined together that existed up to approximately 200 million years ago.

parallel evolution—the independent development within a group of animals of similar adaptations, e.g., the long arms of both platyrrhines and some catarrhines to adapt to a novel feeding strategy.

parapatric hybridization—a form of hybridization that consists of interbreeding at species borders.

parapatric speciation—when a species is widely distributed and a segment of the population is better able to deal with certain environmental conditions and over time natural selection acts on the segmented population, leading to the rise of a new species.

paraphyletic group—a group containing some but not all the known descendants of the common ancestor of the group.

parental investment—the amount of time and energy a parent invests in offspring in order for them to be likely to survive and successfully reproduce themselves.

parous—having produced an offspring.

parsimonious—most likely and least complex explanation.

partnership—having a relationship of joint interest and working toward a common goal. In the terms of conservation efforts, such relationships between people and the countries are the most successful.

patrilocal male—male who remains in the social group into which he was born.

pelage—the fur or hair of a mammal.

pentadactyly—having five fingers and toes.

petrified—having been turned to stone by the process of fossilization where organic material is replaced by inorganic material slowly over time.

petrosal bulla—an inflated area of the petrosal part of the temporal bone surrounding the middle ear structures.

phenotype—the physical appearance of an organism; its observed set of characteristics or traits.

pheromone—a highly volatile chemical perceived by specialized sensory nerves located in the nose.

philopatric—referring to animals that associate on a regular basis with one particular area.

phoneme—the basic sound units of human speech that do not in themselves carry meaning .

photoreceptor—receptor in the retina, in the eye, that is sensitive to light, consisting of two major types, rods and cones.

phylogenetic systematics—the science of classification that involves a systematic examination of specific traits within organisms in order to place them within a branching pattern that illustrates their relatedness to other organisms and their place within an evolutionary lineage, also referred to as cladistics.

phylogeny—the evolutionary lineage of a group of related organisms.

phylum—a level of biological classification that is a taxonomic division within a nested hierarchy of categorical units inferior to kingdom and superior to class.

piloerection—having the body hair stand on end.

pinna—the external part of the ear that picks up sound vibrations that move in the air (plural: pinnae).

plantigrady—walking on the whole hand and foot surface.

planum temporale—a key location within Wernicke's area of the brain that is involved in language comprehension.

plate tectonics—the movement of continental plates, caused by their interaction with the molten rock of the earth's interior.

platyrrhine monkeys—monkeys that belong to the infraorder Platyrrhini, which includes monkeys found in Mexico and Central and South America.

plesiomorphic trait—a trait that is ancestral i.e., has been retained over a long period of evolutionary time.

pollinators—animals that are actively involved in the dispersal of pollen from the anther to the stigma of a plant.

polymorphic—taking multiple forms; the existence of varied expression of a genetic trait within a species or between species.

polyspecific group—a group that is made up of more than one species.

population density—the size of a specific population in relation to some unit of space; a measure of biomass.

positional behavior—the way a species moves about and its postural adaptation.

precocial—referring to infants born relatively well developed, having completed a good portion of growth and development in the womb before the birth.

prehensile tail—a tail that is capable of grasping hold of objects or substrates while supporting the full body weight.

prehensility—the ability to grasp.

premaxilla—bony part of the upper jaw (maxilla) that houses the incisors.

premolars—teeth that are located behind the canines and in front of the molars that vary in surface complexity from species to species but are primarily used for mastication of food.

primaparous—referring to a female that has given birth once.

primary auditory cortex—an area in the neocortex of the brain that is involved in sound comprehension and the recognition of sounds.

primary hybrid zones—a narrow and persistent hybrid zone, or an area where two species are interbreeding and produce fertile offspring, found along the borders of the living space of two different species.

primary rain forests—forests virtually undisturbed by humans in which trees have matured over many centuries.

primate—an order in the class Mammalia defined by a suite of anatomical and behavioral traits including being large-brained, mostly tree-dwelling mammals, that are highly social. Humans are primates.

primatology—the scientific study of the non-human primates.

pulp cavity—the central portion of a tooth underlying the enamel and dentine where nerves and blood vessels are located.

punctuated equilibrium—a model of evolutionary change characterized by rapid bursts of change, followed by long period of stasis.

quadrumanual—walking on the outer edges of the feet and hands.

quadrupedal—a form of locomotion that involves the use of all four limbs.

radiometric dating—an absolute dating technique based on the decay of naturally occurring unstable compounds called isotopes, which change at set rates into stable forms. The ratio of unstable:stable forms provides a specific date range that is attributed to the object containing these compounds.

reciprocal altruism—behaviors that appear to be costly to the actor's fitness but may be of benefit to the recipient and that then become part of a long-term reciprocal interaction.

reconciliation—a nonaggressive reunion between individuals who have been in conflict.

redirected aggression—when an individual is upset about having a conflict with a dominant individual and the subordinate individual redirects its frustration on a third party.

reintroduction—procedure for when former pets or other captive primates are released into the wild after rehabilitation in the hopes that they will survive and ultimately reproduce, helping to preserve the species. Many captive breeding programs involving species that are threatened with extinction have reintroduction as a goal.

relative age—an age that is established on the basis of a comparison with something else, not established on a measurement scale e.g., you are simply younger or older than a sibling.

relative numerousness—an ability to place different groups of objects that have different quantities into some order based on some set criteria (e.g., 3 apples are fewer than 5 oranges).

reproductive isolating mechanisms—behavioral, morphological, physiological, geographical, or ecological differences that make a successful mating, resulting in fertile offspring unlikely to occur.

reproductive strategy—specific behaviors used by individuals to maximize their successful mating, birthing, and rearing of offspring to ensure that the offspring grow up and will in turn to reproduce.

reproductive success—the level of success an individual has in reproducing and passing its genes on into future generations.

resonating air sac—expandable skin on the throat that resonates during vocalization to amplify the call.

resource partitioning—differences in niche occupation involving diet, timing of activities, positional behaviors, locomotion patterns, social structure, and social organization that facilitate the sharing of a habitat and its resources.

retina—the portion of the eye located at the back of the eyeball and covered with photoreceptors that collects visual signals from the outside world and sends them through the optic nerve to the visual cortex in the brain.

retrovirus—an infectious agent (virus) that incorporates its own DNA into the DNA of its host's cells for replication; typically exhibits a high rate of mutation, consequently can be difficult to treat.

rhinarium—patch of naked and moist skin between the nose and upper lip.

rod—photoreceptors in the eye sensitive to dim light.

root—the portion of a tooth that anchors it into the jaw and has an opening through which nerves and blood vessels pass.

sacculated stomach—a complex stomach that is subdivided into sections of saclike expansions, frequently found in mammals that eat mature leaves; gestation is aided by intense microbial action.

saltation—abrupt transition; in biological terminology, a rapid change in the genetic makeup of a species or population.

scientific method—a methodology used to conduct scientific research in which a research plan is constructed; background research is conducted; replicable, reliable data are collected with control and rigor; the data are analyzed, and hypotheses are rejected, revised, or accepted.

secondary hybrid zones—areas where two allopatric taxa (which share a common ancestry) come into contact and reproduce after having been geographically separated for a long period of time.

secondary rain forests—forests that have regenerated after some natural or human-caused disturbance; contain smaller trees and a denser understory of vegetation than what is found in primary rain forests.

sectorial premolar—a tooth complex that includes an elongated single-cusped premolar that serves as a sharpening stone for the upper canines, keeping the back edge of these teeth razor sharp.

seed predation—the destructive consumption of seeds.

seed shadow—the spatial distribution of seeds away from a parent plant.

semantics—meaning attached to words, vocalizations, and signals.

semibrachiators—primates who are capable of moving through the trees using a suspensory locomotor pattern but do not use this as their primary method of locomotion.

sexual dichromatism—differences in the color scheme of the hair and skin between males and females.

sexual dimorphism—size or form differences in physical characteristics between males and females.

sexual selection—when one sex finds the opposite sex more attractive based on morphological characteristics or behaviors that vary within the species.

shared derived characteristics—traits that are shared by members of two or more different taxonomic groups but are not exhibited in other such groups.

social—living in a communal setting.

social competence—the ability to make friends and allies.

social tool—the manipulation of an individual in such a way that will promote the personal gains or goals of the individual that is doing the manipulation.

sonograph—a graphic representation or illustration of sound.

sound spectrogram—visual representation of vocalizations showing the acoustic structure of individual calls.

speciation—the emergence of a new species.

species concepts—concepts that define what a species is.

sperm competition—when males produce more or better sperm than other males or prohibit the sperm of competitors to fertilize a female.

stasis—the state of remaining unchanged for a long period of time.

stereoscopic vision—overlapping fields of vision that allow for depth perception and three-dimensional sight.

strata—the different layers of rock or soil that have been laid down over time on the earth's crust (singular: stratum).

stratigraphy—the study of the earth's strata.

strepsirhine—one of the two suborders of the Primate order. This group of primates includes lemurs, lorises, and bushbabies.

subalpine—referring to mountainous regions close to tree line.

subfossil—species that have become fossilized during the Pleistocene or Holocene.

sulcus—a furrow in the surface of the neocortex of the brain (plural: sulci).

supralaryngeal tract—the mouth, tongue, larynx, and pharynx.

supraorbital torus—a bony ridge located on the forehead above the eye orbits.

sympatric—a term that describes the geographic distribution of populations that occupy overlapping space.

sympatric hybridization—interbreeding among distinct species that live in the same area and have overlapping ranges.

sympatric speciation—when barriers arise between members of the same population in a continuously distributed species and a new species evolves; rarely observed in the wild.

synapomorphies—shared derived traits.

synchronous—occurring at the same time.

synergistic—when two or more variables have a combined effect that is greater than the sum of what both of their independent effects would be.

symplesiomorphies—shared ancestral traits.

syntax—the way sentences are put together according to specific rules (grammar) and words or morphemes are placed in a predictive order to give comprehension to utterances.

tactile pad—area found at the end of each digit and on the palms and soles of the hands and feet that is dense with nerves and therefore has an increased ability to detect what is being held or touched and provide a better grip.

tapetum lucidum—a reflective structure in the eye that improves the night vision of some nocturnal animals by amplifying the available light.

taphonomy—the study of the fossilization process; what happens to bones after death and until they are fossilized.

taxa—the categories that exist in a taxonomic classification system (singular: taxon).

taxonomy—underlying theory for how any phenomena are classified or organized.

temperate—referring to geographic regions characterized by pronounced seasonality located north of the Tropic of Cancer to the Arctic circle and south of the Tropic of Capricorn to the Antarctic circle.

terrestrial—ground-dwelling.

territorial calls—vocalizations that function to inform conspecifics about the individual's location and where the boundary of its home range is located and convey information about how many are present in the group and how willing they are to defend their territory.

territoriality—when primates exhibit defensive or monitoring behaviors regarding the space that they occupy.

theory of mind—the ability to understand the presence of mental states (e.g., feelings, intentions, knowledge) and recognize that other individuals also have mental states and that the mental states of others may be different from one's own.

time budgets—the amount and distribution of time that is spent on different activities; the activity cycles of primates.

tool—any object in nature that is used to modify another object (e.g., when using a rock to crack a nut, it is no longer just a rock, it is also a tool).

tool manufacture—the modification of a natural object to use as tool.

toothcomb—consists of the incisors and canines of the lower jaw tightly packed together and almost horizontally implanted into the mandible; used for grooming and to gain access to food.

torpor—a type of hibernation consisting of inactivity or dormant behavior that is a strategy for reducing energy demands in environments where food supplies can become severely limited.

transect—to cut across; to survey across a section of land.

transitive inference ability—a quantitative judgment wherein an individual is capable of inferring information about one object based on information about another object or objects, e.g., knowing that *a* is more than *b*, which is more than *c* (a>b>c), he or she should also be able to draw the conclusion that *a* is more than *c* (a>c).

translocation—the removal of an endangered species from one area where it is vulnerable and moved to another area within its historical range.

trial-and-error learning—a form of asocial learning; an individual learns by trying something repeatedly and modifying his or her behavior if it is not successful until he or she finds a technique that works.

trichromatic—having three kinds of photopigments in the retina that provide color vision.

trophic levels—various levels of how organisms gain energy in an ecosystem; levels include producers, decomposers, herbivores, primary carnivores, and secondary carnivores.

tropical—referring to geographic regions located in between the Tropics of Cancer and Capricorn.

ungulate—a mammal that possesses hooves.

vertical clinging and leaping—a mode of locomotion exhibited by primates with long, powerful hindlimbs; consists of leaping from vertical support to vertical support and clinging when they land.

vibrissae—specialized hairs located on the muzzle, around the eyes, and sometimes around the wrists that provide animals with sensory information about their surrounding environment (singular: vibrissa).

visual cortex—located in the occipital lobe of the brain where signals from the eyes are ultimately transported and translated into images.

vomeronasal organ—an accessory olfactory system located above the hard palate of the upper jaw in some animals that helps to distinguish pheromones (scents) that may be present in the air; also known as Jacobson's organ.

Wernicke's area—an area of the human brain, located in the left temporal lobe, that is associated with language comprehension both during speech and reading.

Y-5 pattern—a pattern found in the peaks and valleys on the occlusal surfaces of the molars of apes and humans. Five rounded cusps that are connected by pattern of Y-shaped groves.

zoonoses—the transmission of infectious or noninfectious organisms between animals and humans.

zygomatic bone—the bone that makes up the lower outer portion of the eye orbit and the projection of the cheek; the cheekbone.

References

Abegglen J-J. 1984. On socialization in hamadryas baboons. Lewisburg: Bucknell University Press.

Abernethy KA, White LJT, Wickings EJ. 2002. Hordes of mandrills (*Mandrillus sphinx*): Extreme group size and seasonal male presence. Journal of Zoology London 258:131–137.

Abramovich S, Keller G, Adatte T, Stinnesbeck W, Hottinger L, Stueben D, Berner Z, Ramanivosoa B, Randriamanantenasoa A. 2003. Age and paleoenvironment of the Maastrichtian to Paleocene of the Mahajanga Basin, Madagascar: A multidisciniplinary approach. Marin Micropaleontology 47:17–70.

Achard F, Eva HD, Stibig H-J, Mayaux P, Gallego J, Richards T, Malingreau J-P. 2002. Determination of deforestation rates of the world's humid tropical forests. Science 297:999–1002.

AESOP Project. 2006. Plight of monkeys/apes kept as "pets" *www.aesop-project.org* [Accessed 26 June 2006].

Agetsuma N. 2000. Influence of temperature on energy intake and food selection by macaques. International Journal of Primatology 21(1):103–111.

Aich H, Moos-Heilen R, Zimmerman E. 1990. Vocalizations of adult gelada baboons (*Theropithecus gelada*): Acoustic structure and behavioral context. Folia Primatologica 55:109–132.

Aiello LC, Wheeler P. 1995. Expensive-tissue hypothesis: The brain and digestive system in human and primate evolution. Current Anthropology 36:199–221.

Alberts SC, Altmann J. 2001. Immigration and hybridization patterns of yellow and anubis baboons in and around Amboseli, Kenya. American Journal of Primatology 53:139–154.

Alexander KA, Appel MJ. 1994. African wild dogs (*Lycaon pictus*) endangered by a canine distemper epizootic among domestic dogs near the Masai Mara National Reserve, Kenya. Journal of Wildlife Diseases 30(4):481–485.

Allendorf FW, Leary RF, Spruell P, Wenburg JK. 2001. The problem with hybrids: Setting conservation guidelines. Trends in Ecology and Evolution 16(11):613–622.

Alport LJ. 2004. Comparative analysis of the role of olfaction and the neocortex in primate intrasexual competition. The Anatomical Record Part A 281A:1182–1189.

Altmann J. 1980. Baboon mothers and infants. Cambridge, MA: Harvard University Press.

Altmann SA. 1998. Foraging for survival. Yearling baboons in Africa. Chicago: University of Chicago Press.

Alvarez W, Asaro F. 1990. An extraterrestrial impact: Accumulating evidence suggests an asteroid or comet caused the Cretaceous extinction. Scientific American 263:78–84.

Andresen E. 2001. Effects of dung presence, dung amount and secondary dispersal by dung beetles on the fate of *Micropholis guyanensis* (Sapotaceae) seeds in central Amazonia. Journal of Tropical Ecology 17:61–78.

Andresen E. 2002. Primary seed dispersal by red howler monkeys and the effects of defecation patterns on the fate of dispersed seeds. Biotropica 34:261–272.

Ankel F. 1965. Der Canalis sacralis als Indikator für die Länge der Caudalregion der Primaten. Folia Primatologica 3:263–276.

Apiou F, Rumpler Y, Warter S, Vezuli A, Dutrillaux B. 1996. Demonstration of homoe-ologies between human and lemur chromosomes by chromosome painting. Cytogenetic and Cell Genetics 72:50–52.

Araújo MFP, Lima EM, Pessoa VF. 2006. Modeling dichromatic and trichromatic sensitivity to the color properties of fruits eaten by squirrel monkeys (*Saimiri sciureus*). American Journal of Primatology 68:1129–1137.

Archie EA, Moss CJ, Alberts SC. 2006. The ties that bind: Genetic relatedness predicts the fission and fusion of social groups in wild African elephants. Proceedings of the Royal Society, London B 273:513–522.

Ardrey R. 1976. The hunting hypothesis. New York: Bantam.

Arnason U, Adegoke JA, Bodin K, Born EW, Esa YB, Gullberg A, Nilsson M, Short RV, Xu X, Janke A. 2002. Mammalian mitogenomic relationships and the root of the eutherian tree. Proceedings of the National Academy of Science, USA 99(12):8151–8156.

Arnold K, Zuberbühler K. 2006. The alarm-calling system of adult male putty-nosed monkeys, *Cercopithecus nictitans martini*. Animal Behaviour 72:643–653.

Ashmore-DeClue PC. 1992. Macaques: An adaptive array. Ph.D. dissertation, Washington University, St. Louis, Missouri.

Ashton PS. 1988. Dipterocarp biology as a window to the understanding of tropical forest structure. Annual Review of Ecological Systems 19:347–370.

Atsalis S. 1999. Seasonal fluctuations in body fat and activity levels in a rain-forest species of mouse lemur, *Microcebus rufus*. International Journal of Primatology 20(6):883–910.

Aureli F, de Waal FBM editors. 2000. Natural conflict resolution. Los Angeles: University of California Press.

Austad SN. 1997. Comparative aging and life histories in mammals. Experimental Gerontology 32(1/2):23–38.

Bacon A-M, Long VT. 2001. The first discovery of a complete skeleton of a fossil orang-utan in a cave of the Hoa Binh province, Vietnam. Journal of Human Evolution 41:227–241.

Baker M. 1996. Fur rubbing: Use of medicinal plants by capuchin monkeys (*Cebus capucinus*). American Journal of Primatology 38:263–270.

Balakrishnan CN, Sorenson MD. 2006. Song discrimination suggests premating isolation among sympatric indigobird species and host races. Behavioral Ecology 17:473–478.

Baldwin JD. 1992. Determinants of aggression in squirrel monkeys (*Saimiri*). In Silverberg J, Gray JP editors. Aggression and peacefulness in humans and other primates, pp. 72–99. Oxford: Oxford University Press.

Balko EA. 1998. A behaviorally plastic response to forest composition and logging disturbances by *V. variegata variegata* in Ranomafana National Park, Madagascar. Ph.D. dissertation, SUNY-CESF, Syracuse, New York.

Barrett L, Henzi PS. 2000. Are baboon infants Sir Phillip Sydney's offspring? Ethology 106:645–658.

Barrett L, Henzi PS, Weingrill T, Lycett JE, Hill RA. 2000. Female baboons do not raise the stakes but they give as good as they get. Animal Behaviour 59:763–770.

Bartlett TQ. 1999. Socio-ecology of the white-handed gibbon in Khao Yai National Park, Thailand. Ph.D. dissertation. Washington University, St. Louis.

Bartlett TQ. 2003. Intragroup and intergroup social interactions in white-handed gibbons. International Journal of Primatology 24(2):239–259.

Bartlett TQ. 2007. The Hylobatidae: Small apes of Asia. In Campbell CJ, Fuentes A, MacKinnon KC, Panger M, Bearder SK editors. Primates in perspective, pp. 274–289. Oxford, UK: Oxford University Press.

Bartlett TQ, Sussman RW, Cheverud JM. 1993. Infant killing in primates: A review of observed cases with specific reference to the sexual selection hypothesis. American Anthropology 95:958–990.

Barton NH. 2001. The role of hybridization in evolution. Molecular Ecology 10:551–568.

Barton NH, Hewitt GM. 1985. Analysis of hybrid zones. Annual Review of Ecological Systems 16:113–148.

Barton RA. 2006a. Primate brain evolution: Integrating comparative, neurophysiological, and ethological data. Evolutionary Anthropology 15:224–236.

Barton RA. 2006b. Olfactory evolution and behavioral ecology in primates. American Journal of Primatology 68:545–558.

Barton RA, Whiten A, Strum SC, Byrne RW, Simpson AJ. 1992. Habitat use and resource availability in baboons. Animal Behaviour 43:831–844.

Basabose AK. 2005. Ranging patterns of chimpanzees in a montane forest of Kahuzi, Democratic Republic of Congo. International Journal of Primatology 26(1):33–54.

Bass WM. 2005. Human osteology: A laboratory and field manual. 5th Edition. Columbia: Missouri Archaeological Society.

Beard KC. 1998. A new genus of Tarsiidae (Mammalia: Primates) from the middle Eocene of Shanxi Province, China, with notes on the historical biogeography of tarsiers. Bulletin of the Carnegie Museum of Natural History 34:260–277.

Beard KC. 2002. Basal anthropoids. In Hartwig WC editor. The primate fossil record, pp. 133–149. Cambridge, UK: Cambridge University Press.

Beard KC, Qi T, Dawson MR, Wang B, Li C. 1994. A diverse new primate fauna from middle Eocene fissure-fillings in southeastern China. Nature 368:604–609.

Beard KC, Tong Y, Dawson MR, Wang J, Huang X. 1996. Earliest complete dentition of an anthropoid primate from the late middle Eocene of Shanxi Province, China. Science 272:82–85.

Beard KC, Wang J. 2004. The eosimiid primates (Anthropoidea) of the Heti Formation, Yuanqu Basin, Shanxi and Henan provinces, People's Republic of China. Journal of Human Evolution 46:401–432.

Bearder SK, Honess PE, Ambrose L. 1995. Species diversity among galagos with special reference to mate recognition. In Alterman L, Doyle GA, Izard MK editors. Creatures of the dark, pp. 331–352. New York: Plenum Press.

Bearder SK, Nekaris KAI, Curtis DJ. 2006. A re-evaluation of the role of vision in the activity and communication of nocturnal primates. Folia Primatologica 77(1–2):50–71.

Bearder SK, Nekaris KAI, Buzzell A. 2002. Dangers in the night: Are some nocturnal primates afraid of the dark? In Miller LE editor. Eat or be eaten: Predator sensitive foraging among, primates, pp. 21–43. Cambridge: Cambridge University Press.

Beck BB. 1980. Animal tool behavior. The use and manufacture of tools by animals. New York: Garland STPM.

Beck BB, Kleiman DG, Dietz JM, Castro MI, Carvalho C, Martins A, Rettberg-Beck B. 1991. Losses and reproduction in reintroduced golden lion tamarins (*Leontopithecus rosalia*). Dodo, Journal of Jersey Wildlife Preserve Trust 27:50–61.

Beck BB, Stoinski TS, Ballou J. 2002. The effects of pre-release environments on survivorship in reintroduced golden lion tamarins. In Kleiman DG and Rylands AB editors. Lion tamarins: Biology and conservation, pp. 283–300. Washington DC: Smithsonian Institution Press.

Begun DR. 2002. European hominoids. In Hartwig WC editor. The primate fossil record, pp. 339–368. Cambridge: Cambridge University Press.

Begun DR, Ward CV, Rose MD. 1997. Events in hominoid evolution. In Begun DR, Ward CV, Rose MD editors. Function, phylogeny and fossils: Miocene hominoid origins and adaptations, pp. 389–415. New York: Plenum Press.

Bell RHV. 1971. A grazing ecosystem in the Serengeti. Scientific American 225(1):86–93.

Benefit BR. 1999. *Victoriapithecus*, the key to Old World monkey and catarrhine origins. Evolutionary Anthropology 7:155–174.

Benefit BR, McCrossin MC. 2002. The Victoriapithecidae, Cercopithecoidea. In Hartwig WC editor. The primate fossil record, pp. 241–254. Cambridge, UK: Cambridge University Press.

Bennett ATD. 1996. Do animals have cognitive maps? The Journal of Experimental Biology 199:219–224.

Bennett EL, Sebastian AC. 1988. Social organisation and ecology of proboscis monkeys *Nasalis larvatus* in mixed costal forest in Sarawak. International Journal of Primatology 9:233–255.

Bennett J. 1992. A glut of gibbons in Sarawak: Is rehabilitation the answer? Oryx 26:157–164.

Benton MJ. 1998. Molecular and morphological phylogenies of mammals: Congruence with stratigraphic data. Molecular Phylogenetics and Evolution 9(3):398–407.

Bercovitch F. 1988. Coalitions, cooperation and reproductive tactics among adult male baboons. Animal Behaviour 36:1198–1209.

Bercovitch F. 1992. Re-examining the relationship between rank and reproduction in male primates. Animal Behaviour 44:1168–1170.

Bicca-Marques JC, Garber PA. 2003. Experimental field study of the relative costs and benefits to wild tamarins (*Saguinus imperator* and *Saguinus fuscicollis*) of exploiting contestable food patches as single- and mixed- species troops. American Journal of Primatology 60:139–153.

Bicca-Marques JC, Garber PA. 2004. Use of spatial, visual, and olfactory information during foraging in wild nocturnal and diurnal anthropoids: A field experiment comparing *Aotus*, *Callicebus*, and *Saguinus*. American Journal of Primatology 62:171–187.

Bicca-Marques JC, Garber PA. 2005. Use of social and ecological information in tamarin foraging decisions. International Journal of Primatology 26(6):1321–1344.

Birkinshaw CR. 1999. Use of millipedes by black lemurs to anoint their bodies. Folia Primatologica 70:170–171.

Birkinshaw CR, Colquhoun IC. 1998. Pollination of *Ravenala madagascariensis* and *Parkia madagascariensis* by *Eulemur macaco* in Madagascar. Folia Primatologica 69:252–259.

Biro D, Matsuzawa T. 2001. Chimpanzee numerical competence: Cardinal and ordinal skills. In Matsuzawa T editor. Primate origins of human cognition and behavior, pp. 199–225. New York: Springer.

Block M. 1991. Language, anthropology and cognitive science. Man 26:183–198.

Bloomsmith MA, Alford PL, Maple TL. 1988. Successful feeding enrichment for captive chimpanzees. American Journal of Primatology 16:155–164.

Blum D. 1994. The monkey wars. New York: Oxford University Press.

Blurton Jones N. 1993. The lives of hunter-gatherer children: Effects of parental behavior and parental reproductive strategy. In Periera ME, Fairbanks LA editors. Juvenile primates. Life history, development and behavior, pp. 309–326. Oxford, UK: Oxford University Press.

Boesch C. 1991. Teaching among wild chimpanzees. Animal Behaviour 41(3):530–532.

Boesch C. 1994. Cooperative hunting in wild chimpanzees. Animal Behaviour 48:653–667.

Boesch C, Boesch H. 1989. Hunting behavior of wild chimpanzees in the Taï National Park. American Journal of Physical Anthropology 78:547–573.

Boesch C, Boesch-Ackermann H. 2000. The chimpanzees of the Taï Forest. Behavioral ecology and evolution. Oxford, UK: Oxford University Press.

Boesch C, Marchesi P, Marchesi N, Fruth B, Joulian F. 1994. Is nut cracking in wild chimpanzees a cultural behavior? Journal of Human Evolution 26:325–338.

Boinski S. 1988. Use of a club by a wild white-faced capuchin (*Cebus capucinus*) to attack a venomous snake (*Bothrops asper*). American Journal of Primatology 14:177–179.

Boinski S. 1989. The positional behavior and substrate use of squirrel monkeys: Ecological implications. Journal of Human Evolution 18:659–677.

Boinski S. 1996. Vocal coordination of troop movements in squirrel monkeys (*Saimiri oerstedi* and *S. sciureus*) and white-faced capuchins (*Cebus capucinus*). In Norconk MA, Rosenberger AL, Garber PA editors. Adaptive radiation of neotropical primates, pp. 251–269. New York: Plenum Press.

Boinski S. 1999. The social organization of the squirrel monkeys: Implications for ecological models of social evolution. Evolutionary Anthropology 8:101–112.

Boinski S, Sughrue K, Selvaggi L, Quatrone R, Henry M, Cropp S. 2002. An expanded test of the ecological model of primate social evolution: Competitive regimes and female bonding in three species of squirrel monkeys (*Saimiri oerstedii*, *S. boliviensis*, and *S. sciureus*). Behaviour 139:227–261.

Boinski S, Treves A, Chapman CA. 2000. A critical evaluation of the influence of predators on primates: Effects on group travel. In Boinski S, Garber PA editors. On the move: How and why animals travel in groups, pp. 43–72. Chicago: University of Chicago Press.

Boonratana R. 2000. Ranging behavior of proboscis monkeys (*Nasalis larvatus*) in the lower Kinabatangan, Northern Borneo. International Journal of Primatology 21(3):497–518.

Borries K, Launhardt C, Epplen JT, Epplen P, Winkler C. 1999. DNA analyses support the hypothesis that infanticide is adaptive in langur monkeys. Proceedings of the Royal Society, London B 266:901–904.

Bowen-Jones E. 1998. A review of the commercial bushmeat trade with emphasis on central/West Africa and the great apes. In Report for the Ape Alliance. Cambridge, UK: Fauna & Flora International. *www.4apes.com/bushmeat/report/bushmeat.pdf* [accessed 27 August 2007].

Bower JM, Parsons LM. 2003. Rethinking the "lesser brain." Scientific American 289(2):40–47.

Boysen ST, Hallberg KI. 2000. Primate numerical competence: Contributions toward understanding nonhuman cognition. Cognitive Science 24(3):423–443.

Brack M. 1987. Agents transmissible from simians to man. Berlin: Springer-Verlag.

Bradshaw GA, Schore AN, Brown JL, Poole JH, Moss CJ. 2005. Elephant breakdown. Nature 433:807.

Brain C, Bohrmann R. 1992. Tick infestation of baboons (*Papio ursinus*) in the Namib desert. Journal of Wildlife Diseases 28(2):188–191.

Brain C, Mitchell D. 1999. Body temperature changes in free-ranging baboons (*Papio hamadryas ursinus*) in the Namib desert, Namibia. International Journal of Primatology 20(4):585–598.

Brand G, Millot J-L. 2001. Sex differences in human olfaction: Between evidence and enigma. Quarterly Journal of Experimental Psychology 54B(3):259–270.

Brandon-Jones D, Eudey AA, Geissmann T, Groves CP, Melnick DJ, Morales JC, Shekelle M, Stewart C-B. 2004. Asian primate classification. International Journal of Primatology 25:97–164.

Breuer T, Ndoundou-Hockemba M, Fishlock V. 2005. First observation of tool use in wild gorillas. PloS Biology 3(11):1–3 (*www.plosbiology. org*, DOI: 10.1371/journal.pbio.0030380).

Briggs JC. 2003. The biogeographic and tectonic history of India. Journal of Biogeography 30:381–388.

Britt A, Welch C, Katz A, Iambana B, Porton I, Junge R, Crawford G, Williams C, Haring D. 2004. The re-stocking of captive-bred ruffed lemurs (*Varecia variegata variegata*) into the Betampona Reserve, Madagascar: Methodology and recommendations. Biodiversity and Conservation 13:635–657.

Brockington D. 2002. Fortress conservation. The preservation of the Mkomazi game reserve, Tanzania. Bloomington: Indiana University Press.

Bromham L, Phillips MJ, Penny D. 1999. Growing up with dinosaurs: Molecular dates and the mammalian radiation. Trends in Evolution and Ecology 14(3):113–118.

Brown P, Sutikna T, Morwood MJ, Soejono RP, Jatmiko, Wayhu Saptomo E, Rokus Awe Due. 2004. A new small-bodied hominin from the Late Pleistocene of Flores, Indonesia. Nature 431:1055–1061.

Brown S. 2006. The west develops a taste for bushmeat. New Scientist 2559:8.

Brumm A, Aziz F, van den Bergh GD, Morwood MJ, Moore MW, Kurniawan I, Hobbs DR, Fullagar R. 2006. Early stone technology on Flores and its implications for *Homo floresiensis*. Nature 441:624–628.

Brunet M, Guy, F, Pilbeam D, Mackaye HT, Likius A, Ahounta D, Beauvilain A, Blondel C, Bocherens H, Boisserie J-R, de Bonis, L, Coppens Y, Dejax J, Denys C, Duringer P, Eisenmann V, Fanone G, Fronty P, Geraads D, Lehmann T, Lihoreau F, Louchart A, Mahamat A, Merceron G, Mouchelin G, Otero O, Pelaez Campomanes P, Ponce de Leon M, Rage J-C, Sapanet M, Schuster M, Sudre J, Tassy P, Valentin X, Vignaud P, Viriot L, Zazzo A, Zollikofer C. 2002. A new hominid from the Upper Miocene of Chad, Central Africa. Nature 418:145–151.

Buchan JC, Alberts SC, Silk JB, Altmann J. 2003. True paternal care in a multi-male primate society. Nature 425:179–181.

Buchanan-Smith HM. 1999. Tamarin polyspecific associations: Forest utilization and stability of mixed-species groups. Primates 40(1):233–247.

Burney DA. 1999. Rates, patterns, and processes of landscape transformation and extinction in Madagascar. In MacPhee RDE editor. Extinctions in near time: Causes, contexts, and consequences, pp. 145–164. New York: Plenum/Kluwer.

Burney DA, Ramilisonina. 1998. The kilopilopitsofy, kidoky, and bokyboky: Accounts of strange animals from Belo-sur-Mer, Madagascar, and megafaunal "extinction window." American Anthropologist 100:957–966.

Buzzard PJ. 2006a. Ecological partitioning of *Cercopithecus campbelli, C. petaurista*, and *C. diana* in the Taï Forest. International Journal of Primatology 27(2):529–558.

Buzzard PJ. 2006b. Ranging patterns in relation to seasonality and frugivory among *Cercopithecus campbelli, C. petaurista*, and *C. diana* in the Taï Forest. International Journal of Primatology 27(2):559–573.

Byrne RW. 1995. The thinking ape. Evolutionary origins of intelligence. Oxford, UK: Oxford University Press.

Byrne RW. 2006. Parsing behavior: A mundane origin for an extraordinary ability? In Levinson SC, Enfield NJ editors. The roots of human sociality: Culture, cognition and interaction, pp. 478–505. Oxford, UK: Berg Publisher.

Byrne RW, Whiten A. 1985. Tactical deception of familiar individuals in baboons (*Papio ursinus*). Animal Behaviour 33:669–673.

Byrne RW, Whiten A. 1988. Machiavellian intelligence. Social expertise and the evolution of intellect in monkeys, apes and humans. Oxford, UK: Clarendon.

Byrne RW, Whiten A, Henzi SP. 1989. Social relationships of mountain baboons: Leadership and affiliation in a nonfemale-bonded monkey. American Journal of Primatology 18:191–207.

Cain ML, Milligan BG, Strand AE. 2000. Long-distance seed dispersal in plant populations. American Journal of Botany 87:1217–1227.

Call J. 2000. Representing space and objects in monkeys and apes. Cognitive Science 24(3):397–422.

Calsbeek R, Smith TB. 2003. Ocean currents mediate evolution in island lizards. Nature 426:552–555.

Calvin WH. 1983. A stone's throw and its launch window: Timing precision and its implications for language and hominid brains. Journal of Theoretical Biology 104:121–135.

Cameron DW. 1997. A revised systematic scheme for the Eurasian Miocene fossil Hominidae. Journal of Human Evolution 33:449–477.

Campbell CJ. 2000. Fur rubbing behavior in free-ranging black-handed spider monkeys (*Ateles geoffroyi*) in Panama. American Journal of Primatology 51:205–208.

Campbell CJ, Fuentes A, MacKinnon KC, Panger M, Bearder SK editors. 2007. Primates in perspective. Oxford, UK: Oxford University Press.

Candland DK. 1987. Tool use. Comparative Primate Biology vol. 2B: Behavior, cognitive, and motivation, pp. 85–103. New York: Alan R Liss, Inc.

Cartmill M. 1972. Arboreal adaptations and the origin of the order Primates. In Tuttle R editor. The functional and evolutionary biology of primates, pp. 97–122. Chicago: Aldine.

Cartmill M. 1992. New views on primate origins. Evolutionary Anthropology 1(3):105–111.

Cauvin J. 2000. The birth of the gods and the origins of agriculture. Cambridge, UK: Cambridge University Press.

Cavalier-Smith T. 2002. The neomuran origin of archaebacteria, the negibacterial root of the universal tree and bacterial megaclassification. International Journal of Systematic and Evolutionary Microbiology 52:7–76.

Censky EJ, Hodge K, Dudley J. 1998. Over-water dispersal of lizards due to hurricanes. Nature 395:556.

CERCOPAN [Centre for education, research and conservation of primates and nature] *www.cercopan.org* [Accessed 13 August 2007]

Cerling TE, Harris JM. 1999. Carbon isotope fractionation between diet and bioapatite in ungulate mammals and implications for ecological and paleoecological studies. Oecologica 120 (3):347–363.

Chaimanee Y, Jolly D, Benammi M, Tafforeau P, Duzer D, Moussa I, Jaeger J-J. 2003. A middle Miocene hominoid from Thailand and orang-utan origins. Nature 422:61–65.

Chaimanee Y, Suteethorn V, Jintasakul P, Vidthayanon C, Marandat B, Jaeger J-J. 2004. A new orang-utan relative from the late Miocene of Thailand. Nature 427:439–441.

Chalise MK. 2001. Crop raiding by wildlife, especially primates, and indigenous practices for crop protection in Lakuwa area, East Nepal. Asian Primates 7(3–4):4–9.

Champoux M, Metz B, Suomi SJ. 1991. Behavior of nursery/peer-reared and mother-reared rhesus monkeys from birth through 2 years of age. Primates 32(4):509–514.

Chapman CA. 1995. Primate seed dispersal: Coevolution and conservation implications. Evolutionary Anthropology 4:74–82.

Chapman CA, Balcomb SR, Gillespie TR, Skorupa JP, Struhsaker TT. 2000. Long-term effects of logging on African primate communities: A 28-year comparison from Kibale National Park, Uganda. Conservation Biology 14:207–217.

Chapman CA, Chapman LJ, Glander KE. 1989. Primate populations in northwestern Costa Rica: Potential for recovery. Primates 10:37–44.

Chapman CA, Chapman LJ, Rode KD, Hauck EM, McDowell LR. 2003. Variation in the nutritional value of primate foods: Among trees, time periods, and areas. International Journal of Primatology 24(2):317–333.

Chapman CA, Gautier-Hion A, Oates JF, Onderdonk DA. 1999. African primate communities: Determinants of structure and threats to survival. In Fleagle JG, Janson C, Reed KE editors. Primate communities, pp. 1–37. Cambridge, UK: Cambridge University Press.

Chapman CA, Gillespie TR, Goldberg TL. 2005a. Primates and the ecology of their infectious diseases: How will anthropogenic changes affect host-parasite interactions? Evolutionary Anthropology 14:134–144.

Chapman CA, Lambert JE. 2000. Habitat alteration and the conservation of African primates: Case study of Kibale National Park, Uganda. American Journal of Primatology 50:169–185.

Chapman CA, Lawes MJ, Eeley HAC. 2006. What hope for African primate diversity? African Journal of Ecology 44:116–133.

Chapman CA, Russo SE. 2007 Primate seed dispersal: Linking behavioral ecology with forest community structure. In Campbell CJ, Fuentes A, MacKinnon KC, Panger M, Bearder SK editors. Primates in perspective, pp. 510–525. Oxford, UK: Oxford University Press.

Chapman CA, Struhsaker TT, Lambert JE. 2005b. Thirty years of research in Kibale National Park, Uganda, reveals a complex picture for conservation. International Journal of Primatology 26:539–555.

Chappell J, Kacelnik A. 2002. Tool selectivity in a non-primate, the New Caledonian crow (*Corvus moneduloides*). Animal Cognition 5:71–78.

Cheney DL. 1986. Interactions and relationships between groups. In Smuts BB, Cheney DL, Seyfarth RB, Wrangham RW, Struhskaer TT editors. Primate societies, pp. 267–281. Chicago: University of Chicago Press.

Cheney DL, Seyfarth RM. 1990. How monkeys see the world. Chicago: University of Chicago Press.

Cheney DL, Seyfarth RM, Silk JB. 1995. The role of grunts in reconciling opponents and facilitating interactions among adult female baboons. Animal Behaviour 50:249–257.

Chevalier-Skolnikoff S. 1990. Tool use by wild Cebus monkeys at Santa Rosa National Park, Costa Rica. Primates 31:375–383.

The Chimpanzee Sequencing and Analysis Consortium. 2005. Initial sequence of the chimpanzee genome and comparison with the human genome. Nature 437:69–87.

Chomsky N. 1975. Reflections on language. New York: Pantheon Press.

Chomsky N. 1986. Knowledge of language: Its nature, origin and use. New York: Praeger.

Ciochon RL, Gunnell GF. 2002. Chronology of primate discoveries in Myanmar: Influences on the anthropoid origins debate. Yearbook of Physical Anthropology 45:2–35.

Ciochon RL, Long VT, Larick R, González L, Grün R, de Vos J, Yonge C, Taylor L, Yoshida H, Reagan M. 1996. Date co-occurance of *Homo erectus* and *Gigantopithecus* from Tham Khuyen Cave, Vietnam. Proceedings of the National Academy of Science, USA 93:3016–3020.

Ciochon RL, Olsen J, James J. 1990a. Other origins: The search for the giant ape in human prehistory. New York: Bantam Books.

Ciochon RL, Piperno DR, Thompson RG. 1990b. Opal phytoliths found on the teeth of the extinct ape *Gigantopithecus blacki*: Implications for paleodietary studies. Proceedings of the National Academy of Science, USA 87:8120–8124.

Clack JA. 2002. An early tetrapod from "Romer's Gap." Nature 418:72–76.

Clark CJ, Poulsen JR, Parker VT. 2001. The role of arboreal seed dispersal groups on the seed rain of a lowland tropical forest. Biotropica 33(4):606–620.

Clark E, Reichard UH, Zuberbühler K. 2006. The syntax and meaning of wild gibbon song. PLoS ONE 1(1): e73 DOI:10.1371/journal.pone.0000073.

Clutton-Brock TH. 1977. Appendix 1: Methodology and measurement. In Clutton-Brock TH editor. Primate ecology: Studies of feeling and ranging behaviour in lemurs, monkeys and apes, pp. 585–590. London: Academic Press.

Clutton-Brock TH, Harvey PH. 1977. Primate ecology and social organization. Journal of Zoology, London 183:1–39.

Clutton-Brock TH, Harvey PH. 1980. Primates, brains and ecology. Journal of Zoology, London 190:309–323.

Codron D, Lee-Thorp JA, Sponheimer M, de Ruiter D, Codron J. 2006. Inter- and intrahabitat dietary variability of chacma baboons (*Papio ursinus*) in South African savannas based on fecal $\partial^{13}C$, $\partial^{15}N$, and %N. American Journal of Physical Anthropology 129:204–214.

Collins AC. 2004. Atelinae phylogenetic relationships: The trichotomy revived? American Journal of Physical Anthropology 124:285–296.

Collins DA. 1984. Spatial patterns in a troop of yellow baboons (*Papio cynocephalus*) in Tanzania. Animal Behaviour 32:536–553.

Collinson AS. 1988. Introduction to world vegetation. Boston: George Unwin & Hyman.

Colmenares F, Hofer H, East ML. 2000. Greeting ceremonies in baboons and hyenas. In Aureli F, de Waal FBM editors. Natural conflict resolution, pp. 94–96. Los Angeles: University of California Press.

Connell JH. 1978. Diversity in tropical rain forests and coral reefs. Science 199:1302–1310.

Connor RC, Mann J, Tyack PL, Whitehead H. 1998. Social evolution in toothed whales. Trends in Ecology and Evolution 13(6):228–232.

Conroy GC. 1987. Problems in body weight estimation in fossil primates. International Journal of Primatology 8:115–137.

Conroy GC. 1990. Primate evolution. New York: W.W. Norton.

Conroy GC. 1999. Reconstructing human origins. A modern synthesis. New York: W.W. Norton.

Conservation International. 2007. *www.conservation.org* link to: *www.biodiversityhotspots.org/xp/hotspots/ atlantic_forest/pages/default.aspx* [Accessed 20 August 2007].

Corballis MC. 1992. On the evolution of language and generativity. Cognition 44:197–226.

Corballis MC. 2002. From hand to mouth – the origins of language. Princeton, NJ: Princeton University Press.

Costa LP, Reis Leite YL, Mendes SL, Ditchfield AD. 2005. Mammal conservation in Brazil. Conservation Biology 19(3):672–679.

Covert HH. 2002. The earliest fossil primates and the evolution of prosimians: Introduction. In Hartwig WC editor. The primate fossil record, pp. 13–20. Cambridge, UK: Cambridge University Press.

Cowlishaw G. 1999. Predicting the pattern of decline of African primate diversity: An extinction debt from historical deforestation. Conservation Biology 13(5):1183–1193.

Cowlishaw G, Mendelson S, Rowcliffe JM. 2005. Structure and operation of a bushmeat commodity chain in Southwestern Ghana. Conservation Biology 19(1):139–149.

Cracraft J. 1983. The significance of phylogenetic classifications for systematic and evolutionary biology. In Felsenstein J editor. Numerical taxonomy, pp. 1–17. Berlin: Springer.

Cracraft J. 1997. Species concepts in systematics and conservation biology – an ornithological viewpoint. In Claridge MF, Dawah AA, Wilson MR editors. Species: The units of biodiversity, pp. 325–339. New York: Chapman and Hall.

Cramer AE, Gallistel CR. 1997. Vervet monkeys as traveling salesmen. Nature 387:464.

Crawford RL. 2001. Animal Welfare Act. Interpretative summaries. *www.nal.usda.gov* [Accessed 27 August 2007].

Crockett CM, Eisenberg JF. 1986. Howlers: Variation in group size and demography. In Smuts BB, Cheney DL, Seyfarth RM, Wrangham RW, Struhsaker TT editors. Primate societies, pp. 54–68. Chicago: University of Chicago Press.

Curran LM, Trigg SN, McDonald AK, Astiani D, Hardiono YM, Siregar P, Caniago I, Kasischke E. 2004. Lowland forest loss in protected areas of Indonesian Borneo. Science 303:1000–1003.

Curtin RA, Dolhinow P. 1978. Primate social behavior in a changing world. American Scientist 66:468–475.

da Silva JMC, Tabarelli M. 2001. The future of the Atlantic Forest in northeastern Brazil. Conservation Biology 15(4):819–820.

Daeschler EB, Shubin NH, Jenkins FA Jr. 2006. A Devonian tetrapod-like fish and the evolution of the tetrapod body plan. Nature 440:757–763.

Davenport, TRB, Stanley WT, Sargis EJ, De Luca DW, Mpunga NE, Machaga SJ, Olson LE. 2006. A new genus of African monkey, *Rungwecebus*: Morphology, ecology, and molecular phylogenetics. Science 312:1378–1381.

de A. Moura AC, Lee PC. 2004. Capuchin stone tool use in Caatinga dry forest. Science 306:1909.

de Beer G. 1954. Archaeopteryx and evolution. Advances in Science, London 42:160–170.

de Bonis L, Koufos G. 1997. The phylogenetic and functional implications of *Ouranopithecus macedoniensis*. In Begun DR, Ward CV, Rose MD editors. Function, phylogeny and fossils: Miocene hominid evolution and adaptations, pp. 317–326. New York: Plenum Press.

de la Bedoyere C, Campbell B. 2005. No one loved gorillas more. Washington DC: National Geographic.

de Waal FBM 1982. Chimpanzee politics: Power and sex among apes. New York: Harper and Row.

de Waal FBM. 1989. Peacemaking among primates. Cambridge, MA: Harvard University Press.

de Waal FBM. 1996. Conflict as negotiation. In McGrew WC, Marchant LF, Nishida T editors. Great ape societies, pp. 159–172. Cambridge, UK: Cambridge University Press.

de Waal FBM. 1998. Chimpanzee politics: Power and sex among apes. Baltimore: The Johns Hopkins University Press.

de Waal FBM. 1999. Cultural primatology comes of age. Nature 399:635–636.

de Waal FBM. 2000. The first kiss. Foundations of conflict resolution research in animals. In Aureli F, de Waal FBM editors. Natural conflict resolutions, pp. 15–33. Los Angeles: University of California Press.

de Waal FBM. 2001. The ape and the sushi master. New York: Basic Books.

de Waal FBM. 2003. Silent invasion: Imanishi's primatology and cultural bias in science. Animal Cognition 6:293–299.

Deacon TW. 1995. Primate brains and senses. In Jones S, Martin RD, Pilbeam D editors. The Cambridge encyclopedia of human evolution, pp. 109–114. Cambridge, UK: Cambridge University Press.

Dean W. 1995. With broadaxe and firebrand: The destruction of the Brazilian Atlantic Forest. San Francisco: University of California Press.

Deblauwe I, Dupain J, Nguenang GM, Werdenich D, van Elsacker L. 2003. Insectivory by *Gorilla gorilla gorilla* in southern Cameroon. International Journal of Primatology 24(3):493–502.

Deecke VB, Ford JKB, Spong P. 2000. Dialect change in resident killer whales: Implications for vocal learning and cultural transmission. Animal Behaviour 60:629–638.

Defler TR. 2003. Primates de Colombia. Conservación Internacional, Bogotá.

Delfer TR, Rodriguez JV, Hernandez-Camacho JI. 2003. Conservation priorities for Colombian primates. Primate Conservation 19:10–18.

Demment MW, Laca EA. 1991. Herbivory: The dilemma of foraging in a spatially heterogeneous food environment. In Palo RT, Robbins CT editors. Plant defenses against mammalian herbivory, pp. 29–44. Boca Raton, FL: CRC Press.

Detwiler KM, Burrell A, Jolly CJ. 2005. Conservation implications of hybridization in African Cercopithecine monkeys. International Journal of Primatology 26(3):661–684.

DeVore I, Hall KRL. 1965. Baboon ecology. In DeVore I editor. Primate behavior. Field studies of monkeys and apes, pp. 20–52. New York: Holt, Rinehart and Winston.

DeVore I, Washburn SL. 1963. Baboon ecology and human evolution. In Howell FC, Bourlière F editors. African ecology and human evolution, pp. 335–367. New York: Wenner-Gren Foundation.

Dew JL. 2005. Foraging, food choice, and food processing by sympatric ripe-fruit specialists: *Lagothrix lagotrich poeppigii* and *Ateles belzebuth belzebuth*. International Journal of Primatology 26(5):1107–1135.

Di Bitetti MS, Janson CH. 2001. Social foraging and the finder's share in capuchin monkeys, *Cebus apella*. Animal Behaviour 62: 47–56.

Dietz JM, Peres CA, Pinder L. 1997. Foraging ecology and use of space in wild golden lion tamarins (*Leontopithecus rosalia*). American Journal of Primatology 41:289–305.

Di Fiore A, Link A, Stevenson PR. 2006. Scent marking in two western Amazonian populations of woolly monkeys (*Lagothrix lagotricha*). American Journal of Primatology 68(6):637–649.

Di Fiore A, Rodman PS. 2001. Time allocation patterns of lowland woolly monkeys (*Lagothrix lagotricha poeppigii*) in a neotropical *terra firma* forest. International Journal of Primatology 22(3):449–480.

Digby LS, Ferrari SF, Saltzman W. 2007. Callitrichines: The role of competition in cooperatively breeding species. In Campbell CJ, Fuentes A, MacKinnon KC, Panger M, Bearder SK editors. Primates in perspective, pp. 85–105. Oxford, UK: Oxford University Press.

Ding W, Zhao Q-K. 2004. *Rhinopithecus bieti* at Tacheng, Yunnan: Diet and daytime activities. International Journal of Primatology 25(3):583–598.

Dirzo R, Loreau M. 2005. Biodiversity science evolves. Science 310:943.

Dixon AF. 1998. Primate sexuality. Comparative studies of the prosimians, monkeys, apes and human beings. Oxford, UK: Oxford University Press.

Dobzhansky T. 1935. A critique of the species concept in biology. Philosophy of Science 2:344–355.

Dolhinow P. 1977. Normal monkeys? American Scientist 65:266.

Dolhinow P, DeMay MG. 1982. Adoption: The importance of infant choice. Journal of Human Evolution 11:391–420.

Dominy NJ, Duncan BW. 2005. Seed-spitting primates and the conservation and dispersion of large-seeded trees. International Journal of Primatology 26(3):631–649.

Dominy NJ, Garber PA, Bicca-Marques JC, Azevedo-Lopes MAO. 2003. Do female tamarins use visual cues to detect fruit rewards more successfully than do males? Animal Behaviour 66:829–837.

Dominy NJ, Lucas PW. 2001. Ecological importance of trichromatic vision to primates. Nature 410:363–366.

Douglas-Hamilton I. 1972. On the ecology and behaviour of the African elephant: The elephants of Manyara. Ph. D. Thesis, University of Oxford, UK.

Duggen S, Hoernle K, van der Bogaard P, Rüpke L, Morgan JP. 2003. Deep roots of the Messinian salinity crisis. Nature 422:602–606.

Dugmore SJ, Evens CS. 1990. Discrimination of conspecific chemosignals by female ringtailed lemurs, *Lemur catta* L. In Macdonald DW, Müller-Schwarze D, Natynczuk SE editors. Chemical signals in vertebrates 5, pp. 360–366. New York: Plenum Press.

Dunbar RIM. 1984. Reproductive decisions. An economic analysis of gelada baboon social strategies. Princeton, NJ: Princeton University Press.

Dunbar RIM. 1992a. Neocortex size as a constraint on group size in primates. Journal of Human Evolution 22:469–493.

Dunbar RIM. 1992b. Time: A hidden constraint on the behavioural ecology of baboons. Behavioral Ecology and Sociobiology 31:35–49.

Dunbar RIM. 1996. Grooming, gossip, and the evolution of language. Cambridge, MA: Harvard University Press.

Dunbar RIM. 1998. The social brain hypothesis. Evolutionary Anthropology 6:178–190.

Dunbar RIM. 2002. Modeling primate behavioral ecology. International Journal of Primatology 23(4):785–819.

Eisenberg JF, O'Connell MA, August PV. 1979. Density, productivity, and distribution of mammals in two Venezuelan habitats. In Eisenberg JF editor. Vertebrate ecology in the northern neotropics, pp. 187–209. Washington DC: Smithsonian Institution Press.

Elango N, Thomas JW, NISC Comparative Sequencing Program, Yi SV. 2006. Variable molecular clocks in hominoids. Proceedings of the National Academy of Science USA 103(5):1370–1375.

Emery NJ, Clayton NS. 2004. The mentality of crows: Convergent evolution of intelligence in corvids and apes. Science 306:1903–1907.

Enard W, Przeworski M, Fisher SE, Lai CSL, Wiebe V, Kitano T, Monaco AP, Pääbo S. 2002. Molecular evolution of FOXP2, a gene involved in speech and language. Nature 418:869–872.

Enstam KL, Isbell LA. 2007. The guenons (Genus *Cercopithecus*) and their allies: Behavioral ecology of polyspecific associations. In Campbell CJ, Fuentes A, MacKinnon KC, Panger M, Bearder SK editors. Primates in perspective, pp. 252–274. Oxford, UK: Oxford University Press.

Epple G, Belcher AM, Kuderling I, Zeller U, Scolnock L, Greenfield KL, Smith III, AB. 1993. Making sense out of scents: Species differences in scent glands, scent marking behavior, and scent mark composition in the Callitrichidae. In Rylands AB editor. Marmosets and tamarins: Systematics, behaviour and ecology, pp. 123–151. Oxford, UK: Oxford University Press.

Evans BJ, Supriatna J, Melnick DJ. 2001. Hybridization and population genetics of two macaque species in Sulawesi, Indonesia. Evolution 55(8):1686–1702.

Evans CS. 2006. Accessory chemosignaling mechanisms in primates. American Journal of Primatology 68:525–544.

Fa JE. 1984. Structure and dynamics of the Barbary macaque population in Gibraltar. In Fa JE editor. The barbary macaques. A case study in conservation, pp. 263–306. New York: Plenum Press.

Fa JE, Ryan SF, Bell DJ. 2005. Hunting vulnerability, ecological characteristics and harvest rates of bushmeat species in Afrotropical forests. Biological Conservation 121:167–176.

Fa JE, Seymour S, Dupain J, Amin R, Albrechtsen L, Macdonald D. 2006. Getting to grips with the magnitude of exploitation: Bushmeat in the Cross-Sanaga rivers region, Nigeria and Cameroon. Biological Conservation 129:497–510.

Faegri K, Vander Pijl L. 1971. The principles of pollination ecology. 2nd edition. Oxford, UK: Pergamon Press.

Fairbanks LA. 1993. Juvenile vervet monkeys: Establishing relationships and practicing skills for the future. In Periera ME, Fairbanks LA editors. Juvenile primates. Life history, development and behavior, pp. 211–227. Oxford, UK: Oxford University Press.

Fairbanks LA, McGuire MT. 1986. Longterm effects of early mothering behavior on responsiveness to the environment in vervet monkeys. Developmental Psychobiology 21:711–724.

Falk D. 2000. Primate diversity. New York: WW Norton & Company.

Falk D, Hildebolt C, Smith K, Morwood MJ, Sutikna T, Brown P, Jatmiko, Wayhu Saptomo E, Brunsden B, Prior F. 2005. The brain of LB1, *Homo floresiensis*. Science 308:242–245.

Fallon S, Enig MG. 1999. Australian Aborigines – living off the fat of the land. The Weston A. Price Foundation. available at: *www.westonaprice.org/traditional_diets/ australian_aborigines.html* [Accessed 27 August 2007].

Farmer KH. 2002. Pan-African Sanctuary Alliance: Status and range of activities for great ape conservation. American Journal of Primatology 58:117–132.

Fashing PJ. 2007. African Colobine monkeys: Patterns of between-group interaction. In

Campbell CJ, Fuentes A, MacKinnon KC, Panger M, Bearder SK editors. Primates in perspective, pp. 201–224. Oxford, UK: Oxford University Press.

Fashing PJ, Cords M. 2000. Diurnal primate densities and biomass in the Kakamega forest: An evaluation of census methods and a comparison with other forests. American Journal of Primatology 50:139–152.

Fashing PJ, Oates JF. (in press). *Colobus guereza*. In Kingdon J, Happold D, Butynski T editors. The mammals of Africa. London: Academic Press.

Fay JM, Carroll R, Kerbis Peterhans JC, Harris D. 1995. Leopard attack on and consumption of gorillas in the Central African Republic. Journal of Human Evolution 29(1):93–99.

Fearnside PM, Barbosa RI. 2004. Accelerating deforestation in Brazilian Amazonia: Towards answering open questions. Environmental Conservation 31(1):7–10.

Fedigan LM. 1993. Sex differences and intrasexual relations in adult white-faced capuchins (*Cebus capucinus*). International Journal of Primatology 14:853–877.

Fedigan LM, Jack KM. 2001. Neotropical primates in a regenerating Costa Rican dry forest: A comparison of howler and capuchin population patterns. International Journal of Primatology 22:689–713.

Fedigan LM, Pavelka MSM. 2001. Is there adaptive value to reproductive termination in Japanese macaques? A test of maternal investment hypotheses. International Journal of Primatology 22(2):109–125.

Feeley K. 2005. The role of clumped defecation in the spatial distribution of soil nutrients and the availability of nutrients for plant uptake. Journal of Tropical Ecology 21:99–102.

Felsenstein J. 2005. PHYLIP (Phylogeny Inference Package) version 3.65 available at *http://evolution.genetics.washington.edu/ phylip.html* [Accessed 13 August 2007].

Ferrari SF, Iwanaga S, Messias MR, Ramos EM, Ramos PCS, Cruz Neto EHD, Coutinho PEG. 2000. Titi monkeys (*Callicebus* sp., Atelidae: Platyrrhini) in the Brazilian state of Rondônia. Primates 41:229–234.

Ferreira LV, Prance GT. 1998. Structure and species richness of low-diversty floodplain forest on the Rio Tapajós, eastern Amazonia, Brazil. Biodiversity and Conservation 7:585–596.

Fietz J, Ganzhorn JU. 1999. Feeding ecology of the hibernating primate *Cheirogaleus medius*: How does it get so fat? Oecologia 121:157–164.

Finlayson C. 2005. Biogeography and evolution of the genus *Homo*. Trends in Ecology and Evolution 20(8):457–463.

Fisher J, Metz M, Cheney DL, Seyfarth RM. 2001. Baboon responses to graded bark variants. Animal Behaviour 61:925–931.

Fleagle JG. 1999. Primate adaptation and evolution. 2nd edition. New York: Academic Press.

Foer J. 2005. Pushing PhyloCode. Discover 26(4):46–51.

Foerg R, Hoffmann R. 1982. Seasonal and daily activity changes in captive *Cheirogaleus medius*. Folia Primatologica 38:259–268.

Fogassi L, Ferrari PF, Gesierich B, Rozzi S, Chersi F, Rizzolatti G. 2005. Parietal lobe: From action organization to intentional understanding. Science 308:662–667.

Ford SM. 1986. Systematics of the new world monkeys. In Swindler DS, Erwin J editors. Comparative primate biology, Vol. 1, Systematics, evolution, and anatomy, pp. 73–135. New York: Alan R. Liss.

Fossey D, Harcourt AH. 1977. Feeding ecology of free-ranging mountain gorillas (*Gorilla gorilla beringei*). In Clutton-Brock TH editor. Primate ecology: Studies of feeding and ranging behaviour in lemurs, monkeys, and apes, pp. 415–447. New York: Academic Press.

Fouts RS, Fouts DH, van Cantfort TE. 1989. The infant Loulis learns signs from cross-fostered chimpanzees. In Gardner RA, Gardner BT, van Cantfort TE editors. Teaching sign language to chimpanzees, pp. 280–292. Albany, NY: SUNY Press.

Fouts RS, Hirsch AD, Fouts DH. 1982. Cultural transmission of a human language in a chimpanzee mother-infant relationship. In Fitzgerald HE, Mullins JA, Gage P editors. Child nurturance. Studies of development in nonhuman primates, pp. 159–193. New York: Plenum Press.

Fragaszy DM, Visalberghi E, Fedigan LM. 2004. The complete capuchin. The biology of the genus *Cebus*. Cambridge, UK: Cambridge University Press.

Freed BZ. 2007. Social organization in two sympatric lemur species: A lack of dominance. American Journal of Physical Anthropology Supplement 44:110.

Freeman MMR, Bogoslovskaya L, Caulfield RA, Egede I, Krupnik II, Stevenson MG. 1998. Inuit, whaling, and sustainability. Walnut Creek, CA: AltaMira Press.

Fuentes A. 1999. Re-evaluating primate monogamy. American Anthropologist 100:890–907.

Fuentes A. 2002. Patterns and trends in primate pair bonds. International Journal of Primatology 23(5):953–978.

Furuichi T, Hashimoto C, Tashiro Y. 2001. Fruit availability and habitat use by chimpanzees in the Kalinzu Forest, Uganda: Examination of fallback foods. International Journal of Primatology 22:929–945.

Gagneux P, Moore JJ, Varki A. 2005. The ethics of research on great apes. Nature 437:27–29.

Gagneux P, Wills C, Gerloff U, Tautz D, Morin PA, Boesch C, Fruth B, Hohmann G, Ryder OA, Woodruff DS. 1999. Mitochondrial sequences show diverse evolutionary histories of African hominoids. Proceedings of the National Academy of Science, USA. 96:5077–5082.

Galdikas BMF. 1982. Orang-utan tool-use at Tanjung Putting Reserve, Central Indonesian Borneo (Kalimantan Tengah). Journal of Human Evolution 11(1):19–33.

Galdikas BMF. 1995. Reflections of Eden: My years with the orangutans of Borneo. Boston: Little, Brown and Company.

Galef BG. 1988. Imitation in animals. In Galef BG, Zentrall T editors. Social learning: Psychological and biological perspectives, pp. 3–28. Hillsdale, NJ: Lawrence Erlbaum.

Gallup GG Jr. 1991. Toward a comparative psychology of self-awareness: Species limitations and cognitive consequences. In Goethals GR, Strauss J editors. The self: An interdisciplinary approach, pp. 121–135. New York: Springer Verlag.

Gallup GG Jr. 1994. Self-recognition: Research strategies and experimental design. In Parker ST, Mitchell RW, Boccia ML editors. Self-awareness in animals and humans: Developmental prospectives, pp. 35–50. Cambridge UK: Cambridge University Press.

Gannon PJ, Holloway RL, Broadfield DC, Braun AR. 1998. Asymmetry of chimpanzee planum temporale: Humanlike pattern of Wernicke's brain language area homolog. Science 279:220–222.

Ganzhorn JU. 1995. Low-level forest disturbance effects on primary production, leaf chemistry, and lemur populations. Ecology 76(7):2084–2096.

Ganzhorn JU, Fietz J, Rakotovao E, Schwab D, Zinner D. 1999. Lemurs and the regeneration of dry deciduous forest in Madagascar. Conservation Biology 13(4):794–804.

Gao F, Bailes E, Robertson DL, Chen Y, Rodenburg CM, Michael SF, Cummins LB, Arthur LO, Peeters M, Shaw GM, Sharp PM, Hahn BH. 1999. Origin of HIV-1 in the chimpanzee *Pan troglodytes troglodytes*. Nature 397:436–441.

Garber PA. 1987. Foraging strategies among living primates. Annual Review of Anthropology 16:339–364.

Garber PA. 1988. Diet, foraging patterns and resource defense in a mixed-species troop of *Saguinus mystax* and *Saguinus fuscicollis* in Amazonian Peru. Behaviour 105:18–34.

Garber PA. 1989. Role of spatial memory in primate foraging patterns: *Saguinus mystax* and *Saguinus fuscicollis*. American Journal of Primatology 19(4):203–216.

Garber PA. 1993. Feeding ecology and behaviour of the genus *Saguinus*. In Rylands AB editor. Marmosets and tamarins: Systematics, behaviour, and ecology, pp. 273–295. Oxford, UK: Oxford University Press.

Garber PA, Hannon B. 1993. Modeling monkeys: A comparison of computer-generated and naturally occurring foraging patterns in two species of neotropical primates. International Journal of Primatology 14(6):827–852.

Garber PA, Leigh SR. 1997. Ontogenetic variation in small-bodied New World primates: Implications for patterns of reproduction and infant care. Folia Primatologica 68:1–22.

Garber PA, Paciulli LM. 1997. Experimental field study of spatial memory and learning in wild capuchin monkeys (*Cebus capuchinus*). Folia Primatologica 68:236–253.

Gardner RA, Gardner BT. 1969. Teaching sign language to a chimpanzee. Science 165:664–672.

Gause GF. 1934. The struggle for existence. Baltimore: Williams & Wilkins.

Gautier-Hion A. 1971. L'Ecologie du talapoin du Gabon. Terre Vie 25:427–490.

Gautier-Hion A, 1980. Seasonal variations of diet related to species and sex in a community of *Cercopithecus* monkeys. Journal of Animal Ecology 49:237–269.

Gautier-Hion A, Bourlière F, Gautier J-P, Kingdon J. 1988. A primate radiation: Evolutionary biology of the African guenons. New York: Cambridge University Press.

Gautier-Hion A, Maisels F. 1994. Mutualism between a leguminous tree and large African monkeys as pollinators. Behavioral Ecology and Sociobiology 34:203–210.

Gebo DL. 2002. Adapiformes: Phylogeny and adaptation. In Hartwig WC editor. The primate fossil record, pp. 21–43. Cambridge, UK: Cambridge University Press.

Gebo DL, Dagosto M, Beard KC, Qi T. 2001. Middle Eocene primate tarsals from China: Implications for haplorhine evolution. American Journal of Physical Anthropology 116:83–107.

Gebo DL, MacLatchy L, Kityo R, Deino A, Kingston J, Pilbeam D. 1997. A hominoid genus from the Early Miocene of Uganda. Science 276:401–404.

Geissmann T, Orgeldinger M. 2000. The relationship between duet songs and pair bonds in siamangs, *Hylobates syndactylus*. Animal Behavior 60:805–809.

Gheerbrant E, Thomas H, Sen S, Al-Sulaimani Z. 1995. Nouveau primate Oligopithecinae (Simiiformes) de l'Oligocène inférieur de Taqah, Sultanat d'Oman. Comptes Rendís de l'Académie des Sciences, Paris 321:425–432.

Gilbert KA. 1997. Red howling monkey use of specific defecation sites as a parasite avoidance strategy. Animal Behaviour 54:451–455.

Gillespie TR, Chapman CA. 2006. Prediction of parasite infection dynamics in primate metapopulations based on attributes of forest fragmentation. Conservation Biology 20(2):441–448.

Gillespie TR, Chapman CA, Greiner EC. 2005. Effects of logging on gastrointestinal parasite infections and infection risk in African primates. Journal of Applied Ecology 42:699–707.

Ginsberg JR, Alexander KA, Creel S, Kat PW, Mcnutt JW, Mills MGL. 1995. Handling and survivorship of African wild dog (*Lycaon pictus*) in five ecosystems. Conservation Biology 9(3):665–674.

Glander KE. 1980. Reproduction and population growth in free-ranging mantled howling monkeys. American Journal of Physical Anthropology 53:25–36.

Glander KE, Wright PC, Seigler DS, Randrianasolo V, Randrianasolo B.1989. Consumption of cyanogenic bamboo by a newly discovered species of bamboo lemur. American Journal of Primatology 19:119–124.

Godfrey LR, Jungers WL. 2002. Quaternary fossil lemurs. In Hartwig WC editor. The primate fossil record, pp. 97–121. Cambridge, UK: Cambridge University Press.

Godfrey LR, Semprebon GM, Schwartz GT, Burney DA, Jungers WL, Flanagan EK, Cuozzo FP, King SJ. 2005. New insights into old lemurs: The trophic adaptations of the Archaeolemuridae. International Journal of Primatology 26(4):825–854.

Godinot M. 1994. Early north African primates and their significance for the origin of Simiiformes (Anthropoidea). In Fleagle JG, Kay RF editors. Anthropoid origins, pp. 235–295. New York: Plenum Press.

Goldstein SJ. 1984. Feeding ecology of rhesus monkeys (*Macaca mulatta*) in northwestern Pakistan. Ph.D. Thesis, Yale University.

Goodall J. 1964. Tool-using and aimed throwing in a community of free-living chimpanzees. Nature 201:1264–1266.

Goodall J. 1965. Chimpanzees of the Gombe Stream Reserve. In DeVore I editor. Primate behavior. Field studies of monkeys and apes, pp. 425–473. New York: Holt, Rinehart and Winston.

Goodall J. 1971. In the shadow of man. Boston: Houghton Mifflin.

Goodall J. 1986. The chimpanzee of Gombe. Patterns of behavior. Cambridge, MA: The Belknap Press of Harvard University Press.

Goodall J. 1990 Through a window: My thirty years with the chimpanzees of Gombe. Boston: Houghton Mifflin Company.

Goodman M, Porter CA, Czelusniak J, Page SL, Schneider H, Shoshani J, Gunnell G, Groves CP. 1998. Toward a phylogenetic classification of primates based on DNA evidence complemented by fossil evidence. Molecular Phylogenetics and Evolution 9(3):585–598.

Goodman SM, Benstead JP editors. 2003. The natural history of Madagascar. Chicago: University of Chicago Press.

Goodman SM, O'Connor S, Langrand O. 1993. A review of predation on lemurs: Implications for the evolution of social behavior in small, nocturnal primates. In Kappeler PM, Ganzhorn JU editors. Lemur social systems and their ecological basis, pp. 51–66. New York: Plenum Press.

Goosen C. 1987. Social grooming in primates. In Mitchell G, Erwin J editors. Comparative primate biology. Vol. 2 Behaviour, cognition and motivation, pp. 107–131. New York: AR Liss.

Goossen B, Setchell JM, Tchidongo E, Dilambaka E, Vidal C, Ancrenaz M, Jamart A. 2005. Survival, interactions with conspecifics and reproduction in 37 chimpanzees released into the wild. Biological Conservation 123:461–475.

The Gorilla Foundation @ *www.koko.org* [Accessed 3 August 2007].

Gould L. 1992. Alloparental care in free-ranging *Lemur catta* at Berenty Reserve, Madagascar. Folia Primatologica 58:72–83.

Gould L. 1997. Intermale affiliative behavior in ringtailed lemur (*Lemur catta*) at the Beza-Mahafaly Reserve, Madagascar. Primates 38:15–30.

Gould L, Overdorff DJ. 2002. Adult male scent-marking in *Lemur catta* and *Eulemur fulvus rufus*. International Journal of Primatology 23(3):575–586.

Gould L, Sussman RW, Sauther ML. 1999. Natural disasters and primate populations: The effects of a 2-year drought on a naturally occurring population of ringtailed lemurs (*Lemur catta*) in southwestern Madagascar. International Journal of Primatology 20(1):69–84.

Grant BR, Grant PR. 1996. High survival of Darwin's finch hybrids: Effects of beak morphology and diets. Ecology 77:500–509.

Grant PR, Grant BR. 1992. Hybridization of bird species. Science 256:193–197.

Green GM, Sussman RW. 1990. Deforestation history of the eastern rain forests of Madagascar from satellite images. Science 248:212–215.

Green S. 1975. Communication by a graded vocal system in Japanese monkeys. In Rosenblum LA editor. Primate behavior, pp. 1–102. New York: Academic Press.

Greenfield PM, Savage-Rumbaugh SE. 1990. Grammatical combination in *Pan paniscus*: Processes of learning and invention in the evolution and development of language. In Parker ST, Gibson KR editors. "Language" and intelligence in monkeys and apes: Comparative developmental perspectives, pp. 540–578. Cambridge, UK: Cambridge University Press.

Groves C. 2000. What, if anything, is taxonomy? Gorilla Journal 21:12–15.

Groves C. 2001. Primate taxonomy. Washington, DC: The Smithsonian Institution Press.

Groves C. 2004. The what, why and how of primate taxonomy. International Journal of Primatology 25(5):1105–1126.

Grubb P, Butynski TM, Oates JF, Bearder SK, Disotell TR, Groves CP, Struhsaker TT. 2003. Assessment of the diversity of African primates. International Journal of Primatology 24:1301–1357.

Grubb P, Jones TS, Davies AG, Edberg E, Starin ED, Hill JE. 1998. Mammals of Ghana, Sierra Leone and the Gambia. St. Ives, UK: Trendrine Press.

Gunnell GF. 2002. Notharctine primates (Adapiformes) from the early to middle Eocene (Wasatchian-Bridgerian) of Wyoming: Transitional species and the origins of *Notharctus* and *Smilodectes*. Journal of Human Evolution 43:353–380.

Gupta AK. 2004. Origin of agriculture and domestication of plants and animals linked to early Holocene climate amelioration. Current Science 87(1):54–59.

Gursky S. 2003. Lunar philia in a nocturnal primate. International Journal of Primatology 24(2):351–367.

Gursky S. 2007a. Tarsiiformes. In Campbell CJ, Fuentes A, MacKinnon KC, Panger M, Bearder SK editors. Primates in perspective, pp. 73–85. Oxford, UK: Oxford University Press.

Gursky S. 2007b. Primate field studies: The spectral, tarsier. Upper Saddle River, NJ: Pearson Prentice Hall.

Haesler S, Wada K, Nshdejan A, Morrisey EE, Lints T, Jarvis ED, Scharff C. 2004. *FoxP2* expression in avian vocal learners and non-learners. Journal of Neuroscience 24:3164–3175.

Haile-Selassie Y. 2001. Late Miocene hominids from the Middle Awash, Ethiopia. Nature 412:178–181.

Hall KRL, DeVore I. 1965. Baboon social behavior. In DeVore I editor. Primate behavior. Field studies of monkeys and apes, pp. 53–110. New York: Holt, Rinehart and Winston.

Hamilton WD. 1964. The genetic evolution of social behaviour: I and II. Journal of Theoretical Biology 7:1–52.

Hanya G, Kiyono M, Hayaishi S. 2007. Behavioral thermoregulation of wild Japanese macaques: Comparisons between two subpopulations. American Journal of Primatology 69.(7): 802–815.

Hanya G, Kiyono M, Yamada A, Suzuki K, Furukawa M, Yoshida Y, Chijiwa A. 2006. Not only annual food abundance but also fallback food quality determines the Japanese macaque density: Evidence from seasonal variation in home range size. Primates 47:275–278.

Happé F, Booth R, Charlton R, Hughes C. 2006. Executive function deficits in autism spectrum disorders and attention-deficit/hyperactivity disorders: Examining profiles across domains and ages. Brain and Cognition 61:25–39.

Harcourt AH. 1992. Coalitions and alliances: Are primates more complex than non-primates? In Harcourt AH, de Waal FBM editors. Coalitions and alliances in humans and other animals, pp. 445–472. Oxford, UK: Oxford University Press.

Harcourt AH, Greenberg J. 2001. Do gorilla females join males to avoid infanticide? A quantitative model. Animal Behaviour 62:905–915.

Harcourt AH, Purvis A, Liles L. 1995. Sperm competition: Mating systems, not breeding season, affects testes size of primates. Functional Ecology 9:468–476.

Harcourt AH, Stewart KL. 1987. High dominance rank in primate groups requires help from others. In Passera L, Lachaud JP editors. The individual and society, pp. 93–100. Toulouse, France: I.E.C.

Hardie SM. 1998. Mixed-species tamarin groups (*Saguinus fuscicollis* and *Saguinus labiatus* in northern Bolivia. Primate Report 50:39–62.

Harding RSO. 1973. Predation by a troop of olive baboons (*Papio anubis*). American Journal of Physical Anthropology 38:587–592.

Harding RSO. 1981. An order of omnivores: Nonhuman primate diets in the wild. In Harding RSO, Teleki G editors. Omnivorous primates: Gathering and hunting in human evolution, pp. 191–214. New York: Columbia University Press.

Hare B, Call J, Agnetta B, Tomasello M. 2000. Chimpanzees know what conspecifics do and do not see. Animal Behaviour 59:771–785.

Hare B, Call J, Tomasello M. 2001. Do chimpanzees know what conspecifics know? Animal Behaviour 61:139–151.

Hare B, Tomasello M. 2004. Chimpanzees are more skilful in competitive than in cooperative cognitive tasks. Animal Behaviour 68:571–581.

Harlow HF. 1995. Love in infant monkeys. In Eisner T, Wilson EO editors. Animal behavior. Readings from Scientific American, pp. 250–256. San Franscisco: WH Freeman.

Harlow HF, Dodsworth RO, Harlow MK. 1965. Total social isolation in monkeys. Proceedings of the National Academy of Science, USA 54:90–97.

Harlow HF, Zimmermann RR. 1959. Affectional responses in the infant monkey:Orphaned baby monkeys develop strong and persistent attachment to inanimate surrogate mothers. Science 130:421–432.

Harms KE, Wright SJ, Calderón O, Hernández A, Herre EA. 2000. Pervasive density-dependent recruitment enhances seedling diversity in a tropical forest. Nature 404:493–495.

Harris GJ, Chabris CF, Clark J, Urban T, Aharon I, Steele S, McGrath L, Condouris K, Tager-Flusberg H. 2006. Brain activation during semantic processing in autism spectrum disorders via functional magnetic resonance imaging. Brain and Cognition 61:54–68.

Harris M. 1964. The nature of cultural things. New York: Random House.

Harris M. 1979. Cultural materialism: The struggle for a science of culture. New York: Vintage.

Harris TR, Monfort SL. 2003. Behavioral and endocrine dynamics associated with infanticide in a black and white colobus monkey (*Colobus guereza*). American Journal of Primatology 61:135–142.

Harrison T. 2002. Late Oligocene to middle Miocene catarrhines from Afro-Arabia. In Hartwig WC editor. The primate fossil record, pp. 311–338. Cambridge, UK: Cambridge University Press.

Harrison T, Rook L. 1997. Enigmatic anthropoid or misunderstood ape? The phylogenetic status of *Oreopithecus bambolii* reconsidered. In

Begun DR, Ward CV, Rose MD editors. Function, phylogeny and fossils: Miocene hominoid evolution and adaptations, pp. 327–362. New York: Plenum Press.

Hart BL. 1990. Behavioral adaptations to pathogens and parasites: Five strategies. Neuroscience and Biobehavioral Review 14:273–294.

Hart D. 2000. Primates as prey: ecological, morphological, and behavioral relationships between primate species and their predators. Ph.D. dissertation, Washington University, St. Louis, Missouri.

Hart D. 2007. Predation on primates: A biogeographical analysis. In Gursky S, Nekaris K editors. Primate anti-predator strategies, pp. 27–59. New York: Springer.

Hart D, Fegley S. 1994. Social imitation and the emergence of a mental model of self. In Parker ST, Mitchell RW, Boccia ML editors. Self-awareness in animals and humans: Developmental perspectives, pp. 149–165. New York: Cambridge University Press.

Hart D, Sussman RW. 2005. Man the hunted: Primates, predators, and human evolution. New York: Westview Press.

Hartwig W. 2005. Implications of molecular and morphological data for understanding ateline phylogeny. International Journal of Primatology 26(5):999–1015.

Hashimoto C, Tashiro Y, Kimura D, Enomoto T, Ingmanson EJ, Idani G, Furuichi T. 1998. Habitat use and ranging of wild bonobos (*Pan paniscus*) at Wamba. International Journal of Primatology 19(6):1045–1060.

Hauser MD, Carey S. 1998. Building a cognitive creature from a set of primitives: Evolutionary and developmental insights. In Cummins DD, Allen C editors. The evolution of mind, pp. 51–106. Oxford, UK: Oxford University Press.

Hauser MD, Carey S, Hauser LB. 2000. Spontaneous number representation in semi-free-ranging rhesus monkeys. Proceedings of the Royal Society, London. 267:829–833.

Hausfater G. 1975. Dominance and reproduction in baboons (*Papio cynocephalus*): A quantitative analysis. Contributions to Primatology 7:1–50.

Hawkes K, O'Connell JF, Blurton Jones BG, Alvarez H, Charnov EL. 1998. Grandmothering, menopause, and the evolution of human life histories. Proceedings of the

National Academy of Science, USA. 95:1336–1339.

Hayes KJ, Hayes C. 1951. The intellectual development of a home-raised chimpanzee. Proceedings of the American Philosophical Society 95:105–109.

Heesy CP. 2004. On the relationship between orbit orientation and binocular visual field overlap in mammals. The Anatomical Record Part A: 281A:1104–1110.

Heffner RS. 2004. Primate hearing from a mammalian perspective. The Anatomical Record Part A Discoveries in molecular, Cellular and evolutionary biology. 281A:1104–1110.

Henzi SP, Lycett JE, Weingrill T. 1997. Cohort size and the allocation of social effort by female mountain baboons. Animal Behaviour 54:1235–1243.

Heyes CM. 1995. Self-recognition in primates: Further reflections create a hall of mirrors. Animal Behaviour 50:1533–1542.

Heymann EW. 2006. The neglected sense — olfaction in primate behavior, ecology, and evolution. American Journal of Primatology 68:519–524.

Hill CM. 2000. Conflict of interest between people and baboons: Crop raiding in Uganda. International Journal of Primatology 21:299–315.

Hinde RA. 1979. Towards understanding relationships. London: Academic Press.

Hinde RA editor. 1983. Primate social relationships. An integrated approach. Sunderland, MA: Sinauer Associates.

Hladik CM, Charles-Dominique P, Petter JJ. 1980. Feeding strategies of five nocturnal prosimians in the dry forest of the west coast of Madagascar. In Charles-Dominique P, Cooper HM, Hladik A, Hladik CM, Pages E, Pariente GF, Petter-Rousseaux A, Petter JJ, Schilling A editors. Nocturnal Malagasy primates: Ecology, physiology, and behavior, pp. 41–73. New York: Academic Press.

Hladik CM, Gueguen L. 1974. Géophagie et nutrition minérale chez les primates sauvages. Comptes rendus de l'académie des sciences, Paris 279:1393–1396.

Hockett CF. 1963. The problem of universals in language; In Greenberg JH editor. Universals of language. report of a conference held at Dobbs Ferry, New York, April 13–15, 1961 pp. 1–22. New York: MIT Press.

Holmes B. 2006. Meet your ancestors. New Scientist 191(2568):35–39.

Holmes JC, Zohar S. 1990. Pathology and host behavior. In Barnard CJ, Behnke JM. editors. Parasitism and host behavior, pp. 34–63. London: Taylor and Frances.

Hooker JJ, Russell DE, Phélizon A. 1999. A new family of Plesidapiformes (Mammalia) from the Old World lower Paleogene. Palaeontology 42(3):377–407.

Houle A. 1999. The origin of platyrrhines: An evaluation of the Antarctic scenario and the floating island model. American Journal of Physical Anthropology 109:541–559.

Howe HF, Smallwood J. 1982. Ecology of seed dispersal. Annual Review of Ecology and Systematics 13:201–228.

Hrdy SB. 1974. Male-male competition and infanticide among the langurs (*Presbytis entellus*) of Abu, Rajasthan. Folia Primatologica 22:19–58.

Hrdy SB. 1976. Care and exploitation of nonhuman primate infants by conspecifics other than the mother. In Rosenblatt J, Hinde R, Shaw E, Beer C editors. Advances in the study of behavior. Volume 6, pp. 101–158. New York: Academic Press.

Hu Y, Meng J, Wang Y, Li C. 2005. Large Mesozoic mammals fed on young dinosaurs. Nature 433:149–152.

Huang C, Wei F, Li M, Li Y, Sun R. 2003. Sleeping cave selection, activity pattern and time budget of white-headed langurs. International Journal of Primatology 24:813–824.

Huchon D, Douzery EJP. 2001. From the Old World to the New World: A molecular chronicle of the phylogeny and biogeography of Hystricognath rodents. Molecular Phylogenetics and Evolution 20(2):238–251.

Huffman MA. 1997. Current evidence for self-medication in primates: A multidisciplinary perspective. Yearbook of Physical Anthropology 40:171–200.

Huffman MA. 2001. Self-medicative behavior in the African great apes NDI: an evolutionary perspective into the origins of human traditional medicine. Bioscience 51:651–661.

Huffman MA. 2007. Primate self-medication. In Campbell CJ, Fuentes A, MacKinnon KC, Panger M, Bearder SK editors. Primates in perspective, pp. 677–690. Oxford, UK: Oxford University Press.

Huffman MA, Gotoh S, Turner LA, Hamai M, Yoshida K. 1997. Seasonal trends in intestinal nematode infection and medicinal plant use among chimpanzees in the Mahale Mountains, Tanzania. Primates 38:111–125.

Huffman MA, Page JE, Sukhdeo MVK, Gotoh S, Kalunde MS, Chandrasiri T, Towers GHN. 1996. Leaf-swallowing by chimpanzees, a behavioral adaptation for the control of strongyle nematode infections. International Journal of Primatology 17:475–503.

Hugot JP. 1998. Phylogeny of neotropical monkeys: The interplay of morphological, molecular, and parasitological data. Molecular Phylogenetics and Evolution 9(3):408–413.

Hunt G. 1996. Manufacture and use of hook-tools by New Caledonian crows. Nature 379:249–251.

Hunt GR, Gray RD. 2004a. Direct observation of pandanus-tool manufacture and use by a New Caledonian crow (*Corvus moneduloides*). Animal Cognition 7:114–120.

Hunt GR, Gray RD. 2004b. The crafting of hook tools by wild New Caledonian crows. Proceedings of the Royal Society, London B (Biological Letters Supplement) 271:S88–S90.

Hutchinson GE. 1957. Concluding remarks. Cold Spring Harbor Symposium. Quantitative Biology 22:415–427.

Huxley A. 2006. Testing is necessary on animals as well as *in vitro*. Nature 439:138.

ICZN 4th edition. 1999. Available online *www://ICZN.org* [Accessed 28 March 2005].

Ingmanson E. 1996. Tool-using behavior in wild *Pan paniscus*: Social and ecological considerations. In Russon A, Bard K, Parker S editors. Reaching into thought, pp. 190–210. Cambridge, UK: Cambridge University Press.

Isbell LA, Pruetz JD. 1998. Differences between vervets (*Cercopithecus aethiops*) and patas monkeys (*Erythrocebus patas*) in agonistic interactions between adult females. International Journal of Primatology 19:837–855.

Ishida H, Pickford M. 1998. A new late Miocene hominoid from Kenya: *Samburupithecus kiptalami* gen. et sp. nov. Comptes Rendus de l'Académie des Sciences, Paris 325:823–829.

Itani J. 1958. On the acquisition and propagation of a new food habit in the natural group of the Japanese monkey in Takasaki. Primates 1:84–98.

IUCN. 2002. Red list of threatened species. *www.iucn.org* [Accessed 11 May 2006].

IUCN. 2004. Red list of threatened species. *www.iucnredlist.org* [Accessed 11 May 2006].

Izawa K, Nishida T. 1963. Monkeys living in the northern limits of their distribution. Primates 4(2):67–88.

Jablonski NG editor. 1993. *Theropithecus*: The rise and fall of a primate genus. Cambridge, UK: Cambridge University Press.

Jablonski NG. 2002. Fossil Old World monkeys: The late Neogene radiation. In Hartwig WC editor. The primate fossil record, pp. 255–299. Cambridge, UK: Cambridge University Press.

Jablonski NG. 2003. The evolution of the Tarsid niche. In Wright PC, Simons EL, Gursky S editors. Tarsiers, past present and future, pp. 35–49. New Brunswick, NJ: Rutger University Press.

Jablonski NG. 2006. Skin: A natural history. Berkeley: University of California Press.

Jablonski NG, Leakey MG, Kiarie C, Antón M. 2002. A new skeleton of *Theropithecus brumpti* (Primates: Cercopithecidae) from Lomekwi, West Turkana, Kenya. Journal of Human Evolution 43:887–923.

Jacobs GH. 1994/95. Variation in primate color vision: Mechanisms and utility. Evolutionary Anthropology 3(6):196–205.

Jacobs GH, Deegan JF. 2003a. Diurnality and cone photopigment polymorphism in strepsirhines: Examination of linkage in *Lemur catta*. American Journal of Physical Anthropology 122:66–72.

Jacobs GH, Deegan JF. 2003b. Cone pigment variations in four genera of New World monkeys. Vision Research 43:227–236.

Jacobs GH, Deegan JF, Tan Y, Li W-H. 2002. Opsin gene and photopigment polymorphism in a prosimian primate. Vision Research 42:11–18.

Jacobs LL. 1981. Miocene lorisid primates from the Pakistan Siwaliks. Nature 289:585–587.

Jaeger J-J, Thein T, Benammi M, Chaimanee Y, Soe AN, Lwin T, Tun T, Wai S, Ducrocq S. 1999. A new primate from the middle Eocene of Myanmar and the Asian early origin of anthropoids. Science 286:528–530.

Janik VM. 2000. Whistle matching in wild bottlenose dolphins (*Tursiops truncatus*). Science 289:1355–1357.

Janson, CH. 1998. Experimental evidence for spatial memory in foraging wild capuchin monkeys, *Cebus apella*. Animal Behaviour 55:1229–1243.

Janson CH. 2001. Field experiments in primate ecology: The monkeys are always right. American Journal of Primatology 54:107.

Janson CH, Chapman CA. 1999. Resources and primate community structure. In Fleagle JG, Janson CH, Reed KE editors. Primate communities, pp. 237–267. Cambridge, UK: Cambridge University Press.

Janson CH, Di Bitetti MS. 1997. Experimental analysis of food detection in capuchin monkeys: Effects of distance, travel, speed, and resource size. Behavioral Ecology and Sociobiology 41:17–24.

Janson CH, Goldsmith ML. 1995. Predicting group size in primates: Foraging costs and predation risks. Behavioral Ecology and Sociobiology 6:326–336.

Janson CH, Terborgh J, Emmons LH. 1981. Non-flying mammals as pollinating agents in the Amazonian forest. Reproductive Botany 13 (supplement):1–6.

Janson CH, van Schaik CP. 2000. The behavioural ecology of infanticide by males. In van Schaik CP, Janson CH editors. Infanticide by males and its implications, pp. 469–494. Cambridge, UK: Cambridge University Press.

Jarman PJ. 1974. The social organization of antelope in relation to their ecology. Behaviour 48:215–267.

Jensen-Sieman MT, Kidd KK. 2001. Mitochondrial variation and biogeography of eastern gorillas. Molecular Ecology 10:2241–2247.

Jewell PA. 1966. The concept of home range in mammals. Symposium of the Zoological Society, London 18:85–110.

Ji Q, Luo Z-X, Yuan C-X, Wible JR, Zhang J-P, Georgi JA. 2002. The earliest known eutherian mammal. Nature 416:816–822.

Jolly A. 1966. Lemur behavior: A Madagascar field study. Chicago: University of Chicago Press.

Jolly A, Caless S, Cavigelli S, Gould L, Pereira ME, Pitts A, Pride RE, Rabenandrasana HD, Walker JD, Zafison T. 2000. Infant killing, wounding and predation in *Eulemur* and *Lemur*. International Journal of Primatology 21(1):21–40.

Jolly CJ. 1993. Species, subspecies and baboon systematics. In Kimble W, Martin L editors. Species, species concepts and primate evolution, pp. 67–107. New York: Wiley.

Jolly CJ. 2001. A proper study for mankind: Analogies from the Papionin monkeys and their implications for human evolution. Yearbook of Physical Anthropology 44:177–204.

Jolly CJ, Phillips-Conroy JE, Turner TR, Broussard S, Allan JS. 1996. SIV_{agm} incidence over two decades in a natural population of Ethiopian grivet monkeys (*Cercopithecus aethiops aethiops*). Journal of Medical Primatology 25:78–83.

Jones CB. 2005. Behavioral flexibility in primates: Causes and consequences. New York: Springer.

Jones T, Ehardt CL, Butynski TM, Davenport TRB, Mpunga NE, Machanga SJ, De Luca DW. 2005. The highland mangabey *Lophocebus kipunji*: A new species of African monkey. Science 308(5725):1161–1164.

Kaas JH. 1993. The functional organization of somatosensory cortex in primates. Annals of Anatomy 175:509–518.

Kandel E, Schwartz JH, Jessell TM. 2002. Principles of neuroscience. New York: McGraw-Hill.

Kano T. 1989. The sexual behavior of pygmy chimpanzees. In Heltne PG, Marquard LA editors. Understanding chimpanzees, pp. 176–183. Cambridge, MA: Harvard University Press.

Kano T. 1992. The last ape: Pygmy chimpanzee behavior and ecology. Stanford, CA: Stanford University Press.

Kano T. 1996. Male rank order and copulation rate in a unit-group of bonobos at Wamba, Zaïre. In McGrew WC, Marchant LF, Nishida T editors. Great ape societies, pp. 135–145. Cambridge, UK: Cambridge University Press.

Kaplin BA, Moermond TC. 1998. Variation in seed handling by two species of forest monkeys in Rwanda. American Journal of Primatology 45:83–101.

Kappeler PM. 1998. To whom it may concern: The transmission and function of chemical signals in *Lemur catta*. Behavioral Ecology and Sociobiology 42:411–421.

Kasting JF, Holland HD, Kump LR. 1992. Atmospheric evolution: The rise of oxygen. In Schopf JW, Klein C editors. The proterozoic biosphere, pp. 159–163. Cambridge, UK: Cambridge University Press: A Multicidisplinary Study.

Kawai M. 1965. Newly-acquired pre-cultural behavior of the natural troop of Japanese monkeys on Koshima islet. Primates 6(1):1–30.

Kay RF. 1990. The phyletic relationships of extant and fossil Pitheciinae (Platyrrhini, Anthropoidea). Journal of Human Evolution 19:175–208.

Kay RF, Davies AG. 1994. Digestive physiology. In Davies AG, Oates JF editors. Colobine monkeys, pp. 229–249. Cambridge, UK: Cambridge University Press.

Kay RF, Ross C, Williams BA. 1997. Anthropoid origins. Science 275:797–804.

Kay RF, Ungar PS. 1997. Dental evidence for diet in some Miocene catarrhines with comments on the effects of phylogeny on the interpretation of adaptation. In Begun DR, Ward CV, Rose MD editors. Function, phylogeny and fossils: Miocene hominoid evolution and adaptations, pp. 131–151. New York: Plenum Press.

Kellogg WN, Kellogg LA. 1933. The ape and the child: A study of environmental influence on early behavior. New York: Hafner.

Kelly J. 2002. The hominoid radiation in Asia. In Hartwig WC editor. The primate fossil record, pp. 360–384. Cambridge, UK: Cambridge University Press.

Keverne EB, Martensz ND, Tuite B. 1989. Beta-endorphin concentration in cerebrospinal fluid of monkeys are influenced by grooming relationships. Psychoneuroendocrinology 14(1-2):155–161.

Kiiru W. 2004. Eating the unknown. *www.bornfree.org.uk.campanigs/further-activities/bushmeat/* [Accessed 13 May 2007].

King BJ. 1999. Viewed from up close: Monkeys, apes, and language-origins theories. In King BJ editor. The origins of language: What nonhuman primates can tell us, pp. 21–54. Santa Fe, NM: School of American Research Press.

Kingdon J. 1990. Island Africa: Evolution of Africa's animals and plants. New York: Collins.

Kingdon J. 1997. The Kingdon field guide to African mammals. San Diego: Academic Press.

Kinzey W. 1987. Monogamous primates: A primate model for human mating systems. In Kinzey W editor. The evolution of human behavior: Primate models, pp. 105–114. Albany: State University of New York Press.

Kirk EC, Kay RF. 2004. The evolution of high visual acuity in the Anthropoidea. In Ross CF, Kay RF editors. Anthropoid origins: New visions, pp. 539–602. New York: Kluwer/Plenum Press.

Kirkpatrick RC. 2007. The Asian colobines: Diversity among leaf-eating monkeys. In Campbell CJ, Fuentes A, MacKinnon KC, Panger M, Bearder SK editors. Primates in perspective, pp. 186–200. Oxford, UK: Oxford University Press.

Kleiber M. 1961. The fire of life: An introduction to animal energetics. New York: John Wiley.

Kleiman DG, Mallinson JJC. 1998. Recovery and management committees for lion tamarins: Partnership in conservation planning and implementation. Conservation Biology 12(1):27–38.

Kleiman DG, Rylands AB editors. 2002. Lion tamarins: Biology and conservation. Washington DC: Smithsonian Institution Press.

Köhler W. 1927. The mentality of apes. London: Routledge and Kegan Paul.

Kojime T. 1990. Comparison of auditory functions in the chimpanzee and human. Folia Primatologica 55:62–72.

Kolowski JM, Holekamp KE. 2006. Spatial, temporal, and physical characteristics of livestock depredation by large carnivores along a Kenyan reserve border. Biological Conservation 128:529–541.

Kortlandt A. 1995. A survey of the geographical range, habitats and conservation of the pygmy chimpanzee (*Pan paniscus*): An ecological perspective. Primate Conservation 16:21–36.

Krause DW, Maas MC. 1990. The biogeographical origins of late Paleocene-early Eocene mammalian immigrants to the western interior of North America. Geological Society of America Special Papers 243:71–105.

Krebs CJ. 1994. Ecology: The experimental analysis of distribution and abundance. 4th edition. New York: Harper Collins.

Krebs JR, Kacelnik A. 1991. Decision-making. In Krebs JR, Davies NB editors. Behavioral ecology: An evolutionary approach. 3rd edition, pp. 105–136. Oxford: Blackwell Scientific Publications.

Kress RK. 1993. Coevolution of plants and animals: Pollination of flowers by primates in Madagascar. Current Science 65:253–257.

Kress RK, Schatz GE, Andrianifahanana M, Moreland HS. 1994. Pollination of *Ravenala madagascarensis* (Strelitziaceae) by lemurs in Madagascar: Evidence for an archaic coevolutionary system? American Journal of Botany 81:542–551.

Krijgsman W, Hilgen FJ, Raffi I, Sierro FJ, Wilson DS. 1999. Chronology, causes and progression of the Messinian salinity crisis. Nature 400:652–655.

Krishnamani R, Mahaney WC. 2000. Geophagy among primates: Adaptive significance and ecological consequences. Animal Behaviour 59:899–915.

Kroeber AL, Kluckhohn C. 1952. Culture: A critical review of concepts and definitions. Papers of the Peabody Museum of American Archeology and Ethnology 47:41–72.

Krützen M, Mann J, Heithaus MR, Connor RC, Bejder L, Sherwin WB. 2005. Cultural transmission of tool use in bottlenose dolphins. Proceedings of the National Academy of Science, USA 102(25):8939–8943.

Kudo H, Dunbar RIM. 2001. Neocortex size and social network size in primates. Animal Behaviour 62:711–722.

Kumar S, Hedges SB. 1998. A molecular timescale for vertebrate evolution. Nature 392:917–920.

Kummer H. 1968. Social organization of hamadryas baboons. A field study. Chicago: University of Chicago Press.

Kummer H. 1971. Primate societies. Group techniques of ecological adaptations. Chicago: Aldine Publishing Company.

Kummer H. 1995. In quest of the sacred baboon. A scientist's journey. Princeton, NJ: Princeton University Press.

Lambert JE. 1999. Seed handling in chimpanzees (*Pan troglodytes*) and redtail monkeys (*Cercopithecus ascanius*): Implications for understanding hominoid and cercopithecine fruit-processing strategies and seed dispersal. American Journal of Physical Anthropology 109:365–386.

Lambert JE. 2000. The fate of seeds dispersed by African apes and cercopithecines. American Journal of Physical Anthropology (supplement) 30:204.

Lambert JE, Chapman CA, Wrangham RW, Conklin-Brittain NL. 2004. The hardness of cercopithecine foods: Implications for the critical function of enamel thickness in exploiting fallback foods. American Journal of Physical Anthropology 125:363–368.

Lambert JE, Garber PA. 1998. Evolutionary and ecological implication of primate seed dispersal. American Journal of Primatology 45:9–28.

Le Gros Clark WE. 1959. The antecedents of man. Edinburgh: Edinburgh University Press.

Le Gros Clark WE. 1965. History of the primates. Chicago: University of Chicago Press.

Lee PC, Moss CJ. 1999. The social context for learning and behavioural developments among wild African elephants. In Box HO, Gibson KR editors. Mammalian social learning, pp. 102–125. Symposium of the Zoological Society of London 72. Cambridge UK: Cambridge University Press.

Lee RB, DeVore I. editors. 1968. Man the hunter. New York: Aldine Publishing Company.

Leendertz FH, Ellerbrok H, Boesch C, Couacy-Hymann E, Mätz-Rensing K, Hakenbeck R, Bergmann C, Abaza P, Junglen S, Moebius Y, Vigilant L, Formenty P, Pauli G. 2004. Anthrax kills wild chimpanzees in a tropical rainforest. Nature 430:451–452.

Lee-Thorp JA, Sponheimer M, van der Merve NJ. 2003. What do stable isotopes tell us about hominid dietary and ecological niches in the Pliocene? International Journal of Osteoarchaeology 13:104–113.

Lefebvre L, Nicolakakis N, Boire D. 2002. Tools and brains in birds. Behaviour 139:939–973.

Lehman SM, Fleagle JG. editors. 2006. Primate biogeography: Progress and prospects. New York: Springer.

Leigh SR, Setchell JM, Buchanan LS. 2005. Ontogenetic bases of canine dimorphism in anthropoid primates. American Journal of Physical Anthropology 127:296–311.

Leighton, DR. 1987. Gibbons: Territoriality and monogamy. In Smuts BB, Cheney DL, Seyfarth RM, Wrangham RW, Struhsaker TT editors. Primate societies, pp. 135–145. Chicago: University of Chicago Press.

Leroy EM, Kumulungui B, Pourrut P, Rouquet P, Hassanin A, Yaba P, Délicat A, Paweska JT, Gonzalez J-P, Swanepoel R. 2005. Fruit bats as reservoirs of Ebola virus. Nature 438:575–576.

Leroy EM, Rouquet P, Formenty P, Souquière S, Kilbourne A, Forment J-M, Bermejo M, Smit S, Karesh W, Swanepoel R, Zaki SR, Rollin PE. 2004. Multiple Ebola virus transmission events and rapid decline of Central African wildlife. Science 303:387–390.

Leslie A, Sarre A, Filho MS, Buang AB. 2002. Forest certification and biodiversity. ITTO, Tropical Forest Update 12:13–15.

Levine S, Wiener SG, Coe CL. 1993. Temporal and social factors influencing behavioral and hormonal responses to separation in mother and infant squirrel monkeys. Psychoneuroendocrinology 18(4):297–306.

Li Z, Rogers E. 2004. Social organization of white-headed langurs *Trachypithecus leucocephalus* in Fusui, China. Folia Primatologica 75(2):97–100.

Lieberman P. 1975. On the origins of language: An introduction to the evolution of speech. New York: Macmillan.

Lieberman P. 1992. Human speech and language. In Jones S, Martin R, Pilbeam D editors. The Cambridge Encyclopedia of human evolution, pp. 134–137. Cambridge, UK: Cambridge University Press.

Liebig J. 1840. Chemistry in its application to agriculture and physiology. London: Taylor and Walton.

Lindsey PA, Frank LFG, Alexander R, mathieson A, Romanach SS. 2006. Trophy hunting and conservation in Africa: Problems and one potential solution. Conservation Biology 21(3): 880–883.

Link A, de Luna AG. 2004. The importance of *Oenocarpus bataua* (Arecaceae) in the diet of spider monkeys at Tinigua National Park, Colombia. Folia Primatologica 75:391.

Link A, Di Fiore A. 2006. Seed dispersal by spider monkeys and its importance in the maintenance of neotropical rain-forest diversity. Journal of Tropical Ecology 22:235–246.

Linnaeus C. 1758. Systema naturae per regna tria naturae, secundum classes, ordines genera, species cum characteribus, differentris, synonymis, locis. Revised 10th edition. Stockholm: Laurentii Salvii.

Longino JT. 1984. True anting by the capuchin, *Cebus capucinus*. Primates 25:243–245.

Longman KA, Jenik J. 1974. Tropical forest and its environment. London: Longman.

Lozano GA. 1998. Parasitic stress and self-medication in wild animals. Advanced Study in Behavior 27:291–317.

Ludes E, Anderson JR. 1995. "Peat-bathing" by captive white-faced capuchin monkeys (*Cebus capucinus*). Folia Primatologica 65:38–42.

MacFadden BJ. 1980. Rafting mammals or drifting islands? Biogeography of the Greater Antillean insectivores *Nesophontes* and *Solemodon*. Journal of Biogeography 7:11–22.

MacKinnon K, Hatta G, Halim H, Manalik A. 1998. The ecology of Kalimantan. Oxford, UK : Oxford University Press.

MacPhee RDE, Horovits I. 2002. Extinct quaternary platyrrhines of the Greater Antilles and Brazil. In Hartwig WC editor. The primate fossil record, pp. 189–200. Cambridge, UK: Cambridge University Press.

Maestripieri D. 2002. Parent-offspring conflict in primates. International Journal of Primatology 23(4):923–951.

Malenky RK, Stiles EW. 1991. Distribution of terrestrial herbaceous vegetation and its consumption by *Pan paniscus* in Lomako Forest, Zaire. American Journal of Primatology 23:153–169.

Mangel M, Clark CW. 1986. Towards a unified foraging theory. Ecology 67:1127–1138.

Mann A. 1972. Hominid and cultural origins. Man 7:379–386.

Mann J, Connor RC, Tyack PL, Whitehead H editors. 2000. Cetacean societies: Field studies of dolphins and whales. Chicago: University of Chicago Press.

Mann J, Smuts BB. 1998. Natal attraction: Allomaternal care and mother-infant separations in wild bottlenose dolphins. Animal Behaviour 55:1097–1113.

Manson JH. 1999. Infant handling in wild *Cebus capucinus*: Testing bonds between females? Animal Behaviour 57:911–921.

Manson JH. 2007. Mate choice. In Campbell CJ, Fuentes A, MacKinnon KC, Panger M, Bearder SK editors. 2007. Primates in perspective, pp. 447–463. Oxford: Oxford University Press.

Marcus GF, Fisher SE. 2003,UK. FOXP2 in focus: What can genes tell us about speech and language? Trends in Cognitive Sciences 7(6):257–262.

Marini MA, Garcia FI. 2005. Bird conservation in Brazil. Conservation Biology 19(3):665–671.

Marivaux L, Welcomme J-L, Antoine P-O, Métais G, Baloch IM, Benammi M, Chaimanee Y, Ducrocq S, Jaeger J-J. 2001. A fossil lemur from the Oligocene of Pakistan. Science 294:587–591.

Marks J. 2002. What it means to be 98% chimpanzee: Apes, people, and their genes. Los Angeles: University of California Press.

Marler P. 1977. The structure of animal communication sounds. In Bullock TH editor. The recognition of complex acoustic signals, pp. 17–35. Report of Dahlem Workshop, Berlin: Dahlem Konferenzen.

Martin RD. 1986. Primates: A definition. In Wood B, Martin L, Andrews P editors. Major topics in primate and human evolution, pp. 1–31. Cambridge, UK: Cambridge University Press.

Martin RD. 1990. Primate origins and evolution: A phylogenetic reconstruction. London: Chapman & Hall.

Martin RD. 1992. Goeldi and the dwarfs: The evolutionary biology of the small New World monkeys. Journal of Human Evolution 22:367–393.

Martin RD. 1993. Primate origins: Plugging the gaps. Nature 363:223–234.

Martin RD. 2000. Origins, diversity and relationships of lemurs. International Journal of Primatology 21(6):1021–1049.

Martin RD. 2003. Combing the primate record. Nature 422:388 391.

Martin RD. in press. New lights on primate evolution. Berlin: Berlin Abhandler Berl Brandenburg Akademik Wissenshaft.

Martin RD, MacLarnon AM. 1985. Gestation period, neonatal size and maternal investment in placental mammals. Nature 313:220–223.

Marzke MW. 1997. Precision grips, hand morphology, and tools. American Journal of Physical Anthropology 102:91–110.

Matsuo PM. 2005. Environmental education as a tool for conservation of the golden lion tamarin (*Leontopithecus rosalia*) and the Atlantic Forest in Brazil. American Society of Primatology Bulletin 29(4):9–10.

Matsuzawa T. 1990. Form perception and visual acuity in a chimpanzee. Folia Primatologica 55:24–32.

Matsuzawa T. 1991. Nesting cups and metatools in chimpanzees. Behavioral and Brain Sciences 14:570–571.

Matsuzawa T. 2001. Primate foundations of human intelligence: A view of tool use in non-human primates and fossil hominids. In Matsuzawa T editor. Primate origins of human cognition and behavior, pp. 3–25. New York: Springer.

Mayr E. 1942. Systematics and the origin of species. New York: Columbia University Press.

Mayr E. 1963. Animal species and evolution. Cambridge, MA: The Belknap Press of Harvard University.

Mayr E. 1992. Speciational evolution or punctuated equilibria. In Somit A, Peterson S editors. The dynamics of evolution, pp. 21–48. New York: Cornell University Press.

Mayr E, Ashlock PD. 1991. Principles of systematic zoology. 2nd edition. New York: McGraw-Hill.

McBrearty S, Jablonski NG. 2005. First fossil chimpanzee. Nature 437:105–108.

McClintock MK. 1971. Menstrual synchrony and suppression. Nature 229:244–245.

McComb K, Baker L, Moss C. 2006. African elephants show high levels of interest in the skulls and ivory of their own species. Biological Letters 2:26–28.

McComb K, Moss C, Durant SM, Baker L, Sayialel S. 2001. Matriarchs as repositories of social knowledge in African elephants. Science 292:491–494.

McComb K, Moss C, Sayialel S, Baker L. 2000. Unusually extensive networks of vocal recognition in African elephants. Animal Behaviour 59:1103–1109.

McConkey KR. 2000. Primary seed shadow generated by gibbons in the rain forests of Barito Ulu, central Borneo. American Journal of Primatology 52:13–29.

McConkey KR. 2005. Influence of faeces on seed removal from gibbon droppings in a dipterocarp forest in central Borneo. Journal of Tropical Ecology 21:117–120.

McCrossin ML. 1992. New species of bushbaby from the middle Miocene of Maboko Island, Kenya. American Journal of Physical Anthropology 89:215–233.

McCrossin ML, Benefit BR. 1997. On the relationships and adaptations of *Kenyapithecus*, a large-bodied hominoid from the Middle Miocene of eastern Africa. In Begun DR, Ward CV, Rose MD editors. Function, phylogeny, and fossils: Miocene hominoid evolution and adaptation, pp. 241–267. New York: Plenum Press.

McGraw WS. 2005. Update on the search for Miss Waldron's red colobus monkey. International Journal of Primatology 26:605–619.

McGraw WS, Cooke C, Shultz S. 2006. Primate remains from African crowned eagle (*Stephanoaetus coronatus*) nests in Ivory Coast's Tai forest: Implications for primate predation and early hominid taphonomy in South Africa. American Journal of Physical Anthropology 131:151–165.

McGrew WC. 1992. Chimpanzee material culture. Implications for human evolution. Cambridge, UK: Cambridge University Press.

McGrew WC, Marchant LF, Scott SE, Tutin CEG. 2001. Intergroup differences in a social custom of wild chimpanzees: The grooming hand-clasp of the Mahale Mountains. Current Anthropology 42:148–153.

McKee JK. 1992. Observations on the carnivorous activities of chacma baboons at the Buxton Limeworks, Taung District, Bophuthatswana. South African Journal of Science 88:299–300.

McKee JK, Poirier FE, McGraw WS. 2005. Understanding human evolution. 5th Edition. Englewood Cliffs, NY: Prentice Hall.

McKey DS. 1975. The ecology of coevolved seed dispersal syndromes. In Gilbert LE, Raven PH editors. Coevolution of animals and plants, pp. 159–191. Austin: University of Texas Press.

Mehlman PT. 1988. Food resources of the wild Barbary macaque (*Macaca sylvanus*) in high-altitude fir forest, Ghomaran Rif, Morocco. Journal of Zoology, London 214:469–490.

Meijaard E, Wich S. 2007. Putting orang-utan population trends into perspective. Current Biology 17(14):R540.

Meireles CM, Czelusniak J, Schneider MPC, Muniz JAPC, Brigido MC, Ferreira HS, Goodman M. 1999. Molecular phylogeny of ateline New World monkeys (Platyrrhini, Atelinae) based on *y*-globin gene sequences: Evidence that *Brachyteles* is the sister group

of *Lagothrix*. Molecular Phylogenetics and Evolution 12:10–30.

Mendes Pontes AR. 1997. Habitat partitioning among primates in Maracá Island, Roraima, northern Brazilian Amazonia. International Journal of Primatology 18(2):131–157.

Menzel EW. 1971. Communication about the environment in a group of young chimpanzees. Folia Primatologica 15:220–232.

Menzel EW. 1974. A group of young chimpanzees in a one-acre field: Leadership and Communication. In Schrier A, Stollnitz F editors. Behavior of nonhuman primates: Modern research trends, pp. 83–153. New York: Academic Press.

Menzel EW Jr, Davenport RK Jr, Rogers CM. 1963. Effects of environmental restriction upon the chimpanzee's responsiveness in novel situations. Journal of Comparative Physiology Psychology 56:329–334.

Mercader J, Barton H, Gillespie J, Harris J, Kuhn S, Tyler R, Boesch C. 2007. 4,300-year-old chimpanzee sites and the origins of percussive stone technology. Proceedings of the National Academy of Science, USA 104:3043–3048.

Merker S, Groves CP. 2006. *Tarsius lariang*: A new primate species from Western Central Sulawesi. International Journal of Primatology 27(2):465–485.

Michaels MG, Lanford R, Demetris AJ, Chaves D, Brashy K, Fung J, Starzl TE. 1996. Lack of susceptibility of baboons to infection with hepatitis B virus. Transplantation 61(3):350–351.

Miles HL. 1990. The cognitive foundation for reference in a signing orangutan. In Parker ST, Gibson KR editors. "Language" and intelligence in monkeys and apes, pp. 511–539. Cambridge, UK: Cambridge University Press.

Miller ER, Gunnell GF, Martin RD. 2005. Deep time and the search for anthropoid origins. Yearbook of Physical Anthropology 48:60–95.

Miller ER, Simons EL. 1997. Dentition of *Proteopithecus sylviae*, an archaic anthropoid from the Fayum, Egypt. Proceedings of the National Academy of Science, USA 94:13760–13764.

Miller LE editor. 2002. Eat or be eaten. Predator sensitive foraging among primates. New York: Cambridge University Press.

Milner-Gulland EJ, Bennett EL, and the SCB. 2003. Annual Meeting Wild Meat Group. Wild meat: The bigger picture. Trends in Ecology and Evolution 18(7):351–357.

Milton K. 1985. Multimale mating and absence of canine tooth dimorphism in woolly spider monkeys (*Brachyteles arachnoids*). American Journal of Physical Anthropology 68:519–523.

Milton K. 1988. Distribution patterns of tropical plant foods as an evolutionary stimulus to primate mental development. American Anthropologist 83:534–548.

Milton K, May ML. 1976. Body weight, diet, and home range area in primates. Nature 259:459–462.

Mitani JC. 1996. Comparative studies in African ape vocal behavior. In McGrew WC, Marchant LF, Nishida T editors. Great ape societies, pp. 241–254. New York: Cambridge University Press.

Mitani JC, Gros-Louis J. 1995. Species and sex differences in the screams of chimpanzees and bonobos. International Journal of Primatology 16:393–411.

Mitani JC, Rodman P. 1979. Territoriality: The relation of ranging patterns and home range size to defensibility, with an analysis of territoriality among primates species. Behavioral Ecology and Sociobiology 5:241–251.

Mittermeier RA, da Fonseca GAB, Rylands AB, Brandon K. 2005. A brief history of biodiversity conservation in Brazil. Conservation Biology 19(3):601–607.

Mittermeier RA, Konstant WR, Hawkins F, Louis F.E, Langrand O, Ratsimbazafy J, Rasoloarison R, Ganzhorn JU, Rajaobelina S, Tattersall I, Meyers DM. 2006. Lemurs of Madagascar. Washington DC: Conservation Press.

Mittermeier RA, Valladares-Padua C, Rylands AB, Eudey AA, Butynski TM, Ganzhorn JU, Kormos R, Aguiar JM, Walker S. 2006. Primates in peril. The world's 25 most endangered primates 2004–2006. Primate Conservation 20:1–28.

Mivart St. G. 1873. On *Lepilemur* and *Cheirogaleus* and on the zoological rank of the Lemuroidea. Proceedings of the Zoological Society, London 1873:484–510.

Miyamoto MM, Goodman M. 1986. Biomolecular systematics of eutherian mammals: Phylogentic patterns and classification. Systematic Zoology 35:230–240.

Mohnot SM. 1971. Some aspects of social change and infant killing in the hanuman langur, *Presbytis entellus* (Primates: Cercopithecidae) in Western India. Mammalia 35:175–198.

Molino J-F, Sabatier D. 2001. Tree diversity in tropical rain forests: A validation of the intermediate disturbance hypothesis. Science 294:1702–1704.

Molleson L. 2003. The South American bushmeat crisis. *http://www.ippl.org/07-03-22* [Accessed 21 August 2007].

Montague MFA. 1968. Brains, genes, culture, immaturity, and gestation. In Montagu MFA editor. Culture: Man's adaptive dimension, pp. 102–113. London: Oxford University Press.

Moore J. 1996. Savanna chimpanzees, referential models and the last common ancestor. In McGrew WC, Marchant LF, Nishida T editors. Great ape societies, pp. 275–292. Cambridge, UK: Cambridge University Press.

Mootnick A, Groves C. 2005. A new generic name for the Hoolock gibbon (Hylobatidae). International Journal of Primatology 26(4):971–976.

Morwood MJ, Brown P, Jatmiko, Sutikna T, Wayhu Saptomo E, Westaway KE, Rokus Awe Due, Roberts RG, Maeda T, Wasisto S, Djubiantono T. 2005. Further evidence for small-bodied hominins from the Late Pleistocene of Flores, Indonesia. Nature 437:1012–1017.

Moss C. 1988. Elephant memories. Thirteen years in the life of an elephant family. New York: Fawcett Columbine.

Moss CJ. 2001. The demography of an African elephant (*Loxodonta africana*) population in Amboseli, Kenya. Journal of Zoology London 255:145–156.

Moyà-Solà S, Köhler M, Alba DM, Casanova-Vilar I, Galindo J. 2004. *Pierolapithecus catalaunicus*, a new middle Miocene great ape from Spain. Science 306:1339–1344.

Moyà-Solà S, Köhler M, Rook L. 2005. The *Oreopithecus* thumb: A strange case in hominoid evolution. Journal of Human Evolution 49:395–404.

Mulcahy NJ, Call J. 2006. Apes save tools for future use. Science 312:1038–1040.

Myers N, Mittermeier RA, Mittermeier CG, da Fonseca GAB, Kent J. 2000. Biodiversity hotspots for conservation priorities. Nature 403:853–858.

Nakatsukasa M, Ward CV, Walker A, Teaford MF, Kunimatsu Y, Ogihara N. 2004. Tail loss in *Proconsul heseloni*. Journal of Human Evolution 46:777–784.

Nakatsukasa M, Yamanaka A, Kunimatsu Y, Shimizu D, Ishida H. 1998. A newly discovered *Kenyapithecus* skeleton and its implications for the evolution of positional behavior in Miocene East African hominoids. Journal of Human Evolution 34:657–664.

National Science Foundation 2006. American sign language spoken here. *www.nsf.gov/discoveries/disc_summ.jsp?cntn_id=100168&org=NSF* [Accessed 27 August 2006].

Naughton-Treves L. 1998. Predicting patterns of crop damage by wildlife around Kibale National Park, Uganda. Conservation Biology 12(1):156–168.

Naughton-Treves L, Mena JL, Treves A, Alvarez N, Radeloff VC. 2003. Wildlife survival beyond park boundaries: The impact of slash-and-burn agriculture and hunting on mammals in Tambopata, Peru. Conservation Biology 17(4):1106–1117.

Nekaris KAI. 2000. The socioecology of the Mysore slender loris (*Loris tardigradus lydekkerianus*) in Dindigul Tamil Nadu, South India. Ph.D. dissertation, Washington University, St. Louis, Missouri.

Nekaris KAI. 2001. Activity budget and positional behavior of the Mysore slender loris (*Loris tardigradus lydekkerianus*): Implications for slow climbing locomotion. Folia Primatologica 72:228–241.

Nekaris KAI. 2003a. Observation of mating, birthing and parental behaviour in three subspecies of slender loris (*Loris tardigradus* and *Loris lydekkerianus*) in India and Sri Lanka. Folia Primatologica 74:312–336.

Nekaris KAI. 2003b. Spacing system of the Mysore slender loris (*Loris lydekkerianus lydekkerianus*). American Journal of Physical Anthropology 121:86–96.

Nekaris KAI. 2006. Social lives of adult Mysore slender loris (*Loris lydekkerianus lydekkerianus*). American Journal of Primatology 68(12):1171–1182.

Nekaris KAI, Bearder S. 2007. The lorisiform primates of Asia and mainland Africa: Diversity shrouded in darkness. In Campbell CJ, Fuentes A, MacKinnon KC, Panger M, Bearder SK editors. Primates in perspective, pp. 24–45. Oxford, UK: Oxford University Press.

Nekaris KAI, Jayewardene J. 2003. Pilot study and conservation status of the slender loris (*Loris tardigradus* and *Loris lydekkerianus*) in Sri Lanka. Primate Conservation 19:83–90.

Nekaris KAI, Rasmussen DT. 2003. Diet and feeding behavior of Mysore slender lorises. International Journal of Primatology 24:33–46.

Nepstad DC, Verissimo A, Alencar A, Nobre C, Lima E, Lefebvre P, Schlesinger P, Potter C, Moutinho P, Mendoza E, Cochrane M, Brooks V. 1999. Large-scale impoverishment of Amazonian forests by logging and fire. Nature 398:505–508.

Newman TK, Jolly CJ, Rogers J. 2004. Mitochondrial phylogeny and systematics of baboons (*Papio*). American Journal of Physical Anthropology 124:17–27.

Newton PN. 1988. The variable social organization of Hanuman langurs (*Presbytis entellus*), infanticide, and the monopolization of females. International Journal of Primatology 9(1):59–77.

Nielsen MR. 2006. Importance, cause and effect of bushmeat hunting in the Udzungwa Mountains, Tanzania: Implications for community based wildlife management. Biological Conservation 128:509–516.

Nijman V. 2005. Decline of the endemic Hose's langur *Presbytis hosei* in Kayan Mentarang National Park, East Borneo. Oryx 39(2):223–226.

Nishida T. 1968. The social group of wild chimpanzees in the Mahale Mountains. Primates 9:167–224.

Nishida T. 1987. Local traditions and cultural transmissions. In Smuts BB, Cheney DL, Seyfarth RM, Wrangham RW, Struhsaker TT editors. Primate societies, pp. 462–474. Chicago: University of Chicago Press.

Nishida T, Corp N, Hamai M, Hasegawa T, Hiraiwa-Hasegawa M, Hosaka K, Hunt KD, Itoh N, Kawanaka K, Matsumoto-Oda A, Mitani JC, Nakamura M, Norikoshi K, Sakamaki T, Turner L, Uehara S, Zamma K. 2003.

Demography, female life history, and reproductive profiles among the chimpanzees of Mahale. American Journal of Primatology 59(3):99–121.

Nishida T, Hosaka K. 1996. Coalition strategies among adult male chimpanzees of the Mahale Mountains, Tanzania. In McGrew WC, Marchant LF, Nishida T editors. Great ape societies, pp. 114–134. Cambridge, UK: Cambridge University Press.

Nofre C, Tinti JM, Glaser D. 1996. Evolution of the sweetness receptor in primates. II. Gustatory responses of non-human primates to nine compounds known to be sweet in man. Chemical Senses 21:747–762.

Norconk MA. 1990. Introductory remarks: Ecological and behavioral correlates of polyspecific primate troops. American Journal of Primatology 21(2):81–85.

Norconk MA. 2007. Sakis, uakaris, and titi monkeys: Behavioral diversity in a radiation of primate seed predators. In Campbell CJ, Fuentes A, MacKinnon KC, Panger M, Bearder SK editors. Primates in perspective, pp. 123–138. Oxford, UK: Oxford University Press.

Norconk MA, Grafton BW, Conklin-Brittain NL. 1998. Seed dispersal by neotropic seed predators. American Journal of Primatology 45:103–126.

Norton GW, Rhine RJ, Wynn GW, Wynn RD. 1987. Baboon diet: A five-year study of stability and variability in the plant feeding and habitat of Mikumi National Park, Tanzania. Folia Primatologica 48:78–120.

Novacek MJ. 1992. Mammalian phylogeny: Shaking the tree. Nature 356:121–125.

Novak M. 2003. Self-injurious behavior in rhesus monkeys: New insights into its etiology, physiology, and treatment. American Journal of Primatology 59:3–19.

Novak MA, Sigmund K. 2005. Evolution of indirect reciprocity. Nature 437:1291–1298.

Nunes F, Norris RD. 2006. Abrupt reversal in ocean overturning during the Palaeocene/Eocene warm period. Nature 439:60–63.

O'Brien TG. 1991. Male-female social interactions in wedge-capped capuchin monkeys: Benefits and costs of group living. Animal Behaviour 41:555–568.

O'Connell JF, Hawkes K, Blurton Jones NG. 1999. Grandmothering and the evolution of *Homo erectus*. Journal of Human Evolution 36:461–485.

Oates JF. 1978. Water-plant and soil consumption by guereza monkeys (*Colobus guereza*): A relationship with minerals and toxins in the diet? Biotropica 10:241–253.

Oates JF. 1987. Food distribution and foraging behavior. In Smuts BB, Cheney DL, Seyfarth RM, Wrangham RW, Struhsaker TT editors. Primate societies, pp. 197–209. Chicago: University of Chicago Press.

Oates JF, Abedi-Lartey M, McGraw WS, Struhsaker TT, Whitesides GH. 2000. Extinction of a West African red colobus monkey. Conservation Biology 14:1526–1532.

Oates JF, McFarland KL, Groves JL, Bergl RA, Linder JM, Disotell TR. 2003. The Cross River gorilla: Natural history and status of a neglected and critically endangered subspecies. In Taylor AB and Goldsmith ML editors. Gorilla biology: A multidisciplinary perspective, pp. 472–497. Cambridge, UK: Cambridge University Press.

Oates JF, Whitesides GH, Davies AG, Waterman PG, Green SM, Dasilva GL, Mole S. 1990. Determinants of variation in tropical forest primate biomass: New evidence from West Africa. Ecology 71:328–343.

Odum EP. 1963. Ecology. New York: Holt, Rinehart and Winston.

Odum EP. 1971. Fundamentals of Ecology. 3rd edition. Philadelphia: Saunders.

Onderdonk DA, Chapman CA. 2000. Coping with forest fragmentation: The primates of Kibale National Park, Uganda. International Journal of Primatology 21:587–611.

Oppenheimer JR. 1977. Forest structure and its relation to activity of the capuchin monkey (*Cebus*). In Prasad MRN, Kumar TCA editors. Use of non-human primates in biomedical research, pp. 74–84. New Delhi: Indian National Science Academy.

Oppenheimer JR, Lang GE. 1969. *Cebus* monkeys: Effect on branching of *Gustavia* trees. Science 165:187–188.

Overdorff DJ. 1992. Differential patterns in flower feeding by *Eulemur fulvus rufus* and *Eulemur rubriventer* in Madagascar. American Journal of Primatology 28:191–203.

Overdorff D, Parga J. 2007. The new era of primate socioecology: Ecology and intersexual conflict. In Campbell CJ, Fuentes A, MacKinnon KC, Panger M, Bearder SK editors. Primates in perspective, pp. 466–482. Oxford, UK: Oxford University Press.

Packer C, Ikanda D, Kissui B, Kushnir H. 2005. Lion attacks on humans in Tanzania. Nature 436:927–928.

Packer C, Tatar M, Collins A. 1998. Reproductive cessation in female mammals. Nature 392:807–811.

Palagi E, Dapporto L, Borgognini Tarli S. 2005. The neglected scent: On the marking function of urine in *Lemur catta*. Behavioral Ecology and Sociobiology 58:437–445.

The Paleobiology Database @ *http://paleodb.org* [Accessed 3 July 2006].

Palmobit RA. 1996. Pair bonds in monogamous apes: A comparison of the siamang (*Hylobates syndactylus*) and the white-handed gibbon (*Hylobates lar*). Behaviour 133:321–356.

Palmobit RA, Cheney DL, Fischer J, Johnson S, Rendall D, Seyfarth RM, Silk JB. 2000. Male infanticide and defence of infants in wild chacma baboons. In van Schaik CP, Janson CH editors. Infanticide by males and its implications, pp. 123–151. Cambridge, UK: Cambridge University Press.

Palmobit RA, Cheney DL, Seyfarth RM. 2001. Female-female competition for male "friends" in wild chacma baboons (*Papio cynocephalus ursinus*). Animal Behaviour 61:1159–1171.

Paterson HEH. 1978. More evidence against speciation by reinforcement. South African Journal of Science 74:369–371.

Paterson HEH. 1985. The recognition concept of species. In Vrba ES editor. Species and speciation, pp. 21–29. Transvaal Museum Monograph No.4, Pretoria: Transvaal Museum.

Patterson BD, Kasiki SM, Selempo E, Kays RW. 2004. Livestock predation by lions (*Panthera leo*) and other carnivores on ranches neighboring Tsavo National Park, Kenya. Biological Conservation 119:507–516.

Patterson F. 1978. Linguistic capabilities of a lowland gorilla. In Peng FCC editor. Sign language and language acquisition in man and ape, pp. 161–201. Boulder, CO: Westview Press.

Patterson FG. 1984. Self-recognition by *Gorilla gorilla gorilla*. Gorilla 7:2–3.

Patterson FGP, Cohn RH. 1994. Self-recognition and awareness in lowland gorillas. In Parker ST, Mitchell RW, Boccia ML editors. Self-awareness in animals and humans, pp. 273–290. Cambridge, UK: Cambridge University Press.

Patterson F, Linden E. 1981. The education of Koko. New York: Holt, Rinehart and Winston.

Paul A. 1999. The socioecology of infant handling in primates: Is the current model convincing? Primates 40:33–46.

Paul A. 2002. Sexual selection and mate choice. International Journal of Primatology 23(4):877–904.

Paul A, Kuester J, Arnemann J. 1996. The sociobiology of male-infant interactions in Barbary macaques, *Macaca sylvanus*. Animal Behaviour 51:155–170.

Pavelka MSM. 1993. Monkeys of the mesquite: The social life of the south Texas snow monkey. Dubuque, IA: Kendall/Hunt Publishing Company.

Pavelka MSM, Brusselers OT, Nowak D, Behie AM. 2003. Population reduction and social disorganization in *Alouatta pigra* following a hurricane. International Journal of Primatology 24:1037–1055.

Pavelka MSM, Fedigan LM. 1991. Menopause: A comparative life history perspective. Yearbook of Physical Anthropology 34:13–38.

Pereira ME, Fairbanks LA editors. 1993. Juvenile primates. Life history, development and behavior. Oxford, UK: Oxford University Press.

Pereira ME, Macedonia JM. 1991. Ring-tailed lemur anti-predator calls denote predator class, not response urgency. Animal Behaviour 41:543–544.

Peres CA. 1994. Primate responses to phonological changes in an Amazonian terra firme forest. Biotropica 26:98–112.

Peres CA. 2001. Synergistic effects of subsistence hunting and habitat fragmentation on Amazonian forest vertebrates. Conservation Biology 15:1490–1505.

Peres CA, Dolman PM. 2000. Density compensation in neotropical primate communities: Evidence from 56 hunted and nonhunted Amazonian forests of varying productivity. Oecologia 122:175–189.

Perez VR, Godfrey LR, Nowak-Kemp M, Burney DA, Ratsimbazafy J, Vasey N. 2005. Evidence of early butchery of giant lemurs in Madagascar. Journal of Human Evolution 49:722–742.

Perry S. 1996. Female-female social relationships in wild white-faced capuchin monkeys, *Cebus capucinus*. American Journal of Primatology 40:167–182.

Perry S. 1997. Male-female social relationships in wild white-faced capuchin monkeys, (*Cebus capuchinus*). Behaviour 134:477–510.

Perry S, Baker M, Fedigan L, Gros-Louis J, Jack K, MacKinnon KC, Manson JH, Panger M, Pyle K, Rose L. 2003. Social conventions in wild white-faced capuchin monkeys: Evidence for traditions in a neotropical primate. Current Anthropology 44(2):241–268.

Perry S, Rose L. 1994. Begging and transfer of coati meat by white-faced capuchin monkeys, *Cebus capucinus*. Primates 35(4):409–415.

Petrides M, Cadoret G, Mackey S. 2005. Orofacial somatomotor responses in the macaque monkey homologue of Broca's area. Nature 435:1235–1238.

Petter JJ. 1978. Ecological and physiological adaptations of five sympatric nocturnal lemurs to seasonal variations in food production. In Chivers DJ, Joysey KA editors. Recent advances in primatology, pp. 211–223. New York: Academic Press.

Pettigrew JD. 1986. Flying primates? Megabats have the advanced pathway from eye to midbrain. Science 231:1304–1306.

Philipp MT, Purcell JE, Martin DS, Buck WR, Plauché GB, Ribka EP, DeNoel P, Hermand P, Leiva LE, Bagby GJ, Nelson S. 2006. Experimental infection of rhesus macaques with *Streptococcus pneumoniae*: A possible model for vaccine assessment. Journal of Medical Primatology 35:113–122.

Phillips-Conroy JE, Jolly CJ. 1986. Changes in the structure of the baboon hybrid zone in the Awash National Park, Ethiopia. American Journal of Physical Anthropology 71:337–350.

Piaget J. 1952. The origins of intelligence in children. New York: Norton.

Pianka ER. 1994. Evolutionary ecology. 5th edition. New York: Harper Collins.

Pilbeam D. 1982. New hominoid skull material from the Miocene of Pakistan. Nature 295:232–234.

Pilbeam D, Rose MD, Barry JC, Shah SMI. 1990. New *Sivapithecus* humeri from Pakistan and the relationship of *Sivapithecus* and *Pongo*. Nature 348:237–239.

Pilgrim G. 1927. A new *Sivapithecus* palate, and other primate fossils from India. Memoirs of the Geological Survey of India 14:1–26.

Pillans B, Williams M, Cameron D, Patnaik R, Hogarth J, Sahni A, Sharma JC, Williams F,
Bernor RL. 2005. Revised correlation of the Haritalyangar magnetostratigraphy, Indian Siwaliks: Implications for the age of the Miocene hominids *Indopithecus* and *Sivapithecus*, with a note on a new hominid tooth. Journal of Human Evolution 48:507–515.

Pimley ER, Bearder SK, Dixson AF. 2005a. Social organization of Milne-Edward's potto. American Journal of Primatology 66(4):317–330.

Pimley ER, Bearder SK, Dixson AF. 2005b. Home range analysis of *Perodicticus potto edwardsi* and *Sciurocheirus cameronensis*. International Journal of Primatology 26(1):191–206.

Pinker S. 1994. The language instinct. London: Allen Lane.

Pinker S, Bloom P. 1990. Natural selection and natural language. Behavioral and Brain Sciences 13:707–784.

Polaszek A. 2005. A universal register for animal names. Nature 437:477.

Pollick AS, de Waal FBM. 2007. Ape gestures and language evolution. Proceedings of the National Academy of Science, USA 104(19)8184–8189.

Poole JH, 1987. Rutting behavior in African elephants: The phenomenon of musth. Behaviour 102:283–31.

Poole JH. Tyack PL, Stoeger-Horwath AS, Watwood S. 2005. Elephants are capable of vocal learning. Nature 434:455–456.

Potts R. 1987. Transportation of resources: Reconstructions of early hominid socioecology: A critique of primate models. In Kinzey WG editor. The evolution of human behavior: Primate models pp. 28–47. New York: State University of New York Press.

Povinelli DJ. 2003. Folk physics for apes. The chimpanzee's theory of how the world works. New York: Oxford University Press.

Povinelli DJ, Bering JM, Giambrone S. 2000. Toward a science of other minds: Escaping the argument by analogy. Cognitive Sciences 24(3):509–541.

Povinelli DJ, deBlois S. 1992. Young children's (*Homo sapiens*) understanding of knowledge formation in themselves and others. Journal of Comparative Psychology 106:228–238.

Povinelli DJ, Gallup GG, Eddy TJ, Bierschwale DT, Engstrom MC, Perilloux HK, Toxopeus

IB. 1997. Chimpanzees recognize themselves in mirrors. Animal Behaviour 53:1083–1088.

Povinelli DJ, Nelson KE, Boysen ST. 1992. Comprehension of role reversal by chimpanzees: Evidence of empathy? Animal Behaviour 43:633–640.

Power ML, Oftedal OT, Tardif SD. 2002. Does the milk of callitrichid monkeys differ from that of the larger anthropoids? American Journal of Primatology 56(2):117–127.

Prance GT. 1980. A note on the probable pollination of *Combretum* by *Cebus* monkeys. Biotropica 12:239.

Premack D. 1988. "Does the chimpanzee have a theory of mind?" revisited. In Byrne RW, Whiten A editors. Machiavellian intelligence. Social expertise and the evolution of intellect in monkeys, apes, and humans, pp. 160–179. New York: Oxford University Press.

Premack D, Woodruff G. 1978. Does the chimpanzee have a theory of mind? Behavioral and Brain Sciences 4:515–526.

Prince-Hughes D. 2004. Songs of the gorilla nation: My journey through autism. New York: Harmony Books.

Pruetz JD, Bertolani P. 2007. Savanna chimpanzees, *Pan troglodytes verus*, hunt with tools. Current Biology 17:412–417.

Pruetz JD, Isbell LA. 2000. Correlations of food distribution and patch size with agonistic interactions in female vervets (*Chlorocebus aethiops*) and patas monkeys (*Erythrocebus patas*) living in simple habitats. Behavioral Ecology and Sociobiology 49:38–47.

Pusey AE. 1983. Mother-offspring relationships in chimpanzees after weaning. Animal Behaviour 31:363–377.

Pusey AE, Packer C. 1987. Dispersal and philopatry. In Smuts BB, Cheney DL, Seyfarth RM, Wrangham RW, Struhsaker TT editors. Primate societies, pp. 250–266. Chicago: University of Chicago Press.

Radespiel U, Dal Secco V, Drogemuller C, Braune P, Labes E, Zimmermann E. 2002. Sexual selection, multiple mating and paternity in grey mouse lemurs, *Microcebus murinus*. Animal Behaviour 63:259–268.

Radespiel U, Reimann W, Rahelinirina M, Zimmermann E. 2006. Feeding ecology of sympatric mouse lemur species in northwestern Madagascar. International Journal of Primatology 27(1):311–321.

Rae TC. 1999. Mosaic evolution in the origin of the Hominoidea. Folia Primatologica 70:125–135.

Rainforest Action Network *www.ran.org/ info_center* [Accessed 21 August 2007].

Ramstein G, Fluteau F, Besse J, Joussaume S. 1997. Effect of orogeny, plate motion and land-sea distribution on Eurasian climate change over past 30 million years. Nature 386:788–795.

Rasmussen DT. 1990a. Primate origins: Lessons from a neotropical marsupial. American Journal of Primatology 22:263–277.

Rasmussen DT. 1990b. The phylogenetic position of *Mahgarita stevensi*: Protoanthropoid or lemuroid? International Journal of Primatology 11(5):439–469.

Rasmussen DT. 1994. The different meanings of a tarsiod-anthropoid clade and a new model of anthropoid origins. In Fleagle JG, Kay RF editors. Anthropoid origins, pp. 335–360. New York: Plenum Press.

Rasmussen DT. 2002. Early catarrhines of the African Eocene and Oligocene. In Hartwig WC editor. The primate fossil record, pp. 203–220. Cambridge, UK: Cambridge University Press.

Rasmussen DT, Conroy GC, Simons EL. 1998. Tarsier-like locomotor specialization in the Oligocene primate *Afrotarsius*. Proceedings of the National Academy of Sciences, USA 95:14848–14850.

Rasmussen DT, Nekaris KA. 1998. Evolutionary history of Lorisiform primates. Folia Primatologica 69(suppl 1):250–285.

Ratsimbazafy JH. 2001. On the brink of extinction and the process of recovery: Response of black-and-white ruffed lemurs (*Varecia variegata variegata*) to disturbances in Manombo forest, Madagascar. Ph.D. dissertation, State University of New York, Stony Brook, New York.

Ratsimbazafy JH. 2002. How do black and white ruffed lemurs still survive in a highly disturbed habitat? Lemur News 7:7–10.

Rawlins RG, Kessler MJ editors. 1986. The Cayo Santiago macaques: History, behavior and biology. Albany: State University of New York Press.

Redmond I. 2006. The primate pet trade and its impact on biodiversity conservation. In Born to be wild. Primates are not pets, pp. 10–17. The International Fund for Animal Welfare. *www.IFAW.org* [Accessed 21 August 2007].

Redmond I, Juniper A. 2005. The oil for ape scandal. How palm oil is threatening orangutan survival. Research Report September 2005. *www.foe.co.uk* [Accessed 2 May 2006].

Regan BC, Julliot C, Simmen B, Vienot F, Charles-Dominique P, Mollon JD. 2001. Fruits, foliage and the evolution of primate colour vision. Philosophical Transactions of the Royal Society, London. B. 356:229–283.

Reichard U. 1995. Extra-pair copulations in a monogamous gibbon (*Hylobates lar*): Agonism, affiliation, and the concept of infanticide. Ethology 100:99–112.

Remis MJ. 1997a. Ranging and grouping patterns of a Western lowland gorilla group at Bai Hokou, Central African Republic. American Journal of Primatology 43(2):111–133.

Remis MJ. 1997b. Western lowland gorillas (*Gorilla gorilla gorilla*) as seasonal frugivores: Use of variable resources. American Journal of Primatology 43:87–109.

Remis MJ. 2002. Food preference among captive western gorillas (*Gorilla gorilla gorilla*) and chimpanzees (*Pan troglodytes*). International Journal of Primatology 23(2):231–249.

Rendall D, Seyfarth RM, Cheney DL. 2000. Proximate factors mediating "contact" calls in adult female baboons (*Papio cynocephalus ursinus*) and their infants. Journal of Comparative Psychology 114:36–46.

Rendall D, Seyfarth RM, Cheney DL, Owren MJ. 1998. The meaning and function of grunt variants in baboons. Animal Behaviour 57:583–592.

Retallack GJ, Bestland EA, Dugas DP. 1995. Miocene paleosols and habitats of *Proconsul* on Rusinga Island, Kenya. Journal of Human Evolution 29:53–91.

Retallack GJ, Wynn JG, Benefit BR, McCrossin ML. 2002. Paleosols and paleoenvironments of the middle Miocene, Maboko Formation, Kenya. Journal of Human Evolution 42:659–703.

Ribon R, Simon JE, de Mattos GT. 2003. Bird extinctions in Atlantic Forest fragments of the Viçosa Region, southeastern Brazil. Conservation Biology 17(6):1827–1839.

Richard A. 1970. A comparative study of the activity patterns and behavior of *Alouatta villosa* and *Ateles geoffroyi*. Folia Primatologica 12:241–263.

Richard AF. 1985. Primates in nature. New York: WH Freeman and Company.

Richard AF, Dewar RE, Schwartz M, Ratsirarson J. 2002. Life in the slow lane? Demography and life histories of male and female sifaka (*Propithecus verrreauxi verreauxi*). Journal of Zoology 256:421–436.

Richard AF, Goldstein SJ, Dewar RE. 1989. Weed macaques: The evolutionary implications of macaque feeding ecology. International Journal of Primatology 10:569–594.

Richards PW. 1996. The tropical rain forest. 2nd edition. Cambridge, UK: Cambridge University Press.

Richman B. 1987. Rhythm and melody in gelada vocal exchanges. Primates 28(2):199–223.

Ricklefs RE. 1973. Ecology. Portland, OR: Chiron Press.

Riesenberg LH, Buerkle CA. 2002. Genetic mapping in hybrid zones. The American Naturalist 159 (supplement):S36–S50.

Rizzolatti G, Arbib MA. 1998. Language within our grasp. Trends in Neuroscience 21(5):188–194.

Robbins MM. 1995. A demographic analysis of male life history and social structure of mountain gorillas. Behaviour 132:21–48.

Robbins MM. 2007. Gorillas: Diversity in ecology and behavior. In Campbell CJ, Fuentes A, MacKinnon KC, Panger M, Bearder SK editors. Primates in perspective, pp. 305–321. Oxford, UK: Oxford University Press.

Robbins MM, McNeilage A. 2003. Home range and frugivory patterns of mountain gorillas in Bwindi Impenetrable National Park, Uganda. International Journal of Primatology 24(3):467–491.

Robinson JG. 2005. Bushmeat crisis task force. Bulletin February/March *www.bushmeat.org/bulletin* [Accessed 27 May 2006].

Robinson JG, Bennett EL. 2002. Will alleviating poverty solve the bushmeat crisis? Oryx 36(4):332.

Robinson JG, Bennett EL. 2004. Having your wildlife and eating it too: An analysis of hunting sustainability across tropical ecosystems. Animal Conservation 7:397–408.

Rose K. 1995. The earliest primates. Evolutionary Anthropology 3(5):159–173.

Rose LM. 1998. Behavioral ecology of white-faced capuchins (*Cebus capuchinus*) in Costa

Rica. Ph.D. dissertation Washington University, St. Louis, Missouri.

Rose MD. 1994. Quadrupedalism in some Miocene catarrhines. Journal of Human Evolution 26:387–411.

Rosenberger AL, Setoguchi T, Shigehara N. 1990. The fossil record of callitrichine primates. Journal of Human Evolution 19:209–236.

Ross C. 2001. Park and ride? Evolution of infant carrying in primates. International Journal of Primatology 22(5):749–771.

Ross CF. 2000. Into the light: The origin of Anthropoidea. Annual Review of Anthropology 29:147–194.

Ross CF, Williams B, Kay RF. 1998. Phylogenetic analysis of anthropoid relationships. Journal of Human Evolution 35:221–306.

Rouquet P, Forment J-M, Bermejo M, Kilbourne A, Karesh W, Reed P, Kumulungui B, Yaba P, Délicate A, Rollin PE, Leroy EM. 2005. Wild animal mortality monitoring and human Ebola outbreaks, Gabon and Republic of Congo, 2001–2003. Emerging Infectious Diseases 11(2):283–290.

Rowe N. 1996. The pictorial guide to the living primates. New York: Pogonias Press.

Rowell TE, Mitchell BJ. 1991. Comparison of seed dispersal of guenons in Kenya and capuchins in Panama. Journal of Tropical Ecology 7:269–274.

Rumbaugh DM. 1977. Language learning by a chimpanzee: The Lana project. New York: Academic Press.

Rumbaugh D, McCormack C. 1967. The learning skills of primates: A comparative study of apes and monkeys. In Stark D, Schheider R, Ruhn HJ editors. Progress in primatology, pp. 289–306. Stuttgart: Gustav Fisher Verlag.

Rylands AB, Brandon K. 2005. Brazilian protected areas. Conservation Biology 19(3):612–618.

Sackett GP, Ruppenthal GC, Davis AE. 2002. Survival, growth, health, and reproduction following nursery rearing compared with mother rearing in pigtailed monkeys (*Macaca nemestrina*). American Journal of Primatology 56:165–183.

Saj TL, Sicotte P, Paterson JD. 2001. The conflict between vervet monkeys and farmers at the forest edge in Entebbe, Uganda. African Journal of Ecology 39:195–199.

Santiago ML, Lukasik M, Kamenya S, Li Y, Bibollet-Ruche F, Bailes E, Muller MN, Emery M, Goldenberg DA, Lwanga JS, Ayouba A, Nerrienet E, McClure HM, Heeney JL, Watts DP, Pusey AE, Collins DA, Wrangham RW, Goodall J, Brookfield JFY, Sharp PM, Shaw GM, Hahn BH. 2003. Foci of endemic simian immunodefieciency virus infection in wild-living Eastern chimpanzees (*Pan troglodytes schweinfurthii*). Journal of Virology 77(13):7545–7562.

Santos LR, Barnes JL, Mahajan N. 2005. Expectations about numerical events in four lemur species *Eulemur fulvus, Eulemur mongoz, Lemur catta* and *Varecia rubra*. Animal Cognition 8:253–262.

Sanz CM, Morgan DB. 2007. Chimpanzee tool technology in the Goualougo triangle, Republic of Congo. Journal of Human Evolution 52:420–433.

Sapolsky R. 2001. A primate's memoir: A neuroscientist's unconventional life among the baboons. New York: Scribner.

Sapolsky R. 2004a. Social status and health in humans and other animals. Annual Review of Anthropology 33:393–418.

Sapolsky R. 2004b. Why zebras don't get ulcers: A guide to stress, stress-related diseases and coping. New York: Holt.

Sauther ML. 1989. Antipredator behavior in troops of free-ranging *Lemur catta* at Beza Mahafaly Special Reserve, Madagascar. International Journal of Primatology 10:595–606.

Sauther ML. 1993. Resource competition in wild populations of ring-tailed lemurs (*Lemur catta*): Implications for female dominance. In Kappler PM, Ganzhorn JU editors. Lemur social systems and their ecological basis, pp. 135–152. New York: Plenum.

Sauther ML. 1998. Interplay of phenology and reproduction in ringtailed lemurs: Implication for ringtailed lemur conservation. Folia Primatologica 69 Supplement 1:309–320.

Sauther ML, Sussman RW, Gould L. 1999. The socioecology of ringtailed lemurs: Thirty five years of research. Evolutionary Anthropology 8:120–132.

Savage-Rumbaugh SE, Lewin R. 1994. Kanzi: The ape at the brink of the human mind. New York: John Wiley & Sons.

Savage-Rumbaugh SE, Shanker SG, Taylor TJ. 1998. Apes, language, and the human mind. New York: Oxford University Press.

Sawaguchi T. 1992. The size of the neocortex in relation to ecology and social structure in monkeys and apes. Folia Primatologica 58:131–145.

Schemske DW. 2000. Understanding the origin of species. Evolution 54(3):1069–1073.

Scheumann M, Call J. 2006. Sumatran orangutans and a yellow-cheeked crested gibbon know what is where. International Journal of Primatology 27(2): 575–602.

Schick KD, Toth N, Garufi G, Savage-Rumbaugh SE, Rumbaugh DM, Sevcik RA. 1999. Continuing investigations into the stone toolmaking and tool-using capabilities of a bonobo (*Pan paniscus*). Journal of Archaeological Science 26:821–832.

Schidlowski M. 2001. Carbon isotopes as biogeochemical recorders of life over 3.8 Ga of earth history: Evolution of a concept. Precambrian Research 106:117–134.

Schino G. 2001. Grooming, competition and social rank among female primates: A meta-analysis. Animal Behaviour 62:265–271.

Schino G, Speranza L, Ventura R, Troisi A. 2003. Infant handling and maternal response in Japanese macaques. International Journal of Primatology 24(3):627–638.

Schmid J. 2001. Daily torpor in free-ranging gray mouse lemurs (*Microcebus murinus*) in Madagascar. Intenational Journal of Primatology 22(6):1021–1031.

Schneider H, Schneider MPC, Sampaio I, Haradad ML, Stanhope M, Czelusniak J, Goodman M. 1993. Molecular phylogeny of the New World monkeys (Platyrrhini, Primates). Molecular Phlogenetics and Evolution 2:225–242.

Schoener TW. 1971. Theory of feeding strategies. Annual Review and Ecological Systematics 2:369–404.

Schupp EW, Milleron T, Russo SE. 2002. Dissemination limitation and the origin and maintenance of species-rich tropical forests. In Levey D, Silva WR, Galetti M editors. Seed dispersal and frugivory: Ecology, evolution and conservation, pp. 19–33. Wallingford, UK: CABI Publishing.

Schuster M, Duringer P, Ghienne J-F, Vignaud P, Mackaye HT, Likius A, Brunet M. 2006. The age of the Sahara desert. Science 311:821.

Schwartz JH. 1984. The evolutionary relationships of man and orang-utans. Nature 308:501–505.

Schwartz JH. 1987. The red ape: Orang-utans and human origins. Boston: Houghton Mifflin Company.

Schwartz JH. 2003. How close are the similarities between *Tarsius* and other primates? In Wright PC, Simons EL, Gursky S editors. Tarsiers. Past, present and future, pp. 50–96. New Brusnwick, NJ: Rutgers University Press.

Schwartz JH. 2005. The red ape: Orangutans and human origins – revised edition. Cambridge MA: Westview Press.

Scotese CR. 2000. The Paleomap project. *http://www.scotese.com* [Accessed 13 August 2007].

Scotese CR. 2001. Atlas of earth history Arlington: (Paleomap Project). of Texas.

Scott TR, Plata-Salaman CR. 1999. Taste in the monkey cortex. Physiology and Behavior, 67(4):489–511.

Seiffert ER, Simons EL, Attla Y. 2003. Fossil evidence for an ancient divergence of lorises and galagos. Nature 422:421–424.

Seiffert ER, Simons EL, Fleagle JG. 2000. Anthropoid humeri from the late Eocene of Egypt. Proceedings of the National Academy of Sciences, USA 97:10062–10067.

Semaw S, Rogers MJ, Quade J, Renne PR, Butler RF, Dominguez-Rodrigo M, Stout D, Hart WS, Pickering T, Simpson SW. 2003. 2.6-million-year-old stone tools and associated bones from OGS-6 and OGS-7, Gona, Afar, Ethiopia. Journal of Human Evolution 45:169–177.

Senut B, Pickford M, Gommery D, Mein P, Cheboi K, Coppens Y. 2001. First hominid from the Miocene (Lukeino Formation, Kenya). Comptes rendus de l'Academie des sciences, Paris 332:137–144.

Seyfarth RM, Cheney DL, Marler P. 1980. Vervet monkey alarm calls: Semantic communications in a free-ranging primate. Animal Behaviour 28:1070–1094.

Shalev M. 2001. President Clinton signs the Chimpanzee Health Improvement, Maintenance and Protection Act. Laboratory Animals (New York) 30(2):15–16.

Shelford VE. 1913. Animal communities in temperate America. Chicago: University of Chicago Press.

Shimooka Y. 2005. Sexual differences in ranging of *Ateles belzebuth belzebuth* at La Macarena, Colombia. International Journal of Primatology 26:385–406.

Shoshani J. 1986. Mammalian phylogeny: Comparison of morphological and molecular results. Molecular Biology and Evolution 3(3):222–242.

Shoshani J, Groves CP, Simons EL, Gunnell GF. 1996. Primate phylogeny: Morphological vs molecular results. Molecular Phylogenetics and Evolution 5(1):102–154.

Shu W, Cho JY, Jiang Y, Zhang M, Weisz D, Elder GA, Schmeidler J, de Gasperi R, Gama Sosa MA, Rabidou D, Santucci AC, Perl D, Morrisey E, Buxbaum JD. 2005. Altered ultrasonic vocalization in mice with a disruption in the *Foxp2* gene. Proceedings of the National Academy of Science, USA 102(27):9643–9648.

Shu W, Yang H, Zhang L, Lu MM, Morrisey EE. 2001. Characterization of a new subfamily of winged-helix/forkhead (Fox) genes that are expressed in the lung and act as transcriptional repressors. Journal of Biological Chemistry 276:27488–27497.

Shumaker R. 2006. *www.iowagreatapes.org* [Accessed 13 August 2007].

Sigé B, Jaeger J-J, Sudre J, Vianey-Liaud M. 1990. *Altiatlasius koulchii* n. gen. et sp., primate omomyidé du Paléocène supérieur du Maroc, et les origins des euprimates. Palaeontographica Abt A 214:31–56.

Sigg H, Stolba A. 1981. Home range and daily march in a hamadryas baboon troop. Folia Primatologica 36:40–75.

Silk JB. 2000. The function of peaceful post-conflict interactions. An alternate view. In Aureli F, de Waal FBM editors. Natural conflict resolution, pp. 179–181. Los Angeles: University of California Press.

Silk JB, Alberts SC, Altmann J. 2003a. Social bonds of female baboons enhance infant survival. Science 302:1231–1234.

Silk JB, Brosnan SF, Vonk J, Henrich J, Povinelli DJ, Richardson AS, Lambeth SP, Mascaro J, Schapiro SJ. 2005. Chimpanzees are indifferent to the welfare of unrelated group members. Nature 437:1357–1359.

Silk JB, Rendall D, Cheney DL, Seyfarth RM. 2003b. Natal attraction in adult female baboons (*Papio cynocephalus ursinus*) in the Moremi Reserve, Botswana. Ethology 109:627–644.

Silva BTF, Sampaio MIC, Schneider H, Schneider MPC, Montoya E, Encarnación F, Salzano FM. 1992. Natural hybridization

between *Saimiri* taxa in the Peruvian Amazonia. Primates 33(1):107–113.

Silvestri G. 2005. Naturally SIV-infected sooty mangabeys: Are we closer to understanding why they do not develop AIDS? Journal of Medical Primatology 34(5–6):243–252.

Simons EL. 1968. Hunting the "dawn apes" of Africa. Discovery 4:19–32.

Simons EL. 1987. New faces of *Aegyptopithecus* from the Oligocene of Egypt. Journal of Human Evolution 16:273–289.

Simons EL. 1989. Description of two genera and species of late Eocene Anthropoidea from Egypt. Proceedings of the National Academy of Science, USA 86:9956–9960.

Simons EL. 1992. Diversity in the early tertiary anthropoidean radiation in Africa. Proceedings of the National Academy of Science, USA 89:10743–10747.

Simons EL. 1995. Egyptian Oligocene primates: A review. Yearbook of Physical Anthropology 38:199–238.

Simons EL. 2003. The fossil record of tarsier evolution. In Wright PC, Simons EL, Gursky S editors. Tarsiers. Past, present and future, pp. 9–49. New Brunswick, NJ: Rutgers University Press.

Simons EL, Rasmussen DT. 1994. A whole new world of ancestors: Eocene anthropoideans from Africa. Evolutionary Anthropology 3:128–139.

Simpson GG. 1944. Tempo and mode in evolution. New York: Columbia University Press.

Simpson GG. 1961. Principles of animal taxonomy. New York: Columbia University Press.

Singer P, Cavalieri P. editors. 1993. The great ape project. New York: St. Martin's Griffin.

Singleton M. 2000. The phylogenetic affinities of *Otavipithecus namibiensis*. Journal of Human Evolution 38:537–573.

Sinha A, Datta A, Madhusudan MD, Mishra C. 2005. *Macaca munzala*: A new species from Western Arunachal Pradesh, Northeastern India. International Journal of Primatology 26(4):977–989.

Skorupa JP. 1988. The effect of selective timber harvesting on rain-forest primates in Kibale Forest, Uganda. Ph.D. dissertation, University of California, Davis.

Small MF. 1998. Ms Monkey. In Ciochon RL, Nisbett RA editors. The primate anthology. Essays on primate behaviour, ecology and conservation from natural history, pp. 56–59. Upper Saddle River, NJ: Prentice Hall.

Smith GE. 1913. The evolution of man. Annual report of the board of regents of the Smithsonian Institution 1912:553–572.

Smith PF, Konings A, Kornfield I. 2003. Hybrid origin of a cichlid population in lake Malawi: Implications for genetic variation and species diversity. Molecular Ecology 12:2497–2504.

Smith T. 2006. Individual olfactory signatures in common marmosets (*Callithrix jacchus*). American Journal of Primatology 68(6):585–604.

Smith WJ. 1977. The behavior of communication: An ethological approach. Cambridge, MA: Harvard University Press.

Smith WJ. 1981. Referents of animal communication. Animal Behaviour 29:1273–1275.

Smithsonian National Zoological Park. Golden Lion Tamarin Conservation Program. *http://nationalzoo.si.edu/ConservationAndScience/EndangeredSpecies/GLTPProgram* [Accessed 26 March 2006].

Smolker R, Richards A, Conner R, Mann J, Berggren P. 1997. Sponge carrying by dolphins (Delphinidae, *Tursiops* sp.): A foraging specialization involving tool use? Ethology 103:454–465.

Smuts BB. 1985. Sex and friendship in baboons. New York: Aldine de Gruyter.

Smuts BB. 1987. Sexual competition and mate choice. In Smuts BB, Cheney DL, Seyfarth RM, Wrangham RW, Struhsaker TT editors. Primate societies, pp. 385–399. Chicago: University of Chicago Press.

Smuts BB, Smuts RW. 1993. Male aggression and sexual coercion of females in nonhuman primates and other mammals: Evidence and theoretical implications. Advances in the Study of Behavior 22:1–63.

Snowdon C. 1990. Language capacities of nonhuman animals. Yearbook of Physical Anthropology 33:215–243.

Sommer V. 1994. Infanticide among the langurs of Jodhpur: Testing the sexual selection hypothesis with long-term record. In Parmigiani S, vom Saal F editors. Infanticide and parental care. pp. 155–198. London: Harwood Academic Publishers.

Southwick CH, Beg MA, Siddiqi MR. 1965. Rhesus monkeys in North India. In DeVore I editor. Primate behavior: Field studies of monkeys and apes, pp. 111–159. New York: Holt, Rinehart and Winston.

Stanford CB. 1991. The capped langur in Bangladesh: Behavioral ecology and reproductive tactics. Contributions to Primatology 26:1–179.

Stanford CB. 1999. The hunting apes: Meat eating and the origins of human behavior. Princeton, NJ: Princeton University Press.

Stanford CB, Nkurunungi JB. 2003. Behavioral ecology of sympatric chimpanzees and gorillas in Bwindi Impenetrable National Park, Uganda: Diet. International Journal of Primatology 24(4):901–918.

Stanford CB, Wallis J, Matama H, Goodall J. 1994. Patterns of predation by chimpanzees on red colobus monkeys in Gombe National Park, Tanzania, 1982–1991. American Journal of Physical Anthropology 94:213–228.

Steiper ME, Young NM, Sukarna TY. 2004. Genomic data support the hominoid slowdown and an early Oligocene estimate for the hominoid-cercopithecoid divergence. Proceedings of the National Academy of Science, USA 101(49):17021–17026.

Sterling EJ. 1993. Patterns of range use and social organization in aye-ayes (*Daubentonia madagascariensis*) on Nosy Mangabe. In Kappeler PM, Ganzhorn JU editors. Lemur social systems and their ecological basis, pp. 1–10. New York: Plenum Press.

Sterling EJ, Nguyen N, Fashing PJ. 2000. Spatial patterning in nocturnal prosimians: A review of methods and relevance to studies of sociality. American Journal of Primatology 51:3–19.

Stern K, McClintock MK. 1998. Regulation of ovulation by human pheromones. Nature 392:177–179.

Stevens JR, Hauser MD. 2004. Why be nice? Psychological constraints on the evolution of cooperation. Trends in Cognitive Sciences 8(2):60–65.

Stevenson PR, Castellanos MC, Pizarro JC, Garavito M. 2002. Effects of seed dispersal by three ateline monkey species on seed germination at Tinigua National Park, Colombia. International Journal of Primatology 23:1187–1204.

Stevenson PR, Link A, Ramirez BH. 2005. Frugivory and seed fate in *Bursera inverse* at Tinigua National Park, Colombia:

Implications for primate conservation. Biotropica 37:431–438.

Stewart CB, Disotell TR. 1998. Primate evolution: In and out of Africa. Current Biology 8(16):R 582–588.

Stewart KJ, Harcourt AH. 1987. Gorillas: Variation in female relationships. In Smuts BB, Cheney DL, Seyfarth RM, Wrangham RW, Struhsaker TT editors. Primate societies, pp. 155–164. Chicago: University of Chicago Press.

Stoinski TS, Beck BB, Bloomsmith MA, Maple TL. 2003. A behavioral comparison of captive-born, reintroduced golden lion tamarins and their wild-born offspring. Behaviour 140:137–160.

Stokes EJ. 2004. Within-group social relationships among females and adult males in wild Western lowland gorillas (*Gorilla gorilla gorilla*). American Journal of Primatology 64:233–246.

Strier KB. 1992. *Atelinae* adaptations: Behavioral strategies and ecological constraints. American Journal of Physical Anthropology 88:515–524.

Strier KB. 1994a. Brotherhoods among atelines: Kinship, affiliation, and competition. Behaviour 130:151–167.

Strier KB. 1994b. Myth of the typical primate. Yearbook of Physical Anthropology 37:233–271.

Strier KB. 2007. Primate behavioral ecology. 3rd Edition. Boston: Allyn and Bacon.

Struhsaker TT. 1967. Auditory communication among vervet monkeys (*Cercopithecus aethiops*). In Altmann SA editor. Social communication among primates, pp. 281–324. Chicago: University of Chicago Press.

Struhskaer TT. 1975. The red colobus monkey. Chicago: University of Chicago Press.

Struhsaker TT, Leakey M. 1990. Prey selectivity by crowned hawk-eagles on monkeys in the Kable Forest, Uganda. Behavioral Ecology and Sociobiology 26:435–443.

Struhskaer TT, Leland L. 1979. Socioecology of five sympatric monkey species in the Kibale Forest, Uganda. In Rosenblatt J, Hinde RA, Beer C, Busnel MC editors. Advances in the study of behavior, Vol. 9. pp. 158–228. New York: Academic Press.

Strum SC. 1975. Life with the Pumphouse gang: New insights into baboon behavior. National Geographic 14:672–691.

Strum SC. 1983. Baboon cues for eating meat. Journal of Human Evolution 12:327–336.

Strum SC. 1987. Almost human. A journey into the world of baboons. New York: Random House.

Strum SC. 2005. Measuring success in primate translocation: A baboon case study. American Journal of Primatology 65:117–140.

Suarez SA. 2006. Diet and travel costs for spider monkeys in a nonseasonal, hyperdiverse environment. International Journal of Primatology 27(2):411–436.

Sugardjito J, Nuhuda N. 1981. Meat-eating behavior in wild orangutans. Primates 22:414–416.

Sulkowski GM, Hauser MD. 2001. Can rhesus monkeys spontaneously subtract? Cognition 79:239–262.

Supriatna J. 1991. Hybridization between *M. maurus* and *M. tonkeana*: A test of species status using behavioral and morphogenetic analysis. Ph.D. dissertation. University of New Mexico, Albuquerque, New Mexico.

Susman RL. 1987. Pygmy chimpanzees and common chimpanzees: Models for the behavioral ecology of the earliest hominids. In Kinzey WG editor. The evolution of human behavior: Primate models, pp. 105–114. New York: State University of New York Press.

Susman RL. 2005. *Oreopithecus*: Still apelike after all these years. Journal of Human Evolution 49:405–411.

Sussman RW. 1977. Socialization, social structure, and ecology of two sympatric species of lemur. In Chevalier-Skolnikoff S, Poirier F editors. Primate bio-social development: Biological, social, and ecological determinants, pp. 515–529. New York: Garland.

Sussman RW. 1991a. Demography and social organization of free-ranging *Lemur catta* in the Beza Mahafaly Reserve, Madagascar. American Journal of Physical Anthropology 84:43–58.

Sussman RW. 1991b. Primate origins and the evolution of angiosperms. American Journal of Primatology 23(4):209–223.

Sussman RW. 1999. Primate ecology and social structure. Volume 1: Lorises, lemurs, and tarsiers. Boston: Pearson Custom Publishing.

Sussman RW. 2000. Primate ecology and social structure. Volume 2: New World monkeys. Boston: Pearson Custom Publishing.

Sussman RW, Cheverud JM. Bartlett TQ. 1995. Infant killing as an evolutionary strategy: Reality or myth? Evolutionary Anthropology 3:149–151.

Sussman RW, Garber PA, Cheverud JM. 2005. Importance of cooperation and affiliation in the evolution of primate sociality. American Journal of Physical Anthropology 128:84–97.

Sussman RW, Raven PH. 1978. Pollination by lemurs and marsupials: An archaic coevolutionary system. Science 200:731–736.

Sussman RW, Tattersall I. 1976. Cycles of activity, group composition, and diet of *Lemur mongoz mongoz* Linnaeus,1766 in Madagascar. Folia Primatologica 26:270–283.

Suzuki A. 1965. An ecological study of wild Japanese monkeys in snowy areas: Focused on their food habits. Primates 6:31–72.

Swedell L. 2000a. Social behavior and reproductive strategies of female hamadryas baboons, *Papio hamadryas hamadryas*, in Ethiopia. Ph.D. Thesis. Columbia University, New York.

Swedell L. 2000b. Two takeovers in wild hamadryas baboons. Folia Primatologica 71:169–172.

Swedell L. 2002. Affiliation among females in wild hamadryas baboons (*Papio hamadryas hamadryas*). International Journal of Primatology 23(6):1205–1226.

Swindler DR. 1998. Introduction to primates. Seattle: University of Washington Press.

Swindler DR. 2002. Primate dentition. An introduction to the teeth of non-human primates. Cambridge, UK: Cambridge University Press.

Swofford DL. 2001. PAUP*: Phylogenetic analysis using parsimony (* and other methods). Version 4. Sunderland, MA: Sinauer.

Symons DK. 2004. Mental state discourse, theory of mind, and the internalization of self-other understanding. Developmental Review 24:159–188.

Tabuce R, Mahboubi M, Tafforeau P, Sudre J. 2004. Discovery of a highly-specialized plesiadapiform primate in the early-middle Eocene of northwestern Africa. Journal of Human Evolution 47:305–321.

Taglialatela JP, Savage-Rumbaugh SE, Baker LA. 2003. Vocal production by a language-competent *Pan paniscus*. International Journal of Primatology 24(1):1–17.

Takahashi H. 1997. Huddling relationships in night sleeping groups among wild Japanese macaques in Kinkazan Island during winter. Primates 38(1):57–68.

Takai M, Anaya F, Shigehara N, Setoguchi T. 2000. New fossil materials of the earliest New World monkey, *Branisella boliviana*, and the problem of platyrrhine origins. American Journal of Physical Anthropology 111:263–281.

Tan CL. 1999. Group composition, home range size, and diet of three sympatric bamboo lemur species (Genus *Hapalemur*) in Ranomafana National Park, Madagascar. International Journal of Primatology 20(4):547–566.

Tan Y, Li W-H. 1999. Trichromatic vision in prosimians. Nature 402:36.

Tavaré S, Marshall CR, Will O, Soligo C, Martin RD. 2002. Using the fossil record to estimate the age of the last common ancestor of extant primates. Nature 416:726–729.

Teaford MF, Maas MC, Simons EL. 1996. Dental microwear and microstructure in Early Oligocene primates from the Fayum, Egypt: Implications for diet. American Journal of Physical Anthropology 101: 527–543.

Tebbich S, Bshary R. 2004. Cognitive abilities related to tool use in the woodpecker finch, *Cactospiza pallida*. Animal Behaviour 67:689–697.

Templeton AR. 1989. The meaning of species and speciation: A genetic perspective. In Otte D, Endler JA editors. Speciation and its consequences, pp. 3–27. Sunderland, MA: Sinauer.

Templeton AR. 1998. Species and speciation. Geography, population structure, ecology and gene trees. In Howard DJ, Berlocher SH editors. Endless form. Species and speciation, pp. 32–43. Oxford, UK: Oxford University Press.

Terborgh J. 1983. Five New World primates. Princeton, NJ: Princeton University Press.

Terborgh J. 1986. Keystone plant resources in the tropical forest. In Soulé ME editor. Conservation biology: The science of scarcity and diversity, pp 330–344. Sunderland: Sinauer.

Terborgh J, Pitman N, Silman M, Schichter H, Nunez PV. 2002. Maintenance of tree diversity in tropical forests. In Levey DJ, Silva WR, Galetti M editors. Seed dispersal and frugivory: Ecology, evolution and conservation, pp. 1–17. New York: CABI Publishing.

Terrace HS. 1987. Nim. New York: Columbia University Press.

Terrace HS, Petitto LA, Sanders RJ, Bever TG. 1979. Can an ape create a sentence? Science 206:891–902.

Theron W. 2003. *www.animalsentience.com/features/elephants_mourning_their_fallen.htm.* [Accessed 19 march 2006].

Tolman EC. 1948. Cognitive maps in rats and men. Psychological Review 55:189–208.

Tomasello M. 1990. Cultural transmission in the tool use and communicatory signalling of chimpanzees? In Parker S, Gibson K editors. Language and intelligence in monkeys and apes: Comparative developmental perspectives, pp. 274–311. Cambridge, UK: Cambridge University Press.

Tomasello M, Call J. 1997. Primate cognition. New York: Oxford University Press.

Tomasello M, Kruger A, Ratner H. 1993. Cultural learning. Behavioral Brain Sciences 16:495–552.

Torigoe T. 1985. Comparison of object manipulation among 74 species of non-human primates. Primates 26(2):182–194.

Torres de Assumção CT. 1981. *Cebus apella* and *Brachyteles arachnoids* (Cebidae) as potential pollinators of *Mabea fistulifera* (Euphorbiaceae). Journal Mammal 62:386–388.

Toth N, Schick KD, Savage-Rumbaugh SE, Sevcik RA, Rumbaugh DM. 1993. Pan the tool-maker: Investigations into the stone tool-making and tool-using capabilities of a bonobo (*Pan paniscus*). Journal of Archaeological Sciences 20:81–91.

Treves A. 1997. Primate natal coats: A preliminary analysis of distribution and function. American Journal of Physical Anthropology 104:47–70.

Treves A. 1999. Has predation shaped the social systems of arboreal primates? International Journal of Primatology 20:35–67.

Treves A, Chapman CA. 1996. Conspecific threat, predation avoidance, and resource defence: Implications for grouping in langurs. Behavioral Ecology and Sociobiology 39:45–53.

Trivers RL. 1971. The evolution of reciprocal altruism. Quarterly Review of Biology 46:35–57.

Trivers RL. 1972. Parental investment and sexual selection. In Campbell B editor. Sexual selection and the descent of man, 1871–1971, pp.136–179. Chicago: Aldine.

Turelli M, Barton NH, Coyne JA. 2001. Theory and speciation. Trends in Ecology and Evolution 16(7):330–343.

Turner IM. 2001. The ecology of trees in the tropical rain forest. Cambridge, UK: Cambridge University Press.

U.S. Department of Agriculture. 1991. Animal welfare standards. Federal Register 56:6495–6505.

U.S. Department of Agriculture. 1999. Animal welfare: Draft policy on environment enhancement for nonhuman primates. Federal Register 64(135):38145–38150.

U.S. Department of Agriculture. *www.nal.usda.gov/awic/legislat/awabrief.htm#Q9* [Accessed 22 August 2007].

Umiltà MA, Kohler E, Gallese V, Fogassi L, Fadiga L, Keysers C, Rizzolatti G. 2001. I know what you are doing: A neurophysiological study. Neuron 31:155–165.

Utami SS, van Hooff JARAM. 1997. Meat-eating by adult female Sumatran orangutan (*Pongo pygmaeus albelii*). American Journal of Primatology 43:159–165.

Valderrama X, Robinson JG, Attygalle AB, Eisner T. 2000. Seasonal anointment with millipedes in a wild primate: A chemical defense against insects. Journal of Chemical Ecology 26:2781–2790.

van Roosmalen MGM, van Roosmalen T, Mittermeier RA, Rylands AB. 2000. Two new species of marmoset, Genus *Callithrix erxleben*, 1777 (Callitrichidae, Primates), from the Tapajos/Madeira interfluvium, South Central Amazonia, Brazil. Neotropical Primates 8(1):2–18.

van Schaik CP. 1986. Phenological changes in a Sumatran rainforest. Journal of Tropical Ecology 2:327–347.

van Schaik CP. 1989. The ecology of social relationships amongst female primates. In Standen V, Foley RA editors. Comparative socioecology: The behavioral ecology of humans and other mammals, pp. 195–218. Oxford, UK: Blackwell.

van Schaik CP, Ancrenaz M, Borgen G, Galdikas B, Knott CD, Singlcton I, Suzuki A, Utami SS, Merrill M. 2003a. Orangutan cultures and the evolution of material culture. Science 299:102–105.

van Schaik CP, Aureli F. 2000. The natural history of valuable relationships in primates. In Aureli F, de Waal FMB editors. Natural conflict resolutions, pp. 307–333. Los Angeles: University of California Press.

van Schaik CP, Fox EA, Fechtman LT. 2003b. Individual variation in the rate of use of tree-hole tools among wild orang-utans: Implications for hominin evolution. Journal of Human Evolution 44:11–23.

van Schaik CP, Fox EA, Sitompul A. 1996. Manufacture and use of tools in wild Sumatran orangutans. Naturwissenschaften 83:186–188.

van Schaik CP, Janson CH editors. 2000. Infanticide by males and its implications. Cambridge, UK: Cambridge University Press.

van Valen L. 1976. Ecological species, multispecies and oaks. Taxon 25:233–239.

Vargha-Khadem F, Gadian DG, Copp A, Mishkin M. 2005. FOXP2 and the neuroanatomy of speech and language. Nature Reviews/ Neuroscience 6:131–138.

Vauclair J. 1990. Processus cognitifs elabores: Etude des representations mentales chez le babouin. In Roeder JJ, Anderson JR editors. Primates. Recherches actuelles, pp. 170–180. Paris: Masson.

Vezuli A, Hauwy M, Warter S, Rumpler Y. 1997. Chromosome painting: An available method to test the chromosomal changes during evolution of lemurs. Cytogenetic Cell Genetics 78:147–152.

Vickers NJ. 2000. Mechanisms of animal navigation in odor plumes. Biological Bulletins 198:203–212.

Visalberghi E, Limongelli L. 1994. Lack of comprehension of cause-effect relationships in tool-using capuchin monkeys (*Cebus apella*). Journal of Comparative Psychology 108:15–22.

Visalbergi E, Trinca L. 1989. Tool use in capuchin monkeys: Distinguishing between performing and understanding. Primates 30:511–521.

Wada K. 1980. Seasonal home range use by Japanese monkeys in the snowy Shiga Heights. Primates 21:468–483.

Wada K, Tokida E. 1981. Habitat utilization by wintering Japanese monkeys (*Macaca fuscata fuscata*) in the Shiga Heights. Primates 22(3):330–348.

Wakibara JV, Huffman MA, Wink M, Reich S, Aufreiter S, Hancock RGV, Sodhi R,

Mahaney WC, Russel S. 2001. The adaptive significance of geophagy for Japanese macaques (*Macaca fuscata*) at Arashiyama, Japan. International Journal of Primatology 22(3):495–520.

Walker AC. 1997. *Proconsul* function and phylogeny. In Begun, DR, Ward CV, Rose MD editors. Function, phylogeny and fossils: Miocene hominoid evolution and adaptation, pp. 209–224. New York: Plenum Press.

Wallace R, Gomez H, Felton A, Felton AM. 2006. On a new species of titi monkey, genus *Callicebus thomas* (Primates, Pitheciidae), from western Bolivia with preliminary notes on distribution and abundance. Primate Conservation 20:29–39.

Wallman J. 1992. Aping language. Cambridge, UK: Cambridge University Press.

Walsh MM, Lowe DR. 1985. Filamentous microfossils from the 3,500-Myr-old Onverwacht Group, Barberton Mountain Land, South Africa. Nature 314:530–532.

Walters JR. 1987. Transition to adulthood. In Smuts BB, Cheney DL, Seyfarth RM, Wrangham RW, Struhsaker TT editors. Primate societies, pp. 358–369. Chicago: University of Chicago Press.

Walters JR, Seyfarth RM. 1987. Conflict and cooperation. In Smuts BB, Cheney DL, Seyfarth RM, Wrangham RW, Struhsaker TT editors. Primate societies, pp. 306–317. Chicago: University of Chicago Press.

Wang BC, Smith TB. 2002. Closing the seed dispersal loop. Trends in Ecology and Evolution 17:379–385.

Wang D, Ran W, Jin T, Pan W. 2005. Population census of the white-headed langur (*Trachypithecus leucocephalus*) at Longrni Karst Hills, Guangxi, China. Primates 46(3):219–222.

Wang E, Milton K. 2003. Intragroup social relationships of male *Alouatta palliata* on Barro Colorado Island, Republic of Panama. International Journal of Primatology 24(6):1227–1243.

Ward CV, Walker A, Teaford MF. 1991. *Proconsul* did not have a tail. Journal of Human Evolution 21:215–220.

Washburn SL. 1951. The new physical anthropology. Transactions of the New York Academy of Science, Series II 13:298–304.

Washburn SL. editor. 1961. Social life of early man. Chicago: Aldine.

Washburn SL, DeVore I. 1961. The social life of baboons. Scientific American 204(6):62–71.

Watts DP. 1994. Social relationships of immigrant and resident female mountain gorillas, II. Relatedness, residence, and relationships between females. American Journal of Primatology 32:13–30.

Watts DP, Muller M, Amsler SJ, Mbabazi G, Mitani JC. 2006. Lethal intergroup aggression by chimpanzees in Kibale National Park, Uganda. American Journal of Primatology 68(2):161–180.

Watts DP, Pusey AE. 1993. Behavior of juvenile and adolescent great apes. In Pereira ME, Fairbanks LA editors. Juvenile primates. Life history, development, and behavior, pp. 148–167. New York: Oxford University Press.

Watts ES editor. 1985. Nonhuman primate models for human growth and development. New York: Alan R. Liss.

Webb CO, Peart DR 2001. High seed dispersal rates in faunally intact tropical rain forest: Theoretical and conservation implications. Ecology Letters 4:491–499.

Wehner R. 1992. Arthropods. In Papi F editor. Animal homing, pp. 45–144. London: Chapman & Hall.

Welker C. 1973. Ethological significance of the urine washing by *Galago crassicaudatus* E. Geoffroy, 1812 (Lorisiformes: Galagidae). Folia Primatologica 20:429–452.

Weller A, Weller L. 1997. Menstrual synchrony under optimal conditions: Bedouin families. Journal of Comparative Psychology 111:143–151.

Westergaard GC, Lundquist AL, Haynie MK, Kuhn HE, Suomi SJ. 1998. Why some capuchin monkeys (*Cebus apella*) use probing tools (and others do not). Journal of Comparative Psychology 112(2):207–211.

Westermeier RL, Brawn JD, Simpson SA, Esker TL, Jansen RW, Walk JW, Kershner EL, Bouzat JL, Paige KN. 1998. Tracking the long-term decline and recovery of an isolated population. Science 282:1695–1698.

Wheatley BP. 1999. The sacred monkeys of Bali. Prospects Heights, IL: Waveland Press.

White FJ. 1996. Comparative socio-ecology of *Pan paniscus*. In McGrew WC, Marchant LF, Nishida T editors. Great ape societies, pp. 29–41. Cambridge, UK: Cambridge University Press.

White TD, Harris JM. 1997. Suid evolution and correlation of African hominid localities. Science 198:13–21.

Whiten A. 2000. Primate culture and social learning. Cognitive Science 24(3):477–508.

Whiten A, Byrne RW editors. 1997. Machiavellian intelligence II. Extensions and evaluations. Cambridge, UK: Cambridge University Press.

Whiten A, Custance DM, Gomez J-C, Teixidor P, Bard KA. 1996. Imitative learning of artificial fruit processing in children (*Homo sapiens*) and chimpanzees (*Pan troglodytes*). Journal of Comparative Psychology 110:3–14.

Whiten A, Goodall J, McGrew WC, Nishida T, Reynolds V, Sugiyama Y, Tutin CEG, Wrangham RW, Boesch C. 1999. Cultures in chimpanzees. Nature 399:682–685.

Whitham JC, Maestripieri D. 2003. Primate rituals: The function of greetings between male Guinea baboons. Ethology 109:847–859.

Whitmore TC. 1984. Tropical rain forests of the Far East. 2nd edition. Oxford, UK: Clarendon Press.

Whitten AJ. 1982. Home range use by Kloss gibbon (*Hylobates klossii*) on Siberut island, Indonesia. Animal Behaviour 30:182–198.

Wich SA, Utami-Atmoko SS, Mitra Setja TM, Rijksen HD, Schürmann C, van Hooff JARAM, van Schaik CP. 2004. Life history of wild Sumatran orangutans (*Pongo abelii*). Journal of Human Evolution 47(6):385–398.

Wich SA, van Schaik CP. 2000. The impact of El Niño on mast fruiting in Sumatra and elsewhere in Malaysia. Journal of Tropical Ecology 16:563–577.

Wiens F, Zitzmann A. 2003. Social structure of the solitary slow loris *Nycticebus coucang* (Lorisidae). Journal of Zoology 261:35–46.

Wilkie DS, Starkey M, Abernethy K, Effa EN, Telfer P, Godoy R. 2005. Role of prices and wealth in consumer demand for bushmeat in Gabon, Central Africa. Conservation Biology 19(1):268–274.

Wilmé L, Goodman SM, Ganzhorn JU. 2006. Biogeographic evolution of Madagascar's microendemic biota. Science 312:1063–1065.

Wolfe ND, Heneine W, Carr JK, Garcia AD, Shanmugam V, Tamoufe U, Torimiro JN, Prosser AT, LeBreton M, Mpoudi-Ngole E, McCutchan FE, Birx DL, Folks TM, Burke

DS, Switzer WM. 2005. Emergence of unique primate T-lymphotropic viruses among central African bushmeat hunters. Proceedings of the National Academy of Science, USA 102(22):7994–7999.

Wolfe ND, Switzer WM, Carr JK, Bhullar VB, Shanmugam V, Tamoufe U, Prosser AT, Torimiro JN, Wright A, Mpoudi-Ngole E, Mccutchan FE, Birx DL, Folks TM, Burke DS, Heneine W. 2004. Naturally acquired simian retrovirus infections in central African hunters. Lancet 363:932–937.

Wood Jones F. 1916. Arboreal man. London: Edward Arnold.

Woodroffe R, Lindsey P, Romanach S, Stein A, ole Ranah, SMK. 2005. Livestock predation by endangered African wild dogs (*Lycaon pictus*) in northern Kenya. Biological Conservation 124:225–234.

Woodruff G, Premack D. 1981. Primitive mathematical concepts in the chimpanzee: Proportionality and numerosity. Nature 293:568–570.

Wrangham RW. 1980. An ecological model of female-bonded primate groups. Behaviour 75:262–300.

Wrangham RW. 1983. Social relationships in comparative perspective. In RA Hinde. Primate social relationships, pp. 325–334. Oxford, UK: Blackwell.

Wrangham RW. 1987. African apes: The significance of African apes for reconstructing human social evolution. In Kinzey WG editor. The evolution of human behavior: Primate models, pp 51–71. New York: State University of New York Press.

Wrangham RW, Conklin-Brittain N, Hunt KD. 1998. Dietary response of chimpanzees and cercopithecines to seasonal variation in fruit abundance. I. Antifeedants. International Journal of Primatology 19(6):949–970.

Wright PC. 1990. Patterns of paternal care in primates. International Journal of Primatology 11:89–102.

Wright PC. 1994. Night watch on the Amazon. Natural History 103:44–51.

Wright PC. 1996. The neotropical primate adaptation to nocturnality: Feeding in the night (*Aotus nigriceps* and *A. azarae*). In Norconk MA, Rosenberger AL, Garber P editors. Adaptive radiations of neotropical primates, pp. 369–382. New York: Plenum Press.

Wright PC, Martin LB. 1995. Predation, pollination and torpor in two nocturnal prosimians: *Cheirogaleus major* and *Microcebus rufus* in the rain forest of Madagascar. In Izard K, Alterman L, Doyle GA, editors. Creatures of the dark: The nocturnal prosimians, pp. 45–60. New York: Plenum.

Wright RVS. 1972. Imitative learning of a flaked-tool technology: The case of an orangutan. Mankind 8:296–306.

Wright SJ. 2005. Tropical forests in a changing environment. Trends in Ecology and Evolution 20(10):553–560.

Wright TE, Toft CA, Enkerlin-Hoeflich E, Gonzalez-Elizondo J, Alboronoz M, Rodríguez-Ferraro A, Rojas-Suárez F, Sanz V, Trujillo A, Beissinger SR, Berovides AV, Gálvez AX, Brice AT, Joyner K, Eberhard J, Gilardi J, Koenig SE, Stoleson S, Martuscelli P, Meyers JM, Renton K, Rodríguez AM, Sosa-Asanza AC, Vilella FJ, Wiley JW. 2001. Nest poaching in Neotropical parrots. Conservation Biology 15:710–720.

Wyner YM, Johnson SE, Stumpf RM, Desalle R. 2002. Genetic assessment of a white-collared x red-fronted lemur hybrid zone at Andringitra, Madagascar. American Journal of Primatology 67:51–66.

Xu X, Zhou Z, Wang X, Kuang X, Zhang F, Du X. 2003. Four-winged dinosaurs from China. Nature 421:335–340.

Yamagiwa J, Maruhashi T, Yumoto T, Mwanza N. 1996. Dietary and ranging overlap in sympatric gorillas and chimpanzees in Kahuzi-Biega National Park, Zaïre. In McGrew WC, Marchant LF, Nishida T editors. Great ape societies, pp. 82–98. Cambridge, UK: Cambridge University Press.

Yeager CP. 1991. Possible antipredator behavior associated with river crossings by proboscis monkeys (*Nasalis larvatus*). American Journal of Primatology 24:61–66.

Yeager CP. 1997. Orangutan rehabilitation in Tanjung Puting National Park, Indonesia. Conservation Biology 11(3):802–805.

Yerkes RM. 1925. Almost human. New York: Century.

Yerkes RM, Yerkes AW. 1929. The great apes: A study of anthropoid life. New Haven: Yale University Press.

Yoder AD. 1997. Back to the future: A synthesis of strepsirrhine systematics. Evolutionary Anthropology 6:11–22.

Yoder AD. 2003. The phylogenetic position of genus *Tarsius*: Whose side are you on? In Wright PC, Simons EL, Gursky S editors. Tarsiers. Past, present and future, pp. 161–175. New Brunswick, NJ: Rutgers University Press.

Yoder AD, Yang Z. 2000. Estimation of primate speciation dates using local molecular clocks. Molecular Biology and Evolution 17 (7):1081–1090.

Young JM, Trask BJ. 2002. The sense of smell: Genomics of vertebrate odorant receptors. Human Molecular Genetics 11(10):1153–1160.

Young NM, MacLatchy L. 2004. The phylogenetic position of *Morotopithecus*. Journal of Human Evolution 46:163–184.

Zahavi A. 1977. The testing of a bond. Animal Behaviour 25:246–247.

Zhang S-Y. 1995. Activity and ranging patterns in relation to fruit utilization by brown capuchins (*Cebus abella*) in French Guiana. International Journal of Primatology 16:489–507.

Zihlman A. 1996. Reconstructions reconsidered: Chimpanzee models and human evolution. In McGrew WC, Marchant LF, Nishida T editors. Great ape societies, pp. 293–304. Cambridge, UK: Cambridge University Press.

Zihlman A, Cronin JE, Cramer DL, Sarich VM. 1978. Pygmy chimpanzee as a possible prototype for the common ancestor of humans, chimpanzees, and gorillas. Nature 275:744–746.

Zimmermann E, Vorobieva E, Wrogemann D, Hafen T. 2000. Use of vocal fingerprinting for specific discrimination of gray (*Microcebus murinus*) and rufous mouse lemurs (*Microcebus rufus*). International Journal of Primatology 21(5):837–852.

Zito M, Evans S, Weldon PJ. 2003. Owl monkeys (*Aotus* spp.) self-anoint with plants and millipedes. Folia Primatologica 74:159–161.

Zuberbühler K. 2000a. Referential labelling in Diana monkeys. Animal Behaviour 59:917–927.

Zuberbühler K. 2000b. Interspecies semantic communication in two forest primates. Proceedings of the Royal Society, London B. 267:713–718.

Zuberbühler K. 2002. A syntactic rule in forest monkey communication. Animal Behaviour 63:293–299.

Zuberbühler K, Noë R, Seyfarth RM. 1997. Diana monkey long-distance calls: Messages for conspecifics and predators. Animal Behaviour 53:589–604.

Zucker EL, Clarke MR. 1998. Agonistic and affiliative relationships of adult female howlers (*Alouatta palliata*) in Costa Rica over a 4-year period. International Journal of Primatology 19(3):433–449.

Zuckerman S. 1932. The social life of monkeys and apes. London: Kegan Paul.

Credits

Chapter 1

Page 2, © Pamela Ashmore, University of Missouri - St. Louis; page 3, © Pia Nystrom, University of Sheffield; photo donated by Mike Keithly; page 4, Carrie A. Kouri; page 6, © Pia Nystrom, University of Sheffield; page 7, Fitzpatrick KA, Carlson M, Charlton J (1982) Topography, cytoarchitecture and sulcal patterns in primary somatic sensory cortex of the prosimian primate Perodicticus potto.. J Compu Neurol 204:296-310; © Pia Nystrom/ University of Sheffield; page 8, Theodora Eleftheriou; © Pia Nystrom/ University of Sheffield; page 9, James F. Campbell; page 10, © Pia Nystrom/ University of Sheffield; page 11, Stefan Merker, University of Mainz, Germany see more images at www.tarsier.de; page 13, © Sandro Vannini / CORBIS All Rights Reserved; page 14, © Bettmann/CORBIS All Rights Reserved; page 15, © Dean Conger / CORBIS All Rights Reserved; page 16, Michelle L. Sauther; page 20, © Kennan Ward / CORBIS All Rights Reserved; Anthro-Photo File/Richard Wrangham.

Chapter 2

Page 26, Illustrations by Stephen D. Nash/Conservation International; page 43, Benjamin Z. Freed; © Nigel J. Dennis / Gallo Images / CORBIS All Rights Reserved; © Pia Nystrom/ Universit of Sheffield; page 45, © Pia Nystrom/ University of Sheffield; family of lemurs from San Francisco safari tour by Randy T. Ashmore; page 46, Dr. Lisa Gould PhD; page 47, © Pia Nystrom, University of Sheffield; David Haring/Duke Lemur Center; Fitzpatrick KA, Carlson M, Charlton J (1982) Topography, cytoarchitecture and sulcal patterns in primary somatic sensory cortex of the prosimian primate Perodicticus potto.. J Compu Neurol 204:296-310; page 48, K.A.I. Nekaris; photo by Sharon Gursky; page 49, © Pia Nystrom/ University of Sheffield; page 50, © Pia Nystrom/ Unviersity of Sheffield; page 51, © Pia Nystrom/ Unviersity of Sheffield; Volker Sommer; page 53, © T. Q. Bartlett; © Martin Harvey / CORBIS All Rights Reserved; page 54, © Pia Nystrom/ University of Sheffield; Swales, C. and Swales, D.; page 55, © Pia Nystrom/ University of Sheffield; by Jorge Martinez-Contreras; page 56, © Pia Nystrom/ University of Sheffield; page 57, © Pia Nystrom/ University of Sheffield; page 58, © Pia Nystrom/ University of Sheffield; by Randy T. Ashmore; Nick Robl; courtesy of Liza Veig; page 59, © Kevin Schafer / CORBIS All Rights Reserved; © Kevin Schafer / CORBIS All Rights Reserved; page 60, Hamilton Osorio; Billy Kaysing; © Pia Nystrom, University of Sheffield.

Chapter 3

Page 66, © Keren Su / CORBIS All Rights Reserved; Sukree Sukplang/Corbis/Reuters America LLC; © Pamela Ashmore, University of Missouri - St. Louis; page 68, photo courtesy of Vernon Reynolds; © Pamela Ashmore, University of Missouri - St. Louis; page 71, © Pia Nystrom, University of Sheffield; page 72, © Pia Nystrom, University of Sheffield; page 73, © Pia Nystrom, University of Sheffield; page 74, © Steve Kaufman / CORBIS All Rights Reserved; page 75, © Yann Arthus-Bertrand / CORBIS All Rights Reserved; page 81, © Pia Nystrom, University of Sheffield; page 90, Nick Robl; courtesy of Liza Veiga.

Chapter 4

Page 92, © Pia Nystrom, University of Sheffield; page 93, Rebecca Harrison; © Pia Nystrom, University of Sheffield; Christof Wermter/Corbis Zefa Collection; page 95, © Pia Nystrom, University of Sheffield; page 96, © Pia Nystrom, University of Sheffield; page 97, © Pia Nystrom, University of Sheffield; page 98, © Pia Nystrom, University of Sheffield; page 99, photo by Karin Enstam Jaffe; page 102, © Pia Nystrom, University of Sheffield; page 103, © Pia Nystrom, University of Sheffield; page 107, Richard Byrne; page 109, © Pia Nystrom, University of Sheffield; page 110, Swales, C. and Swales, D.; Benjamin Z. Freed; page 111, © Pia Nystrom, University of Sheffield; page 117, © Pia

Nystrom, University of Sheffield; Billy Kaysing; page 119, K.A.I. Nekaris, photo by Sharon Gursky; page 121, © Pia Nystrom, University of Sheffield; page 124, © Pia Nystrom, University of Sheffield; page 128, Lisa Gould.

Chapter 5

Page 140, Colin Keates © Dorling Kindersley; page 142, © Pia Nystrom, University of Sheffield; page 155, © Robert Pickett / CORBIS All Rights Reserved; Timothy Laman/ Getty - National Geographic Society; © Pia Nystrom, University of Sheffield; page 159, Illustrations by Stephen D. Nash/Conservation International; © Pia Nystrom, University of Sheffield; page 164, Photograph © Chris Beard, Carnegie Museum of Natural History; page 171, Professor Masanaru Takai; page 176, Anthro-Photo File/APC00_1987; page 178, Alan Walker; page 185, Brenda R. Benefit; page 189, Professor Nina G. Jablonski; page 190, Professor Nina G. Jablonski; page 191, Brenda R. Benefit; page 193, reprinted with permission of G.J. Retallack; page 194, reprinted with permission of G.J. Retallack.

Chapter 6

Page 205, John Dominis/Getty Images/Time Life Pictures; page 208, Professor David Baum; page 210, Nick Robl; page 215, © Pia Nystrom, University of Sheffield; page 216, © Pia Nystrom, University of Sheffield; page 231, Benjamin Z. Freed.

Chapter 7

Page 236, © Pia Nystrom, University of Sheffield; page 240, photo by Sharon Gursky; page 242, © T. Q. Bartlett; page 243, Theodora Eleftheriou; page 244, © Pia Nystrom, University of Sheffield; page 245, Theodora Eleftheriou; page 247, Theodora Eleftheriou; page 249, Swales, C. and Swales, D.; page 251, © Nigel J. Dennis / Gallo Images / CORBIS All Rights Reserved; page 254, photo by Larissa Swedell; © Pia Nystrom, University of Sheffield.

Chapter 8

Page 260, © Pia Nystrom, University of Sheffield; page 266, photo taken by Amy-Rose Carmel Thomas at Trentham Monkey Resort; page 268, © Fernando Colmenares; page 271, © Pia Nystrom, University of Sheffield; page 273, © Pia Nystrom, University of Sheffield; page 276, © Pia Nystrom, University of Sheffield; page 277, © Pia Nystrom, University of Sheffield; page, 279, Nina Leen/Getty Images/Time Life Pictures; page 280, © Pia Nystrom, University of Sheffield; page 281, © Pia Nystrom, University of Sheffield; page 283, photo by Karin Enstam Jaffe; Craig Stanford/Jane Goodall Research Center; page 287, © Pia Nystrom, University of Sheffield; page 289, © Pia Nystrom, University of Sheffield; page 290, Lisa Gould; page 291, photo taken by Amy-Rose Carmel Thomas at Trentham Monkey Resort; page 292, © Pia Nystrom, University of Sheffield.

Chapter 9

Page 302, © Pia Nystrom, University of Sheffield; page 303, David Haring/Duke Lemur Center; Lisa Gould; page 305, © Pia Nystrom, University of Sheffield; page 306, Alba Perez-Ruiz; page 307, © Pia Nystrom, University of Sheffield; page 306, © Bettmann/CORBIS All Rights Reserved; Terrace/Anthro-Photo File; page 317, © Bettmann/CORBIS All Rights Reserved; © Anna Clopet/ CORBIS All Rights Reserved.

Chapter 10

Page 327, © Pia Nystrom, University of Sheffield; page 331, photo: Jim Anderson, University of Stirling; page 332, photo courtesy of Cognitive Evolution Group, University of Louisiana at Lafayette; page 337, © Pia Nystrom, University of Sheffield; page 339, Gerry Ellis/Getty Images, Inc. - Minden Pictures; page 342, Roy Toft/Getty - National Geographic Society.

Chapter 11

Page 355, Mary S. Willis; page 357, © Pamela Ashmore, University of Missouri - St. Louis; page 360, L. Albretchsen; R. Fulconis; page 363, Donna Hart; page 364, Mary S. Willis ; page 366, © Pamela Ashmore, University of Missouri - St. Louis; © Pia Nystrom, University of Sheffield; page 369, Swales, C. and Swales, D.; page 372, © Pamela Ashmore, University of Missouri - St. Louis; page 375, © Pia Nystrom, University of Sheffield; page 376, © Pia Nystrom, University of Sheffield; page 379, © Kevin Schafer / CORBIS All Rights Reserved; page 380, © Pia Nystrom, University of Sheffield; © Yann Arthus-Bertrand / CORBIS All Rights Reserved.

Index

445